Economic Challenges of Pension Systems

Marta Peris-Ortiz • José Álvarez-García
Inmaculada Domínguez-Fabián • Pierre Devolder
Editors

Economic Challenges of Pension Systems

A Sustainability and International Management Perspective

Springer

Editors
Marta Peris-Ortiz
Department of Business Organization
Universitat Politècnica de València
Valencia, Spain

Inmaculada Domínguez-Fabián
Financial Economics and Accounting
University of Extremadura
Cáceres, Spain

José Álvarez-García
Department of Financial Economics and Accounting
University of Extremadura
Cáceres, Spain

Pierre Devolder
Institute of Statistics, Biostatistics and Actuarial Science (ISBA)
Université Catholique de Louvain
Louvain-la-Neuve, Belgium

ISBN 978-3-030-37911-7 ISBN 978-3-030-37912-4 (eBook)
https://doi.org/10.1007/978-3-030-37912-4

This Springer imprint is published by the registered company Springer Nature Switzerland AG
The registered company address is: Gewerbestrasse 11, 6330 Cham, Switzerland

Foreword

Pension systems face a series of challenges. The first, demographic change, is well known. Life expectancy is rising, and in many countries, fertility is declining. As a result, populations are ageing. Globally, about 1 in 10 people are over 60 years old today; by 2050, the figure will be 1 in 5. Much of this is good news – people are living longer healthy lives – but it also poses problems for financing pensions.

Second, and less widely known, is the changing nature of labour-market relationships.

More than in the past, people are not necessarily in full-time employment for the whole of their career; they have spells of full-time and part-time work and self-employment and spells outside the labour force. That fluidity poses problems for systems that rely on contributions tied to employment.

A third challenge is uncertainty: economic (another economic crisis?), political (instability in the Middle East), environmental (climate change), social (population ageing) and technical (nuclear safety), as well as those connected with the prospective UK departure from the European Union and those connected with the new US administration.

Each of these challenges has profound implications for pension design – the agenda of this book.

Demographic change. What does demographic change suggest for good pension design? A starting point is to note that there are four (and only four) ways of addressing a problem of pension finance:

- Lower monthly pensions, i.e. reducing the living standards of pensioners
- Higher contributions, i.e. reducing the living standards of workers
- Later retirement with no compensating increase in pensions: this approach cuts benefits not by reducing living standards in retirement but by reducing the duration of retirement
- Increasing output, by increasing investment in physical and human capital (thus raising labour productivity) and/or by increasing the number of workers, e.g. through immigration

If the design of pensions in the nineteenth century had related retirement age to life expectancy, there would be much less pressure on pension finance today. The obvious policy is for pensionable age to rise in a rational way as life expectancy increases. The argument for doing so is all the stronger because many people enjoy their work and may not want to retire, not least because jobs today are generally less physically demanding than in the past. Thus, it is both necessary and desirable that in many countries, pension age has already increased or is set to do so.

The main approach to declining fertility are policies to increase saving. Consumption by pensioners during longer retirements must rely on growing output. But a declining workforce will exert downward pressure on output unless offset by other factors. An appropriate response to fewer workers is to make each individual worker more productive through investment in physical capital and human capital.

It is widely believed, but mistaken to think, that increased saving necessarily implies a move towards full-funded individual accounts. That is one way but not the only way. A series of major market failures (Barr 2012, Chap. 7; Barr and Diamond 2008, 2010) calls into question the simple model of choice and competition and creates strong arguments for forms of saving that are reliable, trusted and cheaply administered and involve limited or no choice for workers. Specific lessons include that:

- Voluntarism plus public education are insufficient. Automatic enrolment into a pension plan is more effective: once automatically enrolled, most people will stay with the plan.
- In sharp contrast with simple theory, keep choices simple, for example, offering only a small number of clearly differentiated funds. This type of constrained choice is a deliberate and welfare-enhancing design feature.
- Design a good default option for people who make no choice.
- Different countries arrange saving in different ways.
- Australia and Chile have mandatory membership of individual accounts, with individual choice from a fairly large number of providers.
- New Zealand has auto-enrolment in simple, cheaply administered savings accounts, again with a wide choice of providers.
- The UK is phasing in pensions organized via the National Employment Savings Trust (NEST pensions) in which workers are auto-enrolled in a system which deliberately gives them only limited choice.
- The Netherlands has a system of fully funded occupational pensions, membership of which is mandatory for workers in the industry.
- In Canada, the state defined benefit pension is partially funded, aiming to cover about 25% of benefit payments from funding. The funds are managed at arm's length from government.

It is also possible to arrange additional saving outside the pension system. For example, Norway has a PAYG pension system complemented by a sovereign wealth fund, one of whose purposes is tax smoothing to accommodate the baby boomer generation of pensioners.

More fluid labour-market relations. With long-term, full-time employment less prevalent than in the past, a typical worker has a less complete contributions record. The contributory principle no longer provides the coverage it once did. The conclusion in a growing number of countries is to introduce a non-contributory pension (also called a social pension or a citizen's pension) based on age and residence but without a contributions test. The main purpose of such a pension is to provide poverty relief as a complement to the consumption smoothing provided by contributory earnings-related pensions.

The argument for non-contributory pensions is that they strengthen poverty relief: they can cover everybody and can pay a pension high enough to provide genuine poverty relief. They also have advantages in terms of gender balance, since women tend to have more fragmented contributions records.

A range of instruments helps to make non-contributory benefits affordable, notably (*a*) the size of the monthly pension and (*b*) the age at which the pension is first paid. It is possible also (*c*) to subject the pension to an affluence test, such that the best-off do not receive the benefit.

OECD countries with non-contributory pensions include Australia, Canada, Chile, the Netherlands and New Zealand.

Risk-sharing. Individuals face risks, including over their future earnings and health, and pension systems face economic, demographic and political risks. Separately, pension systems need to adjust to social change, for example, common pension rules for men and women. The question for pension design is where risks should fall. In a pure defined contribution plan, risk falls on the individual worker; in a pure defined benefit plan, risk falls on the plan sponsor, e.g. the firm or industry. In a defined-benefit state system which cannot borrow, risk falls on contributors (since the only way to finance any deficit is through higher contributions). In a defined-benefit state system which can borrow, risk can be shared with past, current and future taxpayers via government borrowing.

In assessing risk-sharing, however, it is necessary to look not just at a particular part of the pension system but at the system as a whole. Thus, a country with a generous non-contributory pension and a small defined contribution system will share risk more widely than one with a small non-contributory pension and major reliance on a defined-contribution element.

The three challenges – incomplete contribution records, demographic change and uncertainty – emerge repeatedly in the chapters in this book which look at the different ways, good and bad, in which a wide range of countries grapple with them.

Professor of Public Economics, London School of Economics and Political Science (LSE), London, UK

Nicholas Barr

References

Barr, N. (2012). *The economics of the welfare state*. 5th edition. Oxford University Press.
Barr, N., & Diamond, P. (2008). *Reforming pensions: Principles and policy choices*. Oxford University Press.
Barr, N., & Diamond, P. (2010). *Pension reform: A short guide*. Oxford University Press.

In Chinese: Shanghai: Truth and Wisdom Press, 2013. http://www.amazon.cn/gp/aw/d/B00GQT8B0K
In Spanish: *La reforma necesaria: El futuro las pensiones*. Madrid: El Hombre del Tres, 2012. ISBN 978-84-940161-4-1, http://www.elhombredeltres.es/index.php/la-reforma-necesaria-2
In Polish: *Reformy systemu emerytalnego: Krotki przewodnik*. Polskie Towarzystwo Ekonomiczne. ISBN 978-83-88700-7

Preface

Given the current economic context, which highlights the relevance of pension systems to ensure both the well-being of individuals and the development of countries, and given the new demographic reality in industrialized countries, indicating an increase in the retired population, a drop in the birth rate and a progressive increase in life expectancy, it is essential that the future of public pensions should be addressed with urgency and with the greatest possible comprehensiveness, joining the efforts of all the actors involved on its development. Societies evolve, and this raises the need to modernize or adapt pension legislation, evidenced by the reforms undertaken in recent years in practically all developed economies to face the great economic challenge of pensions.

Nowadays, there is a broad consensus on the main characteristics of public pension systems: they must be sustainable, adequate and equitable. These are characteristics, first, of difficult fulfilment in themselves, which poses great challenges for the countries that pretend to carry them out; but, second and also important, they are characteristics of difficult conjunction, because it is a task for giants to match all three at the same time, and very few countries can boast of it. The economic crisis that has plagued all world economies over the past decade has had very negative effects on state incomes, while spending, especially social spending, has been maintained and even increased, and pensions are the main component of such expenditure.

The issues of financial sustainability are basically related to income in three different types. First, defined benefit schemes have a formula or an indexing factor that directly relates income from contributions to individual income pensions. Second, in point systems, individuals earn pension points for every contribution they make and then convert points into a retirement pension. Third, in notional defined contribution schemes, pensions depend on the amount of contributions made and the theoretical interest credited to the individual accounts.

With regard to the adequacy of pensions, the importance lies in the fact that it is a relative concept, and more in reference to pensions, since it is not possible to achieve a single figure valid for all countries and systems without taking into account the characteristics and peculiarities of each one of them.

Equity issues go beyond the definition of the concept itself, although three types can be established, with three different ways of achieving them. The first is the contributory equity, which would require reforms both in how to calculate the regulatory base and in the current scale of determination of the replacement rate for quoted years. The second is the intra-generational actuarial equity, which would mean balancing the penalties and premiums for access to retirement at different ages. And the third is the intergenerational actuarial equity, which would imply incorporating the dynamic evolution of life expectancy in the calculation of the initial pension.

This book aims to cover several objectives: first of all, to inform the reader about one of the greatest economic challenges faced by absolutely all governments in the world, the economy of the elderly; moreover, to offer different views on the different situations and solutions that a vast majority of public pension systems have solved; and, last but not least, to extend a perspective on what different world experts think in these issue schemes from the perspective of analysing their own public pension systems. In this sense, this book aims to be an essential reference and discussion manual, complementing existing ones, for the academic, business context and professionals of sector.

The authors of this book provide a broad overview on all these issues. The book starts with a few but very important words from Professor Mr. Nicholas Barr, who gives his particular vision of the main challenges actually faced by the public pension systems and some of the reasons why it is important to mitigate their effects to try to solve the situation. The demographic change is one of the most known one, but not the only. Mr. Barr introduces the discussion about the labour-market relations and its fluidity, due basically to the full-time employment less prevalence than in the past decades. At the same time, he briefly talks about the risk-sharing between men and women, in order to assess the social change and the consequences of the incorporation of the women to the labour market. It is definitely a very clever vision of the current pension systems situation.

The book begins with five chapters where the challenges faced by pension systems are exposed: the economic crisis, the demographic changes, the changes in the labour market and the economic growth and wealth.

In Chapter 1, the authors, Mr. Jose Álvarez, Mr. Amador Durán, Ms. Marta Peris and Ms. María de la Cruz del Río, present the current state of scientific production on public pension systems through a comparative bibliometric study of indexed documents in WoS and Scopus databases. In the same way, there are treated aspects such as correlation between growth, coverage, overlap, dispersion and concentration of articles.

Chapter 2, written by Ms. Estefania Alaminos, Ms. Mercedes Ayuso and Ms. Montserrat Guillen, present an applied view of the evolution of the main demographic indicators in order to identify the challenges present in the design of the public pension systems, as well as its sustainability, especially important in defined benefit schemes.

In Chapter 3, Mr. Robert Meneu, Mr. Borja Encinas and Ms. María de la Cruz del Río present the effects of the economic crisis in the public pension systems, in terms of economic growth versus employment and contributions, assessing that economic growth alone will not be enough to ensure the financial sustainability of the pensions in the long term. Chapter 4, written by Mr. Enrique Devesa and Mr. Rafael Domenech, provides the relationship between pensions, welfare and economic growth, analysing the effects of pay-as-you-go (PAYGO) and funded pension systems on welfare and providing six important conclusions about the debate on the choice between alternative systems.

In Chapter 5, Mr. Filip Chybalski attempts to answer the question about the linkage between pension system designs and the labour market participation in European countries, using selected statistical and econometric tools to analyse the empirical data.

The second block includes three chapters, where the main aspects that must be assessed in a pension system are included: sustainability, adequacy and equity.

Sustainability is one of the main characteristics of the public pension systems. In Chapter 6, Mr. Enrique Devesa, Ms. Beatriz Rosado and Mr. José Álvarez review the main instruments and indicators used to measure it on the PAYGO systems, distinguishing between defined contribution and defined benefit ones.

Chapter 7, written by Mr. Rober Meneu, Mr. Borja Encinas and Ms. Inmaculada Domínguez, centers on the equity of public pension systems, particularly on the concept of the actuarial equity through the internal rate of return and the contributory effort analysis, while Chapter 8, authored by Ms. Marta Peris and Mr. Carlos Rueda, focuses on the adequacy of the pension systems, describing the concept by its multiple dimensions, the single indicators used to measure it and the synthetic indicators way to give adequate information.

Once exposed, the challenges and the aspects that the pension systems must safeguard, are developed in five different international chapters of pension system models.

Chapter 9, written by Mr. John Turner, Mr. Gerard Huges, Ms. Agnieszka Chlon-Dominczak and Mr. David Rajnes, describes the international experience in the use of one particular form of insurance against poverty at advanced ages, the Longevity Insurance Benefits for Social Security, focusing on the programmes established in Ireland, Poland and China, as well as considering proposals for the provision of these benefits in Canada and the United States.

In Chapter 10, Mr. Frédéric Gannon, Ms. Florence Legros and Mr. Vincent Touzé discuss the history and properties of one of the oldest pension point systems, the French one, analysing its actuarial fairness properties of the calculation rule, and propose some similarities and differences with German and Swedish one. Chapter 11, written by Ms. María del Carmen Boado, Ms. Poontavika Naka and Mr. Ole Settergren, presents some of the last lessons learned from the Swedish pension system, one of the most mature NDC systems in the world, together with its actual problems and challenges for the future.

In Chapter 12, Mr. Carmelo Mesa and Mr. Diego Valero provide a perspective from 11 Latin American countries about their recent reforms on capitalization pension systems, offering general guidelines to accomplish increasing pension coverage for all of them and extracting a useful lesson for the regions observed and the world. Chapter 13, written by Mr. Farid Flici and Mr. Frederic Planchet, shows the financial sustainability of the Algerian Retirement System. After the presentation of several international models, two chapters are developed where the defined benefit and defined contribution model and the automatic adjustment mechanisms of the systems are considered, which are some of the best instruments to improve pension systems.

Chapter 14, written by Mr. Pierre Devolder and Mr. Sébastian de Valeriola, presents some alternative architecture for a pension system design based on a mix between defined contribution and defined benefit public pension schemes. In Chapter 15, Ms. Carmen Boado, Mr. Humberto Godínez and Mr. Steven Haberman explore the different mechanisms of automatic balance in pay-as-you-go (PAYGO) pension schemes in terms of financial sustainability and adequacy of benefits.

The role of complementary pensions is studied by Ms. Mercedes Ayuso, Ms. Montserrat Guillen and Mr. Diego Valero in Chapter 16, whose aim in this chapter is to present a comprehensive analysis of the second and third pillars as a complement to the public pension system, as well as the risks faced by them, such as longevity, inflation and interest rates.

Chapter 17, written by Mr. Oscar V. De la Torre, Mr. Evaristo Galeano and Ms. Dora Aguilasocho, and Chapter 18, written by Mr. Francisco López, Ms. Marissa Martínez and Mr. Roberto Joaquín, analyse some of the main aspects of the pension funds and its various aspects, giving a very accurate idea of their configuration, management form and their current development, as well as a current vision of their nowadays situation.

The book ends with two chapters: Chapter 19, written by Ms. Roberta Melis and Alessandro Trudda, and Chapter 20, written by Ms. Inmaculada Domínguez, Mr. Francisco del Olmo and Mr. José Antonio, where new model developments are exhibited and where they try to advance in the reinvention of social security in the face of the challenges they are trying to solve.

These chapters represent an important cross section of the actual research in public pension systems. The problems of pensions dominate the economic problems of the countries and are subject of debates in all countries of the world. Hence, this book is of great interest, which goes beyond showing a typical approach to "pension models". At the same time, the book shows the challenges faced by pension systems and how, with some models in continuous transition, adaptations of public and private systems are being carried out in such different countries, with similar problems related to pensions, such as Italy, Algeria, Mexico, the United States or Spain, among others. The chapters are in some cases eminently technical, others are basically informative or descriptive, a few others contain more opinion, but they all are very interesting works and will make the reader understand that *Economic Challenges of Pension Systems: A Sustainability and International Management*

Perspective has fulfilled its objectives initially described, summarized in one: to report on the importance of public pension systems in today's world.

Finally, the editors wish to express their deep gratitude to all those who have contributed to this publication, especially to the authors of the chapters and all the researchers and academics who collaborated in the double-blind review process.

Valencia, Spain	Marta Peris-Ortiz
Cáceres, Spain	José Álvarez-García
Cáceres, Spain	Inmaculada Domínguez-Fabián
Louvain-la-Neuve, Belgium	Pierre Devolder

Contents

Chapter 1
Public Pension Systems: Bibliometric Study of Academic Publications in Scientific Journals

José Álvarez-García, Amador Durán-Sánchez, Marta Peris-Ortiz, and María de la Cruz del Río-Rama

Abstract One of the main components of the so-called welfare states is *Public Pension Systems*, whose analysis provides an image of a country's politics, economy, demographics and culture. There is now an intense global debate on the future viability and reforms needed to guarantee pension funding, especially in societies with high life expectancy and low birth rates. Thus, the purpose of this chapter is to present the current state of scientific production on *Public Pension Systems* through a comparative bibliometric study of indexed documents in WoS and Scopus databases dealing with aspects such as correlation between growth, coverage, overlap, dispersion and concentration of articles. To do this, and through an advanced search by terms, a representative set of 256 articles until 2015 that formed the ad hoc base of the analysis were selected. In view of the results, the conclusion is that although the WoS and Scopus databases differ in terms of scope, data volume and coverage policies, the documents and the results of their analysis are in many aspects similar with Scopus having greater coverage in the specific area of *Public Pension Systems* by collecting more journals, papers and signatures.

Keywords Public Pension Systems · WoS · Scopus · Bibliometric study · Coverage · Overlap

J. Álvarez-García (✉)
Financial Economy and Accounting Department, University of Extremadura, Cáceres, Spain
e-mail: pepealvarez@unex.es

A. Durán-Sánchez
Economy Department, University of Extremadura, Badajoz, Spain
e-mail: amduransan@unex.es

M. Peris-Ortiz
Department of Business Organization, Universitat Politècnica de València, Valencia, Spain
e-mail: mperis@doe.upv.es

M. C. del Río-Rama
Business Management and Marketing Department, University of Vigo, Ourense, Spain
e-mail: delrio@uvigo.es

M. Peris-Ortiz et al. (eds.), *Economic Challenges of Pension Systems*,
https://doi.org/10.1007/978-3-030-37912-4_1

1.1 Introduction

The so-called welfare states are made up of a set of state institutions providing social policies aimed at protecting citizens from life-cycle risks in the areas of health, education, employment or social security. In 2016, the average social expenditure of the OECD countries was 21% of GDP, France being the country with the highest spending rate (32% $_{/PIB}$) and Turkey, Korea and Mexico the countries that spent the least on social support (below 15% $_{/PIB}$). On average, in OECD, pensions and health services account for two-thirds of total expenditures, with pensions accounting for the highest social expenditure (OECD 2016).

Western countries have long faced a number of economic, demographic and social challenges that are causing growing concerns about the future sustainability of public pension systems, crisis and financial recession, progressive ageing of the population and the inversion of the population pyramid, shorter active phases and longer retirement phases, etc.

Since the middle of 2007, the crisis and its impact have made headlines in all countries. On the one hand, what began as a credit crisis turned into a banking crisis and ended up leading to an employment and public finance crisis. On the other hand, a greater life expectancy and low birth rate increase considerably the dependency rates of an increasingly ageing population. At a global level, the proportion of older people aged 60 and over increased from 9% in 1994 to 12% in 2014 and is projected to reach 21% by 2050. Older people are the fastest growing population group. In 2014, the annual growth rate of the population of over 60 almost tripled the growth rate of the population as a whole. In absolute terms, the number of people over the age of 60 almost doubled between 1994 and 2014, formed predominantly by women. In 2014, there were 85 men per 100 women in the older people group in the world. This sex ratio will increase moderately in the coming decades (United Nations 2014).

As currently configured, and in conjunction with other mechanisms that promote the division of labour, public pension systems favour the existence of inequalities in perceptions between men and women. The average gender gap in pensions in the EU-27 is 39%; 17 out of 27 countries show differences greater than or equal to 30%. The two highest percentages are for Luxembourg (47%) and Germany (44%) and the lowest, Estonia with 4% followed by the Slovak Republic (8%) (Bettio et al. 2013). All these demographic changes are generating a considerable increase in public social spending, as well as a growing concern about the future viability of public pension systems. For this reason, many countries have addressed different reforms; however, not all of them have adopted the same measures.

The Pension Sustainability Index (PSI), which reflects the long-term sustainability of pension systems, shows that China and Thailand have less sustainable systems due to the forecast of their rapid ageing population and a relatively low retirement age. On the opposite side are Australia, Denmark, Sweden, the Netherlands and Norway with well-designed pension systems that put them on a long-term financially sustainable path (Finke and Sabatini 2016).

Due to the interest aroused in the academic world, the main objective of this article is to carry out an analysis of scientific literature published and related to *Public Pension Systems* through a bibliometric study of articles indexed in the WoS and Scopus databases, which allows to determine which has a better coverage of the subject, as well as the overlap between them. In the same way, and as secondary objectives, the objective is to determine how much, who, what, where and how research on *Public Pension Systems* has been done by means of statistical methods and bibliometric indicators.

In order to locate the indexed documents in both WoS and Scopus, an advanced search for terms with a time limit in 2015 was carried out in both databases. As a result, a set of 169 references of WoS and 219 of Scopus were selected, which constitute the ad hoc empirical base of the study and which were further processed through the bibliographic manager Refworks.

This chapter is divided into four main sections. First, and after this introduction, we proceed to the review of the academic literature in order to establish the theoretical framework. Subsequently, Sect. 1.3 describes the methodology of calculations and the tracking strategy used for the selection of references. In Sect. 1.4, the main results obtained in the study of the basic bibliometric indicators, as well as from the analysis of overlap and singularity between the bases, are detailed. Finally, Sect. 1.5 presents the final conclusions reached and the limitations associated with the research.

1.2 Theoretical Framework

In the mid-1990s, the publication of the report "Averting the Old Age Crisis: Policies to Protect the Old and Promote Growth" (World Bank 1994) brought the need to study and discuss financially the viability of pension systems implemented in the world.

In this sense, the rapid demographic changes taking place in Western countries in recent decades have led to the policy of public pension systems being one of the most debated issues within welfare states (Bonoli 2003; Taylor-Gooby 2001). The ageing process caused by the increase in life expectancy and low birth rates makes current public pension systems unsustainable in the long term (Whitehouse and Queisser 2007), a fact that has transcended public opinion. Boeri et al. (2002) found that Germans and Italians are aware that current pension systems are unsustainable and recognize the need to reform them but generally ignore the costs of the system as a whole. In the same way, Janky and Gal (2007) argue that while Europeans are aware of the negative impact of demographic changes on the pension system, they generally continue to oppose reforms. As a consequence, the working-age population loses confidence in the generational agreement that sustains the public pension system. Today's workers expect difficulties in collecting their retirement pensions due to the possible collapse of the system (Breyer and Stolte 2001; Razin and Sadka 2007) and oppose to contributing because they consider that they will not become beneficiaries in the future (Tepe and Vanhuysse 2009). In any case, citizens will accept reforms more readily if they are better informed about the costs and peculiarities of the pension system (Boeri and Tabellini 2005).

With the information currently available, the debate on pension reform is a reasonable concern. The negative effects on the future financial equilibrium of pension systems can only be understood if we accept the hypothesis that the expected growth rate of the GDP will not be enough to compensate for the expected increase in expenditure, considering the current conditions of access to pensions and contribution rates as constant (Ferreiro and Serrano 2011). In a well-known series of comparative studies between OECD countries, Gruber and Wise (1999, 2004, 2005), together with other authors, established that for the majority of developed countries the PAYG social security system includes promises that cannot be kept without significant system reforms. In the absence of reform, current systems are fiscally unsustainable.

The lack of gender equality in pension systems has also been a subject discussed in depth within the academic literature. From this gender perspective, the results are conclusive in terms of inequality between men and women. As Goldin (1993) says, when economists speak of the gender gap these days, they generally refer to systematic differences in the outcomes that men and women achieve in the labour market. These differences are observed in the percentages of men and women in the labour force, the types of jobs they choose and their relative incomes or hourly wages. Many of the studies available (Dahl et al. 2003; Duval 2003; Even and Macpherson 2004; Stark et al. 2005; Monticone et al. 2008; Jefferson 2009; Marin and Zólyomi 2010) show that the pensions they receive are lower than those obtained by men. A second feature that is important in the gender analysis of pensions is the existence of a scope (the labour market), in which the difference in the amounts of women and men's pensions originates, and of a structural factor of gender (the social division of paid and unpaid jobs), which explains the gender gap in the labour market (Vara-Miranda 2011).

Although the challenges facing public pension systems (sustainability, ageing, equity, etc.) have become more apparent since the onset of the economic crisis, many countries had already begun to take various measures aimed at ensuring viability through reforms. The academic literature is not unaware of this fact, and many studies have analysed the reforms carried out in different countries for many years, in Ireland, Abid and O'Donoghue (2014); in Italy, Agudo and García (2011); in France, Aubert (2014); in Germany, Börsch-Supan (2015); in Chile, De Mesa and Mesa-Lago (2006); in the United States, Diamond (2006); or in Spain, Vidal-Melia (2014), among many others.

In most cases, the reform consists of increasing the contribution duration to obtain the full pension, reducing the pension rate or both (Alo 2004). However, in almost all cases, the tendency is towards the adoption of differentiated systems in which public pensions are complemented by individual savings and private pensions, either compulsory or stimulated by incentives (Whitehouse and Queisser 2007). According to Alda-García (2016), the different measures implemented can be divided into two blocks: parametric reforms, those related to the calculation of the public pension (retirement age, base calculation, benefits, etc.), and structural reforms, those that modify the pension system structure. Within the structural reforms, we can differentiate three types at the same time: distribution systems, where workers' contributions finance pensions at that moment; funding systems, where each worker contributes to his or her own public pension; and mixed systems that have characteristics of the two previous ones.

A useful tool when analysing the scientific production on public pension systems, or any other field of knowledge, is *bibliometrics*, capable of measuring the research activity based on the quantitative statistical analysis of the data provided by scientific literature (Sancho 1990).

A common practice in recent years has been the comparison of databases that serve as a documentary source for bibliometrics. In these analyses, using both the relative singularity index (Meyer et al. 1983) and the traditional and relative overlap (Bearman and Kunberger 1977), the coverage of several databases is compared, and the overlap of one base in another one is studied (Pulgarín and Escalona 2007). Since many of the first conclusions reached in the 1960s with this new methodology (Martyn and Slater 1964; Martyn 1967) were finally invalidated (Bost 1968), later studies began to differentiate between overlapping of primary sources (Bourne et al. 1969), overlapping of secondary sources (Bearman and Kunberger 1977) and multiple overlapping (Poyer 1984). Finally, the first review on overlapping was published in 1990 (Gluck 1990).

Since the appearance of Scopus in 2004, there are many examples of papers of this type, which compare it with WoS and whose objective is to identify which of the two products responds better to users' needs. Highlights the study carried out by Goodman and Deis (2005) and the subsequent review (Goodman and Deis 2007), where such diverse aspects as prices, content and time coverage, updating, document types, search facilities, access, etc. are compared, and where it is concluded that Scopus has a greater selection of journals while WoS provides greater coverage over time, therefore they are considered complementary products (Escalona et al. 2010). Fingerman (2006) considered that Scopus have an advantage over WoS due to including, in addition to articles, other documentary types such as books or conference proceedings. In response, later versions of WoS included two new reference databases of conference proceedings.

In articles such as Bakkalbasi et al. (2006) and Neuhaus and Daniel (2008), it is recommended to carry out this type of analysis in specific areas of study in order to determine which of the bases works better in each case, as this will depend on the discipline and time period analysed. Thus, studies such as Mingers and Lipitakis (2010) conclude that WoS coverage is worse in the area of business administration and management, and Santa and Herrero-Solana (2010) found that Scopus had greater journal coverage when analysing the scientific production of the main countries of Latin America and the Caribbean.

Beyond the differences in scope, data volume and coverage policies, studies generally show a good correlation between WoS and Scopus due to the large number of journals indexed by both databases (Gavel and Iselid 2008).

1.3 Methodology

This section describes the process followed for the preparation of the comparative study between the multidisciplinary databases WoS and Scopus in relation to the scientific production on *Public Pension Systems*. The objective was not to assess the content quality of the selected papers but to perform a descriptive-quantitative analysis of the papers by means of bibliometric indexes.

Because the access to the entire scientific production is an unreachable goal, any bibliometric analysis is limited by the availability, relevance and reliability of information (Rueda et al. 2007). Bibliographic databases are the main source of information used by many scientific studies; the validity of the results obtained will depend largely on the adequate selection and coverage of the study area (Norris and Oppenheim 2007). This fact makes WoS and Scopus the bases of our study, since both appear frequently as documentation sources in the scientific literature.

Following the outline of similar studies, only articles published in scientific journals are analysed for the development of bibliometric indicators, since these are the main means of transmitting the results of an investigation (Maltrás-Barba 2003) and constitute a representative sample of the academic activity at international level (Benavides-Velasco et al. 2011). Thus, comments, conference reports, press articles, editorials, notes, letters or errata contained in WoS or Scopus are excluded.

In order to delimit the results of the search to the field of *Public Pension Systems*, we opted to use the search equation modality, which has the advantage of enabling to reach journals classified within all thematic fields of knowledge resulting the search more comprehensive (Corral and Cànoves 2013). After debugging the documents not related to the study area, the ad hoc database (169 references in WoS and 219 in Scopus) was performed, on which the calculation of each of the variables necessary in obtaining bibliometric indicators was made.

1.3.1 Methodology of Calculations

There are two main procedures to perform overlap calculations: based on the primary sources that cover the secondary sources or using the documents (articles in our case) that the sources contain. On the one hand, in the first procedure we have the problem of the different indexing policies followed by each database; while some transfer all the sources, others do so in a more selective way (Pao 1993). On the other hand, the latter requires a greater effort when comparing databases. This chapter analyses the overlap between WoS and Scopus bases in the research area of *Public Pension Systems* following both procedures.

(a) *Meyer's Index*

It is also called the relative index of singularity or peculiarity, which was developed by Meyer et al. (1983) and evaluates the follow-up that a database performs on a certain subject, interpreting the result as the degree to which a database covers that specialty (Pulgarín and Escalona 2007). In this indicator, single documents (or primary sources) contained in a single database are the ones with the highest weight, whose weight will be reduced progressively for duplicate documents, triplicate documents, etc., depending on the number of bases to be compared. The higher the value of the index, the greater the singularity of the database, that is, it will collect a greater number of documents or single sources (Costas et al. 2008).

$$\text{Meyer's Index} = \frac{\sum \text{Sources} * \text{Weight}}{\text{Total sources}}$$

(b) *Traditional Overlap (TO)*

To measure the overlap percentage between two databases, or degree of similarity, traditional overlap (TO), defined by Gluck (1990), is used and the calculation is done using the following expression:

$$\%\text{TO} = 100 * \frac{|A \cap B|}{||A \cup B|}$$

The greater the TO, the greater the degree of similarity between the bases, that is, a coefficient of 0.3 shows a similarity of 30% or a difference of 70% between them, which would imply that when searching only one of the bases, we would find 70% of single sources.

(c) *Relative Overlap*

It was originally used by Bearman and Kunberger (1977). It measures the % of coverage of a database A, compared with another one, B.

$$\%\text{Overlap in A} = 100 * \left(\frac{|A \cap B|}{|A|}\right) \quad \%\text{Overlap in B} = 100 * \left(\frac{|A \cap B|}{|B|}\right)$$

The result is interpreted as the percentage of documents (or sources) that base A covers of base B.

1.4 Results

As we can see in Fig. 1.1, the scientific paper is the type of document mostly chosen by researchers when it comes to publicizing their work, 81% of cases in Scopus and 73% in WoS. Therefore, from this point the results obtained are based exclusively on the analysis of the selected articles.

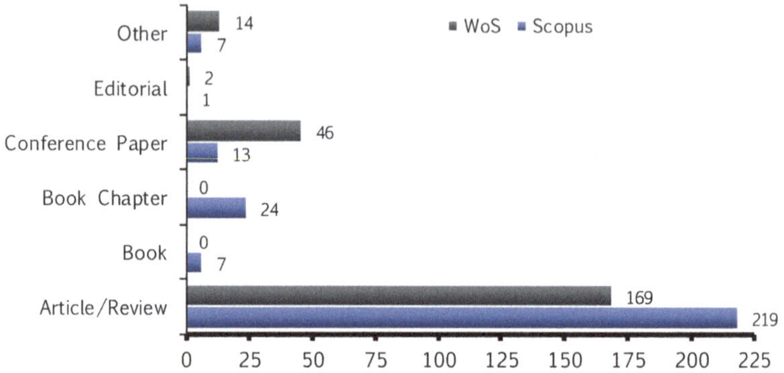

Fig. 1.1 Selection by type of documents in WoS and Scopus. (*Source:* Own elaboration)

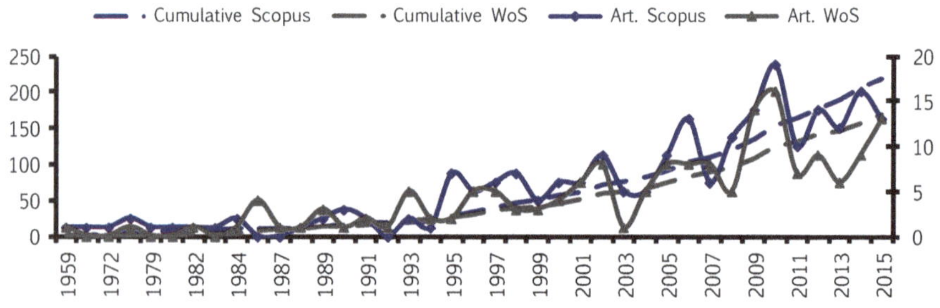

Fig. 1.2 Evolution and cumulative growth of the number of articles published. (*Source:* Own elaboration)

1.4.1 Volume Indicators

As a result of the search for articles related to *Public Pension Systems* within the selected databases and time limit in 2015, a total of 169 articles were obtained in 115 journals for WoS and 219 articles in 152 journals, which form the ad hoc empirical base on which the bibliometric analysis is based. Figure 1.2 shows how the graphs of the production of both bases run parallel over the years, showing some proportionality in the number of articles collected. Cumulative growth reflects a similar evolution until 1997, when Scopus began to accumulate more papers than its competitor, a difference which increases with time.

When organizing the annual distribution of the number of articles present in WoS compared to Scopus (Fig. 1.3), we verified the existence of a correlation between the annual production of both bases and their fit to a line of correlation coefficient equal to 0.88 ($R^2 = 0.7782$).

From the set of selected articles, *Population aging and the rising cost of public pensions* (Bongaarts 2004) with 63 citations in Scopus and 46 in WoS and *Retirement, pensions, and aging, Journal of Public Economics* (Heijdra and Romp 2009) with 34 and 23 citations, respectively, stand out due to the number of citations received (Table 1.1). However, there are also articles with a large number of citations

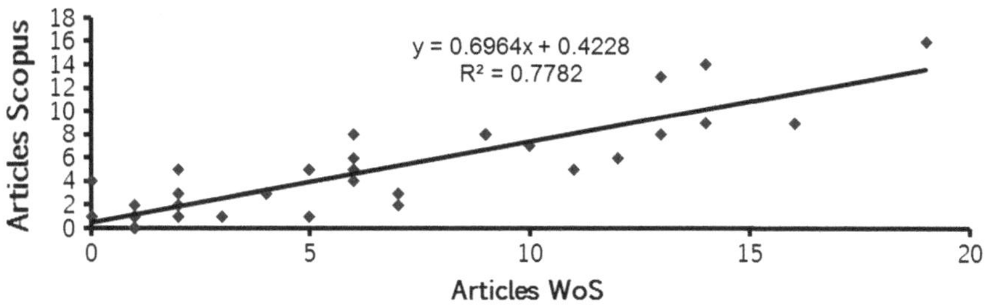

Fig. 1.3 Correlation between the number of articles published. (*Source:* Own elaboration)

Table 1.1 Ranking of articles by no. of citations

	Scopus		WoS	
Article	Ranking	Citations	Ranking	Citations
Bongaarts, J. (2004). Population aging and the rising cost of public pensions. *Population & Development Review*, 30(1), 1–23	1	63	1	46
Beattie, R., & McGillivray, W. (1995). A risky strategy: Reflections on the World Bank Report Averting the old age crisis. *International Social Security Review*, 48(3–4), 5–22	2	44	–	–
Heijdra, B.J., & Romp, W.E. (2009). Retirement, pensions, and ageing. *Journal of Public Economics*, 93(3–4), 586–604	3	34	6	23
Brunner, J.K. (1996). Transition from a pay-as-you-go to a fully funded pension system: The case of differing individuals and intragenerational fairness. *Journal of Public Economics*, 60(1), 131–146	4	33	3	27
De Mesa, A.A., & Mesa-Lago, C. (2006). The structural pension reform in Chile: Effects, comparisons with other Latin American reforms, and lessons. *Oxford Review of Economic Policy*, 22(1), 149–167.	5	31	10	19
Lynch, J., & Myrskylae, M. (2009). Always the third rail? Pension income and policy preferences in European democracies. *Comparative Political Studies*, 42(8), 1068–1097	6	30	2	29
Scholten, U., & Thum, M. (1996). Public pensions and immigration policy in a democracy. *Public Choice*, 87(3–4), 347–361	7	30	4	26
Green, D.A., & Riddell, W.C. (1993). The economic-effects of unemployment-insurance in Canada: An empirical-analysis of UI disentitlement. *Journal of Labor Economics*, 11(1), 96–147	–	–	5	23

Source: Own elaboration

that are only present in one database, such as *A risky strategy: Reflections on the World Bank Report Averting the old age crisis* (Beattie and McGillivray 1995) in Scopus (44) or *The economic-effects of unemployment-insurance in Canada: An empirical analysis of UI disentitlement* (Green and Riddell 1993) in WoS (23).

1.4.2 Overlap and Singularity

As we have seen, WoS identified 115 journals and 169 articles, compared to 152 and 219, respectively, of Scopus. The two databases analysed provided 256 different articles published in 177 journals. Of the total, 124 (48.44%) are single documents, collected in only one of the databases, and 132 (51.56%) are overlapping or shared by both (Fig. 1.4).

The percentage of traditional overlap (%TO) of sources between WoS and Scopus (Gluck 1990) was 50.8%.

$$\%TO_{\text{sources}} = 100 * \left(\frac{|\text{WoS} \cap \text{Scopus}|}{|\text{WoS} \cup \text{Scopus}|}\right) \Rightarrow \%TO_{\text{sources}} = 100 * \frac{90}{25 + 62 + 90}$$
$$\Rightarrow \%TO_{\text{sources}} = 50.8\%$$

This result can be interpreted as that between WoS and Scopus; there is a 50.8% similarity or a 49.2% disparity in relation to primary sources on Public Pensions Systems. Regarding the articles, we find a %TO close to the sources percentage, $\%TO_{\text{articles}} = 51.6\%$.

To measure the coverage percentage of WoS over Scopus and vice versa, we use relative overlap (Bearman and Kunberger 1977). That is, Scopus covers 78% of WoS sources on *Public Pension Systems*. $\%TO_{\text{sources}}$ Scopus = 59%, 19% less compared to the WoS overlap.

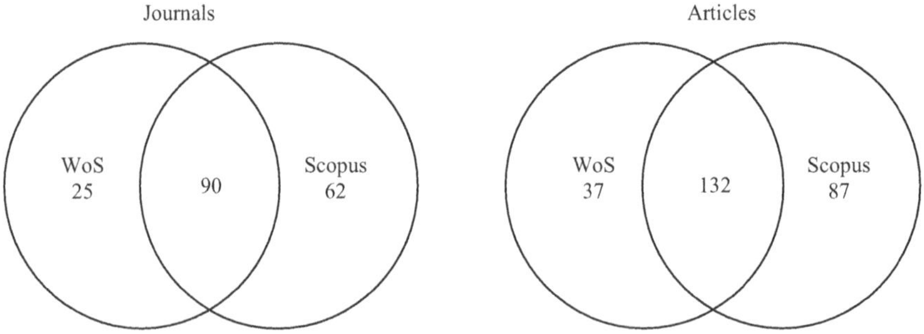

Fig. 1.4 Overlap data between WoS and Scopus. (*Source:* Own elaboration)

Table 1.2 Singularity of WoS and Scopus

	% Single documents		Meyer's index	
Databases	Journals	Articles	Journals	Articles
WoS	21.74%	21.89%	0.61	0.61
Scopus	40.79%	39.73%	0.70	0.70

Source: Own elaboration

Table 1.3 Lotka

			Scopus		WoS	
PI	Producers class	No. articles	No. authors	% authors	No. authors	% authors
PI ≥1	Large	$n \geq 10$	0	0%	0	0%
0 < PI <1	Medium	$2 < n < 9$	34	11%	34	14%
PI = 0	Occasional	$n = 1$	275	89%	205	86%

Source: Own elaboration
Productivity index

$$\%TO_{\text{sources}}\ \text{WoS} = 100 * \left(\frac{|\text{WoS} \cap \text{Scopus}|}{|\text{WoS}|}\right) \Rightarrow \%TO_{\text{sources}}\ \text{WoS} = 100 * \frac{90}{115} = 78\%$$

With respect to the articles,

$$\%TO_{\text{articles}}\ \text{WoS} = 100 * \frac{132}{169} = 78\%; \%TO_{\text{sources}}\ \text{Scopus} = 100 * \frac{132}{219} = 60\%$$

The differences between the overlapping of sources and articles can be explained by the different indexation policies followed by the databases. Although some journals are included in the two databases, all of their documents may not be transferred to each of the databases (Costas et al. 2008).

The database singularity analysis was done using the percentage of single documents present in each database and Meyer's index, which includes the degree of overlap between the bases. The results (Table 1.2) show a greater singularity of Scopus with 40.79% of journals and 39.72% of singles articles and a Meyer's index of about 0.70 for both journals and articles.

1.4.3 Authors

Lotka's law and its productivity index (PI) calculation allow us to differentiate between authors with more than ten published articles (so-called large ones), those with a production between two and nine articles (medium) and authors with a single article (occasional).

Table 1.3 shows that 89% of the authors of Scopus and 86% of WoS are occasional authors with a single article. As a consequence, average productivity in

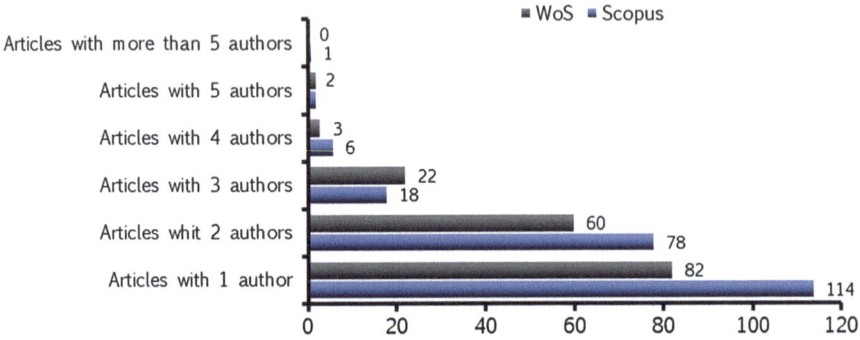

Fig. 1.5 Collaboration index. (*Source:* Own elaboration)

both bases is low, with a value of 1.18 in Scopus and 1.21 in WoS. The most productive authors are Verbon, H.A.A., with 5 articles in Scopus and 65 in WoS, followed by Kolmar, M. (4–4); Börsch-Supan, A. (4–3); Breyer, F.; Kolmar, M. (4–3); and Mesa-Lago, C. (4–3).

In addition, 52% of the articles on *Public Pension Systems* of Scopus and 51% of WoS are signed by a single author and only 12% and 16%, respectively, by more than 2 authors (Fig. 1.5). Thus, the co-authorship index (number of signatures per article) was 1.66 for Scopus and 1.72 for WoS.

The affiliation data of the authors of articles related to *Public Pension Systems* shown in Table 1.4 indicate that United States and Germany, followed by the United Kingdom, Spain and Canada, are the main affiliation countries in both databases. The United States stands out with 81 authorships of 77 authors from 48 different centres, according to Scopus, and 69 authorships by 64 authors from 44 centres based on WoS.

1.4.4 Journals

Scopus' 219 articles were published in 152 different journals, of which 118 (78%) did so on a single occasion. With respect to WoS, the 169 articles are collected in 115 journals, 26 of them (23%) collect more than one work.

According to Bradford's law (Bradford 1934), a small number of journals concentrate most of the published articles on a particular topic, which allows identifying the core of journals most used by authors to publicize their work. Table 1.5 shows the *International Social Security Review*, *Journal of Population Economics* and *Journal of Pension Economics and Finance* as the journals where more articles have been published.

With respect to the main thematic areas which the studies on *Public Pension Systems* can be classified into (Table 1.6), we observe that the majority of the articles

Table 1.4 Main countries of affiliation of authors

	Scopus				WoS			
Country	Ranking	Centres	Authors	Authorships	Ranking	Centres	Authors	Authorships
United States	1	48	77	81	1	44	64	69
Germany	2	23	32	43	2	17	25	39
United Kingdom	3	14	25	29	5	7	13	14
Spain	4	12	21	33	3	10	22	27
France	5	13	17	18	8	5	9	13
Canada	6	9	14	16	4	8	19	21
Japan	7	9	13	14	9	8	9	10
Italy	8	7	11	12	13	3	4	4
Netherlands	9	6	11	15	6	7	12	16
Sweden	10	6	10	13	7	5	10	15
Romania	26	1	2	2	10	4	7	7

Source: Own elaboration

Table 1.5 Ranking of the most relevant journals

Journal	Scopus			WoS		
	Ranking	Articles	% on/total	Ranking	Articles	% on/total
International Social Security Review	1	7	3.20%	–	–	–
Journal of Population Economics	2	7	3.20%	1	8	4.73%
Journal of Pension Economics and Finance	3	6	2.74%	2	7	4.14%
Journal of Public Economics	4	6	2.74%	3	6	3.55%
International Tax and Public Finance	5	5	2.28%	4	5	2.96%
Public Choice	6	4	1.83%	5	4	2.37%
Pensions	6	4	1.83%	–	–	–
World Development	6	4	1.83%	7	3	1.78%

Source: Own elaboration

fall into three fundamental areas: *social sciences* with 95 articles in Scopus and 23 In WoS, *economics and finance* with 77 and 106, and *business and management* with 22 and 22 articles, respectively.

Two main issues are discussed in the articles on *Public Pension Systems*: their reforms and sustainability. Academic literature also reflects other problems that future governments must face: population ageing and immigration, public systems versus privatization or gender inequalities as shown in Table 1.7.

1.5 Conclusions

Until 2004, WoS was the main source of bibliographic documentation with an international and multidisciplinary nature. With the appearance of Scopus in 2004, the need to clarify which of the two products provides greater information possibilities in each area of knowledge arises, when it comes to formulating investigation. Thus, the main objective of this chapter was to perform a bibliometric analysis of the scientific literature published on *Public Pension Systems* comparing the coverage and overlap of both databases while responding to how much, where, what, who and how research is done in this field.

From the detailed analysis of the results obtained, we are able to present our main conclusions.

The article, the same as in other areas of knowledge, is the documentary modality chosen by researchers when it comes to publicizing their work on *Public Pension Systems*. The production of articles in Scopus and WoS shows a similar evolution until 1997, year in which Scopus begins to accumulate a greater number of papers than its competitor, a difference that will increase with time. In general, the work

Table 1.6 Main thematic areas

	Scopus				WoS			
Areas Scopus	Articles	% on/total	Journals	% on/total	Articles	% on/total	Journals	% on/total
Social sciences	95	43.38%	62	40.79%	23	8.58%	17	9.55%
Economics and finance	77	35.16%	50	32.89%	106	39.55%	65	36.52%
Business and management	22	10.05%	14	9.21%	22	8.21%	11	6.18%

Source: Own elaboration

Table 1.7 Classification of total articles according to the topic addressed

Topic	Authors
Reforms of *Public Pension Systems* (types, causes, consequences, case studies, etc.)	Abid and O'Donoghue (2014), Agudo and García (2010b, 2011), Arenas and Bertranou (1997), Aubert (2014), Babich and Beland (2009), Béland and Yu (2004), Béland and Waddan (2014), Booth (2013), Börsch-Supan (2005, 2015), Bütler (2000), Cashu (2000), Datz and Dancsi (2013), De Mesa and Mesa-Lago (2006), Diamond (2006), Díaz-Giménez and Díaz-Saavedra (2009), Ferreiro and Serrano (2011, 2012), Fletcher and Schipke (2007), French and Jones (2012), Gil et al. (2008), Gorgiladze and Gerzmava (2014), Güth et al. (2002), Hautzinger and Konanz (1979), He (2008), Hills (2006), Holzmann (1988), Horwitz and Horwitz (2014), Jaime-Castillo (2013), Karlström et al. (2011), Kato (1991), Kemmerling and Neugart (2009), Kincaid (1976), Liu (2000), Mantovani et al. (2006), Mesa-Lago (2002, 2009), Mierzejewski (2015), Miles and Iben (2000), Muller (2002), Nisticò and Bevilacqua (2013), Okamoto (2010), Pagán (2004), Peinado and Serrano (2012), Richardson and Seligman (2005), Sánchez-Martín (2010), Schnabel (2015), Schrenker (2009), Sefton et al. (2008), Škember (2005), Sundén (2006), Takayama (1995), Vidal-Melia (2014), Von Weizsäcker (1995), Withers (1976), Yoon and Talmain (2001)
Viability of *Public Pension Systems* (privatization, time and amount, financing, modalities: public, private, mixed, etc.)	Agudo and García (2010a), Aguirregabiria (2010), Anderson and Becker (1999), Asthana (2008), Augier et al. (1995), Aydede (2010), Bagchi (2015), Baker et al. (2004), Barba (2006), Bayar (2013), Boado-Penas et al. (2011), Booth and Niemietz (2014), Borgmann and Heidler (2007), Börsch-Supan (2000), Borsch-Supan and Reil-Held (2001), Brouchard and Garon (2014), Breyer (2010), Breyer and Kolmar (2002), Breyer and Hupfeld (2010), Brunetta and Cazzola (2003), Brunner (1996), Burtless et al. (2012), Bütler (2002b), Buziernescu et al. (2006), Chauveau and Loufir (1994), Choi and Hwang (2015), Cigno (2010), Cobo-Reyes and Díaz-Saavedra (2010), Cong et al. (2015), Crawford et al. (2014), Crossan et al. (2011), Disney and Whitehouse (1993), Domínguez-Fabián and Encinas-Goenechea (2008), Dowd (1987), Eagleton (1976), Ebbesen (1959), Farrar et al. (2012), Felderer (1992), Fenge and Von

(continued)

Table 1.7 (continued)

Topic	Authors
	Weizsäcker (2001, 2010a, 2010b), Fernandez et al. (2015), Foguel et al. (2012), Futagami et al. (2002), Giertz and Papke (2007), Han (2013), Hedesström et al. (2007), Hochman and Williamson (1995), Hofer and Koman (2006), Horioka (1999), Hoskins (1995), Hu and Manning (2010), Hupfeld (2009, 2011), Ippolito (1985), Iwasaki and Sato (2005), Jenkins (1993), Jensen et al. (1996), Jiménez-Ridruejo et al. (2009), Jinno (2008), Johnson (1999), Karlstrom et al. (2004), Kaskarelis (2009), Kennedy (1990), Kim and Klump (2010), Klinger et al. (2013), Kolmar (2001, 1997, 2007), Lambrecht et al. (2005), Lang (1990), Le Garrec (2012), Lechevalier (2003), Legendre et al. (2011), López Golpe and Reig Botella (2014), Lynch and Myrskylä (2009), Madrid (2005), Matkin and Chen (2015), Maurer et al. (2009), Mesa-Lago (2006), Metzger (2013), Michl (2006), Milligan and Schirle (2008), Milonas et al. (2009), Mitchell (1984), Moreno et al. (2010), Mumy (1985), Niggle (2003), Nikolova and Graham (2014), Nisticò (2013), Novy-Marx and Rauh (2014, 2011), Overbye (1998), Paddison (2007), Palme et al. (2007), Post et al. (2014), Preda and Grigoraş (2011), Rad (2014), Rajnes (2010), Ranerup and Norén (2015), Rangel and Saboia (2015), Reece and Sam (2012), Regúlez-Castillo and Vidal-Meliá (2012), Rürup (2002), Sabelhaus (1997), Sahin (1997), Salminen (1967), Schneider and Damanpour (2002), Scholten and Thum (1996), Scholtz (1989), Schwab (1995), Schwarz (1985), SeLdon (1994), Shao (2010), Simonovits (2015), St-Amant and Garon (2015), Stanovnik and Kukar (1995), Stanovnik et al. (2015), Takayama and Kitamura (2009), Van der Heijden et al. (1997), Van Dalen and van Praag (1993), Velkova (2008), Verbon (1988, 1987), Von Weizsacker (1989a, b), Wang and Davis (2003), Weise (1972), Willborn (1998), Williamson (2001), Yakymova (2013), Yang et al. (2012, 2010), Zuber et al. (2007)
Challenges faced by *Public Pension Systems* (ageing, immigration, economic crisis, etc.)	Anton Carp and Gorbe Persa (2010), Artu (2006), Beattie and McGillivray (1995), Bennett et al. (1998), Blake and Mayhew (2006), Bongaarts (2004), Booth (2008), Borgy and Chojnicki (2009), Bourdelais (1994), Breyer and Stolte (2001), Cabo and García-González

(continued)

Table 1.7 (continued)

Topic	Authors
	(2014), Carrière et al. (2015), Caselli et al. (2003), Chauveau and Loufir (1996), Demeny (2012), Du Granrut (2006), Foot and Venne (2005), Fritz (1981), Green (1997), Green and Riddell (1993), Haan and Prowse (2014), Heijdra and Romp (2009), Henrik (1998), Henripin (2009), Hills (2006), Hirte (1999), Hong and Lee (2012), Horioka et al. (2007), INGENUE Team (2002), Ishikawa (1988), Jensen and Nielsen (1991, 1993), Lacomba and Lagos (2010, 2007), Lassila and Valkonen (2008), Le Garrec (2015), Leibfritz (1996), MacKellar and Horlacher (2000), Miyazato (2010), Ong et al. (2013), Padilla (2011), Pecchenino and Pollard (2005), Peters (1991), Reynolds and Crimmins (2010), Rürup (1996), Sambt and Cok (2008), Sanderson and Scherbov (2010), Schneider (1998), Segu-í-Cosme (2015), Shaw (2002), Shelton (2008), Vanston (1998), Vásquez Colmenares (2013), Verbon (1990), Wise (2005), Zdravković et al. (2012)
Inequality in the Public Pension System due to gender issues	Bütler (2002a), Chen and Turner (2015), Dion (2006), Gonzalez-Rabanal (2012), Jankowski (2011), Pfaff (1981), Rosenberger (1991), Vara-Miranda (2013)

Source: Own elaboration

collected in Scopus receives a greater number of citations than WoS. However, there are articles with a high number of citations, which are only present in one of them. In both bases, *Population aging and the rising cost of public pensions* (Bongaarts 2004) is the most prominent article. Scopus is also the base that has a greater degree of singularity, that is, it contains a greater number of single articles, covering more than two-thirds of WoS articles. In addition, 20% of WoS's single documents give us the measure of the amount of information that would be lost if Scopus was chosen as the only bibliographic base.

On the one hand, a very high percentage of the authors of both bases are occasional (one authorship), resulting in very low average productivity close to 1.2, Verbon, H.A.A., with five articles is the most productive author. On the other hand, a collaboration index below 2 reflects the authors' limited willingness to work jointly. The data affiliation of the authors of articles related to *Public Pension Systems* show that the United States and Germany, followed by United Kingdom, Spain and Canada, are the main affiliation countries in both databases. As in other areas, universities are the centres to which a greater number of authors are affiliated.

With regard to publications, the *International Social Security Review*, the *Journal of Population Economics* and the *Journal of Pension Economics and Finance* are the leading journals that publish articles related to *Public Pension Systems*. With respect to the main thematic areas which the papers can be classified into, we see that the majority of the articles fall into three fundamental areas: social sciences, economics and finance, and business and management. The main issues discussed are those related to sustainability, reform and future challenges to be faced by *Public Pension Systems*: population ageing and immigration, privatization vs public systems or gender inequality.

To conclude, it is worth mentioning that although there is previous work, from 2005 there has been an increase in the number of articles indexed in WoS and Scopus, whose main objective is the sustainability and reform of *Public Pension Systems*. Both databases differ in terms of scope, data volume and coverage policies (Lopez-Illescas et al. 2008), although the documents and the results of their analysis are in many aspects similar. When comparing coverage in the area of *Public Pension Systems*, Scopus wins over WoS by collecting more journals, papers and signatures.

On the one hand, the results should be contextualized within the area of *Public Pension Systems*, taking into account the limitation of defining a specific search profile. On the other hand, the aim was not to carry out a quality analysis of the selected documents, an objective that could be raised in a subsequent investigation, but a descriptive-quantitative analysis. In order to expand the research, it would be interesting to extend the comparative study to other databases and perform an analysis of citations, such as those carried out in other areas of knowledge.

References

Abid, Y., & O'Donoghue, C. (2014). Irish citizens' attitudes to pension reform and redistribution. *Social Policy and Society, 13*(2), 203–220.

Agudo, L. F., & García, M. A. (2010a). The Republic of Ireland: A young country, but is it young enough to avoid future problems in public pensions? *Pensions: An International Journal, 15*(4), 259–267.

Agudo, L. F., & García, M. A. (2010b). The reform of some European public pension systems: Spain, Italy and Sweden: A breakthrough? *Pensions: An International Journal, 15*(4), 297–304.

Agudo, L. F., & García, M. A. (2011). Pension reform in Italy: Description and evaluation. *Pensions, 16*(2), 96–106.

Aguirregabiria, V. (2010). Another look at the identification of dynamic discrete decision processes: An application to retirement behavior. *Journal of Business & Economic Statistics, 28*(2), 201–218.

Alda-García, M. (2016). La última reforma del Sistema Público de Pensiones en España: de la ampliación a los 67 años al Factor de sostenibilidad. *Análisis Financiero, 130*, 62–77.

Alo, O. (2004). *Current pension reforms: Implications for career development in the public and private sectors*. A paper presented at the 2nd State Conference of the Lagos State Branch of the Chartered Institute of Personnel Management of Nigeria (CIPMN).

Anderson, K. H., & Becker, C. M. (1999). Post-soviet pension systems, retirement, and elderly poverty: findings from the Kyrgyz Republic. *MOCT-MOST: Economic Policy in Transitional Economies, 9*(4), 459–478.

Anton Carp, A., & Gorbe Persa, I. (2010). The ageing cost analysis in the Romanian social insurances' reform. *Metalurgia International, 15*, 95–99.

Arenas, A. D. M., & Bertranou, F. (1997). Learning from social security reforms: Two different cases, Chile and Argentina. *World Development, 25*(3), 329–348.
Artu, P. (2006). Ageing and the government budget deficit. *Retraite et Societe, 47*(1), 35–63.
Asthana, S. (2008). Earnings management, expected returns on pension assets, and resource allocation decisions. *Journal of Pension Economics & Finance, 7*(2), 199–220.
Aubert, P. (2014). The impact of French retirement reforms on the predictability of the amount of pension. *Revue D'economie Polilique, 124*(1), 1–21.
Augier, L., Chauveau, T., & Loupias, C. (1995). The role of the public pension system in a model of optimal-growth with overlapping generations. *Revue Economique, 46*(2), 195–215.
Aydede, Y. (2010). Expected social security wealth simulations and implicit rate of return calculations for the Turkish PAYG system. *Journal of Economic and Social Measurement, 35*(1, 2), 85–126.
Babich, K., & Beland, D. (2009). Policy change and the politics of ideas: The emergence of the Canada/Quebec pension plans. *Canadian Review of Sociology/Revue Canadienne de Sociologie, 46*(3), 253–271.
Bagchi, S. (2015). Labor supply and the optimality of Social Security. *Journal of Economic Dynamics and Control, 58*, 167–185.
Baker, A. J., Logue, D. E., & Rader, J. S. (2004). *Managing pension and retirement plans: A guide for employers, administrators, and other fiduciaries*. Oxford: Oxford University Press.
Bakkalbasi, N., Bauer, K., Glover, J., & Wang, L. (2006). Three options for citation tracking: Google Scholar, Scopus and Web of Science. *BMC Biomedical Digital Libraries, 3*(7), 1–8. Available in: http://www.bio-diglib.com/content/pdf/1742-5581-3-1.pdf.
Barba, A. (2006). Viability of pay-as-you-go pension systems: a demand side perspective. *Review of Political Economy, 18*(3), 413–425.
Bayar, Y. (2013). Financial sustainability of pension systems in the European Union. *European Research Studies, 16*(3), 43–60.
Bearman, T. C., & Kunberger, W. A. (1977). *A study of coverage overlap among fourteen major science and technology abstracting and indexing services*. Philadelphia: National Federation of Abstracting and Indexing Services.
Beattie, R., & McGillivray, W. (1995). A risky strategy: Reflections on the World Bank Report averting the old age crisis. *International Social Security Review, 48*(3–4), 5–22.
Béland, D., & Waddan, A. (2014). Policy change in flat pensions: Comparing Canada and the UK. *Canadian Public Administration, 57*(3), 383–400.
Béland, D., & Yu, K. M. (2004). A long financial march: pension reform in China. *Journal of Social Policy, 33*(2), 267–288.
Benavides-Velasco, C. A., Guzmán-Parra, V., & Quintana-García, C. (2011). Evolución de la literatura sobre empresa familiar como disciplina científica. *Cuadernos de Economía y Dirección de la Empresa, 14*(2), 78–90.
Bennett, N. G., Bloom, D. E., & Ivanov, S. F. (1998). Demographic implications of the Russian mortality crisis. *World Development, 26*(11), 1921–1937.
Bettio, F., Tinios, P., & Betti, G. (2013). *The gender gap in pensions in the EU*. Online: http://ec.europa.eu/justice/gender-equality/files/documents/130530_pensions_en.pdf. Accessed 22 Dec 2016.
Blake, D., & Mayhew, L. (2006). On the sustainability of the UK state pension system in the light of population ageing and declining fertility. *The Economic Journal, 116*(512), 286–305.
Boado-Penas, M. D. C., Settergren, O., & Vidal-Meliá, C. (2011). El balance actuarial del sistema de reparto. Modelo 'sueco'frente a modelo 'EE. UU.': posible aplicación al caso español. *Spanish Journal of Finance and Accounting/Revista Española de Financiación y Contabilidad, 40*(149), 97–123.
Boeri, T., & Tabellini, G. (2005). *Does information increase political support for pension reform?* Discussion Paper (vol. 5319). London: Centre for Economic Policy Research.
Boeri, T., Borsch-Supan, A., & Tabellini, G. (2002). Pension reforms and the opinions of European citizens. *American Economic Review, 92*, 396–401.

Bongaarts, J. (2004). Population aging and the rising cost of public pensions. *Population and Development Review, 30*(1), 1–23.

Bonoli, G. (2003). Two worlds of pension reform in Western Europe. *Comparative Politics, 35*(4), 399–416.

Booth, P. (2008). The young held to ransom–a public choice analysis of the UK state pension system. *Economic Affairs, 28*(1), 4–10.

Booth, P. (2013). State pension reform in a public choice framework. *North American Actuarial Journal, 17*(1), 82–97.

Booth, P., & Niemietz, K. (2014). *Growing the UK pension pot: The case for privatisation*. IEA, London, UK, Institute of Economic Affairs.

Borgmann, C., & Heidler, M. (2007). Volatility of social security wealth: Political risks of benefit-rule changes in Germany. *FinanzArchiv: Public Finance Analysis, 63*(1), 83–106.

Borgy, V., & Chojnicki, X. (2009). Labor migration: macroeconomic and demographic outlook for Europe and neighborhood regions. *Economie Internationale, 3*, 115–153.

Börsch-Supan, A. (2000). Incentive effects of social security on labor force participation: evidence in Germany and across Europe. *Journal of Public Economics, 78*(1), 25–49.

Börsch-Supan, A. (2005). *The 2005 pension reform in Finland*. Finnish Centre for Pensions, Working Papers 2005:1.

Börsch-Supan, A. (2015). Lessons learned from the 1972 pension reform. *Wir Tschaftsdienst, 95* (1), 16–21.

Borsch-Supan, A., & Reil-Held, A. (2001). How much is transfer and how much is insurance in a pay-as-you-go system? The German Case. *The Scandinavian Journal of Economics, 103*(3), 505–524.

Bost, W. E. (1968). Test of abstracts journals. *Journal of Documentation, 24*(1), 61.

Bourdelais, P. (1994). The young, the elderly and retirement the french state pension system and the issue of an aging population in historical-perspective. *Histoire, 1*(176), 74–75.

Bourne, C. P., Kasson, M. S., & North, J. B. (1969). *Overlappig coverage of bibliography of agricultura by fifteen other secondary sources*. USA: Goverment Research and Develpment Report, Bradford.

Bradford, S. C. (1934). Sources of information on specific subjects. *Engineering, 137*, 85–86.

Breyer, F. (2010). Rentenversicherung zwischen Nachhaltigkeit und Gerechtigkeit. *Zeitschrift Für Die Gesamte Versicherungswissenschaft, 99*(5), 569–583.

Breyer, F., & Hupfeld, S. (2010). On the fairness of early-retirement provisions. *German Economic Review, 11*(1), 60–77.

Breyer, F., & Kolmar, M. (2002). Are national pension systems efficient if labor is (im) perfectly mobile? *Journal of Public Economics, 83*(3), 347–374.

Breyer, F., & Stolte, K. (2001). Demographic change, endogenous labor supply and the political feasibility of pension reform. *Journal of Population Economics, 14*, 409–424.

Brouchard, P. A., & Garon, J. D. (2014). Optimal redistributive pensions with temptation and costly self-control. In *International Tax and Public Finance forthcoming*, (No. 1311). Department of Economics, Queen's University.

Brunetta, R., & Cazzola, G. (2003). *Nota per una "Maastricht delle pensioni"*. Work in progress per il semestre di presidenza italiana dell'Unione europea.

Brunner, J. K. (1996). Transition from a pay-as-you-go to a fully funded pension system: the case of differing individuals and intragenerational fairness. *Journal of Public Economics, 60*(1), 131–146.

Burtless, G., Whitehouse, E., & Toft, C. (2012). *Pension reform, retirement ages, and labour supply in the United States and the European Union (EU15) 1950-2060*. Working Paper, University of Kassell.

Bütler, M. (2000). The political feasibility of pension reform options: the case of Switzerland. *Journal of Public Economics, 75*(3), 389–416.

Bütler, M. (2002a). The political feasibility of increasing the retirement age: lessons from a ballot on the female retirement age. *International Tax and Public Finance, 9*(4), 349–365.

Bütler, M. (2002b). Tax–benefit linkages in pension systems: a note. *Journal of Public Economic Theory, 4*(3), 405–415.
Buziernescu, R., Drăcea, R., & Burnea, R. (2006). *Tax havens between theory and practice.* "Finance, Banking and Insurance", no. 12 December 2006.
Cabo, F., & García-González, A. (2014). The endogenous determination of retirement age and social security benefits. *Macroeconomic Dynamics, 18*(1), 93–113.
Carrière, Y., Légaré, J., Léger St-Cyr, M., Ronteix, C., & Diaconu, V. (2015). Policy brief no. 21-an increasing age at retirement may amplify socioeconomic inequalities. *Population Change and Lifecourse Strategic Knowledge Cluster Research/Policy Brief, 1*(6), 6.
Caselli, G., Peracchi, F., Barbi, E., & Lipsi, R. M. (2003). Differential mortality and the design of the Italian system of public pensions. *Labour, 17*(s1), 45–78.
Cashu, I. (2000). The politics and policy trade-offs of reforming the public pension system in post-communist Moldova. *Europe-Asia Studies, 52*(4), 741–757.
Chauveau, T., & Loufir, R. (1994). Demographic transition and social security policies in France: a welfare analysis. OFCE Working Paper No. 94.2. In J. Janssen, C. H. Skiadas, & C. Zopounidis (Eds.), *Advances in stochastic modelling and data analysis*. Amsterdam: Kluwer.
Chauveau, T., & Loufir, R. (1996). The future of public pensions in Japan. *Keio Economic Studies, 33*, 71–92.
Chen, T., & Turner, J. A. (2015). Fragmentation in social security old-age benefit provision in China. *Journal of Aging & Social Policy, 27*(2), 107–122.
Choi, R., & Hwang, B. D. (2015). Influence factors on health and medical of retirees expense to public pension recipients. *Health Policy and Management, 25*(2), 80–89.
Cigno, A. (2010). How to avoid a pension crisis: a question of intelligent system design. *CESifo Economic Studies, 56*(1), 21–37.
Cobo-Reyes, R., & Díaz-Saavedra, J. (2010). La percepción de los trabajadores de la normativa del sistema público de pensiones. El caso español. *Revista Internacional de Sociología, 68*(3), 775–795.
Cong, Y., Frank, H. A., Gianakis, G., & Guo, H. (2015). Critical issues in the transition from the defined benefit to the defined contribution pension model: Perceptions from Florida Municipal Finance and Human Resource Directors. *Review of Public Personnel Administration, 35*(4), 333–351.
Corral, J. A., & Cànoves, G. (2013). La investigación turística publicada en revistas turísticas y no turísticas: análisis bibliométrico de la producción de las universidades catalanas. *Cuadernos de Turismo, 31*(1), 55–81.
Costas, R., Moreno, L., & Bordons, M. (2008). Solapamiento y singularidad de MEDLINE, WoS e IME para el análisis de la actividad científica en una región en Ciencias de la Salud. *Revista Española de Documentación Científica, 31*(3), 327–343.
Crawford, R., Keynes, S., & Tetlow, G. (2014). *From me to you? How the UK state pension system redistributes (No. W14/20).* IFS Working Papers.
Crossan, D., Feslier, D., & Hurnard, R. (2011). Financial literacy and retirement planning in New Zealand. *Journal of Pension Economics & Finance, 10*(4), 619–635.
Dahl, S. A., Nilsen, O. A., & Vaage, K. (2003). Gender differences in early retirement behaviour. *European Sociological Review, 19*, 179–198.
Datz, G., & Dancsi, K. (2013). The politics of pension reform reversal: a comparative analysis of Hungary and Argentina. *East European Politics, 29*(1), 83–100.
De Mesa, A. A., & Mesa-Lago, C. (2006). The structural pension reform in Chile: Effects, comparisons with other Latin American reforms, and lessons. *Oxford Review of Economic Policy, 22*(1), 149–167.
Demeny, P. (2012). Geopolitical aspects of population in the twenty-first century. *Population and Development Review, 38*(4), 685–705.
Diamond, P. A. (2006). The public pension reform debate in the United States and international experience. *Risk Management and Insurance Review, 9*(1), 9–35.

Díaz-Giménez, J., & Díaz-Saavedra, J. (2009). Delaying retirement in Spain. *Review of Economic Dynamics, 12*(1), 147–167.

Dion, M. (2006). Globalización, tipo de régimen político y gasto social en países de ingresos medios, 1980-1999. *Política y Gobierno, 13*(1), 11–49.

Disney, R., & Whitehouse, E. (1993). The earnings-related state pension, indexation and lifetime redistribution in the uk. *Review of Income and Wealth, 39*(3), 257–278.

Domínguez-Fabián, I., & Encinas-Goenechea, B. (2008). Inmigración y solvencia financiera del sistema público de pensiones tras la regularización de 2005. *Revista de Economía Aplicada, 16* (1).

Dowd, J. J. (1987). Justice in old age: An analysis of corporatist social theory. *Social Justice Research, 1*(4), 477–499.

Du Granrut, C. (2006). Le système de retraite aux États-Unis: l'heure de vérité? *Futuribles-Paris, 316*, 21.

Duval, R. (2003). *The retirement effects of old-age pension and early retirement schemes in OECD countries*. Economics Department Working Paper 370. OECD.

Eagleton, T. (1976). Runaway public pension systems. In *Conference board record* (vol. 13, no. 4, pp. 22–24). New York: Conference Board Inc.

Ebbesen, S. (1959). General rules for public pension systems. *Maanedsskrift for Praktisk Lægegerning og Social Medicin, 37*(2), 81.

Escalona, M. I., Lagar, P., & Pulgarín, A. (2010). Web of Science vs. Scopus: un estudio cuantitativo en Ingeniería Química. *Anales de Documentación, 13*, 159–175.

Even, W. E., & Macpherson, D. A. (2004). When will the gender gap in retirement income narrow? *Southern Economical Journal, 71*, 182–200.

Farrar, S., Moizer, J., & Hyde, M. (2012). The value of incentives to defer the UK state pension. *Pensions: An International Journal, 17*(1), 46–62.

Felderer, B. (1992). Does a public pension system reduce savings rates and birth rates? *Journal of Institutional and Theoretical Economics (JITE)/Zeitschrift für die gesamte Staatswissenschaft, 148*, 314–325.

Fenge, R., & Von Weizsäcker, J. (2001). Compulsory savings: Efficiency and redistribution on the interaction of means tested basic income and public pensions. *International Tax and Public Finance, 8*(4), 637–652.

Fenge, R., & Von Weizsäcker, J. (2010a). Mixing Bismarck and child pension systems: an optimum taxation approach. *Journal of Population Economics, 23*(2), 805–823.

Fenge, R., & Von Weizsäcker, J. (2010b). Public pension systems and distortions of intra-EU mobility: the Lodge Test. *Journal of Pension Economics & Finance, 9*(2), 263–275.

Fernandez, P., Ortiz Pizarro, A., Fernandez Acin, P., & Fernández Acín, I. (2015). *Rentabilidad De Los Fondos De Pensiones En España. 1999-2014 (Return of Pension Funds in Spain. 1999-2014).*

Ferreiro, J., & Serrano, F. (2011). Uncertainty and pension systems reforms. *Journal of Economic Issues, 45*(2), 317–322.

Ferreiro, J., & Serrano, F. (2012). Expectations, uncertainty and institutions. An application to the analysis of social security reforms. *International Review of Applied Economics, 26*(2), 253–266.

Fingerman, S. (2006). Web of science and scopus: current features and capabilities. *Issues in Science and Technology Librarianship, 48*. Online: http://www.istl.org/06fall/electronic2.html. Accessed 8 Jan 2017.

Finke, R., & Sabatini, M. (2016). *Pension sustainability index 2016*. Germany: Allianz SE, Munich.

Fletcher, K., & Schipke, A. (2007). *Pension reform*. Occasional paper-international monetary fund, 257, 23.

Foguel, M. N., Moreira, A., & Santos, D. (2012). Impacto do Plano Simplificado de Previdência Social sobre as contribuições voluntárias ao sistema de previdência. *Estudos Econômicos (São Paulo), 42*(4), 639–669.

Foot, D. K., & Venne, R. A. (2005). Awakening to the intergenerational equity debate in Canada. *Journal of Canadian Studies, 39*(1), 5–22.

French, E., & Jones, J. (2012). Public pensions and labor supply over the life cycle. *International Tax and Public Finance, 19*(2), 268–287.
Fritz, D. (1981). The growing challenges of providing pensions to state and local civil servants in an aging society. *International Journal of Public Administration, 3*(4), 405–422.
Futagami, R., Kamada, K., & Tachibanaki, T. (2002). Income redistribution effect of public pensions between dynastic families. *Review of Income and Wealth, 48*(2), 235–244.
Gavel, Y., & Iselid, L. (2008). Web of Science and Scopus: a journal title overlap study. *Online Information Review, 32*(1), 8–21.
Giertz, J. F., & Papke, L. E. (2007). Public pension plans: Myths and realities for state budgets. *National Tax Journal, 60*, 305–323.
Gil, J., Lopez-Garcia, M. A., Onrubia, J., Patxot, C., & Souto, G. (2008). A projection model of the contributory pension expenditure of the spanish social security system: 2004-50. *Hacienda Pública Española, 3*(182), 75–114.
Gluck, M. (1990). A review of journal coverage overlap with an extension to the definition of overlap. *Journal of the American Society for Information Science, 41*(1), 43–60.
Goldin, C. (1993). *Gender gap. The concise Encyclopedia of economics, library of economics and liberty*. http://www.econlib.org/library/Enc1/GenderGap.html. Accessed 15 December 2016.
Gonzalez-Rabanal, M. D. L. C. (2012). Is it possible to avoid gender discrimination in employment pension plans and funds? *International Journal of Interdisciplinary Social Sciences, 6*(8), 114–124.
Goodman, D., & Deis, L. (2005). Web of science (2004 version) and scopus. *The Charleston Advisor, 6*(3), 5–21.
Goodman, D., & Deis, L. (2007). Update on scopus and web of science. *The Charleston Advisor, 7* (3), 15–18.
Gorgiladze, L., & Gerzmava, O. (2014). Problems of reforming pension schemes of the Georgian population. *Georgian Medical News, 237*, 84–92.
Green, D. (1997). Pensions, class and capital: An international perspective. *Review of Radical Political Economics, 29*(3), 144–155.
Green, D. A., & Riddell, W. C. (1993). The economic-effects of unemployment-insurance in Canada - an empirical-analysis of UI disentitlement. *Journal of Labor Economics, 11*(1), 96–147.
Gruber, J., & Wise, D. A. (1999). Introduction and summary. In J. Gruber & D. A. Wise (Eds.), *Social security and retirement around the World* (pp. 1–35). Chicago: University of Chicago Press.
Gruber, J., & Wise, D. A. (2004). Introduction and summary. In J. Gruber & D. A. Wise (Eds.), *Social security programs and retirement around the world: Micro-estimation* (pp. 1–35). Chicago: University of Chicago Press.
Gruber, J., & Wise, D. A. (2005). *Social security programs and retirement around the world: Fiscal implications*. Working Paper 11290. Cambridge: NBER.
Güth, W., Offerman, T., Potters, J., Strobel, M., & Verbon, H. A. (2002). Are family transfers crowded out by public transfers? *The Scandinavian Journal of Economics, 104*(4), 587–604.
Haan, P., & Prowse, V. (2014). Longevity, life-cycle behavior and pension reform. *Journal of Econometrics, 178*, 582–601.
Han, K. J. (2013). Saving public pensions: Labor migration effects on pension systems in European countries. *Social Science Journal, 50*(2), 152–161.
Hautzinger, H., & Konanz, W. (1979). Ein dynamisches Simulationsmodell der langfristigen Rentenfinanzierung. *Zeitschrift für Operations Research, 23*(8), B221–B245.
He, L. (2008). The distributional effects of public pension reform in urban China. *Frontiers of Economics in China, 3*(2), 255–276.
Hedesström, T. M., Svedsäter, H., & Gärling, T. (2007). Determinants of the use of heuristic choice rules in the Swedish Premium Pension Scheme: An internet-based survey. *Journal of Economic Psychology, 28*(1), 113–126.

Heijdra, B. J., & Romp, W. E. (2009). Retirement, pensions, and ageing. *Journal of Public Economics, 93*(3–4), 586–604.
Henrik, J. (1998). Recent research on public pension systems. A review. *Labour Economics, 5*(1), 91–108.
Henripin, J. (2009). Aging and the necessity of a radical reform of the Canadian Pension System. *Canadian Studies in Population, 36*(1–2), 17–36.
Hills, J. (2006). A new pension settlement for the twenty-first century? The UK Pensions Commission's analysis and proposals. *Oxford Review of Economic Policy, 22*(1), 113–132.
Hirte, G. (1999). Raising the retirement age–Why should anybody lose?/Anhebung des Rentenzugangsalters–Muss es Verlierer geben? *Jahrbücher für Nationalökonomie und Statistik, 219*(3–4), 393–408.
Hochman, G., & Williamson, I. B. (1995). The Brazilian public pension system: Policy changes, political effects. *International Social Security Review, 48*(2), 31–47.
Hofer, H., & Koman, R. (2006). Social security and retirement incentives in Austria. *Empirica, 33* (5), 285–313.
Holzmann, R. (1988). Ageing and social-security costs. *European Journal of Population/Revue européenne de Démographie, 3*(3), 411–437.
Hong, J., & Lee, K. (2012). The aging work force in Korea. *International Archives of Occupational and Environmental Health, 85*(3), 253–260.
Horioka, C. Y. (1999). Japan's public pension system: What's wrong with it and how to fix it. *Japan and the World Economy, 11*(2), 293–303.
Horioka, C. Y., Suzuki, W., & Hatta, T. (2007). Aging, savings, and public pensions in Japan. *Asian Economic Policy Review, 2*(2), 303–319.
Horwitz, A., & Horwitz, H. (2014). Politics and policies. *Journal of Insurance Medicine (New York, NY), 44*(1), 49–52.
Hoskins, D. D. (1995). In defense of public pension systems. *Ageing International, 22*(2), 23–26.
Hu, A., & Manning, P. (2010). The global social insurance movement since the 1880s. *Journal of Global History, 5*(1), 125–148.
Hupfeld, S. (2009). Rich and healthy—better than poor and sick?: An empirical analysis of income, health, and the duration of the pension benefit spell. *Journal of Health Economics, 28*(2), 427–443.
Hupfeld, S. (2011). Non-monotonicity in the longevity–income relationship. *Journal of Population Economics, 24*(1), 191–211.
INGENUE Team. (2002). A long—term model for the world economy. In *Market imperfections and macroeconomic dynamics* (pp. 51–73). Springer US, Berlin, Germany.
Ippolito, R. A. (1985). The labor contract and true economic pension liabilities. *The American Economic Review, 75*(5), 1031–1043.
Ishikawa, T. (1988). Saving and labor supply behavior of aged households in Japan. *Journal of the Japanese and International Economies, 2*(4), 417–449.
Iwasaki, I., & Sato, K. (2005). Private pension funds in Hungary. *Acta Oeconomica, 55*(3), 287–315.
Jaime-Castillo, A. M. (2013). Public opinion and the reform of the pension systems in Europe: the influence of solidarity principles. *Journal of European Social Policy, 23*(4), 390–405.
Jankowski, J. (2011). Caregiver credits in France, Germany, and Sweden: lessons for the United States. *Social Security Bulletin, 71*, 61–76.
Janky, B., & Gal, R. I. (2007). *Public opinion on pension systems in Europe*. European Network of Economic Policy Research Institutes Research Report, No. 36.
Jefferson, T. (2009). Women and retirement pensions: A research review. *Feminist Economics, 15* (4), 115–145.
Jenkins, M. (1993). Extending social security protection to the entire population: Problems and issues. *International Social Security Review, 46*(2), 3–20.
Jensen, S. H., & Nielsen, S. B. (1991). Population aging in a small open economy with a public pension system. *Nationalokonomisk Tidsskrift, 129*(3), 288–302.

Jensen, S. E., & Nielsen, S. B. (1993). Aging, intergenerational distribution and public pension systems. *Public finance/Finances publiques, 48*, 29–42.
Jensen, S. E. H., Nielsen, S. B., Pedersen, L. H., & Sørensen, P. B. (1996). Tax policy, housing and the labour market: An intertemporal simulation approach. *Economic Modelling, 13*(3), 355–382.
Jiménez-Ridruejo, A. Z., Arribas, C. B., Díaz, J. L., Lago, C. L., & Sumaza, C. R. (2009). El efecto de la inmigración en la sostenibilidad a largo plazo del sistema de pensiones en España. *Hacienda Pública Española, 188*(1), 74–121.
Jinno, M. (2008). Is it beneficial for households without children to subsidy the cost of rearing children to increase pension benefits? *Economics Bulletin, 8*(9), 1–7.
Johnson, R. W. (1999). *The gender gap in pension wealth: Is women's progress in the labor market equalizing benefits? Brief series 1, Retirement Project.* Washington, DC: Urban Institute.
Karlstrom, A., Palme, M., & Svensson, I. (2004). A dynamic programming approach to model the retirement behaviour of blue-collar workers in Sweden. *Journal of Applied Econometrics, 19*(6), 795–807.
Karlström, A., Palme, M., & Svensson, I. (2011). Assessing the welfare change from a pension reform. *International Tax and Public Finance, 18*(6), 634–657.
Kaskarelis, I. A. (2009). On state pensions and social security systems. *Foresight, 11*(1), 5–8.
Kato, J. (1991). Public pension reforms in the United States and Japan: a study of comparative public policy. *Comparative Political Studies, 24*(1), 100–126.
Kemmerling, A., & Neugart, M. (2009). Financial market lobbies and pension reform. *European Journal of Political Economy, 25*(2), 163–173.
Kennedy, B. R. (1990). Financial consistency in longitudinal microsimulation: homemaker pensions re-examined. *Review of Income and Wealth, 36*(2), 215–221.
Kim, S., & Klump, R. (2010). The effects of public pensions on private wealth: evidence on the German savings puzzle. *Applied Economics, 42*(15), 1917–1926.
Kincaid, J. (1976). Recent developments in British pensions. *Industrial Gerontology, 3*(1), 41–56.
Klinger, S., Bonin, H., Horn, G. A., HerzogStein, A., Ehing, D., & Raffelhüschen, B. (2013). Erwerbstätigkeit auf Rekordniveau – Ergebnis richtiger Arbeitsmarktpolitik? *Wirtschaftsdienst, 93*(3), 143–158.
Kolmar, M. (1997). Intergenerational redistribution in a small open economy with endogenous fertility. *Journal of Population Economics, 10*(3), 335–356.
Kolmar, M. (2001). Optimal intergenerational redistribution in a two-country model with endogenous fertility. *Public Choice, 106*(1), 23–51.
Kolmar, M. (2007). Beveridge versus Bismarck public-pension systems in integrated markets. *Regional Science and Urban Economics, 37*(6), 649–669.
Lacomba, J. A., & Lagos, F. M. (2007). Political election on legal retirement age. *Social Choice and Welfare, 29*(1), 1–17.
Lacomba, J. A., & Lagos, F. (2010). Immigration and pension benefits in the host country. *Economica, 77*(306), 283–295.
Lambrecht, S., Michel, P., & Vidal, J. P. (2005). Public pensions and growth. *European Economic Review, 49*(5), 1261–1281.
Lang, G. (1990). Intergenerational contracts and their decomposition: An extension. *Journal of Economics, 52*(2), 177–189.
Lassila, J., & Valkonen, T. (2008). *Suomen työeläkejärjestelmän stokastinen kedtävyysanalyysi (No. 1137).* ETLA discussion paper.
Le Garrec, G. (2012). Social security, income inequality and growth. *Journal of Pension Economics & Finance, 11*(1), 53–70.
Le Garrec, G. (2015). Increased longevity and social security reform: questioning the optimality of individual accounts when education matters. *Journal of Population Economics, 28*(2), 329–352.
Lechevalier, A. (2003). The dynamics of the federal and social pact in Germany. *Sociétés Contemporaines, 3*, 33–56.

Legendre, B., Mage, S., Briard, K., Duc, C., & de Freitas, N. E. M. (2011). Aléas de carrière et pension de retraite. *Economie et Statistique, 441*(1), 145–158.
Leibfritz, W. (1996). Generational accounting: an international comparison. *Intereconomics, 31*(2), 55–61.
Liu, L. (2000). Public pension reform in Japan. *Social Security Bulletin, 63*, 99.
López Golpe, J., & Reig Botella, A. (2014). El sistema público de pensiones. *Revista Galega de Economía, 23*(1), 115–135.
Lopez-Illescas, C., Moya-Anegon, F., & Moed, H. F. (2008). Coverage and citation impact of oncological journals in the web of science and scopus. *Journal of Informetrics, 2*(4), 304–316.
Lynch, J., & Myrskylä, M. (2009). Always the third rail? Pension income and policy preferences in European democracies. *Comparative Political Studies, 42*(8), 1068–1097.
MacKellar, L., & Horlacher, D. (2000). Population ageing in Japan: A brief survey. *Innovation: The European Journal of Social Science Research, 13*(4), 413–430.
Madrid, R. L. (2005). Ideas, economic pressures, and pension privatization. *Latin American Politics and Society, 47*(2), 23–50.
Maltrás-Barba, B. (2003). *Los indicadores bibliométricos: Fundamentos y aplicación al análisis de la ciencia*. Asturias: Trea.
Mantovani, D., Papadopoulos, F., Sutherland, H., & Tsakloglou, P. (2006). Pension incomes in the European Union: policy reform strategies in comparative perspective. In *Micro-simulation in action* (pp. 27–71). Emerald Group Publishing Limited, Bingley, United Kingdom.
Marin, B., & Zólyomi, E. (Eds.). (2010). *Women's work and pensions: what is good, what is best?* Vienna: Ashgate.
Martyn, J. (1967). Tests on abstracts journals: coverage overlap and indexing. *Journal of Documentation, 23*(1), 45–70.
Martyn, J., & Slater, M. (1964). Tests on abstracts journals. *Journal of Documentation, 20*(4), 212–235.
Matkin, D. S., & Chen, G. (2015). The consolidation of state-administered public pension systems in Us states. *Journal of Public Budgeting, Accounting & Financial Management, 27*(4), 455.
Maurer, R., Mitchell, O. S., & Rogalla, R. (2009). Reforming the German civil servant pension plan. In Mitchell, O.S. & Anderson, G. (eds.), *The future of public employee retirement systems*, pp. 115–142. New York: Oxford University Press.
Mesa-Lago, C. (2002). Myth and reality of pension reform: the Latin American evidence. *World Development, 30*(8), 1309–1321.
Mesa-Lago, C. (2006). Private and public pension systems compared: An evaluation of the Latin American experience. *Review of Political Economy, 18*(3), 317–334.
Mesa-Lago, C. (2009). *Efectos de la crisis global sobre la seguridad social de salud y pensiones en América Latina y el Caribe y recomendaciones de políticas*. CEPAL, Santiago de Chile, Chile.
Metzger, S. (2013). Making sausage no one wants to eat: Options for restructuring Illinois's pension debt. *University of Illinois Law Review, 2013*, 1251.
Meyer, D. E., Mehlman, D. W., Reeves, E. S., Origoni, R. B., Evans, D., & Sellers, D. W. (1983). Comparison study of overlap among 21 scientific databases in searching pesticide information. *ERIC Online Review, 7*(1), 33–43.
Michl, T. R. (2006). Comments on Cesaratto's 'Transition to fully funded pension schemes: a non-orthodox criticism'. *Cambridge Journal of Economics, 30*(6), 981–984.
Mierzejewski, A. C. (2015). Paradigm shift: the reform of the German Public Pension System in 2001. *Journal of Policy History, 27*(4), 695–721.
Miles, D., & Iben, A. (2000). The reform of pension systems: Winners and losers across generations in the United Kingdom and Germany. *Economica, 67*(266), 203–228.
Milligan, K., & Schirle, T. (2008). Working while receiving a pension: Will double dipping change the elderly labour market? In Abbott (ed.), *Retirement Policy Issues in Canada*, 337–352. Bloomington, United States.
Milonas, N. T., Papachristou, G. A., & Roupas, T. A. (2009). Fund management and its effect in the Greek social security system. *Journal of Pension Economics & Finance, 8*(4), 485–500.

Mingers, J., & Lipitakis, E. (2010). Counting the citations; a comparison of *Web of Science* and *Google Scholar* in the field of business and management. *Scientometrics, 85*(2), 613–625.

Mitchell, O. S. (1984). Financial aspects of the United-States Pension System-Bodie, Z, Shoven, Jb. *Journal of Economic Literature, 22*(4), 1677–1678.

Miyazato, N. (2010). The optimal size of Japan's public pensions: An analysis considering the risks of longevity and volatility of return on assets. *Japan and the World Economy, 22*(1), 31–39.

Monticone, C., Ruzik, A., & Skiba, J. (2008). *Women's pension rights and survivor's benefits. A comparative analysis of EU members states and candidate countries*. ENEPRI Research Report, NO. 53.

Moreno, R., Martín, Á., & Ortiz, F. (2010). Political economy of the reform of the Colombian pension system. *Revista de Economía Institucional, 12*(22), 167–192.

Muller, K. (2002). Beyond privatization: Pension reform in the Czech Republic and Slovenia. *Journal of European Social Policy, 12*(4), 293–306.

Mumy, G. E. (1985). The role of taxes and social security in determining the structure of wages and pensions. *Journal of Political Economy, 93*(3), 574–585.

Neuhaus, C., & Daniel, H. D. (2008). Data sources for performing citation analysis: An overview. *Journal of Documentation, 64*(2), 193–210.

Niggle, C. (2003). Globalization, neoliberalism and the attack on social security. *Review of Social Economy, 61*(1), 51–71.

Nikolova, M., & Graham, C. (2014). Employment, late-life work, retirement, and well-being in Europe and the United States. *IZA Journal of European Labor Studies, 3*(1), 5.

Nisticò, S. (2013). Financing pay-as-you-go public pension systems: some notes in the light of the classical-type theory of income distribution. *Review of Political Economy, 25*(3), 426–443.

Nisticò, S., & Bevilacqua, M. (2013). Notional defined contribution (NDC) pension schemes and income patterns. *Economics: The Open-Access, Open-Assessment E-Journal, 7*(2013–29), 1–24.

Norris, M., & Oppenheim, C. (2007). Comparing alternatives to the Web of Science for coverage of the social sciences' literature. *Journal of Infometrics, 1*(2), 161–169.

Novy-Marx, R., & Rauh, J. D. (2011). Policy options for state pension systems and their impact on plan liabilities. *Journal of Pension Economics & Finance, 10*(2), 173–194.

Novy-Marx, R., & Rauh, J. D. (2014). Linking benefits to investment performance in US public pension systems. *Journal of Public Economics, 116*, 47–61.

OECD. (2016). *Society at a glance 2016: OECD social indicators*. Paris: OECD Publishing. https://doi.org/10.1787/9789264261488-en.

Okamoto, A. (2010). Public pension reform in Japan. *Economic Analysis and Policy, 40*(2), 179–208.

Ong, R., Jefferson, T., Wood, G., Haffner, M., & Austen, S. (2013). *Housing equity withdrawal: uses, risks, and barriers to alternative mechanisms in later life.* Australian Housing and Urban Research Institute Final Report Series, 153, pp. 1–92.

Overbye, E. (1998). The politics of voluntary and mandatory pensions in the Nordic countries. *Labour, 12*(1), 169–189.

Paddison, O. (2007). Social protection in the English-speaking Caribbean. *CEPAL Review, 2007*, 101.

Padilla, J. M. (2011). Comentario a la jurisprudencia sobre el tope de pensiones del imss a 10 smdf. *Revista Latinoamericana de Derecho Social*, (12), 193–206.

Pagán, J. A. (2004). Reformas al sistema de seguridad social y el mercado laboral en los Estados Unidos y Canadá. *El Trimestre Económico, 71*(284), 943–962.

Palme, M., Sundén, A., & Söderlind, P. (2007). How do individual accounts work in the Swedish pension system? *Journal of the European Economic Association, 5*(2–3), 636–646.

Pao, M. L. (1993). Term and citation retrieval: A field study. *Information Processing and Management, 29*(1), 95–112.

Pecchenino, R. A., & Pollard, P. S. (2005). Aging, myopia, and the pay-as-you-go public pension systems of the G7: A bright future? *Journal of Public Economic Theory, 7*(3), 449–470.

Peinado, P., & Serrano, F. (2012). A dynamic analysis of the effects on pensioners' welfare of social security reforms. *Journal of Pension Economics & Finance, 11*(1), 71–87.
Peters, W. (1991). Public pensions in transition. *Journal of Population Economics, 4*(2), 155–175.
Pfaff, A. B. (1981). Income as a condition of self care in the aged. *Zeitschrift für Gerontologie, 15*(3), 158–167.
Post, T., Gründl, H., Schmit, J. T., & Zimmer, A. (2014). The impact of investment behaviour for individual welfare. *Economica, 81*(321), 15–47.
Poyer, R. K. (1984). Journal article overlap among index medicus, science citation index, biological abstracts, and chemical abstracts. *Bulletin of the Medical Library Association, 72*(4), 353–357.
Preda, M., & Grigoraş, V. (2011). The public pension system in Romania: Myths and facts. *Transylvanian Review of Administrative Sciences, 7*(32), 235–251.
Pulgarín, A., & Escalona, M. A. (2007). Medida del solapamiento en tres bases de datos con información sobre Ingeniería. *Anales de Documentación, 10*, 335–344.
Rad, N. S. (2014). Conceptualization of a demographically stable model of the pension system and economic activity of third age' people: interaction context. *Проблеми економіки, 3*, 151–158.
Rajnes, D. (2010). Permanent disability social insurance programs in Japan. *Social Security Bulletin, 70*, 61.
Ranerup, A., & Norén, L. (2015). How are citizens' public service choices supported in quasi-markets? *International Journal of Information Management, 35*(5), 527–537.
Rangel, L. A., & Saboia, J. (2015). O regime de previdência dos servidores públicos: Implicações distributivas com base na instituição de um teto nos valores dos benefícios e da criação da FUNPRESP. *Nova Economia, 25*(3), 575–594.
Razin, A., & Sadka, E. (2007). Aging population: The complex effect of fiscal leakages on the politico-economic equilibrium. *European Journal of Political Economy, 23*(2), 564–575.
Reece, C., & Sam, A. G. (2012). Impact of pension privatization on foreign direct investment. *World Development, 40*(2), 291–302.
Regúlez-Castillo, M., & Vidal-Meliá, C. (2012). Individual information for pension contributors: Recommendations for Spain based on international experience. *International Social Security Review, 65*(2), 1–27.
Reynolds, S. L., & Crimmins, E. M. (2010). Trends in the ability to work among men and women in the older American population: 1997–2007. *European Journal of Ageing, 7*(4), 249–256.
Richardson, D. P., & Seligman, J. S. (2005). Optimal retirement portfolios: Social security personal accounts in the context of the four pillars. *The Geneva Papers on Risk and Insurance-Issues and Practice, 30*(4), 565–580.
Rosenberger, N. (1991). Gender and the Japanese state: Pension benefits creating difference. *Anthropological Quarterly, 64*, 178–193.
Rueda, G., Gerdsri, P., & Kocaoglu, D. F. (2007). Bibliometrics and social network analysis of the nanotechnology field. In *PICMET'07–2007 Portland international conference on management of engineering & technology* (pp. 2905–2911). IEEE.
Rürup, B. (1996). Demands on the legal pension security system based on the demographic change. *Zeitschrift fur Gerontologie und Geriatrie, 29*(1), 42–45.
Rürup, B. (2002). The German pension system: status Quo and Reform options. In *Social security pension reform in Europe* (pp. 137–170). University of Chicago Press, Chicago, United States.
Sabelhaus, J. (1997). Public policy and saving in the United States and Canada. *Canadian Journal of Economics, 30*(2), 253–275.
Sahin, I. (1997). Pension expectations as disincentives to job mobility. *Applied Stochastic Models in Business and Industry, 13*(2), 127–148.
Salminen, J. J. (1967). The state's pension system. *Kätilölehti, 72*(12), 508–512.
Sambt, J., & Cok, M. (2008). Demographic pressure on the public pension system. *Informatica, 32*(2), 103–109.
Sánchez-Martín, A. R. (2010). Endogenous retirement and public pension system reform in Spain. *Economic Modelling, 27*(1), 336–349.

Sancho, R. (1990). Indicadores bibliométricos utilizados en la evaluación de la ciencia y la tecnología. *Revisión bibliográfica. Revista Española de Documentación Científica, 13*(3–4), 842–863.
Sanderson, W. C., & Scherbov, S. (2010). Remeasuring aging. *Science, 329*(5997), 1287–1288.
Santa, S., & Herrero-Solana, V. (2010). Cobertura de la ciencia de América Latina y el Caribe en Scopus vs. Web of Science. *Investigación Bibliotecológica, 24*(52), 13–27.
Schnabel, M.W. (2015). *Pension benefit elasticity: An analysis of expected 401 (K) benefits and employee contributions*. Doctoral dissertation, Capella University.
Schneider, O. (1998). Demographic ageing, pension system and macroeconomic performance of the Czech Republic. In S. Griffith (Ed.), *Reforms of the pension system and national savings*. Institute of Economics, Czech National Bank, WP, (84), 71–88.
Schneider, M., & Damanpour, F. (2002). Public choice economics and public pension plan funding: An empirical test. *Administration & Society, 34*(1), 57–86.
Scholten, U., & Thum, M. (1996). Public pensions and immigration policy in a democracy. *Public Choice, 87*(3–4), 347-361.
Scholtz, H. A. (1989). Employees without pension arrangements. *Tijdschrift voor Gerontologie en Geriatrie, 20*(1), 9–24.
Schrenker, M. (2009). Warum fast alle das deutsche Rentensystem ungerecht finden, aber trotzdem nichts daran ändern möchten. *KZfSS Kölner Zeitschrift für Soziologie und Sozialpsychologie, 61* (2), 259–282.
Schwab, S. J. (1995). The diversity of contingent workers and the need for nuanced policy. *Washington and Lee Law Review, 52*(3), 915.
Schwartz, J. D. (1985). Non-fiduciary liability under the employee retirement income security act. *Marquette Law Review, 69*, 561.
Sefton, J., Van de Ven, J., & Weale, M. (2008). Means testing retirement benefits: fostering equity or discouraging savings? *The Economic Journal, 118*(528), 556–590.
Seguí-Cosme, S. (2015). Structural precariousness and the future of pensions in Spain. *Research on Ageing and Social Policy, 3*(1), 2–12.
SeLdon, A. (1994). Saving for life-time risks. *Economic Affairs, 14*(5), 24–26.
Shao, A. J. (2010). El sistema público de pensiones en Taiwán: problemas de igualdad en los sistemas y entre los sistemas. *Revista Internacional de Seguridad Social, 63*(1), 22–39.
Shaw, F. (2002). Is the ageing population the problem it is made out to be? *Foresight, 4*(3), 4–11.
Shelton, C. A. (2008). The aging population and the size of the welfare state: Is there a puzzle? *Journal of Public Economics, 92*(3), 647–651.
Simonovits, A. (2015). Socially optimal contribution rate and cap in a proportional (DC) pension system. *Portuguese Economic Journal, 14*(1–3), 45–63.
Škember, A. (2005). Demographic transition, changes in the structure of labour market and the pension system crisis. *Ekonomski Pregled, 56*(1–2), 103–116.
St-Amant, P. A. B., & Garon, J. D. (2015). Optimal redistributive pensions and the cost of self-control. *International Tax and Public Finance, 22*(5), 723–740.
Stanovnik, T., & Kukar, S. (1995). The pension system in Slovenia: past developments and future prospects. *International Social Security Review, 48*(1), 35–44.
Stanovnik, T., Bejaković, P., & Chłoń-Domińczak, A. (2015). The collection of pension contributions: a comparative review of three Central European countries. *Ekonomska Istraživanja, 28*(1), 1149–1161.
Stark, A., Folbre, N., & Shaw, L. B. (2005). Explorations gender and aging: cross-national contrasts. *Feminist Economics, 11*(2), 163–198.
Sundén, A. (2006). How much do people need to know about their pensions and what do they know?. *Pension reform: Issues and prospects for non-financial defined contribution (NDC) schemes*, Prepared for Conference on NDC Pensions. Sandhamm. Sweeden. September 29–30.325-44.
Takayama, N. (1995). The 1994 Reform Bill for public pensions in Japan: Its main contents and related discussion. *International Social Security Review, 48*(1), 45–65.

Takayama, N., & Kitamura, Y. (2009). How to make the Japanese public pension system reliable and workable. *Asian Economic Policy Review, 4*(1), 97–116.
Taylor-Gooby, P. (2001). Sustaining state welfare in hard times: who will foot the bill? *Journal of European Social Policy, 11*, 133–147.
Tepe, M., & Vanhuysse, P. (2009). Are aging OECD welfare states on the path to the politics of gerontocracy? Evidence from 18 democracies, 1980–2002. *Journal of Public Policy, 29*(1), 1–28.
United Nations. (2014). *La situación demográfica en el mundo, 2014. Informe conciso*. Nueva York: Naciones Unidas.
Van Dalen, H. P., & van Praag, B. (1993). Public pensions, market power, and intergenerational confidence. *Public Finance/Finances publiques, 48*(Supplement), 16–28.
Van der Heijden, E. C., Nelissen, J. H., & Verbon, H. A. (1997). Altruism and fairness in a public pension system. *Journal of Economic Behavior & Organization, 32*(4), 505–518.
Vanston, N. (1998). The economic impacts of ageing. *The OECD Observer, 212*, 10–15.
Vara-Miranda, M. J. (2011). La desigualdad de género en el sistema público de pensiones: el caso de España. *Información Comercial Española, ICE: Revista de Economía, 859*, 119–139.
Vara-Miranda, J. (2013). Gender inequality in the Spanish public pension system. *Feminist Economics, 19*(4), 136–159.
Vásquez Colmenares, P. (2013). Nueva seguridad social y la crisis de las pensiones. *Economía UNAM, 10*(28), 95–101.
Velkova, D. (2008). Changes in the public pension system and their impact on the labor market. *Economic Studies Journal, 2*, 22–59.
Verbon, H. A. (1987). The rise and evolution of public pension systems. *Public Choice, 52*(1), 75–100.
Verbon, H. (1988). The history of transfer payments for the old. In *The evolution of public pension schemes* (pp. 8–36). Berlin: Springer.
Verbon, H. A. (1990). Decision making on old-age transfers. In *Advanced lectures in quantitative economics, Chapter 5*. London: Academic Press.
Vidal-Melia, C. (2014). An assessment of the 2011 Spanish pension reform using the Swedish system as a benchmark. *Journal of Pension Economics & Finance, 13*(3), 297–333.
Von Weizsäcker, R. K. (1989a). *Population trends social security and government finances: political-economic aspects of pension financing*. University of Bonn, Germany, (226). Available in: https://www.popline.org/node/376703
Von Weizsäcker, R. K. (1989b). Demographischer Wandel und staatliche Einkommenssicherung: Eine Inzidenzanalyse/Demographic change and state income support: An incidence analysis. *Jahrbücher für Nationalökonomie und Statistik, 206*, 181–207.
Von Weizsäcker, R. K. (1995). Public pension reform, demographics, and inequality. *Journal of Population Economics, 8*(2), 205–221.
Wang, L., & Davis, O. A. (2003). Freedom and other variables in the choice of public pension systems. *Public Choice, 114*(3), 361–385.
Weise, R. W. (1972). Early retirement under public pension systems in Latin America. *International Social Security Review, 25*(3), 255–265.
Whitehouse, E. R., & Queisser, M. (2007). *Pensions at a glance: Public policies across OECD countries*. Paris: OECD.
Willborn, S. L. (1998). The problem with pension portability. *Nebraska Law Review, 77*(2), 344–835.
Williamson, J. B. (2001). Privatizing public pension systems: Lessons from Latin America. *Journal of Aging Studies, 15*(3), 285–302.
Wise, D. A. (2005). Facing the age wave and economic policy: Fixing public pension systems with healthcare in the wings. *Fiscal Studies, 26*(1), 5–34.
Withers, W. (1976). New-York pension carrousel. *Industrial Gerontology, 3*(3), 167–181.
World Bank. (1994). *Averting the old age crisis: Policies to protect the old and promote growth*. Oxford: Oxford University Press.

Yakymova, L. P. (2013). Modeliuvannia prostorovo-chasovoi dynamiky pensiinoho sotsiumu. Modeling spatio-temporal dynamics of pension society. *Biznes Inform*, (9), 84–89.
Yang, Y., Williamson, J. B., & Shen, C. (2010). Social security for China's rural aged: a proposal based on a universal non-contributory pension. *International Journal of Social Welfare, 19*(2), 236–245.
Yang, J., Tang, J., & Tang, Y. (2012). Pension model and pension facilities planning based on the "continuum of care" concept. *City Planning Review, 5*, 007.
Yoon, Y., & Talmain, G. (2001). Endogenous fertility, endogenous growth and public pension system: Should we switch from a pay-as-you-go to a fully funded system? *The Manchester School, 69*(5), 586–605.
Zdravković, A., Domazet, I., & Nikitović, V. (2012). Impact of demographic ageing on sustainability of public finance in Serbia. *Stanovnistvo, 50*(1), 19–44.
Zuber, S., Bommier, A., Bourdieu, J., & Suwa-Eisenmann, A. (2007). Public education and old-age insurance transfers in France (1850–2000): A generational profile. *Economie & Prévision, 4*, 1–17.

Chapter 2
Demographic and Social Challenges in the Design of Public Pension Schemes

Estefanía Alaminos, Mercedes Ayuso, and Montserrat Guillen

Abstract Demographic changes and social transformations affect the design of public pension systems. Population ageing and factors such as the progressive reduction in fertility rates and the increase in longevity have a direct impact on the sustainability of public pensions, especially in defined-benefit schemes. The study of longer life expectancy requires an analysis of its effects on specific issues such as pension adequacy (both contributory and non-contributory pensions), pensioners receiving several public benefits simultaneously (for instance, retirement and widow/widower's pensions) and the availability of sufficient financial resources to meet health and long-term care costs during retirement. This chapter presents an applied view of the evolution of the main demographic indicators and their effect on pension systems, based on previous studies carried out by the authors.

Keywords Ageing · Welfare state · Pension adequacy · Social challenges

2.1 Introduction

Population ageing has triggered a series of reforms in public pension systems across the globe in recent years. This increase in life expectancy, in combination with the reduction in fertility rates – below the population replacement rate of 2.1 children per woman – has called into question the sustainability of public pension systems, especially for pay-as-you-go defined-benefit schemes, which are highly conditioned by demographic conditions. The most common measure implemented in these recent reforms in the OECD countries has been to increase the statutory retirement age. Additional measures introduced into public pension systems across the OECD have sought to promote active ageing, working longer and the tightening of early retirement provisions (OECD 2015).

E. Alaminos · M. Ayuso (✉) · M. Guillen
Department of Econometrics, University of Barcelona, Barcelona, Spain
e-mail: ealaminos@ub.edu; mayuso@ub.edu; mguillen@ub.edu

M. Peris-Ortiz et al. (eds.), *Economic Challenges of Pension Systems*,
https://doi.org/10.1007/978-3-030-37912-4_2

However, these reforms have all been based on projected expenditures that depend solely on population projections (Actuarial Association of Europe 2016). These institutional population projections are, in turn, founded on assumptions about the evolution of conventional demographic measures. Traditional demographic indicators – based on chronological ages, such as life expectancy, the old-age dependency rate and median age – are expected to increase in future decades because of the increase in longevity. However, various authors have developed new measures based on prospective ages. In 2005, Sanderson and Scherbov introduced a new concept of age founded on remaining years of life rather than on the years that a person has already lived. Using this concept, they have rescaled certain measures related to population ageing – including old-age dependency rates and median ages – concluding that conventional measures typically extrapolate projections and, so, create concern about the sustainability of public pension schemes (Disney 2000). When rescaling these indicators to remaining lifetimes, however, the results obtained do not foresee such increases in longevity and, in some cases, they even remain stable. Thus, concerns regarding the long-term sustainability of pension systems need to be treated with caution and take into consideration different approximations of population projections (Sanderson and Scherbov 2005).

However, the goal of pension policies is not only to guarantee the long-term financial sustainability of the system but also to improve pension adequacy. Public pensions are the main source of income for the elderly across the OECD countries accounting, on average, for around 59% of their budget (OECD 2015). Elderly women are, on average, more exposed to risks of poverty than their male counterparts, owing to their longer longevity and lower pension entitlements (European Commission 2016). Their longer longevity, in turn, means they will live more years in old age, making them more likely to live alone (Lodovici et al. 2015; Alaminos and Ayuso 2015; Uribe et al. 2015; Chuliá et al. 2016). As such, female budgets are more vulnerable to pension indexation because they are paid for a longer period (Määttänen et al. 2014; Lodovici et al. 2015; European Commission 2016). Moreover, women are more likely than men to face daily limitations – either physical or mental – and, therefore, to have to meet the associated long-term care costs (WHO 2011; Guillen and Comas-Herrera 2012; Alaminos et al. 2016; Piulachs et al. 2016).

The lives of individuals are directly affected by the socio-demographic changes that societies have undergone in recent decades. Family structures have been modified by the reduction in fertility rates and by changes in life priorities. Lower fertility rates mean fewer children per woman and, hence, smaller families. Moreover, with a higher female participation in labour markets, individuals tend to postpone the moment of starting a family until their working career is secure (OECD 2011a).

Changes in family structure are also associated with subjective well-being in old age (Pinquart and Sörensen 2000). Elderly people enjoying a good social network are more likely to live healthier than their lone counterparts. Indeed, active ageing would seem to be the best medicine for happy ageing (Holzmann 2013b).

The aim of this chapter is to present evidence of the new challenges that public pension schemes have to face both today and tomorrow. In so doing, we focus on issues related both to demographics and to society. The chapter is structured as follows. In Sect. 2.2, we review the main demographic indicators, highlighting new measures specifically adjusted to remaining years of life. In Sect. 2.3, we present our analysis of the European population in terms of marital status, family structure and household composition. Finally, Sect. 2.4 analyses different indicators of well-being among the elderly.

2.2 New Demographic Indicators on Which to Base Pension Reforms

2.2.1 Traditional Indicators of Population Ageing

Population ageing can be measured in terms of the evolution of four indicators: (i) number of older people; (ii) share of older people over the total population, old-age share; (iii) demographic old-age dependency ratio; and (iv) median age (Ayuso et al. 2015). All these traditional ageing measures are predicted to rise over the next few decades, especially among those aged 80 and above.

Thus, according to Eurostat's population projections (EUROPOP2013), the EU-28 population aged 80 years or more is expected to increase from 3,255,964 in 2015 to 5,003,773 in 2080, reaching a peak in 2050 with 5,535,357 individuals (Eurostat 2016d). The proportion of elderly people in the EU-28, above all those aged 80 years and above, is expected to increase from 5.30% in 2015 to 12.30% in 2080 (Fig. 2.1). The old-age dependency ratio – defined as the proportion of the

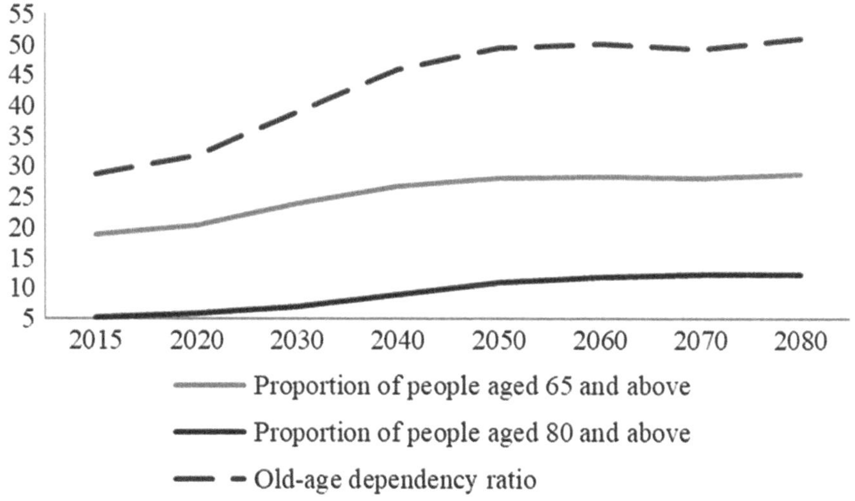

Fig. 2.1 Projected proportions of people aged 65 and above and 80 and above (%). Projected old-age dependency ratio. EU-28. (*Source:* proj_13ndbims, Eurostat database (last update 08.12.16))

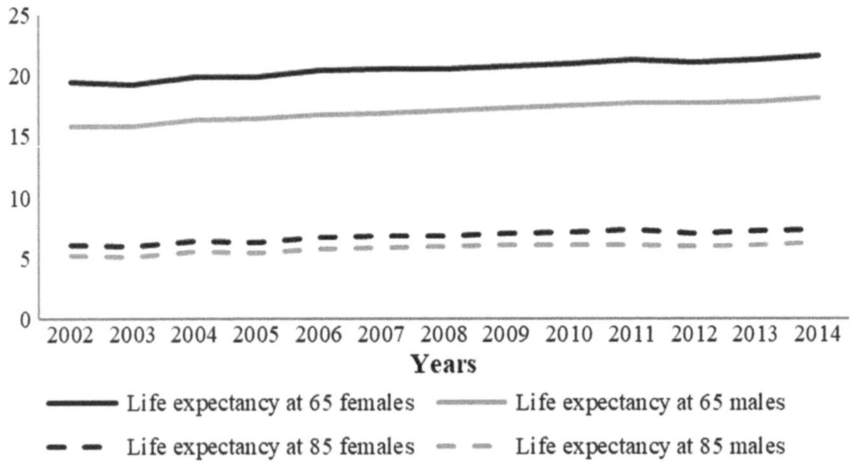

Fig. 2.2 Life expectancy at the age of 65 and 85 by gender for the EU-28 average (in years), 2002–2014 series. (*Source:* demo_mlexpec, Eurostat database (last update 01.12.16))

population aged 65 and over in relation to the population aged 15–64 years – is also expected to increase from 28.80% in 2015 to 51.00% in 2080 (Fig. 2.1). Finally, the median age of the population – the age which divides a population into two groups of equal size, one of them being younger than this age and the other older – is also projected to rise from 42.40 years in 2015 to 46.40 years in 2080.

Adopting Eurostat's methodology, life expectancy can be calculated for any age. However, in line with the specific purpose of this chapter, we focus on life expectancy at older ages, that is, at 65 and 85. Figure 2.2 shows life expectancy at these two ages by gender in the European Union (EU-28 average). Over the last decade, not only has life expectancy at birth increased but it has also increased at advanced ages.[1] This represents the great advances made by society, indicative of the improvement in living standards, in lifestyle and in socio-economic levels, and of the advances in medicine and healthcare, which have reduced mortality rates in both genders.

Figure 2.2 shows that while the life expectancy of the elderly has increased for both genders, women always present longer life spans. Over the 12-year series, the gender gap at 65 has fallen slightly (from 3.7 years in 2002 to 3.4 in 2014); however, the gender gap at 85 years has risen slightly (from 0.9 years in 2002 to 1.1 years in 2014).

[1]Note the gender gap at advanced ages is not as great as it is at birth.

2.2.2 Alternative Indicators of Population Ageing

The traditional measures of population ageing described in the previous section are based on the individual's chronological age and assume that their age-specific characteristics do not change over time or from one location to another (Sanderson and Scherbov 2007, 2010, 2015). However, these characteristics are known to vary over time and space, which led Sanderson and Scherbov to suggest reformulating traditional ageing measures so that they are based on prospective age as opposed to chronological age. Thus, while chronological age is based on the number of years that an individual has lived, prospective age is concerned with the individual's remaining life expectancy. For instance, conventional indicators measure the number of individuals getting older at ages 65 or 85, whereas prospective indicators consider people becoming old when they are expected to live for 10 or 20 more years. Figure 2.3 shows the differences between conventional and prospective median ages in Western Europe between 1960 and 2050. As can be seen, the conventional median age presents a growing trend, but Sanderson and Scherbov seek to demonstrate that when using a prospective measure the result is not the same. Indeed, the prospective median age is expected to have fallen by 2050. Likewise, in the case of the old-age dependency ratio (Fig. 2.4), the prospective indicator is not expected to grow as fast as the conventional measure.

It is not the intention for prospective measures to replace conventional indicators; rather, they should complement each other. Traditional measures based solely on chronological age do not assume that life expectancy is influenced by factors such as disability rates or remaining life expectancy. Moreover, conventional measures foresee an increase in longevity. Prospective indicators, in contrast, seek to slow

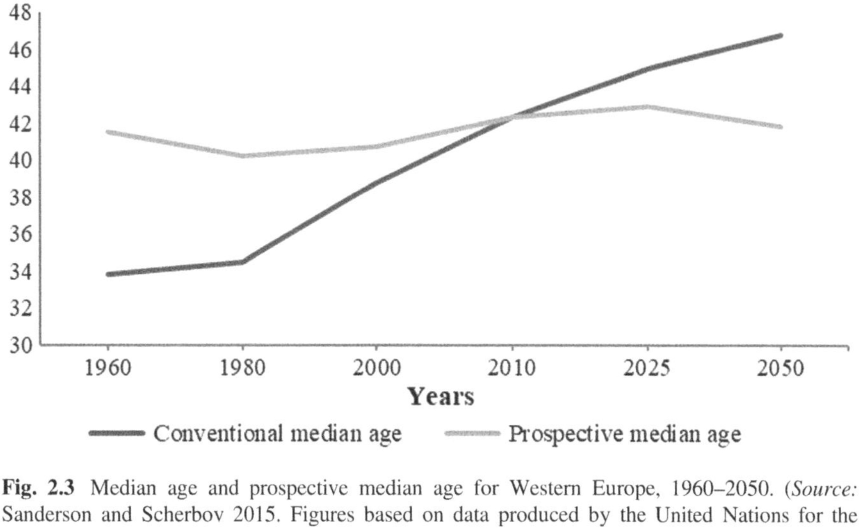

Fig. 2.3 Median age and prospective median age for Western Europe, 1960–2050. (*Source:* Sanderson and Scherbov 2015. Figures based on data produced by the United Nations for the 2012 volume of World Population Prospects)

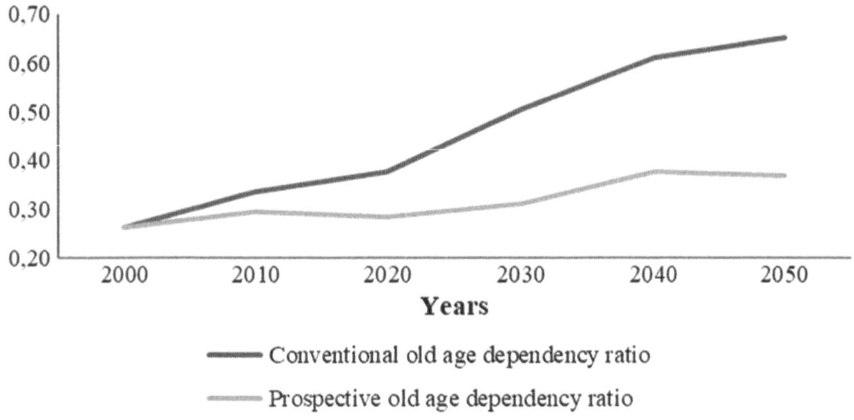

Fig. 2.4 Conventional and prospective old-age dependency ratio for Germany, 2000–2050. (*Source:* Sanderson and Scherbov 2007)

down the ageing process by making more moderate, or even decreasing, predictions, which need to be taken into account when making political decisions linked to the future evolution of population ageing.

2.2.3 Other Indicators of Population Ageing

In this section, we describe the evolution of other indicators based on disability rates and remaining life expectancy: namely, healthy life years and expected number of years in retirement.

Since the publication of the Stiglitz-Sen-Fitoussi Report (2009), new indicators of well-being have been used in policymaking, and GDP is no longer the sole measure of social progress. For example, from the perspective of the individual, health status is an indicator of quality of life (OECD 2011c), but the increase in life expectancy (Fig. 2.2) does not include any evidence as to how many years an individual lives in good health. An indicator of the relative health status of a population is that of healthy life years (or disability-free life expectancy), which seeks to measure the number of years an individual lives in good health rather than measuring the length of life until death – as is the case of life expectancy (Eurostat 2016a). In the case of the EU-28, this measure is calculated using data from mortality statistics (Eurostat demographic database) and from the European Union Statistics on Income and Living Conditions (EU-SILC)[2] (Fig. 2.5).

Eurostat uses three indicators of healthy life years: healthy life years at birth, healthy life years at 50 and healthy life years at 65. In the EU-28 in 2014, healthy life

[2]The data used from the EU-SILC are self-perceived activity limitations data.

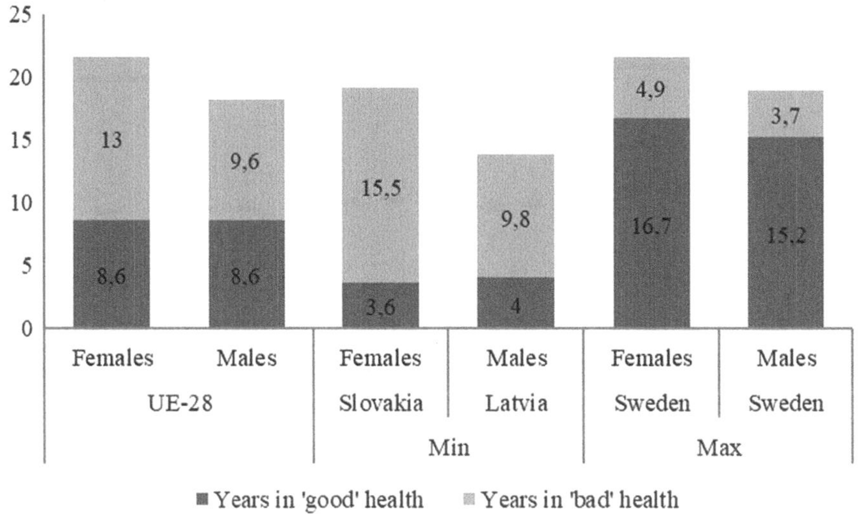

Fig. 2.5 Life expectancy at the age of 65 by gender in 2014 shown as the number of years lived in 'good' (healthy life years) and 'bad' health. Data for the EU-28 average and for countries with the minimum and maximum results at this age. (*Source:* hlth_hlye, Eurostat database (last update 22.04.16))

years at birth was 61.40 years for men and 61.80 years for women (Eurostat 2016a), which as percentages of total life expectancy represent 78.60 and 73.90%, respectively. At the age of 50, healthy life years for men stood at 17.40 and at 17.80 for women, which in relative percentage terms of total life expectancy was 57.70 and 50.90%, respectively. At the age of 65, the healthy life year's indicator was the same for both genders (8.60 years); however, in relative percentage terms of total life expectancy, the gender gap was notorious with elderly women being expected to live 39.81% of their total life expectancy in good health and men 47.25%.

Figure 2.5 shows, in the case of total life expectancy at 65, the number of years lived in 'good' (healthy life years) or 'bad' health in 2014. The EU-28's average by gender shows that women have a higher life expectancy at 65 than men; however, as noted, the proportion of those years lived in good health stands at 39.81% compared to 47.25% in the case of men. Thus, the additional years that women live are lived in poor health conditions (Crimmins et al. 2011; Thorslund et al. 2013; Lindahl-Jacobsen et al. 2013), in what the literature has called the 'male-female health-survival paradox' (Case and Paxson 2005; OECD 2011a; Alberts et al. 2014; among others). The EU member state that presents the lowest number of healthy life years is Slovakia in the case of women and Latvia in the case of men. Slovakian women aged 65 live 18.85% of their remaining lives in good health, while men in Latvia aged 65 live 28.99% of their remaining lives in good health. Note that in these extreme cases, the gender gap is higher than that of the EU-28 average. In contrast, Sweden presents a higher number of healthy life years for both genders. In the case of

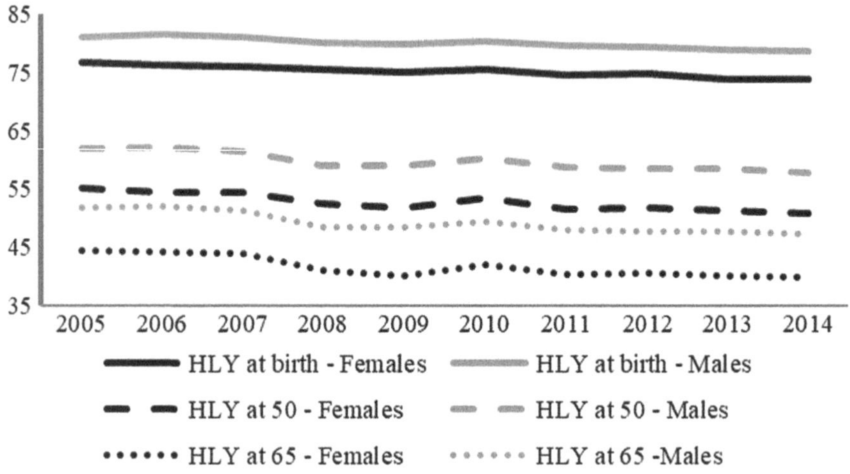

Fig. 2.6 Healthy life years (HLY) as a percentage of total life expectancy (%), time series 2005–2014. (*Source:* hlth_hlye, Eurostat database, (last update 22.04.16). EU-27: 2005–2009; EU-28: 2010–2014)

females, total life expectancy at 65 is the same as that for the EU-28 average; however, Swedish women live more years in good health than the women in the rest of Europe (16.7 vs. 8.6 years), giving a relative percentage of total life expectancy of 77.31%. Swedish men aged 65 live 80.42% of their remaining lives in good health. In all cases, men enjoy more years without health limitations than women, despite the fact that the latter always present a higher life expectancy at 65.

In terms of life expectancy, women usually live longer than men (5.50 years, on average, in 2014 if we consider life expectancy at birth and 3.40 years if considered at 65). However, as seen, these additional years of life are typically marked by some kind of activity limitation. Gender gaps in healthy life years are not as great as they are in terms of life expectancy. In relative terms, the number of healthy life years as a percentage of total life expectancy indicates that women enjoy fewer years of healthy life than men (Fig. 2.6). Despite the fact that the gender gap in healthy life years as a percentage of total life expectancy has remained steady over the last decade, the percentage has followed a slightly downward trend. This can be explained by the fact that although life expectancy has increased, the number of years lived in good health has remained constant, even falling slightly in some cases.

The fact that the additional years of life women live are accompanied by some type of daily limitation means governments not only have to consider the adequacy of their public pensions for the elderly (including, retirement and survivors' pensions), but they also need to implement long-term care systems that cover all the requirements of the population with some degree of dependency. However, the healthy life year's indicator cannot yet provide a proper time series to describe the trend followed by this measure over the last few decades.

A further indicator based on remaining life expectancy is that of the expected number of years in retirement, as used by the OECD. This indicator measures the

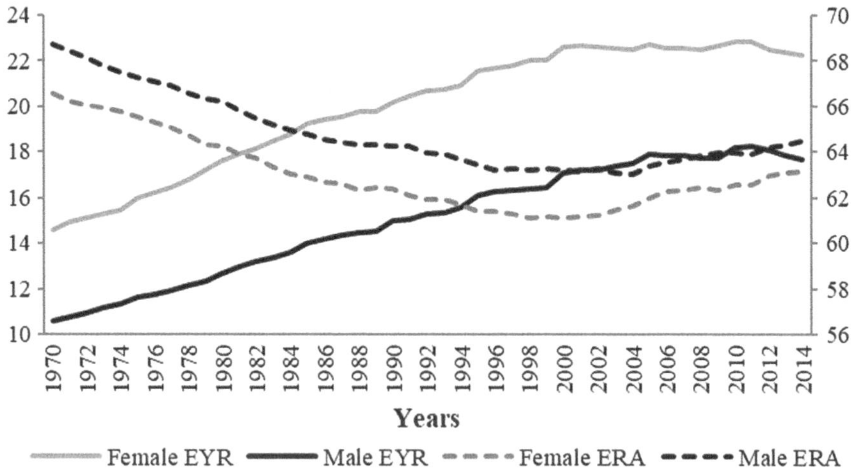

Fig. 2.7 Expected number of years in retirement (EYR) and effective retirement age (ERA) by gender. OECD average, 1970–2014 series. (*Source:* OECD 2015. Left *y*-axis: EYR; right *y*-axis: ERA)

number of years an individual is expected to live between exiting the labour market and death (OECD 2015). The OECD average increased between 1970 and 2014 (Fig. 2.7) due to two factors: first, the effective labour market exit age has fallen over recent decades (in males from 68.73 in 1970 to 64.46 in 2014, and in females from 66.59 to 63.16) and, second, life expectancy has increased (Fig. 2.2). Both genders have experienced an increase in their retirement life span, although there is evidence of a gender gap here too. For women, the average retirement span is 22 years, while for men it is around 18 years. This longer retirement life span makes women, in particular, more vulnerable, as it means they will probably have to live longer with an associated disease and with less income than their male counterparts. Note that the effective retirement age for both males and females experienced a sharp fall during the 1990s and early 2000s for a number of reasons. Some policies targeted a reduction in labour supply, e.g. the promotion of early retirement; others a reduction in labour demand, e.g. reducing incentives for maintaining low-skilled older workers in the labour market (Duval 2003).

2.3 New Family Structures

2.3.1 Changes in Family Patterns

Family structures have been in a constant process of change since the 1960s (OECD 2011b). From the vantage point of society, the role played by women has been crucial. The gains in female educational attainment and the increase in the female

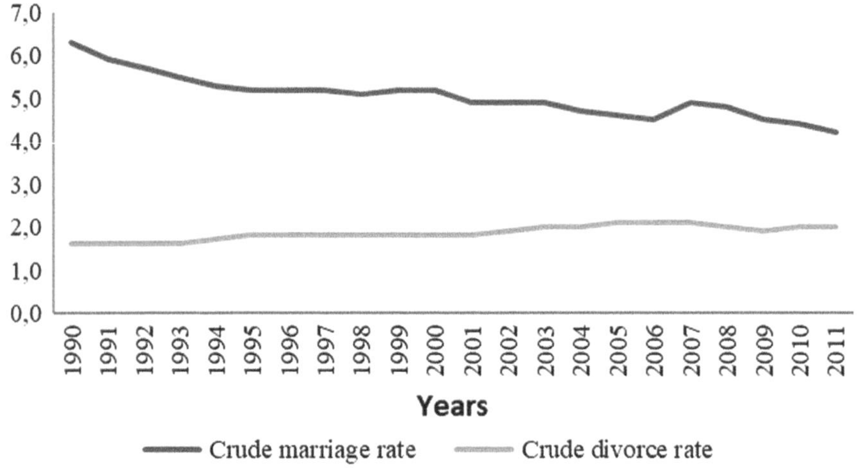

Fig. 2.8 Average crude marriage and divorce rates (per 1000 inhabitants), EU-28, 1990–2011 (*Source:* Marriage (demo_nind) and divorce (demo_ndivind) statistics (Eurostat 2016c))

workforce have delayed the age at which mothers have their first child and increased the childlessness rate. Today, women have the opportunity to fulfil their professional aspirations; thus, there have been changes in life priorities, with women postponing the age at which they form a family. From the demographic perspective, the fall in fertility rates combined with the increase in longevity has led to societies with fewer children and more elderly individuals than a few decades ago (OECD 2011a).

In recent decades, there have also been changes in partnership patterns (Fig. 2.8). Marriage rates have fallen and divorce rates have risen. In the EU-28, the average crude marriage rate has dropped from 6.3 marriages per 1000 persons in 1990 to 4.2 in 2011. In the case of crude divorce rates, the European average has increased from 1.6 divorces per 1000 persons in 1990 to 2.0 in 2011. Moreover, the average age at which first marriage occurs has been delayed, rising to over 30 for men (32.10 years) and almost 30 for women (29.50 years) in 2014. Both series have followed a growing trend over the last few decades.

Furthermore, new family patterns have emerged in European and OECD countries. The decline in marriage has been accompanied by new partnership types, including civil partnerships, cohabitation (or consensual unions) – a situation in which a couple live together in the same household but neither as a married couple nor in a registered partnership – 'living apart together' and 'weekend relationships'[3], the last two relationships being characterised by the fact that each partner maintains their own residence. These new forms of partnership are emerging primarily among younger generations, who are more likely to cohabit than previous cohorts (OECD 2011a; European Union 2015).

[3]All these new classes of partnership represent a significant challenge for conducting statistical analyses in this field (OECD 2016).

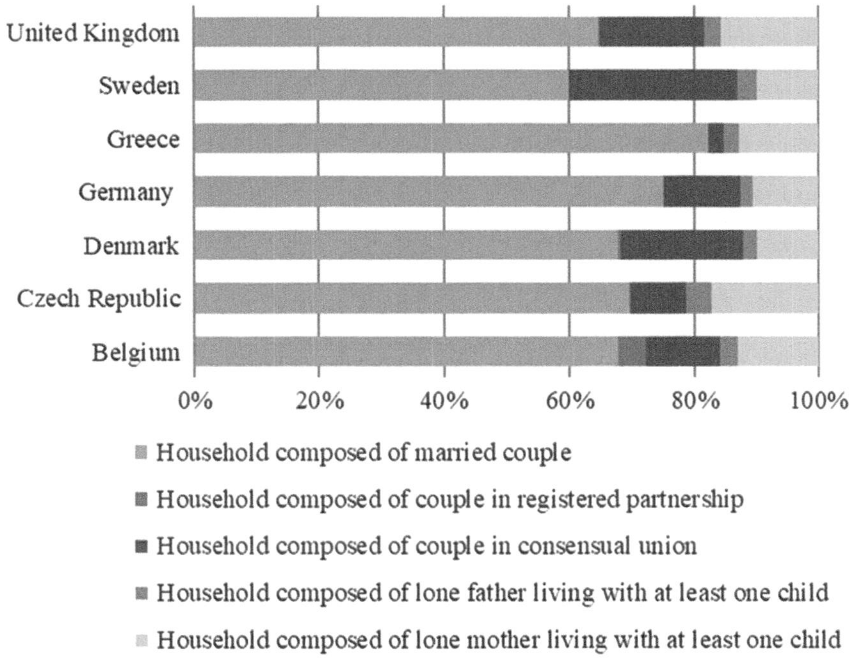

Fig. 2.9 Partnership types in selected EU member states, 2011. (*Source:* cens_11fts_r3, European Population and Housing Census 2011 (Eurostat 2012))

The European 2011 Population and Housing Census (Eurostat 2012) classifies families according to the following types: household composed of married couple, household composed of couple in registered partnership, household composed of couple in consensual union,[4] household composed of lone father living with at least one child and household composed of lone mother living with at least one child.

Figure 2.9 shows the proportion of each partnership type for the European countries for which data are available on all types. The data show that marriage is the most frequent of the unions with registered partnerships being the least frequent. The number of single parents living with at least one child has increased in recent decades – most notably in the case of lone mothers – accounting for more than 10% of household types. These families present the greatest risk of finding themselves in vulnerable situations (Bauman 2002; Gornick and Jäntti 2009; Bradshaw and Chzhen 2011; OECD 2011a; Kramer et al. 2016). Of the two, mother-only families are more likely to be below the poverty line than father-only families (Lewis 1997; Christopher 2005; Kramer et al. 2016).

Despite the changes in the living arrangements of Europeans, the distribution of the population aged over 20 by marital status shows that marriage is the most

[4]These first three types of family include couples without children, couples with at least one resident child under 25 years of age and couples with a youngest resident child aged 25 or older.

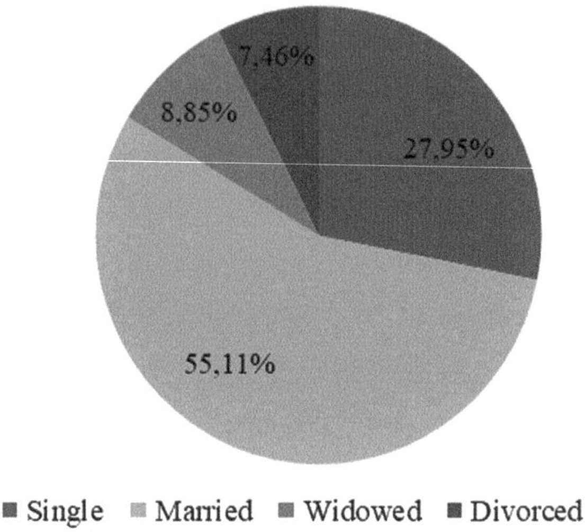

Fig. 2.10 Marital status distribution among European population over the age of 20, EU-28, 2011. (*Source:* cens_11mr_r3, European Population and Housing Census 2011 (Eurostat 2012). Note that the total sum does not add up to 100% as we do not consider those who are unclassified)

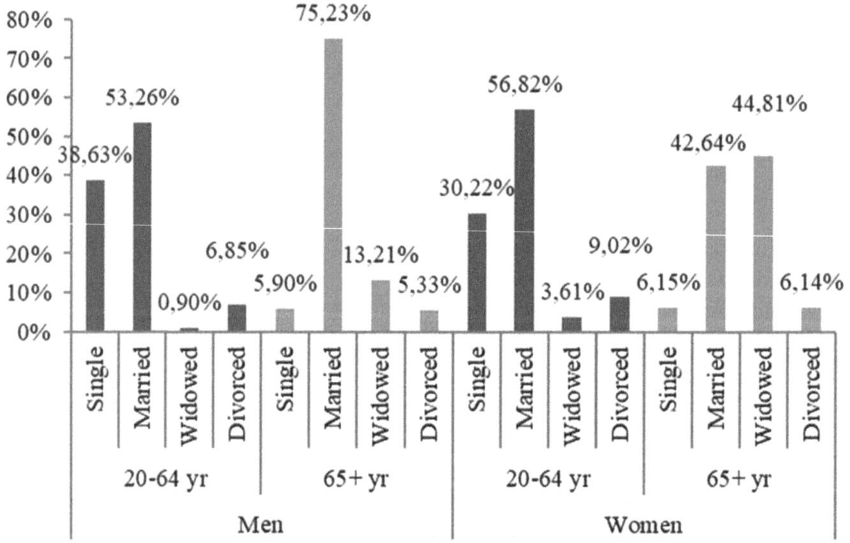

Fig. 2.11 Marital status distribution among European population by gender and age group, 2011. (*Source:* cens_11mr_r3, European Population and Housing Census 2011 (Eurostat 2012))

frequent arrangement (Fig. 2.10). In 2011, 55.10% of the European population aged over 20 was married, followed by those that were single (i.e. those that had never been married), representing 27.97% of the population over the age of 20. Widows/ widowers and divorcees represent 8.85 and 7.46%, respectively, of the total population.

As for the distribution of the population by gender and age group (Fig. 2.11), there is no notable difference between genders aged between 20 and 64. Among the total population, married couples constitute the largest group (53.26% for men and 56.82% for women), followed by singles (38.63 and 30.22%, respectively). Note that there are more widows than widowers (3.61% vs. 0.90%). However, in the cohorts aged 65 and over, there is a marked difference between genders. Elderly men are mostly married (75.23%), there being considerably fewer widowers (13.21%) and singles (5.90%). However, elderly women are mainly widows (44.81%) or married (42.64%). Note that in this case, widows constitute the largest group because of the higher life expectancy of women at advanced ages. These figures indicate that women are more likely to live alone in old age than men (Oeppen and Vaupel 2002; Vaupel and Kistowski 2005; Ayuso and Holzmann 2014; Alaminos and Ayuso 2015).

2.3.2 *Household Composition*

Among Europeans, the most common types of private households by size are those composed of a single individual or by two persons, each of which accounts for a third of the total (Fig. 2.12). Households formed by five or more individuals are the least frequent, accounting for 6.30% in 2015. Between 2007 and 2015, there has been an increase in the proportion of individuals living alone, rising from 30.00% to 32.20%, respectively. Households made up of two individuals have also grown, but at a slower rate than one-person households (from 30.10% in 2007 to 31.30% in 2015). However, while one- and two-person households are becoming more common in Europe, larger households are becoming less frequent. Three-person households have decreased their share in recent years (from 17.20% to 16.40% during the

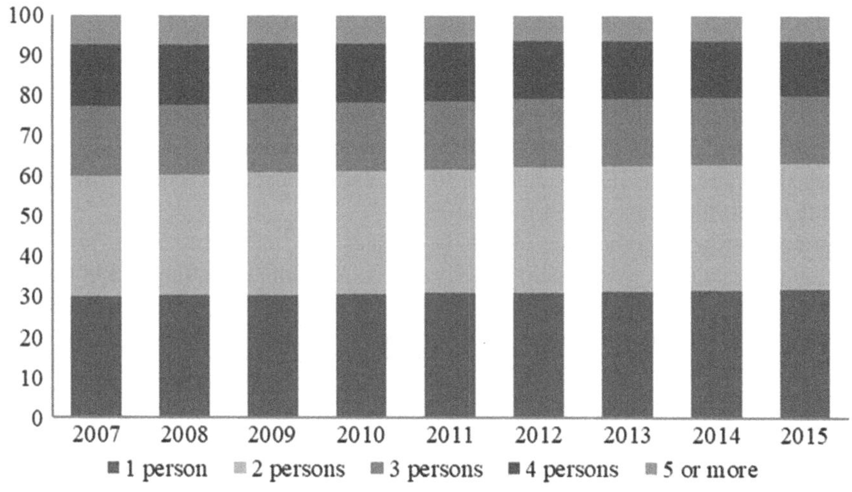

Fig. 2.12 Household composition in percentage (%) in Europe by number of persons, 2007–2015. (*Source:* ilc-lvph03, EU-SILC, Eurostat 2016b. EU-27: 2007–2009; EU-28: 2010–2015)

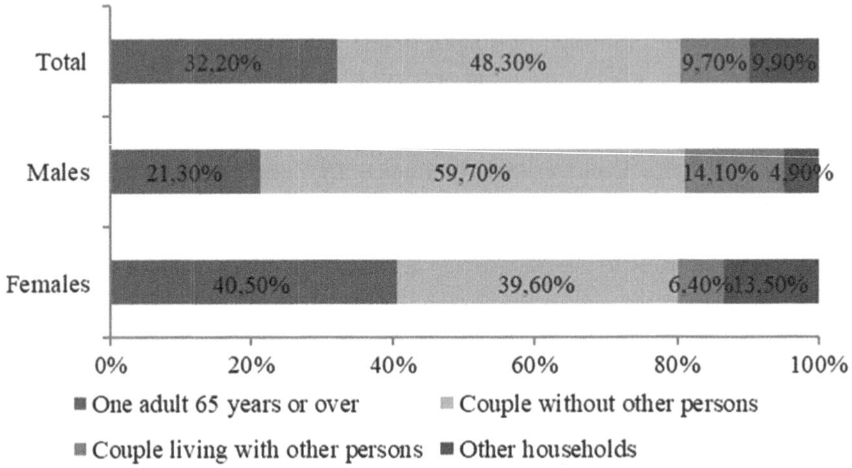

Fig. 2.13 Distribution of the population aged 65 and over by type of household, EU-28, 2015. (*Source:* ilc_lcps30, EU-SILC, Eurostat 2016b)

time series analysed); however, greater reductions have been suffered by households with more occupants, in particular those comprising four individuals. In 2015, the average household size in the EU-28 was 2.3 persons. Household size has fallen or remained steady in all European countries over the last decade (2005–2015 series, Eurostat 2016b). In Belgium, Croatia,[5] Demark and Poland, for example, household size has remained stable at 2.3, 2.8, 2.0 and 2.8 persons, respectively. In contrast, Bulgaria has experienced the sharpest fall, from 2.9 persons in 2005 to 2.5 in 2015.

Figure 2.13 shows the distribution of the EU-28 population aged 65 and over by household type in 2015. Given the importance of the elderly to the discussion conducted here, and as they are the main recipients of social security benefits, the study of these cohorts is of particular relevance. According to EU-SILC[6] data, in 2015 Europe's elderly members lived primarily in couples (48.30%) or alone (32.20%). This distribution however shows a gender difference. Men aged over 65 lived mainly with a partner (59.70%). The proportion of men living alone represented one fifth of the total (21.30%), while households comprising more than two individuals accounted for 14.10%.

In contrast, a predominance of elderly females lived alone (40.50%), in a proportion that is almost twice that of elderly males. As seen above, the distribution of the elderly population by marital status (Fig. 2.11) indicated that women tend to live on their own,[7] whereas men are mostly married. Studies on this subject present

[5]Joined the EU in 2013 – data only available from 2010.

[6]European Union Statistics on Income and Living Conditions (EU-SILC).

[7]Our description of the distribution of the population by marital status showed that among elderly women, widows, singles and divorcees accounted for 57.10%, while married women represented just 42.64% of the total.

evidence indicating that elderly women often prefer to live alone on becoming widows rather than moving into the home of a relative (Kramarow 1995; Chandler et al. 2004). Moreover, many women who never married and became emancipated continued to live with their ascendants until they died, at which point they became one-person households (López Doblas 2005). Elderly women living with a spouse constitute 39.60% of households across the EU, while those living with their spouse and more persons are less than half that of their male counterparts (6.40 vs. 14.10%, respectively).

In the final category, that of other households, these represented 13.50% in the case of elderly females and just 4.90% in that of males. The higher share among females can be attributed to the elderly living with their extended family. The EU-SILC data show that Southern and Eastern European and the Baltic countries present higher shares of this kind of household (e.g. 29.60% in Poland, 29.60% in Latvia, 27.80% in Croatia, 26.20% in Slovakia and 24.90% in Spain). Indeed, Iacovou and Skew (2011) report that in Southern and Eastern European countries extended-family households made up of a multigenerational family, in which a couple live with both children and parents, are more typical than in other European cultures. Thus, elderly widows are likely to end up living in their children's households (Fokkema and Liefbroer 2008).

2.4 Well-Being Indicators Among the Elderly Population

2.4.1 Heterogeneity in Longevity by Marital Status

Following the recommendations of the Stiglitz, Sen and Fitoussi Report (2009), the OECD established a framework for measuring individual well-being in 2011 (OECD 2011c). This framework comprises a series of indicators based on different dimensions of people's well-being, which can be classified in two general areas: quality of life (health status, work-life balance, education and skills, social, connections, civic engagement and governance, environmental quality, personal security and subjective well-being) and material conditions (income and wealth, jobs and earnings, and housing).

The quality of the social network in old age is associated with subjective well-being (Pinquart and Sörensen 2000). Different social networks, such as marital status – marriage – and family ties, are positively linked to life satisfaction and happiness and have an influence on health status (Helliwell and Putnam 2004). Since health perception is considered a predictor of mortality (Menec et al. 1999), an association can be found between marital status and longevity.

Recent studies have established marital status as one of the most important factors affecting individual welfare in old age (European Union 2014). Furthermore, among the socio-economic indicators, marital status is considered an influence on longevity

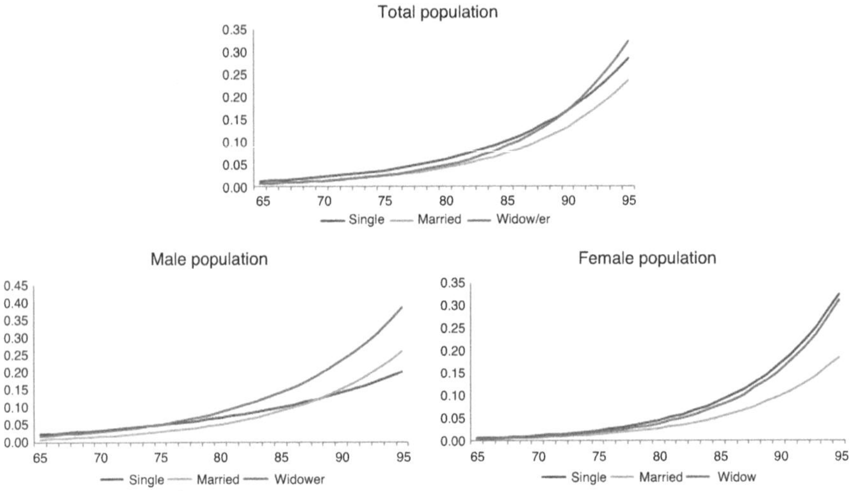

Fig. 2.14 Estimated death probabilities by marital status, age and gender in 2011. Total, male and female Spanish population aged 65 and over. (*Source:* Alaminos and Ayuso (2015, 2019))

(Ayuso et al. 2016). The positive links that married individuals develop, thanks to social interactions, produced mostly by family ties, help them to live in better health. According to survival theories, marriage is associated with greater longevity (Kaplan and Kronick 2006). At old ages, in particular, being married translates into broader social connections and, therefore, more positive feelings (Holzmann 2013a) that have a positive influence on health status (Robards et al. 2012). In old age, the probability of being alone increases (Abellán García and Pujol Rodríguez 2016). Lone elderly people present higher probabilities of death than their peers living in a couple (Manzoli et al. 2007; Ng et al. 2015; Alaminos and Ayuso 2015). On occasions, the feelings of loneliness experienced by the elderly that live alone would appear to account for these higher probabilities of death (Gove 1973).

The probabilities of death for the elderly Spanish population by age, gender and marital status[8] are shown in Fig. 2.14. Regardless of gender, married couples present lower death probabilities than those that live alone. Among this latter group, single people present higher death probabilities than widows/widowers until the age of 90, at which point the latter begin to show higher probabilities. By gender, probabilities of death among men are higher among widowers and those that are married (Alaminos and Ayuso 2015), whereas single women present higher death rates than single men.

[8]Probabilities are estimated in line with the methodology described in Alaminos and Ayuso (2015, 2019).

2.4.2 Active Ageing

The subjective well-being of the elderly can be enhanced by promoting their active ageing. In this regard, policymakers should target the individual's welfare rather than the system as a whole. Among the key factors identified for ensuring happiness in old age, two stand out: having an objective in life and maintaining social interactions (Holzmann 2013b). Since retirement is a transition between two stages in life, conceiving retirement as a specific, punctual event (rather than a gradual process) is perhaps not the best way to achieve well-being in old age.

Workers who remain in the workforce beyond their official retirement age present higher levels of life satisfaction and report better well-being than their retired peers (Graham 2014). Furthermore, later-life work contributes to maintaining and enhancing an individual's social network and providing a sense of purpose in life (Holzmann 2013a; Nikolova and Graham 2014). Indeed, some researchers report that elderly individuals who extend their working life increase their well-being, while those pressed into involuntary retirement suffer a fall in their levels of well-being (Calvo 2006; Bonsang and Klein 2012; Nikolova and Graham 2014).

Aside from benefitting workers, the concept of gradual retirement may also be propitious for employers and governments (Derviş 2013; Nikolova and Graham 2014). In the context of high levels of unemployment and an ageing population, public pension systems face obvious problems of sustainability. One way of addressing this could be to offer phase-in retirement programs so that employees gradually stop working and do not leave the labour market (and so continue to pay their taxes) until the age of 70. An additional advantage is that older employees are an excellent source of experience and can help train younger employees. However, the attitude of employers towards later-time workers is often blind to these benefits. Employers tend to consider older workers as a burden rather than as an opportunity, hence the low rates of old-age employment in Europe and labour markets that do not promote the hiring of the elderly (van Dalen et al. 2010). However, some studies suggest that later-life employees present higher levels of productivity than workers in other cohorts (Burtless 2013; Holzmann 2013b). Overall, the evidence seems to show that the active elderly present lower death probabilities and less likelihood of suffering mental and physical illnesses (Everard et al. 2000; Siegrist et al. 2004; Calvo 2006).

An alternative form of employment after reaching the statutory retirement age is offered by the so-called bridge jobs, carried out by elderly workers once they have retired (Ruhm 1990). Working part-time may also be considered the equivalent of bridge employment (Beehr and Bennett 2014). Bridge jobs help retirees achieve a better work-life balance during retirement and to stay active both socially and productively. Furthermore, such employment can bolster the individual's public retirement pension by providing an extra source of income (Hébert and Luong 2008). All in all, partial retirement can help cushion the consequences retirement may have on a retiree's well-being, improving his or her degree of life satisfaction (Dingemans and Henkens 2015).

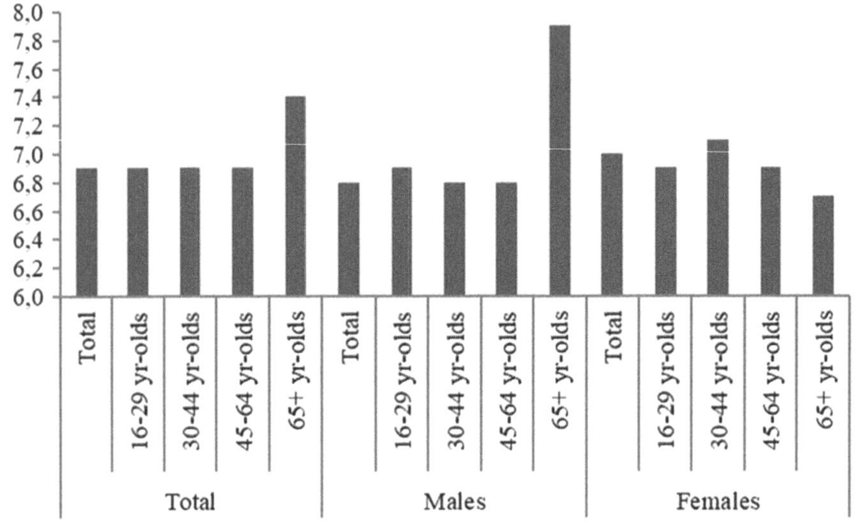

Fig. 2.15 Average job satisfaction by age and gender. Spain, 2013. (*Source:* Life Conditions Survey (Spanish Statistical Office 2014). Average satisfaction scales from 0 to 10, being 0 the worst score and 10 the better one. Only people in employment were surveyed)

However, the positive levels reached by indicators of well-being among elderly workers may be biased for a various reasons (Graham 2014). First, healthier workers are more likely to remain active after the statutory retirement age. Second, more highly skilled and motivated workers tend to remain in the labour force until more advanced ages. Finally, individuals that are happiest in their work are more likely to continue working into retirement. An example of this last point can be found in the Spanish population. Figure 2.15 shows the average job satisfaction by age and gender, according to the Life Conditions Survey (Spanish Statistical Office 2014). Employees aged 65 and over reported higher levels of satisfaction than the mean for all other age cohorts (7.40 vs. 6.90, respectively). By gender, elderly men reported a higher degree of satisfaction than the mean for all other cohorts (7.90 vs. 6.80) and then women of the same age (7.90 vs. 6.70). Note that elderly women reported lower levels of job satisfaction than women at any other age. This might be attributable to the fact that women are likely to be entitled to less money in terms of public pension payments than men of a similar age (Alaminos and Ayuso 2015) and, as such, are obliged to remain in the workforce after passing the statutory retirement age. The European average – regardless of gender – presents similar levels of satisfaction to those presented by the Spanish population (Eurostat 2013). Thus, workers aged 65–74 in Europe report a level of job satisfaction of 7.3 compared to a mean of 7.1 at younger ages.

2.5 Conclusions and Discussion

Recent reforms to public pension systems have been implemented in order to tackle the problems of ageing. These reforms have employed traditional measures of ageing based on chronological ages; however, various studies, most notably Sanderson and Scherbov (2007), have introduced new measures of remaining lifetimes to show that population ageing is unlikely to be as rapid as predictions based on traditional indicators claim. These new prospective indicators seek to complement traditional measures, so that policymakers need to consider both when making population projections on which to base long-term pension policy design.

There is little doubt that the increase in the number of those aged 65 and over (or whatever the corresponding retirement age might be) together with higher levels of female workforce participation will raise the number of individuals entitled to public retirement pensions in the future. Moreover, in some countries, such as Spain, greater longevity is associated with an increase in the number of beneficiaries, especially among females, with entitlement to a survivor's pension. Thus, we can expect an increase in the number of beneficiaries of more than one public pension (Alaminos and Ayuso 2015). From the point of view of the sustainability of the pension system, this means paying more pension entitlements for longer. From the perspective of the individual, this situation flouts the principle of actuarial equity. The fall in the number of marriages, combined with the rise in the number of people living alone, will mean that a greater number of people in the future will only be entitled to their own retirement pension. Survivors' pensions might therefore be inequitable for elderly singles – especially in the case of women – who can only depend on their own retirement pensions (Arza 2015; Alaminos and Ayuso 2019). Elderly people living alone are more likely to be at risk of poverty than those that live in a couple (OECD 2014), because of their lower pension entitlement, lack of family ties and worse health (OECD 2011b). Hence, new policies need to target individuals rather than the population as a whole.

In the last few decades, there has been an increase in the number of one-person households. In part, this increase appears to be a consequence of an ageing population, and the share of people living alone seems set to grow even more over the next few decades according to OECD projections (OECD 2011a). Moreover, elderly women are more likely to live alone than men. Given that in some countries (e.g. Spain) older women are entitled to lower pensions than men (as a result of their shorter labour careers) and are more likely to suffer disabilities, special policies need to be pursued.

The emergence of new family structures also needs to be taken into consideration in formulating new social policies. Legislation governing public pension schemes needs to reflect these changes by introducing new ways of accessing benefits (Mattil 2006).

Finally, well-being in old age plays a vital role among the elderly, with social networks – constituted by family members and/or work colleagues – being the most important variable affecting their levels of subjective well-being. In this regard, active ageing appears to be crucial for happy ageing (Calvo 2006; Holzmann 2013b).

Acknowledgments The study was supported by ICREA Academia, the Spanish Ministry of Economy and Competitiveness and the ERDF under grants ECO2015-66314-R and ECO2016-76203-C2-2-P.

References

Abellán García, A., & Pujol Rodríguez, R. (2016). *Un perfil de las personas mayores en España, 2016. Indicadores estadísticos básicos. Informes del envejecimiento en red 14.*

Actuarial Association of Europe. (2016). *The ageing of the EU – Implications for pensions.* A discussion paper. Brussels.

Alaminos, E., & Ayuso, M. (2015). Una estimación actuarial del coste individual de las pensiones de jubilación y viudedad: Concurrencia de pensiones del Sistema de la Seguridad Social español. *Estudios de Economía Aplicada, 33*(3), 817–838.

Alaminos, E., & Ayuso, M. (2019). Marital status, gender, mortality and pensions: the disadvantages of being single in old age. *Revista Española de Investigaciones Sociológicas, 165*, 3–24.

Alaminos, E., Ayuso, M., & Guillen, M. (2016). An estimation of the individual illiquidity risk for the elderly Spanish population with long-term care needs. In *Modelling and simulation engineering, economics and management. Lecture Notes in Business Information Processing*, 254, 71–81.

Alberts, S. C., Archie, E. A., Gesquiere, L. R., Altmann, J., Vaupel, J. W., & Christensen, K. (2014). The male-female health-survival paradox: A comparative perspective on sex differences in aging and mortality. In Committee on Population; Division of Behavioral and Social Sciences and Education; National Research Council, M. Weinstein, & M. A. Lane (Eds.), *Sociality, hierarchy, health: Comparative biodemography: A collection of papers.* Washington, DC: National Academies Press (US); Sep 22. 15. Available from: https://www.ncbi.nlm.nih.gov/books/NBK242444/#.

Arza, C. (2015). *Protecting women's income security in old age. Toward gender-responsive pension systems. UN Women Policy Brief No. 3.* New York: UN Women.

Ayuso, M., & Holzmann, R. (2014). Longevidad: un breve análisis global y actuarial. *Documentos de trabajo Instituto BBVA de Pensiones, 1*, 1–14.

Ayuso, M., Bravo, J. M., & Holzmann, R. (2015). *Population projections revisited: Moving beyond convenient assumptions on fertility, mortality and migration.* Instituto BBVA de Pensiones - Working Paper N° 10/2015, March. Madrid: BBVA.

Ayuso, M., Bravo, J. M., & Holzmann, R. (2016). *On the heterogeneity in longevity among socioeconomic groups: Scope, trends, and implications for earning-related pension schemes.* IZA Discussion Paper 10060, 1–33.

Bauman, K. J. (2002). Welfare, work and material hardship in single parent and other households. *Journal of Poverty, 6*(1), 21–40.

Beehr, T., & Bennett, M. (2014). Working after retirement: Features of bridge employment and research directions. *Work, Aging and Retirement, 1*(1), 112–128.

Bonsang, E., & Klein, T. J. (2012). Retirement and subjective well-being. *Journal of Economic Behaviour & Organization, 83*(3), 311–329.

Bradshaw, J., & Chzhen, Y. (2011). Lone parent families: Poverty and policy in comparative perspective. In Almeda Samaranch, E. and Di Nella, D. (Eds.) *Bienestar, protección social y monoparentalidad. Colección familias monoparentales y diversidad familiar*, 11(2), 25–46. Barcelona: Copalqui Editorial.

Burtless, G. (2013). The impact of population aging and delayed retirement on workforce productivity. Center for Retirement Research at Boston College Working Paper, 11, 1–45.
Calvo, E. (2006). *Does working longer make people healthier and happier?* MPRA Paper No 5606, 1–9.
Case, A., & Paxson, C. (2005). Sex differences in morbidity and mortality. *Demography, 42*(2), 189–214.
Chandler, J., Williams, M., Maconachie, M., Collett, T., & Dodgeon, B. (2004). Living alone: Its place in household formation and change. *Sociological Research Online, 9*(3), 42.
Christopher, K. (2005). A 'pauperization of motherhood'? Single motherhood and women's poverty over time. *Journal of Poverty, 9*(3), 1–23.
Chuliá, H., Guillen, M., & Uribe, J. M. (2016). Modeling longevity risk with generalized dynamic factor models and vine-copulae. *ASTIN Bulletin, 46*(1), 165–190.
Crimmins, E. M., Kim, J. K., & Solé-Auró, A. (2011). Gender differences in health: Results from SHARE, ELSA and HRS. *European Journal of Public Health, 21*, 81–91.
Derviş, K. (2013). *The next social contract.* Project Syndicate. http://www.project-syndicate.org/commentary/redefiningthe-life-of-work-by-kemal-dervi.
Dingemans, E., & Henkens, K. (2015). How do retirement dynamics influence mental well-being in later life? A 10-year panel study. *Scandinavian Journal of Work Environment and Health, 41*, 16–23.
Disney, R. (2000). Crises in Public Pension Programmes in OECD: What are the reform options? *The Economic Journal, 110*(461), 1–23.
Duval, R. (2003). *The retirement effects of old-age pension and early retirement schemes in OECD countries, OECD Economics Department Working Papers, No. 370.* Paris: OECD Publishing.
European Commission. (2016). *European semester: Thematic factsheets – Adequacy and sustainability of pensions – 2016.*
European Union. (2014). *Population aging in Europe: Facts, implications and policies. Outcomes of EU-funded research.* Luxembourg: Directorate-General for Research and Innovation. Social Sciences and Humanities. European Commission: Publications Office of the European Union.
European Union. (2015). *People in the EU: Who are we and how do we live?* Luxembourg: Eurostat statistical books.
Eurostat. (2012). Population and housing census 2011.
Eurostat. (2013). *Average rating of satisfaction by domain, sex, age and educational attainment level.* Personal well-being indicators (ilc-pwb). Last updated 15 Sept 2016.
Eurostat. (2016a). *Healthy life years statistics.* Eurostat, statistics explained.
Eurostat. (2016b). *Living conditions (ilc_lv).* Population and social conditions.
Eurostat. (2016c). *Marriage indicators (last view: 20/12/2016).*
Eurostat. (2016d). *EUROPOP2013 Population projections (proj_13n).* Population and social conditions.
Everard, K. M., Lach, H. W., Fisher, E. B., & Baum, C. M. (2000). Relationship of activity and social support to the functional health of older adults. *Journal of Gerontology: Social Sciences, 55*(4), S208–S212.
Fokkema, T., & Liefbroer, A. C. (2008). Trends in living arrangements in Europe: Convergence or divergence? *Demographic Research, 19*(36), 1351–1418.
Gornick, J., & Jäntti, M. (2009). Child poverty in upper-income countries: Lessons from the Luxembourg income study. In S. Kamerman & A. Ben-Ariel (Eds.), *From child welfare to child well-being: An international perspective on knowledge in the service of policy making.* New York: Springer.
Gove, W. R. (1973). Sex, marital status and mortality. *American Journal of Sociology, 79*(1), 45–67.
Graham, C. (2014). *Late-life work and well-being* (p. 107). IZA World of Labor.
Guillen, M., & Comas-Herrera, A. (2012). How much risk is mitigated by LTC protection schemes? A methodological note and a case study of the public LTC system in Spain. *The Geneva Papers on Risk and Insurance- Issues and Practice, 37*, 712–724.

Hébert, B. P., & Luong, M. (2008). *Bridge employment*. Perspectives on Labour and Income, November, Statistics Canada, Catalogue no. 75-001.
Helliwell, J. F., & Putnam, R. D. (2004). The social context of well-being. *Philosophical Transactions of the Royal Society B, 359*, 1435–1446.
Holzmann, R. (2013a). An optimistic perspective on population aging and old-age financial protection. *Malaysian Journal of Economic Studies, 50*(2), 107–137.
Holzmann, R. (2013b). *A provocative perspective on population aging and old-age financial protection*. Center for Economic Studies and Ifo Institute. World Bank. IZA Discussion paper No. 7571.
Iacovou, M., & Skew, A. J. (2011). Household composition across the new Europe: Where do the new member states fit in? *Demographic Research, 25*(14), 465–490.
Kaplan, R. M., & Kronick, R. G. (2006). Marital status and longevity in the United States population. *Journal of Epidemiology and Community Health, 60*(9), 760–765.
Kramarow, E. A. (1995). The elderly who live alone in the United States: Historical perspectives on household change. *Demography, 32*(3), 335–352.
Kramer, K. Z., Myhra, L. L., Zuiker, V. S., & Bauer, J. W. (2016). Comparison of poverty and income disparity of single mothers and fathers across three decades. *Gender Issues, 33*(1), 22–41.
Lewis, J. (Ed.). (1997). *Lone Mothers in European Welfare Regimes: Shifting policy logics*. London: Jessica Kingsley.
Lindahl-Jacobsen, R., Hanson, H. A., Oksuzyan, A., Mineau, G. P., Christensen, K., & Smith, K. R. (2013). The male-female health-survival paradox and sex differences in cohort life expectancy in Utah, Denmark, and Sweden 1850-1910. *Annuals of Epidemiology, 23*(4), 161–166.
Lodovici, M. S., Patrizio, M., Pesce, F., & Roletto, E. (2015). *Elderly women living alone: An update of their living conditions*. Brussels: European Parliament. Brussels: European Union.
López Doblas, J. (2005). *Personas mayores viviendo solas: la autonomía como valor en alza*. Madrid: Instituto de Mayores y Servicios Sociales (IMSERSO).
Määttänen, N., Võrk, A., Piirits, M., Gal, R. I., Jarocinska, E., Ruzik, A., & Nijman, T. (2014). *The impact of living and working longer on pension income in five European countries: Estonia, Finland, Hungary, the Netherlands and Poland*. NETSPAR Discussion Paper Series.
Manzoli, L., Villari, P., Pirone, G. M., & Boccia, A. (2007). Marital status and mortality in the elderly: A systematic review and meta-analysis. *Social Science & Medicine, 64*(1), 77–94.
Mattil, B. (2006). *Pension systems. Sustainability and distributional effects in Germany and the United Kingdom. Contributions to Economics*. Heidelberg, Berlin: Springer.
Menec, V. H., Chipperfield, J. G., & Perry, R. R. (1999). Self-perceptions of health: A prospective analysis of mortality, control, and health. *Journal of Gerontology: Psychological Sciences, 54B* (2), 85–93.
Ng, T. P., Jin, A., Feng, L., Nyunt, M. S., Chow, K. Y., Feng, L., & Fong, N. P. (2015). Mortality of older persons living alone: Singapore longitudinal aging studies. *BMC Geriatrics, 15*, 126.
Nikolova, M., & Graham, C. (2014). Employment, late-life work, retirement, and well-being in Europe and the United States. *IZA Journal of European Labor Studies, 3*, 5.
OECD. (2011a). *Doing better for families*. Paris: OECD Publishing.
OECD. (2011b). *The future of families to 2030*. Paris: OECD Publishing.
OECD. (2011c). *How's life? Measuring well-being*. Paris: OECD Publishing.
OECD. (2014). *Society at a glance 2014: OECD social indicators*. Paris: OECD Publishing.
OECD. (2015). *Pensions at a glance 2015: OECD and G20 indicators*. Paris: OECD Publishing.
OECD. (2016). *Cohabitation rate and prevalence of other forms of partnership*. OECD Family Database (updated 27 Nov 2016).
Oeppen, J., & Vaupel, J. W. (2002). Broken limits to life expectancy. *Science, 296*(5570), 1029–1031.
Pinquart, M., & Sörensen, S. (2000). Influences of socioeconomic status, social network, and competence on subjective well-being in later life: A meta-analysis. *Psychology and Aging, 15* (2), 187–224.

Piulachs, X., Alemany, R., & Guillen, M. (2016). Joint modelling of survival and emergency medical care usage in Spanish insureds aged 65. *PLoS One, 11*(4), e0153234.
Robards, J., Evandrou, M., Falkingham, J., & Vlachantoni, A. (2012). Marital status, health and mortality. *Maturitas, 73*(4), 295–299.
Ruhm, C. J. (1990). Bridge jobs and partial retirement. *Journal of Labor Economics, 8*(4), 482–501.
Sanderson, W. C., & Scherbov, S. (2005). Average remaining lifetimes can increase as human populations age. *Nature, 435*(7043), 811–813.
Sanderson, W. C., & Scherbov, S. (2007). A new perspective on population aging. *Demographic Research, 16*, Article 2, 27–58.
Sanderson, W. C., & Scherbov, S. (2010). Remeasuring aging. *Science, 329*(5997), 1287–1288.
Sanderson, W. C., & Scherbov, S. (2015). Faster increases in human life expectancy could lead to slower population aging. *PLoS One, 10*(4), e0121922.
Siegrist, J., von dem Knesebeck, O., & Pollack, C. E. (2004). Social productivity and well-being of older people: A sociological exploration. *Social Theory and Health, 2*(1), 1–17.
Spanish Statistical Office. (2014). *Módulo Bienestar - Módulo 2013*. Encuesta de Condiciones de Vida.
Stiglitz, J., Sen, A., & Fitoussi, J. P. (2009). *Report of the commission on the measurement of economic performance and social Progress*. Paris. Available online from the Commission on the Measurement of Economic Performance and Social Progress: http://www.stiglitz-sen-fitoussi.fr/en/index.htm.
Thorslund, M., Wastesson, J. W., Agahi, N., Lagergren, M., & Parker, M. G. (2013). The rise and fall of women's advantage: A comparison of national trends in life expectancy at age 65 years. *European Journal of Ageing, 10*, 271–277.
Uribe, J. M., Chuliá, H., & Guillen, M. (2015). Asymmetric uncertainty of mortality and longevity in the Spanish population. *Advances in Intelligent Systems and Computing, 377*, 279–287.
van Dalen, H. P., Henkens, K., Henderikse, W., & Schippers, J. (2010). Do European employers support later retirement? *International Journal of Manpower, 31*(3), 360–373.
Vaupel, J. W., & Kistowski, K. G. (2005). Broken limits to life expectancy. *Ageing Horizons, 3*, 6–13.
World Health Organization (WHO). (2011). *Global health and aging*. US National Institute of Aging.

Chapter 3
The Public Pension Systems and the Economic Crisis

Borja Encinas-Goenechea, Robert Meneu-Gaya, and María de la Cruz del Río-Rama

Abstract Concern about the long-term sustainability of European public pension systems has been a permanent feature for decades due to the unstoppable ageing of the population, but demographic change is not the only factor of concern. A deep economic and financial crisis has been added to this structural problem, whose impact on economic growth and job creation has further aggravated the situation. The combination of these two challenges has created a "perfect storm", which is forcing most European countries to introduce far-reaching reforms in their pension systems with the aim of ensuring their sustainability. This chapter analyses the main measures that the different EU-28 countries have addressed since the beginning of the crisis to ensure the sustainability of their pensions. The wide range of measures taken include delaying the retirement age and introducing sustainability factors and automatic adjustment mechanisms.

Keywords Economic crisis · Demographic ageing · Pension reform · Sustainability

B. Encinas-Goenechea (✉)
Department of Finance and Accounting, University of Extremadura, Badajoz, Extremadura, Spain
e-mail: bencinas@unex.es

R. Meneu-Gaya
Department of Financial Economics and Actuarial, University of Valencia, Valencia, Spain
e-mail: robert.meneu@uv.es

M. C. del Río-Rama
Department of Business Organisation and Marketing, University of Vigo, Ourense, Galicia, Spain
e-mail: delrio@uvigo.es

M. Peris-Ortiz et al. (eds.), *Economic Challenges of Pension Systems*,
https://doi.org/10.1007/978-3-030-37912-4_3

3.1 Introduction

The financial sustainability of public pension systems in Europe is under debate. The concern is widespread because all European countries are witnessing a slow but steady ageing of their population due to, on the one hand, the progressive increase in life expectancy and, on the other hand, the decreasing birth rate. In addition, according to all demographic projections, this ageing will increase over the next few decades. In particular, according to Eurostat (projection EUROPOP2013), in the year 2060, 28.4% of the population of the EU-28 will be over 65, compared to a percentage of 18.9% in 2015.

The social and economic implications of this demographic phenomenon, unprecedented in the history of mankind, are manifold (labour market, productivity, health care, care for dependency, etc.) and, therefore, is considered one of the most important challenges facing all European countries in the coming decades. However, one of the issues that most concerns European governments is the impact that this demographic phenomenon can have on the sustainability of pension systems.[1] In this sense, according to the European Commission (2015), the component that explains almost exclusively the increase in pension expenditure on GDP in the period 2013–2060 is population ageing measured by the dependency ratio. In fact, the remaining economic and endogenous factors of the system which pension expenditure on GDP depend on have a positive effect and tend to compensate, totally or partially, for the demographic effect.

In addition to demographic problems, there is the financial and economic crisis, whose impact is being experienced in all economic and social spheres and, particularly, in the area of pension systems.[2] This crisis, among other things, has led to a decline in GDP, decreasing employment, as well as a lack of growth and even lower wages, with all these circumstances causing a decline in income from social contributions, while pension expenditure continues its upward trend due to the unstoppable ageing of the population. For example, in Spain, one of the European countries hardest hit by the crisis in terms of economic activity and job destruction, the social security deficit forecasted for the mid 20s has moved to the present.[3] As Jiménez (2013) points out, the crisis has done in just 4 years what demography should have done in 15 years. In short, the combination of these two challenges, a structural one of demographic origin and another one of economic origin, represents a "perfect

[1]The effects of ageing on pensions have been well known since the early 1990s, when international institutions such as the European Commission, the OECD and the World Bank made the first projections and highlighted the need to initiate reforms to deal with their financial sustainability problem.

[2]In addition to the demographic evolution, there are other factors such as economic growth and job creation, without which pension systems based on the distribution principle would be unsustainable due to insufficient resources (contributions) to finance pension benefits.

[3]In the period 2007–2015, the Spanish social security accounts changed from a surplus of 1.36% of GDP to a large deficit of 1.54% of GDP.

storm" for European public pension systems due to their negative impact, respectively, on their main expenditure and income items.

The concern in Europe about the impact of the crisis was evident at the beginning of the crisis. As early as 2009, the European Commission highlighted in its communication on ageing that the economic crisis could aggravate the economic effects of population ageing on pensions due to the sharp and rapid decline in economic activity and its effects on employment (European Commission 2009a). For pay-as-you-go systems, which are the majority of European systems, the slowdown in the real economy produces additional budgetary pressures on their funding.

A year later, in 2010, the European Commission reaffirmed its concern about the consequences of the crisis on pensions. The Green Paper on pensions (European Commission 2010a) states that population ageing is taking place faster than expected and that with current demographic trends the situation is unsustainable, unless, seeing that we live longer, we also work longer. That is to say, the problem of European pension systems is not so much the increase in longevity but the fact that their operating rules have not adapted to changes in individuals' life cycles adequately. In addition to this demographic challenge, the report points out that the economic crisis has aggravated, even more so, the financial situation of pension systems because of its impact on the capacity to create employment in Europe.

Interest and concern about the sustainability of public pensions is not a recent issue. Most EU-28 countries have been introducing substantial pension reforms in their pensions systems for decades to protect them from the challenge of ageing. However, the crisis has revitalized this debate and has forced all European governments to embark on an unprecedented reform, not only because of the speed with which the reforms have been carried out but also because of their intensity.

This paper analyses how European countries have responded to the crisis in order to strengthen their pension systems. This chapter is organized as follows. After this introduction, the following section analyses the magnitude of the crisis in terms of GDP and job creation, which are two key elements for the sustainability of pensions based on the pay-as-you-go system. Section 3.3 briefly describes the different pension models that exist in European countries. Section 3.4 examines the main reform measures implemented in Europe. The chapter ends with a brief conclusion.

3.2 Magnitude of the Economic Crisis in the EU: An Overview

The global financial and economic crisis that began in the US mortgage market has had very negative consequences on the economy of the EU-28. As will be seen throughout this section, lower GDP growth, negative employment trends and stagnation and even lower wages recorded since the beginning of the crisis have resulted in a fall in income from social contributions, which is the main source of funding for European pension systems. In addition to these relevant factors, pension expenditure has maintained its structural upward trend due to the ageing population, which has led to strong financial tensions in most European countries. In summary, the crisis has duplicated the already complicated equation between ageing and the sustainability of European public pensions.

From the economic activity point of view, the reduction of real GDP in the United States (0.3%) and the low growth rate in the EU-28 (0.4%) in 2008 marked the beginning of a deep and long economic recession. In 2009, real GDP fell by 4.4% in the EU-28 while decreasing by 2.8% in the United States. The recovery in EU-28 caused real GDP to increase by 2.1% in 2010, followed by a further increase of 1.7% in 2011. Subsequently, GDP decreased again by 0.5% in 2012 and remained static in 2013 (0.2%) before accelerating its growth in 2014 (1.6%) and 2015 (2.2%).

The impact of the crisis has been very uneven in the different Member States. After a decrease in all EU-28 countries, except Poland, in 2009, economic growth resumed in 24 countries in 2010 and continued in 2011. However, in 2012 this progress was reversed, just under half (13) of EU Member States experienced economic expansion, while in 2013 this figure increased to 17 and in 2014 to 25. In 2015, the highest growth rates were recorded in Ireland (26.3%),[4] Malta (7.4%), Czech Republic (4.5%), Sweden (4.1%) and seven other countries achieving growth rates above 3%. By contrast, the French (1.3%), Austrian (1%), Italian (0.7%) and Finnish (0.2%) economies were the only ones that grew below 1.5%, and only the Greek one registered a slight fall in GDP of 0.2%.

The extent of the crisis is reflected in the overall evolution of real GDP for the period 2008–2015. For the EU-28 as a whole, the final balance of this period was a low average annual growth of 0.4%. By country, the highest average annual growth rates were recorded in Malta (3.6%), Poland (3.2%), Ireland (3.1%) and Slovakia (2.1%). However, the depth of the crisis and the slow recovery rate meant that for a total of ten countries, the overall evolution of real GDP for the period 2008–2015 was negative and consequently has not yet reached the levels of real GDP before the crisis. Table 3.1 shows the countries that, since the beginning of the crisis, have achieved the highest and lowest average growth rates in their GDP.

The economic slowdown has a very negative impact on the budgetary balance of pension systems due to income stability and increase in expenditure (both expressed as a rate of GDP). In fact, on the one hand, the GDP growth rate is equal to the growth rate of the labour factor (number of contributors) plus the apparent labour productivity (directly related to wages and, ultimately, to the contribution bases); therefore, the income from contributions evolves in the same direction and at a rate similar to that of GDP. On the other hand, pension expenditure is changing in the

[4]The extraordinary growth of Ireland in 2015 is partly fictitious because it was due to the fact that many multinational companies, especially in the technology sector, moved their headquarters to Ireland for tax reasons. However, the GDP, which excludes the contribution of multinationals, also registered a significant growth rate close to 19%.

Table 3.1 EU-28 countries with the highest and lowest average real GDP growth

	2008	2009	2010	2011	2012	2013	2014	2015	Average 2008–2015
EU-28	0.4	−4.4	2.1	1.7	−0.5	0.2	1.6	2.2	0.4
Countries with the highest economic growth (2008–2015)									
Malta	3.3	−2.5	3.5	1.4	2.7	4.6	8.4	7.4	3.6
Poland	4.2	2.8	3.6	5.0	1.6	1.4	3.3	3.9	3.2
Ireland	−4.4	−4.6	2.0	0.0	−1.1	1.1	8.5	26.3	3.1
Slovakia	5.6	−5.4	5.0	2.8	1.7	1.5	2.6	3.8	2.1
Luxembourg	−0.8	−5.4	5.8	2.0	0.0	4.2	4.7	3.5	1.7
Romania	8.5	−7.1	−0.8	1.1	0.6	3.5	3.1	3.7	*1.5*
Bulgaria	6.0	−3.6	1.3	1.9	0.0	0.9	1.3	3.6	*1.4*
Sweden	−0.6	−5.2	6.0	2.7	−0.3	1.2	2.6	4.1	1.3
Countries with the lowest economic growth (2008–2015)									
Greece	−0.3	−4.3	−5.5	−9.1	−7.3	−3.2	0.4	−0.2	*−3.7*
Croatia	2.1	−7.4	−1.7	−0.3	−2.2	−1.1	−0.5	1.6	−1.2
Italy	−1.1	−5.5	1.7	0.6	−2.8	−1.7	0.1	0.7	−1.0
Cyprus	3.9	−1.8	1.3	0.3	−3.2	−6.0	−1.5	1.7	*−0.7*
Latvia	−3.6	−14.3	−3.8	6.2	4.0	2.9	2.1	2.7	−0.7
Portugal	0.2	−3.0	1.9	−1.8	−4.0	−1.1	0.9	1.6	*−0.7*
Finland	0.7	−8.3	3.0	2.6	−1.4	−0.8	−0.7	0.2	−0.6
Spain	1.1	−3.6	0.0	−1.0	−2.9	−1.7	1.4	3.2	*−0.5*

Source: Eurostat

Table 3.2 Pension expenditure on GDP in the EU-28 countries most affected by the crisis

	2007	2014	Change 2007–2014
Greece	12.3	17.1	4.8
Cyprus	6.0	10.5	4.5
Spain	9.0	12.8	3.8
Portugal	12.2	15.6	3.4
Latvia	4.9	7.9	3.0
Finland	10.4	13.4	3.0
Italy	14.0	16.5	2.5
Croatia	9.3[a]	11.0	1.7
EU-28	11.4[b]	12.6	1.2

Source: Eurostat
[a]Figure related to 2008
[b]Figure related to the EU-27

opposite direction: the lower the economic growth, the lower the employment rate and labour intensity and the higher the pension expenditure on GDP (Table 3.2).[5]

[5]See the breakdown of pension expenditure on GDP carried out in the European Commission (2015) to see the factors that influence its evolution.

The consequences of the crisis have also been experienced in the European labour market. From the point of view of the financial equilibrium of pay-as-you-go systems, employment growth is an essential element in ensuring that the system receives sufficient income each year to finance its pension obligations. As a result, employment contraction caused by the crisis has further worsened the precrisis poor prospects on the financial situation of European pension systems. In this context, the implementation of policies aimed at achieving sustained growth and adequate levels of employment are the basic element to ensure the future of pensions in Europe.

In 2008, the EU-28 employment rate for people aged between 15 and 64 reached a maximum rate of 65.7% and decreased in the following years to 64.1% in 2010. This decline during the first years of the crisis (a drop of 1.6%) was followed by a period of stability that lasted until 2013. In 2014 and 2015, the employment rate began an upward trend again, which was observed before the crisis, with a growth rate of 0.8 and 0.7%, respectively, reaching 65.6%.

The analysis by country allows us to observe the considerable differences that have been registered in the labour market performance of the different European countries. Only 12 Member States increased their employment rate, and in some cases there were slight variations. The highest increases were seen in Malta (8.4%) and Hungary (7.5%) and were also significant in Germany, the Czech Republic and Poland, which reached increases greater than 3.5 pp. For the rest of the countries, there was a negative trend, especially in Greece, whose employment rate declined from 61.4% in 2008 to 50.8% in 2015. There were also significant declines (above 4%) in the employment rates of Cyprus, Spain, Ireland, Croatia, Portugal and Denmark (Table 3.3).

Note that although employment levels in the EU-28 remained virtually unchanged in the period 2008–2015 (the employment rate in 2015 was only 0.1% below its 2008 level). These figures should be dealt with caution because in most countries, the increase in employment rates was not due to an increase in the employed population but to a decline in the population aged 15–64 caused by population ageing. Consequently, the impact of the crisis on the number of contributors was more severe than reflected by employment rates. In particular, in the EU-28 as a whole, the employed population at the end of 2015 was 3.8 million less than in 2008. By country, only nine countries had a higher number of employees in 2005 than at the beginning of the crisis, where Germany and the United Kingdom stand out from the rest.

The analysis of the consequences of the economic recession on the labour market should focus not only exclusively on the amount of employment but also on the quality of employment. For this reason, another aspect that should be analysed is how the distribution of full-time and part-time employment evolved. At the beginning of the crisis, the percentage of part-time employment over total employment (part-time rate) was 17.5% in the EU-28, compared with 19.6% in 2015.

The trend for the EU-28 as a whole is repeated in almost all Member States (only Croatia, Poland and Sweden recorded a drop in their part-time employment), which indicates that part-time work is consolidating as a more structural element of the European labour market. The largest increases, above 4 pp, took place in the labour

Table 3.3 EU-28 countries with the highest and lowest variation in employment rates

	2008	2009	2010	2011	2012	2013	2014	2015	Change 2008–2015
EU-28	65.7	64.4	64.1	64.2	64.1	64.1	64.9	65.6	−0.1
Countries with the highest employment rate growth (2008–2015)									
Malta	55.5	55.3	56.2	57.9	59.1	60.8	62.3	63.9	8.4
Hungary	56.4	55.0	54.9	55.4	56.7	58.1	61.8	63.9	7.5
Germany	70.1	70.3	71.1	72.7	73.0	73.5	73.8	74.0	3.9
Poland	59.2	59.3	58.9	59.3	59.7	60.0	61.7	62.9	3.7
Czech Republic	66.6	65.4	65.0	65.7	66.5	67.7	69.0	70.2	3.6
Lithuania	64.4	59.9	57.6	60.2	62.0	63.7	65.7	67.2	2.8
Luxembourg	63.4	65.2	65.2	64.6	65.8	65.7	66.6	66.1	2.7
Romania	59.0	58.6	60.2	59.3	60.2	60.1	61.0	61.4	2.4
Countries with the lowest employment rate growth (2008–2015)									
Greece	61.4	60.8	59.1	55.1	50.8	48.8	49.4	50.8	−10.6
Cyprus	70.9	69.0	68.9	67.6	64.6	61.7	62.1	62.7	−8.2
Spain	64.5	60.0	58.8	58.0	55.8	54.8	56.0	57.8	−6.7
Denmark	77.9	75.3	73.3	73.1	72.6	72.5	72.8	73.5	−4.4
Croatia	60.0	59.4	57.4	55.2	53.5	52.5	54.6	55.8	−4.2
Ireland	67.4	61.9	59.6	58.9	58.8	60.5	61.7	63.3	−4.1
Portugal	68.0	66.1	65.3	63.8	61.4	60.6	62.6	63.9	−4.1
Slovenia	68.6	67.5	66.2	64.4	64.1	63.3	63.9	65.2	−3.4

Source: Eurostat

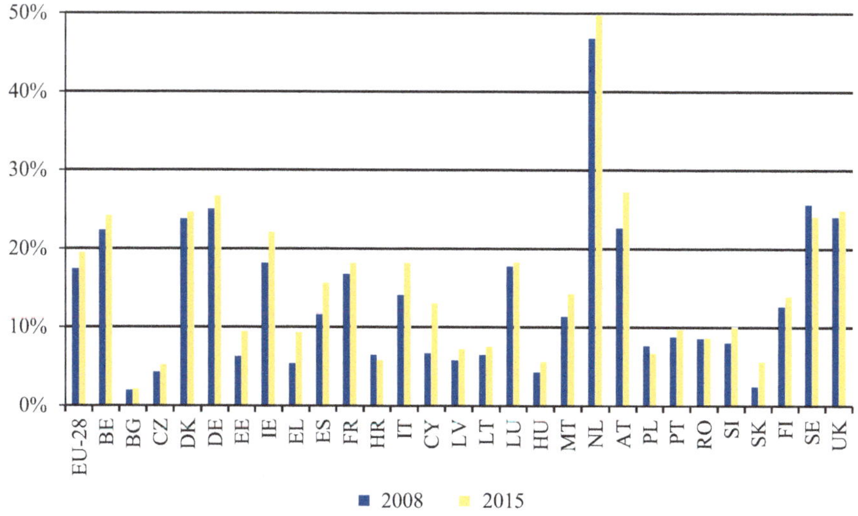

Fig. 3.1 Part-time employment rate in EU-28 countries (2008–2015). (*Source*: Eurostat)

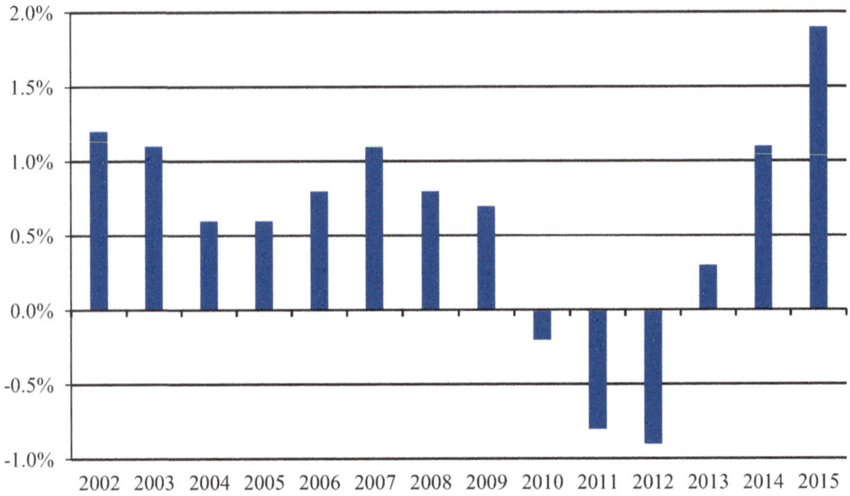

Fig. 3.2 Annual average real wage growth EU-28. (*Source*: ILO (2016))

markets of Ireland, Spain, Italy, Cyprus and Austria (Fig. 3.1). As a result, the fall in the number of employed people together with the greater importance of part-time employment reduced the hours contributed to the social security.

Another dimension of the labour market relevant to the sustainability of pensions is the evolution of wages. Since 2008, there are many European countries that have seen a drastic reduction in real wages. According to ILO data (2016), average real wages in the EU-28 fell sharply in the period 2010–2012, with similar growth to the precrisis years (Fig. 3.2). However, since the beginning of the crisis, real wages have been very different between European countries. For example, in France and Germany, they increased (6% and 7%, respectively,) while in the other two major European economies, Italy and the United Kingdom, there was also a decline, of 6% and 7%, respectively. With regard to the Eurozone countries most affected by the crisis and having undergone strong austerity measures, there are also some significant differences. In Portugal, the average real wages increased by 3%, while in Ireland and Spain they decreased by 1% and 2%, respectively. But above all, we must highlight the case of Greece that accumulates a drop of 25% since the wage levels of 2007.

3.3 Typology of Pensions Systems

Undoubtedly one of the pending issues in the European convergence process is public pensions. In fact, it can be said that until today, the harmonization of European pension systems is practically non-existent. For Morales (2010), the fundamental cause of this lack of integration lies in the Member States' reluctance to give up their powers in this matter due to the high level of political impact that everything related to social protection, in general, has and pension systems, in particular. But precisely because of this, establishing a public pension system that is mainly common to all European countries would lead to moving away from political conditions, which would lead to greater transparency and ensure the sustainability of the pension system from a financial point of view. At the same time, it would lead to greater economic and financial integration and, in addition, would avoid a great number of problems arising from the recognition of rights by the different countries in which the same worker would be able to contribute.

Thus, as outlined in the White Paper on pensions (European Commission 2012a), Member States are primarily responsible for the design of their public pension systems. However, the Treaty on the Functioning of the European Union states that the EU shall support and complement activities of the Member States in the fields of social security and social protection of workers (Article 153). Therefore, in recent years, the EU has promoted a set of actions, such as the creation of a common framework for discussion and information that helps to find individual solutions to the joint problems that threaten the sustainability of the pension systems of each country.[6]

As Jimeno (2000) points out, since Otto Von Bismarck introduced public pensions in Germany, all countries have implemented, to a greater or lesser extent, public pension systems. In general, the aim of these systems is similar in all countries: on the one hand, the guarantee of a minimum income for all individuals and, on the other hand, the continued payment of wages, or a proportion of it that allows to sustain a sufficient standard of living when the retirement age is reached by those who have previously contributed to the system.

Although their design and organization differ in many respects from one country to another, there are certain common characteristics that allow them to be classified in a homogeneous way according to two criteria: (1) according to the form of financing and (2) according to the principle governing the determination of the pension amount.

Depending on the form of financing, it is usually differentiated between pay-as-you-go systems and funded systems.[7] Pay-as-you-go systems are based on the principle of permanent intergenerational solidarity, i.e. the retirement pensions of each generation are financed by the social contributions made by subsequent generations who are active at that moment, and not by the contributions the generations already retired made in their day. It is therefore a question of workers transferring a share of their income to retirees, with the promise (intergenerational agreement) that this process will continue in the future, i.e. when they retire, the new assets in the

[6]At present the main framework of action by the EU institutions in the field of pensions is the open method of coordination (OMC), whose purpose is to help countries develop their own national policies to ensure adequate and sustainable pensions in the long term.

[7]A detailed analysis of PAYG and funded systems and the comparison between them from different perspectives can be seen in Zubiri (2014).

labour market will pay their pensions. The sustainability of these systems is very sensitive to the population growth of assets and to the economic growth since both tend to increase the contributions with which to pay pensions. Conversely, funded systems are long-term savings systems in which each worker finances his pension through his own savings that are accumulated in an individual account, which is invested in financial markets until retirement and the balance will be used to finance the future payment of his own pension. In short, a funded system does not produce intergenerational income transfers, which in turn does occur in PAYG systems.

A second way of classifying pension systems is depending on how the pension amount is calculated, which allows differentiating between defined benefit systems and defined contribution systems. In defined benefit systems, the amount of the retirement pension amount is fixed in advance, on the basis of the worker's employment record, i.e. it depends on his wages, his years of contribution and his retirement age and does not depend on the development of relevant demographic and macroeconomic factors, such as economic growth or life expectancy. The objective of this system is to ensure that there is a certain relationship between his pension and salary at the end of his working life (Jimeno 2003). On the other hand, in a defined contribution system, workers pay their contributions, as in a defined benefit system, which accumulate in a particular fund or individual accounts, but without knowing, a priori, what the pension amount that he will perceive will be, as it will depend not only on the contributions made during his active stage but also on future factors such as the profitability of accumulated capital or certain demographic or macroeconomic factors, such as life expectancy at the time of retirement.[8]

Although it is common to identify public systems with pay-as-you-go and defined benefit procedures and private systems with capitalization and defined contribution schemes, there are numerous possibilities in practice that combine the four characteristics to different degrees (Garcia et al. 2011). In the EU-28, most Member States have a defined benefit and pay-as-you-go system, where intergenerational solidarity has become the cornerstone of their social security systems, but with significant differences between them in terms of parameters, such as the statutory retirement age, methods of updating contributions and revaluating pensions, rules for calculating pensions, etc. Some countries (Sweden, Italy, Poland and Latvia) have defined contribution schemes that follow a notional account system,[9] and other countries

[8]As will be seen further, since the beginning of the crisis several European countries have introduced some mechanism of automatic adjustment into their defined benefit pension systems, which brings them closer to the functioning of defined contribution schemes.

[9]A notional account can be defined as a virtual account, where the contributions of the individual are and the fictitious returns that these contributions generate throughout their working life collected. The return is calculated according to a notional rate, which can be quite varied, although nearly always related to some economic variable, such as the GDP growth rate, average wages, aggregate wages, contribution income, etc. Thus, when the individual retires, he will receive a pension that depends on his accumulated notional fund and life expectancy. The notional accounts model maintains it's financing through the pay-as-you-go system but incorporates elements of funded systems, such as the financial-actuarial formulas for calculating pensions. A detailed analysis of the advantages and disadvantages of notional accounts can be seen in Devesa et al. (2014).

such as Germany, Slovakia and Romania have adopted a points system[10] that is a variant of the former. Other countries such as Ireland, the Netherlands, the United Kingdom and Denmark provide a basic public pension supplemented by a contributory pension funded by the pay-as-you-go system (Table 3.4).

3.4 The Reform of European Pensions in Times of Crisis

As already mentioned, since the 1990s, pension sustainability has been a matter of concern in most European countries because their populations are among the longest living in the world. After signing the Maastricht Treaty, the introduction of the Euro and the requirement to limit budget deficits and reduce public debt, many countries were forced to undertake major reforms in their social security systems, since pension expenditure represents a significant part of public expenditure. In addition, all the projections available showed its significant growth due to the increase in life expectancy and to the retirement of particularly numerous cohorts, which belong to the baby boom generation. It is therefore not surprising that most European countries have spent more than 20 years introducing reforms in their public pension systems in response to the challenges of ageing.

Although there is a significant heterogeneity among the reforms carried out, they can be classified, depending on their depth, into parametric type reforms and structural reforms. Parametric reforms are those that do not imply a radical change in the social security model but changes in legislation that involve adjustments in the basic parameters of the system, such as an increase in the statutory retirement age or stricter conditions for access to early retirement. On the contrary, structural reforms are more profound changes that have a stronger impact on the system, affecting the model severely and especially the financing system. The following are included as structural reforms in Europe:

- The partial replacement of the PAYG system for the funded system.[11] The mixed funded and PAYG system is inspired by the multi-pillar scheme proposed by the

[10]Under this modality, pensions depend on the number of points workers accumulate during their working lives. In Germany each worker obtains "pensionable points" annually, which depend on the ratio between their annual income and the average income of all taxpayers. For example, if a worker's annual income is equal to the general average income of workers, he is assigned 1 point, but if his income in a year is 25% higher than the workers′ average, he will have 1.25 points for that year. At the time of retirement, accumulated points are multiplied by an index (price of points) that converts them into monetary units. The price of points allows to adapt pensions to demographic and/or economic changes.

[11]No European country has opted for a pure funded system. One of the reasons for the little success of this system is that the public pension system is highly regarded by European citizens, which has ensured sufficient income for many generations of pensioners for decades, and is deeply rooted in the welfare state system (Alonso et al. 2011).

Table 3.4 Public pension systems in the EU-28

	Basic pension	Defined benefit	Notional defined contribution	Points system
Belgium		x		
Bulgaria		x		
Czech Republic		x		
Denmark	x	x		
Germany				x
Estonia		x		
Ireland	x	x		
Greece[a]	x	x	x	
Spain		x		
France[b]		x		x
Croatia				x
Italy			x	
Cyprus				x
Latvia			x	
Lithuania		x		
Luxembourg		x		
Hungary		x		
Malta	x	x		
Netherlands	x	x		
Austria		x		
Poland			x	
Portugal		x		
Romania				x
Slovenia		x		
Slovakia				x
Finland		x		
Sweden			x	
United Kingdom	x	x		

Source: European Commission (2015)
[a]The public supplementary pension funds are NDC since 2015
[b]Point system refers to the ARRCO and AGIRC pension schemes

World Bank in 1994.[12] As stated by Alonso et al. (2011), some European countries followed this scheme in such a way that many of the reforms undertaken were to modify the conditions of the first pillar, reducing their benefits, and to

[12]*Pilar 0*: universal non-contributory scheme which provides a minimum level of protection (social pension). *First pillar*: contributory, pay-as-you-go and defined benefit (proportional to the salary received during the active life). *Second pillar*: contributory and mandatory, defined contribution (individual savings accounts of capitalization). *Third pillar*: contributory and voluntary, of defined contribution.

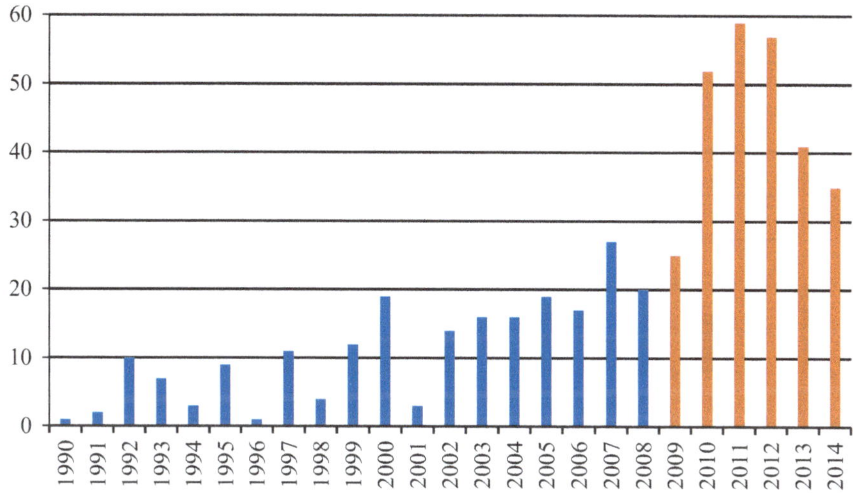

Fig. 3.3 Number of (main) pension measures in the EU since the 1990s. (*Source*: Carone et al. (2016))

complement the pay-as-you-go system with additional contributions to a compulsory or voluntary capitalization account (second and third pillar). This change does have its drawbacks. In addition to the risks inherent in any capitalization system (inflation and insolvency), there is the problem of transition, since the current and future pensions of those who remain in the pay-as-you-go system must continue to be paid. This has been partially resolved by additional contributions for those who enter the new system and partly from the general tax system or from indebtedness. The following EU-28 countries have a compulsory or quasi-compulsory capitalization part in their pension system: Denmark, the Netherlands, Sweden, Poland, Hungary, Slovenia, Latvia, Estonia and Slovakia.

- Change to the notional account system. This is the case in Sweden, Italy, Poland and Latvia.
- The automatic link of some relevant parameters of the PAYG system to the evolution of life expectancy or the economic situation. We will refer to this type of reforms later as this has been one of the most widespread measures in European countries since the economic crisis.

Despite the intensity of the reforms undertaken, the onset of the economic crisis rekindled European countries' concern for the financial health of their public pension systems, so much so that in 2009 an unprecedented wave of reforms began in Europe, in such a way that the need to give priority to reforms of social security systems was imposed in a decisive way in all European governments (Fig. 3.3). Undoubtedly, the recent profusion of reforms is a justified reaction to the financial difficulties encountered by European pension systems, which is provoked by the severe economic deterioration that has been added to growing demographic structural pressures.

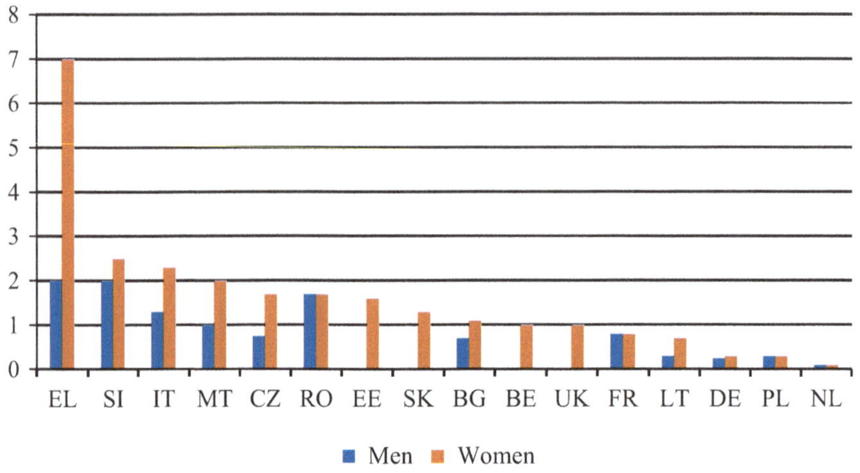

Fig. 3.4 Changes in the statutory retirement age between 2008 and 2013. (*Source*: European Commission (2009b, 2015))

Since 2009, the reforms that have been carried out in the EU-28 have been mainly in the field of parametric changes.[13] It is, therefore, a generation of reforms of lesser extent than many of those promoted in the 1990s and early 2000s. As will be seen further, the measures implemented since the beginning of the crisis are quite varied and in some cases complex. It is therefore increasingly necessary for European social security systems to expand and improve the information they give their citizens about their future pensions so that they can make optimal decisions on issues as crucial as consumption-saving during their active stage or the moment of retirement. Data such as the accumulated contribution made by workers and employers, the probable pension expected or the actuarial balance of the system will not only help in decision-making but also in individuals' awareness of the cost of their pension.

One of the most widely applied parametric measures since the beginning of the crisis has been the gradual delay of the ordinary retirement age (Figs. 3.4 and 3.5). This measure is being implemented progressively over time, so that when it is completed, there will be no EU-28 country (before the crisis there were 11) with a standard retirement age below 65 years, and in many countries, it will be 67 and even 68 years as is the case of the United Kingdom and Ireland.[14] In many countries these increases have been accompanied by measures to equalize the retirement ages of men and women, such as Cyprus, Austria, Slovenia, Italy, Lithuania, the United

[13]A more detailed analysis on the reforms implemented can be seen in the European Commission (2010b, 2012b) and Carone et al. (2016).

[14]In addition, as will be seen further, some countries introduced mechanisms that automatically link the retirement age review to the life expectancy evolution. The implementation of this measure will result in significant increases in retirement ages that in some cases will exceed 70 years.

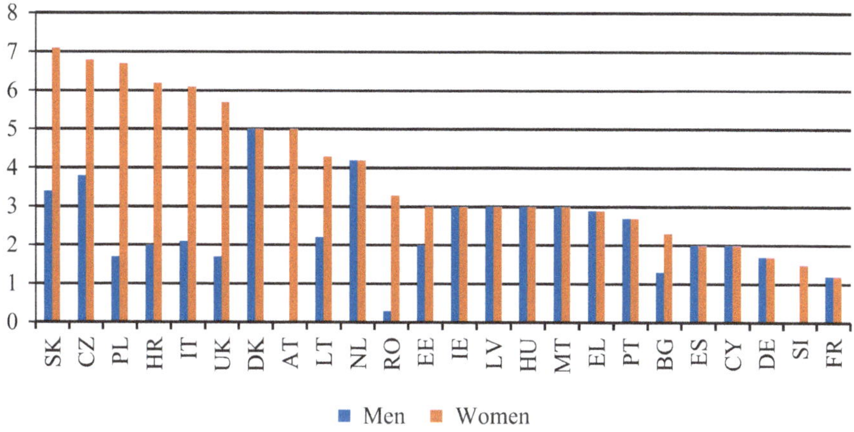

Fig. 3.5 Changes in the statutory retirement age between 2013 and 2040. (*Source*: European Commission (2009b, 2015))

Kingdom and Poland. The only countries that maintain gender differences in their legislation are Bulgaria and Romania.

The increase in the statutory retirement age has two clear effects on the sustainability of pension systems: on the one hand, it reduces pension expenditure by reducing the number of pensioners and, on the other hand, it improves the financial-actuarial balance of the system by extending individuals' working lives and, at the same time, shortening their pensionable stage.[15] However, as pointed out in the opinion of the European Economic and Social Committee on the Green Paper,[16] the mere increase in the statutory retirement age cannot solve the problem of demographic challenges and considers that the effective retirement age[17] should be increased. That is why in many countries this measure has been accompanied by other measures to ensure that the effective retirement age is close to the statutory age. Increasing the age to access to early retirement (Belgium, the Czech Republic, Greece, Italy, the United Kingdom and Bulgaria), increasing the penalty for early retirement[18] (such as Spain and France) and increasing incentives in order to extend

[15]For a pension system to be sustainable, it is necessary for there to be a balance between the income and expenditure for each year, as well as a financial-actuarial balance between the contributions made and the benefits received by the individuals participating in the system, and for this to occur, there must be an adequate relationship between the number of years contributed to the system and the number of years that the pension is received.

[16]Opinion of the European Economic and Social Committee on the subject «Green Paper – towards adequate, sustainable and secure European pension systems ». COM (2010) 365 final.

[17]In 2014, the effective retirement age of men and women in the EU was around 63 years.

[18]For many years, European countries pursued a policy of promoting early retirement as an effective instrument to combat high unemployment rates and to facilitate the access of younger workers to the labour market. As a consequence of this policy, the employment rate of people aged between 55 and 64 fell considerably for several decades. However, the new measures taken reversed this trend. In EU-28, the employment rate of these workers reached 53.3% in 2015 compared to 44.5% in 2007.

the working life beyond the statutory age (e.g. Germany, Austria, Finland, Hungary and Slovakia) are some of the formulas used.

Another reform generally applied in many countries is to increase the number of contribution years that are taken into account to calculate the pension, seeking to strengthen the link between the contributions made and the benefits received. Until recently, in many countries the calculation of pensions was based on the contribution bases of a few years of working life, which involved pensions that were not related to the total contribution effort (contributory inequality), degression of the system[19] and incentives to the informal economy. Progress towards an average calculation base of the whole working life, in addition to improving the equity of the system tends to reduce its generosity and consequently, reduces the pension expenditure.[20] As examples of countries that have applied this measure in the last years are Greece, Czech Republic or Italy, which will take into account the whole working life after their reforms; Spain, which will increase from 15 to 25 years the period for calculating the pension; Austria and France, which will take into account the 20–40 best years and the 15–25 best years, respectively, for calculating the pension; Portugal that changes to a period of 40 years instead of the last 20 years; or Malta, whose pension was based on the best 3 years of contribution within the last 10 years and will take into account the best 10 years within the last 40 years. At present, 18 EU-28 countries are taking full employment as a reference for calculating pensionable entitlement.

The impact of the economic crisis has also forced many countries to change the revaluation criterion of their pensions. In general, countries that used indicators such as wage growth or GDP growth tend to increasingly use the CPI more and more or a combination of the CPI and wages. This measure also has implications for the generosity of the system because price indices tend to grow at rates lower than that of wages or the economy. For example, France switched to using price indices and Portugal to using mixed indices combining prices and economic growth. In Italy, pensions are adjusted annually according to the change in the cost of living, but the percentages applicable to pensions exceeding three times the minimum pension have been reduced. In France, the freezing of pensions, except the lowest pensions, was approved until the end of 2015. In 2011, Spain also approved a freeze on pensions, except the minimum ones. In Austria, the revaluation of pensions in 2013

[19]Systems in which the pension amount is determined according to the contribution bases of a short period of working life produce higher levels of inequality than other systems that take into account longer contribution periods. The reason is that workers with higher wages, generally more skilled, tend to have an increasing wage curve over time, while less skilled workers have greater difficulties in keeping their jobs at the end of their working lives and sometimes find more precarious jobs (Jimeno 2003).

[20]The final effect of this measure on the pension amount is diverse as it depends on the evolution of wages throughout the working life, but, in general, it will imply a lower pension because wages tend to increase with age as one's professional life develops, especially for workers with a higher educational level (Argandoña et al. 2013).

and 2014 was made below the CPI evolution, and in Latvia pensions were frozen between 2009 and 2013.

Some European countries have been more ambitious in reforming their revaluation rules by introducing some mechanism to automatically correct potential financial imbalances produced in the system reducing the revaluation of pensions.[21] The first European countries to introduce these automatic balancing mechanisms before the onset of the economic crisis were Sweden and Germany. In Sweden pension revaluation depends on the evolution of the actuarial balance, a ratio between the present value of the assets and liabilities of the system. If it is lower than one, actuarial imbalance, the revaluation of pensions is reduced, and if it is greater than one, it increases above what is established. Germany has a points system, where the pension depends on the number of points and the value of each point. One of the factors affecting the point value is the dependency ratio of the system, i.e. the existing relationship between pensioners and contributors, so a deterioration in this indicator causes a lower point value and pension.

After the start of the crisis, following the path initiated by Sweden and Germany, several European countries also introduced automatic stabilizers. Luxembourg has implemented pension revaluation since 2013, which may become limited or even annulled depending on the annual ratio between income and expenditure. Hungary introduced a less generous pension indexation system in the 2009 reform, as it depends on the CPI and the nominal wage growth, but the weight of each variable depends on the real GDP growth, so if it does not exceed 3%, pension revaluation will depend only on the CPI. Greece included in the 2010 reform a sustainability clause according to which if long-term projections (year 2060) show an increase in pension expenditure above 2.5 percentage points of GDP compared to 2009, the relevant system parameters will be adjusted so that the increase in expenditure is below that target. The last country to implement a similar mechanism was Spain. Since 2013, there has been a new Pension Revaluation Index (PRI), which links the annual pension growth to the budgetary balance of the social security system in the medium term, giving up the CPI reference used in different ways since 1975. According to de la Fuente et al. (2016), the application of this new mechanism of revaluation implies that pensions in Spain will lose 30% of purchasing power since receiving them (Table 3.5).

The sustainability of public pay-as-you-go systems depends to a large extent on their ability to adapt to demographic change over time. This adaptation must be as automatic as possible so as not to be dependent on political decisions which, due to their high cost,[22] are usually slow and sometimes far from real needs. Therefore, one of the most recent reforms carried out in recent years has been the incorporation of the so-called automatic adjustment mechanisms or sustainability factors into the

[21]This form of automatic pension revaluation implies freeing governments of the responsibility of making sometimes unpopular decisions on the annual increase in pensions.

[22]In increasingly ageing societies, such as European ones, this political cost is increasing due to the increasing importance of pensioners within the whole electorate.

Table 3.5 Fundamental parameters of pension systems in the EU-28 after the latest reforms

Countries	Statutory retirement age		Early retirement	Period calculation of pension	Revaluation of pensions
	Age	Transitional period			
Belgium	65		62	Complete working life	Prices
Bulgaria	M:65; W:63	2012–2020	65	Complete working life	Prices and wages
Czech Republic[a]	63		Statutory age – 5 years	Complete working life	Prices and wages
Denmark[a]	67	2019–2022	Statutory age – 3 years	40 years of residence	Wages
Germany	67	2012–2029	63	Complete working life	Wages adjusted by automatic balance mechanism
Estonia	65	2017–2026	Statutory age – 3 years	Complete working life	Prices and social contributions
Ireland	68	2010–2028	Not possible	---	No rules
Greece[a]	67		Statutory age – 5 years	Complete working life	Prices + GDP (maximum 100% prices)
Spain	67	2013–2027	63	25 years of contribution	IRP (automatic balance mechanism)
France	67	2016–2022	62	25 best years	Prices
Croatia	67	2011–2038	62	Complete working life	Prices and wages
Italy[a]	67		Statutory age – 3 years	Complete working life	Prices
Cyprus[a]	65	2012–2016	Statutory age – 2 years	Complete working life	Prices and wages
Latvia	65	2010–2025	Statutory age – 2 years	Complete working life	Prices and wages
Lithuania	65	2012–2026	Statutory age – 5 years	25 best years	No rules
Luxembourg	65		57	Complete working life	Prices and wages
Hungary	65	2014–2022	Not possible	Complete working life	Prices and wages
Malta	65	2006–2026	61	10 best years in last 40 years	Prices and wages
Netherlands[a]	67	2015–2023	Not possible	50 years of residence	Wages
Austria	65	2024–2033	62	40 best years	Prices
Poland	67	2013–2040	Not possible	Complete working life	Prices and wages
Portugal[a]	66		Temporarily suspended		Prices and GDP

(continued)

Table 3.5 (continued)

Countries	Statutory retirement age		Early retirement	Period calculation of pension	Revaluation of pensions
	Age	Transitional period			
				Complete working life (max. 40 years)	
Romania	M:65; W:63	2011–2030	Statutory age – 5 years	Complete working life	Prices and wages (from 2030 only prices)
Slovenia	65	2013–2020	60	24 best consecutive years	Prices and wages
Slovakia[a]	62		Statutory age – 2 years	Complete working life	Prices and wages (from 2018 pensioners CPI)
Finland	66		63	Complete working life	Prices and wages
Sweden	61–67		Not possible	Complete working life	Wages adjusted by automatic balance mechanism
United Kingdom[b]	68	2018–2028	Not possible	Complete working life	Wages

Source: MISSOC (2016) OECD (2014) and European Commission (2015)
[a]It introduced an automatic mechanism for reviewing the retirement age linked to the life expectancy evolution
[b]The retirement age is planned to have increased to 68 by 2046

design of European pension systems, whereby some parameters of the pension system are linked to the life expectancy evolution, thus adjusting the pension system to the risk of ageing.

Introducing these mechanisms was strongly criticized by the European Economic and Social Committee (2011),[23] stating that "it is the parliaments rather than computers that should take such fundamental decisions on living conditions". However, since the start of the crisis, the number of European countries that have introduced such mechanisms has increased considerably, so there are now ten Member States that have implemented such mechanisms (Table 3.6). The most common case is the relationship between the ordinary retirement age and the life expectancy evolution with the aim of giving the age at which people can retire a more dynamic approach. In this way, it means that individuals belonging to different generations and, therefore, with different life expectancies receive a pension during the same period of time. For example, Italy implemented this mechanism in 2010 to

[23]Opinion of the European Economic and Social Committee on the Annual Growth Survey: anticipation of the EU's overall response to the crisis. COM (2011) 11 final.

Table 3.6 Automatic adjustment mechanisms in EU-28

Countries	Variable which the adjustment depends on	Parameter of the system on which the adjustment falls	Year of entry into force
Denmark	Life expectancy	Retirement age	2030
Greece	Life expectancy	Retirement age	2020
Spain	Life expectancy	Initial pension amount	2019
France	Life expectancy	Contribution years for 100% pension	2009
Italy	Life expectancy	Retirement age	2013
		Minimum contribution years for early retirement	
Cyprus	Life expectancy	Retirement age	2018
Netherlands	Life expectancy	Retirement age	2023
Portugal	Life expectancy	Initial pension amount	2010
		Retirement age	2016
Finland	Life expectancy	Initial pension amount	2010
Slovakia	Life expectancy	Retirement age	2017

Source: European Commission (2015)

index the retirement age to changes in life expectancy at age 65. Following the changes introduced in 2011, the adjustments are every 3 years, the first one in 2013, and are based on average data from the last triennium compared to those of the previous triennium. In Denmark, this mechanism will be activated once the process of delaying the retirement age from 65 to 67 has been completed in 2022, and then it will be linked to the life expectancy evolution at age 60 on the basis of 2020. Other countries that have implemented this mechanism are Cyprus, Slovakia, Greece, the Netherlands and Portugal.

Another option was to adjust the amount of the first pension to life expectancy. If life expectancy at the reference retirement age increases, the sustainability factor implies a decrease in the initial pension. In this way, the present value of the pensions that will be perceived during a retired person's entire life is constant for the same contributory effort, not increasing with the increase in life expectancy. The countries that have implemented such an automatic mechanism are Finland and Portugal. Recently, Spain also incorporated a similar sustainability factor so that from 2019 the amount of the initial pension will be adjusted to the life expectancy evolution at age 67. During the first year of application, the coefficient is obtained as a quotient between life expectancies at 67 years in 2012 and 2017 raised to 1/5. This coefficient will be reviewed every 5 years.

The mechanism implemented in France pursues a similar effect, whereby the number of contribution years required to obtain a full pension increases with the life expectancy at the age of 61, with the idea of maintaining the ratio between the years contributed and years of pension collecting (life expectancy) constant. This relationship has been applied since 2009 starting from the 40 years of contribution that were necessary in 2008, and the generation born in the 1960s is expected to contribute for 41.5 years as a result of the increase in life expectancy.

In addition, Italy introduced an automatic mechanism according to which, since 2013, the number of years required to access to early retirement is adjusted based on life expectancy at age 65.

Finally, note that most of the reforms undertaken have been aimed at improving the budgetary balance of pension systems by reducing their expenditure. Another possibility to reach such a balance is to introduce reforms aimed at increasing revenues by, for example, increasing the contribution rate. However, this type of measure has been quite rare because of the adverse effects it may have on employment. For Meneu and Encinas (2012), the effect of an increase in the contribution rate depends on whether it falls on the employer or the worker. In the former case, it would have adverse effects of opposite sign on the quantity of work demanded since it would imply a higher labour cost, so the final effect would be ambiguous. In the latter case, the system's income would improve but at the expense of lower purchasing power of wages, which could have a negative impact on aggregate consumption and revenue from other tax sources. The few countries that introduced this type of reforms are Cyprus (1.3 percentage points every 5 years between 2009 and 2039) and Bulgaria (1.8 percentage points in 2011). There have also been occasional increases for certain groups. For example, in Italy the contribution rates paid by self-employed workers increased progressively from 20% in 2011 to 24% in 2018, and in Portugal[24] the contribution rate of temporary contracts has increased by 3 pp.

3.5 Conclusions

The financial crisis that began in 2007 has become the worst social and economic crisis of the last decades. Its impact on the real economy and employment has reignited doubts about the sustainability of European public pension systems. The need to contain pension expenditure, which is often one of the main expenditure items in public budgets in European countries, and the obligation to ensure long-term sustainability of pension systems have forced all Member States to introduce reforms.

Although the increase in longevity and the consequent ageing of the population already required a thorough reform of European pension systems, the reality is that it has been the crisis that has increased its urgency and has acted as the drive of this reformist process. Before the crisis, many countries were aware of the need to

[24]In September 2012, the Portuguese government announced its intention to increase social contributions for 2013, but the strong social rejection forced to reverse this decision. Specifically, the measure was to increase employee contributions from 11% to 18% and, at the same time, to reduce entrepreneurs' contributions from 23.75% to 18% to encourage job creation.

respond to the demographic challenge, but their governments were reluctant to assume the political cost of such reforms.

While it is true that the Member States are primarily responsible for the design of their public pension systems, the reforms undertaken following the economic crisis have been driven and guided by the recommendations of the European Commission. It would not be otherwise understood that in a very short period of time, a series of reforms have taken place in all the Member States following a basic model or pattern which complies with the recommendations given by the European Commission and which has basically been to delay the statutory retirement age, to extend the contribution period taken into account for calculating the pension, to equalize the retirement age between men and women, to modify the rules for revaluation of pensions, to restrict access to early retirement and to introduce sustainability factors that link some basic parameters of the system to the retirement age. Each country has obviously applied these recommendations with different intensity according to its needs.

The latest reforms undertaken have focused on ensuring the sustainability of pensions within a more general context of sustainability of public finances. In this sense, the latest projections by the European Commission (2015) foresee that EU pension expenditure for the whole of the EU, in 2060, will be 11%, a figure well below the projected 12.8% 3 years before (European Commission 2012b). However, the situation of a given pension system should not only be assessed from the point of view of its sustainability but should also ensure that it provides for adequate pensions, as is stated, inter alia, in the White Paper on pensions (European Commission 2012a). An example of the problems that may arise from the approved reforms, from the point of view of adequacy, is the change introduced in the revaluation of pensions in Spain. According to de la Fuente et al. (2016), the new indexation rules imply quasi-freezing Spanish pensions, which will result in a loss of purchasing power of 30% from the start of pension collecting. The challenge now is to ensure that the pensions of future retirees are sufficient to enable them to fulfil their main objective, which is to ensure that European workers have a standard of living during retirement comparable to that enjoyed during their working lives.

References

Alonso, J., Doménech, R., & Tuesta, D. (2011). Sistemas públicos de pensiones y la crisis fiscal en la zona euro. Enseñanzas para América Latina. Working Paper BBVA Research, 11/23. https://www.bbvaresearch.com/wp-content/uploads/migrados/WP_1123_tcm346-262717.pdf

Argandoña, A., Díaz-Giménez, J., Díaz-Saavedra, J., & Álvarez, B. (2013). El reparto y la capitalización en las pensiones españolas. Fundación Edad& Vida. http://www.edad-vida.org/fitxers/publicacions/Estudio%20pensiones%20E&V_IESE_final.pdf

Carone, G., Eckefeldt, P., Giamboni, L., Laine, V., & Pamies, S. (2016). Pension Reforms in the EU since the early 2000's: Achievements and challenges ahead. European Economy Discussion Paper, 42. http://ec.europa.eu/economy_finance/publications/eedp/pdf/dp042_en.pdf

De la Fuente, A., García Díaz, M. A., & Sánchez, A. (2016). La salud financiera del sistema público de pensiones español. Análisis retrospectivo, proyecciones de largo plazo y factores de riesgo. FEDEA, Estudios sobre la Economía Española, 2017/04.

Devesa, J. E., Devesa, M., Domínguez, I., Encinas, B., & Meneu, R. (2014). La sostenibilidad de los sistemas públicos de pensiones europeos como pilar fundamental de un nuevo Estado del bienestar. EUROBASK, XII Research Award of Francisco Javier de Landaburu Universitas 2013. http://www.eurobasque.eus/wp-content/uploads/2015/05/libros/UNIVERSITAS_2013.pdf

European Commission. (2009a). Comunicación de la Comisión al Parlamento Europeo, al Consejo, al Comité Económico y Social Europeo y al Comité de las Regiones: Abordar los efectos del envejecimiento de la población de la UE (2009 report on demographic ageing). Brussels, COM (2009) 180 final, of 29 Apr 2009. http://eur-lex.europa.eu/Statutory-content/ES/TXT/PDF/?uri=CELEX:52009DC0180&from=ES

European Commission. (2009b). The 2009 ageing report – Economic and budgetary projections for the EU-27 Member States (2008–2060). European Economy 2/2009.

European Commission. (2010a). Green Paper, en pos de unos sistemas de pensiones europeos adecuados, sostenibles y seguros. Brussels, COM (2010) 365 final, of 7 July 2010. http://eur-lex.europa.eu/LexUriServ/LexUriServ.do?uri=COM:2010:0365:FIN:ES:PDF

European Commission. (2010b). Joint report on pensions: Progress and key challenges in the delivery of adequate and sustainable pensions in Europe. European Economy. Occasional Papers, 71. http://ec.europa.eu/economy_finance/publications/occasional_paper/2010/pdf/ocp71_en.pdf

European Commission. (2012a). White Paper, agenda para una pensiones adecuadas, seguras y sostenibles. Brussels, COM (2012) 55 final, of 16 February 2012. http://eur-lex.europa.eu/LexUriServ/LexUriServ.do?uri=COM:2012:0055:FIN:ES:PDF

European Commission. (2012b). The 2012 ageing report – Economic and budgetary projections for the 27 EU Member States (2010–2060). European Economy 2/2012. http://ec.europa.eu/economy_finance/publications/european_economy/2012/pdf/ee-2012-2_en.pdf

European Commission. (2015). The 2015 ageing report – Economic and budgetary projections for the 28 EU Member States (2013-2060). European Economy 3/2015. http://ec.europa.eu/economy_finance/publications/european_economy/2015/pdf/ee3_en.pdf

European Economic and Social Committe (2011). Opinion of the European Economic and Social Committee on the 'Annual Growth Survey: advancing the EU's comprehensive response to the crisis COM(2011) 11 final. Official Journal of the European Union C 132, 3 may 2011

García, D., Gordo, E., & Manrique, M. (2011). Reformas de los sistemas de pensiones en algunos países de la UEM. Bank of Spain Economic Bulletin, July–August, 119–134. http://www.bde.es/f/webbde/SES/Secciones/Publicaciones/InformesBoletinesRevistas/BoletinEconomico/11/Jul/Fich/art4.pdf

ILO. (2016). Global Wage Report 2016/2017. Wage inequality in the workplace, Geneva, ILO. http://www.ilo.org/wcmsp5/groups/public/%2D%2D-dgreports/%2D%2D-dcomm/%2D%2D-publ/documents/publication/wcms_537846.pdf

Jiménez Martín, S. (2013). Envejecimiento, crisis económica y reforma del sistema de pensiones. Informe IEB sobre Federalismo Fiscal y Finanzas Públicas´13, 54–57.

Jimeno Serrano, J. F. (2000). El sistema de pensiones contributivas en España: Cuestiones básicas y perspectivas en el medio plazo. FEDEA, Working Paper 2000/15. http://documentos.fedea.net/pubs/dt/2000/dt-2000-15.pdf

Jimeno Serrano, J. F. (2003). La equidad intrageneracional de los sistemas de pensiones. *Revista de Economía Aplicada, 11*(33), 5–48. http://www.revecap.com/revista/numeros/33/pdf/jimeno.pdf.

Meneu, R., & Encinas, B. (2012). Valoración de la reforma del sistema de pensiones español de 2011 desde la óptica de la viabilidad financiero-actuarial. Un análisis a través de la MCVL. Ministerio de Empleo y Seguridad Social: FIPROS Awards. http://www.seg-social.es/prdi00/groups/public/documents/binario/174193.pdf

MISSOC (2016). Mutual Information System on Social Protection database [online] Available at: https://www.missoc.org/missoc-database/ [Accessed 11 Sep. 2016].
Morales Ramírez, M. A. (2010). La política de la Unión Europea sobre las pensiones de vejez. Biblioteca Jurídica Virtual del Instituto de Investigaciones Jurídicas de la UNAM. http://www.revistas.unam.mx/index.php/rlds/article/view/24018/22571
OECD. (2014). Pensions outlook 2014. https://doi.org/10.1787/9789264222687-en
Zubiri, I. (2014). Capitalización y reparto: Un análisis comparativo. *Ekonomiaz, 85*, 208–233.

Chapter 4
Pensions, Economic Growth and Welfare in Advanced Economies

Enrique Devesa and Rafael Doménech

Abstract In this chapter, we analyse the effects of PAYG and funded pension systems on welfare. The debate on the choice between alternative systems focuses on their effects on savings, capital accumulation, labour supply, economic growth and inequality and the potential benefits of mixed systems in which a PAYG system with notional accounts is complemented by a funded pensions system. The main findings are as follows. Firstly, the redistribution of income among individuals makes the PAYG system an important part of any mixed system. Secondly, the design of the pension system should efficiently balance incentives and distortions with equality and insurance against individual idiosyncratic risks. Thirdly, funded systems generate positive effects on the savings rate, capital accumulation, productivity and the labour supply. These effects must be taken into account when PAYG systems are improved with notional accounts. Fourthly, in practice, income distribution among older people does not clearly depend on the relative importance of PAYG over funded pensions systems, suggesting that other factors are even more important. Fifthly, there are significant differences between advanced economies in their social preferences regarding the combination of replacement rates in PAYG systems and contributions to funded systems. Lastly, there is no guarantee that, regardless of social preferences, imposing a target of pension expenditure on GDP maximises social welfare.

Keywords Contributiveness · Defined benefit · Defined contribution · Dependency ratio · Economic growth · Efficiency · Funded system · Intergenerational transfers · Life expectancy · National savings rate · Notional account system · Pay-as-you-go · Pensions · Productivity · Redistribution · Replacement ratio · Savings · Social preferences · Sustainability · Welfare

E. Devesa (✉)
Financial and Actuarial Economy Department, University of Valencia, Valencia, Spain
e-mail: Enrique.Devesa@uv.es

R. Doménech
BBVA Research and University of Valencia, Madrid, Spain
e-mail: r.domenech@bbva.com

M. Peris-Ortiz et al. (eds.), *Economic Challenges of Pension Systems*,
https://doi.org/10.1007/978-3-030-37912-4_4

4.1 Introduction

Pensions are a cornerstone of the welfare state that provide a solution to the inherent risks of ageing, providing an adequate level of income to people who leave the labour market because of their age. That is why pension systems need to be evaluated in terms of their ability to simultaneously meet two basic objectives (see, e.g. Holzmann and Heinz 2005):

- To smooth out pensioners' consumption through pensions that are as high as possible while ensuring levels of welfare similar to those that they had while they were working.
- To avoid situations of poverty and social exclusion among pensioners, promoting a fair and efficient redistribution of income between and within generations.

These two objectives are used to assess the efficiency of pension systems in achieving the highest levels of consumption, with as few disincentives to investment, productivity and employment growth as possible, and to contribute to ensuring that inequality within the retired population is equal to or even lower than that among the working population.

As in previous studies (such as Diamond and Orszag 2005; Barr and Diamond 2008; Doménech 2014), the aim of this chapter is to evaluate the theoretical and empirical advantages and disadvantages of pay-as-you-go (PAYG) and funded systems, whether private, public or under mixed management, to achieve the objectives that have just been discussed, using the most recent studies and information available. As it is concluded in the next sections, neither of these two systems is clearly better than the other in the three areas under consideration. As a result, our approach is quite pragmatic and eclectic: PAYG and funded systems complement one another as solutions to the challenge of maximising welfare.

PAYG and funded systems have relative strengths and weaknesses. The existence of market failures, inequality of opportunities, the myopia of economic agents, low levels of financial education or the absence of appropriate financial products, the need for regulation and financial supervision, and the desire to insure workers against idiosyncratic risks make public intervention in the pension system worthwhile. In a world without market imperfections, with equal opportunities and homogeneous individuals, a funded system would be the optimal solution to the problem of intertemporal maximisation of consumption throughout the life cycle (Samuelson 1958, 1975). However, as Samuelson himself and Diamond (2004) argue, the real world is far from that situation. The challenge is therefore to find an appropriate balance between pension systems, with a design and operation that takes into account the potential incentives and distortions that affect the decisions of economic agents.

Figure 4.1 illustrates this dilemma between contributiveness and redistribution in pension systems. The horizontal axis measures the inequality which results from the pension system, and the vertical axis measures the average pension. As discussed in the next section, there are arguments that justify that higher levels of

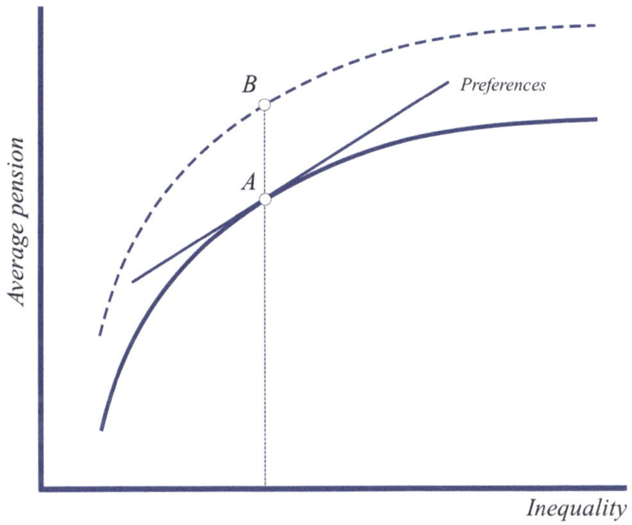

Fig. 4.1 The problem of maximising welfare in pension systems

contributiveness can lead to higher average pensions at the expense of greater inequality in the incomes of pensioners, although possibly with diminishing returns. The straight line with a positive slope represents social preferences, so that the optimum choice is given by the point *A*. This figure also shows that improved efficiency in the economy, in general, and in the pension system, in particular, shifts the frontier of possible choices so that it is possible to achieve a higher average pension without increasing inequality (point *B*).

As discussed in this chapter, the experience of almost all advanced economies suggests that social preferences end up resulting in a combination of different pension systems (PAYG and funded, public and private) as a way of maximising social welfare.

The structure of this chapter is as follows: Section 4.2 examines the effects of distortions and incentives of funded and PAYG pension systems on savings, employment and economic growth. Section 4.3 discusses how the design of pension systems and their sustainability also affect the balance between fairness and efficiency. Section 4.4 takes an in-depth look at the analysis of the dilemma between redistribution, on the one hand, and contributiveness and efficiency, on the other, evaluating the reasons why, when faced with extreme situations, advanced economies end up choosing an intermediate situation between contributiveness and redistribution, albeit with considerable differences across countries. Lastly, Section 4.5 presents the main conclusions of this chapter.

4.2 Pensions, Savings, Employment and Growth: Funded Versus PAYG

One of the issues that continuously appears in debates on pensions is how the design of the pension system affects savings and growth.

One useful classification of pension systems depends on whether they accumulate (funded) or not (PAYG) savings with which to finance the living standards of retirees. PAYG systems are based on an implicit and perpetual intergenerational contract (as argued by Becker and Murphy 1988), so that current contributors pay for the benefits of retirees who are receiving pensions with the expectation that when these workers retire, the contributors of the future will pay their pensions. For this latter condition to be met, it must be assumed that the intergenerational contract is permanent. For their part, funded systems are defined as those in which, at the age of retirement, the actuarial value of insurance premia accumulated during the savings period is equal to the actuarial value of the benefits expected to be received. In the case of an individually funded system, which is the most commonly used form, the equilibrium is planned for each individual.

From a strictly financial and actuarial point of view, there are a number of elements or characteristics that substantially differentiate these two systems. Firstly, the first question is whether the pension system generates *reserves* or not. In PAYG systems, theoretically no reserves are generated, since the premium paid corresponds to the natural premium, i.e. contributions are intended to pay the benefits for the current year. However, many countries set up funds to smooth out the economic cycle: during expansionary times, contributions exceed spending on pensions, and in recessions the opposite occurs. In funded systems, the amount of the reserves generated is obtained by calculating the present actuarial value of future benefits, less the present actuarial value of pending contributions. The return on the savings accumulated depends on how these reserves are managed.

The second differentiating element has to do with the existence or otherwise of *intergenerational transfers*. The PAYG system is based on a full transfer of resources from contributors to pensioners, which does not mean that the system is not contributory. In the funded system, there is no transfer of any type and contributiveness reaches its maximum level. In fact, in the case of PAYG systems with notional accounts, the return on contributions can be as high as in the funded system, although there are endogenous elements that allow the introduction of a certain degree of redistribution,[1] such as the use of actuarial instruments that do not differentiate by gender or the existence of minimum pensions. This system takes into account the contributions actually made to the system, reassessing them according to a predetermined index, and once the time of retirement is reached, the initial pension is calculated by applying a conversion factor, such as life expectancy or the present value of an annuity.

---

[1]In Sect. 4.4, there will be further discussion on the relationship between the ratio to contributions made and redistribution.

The third aspect has to do with whether it is a *defined contribution* or *defined benefit* system. In general, a PAYG contribution system does not guarantee 'a priori' an exact amount of future pensions either to current or future pensioners, as in most cases it depends on the dynamics between pensioners and contributors (dependency ratio) and the evolution of the resources in the system. In this case, the intergenerational contract is based on the principle that the system guarantees a similar effort by each generation that does not necessarily translate into an equal replacement ratio, depending on the evolution of the dependency ratio. A simple way of illustrating this statement is by taking as a starting point the financial equilibrium between the income (I) and pension expenditures (G) over the economic cycle:

$$I = G \Rightarrow \tau wL = p^m P \Rightarrow \frac{p^m}{w} = \tau \frac{L}{P} \tag{4.1}$$

where τ is the tax rate on the average wage (w), L is the number of contributors to social security, p^m is the average pension and P the number of pensioners. When the tax rate is exogenous and constant (τ), so that there is tax smoothing, the system has to adjust the replacement ratio (p^m/w) for changes in the dependency ratio (P/L).[2] On the contrary, for the PAYG system to guarantee a defined benefit (p^m), it needs to move all the demographic risks (which determines the ratio L/P) and economic uncertainties (in employment and wages growth) to the contributors, so that expenditures are exogenous and the system makes taxes (τ) an endogenous variable that adjusts to financially balance the system. For its part, the funded system does not guarantee a defined benefit, unless an additional insurance product is considered, allowing the future pension to be decoupled from the specific performance of the assets in which the pension fund has invested. In addition, increasing life expectancy may lead to benefits that are lower than those initially planned.

Once the main characteristics of the pension systems are explained, we can analyse their interaction with economic growth in two possible directions. Firstly, with regard to the effects of growth on pensions, the traditional way of comparing the PAYG system with the funded system is through internal rates of return. Extending Samuelson's (1958) seminal model to an economy with technical progress in which each working-age generation transfers a percentage τ of its income to the pensioners with whom they coexist, the internal rate of return of the PAYG system is equal to employment growth (n) plus productivity growth (g). In the funded system, the rate of return of a perfectly diversified portfolio is the real interest rate (r), which in the long term is determined by the intertemporal discount rate ($\beta = 1 - \rho$), the coefficient of relative risk aversion (σ) and productivity growth:

[2]The tax rate can be understood broadly as the result of dividing all the income from the social security system (not only social contributions but any other tax with which pensions are financed) by the payroll of the economy as a whole.

$$r = \rho + \sigma g \tag{4.2}$$

For an economy in a dynamically efficient steady-state equilibrium,[3] it is shown that:

$$r = \rho + \sigma g > n + g \tag{4.3}$$

so that the internal rate of return of the PAYG system is lower than that of the funded system: if each generation of workers, rather than allocating a percentage τ of their income to a PAYG system, invested it in the capital market, they would obtain a higher retirement pension.

With regard to the effects in the opposite direction, from pensions on economic activity, the economic literature has analysed the extent to which economic agents change their decisions, mainly on savings and labour supply, depending on the incentives and distortions created by the way in which pensions are financed. Although some critics of funded systems (such as Orszag and Stiglitz 2001) question this argument, traditionally one of the benefits usually granted to the funded system over the PAYG system is the increase in the savings rate (see, e.g. Feldstein 1974, or Lindbeck and Persson 2003). In a closed economy or one with imperfect capital mobility, this higher savings rate in turn implies a higher rate of investment, so that a larger stock of productive capital (physical, technological and human) would be accumulated. Depending on the endogenous growth mechanisms prevailing in the economy, this increased productive capital would not only result in a higher level of GDP per worker but also in a higher rate of productivity growth. An open economy with capital mobility provides the additional possibility of obtaining even higher returns from investing in foreign assets and diversifying risks than from domestic assets.

However, studies that have examined the empirical evidence have not found clear results on the effects of the pension system on national saving. It is true that most advanced economies have a PAYG system complemented by funded systems and that countries with lower replacement ratios in public pension systems show, in general, higher contributions from savings in funded systems (see Doménech 2014). However, this does not necessarily translate into higher domestic savings rates, since individuals may be replacing some forms of savings with others, as pointed out by Feldstein and Liebman (2002). In addition, countries with similar replacement ratios in the public system can show very different contributions to funded systems, which

[3] According to the optimal growth models (see, e.g. Barro and Sala-i-Martin 2003; Blanchard and Fischer 1993), in the steady state the modified golden rule is verified, by which the interest rate is equal to the sum of the discount rate (ρ) and population growth (n), i.e. $r = n + \rho$. In these models, the steady state is dynamically efficient and capital (k) does not accumulate in excess when $r = f'(k) - \delta = \rho + \sigma g > n + g$, where σ is the relative risk aversion coefficient, $f'(k)$ the marginal productivity of capital and δ is the depreciation rate.

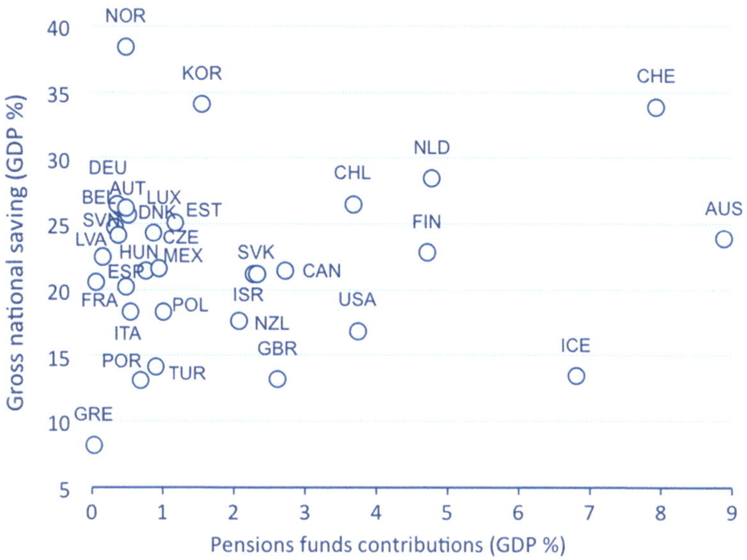

Fig. 4.2 Contributions to funded schemes and national savings rate in the OECD, as a percentage of GDP. Averages between 2007 and 2015. (*Source:* own preparation from data provided by the OECD, AMECO and the World Bank)

may be consistent with problems of incentives or myopia leading to inadequate rates of private savings, something which is acknowledged in the literature (Diamond 2004).

The evidence presented in Fig. 4.2 allows us to observe that there is no clear link between contributions to pension plans and funds in relation to GDP and the national savings rate in OECD countries, using the average of these variables between 2007 and 2015 to eliminate the effects of the economic cycle. This is especially evident in the case of many countries in which contributions to funded schemes do not reach 1% of GDP but which show very low rates of domestic savings (Greece, Italy and Portugal) compared to others with very high savings rates (Norway, Germany, Austria or Denmark). Similarly, it can be seen that some countries with similar rates of national savings have very low contributions to funded systems (Denmark), while others are very high (e.g. Australia. with almost 9% of GDP).

In addition to the effects on the savings rate, the choice of the pension system can also influence the labour supply. To finance the pensions of retired workers, a PAYG system requires taxes that have distorting effects on economic activity. These effects are more or less intense and operate through different mechanisms depending on the type of tax and the way economic agents internalise the relationship between social security contributions and future pensions. The extensive theoretical and empirical literature in existence has shown that the least distortionary taxes are those levied on consumption, followed by those that tax labour income, while the most distortionary are taxes on capital income.[4] Tax distortions can affect both the number of workers employed (known as the extensive margin of the labour market) and the number of hours worked per adult (intensive margin).

Prescott (2004) argues that differences in the tax burden may explain differences in hours worked per adult between the USA and several European countries. Similarly, Rogerson (Rogerson 2006, 2008) has shown that taxation, along with technology, can account for these differences. Meanwhile, Ohanian et al. (2008) present evidence that changes in taxes on labour income account for a significant part of the trend differences in the hours worked in a sample of 21 OECD countries from 1956 to 2004, even when taking into account other explanatory variables, such as unemployment benefits or job protection. However, Pissarides (2007) and Rogerson (2007) have noted that the effects of taxes on employment depend on the specification of the model, which may be appropriate for some countries (the USA and continental Europe), but not for others, such as the Scandinavian countries.

The effects of taxes on employment or unemployment rates have received even more attention than the hours worked per employee. As Doménech and García (2008) and Feldstein and Liebman (2002) argue, the empirical evidence provides a wide range of results, which mainly depend on whether workers internalise or not the public goods and services received in return for the taxes they pay. This is particularly relevant in the case of social contributions, as their distortionary effects will be lower the higher the contributiveness of the system and the greater the perception that the pension is a deferred salary directly linked to those contributions (see Disney 2004, or Melguizo and González-Páramo 2012). In addition to many others benefits, one of the great advantages of notional accounts is precisely that by increasing the contributiveness and the transparency of the system, the distorting effect of social contributions on the demand and supply of labour is reduced. It is no longer perceived as being a tax wedge between the labour cost to the firm and the salary received by the worker (Lindbeck and Persson 2003, or Buyse et al. 2013). Additionally, the distortionary effects may also depend on other factors, such as the age, gender, marital status or income of workers, introducing plenty of individual heterogeneity.

Given the effects that a pension system's design, features and method of funding have on consumption and savings decisions and on the demand and supply of labour, other macroeconomic aggregates (GDP, current account balance, etc.) also end up being affected. As shown by Boscá et al. (2013), the ratio of social security contributions to implicit tax rates on consumption generates a bias towards a current account deficit and negatively affects GDP, employment and capital accumulation in the short and medium term. Depending on social preferences, some countries, such as Denmark, have tried to avoid some of the distortionary effects of social security contributions, by opting to finance public pensions mainly through other taxes.

[4]See, for example, Johansson (2016); Acosta-Ormaechea and Yoo (2012); Mirrlees (2011); Arnold et al. (2011); Boscá et al. (2009); and the references therein.

In short, the choice of a PAYG pension system over a funded system can give rise to different effects on national saving, investment, labour supply and demand and, ultimately, on economic growth, which in the end will have consequences for the standard of living of future pensioners. These effects are so varied and diverse that their final combination does not allow us to draw a crystalline conclusion about the superiority of one system over the other in terms of welfare, as showed by the fact that the empirical evidence is inconclusive. In particular, this because all the aspects that have to do with efficiency, redistribution and social inclusion are just as important as the channels that have been discussed previously, as will be discussed in the next two sections.

4.3 Efficiency and Sustainability

Efficiency within a contributory pension system is a term that needs to be defined, due to the different interpretations that can be given to this concept. Efficiency can be defined as the set of features that make contributions to the pension system attractive and which avoid discouraging participation in the system, thereby increasing the welfare of society as a whole. In line with this definition, Alonso and Pazos (2001) state that, according to the principle of efficiency, the system is intended to affect the behaviour of economic agents (workers and companies) to ensure sufficient contributions and to combat the underground economy.

It is evident that for participation in the system to be attractive, the workers who contribute to it must perceive the system as being fair and equitable. That is why the concept of efficiency is related to fairness, understood in a broad sense. According Devesa et al. (2012), to achieve greater equity in a PAYG defined benefit system, it is necessary to act on the two main elements that determine it: contributiveness and the replacement rate.

With regard to contributiveness, it is essential that the basis on which the initial pension of retiring workers is calculated accurately reflects their social security contributions during the period in which they remained active, for which it is necessary to:

- Take into account the contribution bases throughout their whole working life, preventing two individuals who have made similar tax contributions throughout their working life from receiving different pensions because of the fact that the payments were distributed across different moments in time.
- Avoid using fictitious contribution bases for calculating the regulatory base, which would eliminate the so-called integration of contributory gaps.
- Capitalise the contribution bases until retirement.

As for fairness in the replacement rate,[5] three types of fairness can be considered:

- Actuarial intergenerational fairness, i.e. between individuals of different generations who retire at the same age but in different years. This fairness is achieved by introducing mechanisms to adjust the variation in life expectancy[6] to any of the system parameters, such as the amount of the initial pension, the retirement age or the number of years before obtaining 100% of the pension. The challenge is to maintain dynamically over time the actuarial and financial equilibrium between contributions and pensions. The discussion about which parameter should be adjusted depends on the specific objective pursued,[7] with substantial dispersion among countries that have used a mechanism of this type. For example, in Spain, Portugal and Finland, the choice was made to adjust the amount of the initial pension, with the intention that anyone who does not consider the amount to be received to be sufficient can voluntarily delay retirement in order to increase their retirement pension.
- Actuarial intragenerational fairness refers to individuals of the same generation who retire at different ages. This fairness is broken when the reduction coefficients applied to early retirement are greater than the additional percentages used to retire at a later age than usual. This leads to the paradox that early retirement is more favourable for the pension system than normal age retirement.[8]
- Contributory fairness means that each year of contributions generates equivalent future pension rights, regardless of whether it is above a minimum or maximum number of years.[9]

The proposal to eliminate the inequities of a defined benefit system, made by Devesa et al. (2012), is based on redefining the replacement rate applicable to any individual, consisting of two phases. In the first phase, the replacement rate is set for the base case, that is, an individual who retires with the system's reference

[5]In this chapter, the substitution rate is defined as the ratio between the initial pension and the regulatory base. It is therefore different from the replacement rate, which is the ratio of the initial pension and the last wage before retirement, or the benefit or generosity rate of the system, which is defined as the ratio between the average pension and the average wage of the economy.

[6]Other countries, such as Portugal and Finland, have chosen to use the present value of an annuity, rather than life expectancy. From a financial standpoint, it seems more logical to use the present value of an annuity because it seems to suit the purposes of the coverage given by a retirement pension. In fact, life expectancy is the specific case in the present value of an annuity, when the interest rate used for the valuation is zero.

[7]The choice of one or other parameter is more a preference question than a technical problem, since obtaining the value of the corresponding parameter does not entail any additional difficulty from an actuarial point of view.

[8]For example, in Spain, the reduction coefficients for bringing forward the retirement age vary between 6% and 8% per year, while those who delay retirement find their pension has increased by between 2.5% and 4% per year.

[9]For example, in Spain, having contributed for fewer than 15 years does not lead to any contributory pension, and any years in excess of 37 years of contributions do not generate any additional increase, unless they are added to another set of conditions.

parameters (period, age and years of contributions). Setting this replacement rate is important because it is an economic policy instrument that directly or indirectly affects a great number of elements and also serves to reconcile the adequacy and sustainability objectives of a pension system.[10] The second phase ensures fairness between individuals, by applying different adjustment coefficients in order to ensure intergenerational, intragenerational and contributory fairness as compared to the base case.

To achieve this goal, the following formula is proposed for the replacement rate (ts), in which three variables are involved: the number of full-time equivalent years of social security contributions (y), the year of retirement (t) and the age (x) at which it takes place:

$$\begin{aligned} \mathrm{ts}(t_1, x_1, y_1) &\approx \mathrm{ts}(t_0, x_0, y_0) \frac{a_{x_0}^{(12)}(t_0)}{a_{x_0}^{(12)}(t_1)} \frac{a_{x_0}^{(12)}(t_0)}{a_{x_1}^{(12)}(t_0)} \frac{y_1}{y_0} \\ &= \mathrm{ts}(t_0, x_0, y_0) A(t_1)\, B(x_1)\, C(y_1) \end{aligned} \tag{4.4}$$

where $a_{x_0}^{(12)}(t_0)$ is the current value of a (monthly) income unit payable to an individual aged x_0 retiring in the year t_0. Thus, this expression consists of two parts. One controls the overall level of pensions, through the replacement rate of the base individual (ts), and the other results from multiplying the terms $A(t_1)$, $B(x_1)$ and $C(y_1)$ to ensure fairness between individuals from an intergenerational, intragenerational and contributory perspective, using the respective adjustment coefficients.

The above concepts can be complemented with three additional definitions of fairness provided by the European Commission (2015a):

1. Intergenerational fairness. This notion draws on some of the arguments and methodology from the 'generational equity' discussion. The main idea is to adjust the key variables (e.g. the definition of the active-age population) and retirement (e.g. the pensionable age) so that the old age dependency ratio is kept reasonably constant as population ages.
2. Social fairness. As we adjust to demographic changes, social fairness, according to the Actuarial Association of Europe, could entail taking into account the way cohort-specific life expectancy at effective pension age will change and ensuring that the pension age and the years spent working are adjusted so as to maintain a stable ratio between retirement years and working years. This is one way of implementing the European Commission recommendation that, in response to an ageing population, member states should establish and maintain a better balance between retirement and working years.

[10]Devesa et al. (2012) estimated that the replacement rate would have to be reduced by 35% to make the system sustainable.

3. Actuarial fairness. This concept establishes a closer relationship between the present value of the pensions received during retirement and the contributions paid while the pensioner was working.

Obviously, the challenge is to achieve the right balance between these concepts of equity, without jeopardising the sustainability and adequacy of pensions, to the extent that securing any one of them completely (e.g. actuarial fairness) may be at the expense of not meeting another one (e.g. social fairness).

This challenge leads to another important aspect related to the implications that welfare and economic growth have for the performance and efficiency of the PAYG pension system, depending on whether its sustainability is or is not at risk, and that expectations are generated of future increases in the tax burden that is needed to finance pensions or reductions in the benefit rate. To illustrate this point, we need to go back again to Eq. (4.1), which we will generalise for the case in which the system could currently have a structural deficit:

$$\frac{p^m}{w} \geq \tau \frac{L}{p} \qquad \text{(4.1 bis)}$$

How can economic growth, and therefore the future welfare of society, be affected by the uncertainties generated by the future evolution of the various components of the previous equation? Firstly, the very existence of the structural deficit and doubts about how to eliminate it affect the decisions of the economic agents, which can lead to increased risk premia, the tightening of financial conditions and a negative outlook on the rating of the economy. All this adversely affects investment, job creation and growth. Secondly, even if there is no structural deficit at present, the expectation that one will arise in the future as a result of the increase in the dependency ratio (in terms of Eq. (4.1) through decreases in the ratio *L*/*P*) can lead to the same kinds of uncertainties just described. Thirdly, the decline in the benefit rate (p^m/w) or an increase in the tax burden (τ) to restore the sustainability of the system results in a loss of welfare due to the expectations generated by the implicit contract between generations that are thus dashed. If we opt for a decrease in the future benefit rate, the workers who are financing their current pensions with their contributions see their expectations changed, to the extent that their pensions will lose purchasing power relative to the average future wage, compared to that enjoyed by current pensioners. If we opt for an increase in the tax burden, we only manage to pass this problem on to future taxpayers, while the distortions that result in tax increases can mean lower wages, less employment and ultimately lower pensions.

Figure 4.3 shows the huge heterogeneity among European Union countries in two of the three terms in Eq. (4.1 bis): the benefit rate and the tax burden, which in this figure is approximated by spending on pensions over GDP. The correlation between the two variables is positive, even without correcting for the dependency ratio, which shows clearly that there is no such thing as a free lunch and that the choice of a higher rate of benefit entails the higher levels of tax pressure, unless an increase in the employment rate should allow the necessary resources to be obtained.

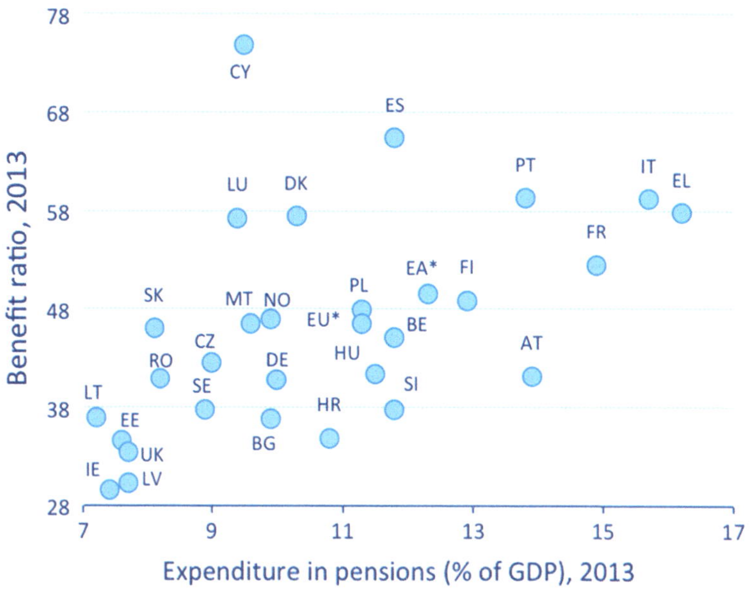

Fig. 4.3 Benefit rate (p^m/w) and pension expenditure as a percentage of GDP in the European Union, 2013. (*Source:* own preparation from data from the European Commission Ageing Report (2015b))

To describe the extent to which increasing the employment rate helps the balance between revenues and expenditures, it is necessary to rewrite Eq. (4.1 bis) as follows:

$$\frac{p^m}{w} \geq \tau \frac{L}{\mathrm{WAP}} \frac{\mathrm{WAP}}{L^{65+}} \frac{L^{65+}}{P} \tag{4.5}$$

where WAP is the working-age population, L/WAP is the employment rate and L^{65+} is the population over 65 years of age, such that WAP/L^{65+} is the inverse of the dependency ratio. Figure 4.4 represents the heterogeneity in 2013 among EU countries in employment rates and dependency ratios. With similar dependency ratios, about 27%, we find countries (e.g. Italy, Spain and Hungary, at one end, and the Nordic countries and Germany on the other) in which differences in employment rates reach more than 20 percentage points, which gives an idea of the scope for improving efficiency and dealing with an ageing population through structural reforms that increase employment rates, thus avoiding further adjustment of the benefit rate or increases in the tax burden.

In addition to reforms that improve labour market regulations and increase competition in product markets (in line with the traditional approach of Blanchard

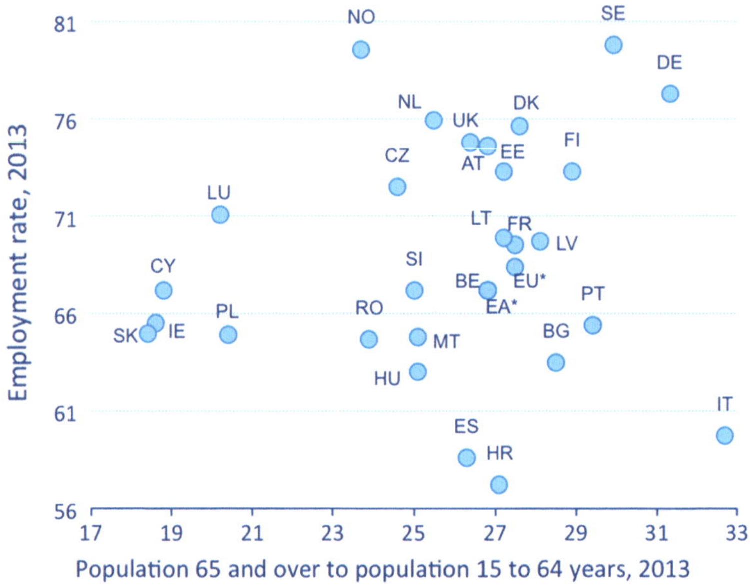

Fig. 4.4 Employment rate (*L*/WAP) and dependence ratio (L^{65+}/WAP) in the European Union, 2013. (*Source:* own preparation using data from Eurostat)

and Giavazzi 2002, or Layard et al. 2005),[11] many of the structural reforms that may be considered in order to increase employment rates also improve the efficiency of the PAYG system. In fact, some of the countries that show higher employment rates have opted for more efficient and less distortionary taxation (e.g. Denmark) or notional accounts (e.g. Sweden).

With regard to taxation, as mentioned in the previous section, the aim is to reduce taxation on labour (e.g. social security contributions) in exchange for increasing indirect taxation, a proposal known as a fiscal devaluation (see, e.g. Boscá et al. 2013, or Farhi et al. 2014).

As for notional accounts, their great advantage is the transparency, simplicity and the improved contributiveness that they involve, which encourages participation in the labour market and reduces taxation distortions on employment. Unlike notional accounts, the PAYG systems in place in many countries do not provide an accurate idea for future pensioners of what the relationship will be between the accumulated contributions made throughout the working life and the annual pension to which they would be entitled, based on their retirement age and life expectancy. If this is added to uncertainty about possible regulatory changes that could reduce system's

[11]Doménech et al. (2016) apply this type of model, in which both workers and companies have the power to set prices and wages in labour markets and products, in order to perform a breakdown of the structural shocks that explain the movements in the unemployment rate in Spain since the mid-1980s.

future contributiveness, the result is that contributions to social security are perceived more as a tax wedge than as deferred salary. Faced with this 'veil' between contributions and pensions, the notional account system operates under the transparent principle that €1 of contribution entitles you to €1 of contributory pension while simultaneously improving the efficiency of the pension system and the labour market and ultimately making participation in the pension system more attractive.

4.4 Redistribution Versus Efficiency and Contributiveness

Although greater efficiency and contributiveness of the pension system has positive effects on economic growth, this does not necessarily translate into increased social welfare. From a welfare perspective, the pension system has to take into account the extent to which it ensures an adequate income upon retirement, in economies that are subject to different imperfections, the myopic behaviour of individuals and shocks that can have permanent effects on the income of workers, with significant distributional consequences. In the absence of such imperfections and disturbances, a purely contributory system would be theoretically efficient and would not generate inequality. However, in the real world, one of the relative advantages that is most often highlighted regarding the PAYG system is its ability to promote a more equitable distribution of income, avoiding situations of relative poverty, reducing the risk of social exclusion and increasing social welfare. At the end of the day, the average income of pensioners is only an incomplete indicator of aggregate welfare, as is GDP per capita, if we do not consider other important aspects, such as the inequality that characterises the distribution of consumption levels. In fact, as shown empirically by Jones and Klenow (2016) for a sample of 152 countries, some economies with lower income per capita than others can achieve similar levels of welfare, as lower inequality compensates for the income gap. Therefore, one of the challenges for the pension system is to achieve the right balance between efficiency and contributiveness, on the one hand, and redistribution, on the other, to maximise social welfare levels.

In general, the total benefit provided by the pension system usually consists of the sum of two sources of income: public and private pensions. While the private part is composed almost entirely of contributory benefits, public pensions can be divided, in turn, into contributory and non-contributory. The ultimate goal of public non-contributory benefits is precisely the reduction of inequality, avoiding situations of relative poverty and social exclusion.

Overall, the consensus is that the contributory part of the PAYG system should be financed by social security contributions, in a clear, simple and transparent way making these contributions a deferred salary. One of the objectives of notional account systems is precisely this. The fact that the workers will receive a high return on the contributions made to the system encourages them to continue making or even increase these contributions. In contrast, a low return may discourage labour supply and contributions to the system, even stimulating the underground economy.

Meanwhile, the consensus is that non-contributory benefits should be financed by taxes. Otherwise, a double redistribution may appear if contributions are also used to finance non-contributory benefits: part of the redistribution would be financed out of workers' contributions and the other, additionally, out of their taxes. For this reason, it seems more appropriate that taxes should finance non-contributory pensions, while the social contributions finance only contributory pensions.[12] However, some countries have gone beyond this principle and even finance part of the contributory pensions with general taxes as a way to further promote employment and economic activity. This is the case of Denmark, where social security contributions barely accounted in 2013 for 0.2% of GDP while spending on pensions reached 10.3% of GDP.

How can we determine the degree of redistribution and contributiveness that will maximise social welfare? To try to answer this question, the first thing to solve is how to measure the degree of contributiveness versus redistribution. It is obvious that if all pensions were equal, regardless of the contributions made during workers' life, contributiveness would be zero and redistribution would be maximum. In contrast, contributiveness would be maximum if pensions were directly proportional to the social contributions made and if non-contributory benefits are absent. Therefore, as an approximation to the system's degree of contributiveness, it seems appropriate to use the ratio of expenditure, less any non-contributory benefit, to total expenditure on pensions. The main problem with this measure is that it leaves out important elements that can also affect the system's degree of contributiveness as, for example, rates of progressive contributions, exemptions in the base of social contributions or maximum pensions, which mean the relationship between the social contributions paid and the pension received is not exactly proportional. All these elements make it difficult to estimate the real contributiveness of the system.

Another alternative way for determining the balance between contributiveness and redistribution is to set a minimum level of benefits. This is one of the main challenges that are already being faced by pension systems. However, it is not an easy problem to solve, because of the inherent difficulty of determining an optimal level of minimum pensions with objective criteria and a design that maximises its positive effects and, at the same time, minimises their distortions and disincentives. When using subjective criteria, social preferences regarding minimum pensions and their funding are very heterogeneous between individuals and, also, may change over time.

This heterogeneity is present in the differences observed across countries, although in practice all public pension systems include a first PAYG pillar, characterised by some kind of redistribution. Since pensions are the main source of income for people aged over 65, the redistribution of the PAYG system facilitates greater fairness in the distribution of income as compared to the funded system. To

[12]Specifically, in Spain, the non-permanent Commission on monitoring and evaluation of the Toledo Pact Agreements on the issue of pensions suggests maintaining this separation of the sources of funding.

the extent that pensions from funded systems are proportional to the savings accumulated, funded systems tend to perpetuate the existing income distribution before reaching retirement age. In fact, savings in a funded system are subject to idiosyncratic shocks throughout workers' careers, affecting disposable income when leaving the labour market. These shocks affect workers' level of income and therefore their level of savings. The funded system is also exposed to shocks in its rate of return, so that people who have saved the same amount during their working life but in different assets can end up obtaining very different levels of income as pensioners. For these reasons, it is often argued that the PAYG system is a good solution to risks in individual decisions that can affect insurance for old age and to the inequality of opportunity (Diamond 2004).

In practice, a measure of the degree of redistribution of the pension system is obtained comparing the inequality of the distribution of national income with that of public pensions, two variables for which we have available information. Based on this comparison, the OECD (2013) has set up a progressivity index (PI) for the mandatory pillar (public or private) of the pension systems of its member countries, based on the proposal made by Musgrave and Thin (1948). Specifically, this index is defined as:

$$\mathrm{PI} = 100 - 100\frac{\mathrm{Gini}^P}{\mathrm{Gini}^W}$$

where Gini^P and Gini^W are the Gini coefficients of public pensions in the mandatory pillar and of national income, respectively. When the progressivity index is zero, the mandatory pillar results in a distribution of pensions that replicates the distribution of income at aggregate level, i.e. $\mathrm{Gini}^P = Gini^W$. Conversely, if pensions were all equal, then $\mathrm{Gini}^P = 0$ and the progressivity index would equal 100.

Figure 4.5 shows the Gini coefficient of pensions and the progressivity index for OECD countries in 2013. As can be seen, in almost all the countries, except Sweden and Hungary, inequality of pensions is lower than that of national income and the progressivity index is positive, with an average of 38.5%. Secondly, there is a clear negative relationship between inequality in the distribution of pensions and the progressivity index. At one extreme, we can find the cases of Ireland and New Zealand, where public mandatory pensions are equal for all pensioners, so that their Gini coefficients are equal to zero. On the other extreme, we find Portugal and Turkey, which have greater inequality in their pensions and a progressivity index close to zero. It is important to note that countries with very different weighting and generosity in their mandatory pension systems have very similar Gini coefficients for public pensions. For example, Austria and Spain have replacement ratios that are much higher than in Germany and the USA but show a distribution of pensions with similar or even greater inequality. The same can be said about the fact that the presence of a compulsory contributory part does not correlate with inequality in the distribution of pensions. For example, the weight of the mandatory funded part in Denmark is slightly higher than in Sweden, where the

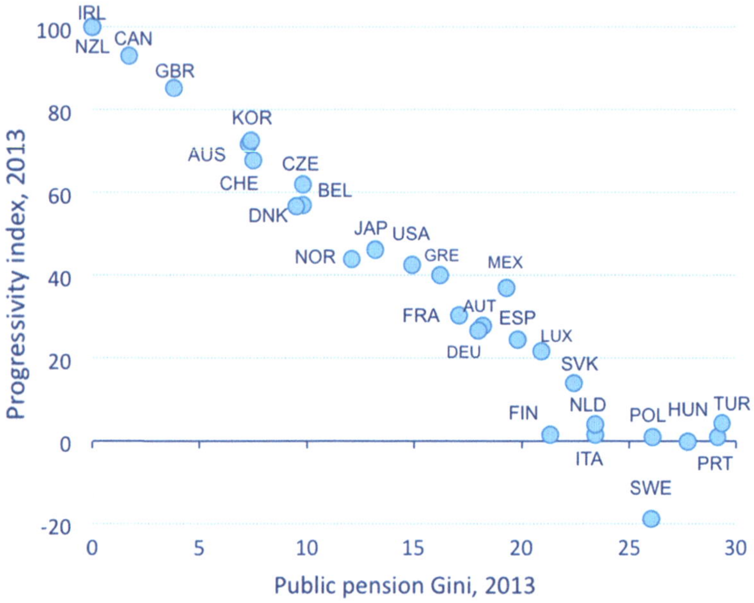

Fig. 4.5 Gini coefficient of public pensions and progressivity index in the OECD in 2013. (*Source:* own preparation from OECD (2013))

public PAYG part is more important, but it achieves greater equality in the distribution of pensions.

In view of these differences, is it better to be in a position closer to Ireland and New Zealand or, conversely, to Portugal or Sweden? The problem is that no normative conclusions can be drawn from the evidence presented in Fig. 4.5, for several reasons. Firstly, because the progressivity index only makes reference to the inequality of the public pension pillar, so it does not take into account the pensions provided by the private system. Some countries where the public pension is equal for all pensioners, independently of their contributions, have a high percentage of workers who also receive private pensions.

Secondly, because there is not enough information to break down the inequality in the total income of pensioners, it is not possible to compute how much of it is explained by the inequality of pensions, whether from public or private sources. At best, we can only calculate the correlation between the two variables, as shown in Fig. 4.6. As can be seen, the correlation between the two variables is zero. Some of the countries with the lowest public pension inequality have higher income inequality after taxes and transfers for the population aged over 65, while in others the opposite is true. As a result, countries that were at the extreme ends of the progressivity index shown in Fig. 4.5 ended up having a similar inequality when all sources of income, transfers and taxes are taken into account.

Lastly, it is necessary to add some additional criteria on how differences in income caused by the pension system end up affecting the welfare of pensioners,

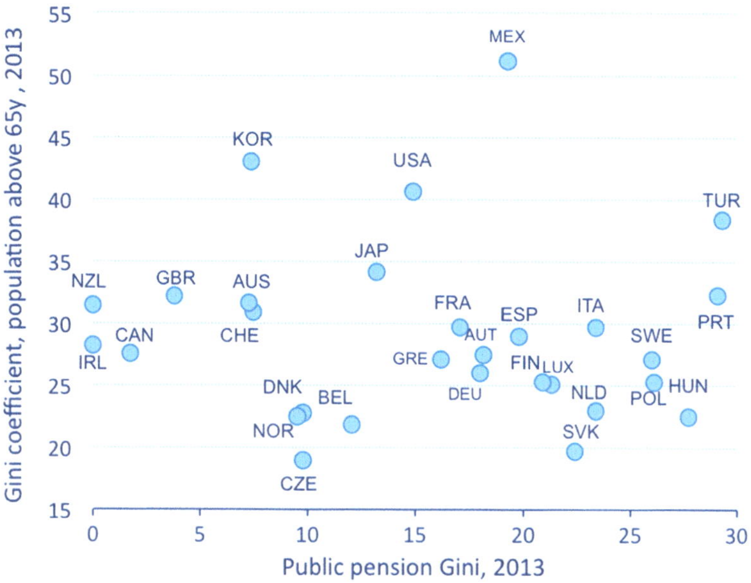

Fig. 4.6 Gini coefficient for public pension and disposable income for the population aged over 65 after taxes and transfers, OECD (2013). (*Source:* own preparation from data from the OECD Income Distribution and Poverty Database)

because it is perfectly possible that greater inequality could be offset by higher pensions. This is illustrated in Fig. 4.7, which shows a measure of inequality in disposable income after taxes and transfers for the population aged 65 and over and its average disposable income. The line with the positive slope represents the iso-welfare curve that crosses the point for the USA, with the combinations of inequality and income (in logarithms) that keep social welfare constant. This line has been obtained using the approach proposed by Jones and Klenow (2016), under the assumption that life expectancy and leisure remain constant.[13] As can be seen, social welfare in the USA is similar to that of Switzerland, Canada or Austria, so that the reduction of inequality in the range represented in Fig. 4.7 leaves social welfare unchanged, despite the fact that average disposable income is 20 percent lower than in the USA.

[13]More specifically, the inequality variable shown in this figure is half the variance of the distribution of disposable income, which have been estimated using the Gini index of income:

$\sigma^2/2 = (2^{0,5}*\text{norminv}((1 + \text{Gini})/2,0,1))/2$

where Gini is the Gini coefficient of disposable income for the population aged 65 and over and norminv is the inverse of the cumulative normal distribution function with mean 0 and unit variance. The income level refers to the average disposable income, after taxes and transfers, of the population aged 65 and over in purchasing power parities of private consumption. The data have been obtained from the OECD *Income Distribution and Poverty Database*. (https://goo.gl/Lefexj)

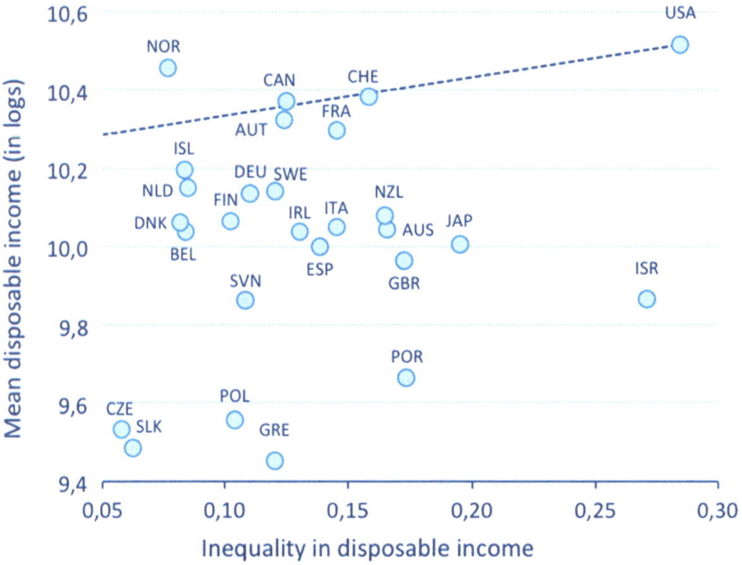

Fig. 4.7 Average and inequality of disposable income after taxes and transfers, for the population aged over 65, in the OECD (2013). The straight line with a positive slope represents the combinations of income and inequality that keep social welfare constant according to the approach proposed by Jones and Klenow (2016). (*Source:* own preparation from data from the OECD Income Distribution and Poverty Database)

In summary, it seems reasonable to think that neither extreme equality (at the expense of a lower contributiveness) nor extreme contributiveness (at the price of greater inequality) is optimal. For example, Le Garrec (2012) shows that greater progressivity in the pension system leads to less inequality but at the cost of lower growth, as a result of disincentives and distortions that we have analysed in the sections above. At the same time, very high inequality also ends up hurting long-term economic growth, as argued by Andrés and Doménech (2015). Therefore, in this trade-off between equality and contributiveness, an intermediate situation will surely allow higher levels of social welfare to be achieved, but ultimately the final choice depends on social preferences and the existing political economy constraints.

4.5 Conclusions

In this chapter, we have analysed the effects of PAYG and funded pension systems on growth and social welfare. The debate on the choice between alternative pension systems has focused on the incentives and distortions they generate, comparing their effects on savings, employment, economic growth and inequality.

The main findings of this analysis are as follows. Firstly, funded systems generate positive effects on the rate of savings, productivity and employment, avoiding many of the distortions generated by taxes. These distortions and incentives should be taken into account when improving the PAYG system with notional accounts, so as to increase the link between social contributions and future pensions. Secondly, the design of the pension system needs to seek an efficient balance between the economic and social effects of distortions and incentives, on the one hand, and equality and insurance against idiosyncratic risks, on the other. The reduction of multiple inefficiencies and distortions through notional accounts can simultaneously lead to higher average pensions in a PAYG system, more equality and increased social welfare. Thirdly, there are sufficient arguments for a well-designed PAYG system to remain a fundamental part of the pension system. The PAYG system is not necessarily an inefficient insurance mechanism but a mechanism of redistribution of income between individuals that funded systems alone cannot satisfy. Fourthly, although there are theoretical arguments for expecting PAYG systems to achieve a more equitable distribution of income among pensioners than funded systems, in practice, equality seems to depend more on other determinants, in particular the efficiency of the labour market. Fifthly, the evidence presented in this chapter shows that there are significant differences among advanced economies in their social preferences regarding the combination of replacement ratios and contributions to the funded system, so there is no guarantee that social welfare is maximised by imposing an objective of pension's expenditure over GDP, independently of those preferences.

In view of the above results, the experience of many economies in central and northern Europe indicates that it is possible to maximise social welfare with average pensions to average wage ratios below 50 percent and low inequality. This requires, firstly, ensuring sustainability and improving the efficiency and contributiveness of the PAYG system, which needs to be a fundamental pillar of the pension system and the welfare state, using notional accounts and minimum pensions that are sufficient to reduce inequality and eliminate the risk of social exclusion. The changes required to move in that direction need to be implemented gradually, but as quickly as possible and with maximum transparency, so that workers can anticipate them and can take decisions that will offset the effects of these changes on their future pensions by prolonging their working lives, improving their skills, increasing their rate of activity and increasing their savings for retirement. And secondly, as some countries already have done, this requires implementing individual funded accounts with automatic enrolment, with contributions from both workers and firms, regardless of whether the management of these accounts is public or private.

Acknowledgements The authors would like to thank the comments by D. Carrasco and E. Marazuela. R. Doménech acknowledges the financial support of research projects CICYT ECO2014-53150 and GVPROMETEO2016-097.

References

Acosta-Ormaechea, S., & Yoo, J. (2012). *Tax composition and growth: A broad cross-country perspective*. WP No. 12–257. International Monetary Fund. http://goo.gl/DvADbz

Alonso, D., & Pazos, M. (2001). Equidad y eficiencia en el sistema español de pensiones: Una revisión crítica (Equity and efficiency in the Spanish pension system: A critical review). Instituto de Estudios Fiscales. P. T. N° 4/10.

Andrés, J., & Doménech, R. (2015). *En Busca de la Prosperidad*. (*In Search of Prosperity*.) Ediciones Deusto. https://goo.gl/jmJPLl

Arnold, J. M., Brys, B., Heady, C., Johansson, Å., Schwellnus, C., & Vartia, L. (2011). Tax policy for economic recovery and growth. *The Economic Journal, 121*(550), F59–F80. http://goo.gl/vU6ok1.

Barr, N., & Diamond, P. (2008). *Reforming pensions: Principles and policy choices*. New York/Oxford: OUP.

Barro, R. J., & Sala-i-Martin, X. (2003). *Economic growth*. Cambridge, MA: The MIT Press.

Becker, G. S., & Murphy, K. M. (1988). Family and the state. *The Journal of Law and Economics, 31*(1), 1–18. https://goo.gl/PpcZ9h.

Blanchard, O., & Fischer, S. (1993). *Lectures on macroeconomics*. Cambridge, MA: The MIT Press.

Blanchard, O., & Giavazzi, F. (2002). Current account deficits in the euro area: The end of the Feldstein-Horioka puzzle? *Brookings Papers on Economic Activity, 2002*, 147–186. http://goo.gl/uCI05l.

Boscá, J. E., Doménech, R., & Ferri, J. (2009). Tax reforms and labor-market performance: An evaluation for Spain using REMS. *Moneda y Crédito, 228*, 145–196. http://goo.gl/2tT4fT.

Boscá, J. E., Doménech, R., & Ferri, J. (2013). Fiscal devaluations in EMU. *Hacienda Pública Española/Review of Public Economics, 206*(3/2013), 27–56. http://goo.gl/KCjtFl.

Buyse, T., Heylen, F., & Van de Kerckhove, R. (2013). Pension reform, employment by age, and long-run growth. *Journal of Population Economics, 26*, 769–809.

Devesa, J. E., Devesa, M., Domínguez, I., Encinas, B., Meneu, R., & Nagore, A. (2012). Equidad y sostenibilidad como objetivos ante la reforma del sistema contributivo de pensiones de jubilación. (Equity and sustainability as objectives in the reform of the contributory retirement pension system). *Hacienda Pública Española, 201*(2/2012), 9–38.

Diamond, P. (2004). Social security. *American Economic Review, 94*(1), 1–24.

Diamond, P. A., & Orszag, P. R. (2005). Saving social security. *The Journal of Economic Perspectives, 19*(2), 11–32.

Disney, R. (2004). Are contributions to public pension programmes a tax on employment? *Economic Policy, 19*, 267–311.

Doménech, R. (2014). Pensiones, bienestar y crecimiento económico. In J. A. Herce (Ed.), *Pensiones: Una reforma medular*. Enero: Fundación de Estudios Financieros y Círculo de Empresarios.

Doménech, R., & García, J. R. (2008). Unemployment, taxation and public expenditure in OECD economies. *European Journal of Political Economy, 24*, 202–217.

Doménech, R., García, J. R., & Ulloa, C. (2016). The effects of wage flexibility on activity and employment in the Spanish economy. WP 16/17 BBVA Research. https://goo.gl/Z57Zyn

European Commission. (2015a). *The 2015 pension adequacy report: Current and future income adequacy in old age in the EU*. Social Protection Committee (SPC) and the European Commission (DG EMPL).

European Commission. (2015b): The *2015 ageing report. Economic and budgetary projections for the 28 EU Member States (2013–2060)*. European Economy 3|2015. https://goo.gl/dywuaW

Farhi, E., Gopinath, G., & Itskhoki, O. (2014). Fiscal devaluations. *The Review of Economic Studies, 81*(2), 725–760. https://goo.gl/wWUKBL.

Feldstein, M. S. (1974). Social security, induced retirement and aggregate capital accumulation. *Journal of Political Economy, 82*(5), 905–926.

Feldstein, M., & Liebman, J. B. (2002). Social security. In A. J. Auerbach & M. Feldstein (Eds.), *Handbook of public economics* (Vol. 4, pp. 2245–2324). Amsterdam: Elsevier. https://goo.gl/cDA0Rm.

Holzmann, R., & Heinz, R. (2005). *Old age income support in the 21st century*. Washington, DC: The World Bank.

Johansson, Å. (2016). *Public finance, economic growth and inequality*. WP 1346. OECD. https://goo.gl/n0JDE2

Jones, C. I., & Klenow, P. J. (2016). Beyond GDP? Welfare across countries and time. *The American Economic Review, 106*(9), 2426–2457. https://goo.gl/Y3t0GM.

Layard, R., Nickell, S., & Jackman, R. (2005). *Unemployment: Macroeconomic performance and the labour market* (2nd ed.). Oxford: Oxford University Press.

Le Garrec, G. (2012). Social security, income inequality and growth. *Journal of Pension Economics and Finance, 11*(1), 53–70. https://goo.gl/zVO5ZD.

Lindbeck, A., & Persson, M. (2003). The gains from pension reform. *Journal of Economic Literature, XLI*, 74–112.

Melguizo, A., & González-Páramo, J. M. (2012). Who bears labour taxes and social contributions? A meta-analysis approach. *SERIEs, Spanish Economic Association, 4*(3), 247–271.

Mirrlees, J. (2011). *Tax by design: The Mirrlees review*. Oxford: Oxford University Press. http://goo.gl/uGN1mb.

Musgrave, R. A., & Thin, T. (1948). Income tax progression 1924–48. *Journal of Political Economy, 56*, 498–514.

OECD. (2013) *Pensions at a Glance*. https://goo.gl/kYSD0u

Ohanian, L., Raffo, A., & Rogerson, R. (2008). Long-term changes in labour supply and taxes: Evidence from OECD countries, 1956–2004. *Journal of Monetary Economics, 55*, 1353–1362.

Orszag, P. R., & Stiglitz, J. E. (2001). Rethinking pension reform: Ten myths about social security systems. In R. Holzmann & J. Stiglitz (Eds.), *New ideas about old age security* (pp. 17–56). Washington, DC: The World Bank. https://goo.gl/nRMBOV.

Pissarides, C. A. (2007). Unemployment and hours of work: The North Atlantic divide revisited. *International Economic Review, 48*(1), 1–36.

Prescott, E. C. (2004). Why do Americans work so much more than Europeans? *Federal Reserve Bank of Minneapolis Quarterly Review, 28*, 2–13.

Rogerson, R. (2006). Understanding differences in hours worked. *Review of Economic Dynamics, 9*, 365–409.

Rogerson, R. (2007). Taxation and market work: Is Scandinavia an outlier? *Economic Theory, 32*, 59–85.

Rogerson, R. (2008). Structural transformation and the deterioration of European labor market outcomes. *Journal of Political Economy, 116*(2), 235–259.

Samuelson, P. A. (1958). An exact consumption-loan model of interest with or without the social contrivance of money. *Journal of Political Economy, 66*, 467–482. https://goo.gl/1s73Ze.

Samuelson, P. A. (1975). Optimal social security in a life-cycle growth model. *International Economic Review, XVI*, 539–544.

Chapter 5
Pension Systems and Labour Market Participation in European Countries

Filip Chybalski

Abstract Many countries all over the world have been facing the problem of deteriorating demographics, forcing reforms of the pension system model as well as its main parameters. An important perspective of the assessment of the financial sustainability of a pension system is the division of current GDP among generations. This results from the macroeconomic rules that determine the pension system functioning. The main factor affecting the sustainability and, therefore, the income adequacy of pensioners in the long run is the relationship between the pension system and the labour market. The timing of retirement determines the border between the working age generation and the generation of pensioners. In this chapter, the author attempts to answer the research question whether empirical data covering European countries confirm that there is a linkage between pension systems design or their selected parameters and the condition of labour markets. This question seems to be crucial for policymakers, especially in countries refraining from a systematic increase in the retirement age or that are even planning to decrease it. The method employed to analyse empirical data is mainly based on selected statistical as well as econometric tools.

Keywords Pension · Retirement · Labour market · Human resources · Generation

5.1 Introduction

Pension reforms across the world are mainly in response to deteriorating demographics. They aim at maintaining the minimum required level of income adequacy under the condition of financial sustainability. These reforms include model changes (from defined benefit (DB) to defined contribution (DC), from unfunded to funded) and changes in some parameters (contributions, benefits, pensionable age) and, as a

F. Chybalski (✉)
Department of Management, Lodz University of Technology, Lodz, Poland
e-mail: filip.chybalski@p.lodz.pl

M. Peris-Ortiz et al. (eds.), *Economic Challenges of Pension Systems*,
https://doi.org/10.1007/978-3-030-37912-4_5

result, they very often affect the relation between state and market in a pension system. This relation is at least of two-dimensional nature. First, it refers to the relation between public and private administration or management in a pension system. Second, it very often determines the relation between the compulsoriness and voluntariness of participation in a pension system. Both these dimensions of the relation between state and market (or between state and market economy) may affect the influence a pension system has on the labour market. The pension policy of a given country may encourage one to stay longer economically active and work beyond the pensionable age (if permitted by the law) or vice versa, it may stimulate earlier retirement. While from the 1970s to 1990s in some countries, especially in Continental Europe, the policy to stimulate jobs growth for the young through encouraging older people to take early retirement was implemented (Gruber et al. 2009; Lefebvre 2012), at the end of the twentieth century this idea turned out to be bankrupt. As noticed by Barr and Diamond (2006), "[t]he common view that early retirement eases unemployment is generally mistaken. From a long historic perspective, developed countries have seen a vast decrease in the average retirement age, yet unemployment has shown no trend decrease". Since 1995, the average pensionable age in OECD countries has been increasing, which is a result of a retreat from "the earlier retirement the better policy" to "the later retirement the better policy". However, it should be noted that although the trend of increasing the pensionable age characterizes the majority of European countries, there are some exceptions where the policy is the opposite. The different paths of pension reforms give cause to study the relationship between a pension system and the labour market, since an effective labour market determines the sustainability of pension system and, therefore, income adequacy in the long term. In this chapter, I try to answer the question whether the design of a pension system or its selected parameters affect the participation of older people in the labour market.

5.2 Literature Review

Barr and Diamond (2006, 2010) indicate that analysing pension systems requires recognition of the trade-off between efficiency in the labour market and the realization of the goals of pension systems (consumption smoothing, insurance, redistribution, poverty alleviation, and others). The link between salary during working life and pension benefits after retirement may affect the decision concerning both the professional career and the timing of retirement. To reduce distortions between the pension system and the labour market, a pension benefit formula should account for most or all of a worker's earnings history. However, the models of a pension system based on a strictly actuarial relationship between contributions and benefits are not the solution to these distortions. This results from many premises, one of the most important of which is that consumption smoothing is not the only goal of a pension system. Another very important social objective, if not the most important one, is poverty alleviation. Therefore, the labour market distortions caused by pension system are unavoidable and minimizing them is not the goal. The goal is to balance labour market efficiency against the objectives of pension systems (Barr and Diamond 2006, 2010).

Nevertheless, consumption smoothing is an important goal of a pension system, the second most important in the dimension of adequacy, next to poverty alleviation. According to the intertemporal choice model by Fisher, households have to make a choice between present and future consumption, taking rather the long- instead of the short-term perspective. They seek to maximize their utility over their whole life cycle and to achieve this goal they refrain from current consumption and transfer it to the future. The division of current income between consumption and saving determines the future consumption, taking also the real interest rate into account (Fisher 1930). On the basis of Fisher's model, Modigliani, Brumberg and Ando proposed the life cycle hypothesis (Modigliani and Brumberg 1954; Ando and Modigliani 1963) and Friedman (1957) proposed his permanent income hypothesis. Both these theories assume that people smooth their consumption over their life cycle. The tool to do this is a pension system, regardless of whether it is more public or private, unfunded or funded, with defined benefits or defined contributions. Decisions concerning the income allocation over the life cycle include inter alia the decision about when to stop the accumulation phase and start the decumulation phase. The borderline between these two phases is, to simplify, convergent with the borderline between the working and retirement period and is determined by the effective retirement age. This way, the labour market and pension system interact on the micro-level. Simultaneously, agents' decisions about retirement and saving aggregate at the macro-level, at which current GDP is divided among generations, including mainly the generation of workers and the generation of pensioners. The division of current GDP affects the future GDP that will be divided by future generations (see Góra 2008; Barr and Diamond 2006). This way, the process of income allocation serving for consumption smoothing over the life cycle, aggregated at the macro-level to the transfers between overlapping generations, may affect the decision about when to leave the labour market. The empirical studies of a life cycle model are, however, inconsistent. Some of them support this theoretical model, others rather not (see, e.g. the review of such studies presented by Blake 2006).

Hernaes (2013), on the basis of a literature review, indicates the fields of possible interactions between a pension system and the labour market. These are retirement incentives, gradual retirement (people may retire slowly, combining pensions with work), family interactions (relationship between the retirement decisions made by wife and husband), financial literacy, knowledge about the pension system and the transparency of its rules, expectations about future benefits, firm impact as well as human capital formation. Feldstein (1974) uses an extended version of the life cycle model to analyse the impact of social security on the agent's decision about retirement and saving. His analysis delivers arguments supporting the life cycle hypothesis, however with the important role of the retirement age as a subject of an economic decision. Feldstein (1995) confirms empirically that public social security reduces private saving. Since social security is an exemplification of the state's involvement in a pension system, the results of studies by Feldstein may suggest that agents take the role of public sector in ensuring the financial security for the elderly into account when making economic decisions about saving and retirement. Thus, it seems justified to account for the possible impact of the proportion between a public mandatory pension system and private voluntary pension plans when analysing the relationship between a pension system (as a whole, including its public as well as private parts) and the labour market. People can make the decision about when to retire on the basis of the state's promise to pay adequate pension benefits or its general involvement in a pension system.

Radl (2013) emphasises the "push-versus-pull dualism" of the mechanisms affecting the decisions about the timing of retirement. The pull approach is based on the conviction that monetary incentives are crucial for the decision about retirement. There are no doubts that the early retirement policy applied in the 1970s resulted in the decline in economic activity among older workers. The push approach is based on the thesis that labour market constraints are more important and dominate over the financial incentives or disincentives of retirement. According to this view, the main drivers for early retirement are unemployment and disabilities (Radl 2013).

Esping-Andersen (1990) delivers arguments that the retirement age, as one of the tools of full-employment policy, may be affected by the welfare state regime. In the liberal regime, the full-employment policy is not as important as in the other regimes (conservative and social-democratic). He empirically proves that GDP growth does not affect the realization of the full-employment policy. Full-employment is a matter of political decisions (Esping-Andersen 1990). This supports the view that the relation between state and market or public and private administration should be taken into account in the analysis of the relationship between a pension system and the labour market. This results from the main criterion used to differentiate between welfare state regimes or pension regimes, which is the relation between state and market in the socio-economic policy realized by the government.

Casamatta and De Paoli (2012) also emphasise the political context of the relation between a pension system and the labour market, indicating the tendency of the political process to encourage agents to retire earlier than optimally. They show that the optimal retirement age requires adjustment to increasing life expectancy (Casamatta and De Paoli 2012). Hansen and Lonstrup (2009) also find a positive relationship between the legal retirement age and life expectancy as required if the legal retirement age is set optimally ex ante. However, if the payroll tax is constant in a given period of time, a constant legal retirement age (or slightly modified) can be justified. This results from the fact that increasing longevity would decrease the public pension annuity rate in the future, which should stimulate capital accumulation (Hansen and Lonstrup 2009). However, this implication seems to require the assumption of rational behaviour on the part of agents, which means the ability to analyse objectively the changes of pension system parameters or economic and demographic variables (as, e.g. increasing longevity and expected incomes). Staubli and Zweimuller (2011) prove that an increase in early retirement age has a positive effect on delaying retirement, however not in a one-for-one relation. According to their findings based on data for Austria, about 30–40% of old-age agents prolong their employment as a result of an increase in the early retirement age. 60–70% of older agents enlarges the unemployment population and is paid unemployment benefits (Staubli and Zweimuller 2011).

Lacomba and Lagos (2009) prove that the model of pension benefit formula – defined contribution or defined benefit – may affect the preferred legal retirement age. They study these two pension plans and show that an increase in the redistribution transfers increases the retirement age in the case of a defined contribution plan, whereas in the case of a defined benefit plan, redistribution decreases retirement age. They conclude that policymakers should take this fact into account when aiming at delaying the legal retirement age. To minimize the degree of compulsion in a pension system based on a defined contribution formula, an increase in the legal retirement age should be achieved with a greater level of redistribution. In the case of defined benefit pension systems, redistribution should be reduced and replaced by a stronger link between lifetime contributions and pension benefits (Lacomba and Lagos 2009).

Another factor that may affect the decision about retirement is occupation. As proved by Saure and Zoabi (2012), occupational distribution is a vital driver force for an average effective age of retirement. This is observed at a cross-country level at which age of retirement differs dependently on the structure of occupations in labour.

5.3 Theoretical and Conceptual Framework

The literature review proves obvious relationships between a pension system and the labour market and indicates possible drivers of the decisions about retirement. The first group of drivers is relatively independent of pension system design and results mainly from the theory of consumption (Fisher 1930; Modigliani and Brumberg 1954, Ando and Modigliani 1963; Friedman 1957; Feldstein 1974). Agents aim at smoothing consumption over the life cycle and achieve this goal through saving, which expresses refraining from current consumption to consume in the future (after retirement). Therefore, the analysis of the timing of retirement should control for incomes and interest rates. From the macroeconomic point of view, the current situation on the labour market expressed by the unemployment rate may be also an important factor determining retirement decisions. An agent, if permitted by law, may use early retirement to avoid unemployment.

Other drivers are strictly connected to pension system design. First, the involvement of the state in a pension system may affect the expected generosity of this system as well as the security of pension guarantees. Additionally, different regimes of welfare state evaluate differently the role of full employment policy. This means that the relation between state and market in a pension system, which is one of the dimensions of the welfare state, may determine the retirement age since it can be used to reduce unemployment. A quite different question is if such a policy is efficient. The majority of empirical studies suggests that it is not. Another important feature of pension system design may be the compulsoriness of participation in pension plans. The greater this participation (measured, e.g. by mandatory public pension contribution), the greater the perceived guarantee of financial security for the elderly after retirement may be which, in turn, may encourage agents to retire earlier. This results, e.g. from the fact that social security generally reduces the private savings rate and similarly may reduce the need to save longer (and retire earlier). However, the opposite situation is also possible, especially if providing that agents are rational. Then, agents may strive to work longer since their private savings are reduced by greater social security.

The generosity of a pension system is the next possible determinant of decisions about retirement. Agents may analyse the current as well as projected generosity of a pension system. Greater generosity, measured as a ratio between pension benefit and salary (with the use of replacement rate) may encourage earlier retirement, and vice versa, lower generosity may stimulate a longer duration of working life.

Other possible drivers refer directly to the technical design of a pension system and include the benefit formula as well as method of benefit financing. As far as benefit formula is concerned, two models or hybrids thereof may be applied. These are defined benefit and defined contribution. The defined benefit formula is usually less linked to contributions paid across the working life, not to mention flat rate formula. In this case, benefits may be correlated to salary history (to the whole period of professional life or a shorter period directly before retirement). In the case of a defined contribution, there is an actuarial balance between contributions and benefits taking the life expectancy at retirement into account. The relation between the benefit formula and the timing of retirement is suggested by Lacomba and Lagos (2009). Additionally, agents aware of the direct link between contributions and benefits as well as between the period of paying contributions (convergent with duration of working life) and the period of being paid benefits may seek to delay retirement to increase pension benefits. In contrast, the defined benefit formula, especially with induced huge redistribution, may discourage prolongation of professional life.

The decision about retirement may be also affected by the method of financing pension benefits (taxes vs. separated contributions). In the case of tax-financed pension systems, financial obligations (liabilities) towards the pensioners are not precisely defined. In such a case, individual pension accounts rather do not exist and pension payment actually seems to be a promise of the government to pay benefits taking public budget constraints into account. In the case of a contribution-financed pension system with individual accounts, liabilities are well and precisely defined. Therefore, contribution-financed pension systems may be perceived as safer in terms of the benefits payment guarantees due to individualisation of liabilities. The opposite perception may characterize tax-financed pension systems, in which guarantees seem more to be a promise. This difference may affect the decision about when to retire.

Taxation of the withdrawal from the private pension scheme may also matter when making decisions about retirement. Taxation may discourage leaving the labour market and therefore stimulate later retirement.

5.4 Methodology and Data

In the empirical study, I use the following variables characterizing employment around retirement age: average effective age of retirement for males and females (AERm and AERf), duration of working life of males and females (DWLm and DWLf), employment rate for males and females aged 55–64 (EMP55-64_m and EMP55-64_f) and employment rate for males and females aged 65–74 (EMP65-74_m and EMP65-74_f). To analyse the relationship between these indicators and pension system design, I use two independent approaches. The first is based on the comparative study of different pension regimes differentiated on the basis of the relation between state and market in pension systems in terms of the labour market indicators mentioned above. In the other approach, I use regression models for these variables with explanatory variables referring to pension system design with controls representing incomes, interest rates as well as the overall labour market condition (unemployment).

The pension regime typology employed in the study originates from work by Marcinkiewicz and Chybalski (2019). They analyse pension regime typologies, especially those by Esping-Andersen (1990), Soede and Vrooman (2008), Krieger and Traub (2008), Rhodes and Natali (2003) and Borsch-Supan (2007), and assess their applicability in terms of adequacy and efficiency comparisons. They also propose a new typology for OECD countries. To distinguish between pension regimes, they apply a quantitative approach based on the variables referring to two dimensions: the extent of involvement of the state and the market in a pension system and the role of voluntary schemes. The set of variables used is as follows (Marcinkiewicz and Chybalski 2019):

X1 – the ratio between the expenditure on old-age pension provision from mandatory public schemes and total expenditure on old-age pensions (public and private mandatory and voluntary private). This measures the share of mandatory and publicly managed schemes in the whole pension system (2011).

X2 – the ratio between the expenditure on old-age pension provisions from mandatory private schemes and total expenditure on old-age pensions (public and private mandatory and voluntary private). This measures the share of mandatory and privately managed schemes in the whole pension system (2011).

X3 – the ratio between the expenditure on old-age pension provisions from voluntary private schemes and total expenditure on old-age pensions (public and private mandatory and voluntary private). This measures the share of privately managed voluntary schemes in the whole pension system (2011).

X4 – measures the contribution of the mandatory public pension system in ensuring retirement income. It is obtained by the formula: $X4 = P1/(P1 + P2 + P3)$.

X5 – measures the contribution of the mandatory private pension system in ensuring retirement income. It is obtained by the formula: $X5 = P2/(P1 + P2 + P3)$.

X6 – measures the contribution of the voluntary pension system in ensuring retirement income. It is obtained by the formula $X6 = P3/(P1 + P2 + P3)$:

where:

P1 denotes the net pension replacement rate from the public pension system.
P2 denotes the net pension replacement rate from the mandatory private pension system.
P3 denotes the net pension replacement rate from the voluntary pension system.

For all the P1–P3 variables, the net replacement rates projected for a person entering labour market in 2012 and earning an average wage (with no career breaks) are employed.

X7 – coverage of mandatory and quasi-mandatory private pension schemes (hereinafter referred to as private mandatory schemes) by type of plan, expressed as a percentage of the working age population (15–64 years) (2011).
X8 – coverage of voluntary private pension schemes by type of plan, expressed as a percentage of the working age population (15–64 years), calculated as the maximum of two values: coverage of voluntary occupational schemes and coverage of voluntary personal schemes (2011).
X9 – the rate of public mandatory pension contribution (if does not exist, X9 = 0) (2012).
X10 – the share of public minimum pension provision in the whole retirement income package in the mandatory system (the first and the second tier according to OECD classification). X10 contains the provision from the first tier, which serves for ensuring an absolute minimum standard of living (2012).
X11 – the share of public ER (earnings related) or DC provision in the whole retirement income package in the mandatory system. This contains the provision from the public part of the second tier (according to OECD classification) (2012).
X12 – the share of private pension provision in the whole retirement package in the mandatory system. This contains the provision from private DB and private DC schemes, thus from the private part of the second tier (2012).

With the application of multivariate statistical analysis (hierarchical clustering, k-means clustering and correlation analysis), Marcinkiewicz and Chybalski identify three following regimes: the regime of voluntary pension schemes (regime I), the regime of significant mandatory participation in private schemes (II regime) and the mandatory public regime (III regime). The I regime includes Canada, Ireland, the Czech Republic, New Zealand, the United Kingdom and the United States. This regime is the most liberal one in terms of participation in compulsory schemes, which exist only in the public part of the system, not in the private one. The share of public expenditure in the whole (public and private) expenditure on pensions is relatively low. In this regime, the minimum pensions paid from the public sector play an important role in the whole retirement income package from the mandatory part of the pension system. The II regime includes Australia, Denmark, Estonia, Iceland, Israel, Netherlands, Poland, the Slovak Republic and Sweden. Here, mandatory private pension schemes play a very important role, whereas in other regimes they do not actually exist. The share of public expenditure on pensions is very similar to this in the I regime, with the exception of CEE countries and Israel. To the III regime belong Austria, Belgium, Finland, France, Germany, Greece, Hungary, Italy, Luxembourg, Portugal, Slovenia, Spain and Turkey. This regime is characterized by the greatest ratio of public expenditure on benefits in the whole pension expenditure. Here, definitely, social security ensured be the state dominates. Participation in the mandatory private schemes almost does not occur and voluntary schemes are of minor interest (Marcinkiewicz and Chybalski 2019).

In the second approach, I estimate regression models for the average effective age of retirement (AERm and AERf), the duration of working life (DWLm and DWLf), the employment rate for the population aged 55–64 (EMP55-64_m and EMP55-64_f) and the employment rate for the population aged 65–74 (EMP65-74_m and EMP65-74_f), separately for males and females in the case of all indicators.

Models are estimated with the application of forward stepwise OLS regression for cross-sectional data from the years 2012, 2013 or 2014 (as available). The estimation procedure starts with the model without predictors (explanatory variables) and then one predictor is added in each subsequent step. To include or eliminate a given variable from the model, F statistics is used as the criterion. The estimation is performed with the use of Statistica software.

The models include the following explanatory variables:

RAm and RAf – pensionable age for males and for females (OECD data from 2014)
ARRm and ARRf – aggregated replacement ratio for males and for females (Eurostat data, 2014)
MoF – method of financing: separate pension contribution, MoF = 1; other, MoF = 0 (OECD data, 2012)
MoMP – modality of mandatory pillars (MoMP = 1 for dominant defined contribution formula, MoMP = 0 for another case)
ToW – taxation of withdrawal from private pension schemes: taxation, ToW = 1; no taxation, ToW = 0 (OECD data, 2012)
PPC – public pension contribution (OECD, World Bank or Pensionfundsonline data, 2013 or 2014)

Control variables: PE, pension expenditure as percentage of GDP (Eurostat data, 2013, for Poland and Greece 2012); ODR, old dependency ratio (Eurostat data, 2013); GDP, GDP per capita of population, in USD, current prices, current PPPs (OECD data, 2013); STIR, short-term interest rate (OECD data, 2013); LTIR, long-term interest rate (OECD data, 2013); UNEMPm and UNEMPf, unemployment rate for males and females (Eurostat data, 2014).

Data used in the analysis covers 21 European countries: Austria, Belgium, the Czech Republic, Denmark, Finland, France, Germany, Greece, Hungary, Iceland, Ireland, Italy, the Netherlands, Norway, Poland, Portugal, Slovakia, Slovenia, Spain, Sweden and the United Kingdom. Data comes from the Eurostat and OECD statistics databases from the years 2012–2014, depending on availability.

5.5 Results

The comparative analysis of the average effective age of retirement and labour market indicators confirms that the relation between the public and private character of a pension system as well as the relation between mandatory and voluntary participation in pension schemes affect the decision about retirement. As a result, a pension system model or, more generally, its "philosophy" (state vs. market involvement or some hybrid solutions) determines the influence of pensions on the labour market (Table 5.1).

The significant differences in the analysed indicators across pension regimes are bolded in Table 5.1. We can observe that in the case of the most social regime where the state dominates in a pension system and the private sector or voluntary schemes are marginalized, the employment rates for older people (aged 55–64 or 65–74 years) both for males and females are lower than in the case of two other regimes in which the market plays a notable role. In the case of the duration of working life or the average effective age of retirement, differences are observable especially for males, less so for females. In the regime of significant voluntary pension schemes and in the regime of significant mandatory participation in private schemes, employment rates for males aged 55–64 are on average 10 p.p. greater than in the mandatory public regime. For women, this difference is quite similar. Medians of this indicator differ even more. For females aged 55–64, the median employment rate for the II regime equals 55.4%, whereas for the III regime it is only 37.7%. This is a substantial disparity in terms of labour market participation. In the case of employment rates for the population aged 65–74, the differences equal on average 6–10 p.p. for males and 2–7 p.p. for females. This proves that a dominant role of the state in a pension system reduces the economic activity of older people.

The results of the second approach based on a regression procedure are presented in Tables 5.2, 5.3, 5.4, and 5.5. I include the best estimated models for forward

Table 5.1 Average effective age of retirement and labour market indicators across pension regimes

Indicator	EMP55-64_m	EMP55-64_f	EMP65-74_m	EMP65-74_f	DWLm	DWLf	AERm	AERf
Mean								
I regime	**65.3**	**48.4**	**16.7**	**8.3**	**39.3**	32.6	**64.3**	61.8
II regime	**65.7**	**54.9**	**19.0**	**11.6**	**38.8**	**35.2**	**64.2**	**62.5**
III regime	54.9	40.6	11.5	5.9	37.4	32.1	62.3	61.5
Median								
I regime	**66.1**	**45.4**	**19.9**	**7.5**	**38.6**	31.6	**64.1**	**62.4**
II regime	**63.3**	**55.4**	**17.2**	**9.6**	36.6	**35.1**	63.3	**62.4**
III regime	53.8	37.7	10.1	5.5	37.1	32.7	62.2	60.8

Source: Own computations

Table 5.2 Regression models for EMP55-64_m and EMP55-64_f variables

Predictors	EMP55-64_m	*p*-value	EMP55-64_f	*p*-value
const.	−80.366	0.115	**−214.041**	**<0.001**
RAm	**2.389**	**0.011**	–	–
RAf	–	–	**4.063**	**<0.001**
ARRm	−33.404	0.108	–	–
MoF	–	–	4.664	0.271
MoMP	5.362	0.254	–	–
ODR	–	–	0.534	0.204
GDP	**<0.001**	0.190	–	–
STIR	1.874	0.135	**3.106**	**0.015**
LTIR	–	–	−0.871	0.195
UNEMPm	−0.555	0.115	–	–
UNEMPf	–	–	**−1.129**	**<0.001**
R^2	0.806		0.885	
R^2 (adjusted)	0.722		0.836	
F (*p*-value)	9.671 ($p < 0.001$)		17.973 ($p < 0.001$)	

Source: Own computations

Table 5.3 Regression models for EMP65-74_m and EMP65-74_f variables

Predictors	EMP65-74_m	*p*-value	EMP65-74_f	*p*-value
Const.	−47.010	0.231	−24.781	0.236
RAm	**1.066**	**0.098**	–	–
RAf	–	–	0.469	0.159
ARRm	−19.220	0.202	–	–
MoF	−4.943	0.142	−3.122	0.105
ToW	**8.354**	**0.013**	**5.271**	**0.012**
STIR	**4.072**	**<0.001**	**2.983**	**<0.001**
UNEMPm	−0.266	0.225	–	–
UNEMPf	–	–	−0.173	0.110
R^2	0.879		0.870	
R^2 (adjusted)	0.827		0.827	
F (*p*-value)	16.954 ($p < 0.001$)		20.127 ($p < 0.001$)	

Source: Own computations

stepwise OLS regression. The predictors that are statistically significant for a p-value not greater than 0.100 are bolded.

The models estimated explain significantly the dependent variables since the *p*-value for *F*-statistics is lower than 0.001. R^2 (ordinary, not adjusted), ranges between 0.637 and 0.879 and is at a satisfactory level. Therefore, the quality of models seems to be sufficient to allow formulation of the following opinions. The employment rate among males at age before retirement is determined by the pensionable age. The simple regression on the employment rate for males aged 55–64 (EMP55-64_m) with pensionable age (RAm) suggests that a 1-year increase in this age causes an

Table 5.4 Regression models for DWLm and DWLf variables

Predictors	DWLm	*p*-value	DWLf	*p*-value
const.	−1.845	0.897	−9.082	0.566
RAm	**0.664**	**0.009**	–	–
RAf	–	–	**0.665**	**0.019**
ARRm	−6.592	0.262	–	–
ToW	**2.885**	**0.040**	**3.326**	**0.067**
STIR	**0.734**	**0.056**	**0.907**	**0.060**
UNEMPm	−0.142	0.145	–	–
UNEMPf	–	–	**−0.259**	**0.012**
R^2	0.742		0.710	
R^2 (adjusted)	0.656		0.637	
F (*p*-value)	8.641 ($p < 0.001$)		9.782 ($p < 0.001$)	

Source: Own computations

Table 5.5 Regression models for AERm and AERf variables

Predictors	AERm	*p*-value	AERf	*p*-value
const.	**43.713**	**0.001**	**19.511**	**0.010**
RAm	**0.321**	**0.072**	–	–
RAf	–	–	**0.701**	**<0.001**
MoF	**−2.217**	**0.013**	–	–
ToW	–	–	**2.799**	**0.004**
GDP	–	–	**<0.001**	**0.031**
STIR	**0.533**	**0.027**	**0.600**	**0.006**
UNEMPf	–	–	−0.090	0.109
R^2	0.724		0.860	
R^2 (adjusted)	0.676		0.813	
F (*p*-value)	14.888 ($p < 0.001$)		18.434 ($p < 0.001$)	

Source: Own computations

increase in the employment rate (EMP55-64_m) of 3.77 p.p. on average (see Fig. 5.1). In the case of women, this effect is even stronger and a 1-year increase in the pensionable age (RAf) results in an average increase in the employment rate (EMP55-64_f) of 4.16 p.p. (Fig. 5.2). Another factor stimulating the economic activity of women at near-retirement age is said to be the short-term interest rate (STIR) and unemployment rate. Both these variables are treated as controls and do not refer to the design or parameters of a pension system, but result from consumption theory (mainly from intertemporal choice model by Fisher) or theory and empirical studies on labour markets. The interest rate stimulates the employment positively, whereas unemployment affects the employment among women at near-retirement age negatively.

The short-term interest rate is a positive driver for employment among both males and females at age 65–74. The same refers to the taxation of withdrawals from

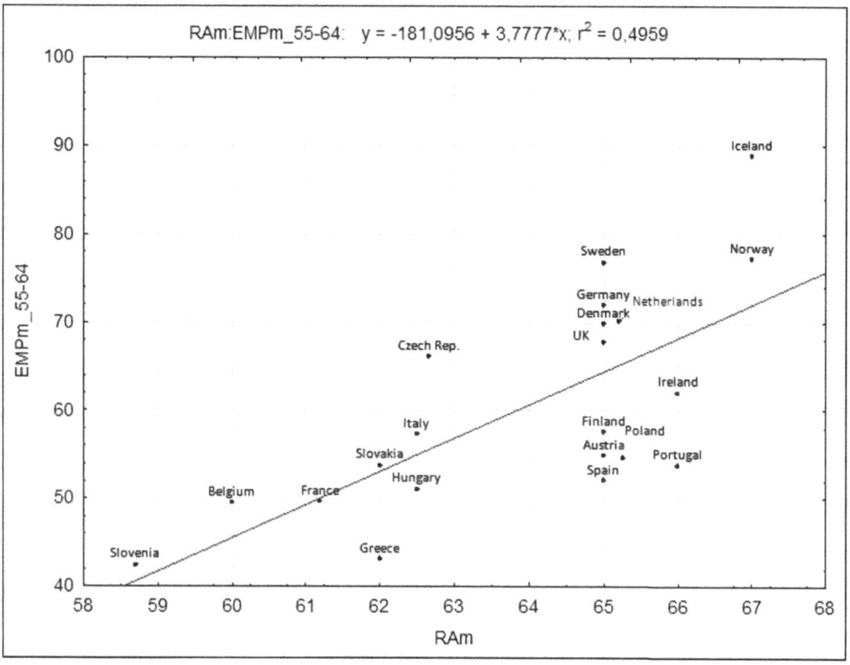

Fig. 5.1 Simple regression on EMP55-64_m with RAm. (*Source:* Own elaboration)

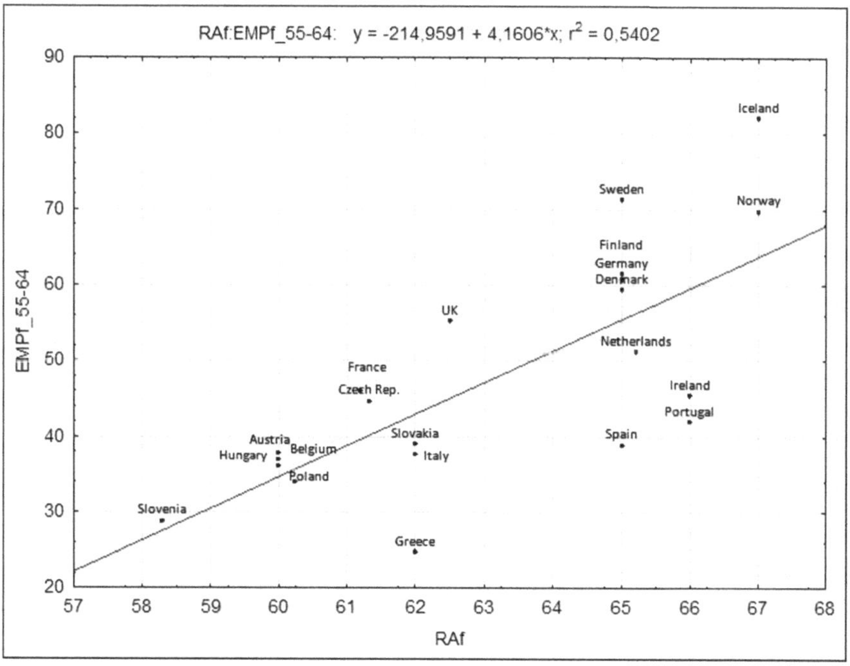

Fig. 5.2 Simple regression on EMP55-64_f with RAf. (*Source:* Own elaboration)

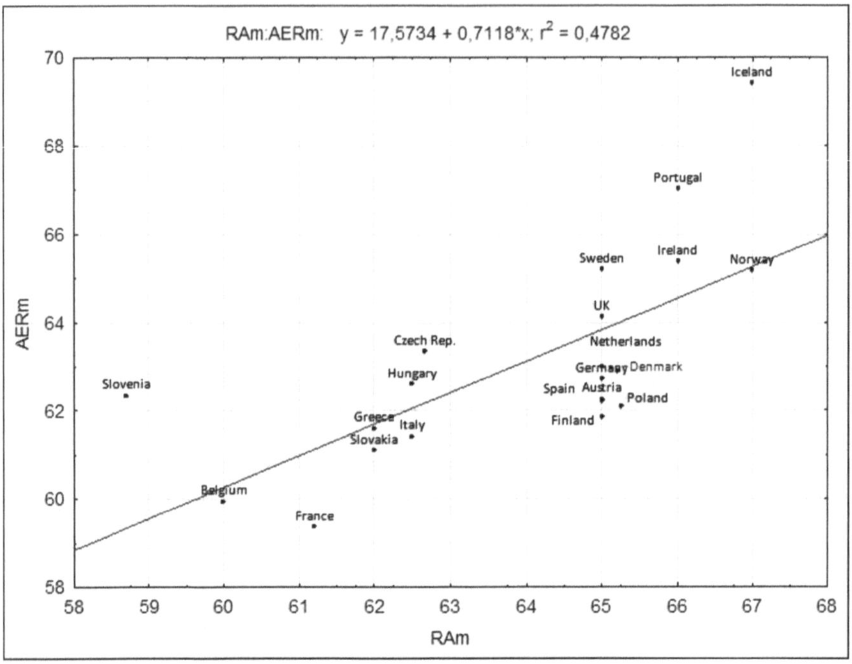

Fig. 5.3 Simple regression on AERm with RAm. (*Source:* Own elaboration)

private pension schemes, which encourages remaining in the labour market longer. The pensionable age does determine the employment rates among older males (aged 65–74) significantly; however in the case of females, this relationship is statistically insignificant.

The duration of working life (DWL) is for both males and females affected by the pensionable age and the short-term interest rate. Additionally, a statistically significant impact of taxation of withdrawals from private pension schemes on duration of working life is also observed for both genders. Males' length of professional life, as opposed to females, seems to be resistant to the overall labour market condition expressed by the unemployment rate.

The average effective age of retirement for both genders (AERm and AERf) is sensitive to pensionable age and the relationship between these variables is quite strong (see Figs. 5.3 and 5.4). In the case of males, a 1-year greater pensionable age results in 0.712-year (8.5-month) later retirement. In the case of females, it is 0.745-year (8.9-month) later retirement. The average effective age of retirement is also positively affected by the short-term interest rate. Additionally, pension systems based on separate contribution financing decrease the average effective age of retirement for males. In the case of females, taxation of withdrawals from private pension schemes delays retirement.

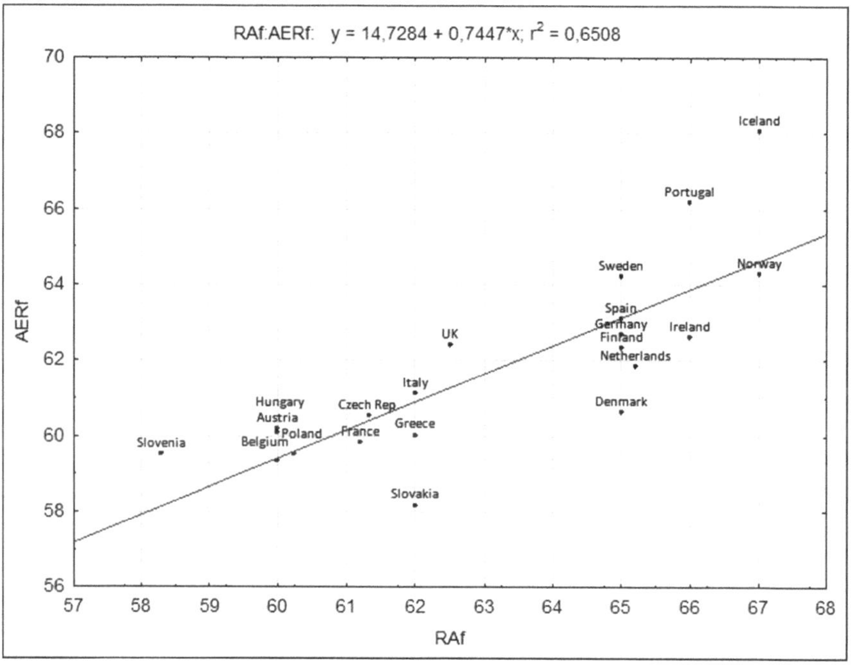

Fig. 5.4 Simple regression on AERm with RAf. (*Source:* Own elaboration)

5.6 Discussion and Conclusions

The study conducted allows some conclusions to be drawn that support selected theoretical approaches to the interactions between the pension system and the labour market or empirical studies presented in the literature. Moreover, the results obtained also indicate other factors that may affect agents' decisions about retirement and, therefore, affect labour market indicators.

The first analysis based on the comparison of selected labour market indicators across pension regimes supports the view by, e.g. Esping-Andersen (1990) that retirement age may be used as one of the tools of full-employment policy which varies across different welfare regimes. I observe that the regime in which the state dominates in a pension system is characterized by a shorter duration of working life and a lower average effective age of retirement, especially in the case of males. However, for those indicators, differences between regimes are not as clear and conclusive as in the case of labour market participation indicators. In terms of these, more liberal and private regimes as the regime of significant voluntary pension schemes (the most liberal one) or the regime of significant mandatory participation in private schemes (an intermediate regime, between regime of significant voluntary schemes and mandatory public regime) are characterized by greater employment rates for older people (aged 55–64 and 65–74) for both genders. This suggests that the significant involvement of the government in a pension system is often linked to the full-employment policy. Simultaneously, agents' retirement behaviour may be affected by such involvement as well. People may perceive the dominant role of the state in a pension system as a guarantee of its income adequacy, at least in the comparison to private pension schemes. Additionally, public pensions are usually (if not always) paid in the form of annuities, whereas benefits paid from private schemes are not as resistant to longevity risk as public ones. Therefore, public social security does not encourage postponement of retirement. This is also indirectly consistent with Feldstein's (1995) findings that public social security reduces private savings. In both cases, the decisions about the timing of retirement as well as private pension savings may be determined by government behaviour. The greater the role of the public sector in social security, the lower private care there is about pensions, expressed, e.g. by lower private saving or earlier retirement.

The regression analysis also confirms that according to Fisher's intertemporal choice model (Fisher 1930) life cycle hypothesis (Modigliani and Brumberg 1954; Ando and Modigliani 1963), supported by Feldstein's (1974) empirical analysis and developed by the induced retirement, the short-term interest rate may affect decisions about when to retire. The greater the interest rate is, the greater the prize for postponing consumption in time is. However, since our analysis addresses the decisions about retirement, the short-term interest rate seems to play a greater role than the long-term one. This results from the fact that an agent making a decision about retirement and choosing between accelerating or delaying exit from the labour market analyses it rather in the short-term and not the long-term perspective. People postpone retirement by 1 or 2 years, not 5 or 10. However, if they stay healthy, physically able to work, they repeat this decision after 1 or 2 years. Nevertheless, they prolong their economic activity for a short period, which does not exclude doing so many times (and few short periods aggregate into a longer one).

Another very important predictor that is statistically significant in the majority of the models estimated is the pensionable age. The legal retirement age affects actual retirement, the duration of working life and, therefore, the participation of older people at near-retirement age in the labour market in a direct manner. The greater the pensionable age, the longer the duration of working life, the later the retirement and the greater the employment rate for population aged 55–64 or 65–74 (males). This conclusion is consistent with the findings by Casamatta and De Paoli (2012), Hansen and Lonstrup (2009) or Staubli and Zweimuller (2011), who show that the optimal retirement age should be linked to increasing life expectancy. My analysis confirms that in the countries with a higher legal retirement age, the effective age of retirement is also higher, which could have been expected. Additionally, to compare two countries with different pensionable ages, in the country in which this age is 1 year greater, people retire on average over 8–9 months later (both males and females). So the effect is not in a one-for-one relation but it is nevertheless significant (one-for-over 0.7).

The current situation on the labour market also matters; however the results suggest that only with regard to females. Women's decisions about retirement seem to be more sensitive to the current labour market condition. The duration of females' working life is negatively correlated to the unemployment rate for this gender. This means that women may use early retirement to avoid unemployment. This is also observed in the case of the employment rate for females aged 55–64, which is negatively linked to unemployment as well. In the case of males, these relationships are not statistically significant.

An interesting conclusion may be drawn from the models in which the predictor ToW (taxation of withdrawals from private pension schemes) is statistically significant. This predictor is rather not taken into account in studies addressing the relations between a pension system and the labour market, whereas my estimates suggest that taxation of withdrawals from private schemes prolongs duration of working life for both genders and delays effective retirement of females. As a result, taxation increases employment rates among the elderly (aged 65–74) for both genders. This phenomenon of "aversion to taxation" requires further and more in-depth studies since its impact on decisions about retirement or on labour market indicators may be determined by the role of voluntary pension plans. One may expect that the lesser the role of private schemes, the lesser the impact of taxation on pension decisions. However, if this effect really matters, the model of taxation of private schemes may become a useful tool for delaying retirement and stimulating the employment of older people.

The analysis does not support the view that the method of financing (MoF: separate contributions vs. taxes) or pension benefit formula (MoMP: defined contribution or others as, e.g. flat rate of defined benefit) affects the duration of working life or effective retirement significantly and, as a result, does not influence labour market indicators. An exception is the average effective age of retirement for males, which is negatively affected by the method of financing – defined contribution decreases effective retirement age. I also did not find a significant relationship between the generosity of a pension system (expressed by replacement rates) and effective retirement. If a replacement rate occurs in a given model, it refers only to males and has a negative parameter, however statistically insignificant. This means that in the case of men, the relationship is negative as expected – the lesser the generosity, the longer the duration of working life and the greater the labour market participation of older males (aged 55–64 and 65–74). However, as stated before, the relationship is too weak to be assessed as statistically significant.

To summarize, the participation of older people in the labour market is not random in nature. It seems to be determined not only by microeconomic factors resulting from the theory of consumption but also by macroeconomic factors (unemployment) and pension system design or parameters. The policy of full employment involving early retirement to unblock vacancies for young people is ineffective and seems to be impossible to realize in today's and future demographic conditioning. Therefore, we can expect the full reverse from early retirement incentives towards a later retirement policy. This study confirms that the main drivers of the duration of working life and effective retirement age and, as a result, determinants of employment rates of the elderly (aged 55–64 and 65–74) are mainly legal retirement age, unemployment or interest rate. However, taxation of withdrawals from private pension schemes seems also to matter in decisions about retirement.

The identified "aversion to taxation" may indicate another tool to stimulate later retirement.

Acknowledgements The paper forms part of the project Intergenerational fairness across welfare state regimes: A comparative cross-country study, funded by the National Science Centre (Poland) under grant number UMO-2016/23/B/HS4/01772.

References

Ando, A., & Modigliani, F. (1963). The life cycle hypothesis of saving: Aggregate implications and tests. *American Economic Review, 53*(1), 55–84.

Barr, N., & Diamond, P. (2006). The economics of pensions. *Oxford Review of Economic Policy, 22* (1), 15–39.

Barr, N., & Diamond, P. (2010). *Pension reform: A short guide*. New York: Oxford University Press.

Blake, D. (2006). *Pension economics*. West Sussex: Wiley.

Borsch-Supan, A. (2007). *European welfare state regimes and their generosity towards the elderly*. MEA discussion paper series, 07128.

Casamatta, G., & De Paoli, C. (2012). Choosing the legal retirement age in presence of unemployment. *Recherches économiques de Louvain, 78*(1), 5–25.

Esping-Andersen, G. (1990). *The three worlds of welfare capitalism*. Princeton: Princeton University Press.

Feldstein, M. (1974). Social security, induced retirement and aggregate capital accumulation. *Journal of Political Economy, 82*, 905–926.

Feldstein, M. (1995). *Social security and saving: New time series evidence*. NBER Working Paper No. 5054. National Bureau of Economic Research, Cambridge.

Fisher, I. (1930). *The theory of interest*. London: Macmillan.

Friedman, M. (1957). *A theory of consumption function*. Princeton: Princeton University Press.

Góra, M. (2008). *Retirement decisions, benefits and the neutrality of pension systems*. ENEPRI research report no. 51.

Gruber, J., Milligan, K., & Wise, D. A. (2009). *Social security programs and retirement around the world: The relationship to youth employment*. Working Paper 14647. National Bureau of Economic Research, Cambridge.

Hansen, C. W., & Lonstrup, L. (2009). *The optimal legal retirement age in an OLG model with endogenous labour supply*. Discussion Papers on Business and Economics No. 5/2009. Department of Business and Economics, University of Southern Denmark, Odense.

Hernaes, E. (2013). *Pension systems and labour supply – Review of the recent economic literature*. Working paper 1/2013. Stiftelsen Frischsenteret for samfunnsøkonomisk forskning Ragnar Frisch Centre for Economic Research.

Krieger, T., & Traub, S. (2008). *Back to Bismarck? Shifting preferences for intragenerational redistribution in OECD pension systems*. Discussion Papers Series No. 001–2008. University of Bremen, Bremen.

Lacomba, J. A., & Lagos, F. (2009). Defined contribution plans vs. defined benefit plan: Reforming the legal retirement age. *Journal of Economic Policy Reform, 12*(1), 1–11.

Lefebvre, M. (2012). Unemployment and retirement in a model with age-specific heterogeneity. *Labour, 26*(2), 137–155.

Marcinkiewicz, E., & Chybalski, F. (2019). A new proposal of pension regimes typology: Empirical analysis of the OECD countries. *Journal of Economic Policy Reform, 22*(1), 84–99.

Modigliani, F., & Brumberg, R. (1954). Utility analysis and the consumption function: An interpretation of cross-section data. In K. Kurihara (Ed.), *Post-Keynesian economics* (pp. 388–436). New Brunswick: Rutgers University Press.

Radl, J. (2013). *Retirement timing and social stratification. A comparative study of labor market exit and age norms in Western Europe*. London: Versita.

Rhodes, M. & Natali, D. (2003). *Welfare regimes and pension reform agendas*. Paper given at the Conference 'Pension reform in Europe: Shared problems, sharing solutions', London, 5 December.

Saure, P., & Zoabi, H. (2012). *Retirement age across countries: The role of occupations*. Working Paper No. 2012–6, Swiss National Bank, Zurich.

Soede, A. & Vrooman, C. (2008). *A comparative typology of pension regimes*. Enepri Research Report No. 54.

Staubli, S. & Zweimuller, J. (2011). *Does raising the retirement age increase employment of older workers?* Discussion Paper Series, IZA DP No. 5863, Bonn.

Chapter 6
Sustainability of Public Pension Systems

José Enrique Devesa-Carpio, Beatriz Rosado-Cebrian, and José Álvarez-García

Abstract The aim of this chapter is to review the main instruments and indicators used to measure the sustainability of PAYG pension systems. It will distinguish between defined contribution and defined benefit systems, due to the various implications that each of them has. It will also be necessary to review the different types of sustainability instruments, for example, those based on cash criteria, financial criteria set by the economic cycle and actuarial criteria. For the actuarial criteria, we will review the criteria of the internal rate of return (IRR) and the actuarial balance. Subsequently, we will review which countries publish official pension system sustainability data and what kind of indicators they choose. We will also use the databases of international organizations to analyse what level of pension system sustainability information is being provided. Finally, we will reflect on the advantages and disadvantages of each of the indicators and set a series of recommendations for the different countries in order to improve the information given on the sustainability of their pension systems.

Keywords Sustainability · Pension system · Internal rate of return · Actuarial balance

6.1 Introduction

Pension systems have been, are and will be one of the essential elements of the welfare state of any developed country, so it is not surprising that governments devote a major budgetary effort to this item and that a large number of researchers

---

J. E. Devesa-Carpio (✉)
Financial and Actuarial Economy Department, University of Valencia, Valencia, Spain
e-mail: Enrique.Devesa@uv.es

B. Rosado-Cebrian · J. Álvarez-García
Department of Financial Economics and Accounting, University of Extremadura, Cáceres, Spain
e-mail: brosado@unex.es; pepealvarez@unex.es

M. Peris-Ortiz et al. (eds.), *Economic Challenges of Pension Systems*,
https://doi.org/10.1007/978-3-030-37912-4_6

are devoted to studying, analysing and developing new methods for their improvement.

Pension systems can be analysed from many points of view and based on different typologies. One of these classifications can be established according to the basic characteristics to which any pension system is subjected: sustainability, adequacy and equity.

All three characteristics are important to achieve a pension system that responds to the needs of the welfare state. However, given the current situation and the demographic and financial challenges that pension systems have to face in the near future, there seems to be growing consensus that sustainability is the first element to be assured, so as to be able to construct the rest of the structure that constitutes the system on that basis.

Two other chapters of this book deal with the problems of defining and studying both the adequacy and equity of pension systems, while in this chapter we will focus on the issue of sustainability. This can also be analysed from several points of view, which will give rise to different definitions, which we will explore throughout the chapter. This implies that different results can even be achieved in the short term, depending on the approach used, although in the long term and corrected by the economic cycle, it seems logical that the methods converge towards a similar diagnosis.

The analysis that will be developed in this chapter will consider, firstly, the different level of sustainability according to whether the system is of defined benefit, defined contribution or mixed and, in turn, according to the actuarial financial system: distribution and capitalization. In Sect. 6.3, the different ways of measuring the sustainability of a pension system will be studied, among which we can mention: the one based on cash criterion, financial methods and those based on actuarial criteria. In Sect. 6.4, we will investigate which countries publish official data on sustainability and what kind of indicators they use and investigate the databases of international organizations in order to analyse what level of information on the sustainability of public pension systems they are providing. In Sect. 6.5, we will reflect on the advantages and disadvantages of each of the indicators and make a series of recommendations for the different countries to improve information on the sustainability of their pension systems, which we consider to be totally necessary. Finally, we will present the conclusions obtained and the bibliography used.

6.2 Sustainability According to the Obligations of the System: Defined Benefit and Defined Contribution

One of the most relevant criteria when analysing the sustainability of a pension system is based on its obligations. According to this criterion, we can distinguish between defined contribution, defined benefit and mixed systems.

6.2.1 Defined Contribution Systems

They are characterized because the amount of the benefit is calculated at the time of retirement and is derived from the accumulation process. It can be considered, from a financial point of view, as a constitution operation, through contributions that are usually periodic and normally respond to a predetermined plan, which does not mean that they must be of a fixed amount. All of this implies that it is a post-determined operation, since the profitability or revaluation index that will be used to capitalize the contributions is unknown beforehand. Therefore, it is a "purely" financial operation, in the sense that no biometric phenomenon is involved, being independent of the age of the participant, although the exponential effect of the compound capitalization law makes the number of years have an important influence on the amount of the accumulated fund. Another question is the formula used to transform the accumulated fund into the pension amount. It is logical to use some type of actuarial instrument, such as the life expectancy or the current value of an annuity.

Defined contribution systems can in turn be divided into (De la Peña 2000):

(a) Pure defined contribution. The contribution is made without any reference, as could be the level of future benefits. Thus, the amount of this contribution will only be known at the time of receiving the amount constituted.
(b) Contribution defined with target benefit. The participant sets the objective to reach a certain economic level and, through an equation of financial equivalence, determines the contribution to be made.
(c) Defined contribution systems can also be differentiated according to the actuarial financial system on which they are based.
(d) In the case of capitalization systems, it can be said that sustainability is almost guaranteed by definition.
(e) In the case of PAYG,[1] it cannot be said that sustainability is guaranteed by definition, but it can be achieved more easily than in a defined benefit, especially taking care when choosing the formula and revaluation rate to transform the accumulated fund into the corresponding pension.

6.2.2 Defined Benefit Systems

They are those in which the amount of the benefit is determined and the amount of the contribution necessary to achieve the objective is calculated through financial or actuarial procedures. From a purely technical point of view, the calculation should take into account the probabilities associated with the contingencies covered. In addition, it is logical that depending on the evolution of the various elements

[1]We are facing what is known in the literature as a system of notional accounts. In this regard you can refer to Devesa and Vidal 2004.

involved, these calculations will be reviewed periodically, in order to readjust the contributions to achieve the desired level of benefits.

As in the previous case, it is appropriate to distinguish according to the actuarial financial system on which it is based:

(a) In capitalization-based systems, sustainability depends on whether the necessary contributions can be made to meet the intended objective and that there is an adequate mechanism to convert the accumulated fund into an annuity of the desired amount, which implies that a certain return should be ensured.
(b) In the PAYG system, sustainability becomes secondary if the appropriate corrective measures are not taken, such as the use of formulas to determine both the initial pension and its subsequent revaluation.

6.2.3 Mixed Benefit Systems

The objective is to determine, simultaneously or separately, the amount of the benefit and the amount of the contribution. The usual thing is to combine the defined contribution for some contingency (e.g. retirement) with the defined benefit for others (such as disability, survivor's pension, orphan's pension). We also include those systems in which a minimum or determined return (or rate of revaluation of contributions) or a minimum or specific level of benefits is "guaranteed".

6.3 Different Ways of Measuring the Sustainability of a Pension System

After the comment in the previous section and given that PAYG systems are more prevalent by their number within public systems, we are going to focus on them.

There is a great and constant concern about the sustainability of this type of system, which is only partly explained by an important characteristic implicit in the system itself: funding commitments as they arise, i.e. on the go.

Although, at first, it may not seem necessary to define the sustainability of a pension system, a review of the literature (see for example Oria and Escudero 2003; Bonoli and Shinkawa 2006; Moral-Arce et al. 2008; Robalino and Bodor 2009; or Conde-Ruiz 2017) shows us that there are different concepts and different ways of naming it (viability, solvency) and some even go as far as stating that there is no need to raise the problem of sustainability of a public pension system because it is a political rather than an economic problem[2]; i.e. sustainability would be guaranteed by definition.

[2]In Spain a manifest was published in 2013, (Manifiesto 2013) signed by jurists and economists known as "In defense of the public pension system", where such a statement was made.

Undoubtedly, the most well-known definition is the so-called financial or cash sustainability, which arises when the cash income (I) and expenses (G) of the pension system are compared over a given time horizon, usually a year. This definition is totally related to the financial equation, or balanced budget, which characterizes any PAYG system.

$$I = G \tag{6.1}$$

If the equation were to be fulfilled annually, that would mean annual decreases or increases, of either the type of contribution (with consequent uncertainty about the labour cost for the company) or the average pension amount. Therefore, it is acceptable for the balanced budget not to be achieved year by year, but over a number of years, thus smoothing the effects of the economic cycle. Many countries have also opted to create a reserve fund that allows them to accumulate surpluses in the high phases of the economic cycle in order to pay the deficits in the lower part of the cycle.

But there are more ways to define the sustainability of a pension system. To that end, we are going to focus on the case of PAYG systems, especially those with defined benefits, which most of the studies are focused on (e.g. Devesa and Devesa 2008a, b, 2010), on one of the following types of study,[3] classified by the main indicator used:

(a) Analysis of the sustainability of the system through the study of the balance based on the pension flow. They try to determine the projection of pension expenditure flows as a percentage of GDP. In this case, it is usual to assume that the contribution income will be constant in relation to GDP. Financial unsustainability is easy to determine, since it relates to the moment when pension expenditure exceeds the income from contributions. It can be considered a relatively simple method, so it is used for an open system, i.e. for a system to which new affiliated people continue to be incorporated with time.
The fact that many countries have provided their systems with reserve funds to avoid fluctuations in the economic cycle has made it necessary to incorporate the surpluses of other years to explain the point of rupture or unsustainability of the system. In Spain, the work by Blanco et al. (2000) and Gil et al. (2007) can be cited for measuring it this way. For example, in Spain, the income level from contributions has historically been an average 10% of GDP, although "the net social contributions" have been an average of 12.65% over the last 12 years for Spain, as can be seen in Table 6.8, and in addition, all the forecasts are expected to continue at those levels over the next 10–15 years. Other countries, on the other hand, maintain radically different levels, such as Denmark (1.29% on average), Sweden (3.73%) or Iceland (3.34%), or cases such as Belgium (16.04%), Germany (16.66%) or France (18.77%), which gives us an idea of

[3]There are several typologies for classification, but we have chosen to present the one that seems best from a financial-actuarial point of view.

the very important difference in the pension systems, applied by each of these groups of countries.

In addition, it should be noted that both an increase in the employment rate and an increase in productivity change the contribution bases to a large extent and, therefore, the cash income, but do not increase the contribution percentage of the GDP.

(b) Analysis of the sustainability of the system through the study of the balance based on the flow of pensions and contributions. This is an extension of the previous case. It is a question of not only determining the pension expenditure flow (as a percentage of GDP) but also the projection of income flow from contributions. With this, it is possible to determine the cash balance of the system for each year and thus accumulate the surpluses or deficits in a fund. With this method, two additional objectives are achieved:

- When making income projections, there is room for quantification, which the modifications of some of the parameters related to the volume of contributions have on the deficit of the system, so as to be able to analyse which are the most efficient measures.
- It allows the incorporation of the accumulated balance in a fund, so that estimates can be made not only of when an annual deficit will be incurred but also of until when there will be a positive balance in the reserve fund, in such a way that the system remains sustainable.

This method also applies to an open system, but also provides more information than the previous one. The main drawback is that it does not consider the sustainability of the system from a perspective closer to that of insurance techniques. In Spain, we can cite the following studies: Herce and Pérez-Díaz (1995), Barea et al. (1996), Serrano et al. (2004), MTAS (2005), Balmaseda et al. (2006), and Jiménez-Ridruejo (2008).

(c) Analysis of the sustainability of the system through the study of implicit debt. Following Van den Noord and Herd (1993), the implicit debt of a pension system, at a time "*t*", can be defined, in a generic way, as the "*t*" value of the commitments assumed by the system up to that moment with its participants, both with pensioners, and those accrued up to that moment by current contributors, since the latter are acquiring the right to perceive a series of benefits in the future, from the moment they enter the system. It would coincide with the single capital which, disbursed in "*t*", would guarantee actuarially the commitments assumed. From the actuarial point of view, the calculation of the implicit debt is made by obtaining the mathematical reserve of the operation. In fact, it is not a true measure of the sustainability of a system, since it is difficult to determine the maximum permissible level of debt that could be assumed. In addition, it would be interesting to make projections of its evolution in order to analyse if an improvement of this indicator is going to take place in the future, but this usually requires the estimation of a high number of hypotheses.

The calculation of the implicit debt entails financing since, for example, the issuance of debt will produce deferred payment, but in exchange for having to pay the corresponding interest.

In this method, the calculation is usually done for a closed system, i.e. a system where the incorporation of new affiliates is not contemplated. In the literature there is a large number of studies that have revolved around this topic, for example: Van den Noord and Herd (1993), Barea and González-Páramo (1996), Abío et al. (1999), Bravo and Uthoff (1999), Gil and Patxot (2002), Holzmann et al. (2004), Gokhale and Smetters (2005), Devesa (2007) and the Committee on Monetary, Financial and Balance of Payments Statistics (2008).

(d) Analysis of the sustainability of the system through the study of the internal rate of return (IRR). Its objective is to determine the profitability that the system offers its participants and to compare it with the GDP growth, to analyse if the system is sustainable. Thus, according to Samuelson (1958), the system will be sustainable when the IRR is at most equal to the country's GDP growth.
In most studies on this subject, the IRR has been calculated considering only the retirement benefit, as in the case of Spain (Bandrés and Cuenca 1998; Monasterio et al. 1996). Others also only take into account the general regime; among them are Gil and López-Casasnovas (1999), Jimeno and Licandro (1999), and Durán (1995) that analyse only a few type individuals. There are authors who obtain the IRR using an approximate formula, such as Devesa et al. (2002). However, in Devesa (2007), a model is developed which enables to obtain the IRR, considering all benefits (retirement, widow's pension, orphan's pension and disability) and all the social security schemes in Spain. The calculations are made for the case of a closed group, and using actuarial instruments, which gives a perspective very far from the simple comparison of cash flows.

(e) Analysis of the sustainability of the system through the study of the financial-actuarial imbalance. It is obtained considering not only future commitments and contributions but also past benefits and contributions. In this way, we have a global and not partial view of the system, as in the case of implicit debt. The difference with the previous method is that, now, the comparison is made in absolute terms and not in relative terms. This indicator shows us the total financial-actuarial imbalance of the system and measures it in currency units. Thus, it is clear that the system will be unsustainable when it gives out a greater amount in current actuarial value than the one received, calculated in an analogous way. It applies to closed systems. It has been used by Devesa and Devesa (2010).

(f) Analysis of the sustainability of the system through the study of the cost per unitary pension. In this case, the cost of giving a currency unit of pension is analysed from the financial-actuarial point of view. It is a relative measure, since it is obtained by dividing the current actuarial value of the contributions by the current actuarial value of pensions. Of course, if the cost is greater than one, the system will be imbalanced. It applies to closed systems. It was applied by Devesa and Devesa (2010), for retirement, disability and benefits for death and survival and also for unemployment, by Devesa et al. (2013).

(g) Analysis of the sustainability of the system through the study of the actuarial balance. According to Boado and Vidal (2008), the actuarial balance of the PAYG pension system is the financial statement that relates the obligations with contributors and pensioners at a certain date, with the magnitudes of the different assets (financial, real, from contributions) that support those obligations. The main purpose of the actuarial balance is to be a true and fair image of the assets of the system at the beginning and end of the financial year and by comparison to determine the result. In Settergren (2003), a broad perspective of the actuarial balance can be seen.

In the first two cases, a financial method is applied, although it is possible to enter survival probabilities, either explicitly or implicitly. They are based on the analysis of the existence of a cash deficit or surplus, although it does not have to be annual, since it can be obtained for a longer period, such as those that correct for the economic cycle.

The remaining methods can be classified as actuarial, since they use actuarial technique tools. They are not directly related to cash deficit or surplus. They are usually applied to the case of closed systems, due to the great complexity of obtaining the values corresponding to the case of open systems, motivated by the overlap of multiple generations.

It should be noted that the methods discussed can be considered complementary between each other and not as alternatives, since each one provides different information on the financial-actuarial health of pension systems.

Since actuarial models are less well-known, we will comment them more in-depth, based on Devesa and Devesa (2008a, b, 2010).

Thus, the starting point is generally obtaining the implicit debt, calculated by using two different methods: the "retrospective method", based on past data, and the "prospective method", based on future information. In addition, it is necessary to distinguish between commitments accumulated to date and commitments with current assets and pensioners.

From the financial point of view, it is a question of calculating the mathematical reserve or financial balance of a financial-actuarial transaction. In the case of pensioners, it is much easier to use the prospective method (current value of future pensions), since the retrospective method (difference between the current value of the total contributions and the current value of the pensions already paid) is very complicated, due to the difficulty of obtaining all the necessary data. However, the assessment of the commitments of assets should be done using the two methods, in order to be able to use that information as a preliminary step before obtaining other indicators. In Fig. 6.1 all the contributions and benefits of the system are shown, although with different criteria in terms of their distribution.

where:

x_e: Age of entry into the system
t: Present moment
x_a: Exit age from the system

If the pension system were actuarially fair for assets, the principle of financial-actuarial equivalence should be fulfilled; i.e. the actuarial value at the moment "t" of

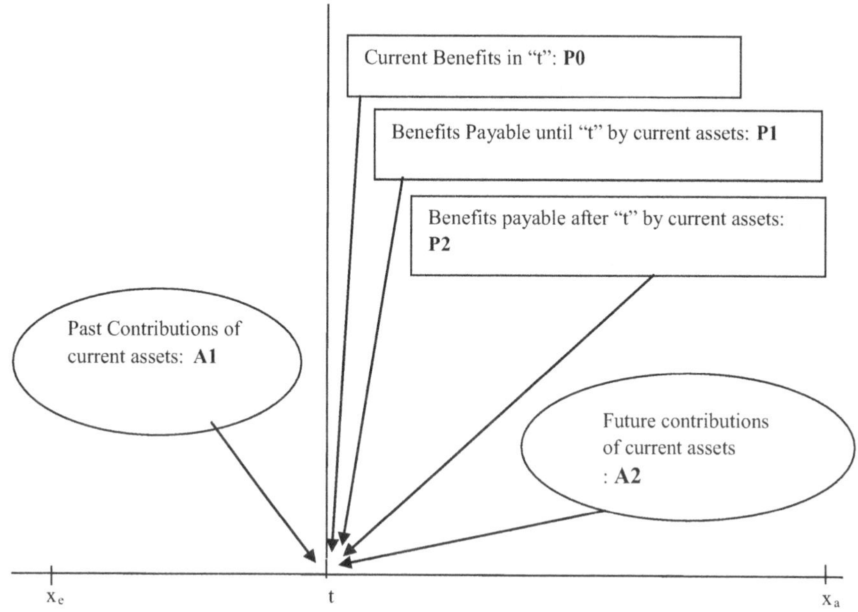

Fig. 6.1 Contributions and benefits of a social security system. (Source: Devesa and Devesa 2008a)

all the contributions of current assets would have to be equal to the actuarial sum at the same moment "*t*" of the benefits that the current assets would receive, i.e.:

$$A1 + A2 = P1 + P2 \tag{6.2}$$

So when solving for A1, we have what has been denominated implicit debt with current assets (D_a):

$$A1 = P1 + P2 - A2 = D_a \tag{6.3}$$

Thus, debt with current assets and pensioners (D) would be obtained by adding to Eq. (6.3) the debt plus current liabilities (D_p):

$$D = D_p + D_a = P0 + A1 = P0 + P1 + P2 - A2 \tag{6.4}$$

The first method is called retrospective (although debt with liabilities is not calculated in this way) and the second one is called prospective.

$$D^R = D_p + D_a = P0 + A1 \quad \text{("retrospective method")} \tag{6.5}$$

$$D^{\mathrm{P}} = D_{\mathrm{p}} + D_{\mathrm{a}} = \mathrm{P0} + \mathrm{P1} + \mathrm{P2} - \mathrm{A2} \quad \text{("prospective method")} \tag{6.6}$$

where:

D: Implicit debt
D^{R}: Implicit debt calculated by the retrospective method
D^{P}: Implicit debt calculated by the prospective method
D_{p}: Implicit debt plus current liabilities
D_{a}: Implicit debt plus current assets

If the system were not actuarially fair, the theoretical debt with assets, calculated by the two methods, would be different, and the difference between the two values will be used as a measure of the financial-actuarial imbalance of the pension system with current assets, so that:

$$\begin{aligned}\mathrm{Imbalance}_{\mathrm{Assets}} &= \mathrm{DT}_{\mathrm{a}}^{\mathrm{P}} - \mathrm{DT}_{\mathrm{a}}^{\mathrm{R}} = \mathrm{P1} + \mathrm{P2} - \mathrm{A1} - \mathrm{A2} \\ &= \begin{cases} > 0 \Rightarrow \text{Deficit} \\ < 0 \Rightarrow \text{Surplus} \\ = 0 \Rightarrow \text{Balance} \end{cases}\end{aligned} \tag{6.7}$$

The actuarial imbalance reflects the actuarial present value difference between the total benefits and the total contributions of the current assets, which allows us to relate it to the cost of the benefit and provides us with much more information than the implicit debt, at least in terms of measuring sustainability. In this sense, Bravo (2000) states that "implicit debt is a useful indicator and is key to knowing the fiscal cost of ending with a PAYG system; however, it is not useful to know if a system is sustainable or not. For example, high implicit debt can continue to be passed on to future generations under reasonable conditions for both workers and retirees, and therefore cannot be considered unsustainable".

On the other hand, the actuarial imbalance bears some resemblance with the concept of expected net present value that is used in the assessment of investment projects, although it differs from it in that it is not calculated at the initial moment of the investment and that past capital is considered in its mathematical formulation, with probability equal to one.

To determine the total imbalance of the system, the imbalance generated by both assets and liabilities would have to be added.

The difficulty of calculating the implicit debt of the current liabilities by the retrospective method makes it very difficult to quantify the imbalance of the liabilities, so that sometimes an estimate is made related to the imbalance of the assets.

According to Devesa and Devesa (2008a, b), one of the great advantages of measuring imbalance is that it is only necessary to make estimates of a few variables, although the method to calculate it from individual microdata involves analysing for each individual that pays into a pension system, the contributions that he makes and the pensions he receives throughout his life. This implies a laborious procedure since you have to know his whole working record and all the pensions that he will receive.[4]

In general terms, lack of data requires the completion of the individuals' working record, estimating the date and amount of the pension to be received, using the probabilities of survival in order to obtain the actuarial equivalence equation and set an interest rate for the valuation of all the previous elements, which becomes a complicated exercise, so that sometimes researchers are forced to choose subsamples to facilitate their task, for example, that of individuals who retire in the year of study, since this allows to know much of their working record and initial pension.

6.4 Indicators of the Sustainability of the Public Pension Systems of the Main Countries

Having analysed the main sustainability measures that come from the academic world, it is convenient to investigate whether these indicators are used by the pension systems of the main countries or others are used. It also analyses why there are divergences between those proposed by some and those applied by others.

We will first analyse the most simple sustainability indicators and then review some of the synthetic indicators proposed by different organisms and companies. It should not be forgotten that one of the reasons why some indicators are used is related to the ease of calculation, but above all, on the condition that they offer homogeneous data for a large number of countries, in order to carry out comparative studies among them.

6.4.1 Most Used Sustainability Indicators by Individual Countries and Supranational Bodies to Measure the Sustainability of Pension Systems

We can list the following:

1. Old-age economic dependency ratio
   It is defined as the ratio between the nonworking population and the working population or working-age population:

[4]For example, in many countries there are microdata of samples, enabling to carry out the calculations. In Spain, for example, they are made from the so-called Continuous Work History Sample, provided to researchers by the social security itself.

$$\text{Old age dependency ratio} = \frac{\text{Population 65 and over}}{\text{Population between 15 and 64}} \tag{6.8}$$

It gives a measure of the average number of individuals that each "theoretical employee" must support, being relevant as it considers the potential growth prospects of GDP per capita. It is an indicator widely used by all countries, but it is a static measure (it is a photograph that changes day by day), relative measure (does not take into account unemployment) and subject to great variations, so it is often used in combination with other indicators or as part of composite synthetic indicators. In most European countries, and especially in the statistics used for cross-country comparison, the following ratio is used:

$$\frac{\text{Population 65 and over}}{\text{Population between 20 and 64}} \tag{6.9}$$

and even how it is done in the European Commission, in Ageing Report (2015):

$$\frac{\text{Population 65 and over}}{\text{Population between 20 and 74}} \tag{6.10}$$

2. Pension expenditure as a percentage of GDP
   It is the most used indicator in the studies of the financial sufficiency of pension systems and in which the effects of the introduced reforms are analysed. The European Commission, for example, produces an ageing report (the *Ageing Report*) every 3 years, where it shows pension expenditure and total expenditure associated with ageing, in terms of GDP, for all member countries, with a time horizon of about 50 years. As discussed in Sect. 6.3, since income of GDP has remained historically stable in most countries, the projection of expenditure implicitly implies a projection of financial equilibrium.
3. Implicit debt
   Although it was already mentioned in Sect. 6.3, it is important to remember that it is the amount that should be allotted by the pension system to fulfil future commitments already generated. While it can be considered an indicator of sustainability, it really is not, because it does not take into account past contributions. It is very difficult to see this data published in the official statistics of many countries.
4. Internal rate of return (IRR)
   It is one of the most used sustainability indicators by the academic world, especially by researchers from the financial and actuarial field. It takes into account both the pensions and contributions of the group considered, and in addition, it has the advantage that it is an indicator in relative terms, so the IRR figure of the subsample can be extrapolated to the whole system, under the assumption that the legislation applied and the behaviour of this group, in terms of contributions and pensions, is the same for the rest of individuals. The IRR is

interpreted as the real profitability in financial-actuarial terms of capital delivered in the form of contributions and received in the form of pensions.

It is not usually used in cross-country comparative studies, due to the difficulty of its calculation, which in some cases is due to lack of transparency of the entities responsible.

5. Financial-actuarial imbalance
   It is an indicator based on the calculation of the implicit but extended debt, with the incorporation of data prior to its calculation. It is defined as the difference between the financial-actuarial sum of the contributions and pensions (past and future) of the selected group. It is interpreted observing that the pension system will not be structurally sustainable when this indicator is negative, because this implies that the system gives out a greater amount of pension in current actuarial value than the one received. If the retirement pension system were to be actuarially in equilibrium, the principle of financial-actuarial equivalence would have to be fulfilled, i.e. the current actuarial value of all contributions of current assets and liabilities would have to be equal to the actuarial present value of all pensions received by the same group. In rare cases, it is also made public by the pension systems themselves.
6. Pension per contribution unit
   This indicator is deduced from the financial actuarial imbalance. It measures the cost of delivering a currency unit of pension for each currency unit of contribution that the system receives, all in actuarial terms. If the pension per unit of contribution is higher than the unit, it means that the system, in financial-actuarial terms, has a structural deficit and is unsustainable. Like the two previous ones, it is not usually made public by the people responsible for the pension system.
7. Actuarial balance
   As mentioned in the previous section, it is the financial statement that relates the obligations with contributors and pensioners at a specific date, with the magnitudes of the different assets (financial, real and from contributions) that support those obligations. The main purpose of the actuarial balance is to be a true and fair view of the assets of the system at the beginning and end of the financial year and by comparison to determine the result. In this case, there are several countries that present the actuarial balance as a policy of transparency, including Sweden, the United States and Japan.
8. Replacement rate
   It is defined as the ratio between the last salary received and the first pension received. This indicator is widely used by the European Commission, OECD and other international bodies for cross-country comparisons, although at the same time it can be said that it is more appropriate as an indicator of adequacy. The decrease in the value of this indicator may lead to the appearance of impoverishment symptoms in the retired generations. For example, the growth of wages and the number of retirees can compensate for a lower substitution rate and, at the same time, increase pension expenditure, so it would not be a good sustainability index.

6.4.2 Indicators Used by International Organizations

The indicators on which information is available from the different countries, and therefore the most used for comparisons between them, are obtained from statistics collected by supranational organizations such as the OECD or the European Commission through Eurostat, which have the undeniable advantage of homogeneity in the data, although with the disadvantage of delay in the publication dates of the various reports and the (relative) outdated data provided. As an additional advantage for the use of these macro-data, it is necessary to point out that they use the projections of the indicators up to years 2050, 2060 and even 2080, which gives greater broadness to the concept. However, they do not use all the sustainability indicators, but instead opt for a small range because of the previously mentioned.

The OECD prefers the "pension expenditure as a % of GDP" indicator as the main sustainability indicator, namely, of financial sustainability.

The European Commission, through Eurostat, in addition to this indicator, also provides the "old-age dependency ratio" as an indicator of sustainability, although it includes it in its "demography" section, but refers to it in its reports (Ageing Report), in relation to "public finances sustainability".

Although the complete data tables (Tables 6.6 and 6.7) are in Annex I, we provide Tables 6.1, 6.2 and 6.3, in which the four countries with the highest value were selected, sorted by the relative ranking of each one of the indicators most used by Eurostat and the OECD for different years.

Table 6.1 Old-age dependency ratio

Real				Projected			
1990		2015		2020		2080	
Country	Data	Country	Data	Country	Data	Country	Data
Sweden	27.7	Italy	33.7	Germany	35.8	Slovakia	68.7
Norway	25.2	Greece	32.4	Finland	35.8	Portugal	68.2
United Kingdom	24.1	Germany	32.0	Italy	34.9	Germany	59.9
Denmark	23.2	Finland	31.3	Greece	34.3	Poland	59.6

Source of Data: Eurostat (Population Projections EUROPOP 2013)

Table 6.2 Expenditure on pensions as % of national GDP

Real				Projected			
2003		2014		2020		2060	
Country	Data	Country	Data	Country	Data	Country	Data
Austria	14.20	Greece	17.10	Austria	15.10	Luxemburg	18.60
Italy	14.10	Italy	16.50	Italy	14.50	Slovenia	18.30
Poland	13.80	Portugal	15.60	France	14.40	Belgium	16.60
Germany	13.10	France	15.20	Finland	14.00	Cyprus	16.40

Source of Data: Eurostat

Table 6.3 Net social contributions as % of national GDP

2004		2015		Increases (2015–2004)		Decreases (2015–2004)	
Country	Data	Country	Data	Country	Data	Country	data
Germany	17.60	France	18.90	Lithuania	2.5	Malta	−1.00
France	17.50	German	16.50	Greece	1.8	Germany	−1.10
Belgium	15.50	Belgium	16.50	Finland	1 5	Romania	−1.50
Austria	15.30	Austria	15.40	Cyprus	1.4	Bulgaria	−2.10

Source of Data: Eurostat

It can be seen that the sustained growth in longevity has led to an increase in the old-age dependency ratio, which measures the number of older people as part of the working-age population in the last 25 years. But it can also be seen how the already ageing European population will have to bear higher dependency ratios in the coming years, as shown by Eurostat's projections for 2080, where countries suffering the most from this effect could see this ratio almost doubled; for example, Germany could increase its old-age dependency ratio by almost 4 points in just 5 years and from 32% in 2015 to 59.9% in 2080.

The interpretation of pension expenditure as a percentage of GDP is not direct, since it depends on many factors, and the pensions paid are of a different nature. But it seems that there is a fairly similar pattern in all European countries when analysing this indicator.

A total of 1683 billion Euros was spent on pensions throughout the EU in 2013 (data excluded Greece and Poland) according to Eurostat data,[5] which represents approximately 12.8% of EU GDP. Expenditures vary considerably from one country to another, although most have grown at a rate of approximately 3% in the last 10 years. Greece, for example, spent 17.10% of GDP on pensions in 2014, more than in any other country, while another three (Italy, Portugal and France) spent 15% of their GDP or more in the same year. Estonia, Lithuania and Ireland spent about 7% of their GDP on pensions, although Eurostat projections for 2060 show that the group of countries spending between 16% and 18% of GDP on pensions will be greater.

In Germany in 2004, social contributions paid were equal to 17.6% of GDP. According to Eurostat data, this percentage has remained stable in recent years and even decreased by about 1% point in 2015. It is one of the few cases in the European environment, as according to Eurostat, in the last 10 years this indicator has increased in all countries, such as France, where it has increased by 1.5% points, as well as in Finland, with even greater increases in Greece and Lithuania. On the other hand, there are cases, such as Bulgaria or Romania, where social contributions account for less percentage of GDP in 2015 than in 2004, such as Bulgaria and Romania and Germany.

[5]http://ec.europa.eu/eurostat/statistics-explained/index.php/Social_protection_statistics_-_pension_expenditure_and_pension_beneficiaries#Expenditure_on_pensions_in_the_EU

In addition, the World Bank published a report on pensions in 2010, called "Green Paper: towards adequate, sustainable and safe European pension systems", where it measures the financial sustainability of the pension systems, using a range of quite broad indicators:

- Demographic structure of the population in 2008 and 2060
- Old-age dependency ratios under different average exit age scenarios
- Change in public pension expenditure as a share of GDP over 2007–2060 (in percentage points)
- Benefit ratios in EU member states in 2007 and 2060
- Changes in theoretical replacement rates for an average wage earner retiring at 65 after 40 years of career between 2006 and 2046 in percentage points
- Standard pension eligibility age and average labour market exit age in EU-27
- Overall female and older workers employment rates in EU-27, 2000–2008, in percentage
- Pension benefit impact of shorter and longer working lives
- Pension benefit impact of career breaks due to unemployment
- Increasing significance of funded pensions

Subsequently, in the report "International patterns of pension provision II: a worldwide overview of facts and figures", World Bank (2012), indicators of financial sustainability of public pension systems are discussed, and among others, like the European Commission and assuming the intention to homogenize data with other entities, they use the "pension expenditure as a % of GDP" and the "old-age dependency ratio" as the main indicators.

6.4.3 Synthetic or Composite Indicators

Synthetic or composite indicators are aggregate indices of simple indicators, which are obtained by weighing these with weights that represent the relative importance that each of them must have in the final aggregate index. Ideally, this aggregation should measure multidimensional concepts that cannot be captured by single indicators individually. However, their construction is not direct and, if not done efficiently, can lead to results that could be misinterpreted or manipulated. The perfection of a composite indicator, as well as the soundness of the messages it transmits, depends both on the methodology used in its construction and, fundamentally, on the quality of the structure and the data used (JRC-EC 2008).

In recent years, synthetic indicators (hereinafter SI) have become one of the most commonly used analytical instruments in practice in many fields of social reality, and in fact, synthetic indicators are already commonly accepted as useful tools for decision-making and communication of information. According to the definition of statistical terms of the OECD, a synthetic indicator can be defined as that combination or mathematical aggregation of the indicators that represent the different components of the concept, which is intended to be evaluated from a starting system, providing its multidimensional evaluation (Saisana and Tarantola 2002).

There are many reasons for using SI. Briefly, it can be summarized into its capacity to facilitate the interpretation of the information by the users and, at the same time, to evaluate complex and multidimensional phenomena in a simple way (Blancas et al. 2011).

From a technical point of view, the construction of a SI involves establishing a mathematical procedure to add a set of individual indicators, often referred to as sub-indicators, to measure multidimensional phenomena that could not be represented by a single measure. A complete review of the procedures for constructing indicators can be seen, among others, in Nardo et al. (2005) and Saisana and Tarantola (2002).

The analysis of the existing literature allows to state that there is no clearly accepted methodology as the most adequate for the construction of a SI. Thus, it should be the analyst who decides and justifies both the procedure to be used according to the analysis that needs to be carried out and the following subjective choices: the choice of the starting indicators, the way to group them, the use or not of a method of data standardization, the choice of such a method, the weighting procedure of the information provided by each indicator and the form of aggregation of such information (Nardo et al. 2005).

To counteract the critical aspects associated with the degree of subjectivity, methodologies have been developed to obtain a SI, reducing the number of decisions that must be taken by the analyst, as evidenced, among others by the work of Munda (2005) or Munda and Nardo (2009). Undoubtedly, the phase in which each individual indicator is weighted and aggregated to determine the unique value that will represent each alternative is the step in which the analyst's subjectivity can affect the process more (Saisana and Tarantola 2002).

There are multiple experiences in the selection of indicators and, in basic terms, can be summarized into the following three (OECD 2014):

- The selected indicators should provide a high degree of approximation on the evolution of the variable object of study.
- These indicators should be operational; that is, they must be easily accessible.
- They must be available in real time, to ensure effective contact with reality.

In order to analyse the sustainability of public pension systems, we have selected two synthetic indicators: the Allianz-Pension Sustainability Index and the Mercer Global Pension Index, which, although it is a global assessment index, has a composite sub-index regarding sustainability.

6.4.3.1 Allianz-Pension Sustainability Index

For the construction of the indicator, a methodology consistent with other proposals is followed (see, e.g. Alonso et al. 2016) and, in a certain way, standardized; i.e. the dimensions are defined, sub-indicators are included in each dimension, a weight is

Table 6.4 The dimension

Demographic	Old-age dependency ratio
Pension system	Level of pension benefit from first pillar and coverage of workforce
	Legal/effective retirement age
	Strength of funded pillar and reserve fund (as % of GDP)
Public finances	Pension payments/GDP
	Public indebtedness/GDP
	Need for welfare support

Source: Allianz-Pensions Sustainability Index

assigned to each one and a value is obtained, to later build a ranking. Each sub-indicator is obtained on the basis of a set of variables, which are shown in Table 6.4, assigning a score of 1–10 to each one, where 1 indicates the worst rating (e.g. high levels of pension debt, high replacement rates, high old-age dependency ratios or low retirement age) and 10 for the best rating.

Finally, the three sub-indicators are combined into a final single score. A score of 1 would indicate that the country urgently needs to reform its pension system, as it is highly unsustainable, while a score of 10 would indicate that the country does not require any reform, as it is perfectly sustainable.

The results are broken down into four sub-indices, depending on the different world regions:

- Western Europe and North America
- Selected countries in Central and Eastern Europe
- Selected countries in Asia
- Selected countries in Latin America, Oceania and Africa

As indicated throughout their report, the factors that would improve the value of the sub-indicators would be:

1. *Demography:*
    - A favourable old-age dependency ratio (low proportion of dependent workers aged 65 or over, in relation to the number of working-age people aged 15–64).
    - Any change in the "work-retirement" ratio is expected to be moderate.
2. *Pension system design:*
    - The public pillar PAYGO system provides modest benefits and covers a large percentage of the population.
    - The retirement age is high or is related with the life expectancy.
    - There is an individually funded pillar supplementing retirement income.
3. *Public finance:*
    - Low fiscal spending on pensions.
    - The state has sufficient resources to increase its debt level, or the burden on the economy, to finance the increase in pension costs.

As for the main conclusions of the ranking, they state that the ten countries with the most sustainable pension systems are (1) Australia, (2) Denmark, (3) Sweden, (4) the Netherlands, (5) Norway, (6) New Zealand, (7) Latvia, (8) Estonia, (9) the United States and (10) Chile, while the ten countries with the most unsustainable pension systems are (1) Thailand, (2) China, (3) Slovenia, (4) Greece, (5) Brazil, (6) Italy, (7) India, (8) Malta, (9) Japan and (10) Spain.

In the conclusions of the 2016 report, they note that "… the expected increase in pension expenditure (as % of GDP) has been successfully reduced and the burden of pension systems on public finances seems to be more under control - although in many countries additional reforms are needed and the reform effort must be maintained- …".

6.4.3.2 Melbourne Mercer Global Pension Index: The Sustainability Sub-index

The Global Pension Index is an annual index published since 2009. It consists of 3 sub-indices: adequacy (40% of the index weight), sustainability (35% of the index weight) and integrity (25%). Its construction is shown in Table 6.5.

It covers almost 60% of the world population, although it only provides data of 27 countries.

The sustainability sub-index includes factors such as the economic importance of private pensions and their number, the total number of pension funds, current and future retirement dates, work of older age groups (55–64 and 65+) and public debt. It does not use the pension expenditure as % of GDP indicator.

Table 6.5 The Global Pension Index

Sub-index	Indicators included	Final weighting
Adequacy	Benefits	40%
	Savings	
	Tax support	
	Benefit design	
	Growth assets	
Sustainability	Coverage	35%
	Total assets	
	Contributions	
	Demography	
	Government debt	
Integrity	Regulation	25%
	Governance	
	Protection	
	Communication	
	Costs	

Source: Melbourne Mercer Global Pension Index

The ranking provided only refers to 27 countries, and the data is based on its collection by the regional offices in each of the countries compared. Despite this, its relevance lies in the homogeneity of its data and the uninterrupted annual evolution since 2009, which is of great importance in cross-country comparisons.

In its 2016 report on sustainability, it states: "... to reduce the direct consequences of population ageing and ensure that pension systems are sustainable, countries must first increase labour participation in older ages; Secondly, increase the retirement age and/or the age or pension age; and thirdly, increase the level and amount of private pension funds established to supplement public pensions in the future".

6.5 Conclusions

This chapter has reviewed the different definitions of sustainability that are used both in the academic world and by the main institutions that are interested in making pensions one of the basic pillars of any pension system.

It has been possible to verify that the range of definitions that can be found on the sustainability of a pension system is quite broad and supports multiple interpretations. In a first classification, three groups of indices can be found: those based on economic and financial criteria, actuarial approaches and composite indicators.

Undoubtedly, the best known are the first ones, since they have the advantage of being more simple to calculate and are more easily understood, but on the other hand, they only offer us a cross-sectional view, i.e. for an annual time horizon or just a few years. However, the actuarial type gives us a longitudinal view of the problem, having special importance those that consider the whole life cycle, because they incorporate very useful information to understand the sustainability of pension systems better. In spite of this, it does not mean that actuarial indicators are better than the others, but must be understood as complementary elements that broaden the global understanding of pension systems.

Composite indicators, which are becoming increasingly important, deserve special mention. They have the advantage of bringing together a set of indices that are relevant for measuring different characteristics of any variable. The only limitation is given by the availability of the data, since it is important to be able to carry out a cross-country comparison. This would allow us to place the relative position of a particular country and determine the way forward in order to achieve a specific objective. One of the problems of composite indicators is the choice of the different indices that are part of it and their weighting, since the different composition could lead to very different results. Therefore, these indicators should adjust their composition depending on the new indices that are appearing and on the inconveniences arising throughout the process.

Throughout the study, it was also observed that many of the theoretical indicators raised from the academic world do not correspond to those used by international organizations, especially actuarial ones. One of the causes can be easy to understand, the difficulty of their calculation, since it takes a lot of microdata to recreate the working lives of the assets, both the contributions and the benefits. The second reason only seems to be explained by the lack of confidence that the authorities of the pension systems have in their own pension systems, especially in what refers to actuarial indicators. This goes against one of the characteristics that all pension systems are supposed to fulfil: transparency.

In view of all this, and as a recommendation, we believe that public pension authorities should calculate or at least facilitate the achievement of all the indicators related to the sustainability of a pension system, as this would lead to greater knowledge of the system itself, facilitating decision-making that would improve its credibility and citizens' confidence, who are the main stakeholders in its good functioning.

Annex I

Table 6.6 Expenditure on pensions (Eurostat)

Expenditure on pensions (EuroStat). Current prices (% of national GDP). 2003–2060 (projected)

													Projected									
2003	2004	2005	2006	2007	2008	2009	2010	2011	2012	2013	2014	Countries	2015	2020	2025	2030	2035	2040	2045	2050	2055	2060
14.2	13.9	13.7	13.6	13.4	13.6	14.5	14.6	14.3	14.5	14.8	14.9	Austria	14.4	15.1	16.1	16.7	16.7	16.5	16.4	16.4	16.4	16.1
11.1	10.9	10.9	10.8	10.5	11.1	11.9	11.8	12.1	12,00	12.5	12.5	Belgium	11.9	13.1	14.5	15.5	16.2	16.5	16.7	16.7	16.8	16.6
:	:	7.4	7.1	6.5	6.7	8.2	8.7	8.1	8.1	8.6	8.8	Bulgaria	8.7	9.2	9.5	9.6	9.7	10.1	10.6	11.1	11.3	11.1
:	:	:	:	:	9.3	10.4	10.6	10.4	10.6	10.9	11,00	Croatia	:	:	:	:	:	:	:	:	:	:
6.1	5.9	6.1	6,00	6,00	6.1	6.6	7.5	7.9	8.6	9.8	10.5	Cyprus	8.7	9.5	10.4	11.1	11.5	12.1	13.1	14.4	15.5	16.4
8.00	7.6	7.7	7.7	7.6	7.8	8.7	8.8	9.2	9.3	9.3	9,00	Czech Republic	8.6	8.7	8.7	8.9	9.2	9.7	10.3	11.00	11.6	11.8
10.9	10.8	10.7	10.4	11.7	11.7	13.1	12.7	12.8	12.8	13.6	14.2	Denmark	10.4	10.8	10.6	10.7	10.5	10.3	10,00	9.6	9.5	9.5
5.9	6,00	5.8	5.9	5.7	6.9	8.9	8.7	7.8	7.6	7.6	7.6	Estonia	7.8	7.7	7.9	8.2	8.1	8.1	8.1	8,00	8,00	7.7
10.8	10.7	10.7	10.7	10.4	10.4	12,00	12.2	12,00	12.5	13,00	13.4	Finland	12.8	14,00	14.9	15.6	15.5	15.2	14.9	14.9	15.1	15.2
12.8	12.8	12.9	13,00	13.1	13.3	14.3	14.3	14.5	14.8	15,00	15.2	France	14.4	14.4	14.5	14.9	15.2	15.2	15.2	15.1	15.1	15.1
13.1	13,00	12.9	12.5	12,00	12,00	12.8	12.4	11.9	11.9	11.9	11.8	Germany	10.5	10.9	11.4	12,00	12.4	12.7	12.8	13,00	13.2	13.4
11.1	11.3	12,00	11.9	12.3	13.1	14.3	14.8	16.4	17.7	16.7	17.1	Greece	14.1	13.7	13.6	14.1	14.6	14.9	15.3	15.4	15,00	14.6
9.1	9.2	9.6	9.8	10.3	10.8	10.9	10.8	10.8	9.4	9.4	9,00	Hungary	11.9	11.5	11.4	11.1	11.4	12.1	12.8	13.5	14.2	14.7
7.1	6.9	6.8	6.6	6.7	6.9	7.8	7.5	8.3	8.5	8.6	9,00	Iceland	:	:	:	:	:	:	:	:	:	:
4.8	4.8	4.8	4.9	5,00	5.9	6.7	6.9	6.7	6.8	6.8	6.4	Ireland	8.3	9,00	9,00	9,00	9.4	10,00	10.6	11.4	11.7	11.7
14.1	14,00	14.1	14,00	14,00	14.3	15.5	15.5	15.5	16.1	16.5	16.5	Italy	14.9	14.5	14.4	14.5	15,00	15.6	15.9	15.7	15,00	14.4
7.2	6.6	6,00	5.7	4.9	5.7	8.3	10.1	8.7	8.3	8.2	7.9	Latvia	7.6	7.3	6.9	6.5	6.4	6.3	6.2	6.4	6.3	5.9
6.7	6.7	6.5	6.3	6.5	7.3	9.5	8.4	7.6	7.6	7.2	7,00	Lithuania	7.4	7.6	7.8	8.4	9.1	9.6	10,00	10.8	11.6	12.1
10.1	9.8	9.7	8.8	8.4	8.7	9.7	9.2	9.2	9.6	9.6	9.4	Luxembourg	9.9	10.8	12.4	14,00	15.4	16.5	17.6	18.1	18.7	18.6
8.2	8.4	8.6	8.7	8.6	8.7	9.2	9.4	9,00	9.2	8.8	8.6	Malta	10.5	10.6	10.3	10.4	10.7	11.4	12.4	13.4	14.8	15.9
12.2	12,00	11.7	11.6	11.5	11.3	12.2	12.4	12.7	13.1	13.2	11.5	Netherlands	6.8	7.4	8.3	9.1	10,00	10.4	10.5	10.4	10.4	10.4
8.5	8.2	7.8	7.4	7.5	7.5	8.6	8.3	8.3	8.5	8.8	9.3	Norway	10.9	11.6	12.3	12.9	13.4	13.7	13.8	13.9	14,00	14.2
13.8	13.1	12.6	12.4	11.5	11.5	12.2	11.8	11.3	11.5	11.9	11.8	Poland	10.7	10.9	11.1	10.9	10.6	10.3	10.1	10,00	9.9	9.6
11.2	11.7	12,00	12.2	12.2	12.7	13.6	13.7	14.4	14.5	15.7	15.6	Portugal	13.3	13.5	13.4	13.2	13.1	13.1	13.2	13.1	12.9	12.7
5.9	6.1	6.2	6,00	6.4	7.5	9.2	9.3	9.1	8.7	8.3	8.2	Romania	9.3	9.2	9.6	10.3	10.9	11.6	12.2	12.8	13.4	13.5

7.2	7.2	7.3	7.2	7.1	7,00	8.3	8.2	8.1	8.3	8.4	8.7	Slovakia	8.1	8.6	9.1	9.5	10,00	10.6	11.3	12.2	13.2	13.2
10.5	10.3	10.2	10.1	9.6	9.5	10.7	11,00	11.2	11.4	11.7	11.2	Slovenia	11.8	12.2	12.5	13.3	14.5	15.8	16.9	17.9	18.3	18.3
8.9	8.9	8.8	8.7	9,00	9.2	10.1	10.5	11.1	11.8	12.6	12.8	SPAIN	10.4	10.6	10.5	10.6	11.3	12.3	13.3	14,00	14,00	13.7
11.4	11.3	11.5	11.1	10.9	11.1	12.2	11.3	11.1	11.6	11.9	11.5	Sweden	9.7	9.6	9.8	10.1	10.2	10.2	9.9	9.9	10.1	10.2
11.8	11.7	11.7	11.3	11.1	10.9	11.5	11.4	11.5	11.6	11.7	11.8	Switzerland	:	:	:	:	:	:	:	:	:	:
9.8	9.7	9.8	9.8	9.8	10.2	11.3	11.4	11.4	11.7	11.5	11.3	United Kingdom	7.4	7,00	7.3	7.7	8,00	8.2	8,00	8.2	8.7	9.2
:	:	**11.6**	**11.5**	**11.4**	**11.6**	**12.6**	**12.6**	**12.6**	**12.6**	**12.7**	**12.6**	**EU 27**	**11.2**	**11.3**	**11.5**	**11.9**	**12.3**	**12.6**	**12.7**	**12.8**	**12.9**	**12.9**

: = not available
Source of Data: Eurostat
Last update: 16.01.2017
Date of extraction: 17 Jan 2017 17:54:24 CET
General Disclaimer of the EC website: http://ec.europa.eu/geninfo/legal_notices_en.htm
Short Description: *The 'Pensions' aggregate comprises part of periodic cash benefits under the disability, old-age, survivors and unemployment functions. It is defined as the sum of the following social benefits: disability pension, early-retirement due to reduced capacity to work, old-age pension, anticipated old-age pension, partial pension, survivors' pension, early- retirement benefit for labour market reasons*

Table 6.7 Old-age dependency ratio (Eurostat)

Old-age-dependency ratio (Eurostat) per 100 persons (1990–2080, projected)																	
1990	1991	1992	1993	1994	1995	1996	1997	1998	1999	2000	2001	2002	2003	2004	2005	2006	2007
22.1	22.2	22.1	22.1	22.2	22.5	22.7	22.8	22.9	22.9	22.9	22.8	22.8	22.7	22.7	23.5	24.3	25,0
22.1	22.5	22.9	23.2	23.5	23.8	24.3	24.7	25,0	25.3	25.5	25.7	25.8	26,0	26.1	26.3	26.2	25.9
19.5	20.1	20.8	21.3	21.8	22.2	22.6	22.7	23.1	23.4	23.8	24,0	25,0	25.1	25.1	25.2	25.3	25.5
:	:	:	:	:	:	:	:	:	:	:	24,0	24.6	25.2	25.6	26,0	26.3	26.5
17.2	17.2	17.3	17.4	17.3	17.2	17.2	17.1	17.1	17,0	17,0	17,0	17.4	17.5	17.6	17.7	17.8	18,0
19,0	19.1	19.1	19.2	19.2	19.3	19.4	19.6	19.7	19.8	19.8	19.7	19.7	19.7	19.7	19.8	20,0	20.3
23.2	23.1	23.1	23,0	22.8	22.7	22.5	22.4	22.3	22.2	22.2	22.2	22.3	22.3	22.5	22.7	22.9	23.2
17.5	17.7	18.2	18.9	19.7	20.2	20.9	21.5	22,0	22.2	22.1	22.4	22.8	23.4	23.8	24.3	24.8	25.5
:	:	:	:	:	:	:	:	:	:	:	23.5	23.9	24.1	24.4	24.7	25,0	25.2
19.8	20,0	20.3	20.5	20.8	21.1	21.5	21.7	21.9	22,0	22.2	22.4	22.7	22.9	23.3	23.8	24,0	24.8
:	21.2	21.6	22,0	22.4	22.7	23.1	23.5	23.8	24,0	24.3	24.5	24.7	24.8	24.9	25.1	25.1	25.1
22,0	21.7	21.8	21.9	22.2	22.5	22.8	23,0	23.2	23.3	23.9	24.5	25.2	25.9	26.8	27.8	28.9	29.9
20.4	20.5	21.1	21.5	22.2	22.7	23.3	23.9	24.4	24.9	25.5	26.2	26.1	26.6	27.1	27.4	27.7	27.9
20,0	20.2	20.4	20.5	20.7	20.9	21.2	21.3	21.6	21.8	22,0	22.2	22.3	22.4	22.6	22.7	22.9	23.2
16.4	16.6	16.7	16.9	17.1	17.3	17.6	17.8	17.9	17.8	17.8	17.8	17.8	17.9	17.9	17.9	17.6	17.2
18.6	18.5	18.3	18.2	18,0	17.8	17.6	17.4	17.2	17,0	16.8	16.6	16.5	16.4	16.3	16.3	16,0	15.7
21.5	22,0	22.4	22.9	23.4	24,0	24.7	25.2	25.8	26.3	26.8	27.4	27.9	28.4	28.8	29.4	30.1	30.5
17.7	17.7	18.6	19.4	20.1	20.5	20.9	21.4	21.8	22,0	22.1	22.3	22.7	23.3	23.8	24.3	24.8	25.4
16.2	16.6	17,0	17.5	18.1	18.5	19,0	19.5	20,0	20.5	20.8	20.9	21.8	22.3	23,0	23.6	24.3	24.7
19.3	19.5	19.7	19.9	20.2	20.6	20.9	21.2	21.3	21.4	21.4	20.7	20.8	20.9	20.8	20.9	20.8	20.7
15.7	15.9	16.1	16.2	16.3	16.4	16.8	17.4	17.6	17.8	17.9	18.1	18.5	18.7	19,0	19.3	19.9	19.9
18.6	18.7	18.8	19,0	19.1	19.3	19.5	19.6	19.8	19.9	20,0	20.1	20.2	20.3	20.5	20.8	21.1	21.5
25.2	25.2	25.2	25.1	24.9	24.8	24.6	24.5	24.2	23.9	23.5	23.2	23,0	22.7	22.5	22.4	22.4	22.2
15.4	15.7	15.9	16.1	16.3	16.6	16.9	17.2	17.4	17.5	17.8	18,0	18.2	18.4	18.6	18.7	18.9	19,0
20,0	20.5	20.9	21.3	21.6	22,0	22.4	22.7	23.1	23.5	23.8	24.2	24.6	24.9	25.3	25.7	26,0	26.3

15.6	15.9	16.6	16.9	17.3	17.6	18,0	18.2	18.7	19,0	19.3	19.6	20.4	20.7	20.7	20.7	21.6	21.5
16,0	16.1	16,0	16.1	16.2	16.3	16.4	16.5	16.6	16.6	16.6	16.5	16.3	16.3	16.3	16.4	16.5	16.7
15.5	15.8	16.1	16.5	17,0	17.4	18,0	18.5	19,0	19.4	19.8	20.2	20.6	21,0	21.4	21.8	22.2	22.7
20.2	20.6	20.9	21.2	21.6	22,0	22.4	22.8	23.3	23.7	24.1	24.5	24.8	24.7	24.4	24,0	24.2	24,0
27.7	27.7	27.7	27.6	27.6	27.4	27.4	27.4	27.3	27.1	26.9	26.8	26.6	26.5	26.4	26.5	26.4	26.4
21.3	21.3	21.4	21.5	21.6	21.7	21.9	22.1	22.3	22.5	22.7	22.9	23.1	23.1	23.2	23.3	23.5	23.8
24.1	24.2	24.3	24.4	24.5	24.5	24.5	24.5	24.5	24.4	24.3	24.3	24.3	24.2	24.2	24.2	24,0	23.9

Old-age-dependency ratio (Eurostat) per 100 persons (1990–2080, projected)

									Projected						
2008	2009	2010	2011	2012	2013	2014	2015	Countries	2020	2030	2040	2050	2060	2070	2080
25.4	25.8	26.2	26.1	26.3	26.8	27.2	27.5	Austria	29.3	37.4	44.3	46.6	50.4	52.3	54.2
25.8	25.9	26,0	26,0	26.4	26.8	27.3	27.8	Belgium	29.5	34.5	37.2	37.9	39.8	41.9	45.1
25.8	26.1	26.5	27,0	27.8	28.5	29.3	30.2	Bulgaria	33.5	38.9	45.3	53.9	58.7	52.9	53.4
26.7	26.8	26.7	26.5	26.7	27.1	27.6	28.3	Croatia	31.7	39.1	43.7	49.1	52.2	53.3	54.6
17.9	17.8	17.8	18,0	18.1	18.8	19.9	21.2	Cyprus	24,0	31.8	36.5	42.3	46.6	43.1	42.5
20.6	21.1	21.7	22.3	23.4	24.6	25.7	26.6	Czech Repblic	31.3	35.2	40.2	48.2	50.3	45.6	47.8
23.6	24.1	24.9	25.7	26.7	27.6	28.3	28.8	Denmark	31.4	36.5	40.5	39.4	41.6	44.9	47.2
25.8	25.8	25.9	26,0	26.5	27.2	27.9	28.7	Estonia	32.4	39.6	45.2	51.4	54.9	48.2	50.8
25.5	25.8	26.1	26.4	26.9	27.5	28.2	28.8	**EU 28**	31.8	39,0	45.9	49.4	50.2	49.3	51,0
24.8	25.2	25.6	26.5	27.7	28.9	30.2	31.3	Finland	35.8	41.3	41.2	41.9	44.9	47.2	49.8
25.2	25.4	25.6	25.9	26.7	27.5	28.4	29.2	France	32.6	39,0	44,0	43.8	42.9	44.2	46.4
30.4	30.9	31.4	31.4	31.4	31.3	31.6	32,0	Germany	35.8	46.8	55.6	57.3	59.2	59.8	59.9
28,0	28.2	28.6	29.2	30,0	30.7	31.6	32.4	Greece	34.3	41.2	53.2	63.6	61.1	56.2	56.8
23.5	23.8	24.2	24.4	24.6	25.1	25.8	26.5	Hungary	30.5	34.4	39.8	47.3	52.4	52.4	52.9
17.1	17.2	17.9	18.4	18.9	19.5	19.9	20.5	Iceland	24.3	32.3	36,0	37.5	38.9	39.1	41.2
15.6	16,0	16.5	17.2	17.9	18.6	19.3	20,0	Ireland	23.2	30.3	38.6	44.8	36,0	32.4	36.9
30.7	30.9	31.2	31.3	32,0	32.7	33.1	33.7	Italy	34.9	40.8	49.9	52.9	53.1	53.6	56.8
25.7	26.2	26.8	27.2	27.6	28.1	28.8	29.5	Latvia	32.1	41.9	47.6	50.5	50.9	39.7	40.2

(continued)

Table 6.7 (continued)

Old-age-dependency ratio (Eurostat) per 100 persons (1990–2080, projected)

									Projected						
2008	2009	2010	2011	2012	2013	2014	2015	Countries	2020	2030	2040	2050	2060	2070	2080
25.2	25.4	25.6	26.6	26.9	27.2	27.5	28.1	Lithuania	31.8	47.3	55.7	51.9	46.2	34.5	34,0
20.6	20.5	20.4	20.3	20.3	20.2	20.4	20.5	Luxembourg	21.6	25.6	29.2	31.6	35.3	40.3	44,0
19.9	20.3	21.4	22.7	23.9	25.1	26.4	27.6	Malta	32.7	40.5	40.7	44.8	50.7	50.7	49,0
21.8	22.3	22.8	23.3	24.4	25.5	26.4	27.2	Netherlands	30.8	40.1	47.1	46.4	47.7	50.5	52.3
22.1	22.1	22.5	22.8	23.3	23.7	24.2	24.5	Norway	26.3	30,0	33.7	35,0	38.8	42.7	46,0
18.9	18.9	19.1	19.1	19.7	20.4	21.2	22.2	Poland	27.1	35.4	40,0	51.9	60.9	59.2	59.6
26.6	27,0	27.5	28.2	28.8	29.4	30.3	31.1	Portugal	34.3	43.1	54.9	64.3	63.9	66,0	68.2
22.6	23.7	23.7	23.7	23.7	23.9	24.3	25.2	Romania	28.4	32.7	41.3	48.5	51.9	49.9	49.6
16.8	17,0	17.3	17.5	17.8	18.4	19,0	19.7	Slovakia	24.3	32.6	40,0	54.2	65.9	65.9	68.7
23.3	23.6	23.8	23.9	24.4	25,0	25.7	26.6	Slovenia	31.7	40.6	47.4	53.9	52.8	48.1	49.7
23.8	24.1	24.6	25.2	25.7	26.3	27.2	27.9	Spain	30.4	39.6	53.5	62.5	53.7	46.5	48.3
26.7	27.1	27.7	28.4	29.2	29.9	30.6	31.1	Sweden	33,0	35.5	37.4	37.5	41.4	41.9	44.5
24.1	24.3	24.7	24.9	25.3	25.7	26.1	26.4	Switzerland	28.7	35.7	40.8	42.5	44.4	45.7	47.8
24,0	24.3	24.6	24.9	25.6	26.4	27,0	27.5	Unit.Ktngdom	29.5	34.9	39.1	40.6	42.7	42.4	44.7

Source of Data: Eurostat - Population projections EUROPOP2013
Last update: 24.11.2016
Date of extraction: 17 Jan 2017 17:39:52 CET
General Disclaimer EC web: http://ec.europa.eu/geninfo/legal_notices_en.htm
Short Description: *This indicator is the ratio between the projected number of persons aged 65 (the age when they are generally economically inactive) and the projected number of persons aged between 15 and 64. The value is expressed per 100 pp of working age (15–64)*

Table 6.8 Net social contributions (Eurostat)

Net social contributions (EuroStat) as a % of GDP 2005–2016												
Countries	2005	2006	2007	2008	2009	2010	2011	2012	2013	2014	2015	2016
EU (28 countries)	12.9	12.8	12.7	13,0	13.5	13.2	13.3	13.4	13.4	13.4	13.2	13.4
EU (27 countries)	13,0	12.8	12.7	13,0	13.5	13.3	13.3	13.4	13.5	13.4	13.2	13.4
Euro area (19 countries)	14.9	14.7	14.5	14.7	15.2	15.1	15.1	15.4	15.5	15.5	15.3	15.4
Euro area (18 countries)	14.9	14.7	14.5	14.7	15.2	15.1	15.2	15.4	15.5	15.5	15.3	15.4
Austria	14.9	14.7	14.5	14.6	15,0	14.9	14.8	14.9	15.2	15.3	15.3	15.5
Belgium	15.3	15.2	15.3	15.8	16.4	16.1	16.3	16.6	16.8	16.7	16.6	16,0
Bulgaria	9.5	8.1	7.7	7.4	7.2	6.6	6.7	6.8	7.4	7.9	7.9	8,0
Croatia	11.6	11.5	11.5	11.7	12.1	11.8	11.6	11.5	11.3	11.8	11.9	11.9
Cyprus	7.5	7.1	6.8	7,0	7.8	8,0	7.9	7.8	7.5	8.2	8.4	8.6
Czech Republic	14.8	15,0	15.1	14.9	14.3	14.6	14.7	14.8	14.8	14.6	14.6	14.9
Denmark	1.5	1.4	1.4	1.3	1.4	1.3	1.3	1.2	1.1	1,0	1,0	1,0
Estonia	10.3	10.1	10.5	11.6	13.1	13,0	11.8	11.4	11.2	11.2	11.6	11.9
Finland	11.6	11.9	11.6	11.6	12.3	12.2	12.2	12.8	12.7	12.8	12.9	13.1
France	17.6	17.7	17.5	17.6	18.3	18.1	18.3	18.5	18.9	19,0	18.8	18.7
Germany	17.4	16.9	16.1	16.1	16.9	16.5	16.4	16.5	16.5	16.5	16.5	16.7
Greece	12.3	11.9	12.4	12.7	12.4	13.1	13.2	13.9	13.5	13.5	13.9	14.2
Hungary	12.4	12.4	13.6	13.5	13,0	12,0	13.1	13,0	13,0	13,0	13.2	13.8
Iceland	3.1	3.2	2.9	2.7	2.9	3.9	3.9	3.6	3.7	3.7	3.6	3.6
Ireland	5.1	5.2	5.4	5.9	6,0	5.7	6,0	5.6	5.8	5.6	4.3	4.3
Italy	12.2	11.9	12.6	13,0	13.5	13.3	13.2	13.4	13.4	13.2	13.3	13.2
Latvia	8.1	8.3	8.1	8.4	9.6	8.9	8.8	8.9	8.7	8.7	8.7	8.7
Liechtenstein	:	:	:	:	:	:	:	:	:	:	:	:
Lithuania	9.2	9.4	9.4	9.9	13.1	12.1	11.5	11.2	11.1	11.4	11.9	12.5
Luxembourg	12.1	11.4	11.3	11.8	13.1	12.2	12.2	12.7	12.4	11.9	11.9	11.9
Malta	7.4	7.2	6.9	7,0	7.1	6.9	7.1	7,0	6.9	6.6	6.4	6.5
Netherlands	13,0	13.7	13.1	14,0	13.4	13.7	14.3	15.2	15.4	15.4	14.6	15.3
Norway	8.7	8.5	8.7	8.6	9.6	9.4	9.3	9.3	9.5	10,0	10.5	10.6
Poland	13.1	13,0	12.7	12.1	12,0	11.9	12.2	13,0	13.4	13.3	13.6	14,0
Portugal	11.6	11.5	11.3	11.6	12.1	11.9	12,0	11.4	12,0	11.8	11.6	11.7
Romania	10.2	10.3	10.4	9.9	10,0	9.3	9,0	8.7	8.6	8.5	8.1	8.1
Slovakia	12.6	11.7	11.7	11.8	12.6	12.3	12.3	12.5	13.5	13.6	14,0	14.3
Slovenia	14.2	14,0	13.7	14,0	14.9	15.2	15,0	15.3	15,0	14.7	14.8	15,0
Spain	12.6	12.6	12.6	12.7	12.9	12.8	12.9	12.7	12.5	12.5	12.3	12.2
Sweden	3.8	3.5	3.5	3.6	3.8	3.6	3.7	3.8	3.8	3.7	3.7	3.7
Switzerland	6.5	6.3	6.2	6.2	6.6	6.4	6.7	6.8	6.8	6.8	6.9	:
United Kingdom	7.6	7.6	7.6	7.8	7.9	7.9	7.9	7.8	7.8	7.6	7.8	8,0

:=not available

Source of Data: Eurostat

Last update: 15.01.2017

Date of extraction: 02 Feb 2017 10:38:59 CEST

Hyperlink to the table: http://ec.europa.eu/eurostat/tgm/table.do?tab=table&init=1&plugin=1&language=en&pcode=tec00019

General Disclaimer: http://ec.europa.eu/geninfo/legal_notices_en.htm

Short Description: Net social contributions (ESA 2010 code D.61) are the actual or imputed contributions made by households to social insurance schemes to make provision for social benefits to be paid

References

Abío, G., Bonin, H., Gil, J., & Patxot, C. (1999). El impacto intergeneracional de la Reforma de las Pensiones en España: Un enfoque de Contabilidad generacional. *Economic Journals ICE (Spanish Commercial Information), 65*, 101–116.

Allianz-Pensions sustainability index. Available at: http://projectm-online.com/app/uploads/Allianz_2016_Pension_Sustainability_Index.pdf

Alonso, J. J., Devesa, J. E., Devesa, M., Domínguez, I., Encinas, B., & Meneu, R. (2016). A proposal of a pension adequacy index for the EU countries. Presentation II workshop on pensions and insurance 2016. Barcelona (Spain), 14 and 15 July 2016.

Balmaseda, M., Melguizo, A., & Taguas, D. (2006). Las reformas necesarias en el sistema de pensiones contributivas en España. Moneda y Crédito, no. 222.

Bandrés, E., & Cuenca, A. (1998). Equidad intrageneracional en las pensiones de jubilación. La reforma de 1997. *Journal of Applied Economics, VI*(18), 119–140.

Barea, J., & González-Páramo, J. M. (1996). *Pensiones y prestaciones por desempleo*. Bilbao: Foundation BBV Documenta.

Barea, J., Carpio, M., & Domingo, E. (1996). *Escenarios de evolución del gasto público en pensiones y desempleo en el horizonte 2020*. Bilbao: Foundation BBV Documenta.

Blancas, F. J., Contreras, I., & Ramírez-Hurtado, J. M. (2011). Construcción de indicadores sintéticos: una aproximación para maximizar la discriminación. *ASEPUMA Annals, 19*, 01–10.

Blanco, A., Montes, J., & Antón, V. (2000). *Modelo para simular escenarios de gasto en pensiones contributivas de jubilación de la seguridad social*. Ministry of Economy and Finance. Working Paper of the General Directorate for Budgetary Analysis and Programming.

Boado, M. C., & Vidal, C. (2008). *El balance actuarial como indicador de la solvencia del sistema de reparto*". Working paper IVIE WP-EC 2008-02.

Bonoli, G., & Shinkawa, T. (Eds.). (2006). *Ageing and pension reform around the world: evidence from eleven countries*. Edward Elgar Publishing, Great Britian.

Bravo, J. (2000). Envejecimiento de la población y sistemas de pensiones. *Journal of CEPAL, 72*, 121–146.

Bravo, J., & Uthoff, A. (1999). Transitional fiscal costs and demographic factors in shifting from unfunded to funded pension in Latin America. Development Finance Series, no. 88, Santiago de Chile. CEPAL.

Committee on Monetary, Financial and Balance of Payments Statistics. (2008). Statistical contribution to the review of the sustainability of public finances – Final report on the statistical measurement of the assets and liabilities of pension schemes in general government, CMFP 08/01/A6.1. Luxembourg. Available at: http://www.cmfb.org/pdf/TF%20on%20Pensions%20-%20Final%20report.pdf

Conde-Ruiz, J. I. (2017). *Medidas para restaurar (o no) la sostenibilidad financiera de las pensiones (No. 2017-04)*. FEDEA.

De la Peña, J. I. (2000). *Planes de Previsión Social*. Madrid: Pirámide.

Devesa, M. (2007). El desequilibrio financiero-actuarial del sistema contributivo de pensiones de la Seguridad Social española. Doctoral Thesis. ISBN: 978-84-370-7067-4. Available at: http://www.tesisenxarxa.net/TDX-1128108-090646/

Devesa, J. E., & Devesa, M. (2008a). *La deuda implícita y el desequilibrio financiero-actuarial de un sistema de pensiones. El caso del Régimen General de la Seguridad Social en España*. Savings Bank Foundation (FUNCAS). Working Paper, no. 429, November.

Devesa, J. E., & Devesa, M. (2008b). Desequilibrio financiero-actuarial en el sistema de pensiones de jubilación del Régimen General. *Journal of Applied Economics, XVI*(46), 85–117.

Devesa, J. E., & Devesa, M. (2010). The cost and actuarial imbalance of pay-as-you-go systems: the case of Spain. *Journal of Economic Policy Reform, 13*(3), 259–276.

Devesa, J. E., & Vidal, C. (2004). Cuentas nocionales de aportación definida (NDC's). ¿Cuál hubiera sido el efecto de su implantación en el sistema de pensiones español? *Moneda y Crédito, 219*, 101–142.

Devesa, J. E., Lejárraga, A., & Vidal, C. (2002). El tanto de rendimiento de los sistemas de reparto. *Journal of Applied Economics, X*(30), 109–132.

Devesa, J. E., Domínguez, I., & Nagore, A. (2013). La sostenibilidad financiera del sistema de desempleo contributivo en España. Análisis comparado 2009-2011. *Annals of Spanish Actuaries, 19*, 155–176.

Durán, A. (1995). Rentabilidad de lo cotizado para pensiones. *Economistas*, no. 68.

European Commission. (2015). *The 2015 ageing report. Underlying Assumptions and Projection Methodologies*. Brussels: European Commission. Directorate-General for Economic and Financial Affairs.

Gil, J., & López-Casasnovas, G. (1999). Redistribution in the Spanish pension system: an approach to its life time effects. EEE-55, FEDEA.

Gil, J., & Patxot, C. (2002). Reformas de la financiación del sistema de pensiones. *Journal of Applied Economics, X*(28), 63–85.

Gil, J., López-García, M. A., Onrubia, J., Patxot, C., & Souto, G. (2007). A projection model of the contributory pension expenditure of the Spanish social security system: 2004-2050. *Spanish Tax Authorities/Journal of Public Economics, 182*, 75–114.

Gokhale, J., & Smetters, K. (2005). *Measuring social security's financial problems"*. NBER Working Paper Series, no. 11060. Available at: http:www.nber.org/papers/w11060.

Herce, J. A., & Pérez-Díaz, V. (directors) (1995). La reforma del sistema público de pensiones en España. Research Service of La Caixa., Studies and reports collection, no. 4.

Holzmann, R., Palacios, R., & Zviniene, A. (2004). *Implicit pension debt: Measurement and scope in international perspective. Social Protection Discussion Paper Series, no. 403*. Washington, DC: The World Bank.

Jiménez-Ridruejo, Z. (coordinator) (2008). El efecto de la inmigración en la sostenibilidad a medio y largo plazo del sistema de pensiones en España. Ministry of Work and Social Affairs. FIPROS.

Jimeno, J. F., & Licandro, O. (1999). La tasa interna de rentabilidad y el equilibrio financiero del sistema español de pensiones de jubilación. *Investigaciones Económicas, XXIII*(1), 129–143.

JRC-EC, Joint Research Centre-European Commission. (2008). *Handbook on constructing composite indicators: Methodology and User guide*. Paris (EU): OECD Publishing.

Manifiesto. (2013). En defensa del sistema público de pensiones. Available at http://documentopensiones.org/

Melbourne Mercer Global Pensions Index. Available at http://www.globalpensionindex.com/wp-content/uploads/MMGPI2016-Report.pdf

Monasterio, C., Sánchez, I., & Blanco, F. (1996). *Equidad y estabilidad del sistema de pensiones en España*. Bilbao: Foundation BBV Documenta.

Moral-Arce, I., Patxot, C., & Souto, G. (2008). La sostenibilidad del sistema de pensiones. Una aproximación a partir de la MCVL. *Journal of Applied Economics, 16*(E1), 29.

MTAS, Ministry of Work and Social Affairs. (2005). *Informe de Estrategia de España en relación con el futuro del sistema de pensiones*. Madrid: MTAS.

Munda, G. (2005). Measuring sustainability: A multi-criterion framework. *Environment, Development and Sustainability, 7*, 117–134.

Munda, G., & Nardo, M. (2009). Noncompensatory and nonlinear composite indicators for ranking countries: A defensible setting. *Applied Economics, 41*, 1513–1523.

Nardo, M., Saisana, M., Saltelli, A., Tarantola, S., Hoffman, A., Giovannini, E. (2005). *Handbook on constructing composite indicators: methodology and user guide*. OECD Statistics Working Papers, Paris: OECD.

OECD Composite Leading Indicators. (2014). Methodological notes for the news release. Available at www.oecd.org/std/leading-indicators/44728410.pdf

Oria, I. Z., & Escudero, C. M. (2003). *El futuro del sistema de pensiones en España*. Ministry of Finance.

Robalino, D. A., & Bodor, A. (2009). On the financial sustainability of earnings-related pension schemes with 'pay-as-you-go' financing and the role of government-indexed bonds. *Journal of Pension Economics and Finance, 8*(02), 153–187.
Saisana, M., & Tarantola, S. (2002). *State of the art report on current methodologies and practices for composite indicator development*. Joint Research Centre, European Commission.
Samuelson, P. A. (1958). An exact consumption-loan model of interest with or without the social contrivance of money. *Journal of Political Economy, 66*, 467–482. https://goo.gl/1s73Ze.
Serrano, F., García, M. A., & Bravo, C. (2004). *El sistema español de pensiones. Un proyecto viable desde un enfoque económico*. Barcelona: Ariel.
Settergren, O. (2003). Financial and inter-generational balance? An introduction to how the Swedish pension system manages conflicting ambitions. *Scandinavian Insurance Quarterly, 2*, 99–114.
Van den Noord P., & Herd, P. (1993). *Pension liabilities in seven major economies*. Working Paper, no. 142. Paris: OECD.
World Bank. (2012). *International patterns of pension provision II: A worldwide overview of facts and figures*. Social Protection and Labor Discussion Paper; No. 1211. Washington, DC: World Bank. Available at https://openknowledge.worldbank.org/handle/10986/13560.

Chapter 7
Equity of Public Pension System

Robert Meneu-Gaya, Borja Encinas-Goenechea, and Inmaculada Domínguez-Fabián

Abstract Fairness is an important feature of pension systems, but it is a wide concept with multiple sides. In this chapter, we try to distinguish some of them with the aim of using the terms in a proper manner. More specifically, we have observed at least five meanings for the notion of fairness when applying to a pension system: justice, equity, neutrality, solidarity and integrity. We explain each sense of fairness and other related concepts. We also provide, when possible, a way to measure each of them, with some figures for a selected European countries.

Keywords Actuarial fairness · Equity · Actuarial neutrality · Solidarity · Integrity · Public pension

7.1 Introduction

The adequacy and the long-term financial sustainability of pensions are the two main aspects when evaluating pension systems. Perhaps, the third most important feature is fairness. Fairness of a pension system may have different senses: justice, equity, neutrality, solidarity and integrity, as the most significant. Sometimes, authors use the same expression with different meanings, so the debate is often confuse. Our aim is to clarify these concepts. We have organized the chapter in five more sections, each one to develop one of the meanings of fairness.

R. Meneu-Gaya (✉)
Department of Mathematics for Economy anf Business, Universitat de València, Valencia, Spain
e-mail: robert.meneu@uv.es

B. Encinas-Goenechea
Department of Financial Economics and Accounting, University of Extremadura, Badajoz, Spain
e-mail: bencinas@unex.es

I. Domínguez-Fabián
Financial Economics and Accounting, University of Extremadura, Cáceres, Spain
e-mail: idomingu@unex.es

M. Peris-Ortiz et al. (eds.), *Economic Challenges of Pension Systems*,
https://doi.org/10.1007/978-3-030-37912-4_7

In an earnings-related pension system, justice means a proper link between contributions and benefits in the sense that what you pay in the working stage is what you get in the retirement stage, assuming a fair rate of return. This meaning can be applied to the pension system as a whole.

If we analyse the behaviour of the pension system among individuals or groups of individuals, we can study if the system offers the same deal to all of them. In this case, the pension system is equitable or impartial. If the pension system has redistribution effects from individuals with specific characteristics towards individuals with other characteristics, the rate of return of contributions differs across groups of individuals. Then, we can investigate if these inequities are socially acceptable (e.g. a higher rate of return for women) or they are the result of a bad design of the system. In the latter case, some reforms to reinforce the equity can be necessary.

In the literature, the notion of neutrality is used as a marginal concept. Neutrality between individuals can work in two circumstances. The first is to compare individuals of the same cohort who retire at different ages and the second is to compare individuals of different cohorts and, then, with different life expectancies. In both cases, neutrality entails some marginal adjustments to provide the same deal to all the individuals: penalizations or incentives for retiring at different ages in the first case and life expectancy factors to automatically adjust pension level to life expectancy improvements in the second case.

The pension system also has a side of solidarity. In this sense, the term fairness refers to social justice, a sociological concept that entails some type of redistribution. Social justice in developed societies includes public services, like health and school, and progressive taxation to ensure equal opportunities. The use of the pension system with redistribution purposes is something controversial but, accepting that the earnings-related part of the system is the most important, many pension systems contain a minimum income provision scheme.

The last sense of fairness that we develop in this chapter is integrity, a broad concept that includes other concepts like transparency, regulatory stability and efficiency, among others. All these features allow people to take optimal decisions about saving and consumption throughout the life cycle and to choose the best moment for retirement.

7.2 Fairness in the Sense of Justice

Perhaps, the most common sense of fairness has to do with the notion of justice. In an earnings-related pension system, justice means a balanced link between contributions and benefits along the entire lifetime and, therefore, actuarial formulations are necessary to evaluate this feature. The most common expression in the literature is actuarial fairness. Using the definition of Queisser and Whitehouse (2006), an actuarially fair pension scheme requires that the present value of lifetime contributions equals the actuarial present value of lifetime benefits at the time of retirement:

$$c\sum_{i=e}^{j-1} w_i(1+r)^{j-i} = p_j A(r,\lambda,s,j,T) \tag{7.1}$$

The left-hand side in (7.1) is the value of contributions at the retirement age, where c is the (constant) contribution rate, w_i are individual earnings at age i, r is the interest rate, e is the age when entering the system and j is the retirement age. The right-hand side in (7.1) is the actuarial present value of benefits (pension wealth), where p_j is the first pension and $A(r, \lambda, s, j, T)$ is the annuity factor. The annuity factor is the actuarial present value at age j of a unit pension, increased by the rate λ (pension indexation) and discounted at an interest rate r, where T is the last age in the life tables and s is the probability vector of being alive at each age conditional of being alive at the retirement age.[1] The concept is defined across the population and only makes sense ex ante. This implies the use of population mortality rates to compute the actuarial present value of benefits and, then, to assess the actuarial fairness of a pension system.

On the other hand, it is known that high-income groups or certain professions have a higher life expectancy, getting a better deal than people with a lower life expectancy. If we take into account differences by social groups in mortality rates when evaluating the actuarial present value of benefits, we get the concept of *social actuarial fairness*. Both concepts require an actuarial equilibrium of contributions and benefits ex ante, but social actuarial fairness allows for differences in life expectancy by social or economic groups when computing the benefits while actuarial fairness does not necessarily take into account these differences. Obviously, social actuarial fairness implies actuarial fairness but the reverse is not true automatically.

The concept of social actuarial fairness implies different contributing rates and/or different formulas to compute the pension for certain social groups with the aim of compensating the expectancy to die earlier. In theory, it is possible to establish different rules, following Eq. (7.1), if we know the specific mortality rates (vector s) for a group of workers but, in practice, this is not the general case. Only private funded schemes use mortality tables by gender when computing the benefits.

The assessment of actuarial fairness depends on the interest rate (r) that equals the present value of accumulated contributions and the actuarial present value of benefits. This interest rate is similar to the internal rate of return (*IRR*) of an investment and must be compared with a benchmark (fair) interest rate. Following the discussion in Queisser and Whitehouse (2006) there are two alternatives to choose the benchmark interest rate. The first is the market rate of return, because this is the return of a defined contribution retirement savings account, which is the private alternative if no public system exists. The second is the riskless interest rate, because

[1] $A(r,\lambda,s,j,T) = \sum_{i=j}^{T}(1+r)^{j-i}(1+\lambda)^{i-j}s_i$

$s_i = \prod_{k=j}^{i}(1-q_k)$, where q_k is the mortality rate from age k to $k+1$ ($q_T = 1$).

this is the interest rate at which the government can move money over time through the long-term government bound.

The first one is usually greater than the second one, but the reason could be the assumption of a higher risk. Consequently, the use of the market interest rate as the reference to assess the actuarial fairness seems acceptable in the case of funded pension schemes and the riskless interest rate appears as the best option in the case of pay-as-you-go pension systems.

The value of r in Eq. (7.1) is also related with the concept of solvency of a pay-as-you-go pension scheme through the Aaron-Samuelson condition (Samuelson 1958; Aaron 1966). In this case, the *IRR* of the system must be compared with the growth rate of the fiscal base (the sum of workforce growth and average earnings growth). In the steady state, if the *IRR* were greater than the growth rate of the fiscal base, the system would be financially unsustainable in the long term. This concept is more developed in Chap. 16 of this book.

Equation (7.1) is easy to implement in pure funded pension schemes because the contributions are invested at the market rate of return and the accumulated capital is converted to a pension flow using the same interest rate and following Eq. (7.1). Then, the internal rate of return, r in Eq. (7.1), is the market rate of return of investments and the system is actuarially fair, assuming that this is the benchmark interest rate. On the contrary, a private funded system is not social actuarially fair because it does not distinguish mortality rates by social or economic groups, although it does by gender.

A notional account system is a pay-as-you-go public system but similar to a funded defined contribution system when computing both the pensionable earnings and the pension entitlements. The accumulated notional capital uses a notional (virtual) interest rate instead of a real one, which can be different of the discount rate to calculate the annuity factor and the pension. Then, in a notional account scheme, the balance equation is:

$$c\sum_{i=e}^{j-1} w_i(1+r_n)^{j-i} = p_j A\left(r_p, \lambda, s, j, T\right) \tag{7.2}$$

where r_n is the notional interest rate for contributions and r_p the discount rate for pensions. Since this is a public system, the riskless interest rate seems to be the suitable reference to assess the fairness of the system. In a notional account scheme, the value of r in Eq. (7.1) is easy to obtain if the notional interest rate used when accumulating the capital is the same with the interest rate used to convert the notional capital into a pension flow $r = r_n = r_p$). In this case, Eq. (7.2) leads to Eq. (7.1), but r can be lower, equal or higher than the riskless interest rate, deriving in an actuarially fair or unfair system. However, in practice, countries with notional accounts use different notional interest rates in both stages and not equal to the riskless interest rate. In this case, the assessment of Eq. (7.1) is more difficult, and individual circumstances can affect the value of r. For example, in Sweden the notional account is indexed annually on average earnings growth while at retirement the annuity factor uses an internal rate of return of 1.6%.

In a defined benefit scheme, actuarial fairness rarely occurs. The first pension depends on some measure of average revalued earnings (*B*), on the number of years of contributions $(j - e)$ and on the accrual rate for each year of service *a*:

$$p_j = B(j - e)a \tag{7.3}$$

To achieve actuarial fairness in a defined benefit system two conditions must occur. First, the measure of average earnings, *B*, should take into account the full career and each yearly earnings should be valorised using the fair interest rate. Then, $B = \frac{\sum_{i=e}^{j-1} w_i(1+r)^{j-i}}{j-e}$, and substituting Eq. (7.3) in (7.1), we get the second condition:

$$\begin{aligned} c\sum_{i=e}^{j-1} w_i(1+r)^{j-i} &= B(j-e)aA(r,\lambda,s,j,T) \\ &= \left(\frac{\sum_{i=e}^{j-1} w_i(1+r)^{j-i}}{j-e}\right)(j-e)aA(r,\lambda,s,j,T) \\ \rightarrow a &= \frac{c}{A(r,\lambda,s,j,T)} \end{aligned}$$

Consequently, the accrual rate, *a*, should be equal to the contribution rate divided by the annuity factor. Under these conditions, Eq. (7.1) is satisfied and the system is actuarially fair. However, in practice, countries with defined benefit schemes do not meet these two conditions. In most countries, the pensionable earnings reference is not the full career and the valorisation variable is prices or wages or a mix of both, but not the riskless interest rate. In addition, the accrual rate not always is constant for each year of service, reflecting redistributive purposes; and its value should be adjusted with mortality improvements to achieve the second condition but this is not the general case, and only recently, a few countries have incorporated sustainability factors.

On the other hand, most part of countries with defined benefit schemes have special rules to qualify for a pension or to compute the pension payment in the case of dangerous or unhealthy jobs. Therefore, these systems reflect partially social differences although we cannot say that a defined benefit scheme is a social actuarially fair system because the special rules do not have an actuarial base.

Although defined benefit systems are not, in general, actuarially fair, recent reforms in most countries tend to reinforce actuarial fairness, for example, moving to a full career as the pensionable earnings reference, linking benefits with life expectancy and changing the valorisation rule of contributions or the indexation rule of pensions.

The evaluation of actuarial fairness through Eq. (7.1), as we have noted, is more difficult in notional account plans with different interest rates in both stages and, especially, in defined benefit schemes. In fact, pension reports by official institutions like European Commission and OECD do not present the value of r. A unique methodology for all countries is quite impossible because of the diversity of pension systems. For example, measuring pension contributions is very problematic due to the variety of contingencies that they cover among countries. However, in our opinion, it is interesting to provide a reasonable methodology to compute the value of r in each country.[2] Although the results are not comparable by countries, they can be compared by periods within each country.

Regarding the data, if microdata are available, it is possible to estimate the internal rate of return of the pension system by aggregation of the contributions and expected benefits of a sample of new pensioners. This collective is the most suitable because they are at the retirement age, but the availability of their history of contributions is problematic. If microdata are not available, a theoretical value of r in Eq. (7.1) can be approached through case study-based calculations for an average or hypothetical worker, similar to the methodology used to compute the theoretical replacement rate.

7.3 Fairness in the Sense of Equity

Equity means the same deal for different groups of people and different individuals within groups. *Actuarial equity* entails the same r in Eq. (7.1) for individuals with different characteristics such as gender, level of earnings, lifetime earnings profile, career length or occupational categories and also for certain groups of workers with special rules (e.g. civil servants or self-employed). Note that the same r among individuals do not imply that this is the fair interest rate. Then, actuarial fairness and actuarial equity is not the same concept. In addition, the concept of actuarial fairness is defined across the population while actuarial equity only makes sense if we evaluate Eq. (7.1) for groups of individuals.

In funded and notional account schemes, actuarial equity in the active stage is ensured by definition (contributory equity), regardless of the level of the market rate of return of investments or the notional interest rate. The reason is that the accumulated capital in the individual account depends on the entire lifetime individual contributions and the interest rate is the same for all individuals. However, in the retirement stage, the pension payment is not based on specific annuity factors for each group, but on mortality rates across the population. Consequently, these systems give a better deal to individuals with higher life expectancy a priori (e.g. women or high-income workers); then, actuarial equity is not absolute.

In defined benefit schemes, actuarial equity is usually infringed in both stages. This is clear in the retirement stage because the pension does not have an actuarial

---

[2] Jimeno and Licandro (1999) and Devesa et al. (2012) attempt to obtain the internal rate of return of the Spanish pension systems.

base. Something similar occurs in the contribution stage because pension entitlements do not proportionally depend on the contribution effort (contributory inequity). Most countries use a measure of earnings that only consider the best years or the last years of the working career. In other cases, multiple accrual rates are applied depending on the career length. The result is that individuals get a different r when assessing Eq. (7.1) according to the earnings profile or the years of service.

Note that the evaluation of equity requires the application of Eq. (7.1) to compute the internal rate of return for each individual or group. Therefore, the same methodological difficulties as in the evaluation of actuarial fairness appear. In addition, if we have overcome these obstacles, we need some consensual measure of inequity. Some typical measures of dispersion are the standard deviation or the coefficient of variation. The comparability of this measure across countries seems problematic because the methodology to compute the internal rate of return is probably different in each country, but it can serve to assess pension reforms within a country from the point of view of equity.

In theory, actuarial equity could be improved establishing special rules, with an actuarial base, for groups of individuals with different life expectancy but, in practice, this is not possible because specific mortality tables are not available by relevant characteristics, except gender.

One special source of inequity is the existence of separate pension schemes for workers of certain sectors. In many countries, employees of the public and private sector have different statutory retirement age, contributory period for a full pension, accrual rates and so on. The result is that the replacement rate is usually higher for civil servants (see OECD 2016) and then, the internal rate of return is also higher than for private sector workers assuming that no differences exist in life expectancy. Recent pension reforms, however, tend to unify both schemes: new public sector workers are covered by the general scheme while the rest remains in the separate scheme.

7.4 Fairness in the Sense of Neutrality

The concept of fairness in the sense of neutrality, impartiality or equity between individuals is closely related with the previous concept of actuarial fairness. Firstly, as population mortality rates are dynamic, the fulfilment of actuarial fairness over time means also dynamic rules of computing the pension. Otherwise, an actuarially fair system can lead to an actuarially unfair system in the future if mortality rates change. In this case, actuarial fairness over time implies the same deal to succeeding generations. Then, actuarial fairness also means *intergenerational actuarial neutrality*. However, this feature could exist without actuarial fairness because this concept has to do with providing the same deal to individuals of different generations through actuarial adjustments linked to improvements in life expectancy. Then, if the system is actuarially unfair and we apply actuarially neutral adjustments for the next generations, the system will remain actuarially unfair. Perhaps, we can say that these are actuarially fair adjustments but this only ensures that the system is neutral or impartial between generations and not necessarily fair.

Although the aim of recent reforms in defined benefit pension systems is ensuring the financial sustainability, some countries have legislated automatic adjustment mechanisms linked to life expectancy that, at the same time, implies a strengthening of the intergenerational actuarial neutrality. Many countries in EU-28 have linked the statutory retirement age to life expectancy (Denmark, Greece, Cyprus, Italy, Netherland, Portugal and Slovakia) while in other countries (Finland, Portugal and Spain) a sustainability or life expectancy factor has been incorporated to the formula when computing the first pension. The exact link between life expectancy and retirement age or pension amount is different in each country but, in any case, it entails a movement towards intergenerational actuarial neutrality. About who bears life expectancy risk in pension schemes see Whitehouse (2007) and about the actuarially neutral way of relate mortality dynamics and pension parameters see Meneu et al. (2016). For example, following the notation in Eq. (7.1), an actuarial neutral adjustment in retirement age in period 1 with respect period 0 must ensure the condition:

$$A(r,\lambda,s_1,j_1,T) = A(r,\lambda,s_0,j_0,T) \tag{7.4}$$

In Eq. (7.4), s_1 is the new vector of conditional survival probabilities in period 1 and j_1 is the retirement age in period 1 that keeps actuarial neutrality. This implies a retirement age adjustment rule in such a way that the actuarial present value of pensions remains constant (see Meneu et al. 2016, for more details).

Table 7.1 shows the age of retirement that keeps constant the annuity factor, following Eq. (7.4), in three selected countries that have legislated an automatic link between retirement age and life expectancy: Denmark, Netherlands and Portugal. It is assumed that the age of reference is 65 years in 2015 in the three countries. The results in Table 7.1 reveal that Denmark expects a higher increase in retirement age because the assumed mortality improvements are also higher, especially for women

Table 7.1 Actuarially neutral adjustment in retirement age j_1 by 5-year period

	Denmark	Netherlands	Portugal
2015	65 y	65 y	65 y
2020	65 y 10 m	66	65 y 9 m
2025	66 y 7 m	66 y 7 m	66 y 3 m
2030	67 y 2 m	67 y 2 m	66 y 10 m
2035	67 y 10 m	67 y 9 m	67 y 4 m
2040	68 y 5 m	68 y 3 m	67 y 10 m
2045	69 y	68 y 10 m	68 y 3 m
2050	69 y 6 m	69 y 3 m	68 y 9 m

Survival probabilities from Eurostat (EUROPOP2013 mortality assumptions). The adjustment is the average of males and females with $r = 2\%$, $\lambda = 0\%$ and $j_0 = 65$.

(Denmark +3.9 years in life expectancy at the age of 65 in 2015–2050 period, Netherlands +3.7 and Portugal +3.4).

On the other hand, an actuarial neutral adjustment in the accrual rate, or in the first pension through Eq. (7.3), must verify:

$$a_1 = \frac{A(r, \lambda, s_0, j, T)}{A(r, \lambda, s_1, j, T)} a_0 \tag{7.5}$$

This type of adjustment consists of multiplying the initial accrual rate by a coefficient equal to the ratio of two annuity factors, with the survival probabilities of the base year in the numerator and the survival probabilities of the revision year in the denominator. Table 7.2 depicts the value of this ratio in three European countries with a legislated automatic accrual rate adjustment: Finland, Portugal and Spain. The specific formula of the adjustment is different in each country and also the year of reference, the age of retirement j and the value of r.[3] However, the results in Table 7.2 are obtained assuming the same parameters, except survival probabilities, in all three countries, with 2015 as the base year. As Table 7.2 shows, the adjustments are very similar in this group of countries because the assumptions about life expectancy improvements are analogous. Note also that the adjustment coefficient decreases faster in the first years than in the last ones, imitating the behaviour of the mortality assumptions in the population projections.

Oksanen (2005) uses a similar concept, *actuarial neutrality across generations*, but from a macroeconomic point of view. With an overlapping generation framework, his condition for actuarial neutrality across generations is that implicit pension debt (present value of next period pension) minus financial reserves of the system remains constant in relative terms. Then, he studies the effects at the macro level of

Table 7.2 Actuarially neutral accrual rate adjustment by 5-year period

	Spain	Finland	Portugal
2015	1.000	1.000	1.000
2020	0.969	0.981	0.972
2025	0.952	0.961	0.953
2030	0.937	0.942	0.934
2035	0.922	0.924	0.917
2040	0.908	0.908	0.901
2045	0.895	0.892	0.886
2050	0.883	0.878	0.872

Survival probabilities from Eurostat (EUROPOP2013 mortality assumptions). The adjustment is the average of males and females with $r = 2\%$ and $\lambda = 0\%$

[3]For example, the age or reference is 62 in Finland, 65 in Portugal and 67 in Spain. In addition, in Spain and Portugal, the adjustment is a ratio of life expectancies instead of a ratio of annuity factors.

an ageing population over different pension systems (totally funded, partially funded or pure PAYG).

The third concept is *intra-generational actuarial neutrality* or actuarial neutrality within generations. This concept has to do with obtaining the same actuarial present value of benefits regardless of the age retirement. Queisser and Whitehouse (2006) refer to this concept with the expression of actuarial neutrality while Belloni and Maccheroni (2013) use the term marginal actuarial fairness. This characteristic compares individuals within the same cohort who retire at different ages.

In order to achieve actuarial neutrality within generations in defined benefit systems, incentives or penalizations when delaying or anticipating the age of retirement must have an actuarial base. Again, this type of actuarial neutrality could occur with or without actuarial fairness, because it only depends on the way in which adjustments for retirement at different ages are calculated.

The expression for an actuarially neutral adjustment emerges when we require that the pension wealth for retiring today is the same as the pension wealth for retiring 1 year later, assuming that no additional pension entitlements have been accrued in that additional year. The pension wealth for an individual who retires at the age of j and receives immediately the pension is the product of the first pension amount (p_j) by the annuity factor. However, if the individual decides to claim the pension 1 year later ($j + 1$), the pension wealth must considerer the probability of die (q_j) before obtaining the pension. Finally, to compare the pension wealth in two periods we also need the discount factor. Then, using the previous notation, we get:

$$\underbrace{p_j A(r,\lambda,s,j,T)}_{\substack{\text{Pension wealth when} \\ \text{retiring at the age } j}} = \underbrace{\frac{p_{j+1} A(r,\lambda,s,j+1,T)\left(1-q_j\right)}{1+r}}_{\substack{\text{Pension wealth when delaying 1 year} \\ \text{the withdrawal of the pension (valued in } j)}} \tag{7.6}$$

From Eq. (7.6) we get the actuarially neutral incentive (α) of delaying from j to $j + 1$ the withdrawal of benefits:

$$\begin{aligned} p_{j+1} &= p_j \frac{A(r,\lambda,s,j,T)}{A(r,\lambda,s,j+1,T)} \frac{1+r}{\left(1-q_j\right)} = p_j(1+\alpha) \\ \rightarrow \qquad \alpha &= \frac{A(r,\lambda,s,j,T)}{A(r,\lambda,s,j+1,T)} \frac{1+r}{\left(1-q_j\right)} - 1 \end{aligned} \tag{7.7}$$

Most countries in the EU have penalties for early retirement and incentives to delay the moment of retirement, but their values do not usually have an actuarial base. For example, the result of Eq. (7.7) would imply variable incentives with age because mortality rates are not constant, while the legislated rule in pension systems consists in a constant bonus per year of delay. In addition, the value of the penalty or

Table 7.3 Annual actuarially neutral adjustments (α) by age

	Germany		Spain	
Age	2015	2035	2015	2035
61	5.9%	5.4%	5.6%	5.2%
62	6.1%	5.6%	5.8%	5.3%
63	6.3%	5.7%	6.0%	5.5%
64	6.5%	5.9%	6.2%	5.7%
65	6.8%	6.1%	6.4%	5.8%
66	7.0%	6.3%	6.6%	6.0%
67	7.3%	6.5%	6.8%	6.2%
68	7.6%	6.8%	7.1%	6.5%
69	7.9%	7.0%	7.4%	6.7%

Survival probabilities from Eurostat (EUROPOP2013 mortality assumptions). α is the average of males and females with $r = 2\%$ and $\lambda = 0\%$

the bonus should be similar in countries with comparable life expectancy but this is not the case and the differences are relevant.

Table 7.3 shows the value of the adjustment in two selected European countries, Germany and Spain, with different life expectancy. Adjustments for deferring the pension at the age of 66 instead of 65 are lower in Spain (6.4%) than in Germany (6.8%) because the life expectancy at the age of 65 is higher (+1.1 years for men and +1.8 years for women). Similarly, if a worker decides to anticipate the retirement at the age of 64, the penalty should be 6.5% in Germany and 6.2% in Spain in 2015. The legislated reduction coefficient is 0.3% per month in Germany, clearly lower than the actuarially neutral, and 1.5–1.875% per quarter in Spain, depending on the contributory period. In Spain, however, the incentive for delaying 1 year the retirement is 2–4%, depending on the contributory period, lower than the actuarially neutral value and discouraging the postponement of retirement.

Note also in Table 7.3 that the extra pension for delaying the retirement one additional year should be increasing with age. In these cases, the cumulative incentives or penalties are multiplicative. Finally, the level of the adjustments is dynamic, with lower values in 2035 than in 2015 as life expectancy improves.

In funded and notional account defined contribution systems, pension payments are computed in an actuarial base, but assuming that the individual is alive at that age. Then, actuarial neutrality is only approximately fulfilled because the actuarial calculations do not consider the mortality rate from age j to age $j + 1$.

Both concepts of intra- and intergenerational actuarial neutrality differ from the concepts of actuarial fairness or actuarial equity in the periods of time that are considered. Actuarial fairness or actuarial equity takes into account the complete lifetime of contributions and pensions while actuarial neutrality only needs marginal adjustments.

7.5 Fairness in the Sense of Solidarity

The concept of *social fairness* in a pension system refers to the solidarity side of the system. The recent reform process tends to reinforce the actuarial fairness and the fiscal sustainability of the pension system but also entails a higher risk of receiving low pensions for groups of workers with low earnings or short careers. In this sense, and following the Actuarial Association of Europe (2016), the fundamental challenge is to find the right balance between actuarial fairness and social justice.

Social fairness works through different mechanisms. Most of the pension systems has a non-earnings-related part that ensures a minimum income provision for older people without sufficient resources: universal flat rate pension, guaranteed pensions, contributory minimum pension or means-tested minimum income. The minimum income provision is an important part of the adequacy of the pension system because of its role in preventing poverty among older people; then, the social solidarity feature of pension systems is closely related with adequacy of pensions.

Social solidarity implies redistribution of income and this happens in pension systems with some type of minimum income provision. There are, however, other mechanisms of redistribution and solidarity: applying a lower indexation for higher pensions, limiting maximum pension, increasing pension rights in the case of unemployment or maternity periods or reducing the statutory retirement age for some unhealthy or dangerous jobs, for example.

The Actuarial Association of Europe, AAE (European Commission 2015b), uses the expression social fairness to require adjustments in the retirement age as life expectancy rises. Keeping constant the ratio between cohort life expectancy at the effective pension age and years of working life completed up the effective pension age gives a measure of fairness of the pension age in maintaining a balance between working and pension life. For example, France applies a *coefficient of proration* to reduce the pension level in a proportion equal to the ratio between the contributory period and the reference career length, which depends on life expectancy. To incorporate social solidarity, we can compute this ratio by cohort, socio-economic group and employment category and/or include periods of unemployment, disability or maternity when computing the working life.

Table 7.4 shows the projected evolution of this ratio in a group of selected European countries. In all these countries except Sweden it is projected a rise in the statutory retirement age. In four countries, Denmark, Greece, Italy and Portugal, exists an automatic link between statutory retirement age and life expectancy. France has an automatic link between life expectancy and the reference career length.

Note in Table 7.4 that the results by countries are irregular, showing that not only the pension policy is important (statutory retirement age) but also the projected individual behaviour (effective exit age) matters.

Intergenerational solidarity is other concept linked to pay-as-you-go pension systems. These retirement schemes allow older people to maintain their living standard after retirement through a redistribution of income from young people. However, population ageing demands some adjustments in key parameters; in other

Table 7.4 Life expectancy at average effective exit age from the labour market over average length of working career by gender (%)

	Males		Females	
	2014	2040	2014	2040
Denmark	39.3	42.1	54.6	52.2
Germany	41.0	44.9	52.2	55.4
Greece	45.2	43.4	53.9	53.6
Spain	49.7	46.2	57.1	52.6
France	56.3	55.4	70.7	67.9
Italy	54.7	47.4	68.7	58.8
Portugal	44.1	44.2	54.1	53.3
Sweden	39.9	45.4	51.8	58.1
UK	40.9	43.8	51.3	51.2

Source: The 2015 Ageing Report (European Commission 2015a)

Table 7.5 65 old-age dependency ratio (%) and age *x* to keep constant the ratio at the initial level

	2015	2040	Age *x*
Denmark	29.4	40.4	69 y 5 m
Germany	32.5	50.3	71 y 4 m
Greece	32.9	59.2	72 y 1 m
Spain	28.3	54.9	72 y 9 m
France	29.8	46.0	71 y 2 m
Italy	34.2	58.1	71 y 5 m
Portugal	31.6	56.4	72 y 1 m
Sweden	31.6	37.7	67 y 7 m
UK	28.0	39.2	69 y 10 m

Source: Population projection EUROPOP2013 (Eurostat)

case, young generations should increase their contributions to bear the extra cost. In the limit, this can imply an excess of solidarity from young to old people, breaking the generational equity. If the extra burden is financed with new government debt, future generations will pay more taxes and lose welfare. Then, to preserve intergenerational solidarity in a reasonable level, it is recommended to establish some automatic mechanism to adjust the retirement age as the population ages.

In this sense, the Actuarial Association of Europe (European Commission 2015b) suggests the concept of intergenerational fairness. The AAE proposes to adjust key variables of work (definition of active age population) and retirement to keep constant the demographic x old-age dependency ratio (people aged x and over/ people aged 16 up to x) or the economic old-age dependency ratio (pensioners/ contributors between 16 and x), where x is the legislated future pension age.

Table 7.5 shows the 65 old-age dependency ratio in 2015 and 2040 and the x value that would keep constant the old-age dependency ratio at the initial level in the same group of European countries as in Table 7.4.

The figures in Table 7.5 are clearly influenced by past demography (fertility and migration) and by mortality assumptions for the future. Logically, the higher the increase in the old-age dependency ratio, the higher the age required in the future to maintain the ratio at the initial level. This is a way to illustrate the demographic change, with serious differences between Spain and Sweden, for example, but it could be partially compensated if economic growth was robust enough. In this case, increasing employment rates, especially in the 55–74 age group, would cause a lesser decline in the economic old-age dependency ratio than in the demographic old-age dependency ratio. For example, according to the 2015 Ageing Report (European Commission 2015a), the old-age dependency ratio (15–64 age group) in Spain will evolve from 27% in 2013 to 54% in 2040 (factor 2) while the economic old-age dependency ratio (15–64 age group) is projected to be 66% in 2040 from 48% in 2013 (factor 1.375). In Sweden, however, it is projected that both ratios will be multiplied by 1.2.

7.6 Fairness in the Sense of Integrity

Integrity is a broad concept that includes a range of features of a pension system. In this sense, fairness means honesty, which can be understood as transparency, regulatory stability, efficiency and so on. Improving these features entails a higher confidence of individuals in their pension system. The integrity side of a pension system appears as the third dimension of the Melbourne Mercer Global Pension Index, after adequacy and sustainability, but focuses on the private sector system (Mercer 2016). However, integrity can be extended to the public pension system.

Transparency implies a set of actuations. Social security authority should publish all the underlying variables that affect the value of certain parameters. For example, valorisation of contributions or indexation of pensions usually depends on consumer price index and/or average wage growth. Recently, some countries have incorporated more complex mechanisms, through sustainability factors, depending on life expectancy, pensioner to contribution ratio, revenues and expenses of the social security system, etc. People should know the current value of these variables and the resulting values for the parameters of the pension system. It would be useful to incorporate these data in an annual report together with an outlook of the current and prospective situation of the main features of the pension system.

In addition, contributors should be provided with individual information about the projected pension level under different scenarios of retirement age, taking into account the past contributions and assuming reasonable values for the variables in the future. This would allow people to take optimal decisions about consumption and saving and about the age of retirement. In this context, the orange envelope of Sweden can be considered a good practice.

At the same time, the pension system should be, to a large degree, free of policy risk. Demographic ageing often triggers pension policy decisions that suppose unanticipated changes in pension rules like qualifying conditions, legal retirement age or pension entitlements. These repeated reforms disturb the process of decision-making by individuals. To prevent this situation, it would be desirable to reach a political consensus about a few automatic adjustment mechanisms, for example, linking some parameters to life expectancy or to the budget balance of the pension system. In this way, unpleasant reforms would be politically easier to adopt and socially more comprehensible.

Efficiency is an important component of the integrity of a pension system. Perhaps, the central side of efficiency has to do with a low level of administration and transaction costs. Public pension schemes usually manage very large size funds, about 10–15% of GDP, so economies of scale are significant. Improvements in management when collecting contributions or paying benefits can lead to important savings. Financial and funds management are more important in funded systems but also in pay-as-you-go schemes with a capital fund. Total management cost as a percentage of total expenses of social security is an indicator that should be monitored and reduced.

Efficiency also means to have adequate tools to fight against fraud. In this sense, it is necessary to innovate, maintain and manage the social security information system, including computer elements and computer applications, as well as ensuring the confidentiality and security of the data. Some actions to prevent fraud include controlling the fulfilment of the contributory obligations, monitoring the contributory debt of companies, checking the requirements to get a pension, supervising the situation of disability pensioners (medical controls), controlling the living of old-age pensioners and so on. An indicator to assess this side of efficiency could be the amount of money collected as a result of inspections.

An efficient use of human and material resources of the social security system provides a better service to citizens. Some indicators that should be observed are the average time between a request and a resolution of a pension, the percentage of pensions controlled and reviewed, the valuation of social security services through surveys, the number of social security employee attending training courses, the quantity and quality of reports and statistics produced, etc.

7.7 Conclusions

In this chapter we have tried to clarify the different meanings of the notion of fairness of a pension system. The most important is the sense of justice or actuarial fairness, which has to do with a balanced relationship between contributions and benefits along the lifetime. Unfortunately, it is difficult to measure the internal rate of return of the flow of contributions and benefits for the overall pension system. However, we think that it is quite plausible to adopt an acceptable methodology to obtain the internal rate of return, on an individual basis, for an assumed hypothetical worker with parameters close to the economy-wide average. We encourage international institutions like European Commission or OECD to promote a consensual methodology.

Comparing the internal rate of return for different individuals or groups of individuals, we can assess the actuarial equity. This sense of fairness means that each individual must get the same deal out of the pension system. This makes sense a priori, using mortality probabilities, because a posteriori who lives longer will get a better deal. Besides the methodological difficulties of computing the internal rate of return, there exists another one: the choice of the most suitable measure of dispersion to compute the inequity. The coefficient of variation of the internal rate of return seems a good indicator of equity. The aim is not to obtain a zero-dispersion value among all the individuals because it could be socially desirable to offer a better deal for certain groups but it would be interesting to reduce differences between some groups and within each group. A recommendation of pension policy in this field is to eliminate special pension rules depending on occupations or economic sectors (e.g. civil servants) except for certain unhealthy or risky jobs with a probably shorter life expectancy.

One way to reach actuarial equity is applying marginal adjustments with an actuarial support in the case of retirement at different ages. This leads to the concept of actuarial neutrality. In funded and notional account schemes this requirement is approximately fulfilled by definition. Then, it is recommended, for defined benefit systems, to establish penalties and incentives in an actuarial neutral way in the case of anticipating or delaying the retirement. We have suggested a formula to compute these corrections and we have shown that current adjustments in some countries are not actuarially neutral. In a similar way, actuarial neutrality can be applied to adjust the first pension for individuals of succeeding generations with higher life expectancy. This policy is an alternative to an increase in retirement age. We have also proposed a formula for this adjustment and we have computed it for three European countries that have legislated a similar rule.

We have also focused our attention in the solidarity side of the pension system. In this context, social fairness is closely related with adequacy, especially in the capacity of preventing poverty among older people. We propose to maintain a component of the pension system that guarantees a minimum pension, if the pensioner does not have other income sources, even in the case of short careers or low earnings contributory history. In addition, to preserve intergenerational solidarity in an adequate level, it is recommended to raise the retirement age in line with life expectancy. In this way, all the society share the extra cost of an ageing population and not only young generations.

Our final recommendations to reach a fair pension system include a set of actions to improve transparency, information to future pensioners, management and fight against fraud. The use of information and communication technologies to manage contributions and benefit payments can lead to important savings in administration and transaction costs. The provision of aggregate information about the fiscal balance and the dynamic evolution of the key parameters of the system allows people to rely more on the public system and to understand some undesirable reform. Finally, delivering individual information about the future pension entitlements helps people to take optimal decisions throughout the life cycle.

References

Aaron, H. J. (1966). The social insurance paradox. *Canadian Journal of Economics and Political Science, 32*, 371–374.

Actuarial Association of Europe. (2016). The Ageing of the EU – implications for pensions, Discussion paper. http://actuary.eu/documents/AAE-The-ageing-of-the-EU_DEF.pdf

Belloni, M., & Maccheroni, C. (2013). Actuarial fairness when longevity increases: an evaluation of the Italian pension system. *The Geneva Papers on Risk and Insurance - Issues and Practice, 38*, 638–674.

Devesa, J. E., Devesa, M., Meneu, R., Nagore, A., Domínguez, I., & Encinas, B. (2012). Equidad y sostenibilidad como objetivos ante la reforma del sistema contributivo de pensiones de jubilación. *Hacienda Pública Española, 201*(2/2012), 9–38.

European Commission. (2015a). The 2015 ageing report - Economic and budgetary projections for the 28 EU Member States (2013-2060). European Economy 3/2015.

European Commission. (2015b). The 2015 Pension adequacy report: Current and future income adequacy in old age in the EU. Volume I.

Jimeno, J. F., & Licandro, O. (1999). La tasa interna de rentabilidad y el equilibrio financiero del Sistema español de pensiones de jubilación. *Investigaciones Económicas, 23*(1), 129–143.

Meneu, R., Devesa, E., Devesa, M., Domínguez, I., Encinas, B. (2016). Adjustment mechanisms and intergenerational actuarial neutrality in pension reforms. *International Social Security Review 69*(1), 87–107.

Mercer. (2016). *Melbourne Mercer Global Pension Index*. Melbourne: Australian Centre for Financial Studies.

OECD. (2016). *OECD pensions outlook 2016*. Paris: OECD Publishing. https://doi.org/10.1787/pens_outlook-2016-en.

Oksanen, H. (2005). Actuarial neutrality across generations applied to public pensions under population ageing: Effects on government finances and national saving. European Economy Economic Papers, no. 230.

Queisser, M., & Whitehouse, E. (2006). *Neutral or fair? actuarial concepts and pension-system design. OECD Social, Employment and Migration Working Papers, no. 40*. Paris: OECD Publishing.

Samuelson, P. (1958). An exact consumption-loan model of interest with or without the social contrivance of money. *The Journal of Political Economy, 66*(6), 467–482.

Whitehouse, E. (2007). *Life-expectancy risk and pensions: who bears the burden? OECD Social, Employment and Migration Working Papers, n° 60*. Paris: OECD Publishing.

Chapter 8
Adequacy of Public Pension Systems

Beatriz Rosado-Cebrian, Marta Peris-Ortiz, and Carlos Rueda-Armengot

Abstract Pensions are the main source of income in old age. Their main value is provided, in most countries, by public pension systems. Therefore, one of the main challenges for governments and policymakers is to enable people to smooth consumption over the life cycle in an appropriate scale. This implies that pensions must be sufficient to prevent poverty and social exclusion, or even to provide enough income allowing to maintain the previous standard of living, and also to limit the gender gap between men and women. In recent years there has been a wave of reforms of public pension systems with the main objective to improve their financial sustainability both in the medium and long term. Many of the measures carried out within these reforms have negative effects on the adequacy of pension systems because they involve, in one way or another, e.g. a decrease in the replacement rate, a lower indexation. Therefore, reconciling the objectives of sustainability and adequacy is a priority challenge for pension policymakers in the coming years. Because of that, the aim of this chapter is to explore the concept of adequacy, different means of its measurement, the indicators used in cross-country studies on adequacy and how that measurement at different moments of time can help to take action in one way or another.

Keywords Public pension systems · Pension policy · Adequacy · Sustainability · Replacement rate · Indexation · Rate of coverage

B. Rosado-Cebrian (✉)
Department of Financial Economics and Accounting, University of Extremadura, Cáceres, Extremadura, Spain
e-mail: brosadot@unex.es

M. Peris-Ortiz · C. Rueda-Armengot
Departamento de Organización de Empresas, Universitat Politècnica de València, Valencia, Spain
e-mail: mperis@doe.upv.es; crueda@doe.upv.es

M. Peris-Ortiz et al. (eds.), *Economic Challenges of Pension Systems*,
https://doi.org/10.1007/978-3-030-37912-4_8

8.1 Introduction

Many countries all over the world have been facing the socio-economic problems caused by deteriorating demographics. The increasing life expectancy which is a very positive phenomena since people live longer and stay healthy longer is accompanied very often by decreasing birth rates. As a result, pension systems have experienced and especially will experience in the future the problem of financial sustainability since the population of pensioners has been increasing and the population of workers has been decreasing. This process expressed by growing dependency ratios threatens the adequacy of pensions, since it is conditioned by a financial balance of a pension system, mainly in the long run. Therefore, many countries have decided to reform their pension systems changing not only some parameters like contribution rates, pension benefits or pension age but also altering the general model by replacing unfunded schemes with funded ones or the defined benefit formula with the defined contribution one. However, today's pension systems have the nature of hybrids rather than the form of pure theoretical models. In the majority of countries, pension reforms aim at strengthening the adequacy of pensions. However, it does not mean an increase in generosity of pensions, but rather the maintenance of pensions at a minimum required level. Therefore, public pension systems seem to evolve in the direction of poverty protection instead of consumption smoothing.

Regardless of the directions of pension reforms, old-age pensions remain one of the main elements of the welfare state, since they are the main source of income after retirement. Consequently, governments face major challenges to make these pensions sustainable and adequate to protect individuals from the poverty at old age (see, e.g. Banks et al. 1998; Bernheim et al. 2000; Fornero et al. 2009; Lusardi and Mitchell 2007; Munnell et al. 2006; or Skinner 2007).

In May 2012 the "Adequacy of pensions in the European Union 2010-2050" report was submitted, conducted by the Directorate General for Employment, Social Affairs and Equal Opportunities Commission and the Social Protection Committee (SPC) of the European Union. This report, focused on analysing the adequacy of pensions, supplemented the Economic Policy Committee (EPC) report on ageing, aimed at sustainability aspects of pensions from a public budget perspective. This report highlighted the main demographic challenge faced by the European society: the progressive increase in life expectancy and the low birth rate. This challenge implies that pension systems need to be adapted periodically to remain sustainable and adequate, and, given the differences between countries, there is no single answer valid for all. In October 2015, the same institution introduced a new version of the report on the adequacy of pensions, entitled "The 2015 Pension adequacy report: current and future income adequacy in old age in the EU", written by the same authors. In addition, all forms of income in the elderly, both public and private, for men and women, are being investigated in the report, pointing out the importance of the pension in relation to other resources available to retirees, including their real estate assets and access to free or subsidized public services.

Trying to reconcile the sustainability of pension systems with the adequacy of pensions, significant advances in the sustainability of pension systems have been achieved through different reforms in the parameters of pension systems. Therefore, the challenge to achieve the consensus between sustainability and adequacy requires significant efforts to promote different solutions in the short, medium and long term (i.e. the extension of working life, delaying retirement, effective health policy, effective education process and updating skills through permanent training and lifelong learning). Adequacy can also be strengthened through additional contributions to supplementary pension schemes. The analysis of changes in the replacement rates shows that the sustainability of public pensions has been achieved through the reduction of future adequacy. The replacement rate of the last salary with respect to the first pension varies greatly throughout countries. However, the dominant role of the state in ensuring pension adequacy seems to become less and less popular and governments strive for reforming pension systems towards a rational mix between the public and private sector. This way, the responsibility for the future benefits is shared between the government, employers, employees and private financial institutions.

All countries with public pension systems have faced, in one way or another, the challenge of sustainability, with reforms, modernizations, adaptations, homogeneous solutions to the countries around them and even testing new systems. But the adequacy of pensions has not been achieved yet in most of them. As the European Commission said on the pension adequacy in its White Paper, "the higher sustainability of public pension expenditure in view of population ageing has been achieved in a partial trade off with the level and security of adequacy (European Commission 2012a, b)".

8.2 Adequacy of Pension Concept

Adequacy is a very complex concept due to its close relationship with actuarial equity and sustainability of a pension system, although the adequacy of pensions is an objective in and of itself.

The key question that arises when investigating the adequacy of pensions is: what is the level (of income, consumption) at which adequacy is achieved? It can be said that the adequacy of retirement income is a relative measure and that there is no single approach, as it depends on the purpose and who uses it (Bajtelsmit et al. 2013).

If we analyse the studies and researches delivered by international institutions conducted in the area of pensions, we can find very homogenous definitions of adequacy. For example, the World Bank defines an adequate pension system as "one which guarantees retirees a level of income enough to protect them from poverty and allow them a certain level of consumption during the rest of their life cycle" (Holzman and Hinz 2005). The European Commission set down that an adequate pension system is one which prevents poverty among the elderly; allows people to maintain, at a reasonable degree, their living standard after retirement; and promotes intra- and intergenerational solidarity (European Commission 2003). The International Labour Organization (ILO 1998) states that the purpose of a pension system is "to ensure an adequate standard of living above the poverty line for the rest of the life of a retiree". The Organization for Economic Cooperation and Development considers an adequate system of pensions as one which replaces the income of a worker to a degree that allows him to maintain a standard of retirement living comparable to that enjoyed during his working life, despite retirement income often not replacing wages (OECD 2013).

Therefore, to summarize the concepts of pension adequacy mentioned before, we can find their common elements. The first one is protection against poverty, and the other one is maintaining a reasonable standard of living. But it is easily deductible that both concepts are relative and this is the main source of its complexity.

8.2.1 Protection Against Poverty

The poverty threshold, both relative and absolute, can vary significantly depending on the country and depending on the economic, demographic and statistical elements that it uses to define it. As a result, the most commonly used indicator is AROPE (At Risk of Poverty or Social Exclusion), which was initially defined by the European Commission and is now widely accepted. This indicator, which in the case of pensions is usually used for the population aged over 65 years, allows to know the measure of the risk of poverty and/or social exclusion that a country has at a given time, so it is considered a static indicator. Given that the pension is the main source of income after that age, to be adequate to meet the basic needs and consumption makes it also a way of fighting against poverty. That is why both concepts are closely linked: greater adequacy means, in a general way, a lower poverty index of the population.

Table 8.1 includes the AROPE 65+ indicators for EU countries in the years 2006–2015. For 17 countries the increasing trends in poverty can be identified, which is a negative phenomenon. In other cases the poverty rate has decreased, especially in Czech Republic, in Hungary or in Poland. Although the economic crisis and the flexibility with which pension systems are adapted to its consequences are main drivers of this deterioration, the reform processes undertaken in some countries in the last years (e.g. in Spain or Ireland), the definitive organization of their pension systems (e.g. Estonia, Lithuania or Slovenia), or even the consolidation of long-standing reforms to improve pension systems (e.g. in Luxembourg, the Netherlands or Switzerland) may have also affected the poverty indicators.

It is important to point out a clear consequence of these data: the difficult reconciliation of sustainability and adequacy objectives when undertaking or consolidating pension reforms.

The concept of "risk of poverty", following the guidelines set out in the Europe 2020 Strategy, has been expanded to consider not only monetary terms (income

Table 8.1 AROPE 65+ indicator (2006–2015) European Union countries

Country	2006	2007	2008	2009	2010	2011	2012	2013	2014	2015
Austria	25.1	24.7	25.9	25.3	26.0	27.1	25.8	25.9	25.4	25.6
Belgium	26.8	27.5	27.0	26.7	26.7	27.8	27.7	26.3	27.5	26.7
Bulgaria	24.7	25.5	27.1	26.4	27.1	27.4	25.9	26.7	27.3	28.4
Croatia	:	:	:	:	30.0	30.7	30.6	29.7	29.9	31.0
Cyprus	21.6	21.0	22.9	23.6	23.5	23.5	23.5	24.3	24.6	25.4
Czech Republic	21.6	20.1	20.0	17.9	18.1	18.0	17.6	16.6	17.2	16.8
Denmark	28.0	27.1	27.8	31.2	29.1	27.9	27.4	27.8	26.9	25.8
Estonia	24.6	25.2	24.7	25.9	24.9	24.9	24.8	25.4	28.4	27.8
Euroarea19	24.8	24.6	24.2	24.4	25.2	25.7	25.2	25.5	25.8	25.6
EU28	:	:	:	:	26.0	26.4	25.8	26.0	26.1	25.9
Finland	28.6	28.9	27.3	26.2	27.0	27.4	26.9	26.4	27.6	26.8
France	24.9	26.4	23.5	24.0	24.9	24.7	23.8	24.4	24.0	23.9
Germany	25.7	24.8	24.2	24.1	24.2	25.1	24.3	24.4	25.0	25.1
Greece	23.4	23.7	23.3	22.7	23.8	24.8	26.8	28.0	26.0	25.5
Hungary	29.6	29.3	30.4	28.9	28.4	29.0	27.3	27.0	26.6	25.7
Iceland	18.5	18.2	19.0	19.7	22.8	23.1	23.1	22.7	21.2	20.6
Ireland	32.8	33.1	34.0	37.5	39.9	39.6	39.3	38.5	37.2	:
Italy	23.7	23.7	23.5	23.3	23.7	24.6	24.5	24.6	24.7	25.4
Latvia	28.0	27.5	30.2	31.0	28.5	26.8	25.7	26.0	27.0	27.3
Lithuania	26.6	25.5	27.4	28.6	31.3	30.2	28.4	30.3	27.5	28.6
Luxembourg	23.6	23.4	23.6	27.0	29.1	27.2	29.0	29.4	27.6	27.2
Macedonia	:	:	:	:	:	:	28.8	26.8	24.8	:
Malta	21.3	21.5	22.9	22.9	23.5	23.2	24.0	23.3	23.8	23.7
Netherlands	21.0	20.6	19.9	20.5	21.1	20.9	20.6	20.8	21.3	22.2
Norway	30.6	27.7	25.6	25.2	26.6	29.6	25.8	26.0	24.8	26.5
Poland	28.6	26.5	25.1	23.6	24.4	24.1	22.9	23.0	23.1	22.9
Portugal	25.1	24.2	24.9	24.3	26.4	25.4	25.3	25.5	26.7	26.4
Romania	:	31.5	30.8	28.7	27.8	29.2	28.8	28.2	28.8	29.3
Serbia	:	:	:	:	:	:	:	31.8	32.6	37.2
Slovakia	20.0	18.2	18.4	17.1	19.8	19.5	20.0	20.1	19.6	19.0
Slovenia	24.2	23.1	23.0	22.0	24.2	24.2	25.2	25.3	25.1	24.8
Spain	24.6	23.7	25.7	26.9	28.8	30.0	29.1	30.0	31.1	30.1
Sweden	29.0	27.5	28.5	26.6	26.7	27.9	27.4	27.1	28.5	26.9
Switzerland	:	22.7	22.2	22.6	22.9	23.4	23.4	22.8	24.3	:
Turkey	27.4	25.8	25.8	26.7	26.5	25.0	25.3	24.8	:	:
United Kingdom	30.1	29.7	28.9	30.4	31.0	30.5	29.7	30.1	29.4	29.2

Source: Eurostat. (updated 15.11.2016, extracted 05.12.2016)
Note: ":" means "data not available"

level) but also using a multidimensional approach to define poverty, incorporating the sub-indicators "poverty risk rate after social transfers", "severe material shortage" and "low labour intensity households". According to the Europe 2020 Strategy, people are considered at risk of poverty and/or social exclusion in the following three situations: (I) living with low incomes (60% of the median equivalent income or per unit of consumption), (II) people suffering severe material deprivation (4 out of 9 defined items) and (III) people living in households with a very low employment intensity (below 20%).[1] Because of this, ensuring a minimum pension income can be considered a solution to avoid the risk of poverty.

In any case, there is no correct answer as to what the minimum pension amount should be, as it depends on a number of different socio-economic factors in each of the countries. However, it is suggested that a minimum pension of about 30% of national average earnings adequately meet the goal of poverty alleviation (Mercer 2016). This level was chosen in 2009 when it was slightly above the average OECD, establishing 27% for pensions in the first quartile of countries, as shown in OECD (2009). The average basic pension in the first 18 OECD countries ranked by its economy (OECD 2015, pp.126) was 20.1%, so a range of 10–30% remains reasonable. However, although this indicator reveals a low income point at which people are at risk of poverty and/or social exclusion, it is still a static and unique measure for a country, state or region, and subject to temporary changes, which is not sufficient to measure the adequacy of pensions or to compare countries on the basis of this measure.

8.2.2 Maintenance of a Reasonable Standard of Living

As in all approaches to the measurement of the adequacy of pensions, the definition of these standards of living has its pros and cons and is subject to considerable debate[2] about what they represent as adequate levels of life and how it can reflect realistically the diversity of ways of living and models that households have, with regard to pensions (Harmer Pension Review 2008). Therefore, it is clear that a "reasonable standard of living" cannot represent the same for different citizens, since it will be given by all the social and economic environmental conditions, as well as the way of life in which each individual has developed his career. Many economists and legislators argue that households do not save enough to maintain an adequate standard of living during retirement and fully trust their future welfare to the amount of the public pension. However, there is no consensus answer to the question about what a reasonable standard of living is, even though it is crucial for designing an efficient pension system and incentives for private savings.

In Binswanger and Schunk (2011), an interesting approach was made to this concept, conducting a survey to retired US and the Netherlands. Their findings indicate that, for the majority, retirement expenses may be at least 80% of expenditure during working life and that the desired replacement rates depend heavily on pre-retirement income levels. In contrast, Banks et al. (2005) already indicated, in his

[1]In the case of being included in two or three conditions, people will be counted only once.

[2]A further discussion of these points can be read in Whiteford and Henman (1998).

study of British pensioners, that the minimum to maintain a reasonable standard of living requirement was to overcome the poverty line.

This may be due to the fact that individuals simply adopt attitudes by default (Beshears et al. 2006) and lack the willpower to save enough (Thaler 1994) or, as indicated by Skinner (2007), the fact that choosing an appropriate savings plan that implements a specific life cycle consumption profile is highly complex due to the widespread lack of specific financial culture.

On the other hand, deducing people's true preferences for their actual retirement options would be difficult even in the absence of this provision, since actual options may be constrained by the presence of a mandatory pension system. This is a particular concern for many European countries, where pension systems have relatively high replacement rates above 70% (see OECD 2007).

In short, it is important to note that the standard of living of retired people, measured by the current level of their pension, depends on the good performance of the public pension system in the past, so that if the change comes, better or worse, the minimum standard of living required will change in the same direction. In addition, the pensioner's wealth, particularly the possession of a house in property and the amount of private savings, has a positive effect on the relative living standards of older people. This entirely means that the standard of living is not a sufficient measure to assess the adequacy of pensions.

8.3 Pension Adequacy Measure Indicators

In order to measure adequacy, it is necessary to consider the situation of both current and future pensioners, since the various reforms in the public pension systems are gradually implemented.

The measurement of the adequacy of pensions is a challenge with several dimensions, including incomes from the three pillars of pensions, alternative sources of income and wealth for the elderly (e.g. housing or work), tax treatment and access of the elderly to services and goods in kind provided by the states. The minimum net security income provisions, or minimum pensions, for those who were unable to contribute sufficiently to pension are very relevant, particularly in the fight against poverty in old age.

Until many years ago, and even today, the measurement of the adequacy of pensions has been made through economic indicators, which allow representing an economic reality in a quantitative and direct way. It is usually an official statistic or a simple ratio, which is a measurement of a variable over a period of time. These indicators have not lost any validity, they are absolutely necessary measurements to approach the concepts they intend to measure, but, as we will see below, given the complexity of the current world and the accumulation of available and necessary information, they become insufficient as a single measure.

Probably the weakness of any evaluation is to find a quantifiable indicator that adequately reflects the objective pursued, and this task is more difficult if it is intended to find a common indicator for several countries in order to be able to compare them. The European Union, through the European System of Integrated Social Protection Statistics (ESSPROS), has invested to achieve this, although in reality the different surveys on the labour force or living conditions carried out through the various statistical institutes in each country are used (Duran-Heras 2012).

Some of the most relevant and most used indicators (also called "first-line" indicators) to measure aspects of pension adequacy, by themselves or in combination with each other, are shown in the following Table 8.2, classified by their different concepts of measurement.

It can be clearly seen that these indicators try to measure the extent to which the income is responsible for the well-being or the poverty of the retiree, now or in the future, which is consistent with the concept of adequacy. The concept of inequalities is included in both the gender gap and income distribution variants, since both can be causes of poverty in pensions. Likewise, the most mentioned indicator is the replacement rate.

The replacement rate, in any of its variants (gross, net, average or aggregate), is one of the indicators traditionally used to measure adequacy. Its usefulness as a single indicator has been questioned in several ways. One of the problems proposed is the determination of the correct amount in the numerator and denominator of the ratio, since there is no consensus on the use of average incomes of the entire labour career, or the average income of the last year, or any other variant of both concepts (Biggs and Springstead 2008; or Grech 2013); some researchers consider the replacement rate an imperfect adequacy measure (e.g. Chybalski and Marcinkiewicz 2015), particularly if it is based exclusively on pension benefits, because today's pensioners may obtain their income from very different sources, including work and capital investments, and this affects their total income and consequently their standard of living. And, even more, it is an imperfect adequacy measure because its focus is from a one-dimensional perspective, as it takes into account a single indicator, the pension wage, and because of the static measure time, the date of retirement. In addition, there are researchers who argue that replacement rate calculations are overly simplistic and potentially inaccurate because they are often based on methodologies limited to pre-retirement cash flow substitution after adjustment for taxes, savings and related expenditures with age and/or work (Van Derhie 2006).

Nevertheless, establishing a minimum replacement rate for each system has become one of the objectives of governments and researchers. For example, the World Bank, in its book *Averting the Old Age Crisis* (1994), suggested that a net replacement rate for workers with average wages and full careers in mandatory pension systems could be any of the following:

- 78% of the average net salary of the working life
- 60% of the gross average salary of the working life
- 53% of the net salary of the last year of working life
- 42% of gross salary of the last year of the working life

Table 8.2 Adequacy first-line indicators

Concept	Indicator	Description
Poverty	AROPE 65+	At risk of poverty or social exclusion is the share of people aged 65+ with an equivalized disposable income (after social transfer) below the at-risk-of-poverty threshold (set at 60% of the national median equivalized disposable income after social transfers)
	Severe material deprivation	It measures the percentage of the population that cannot afford at least three of the following nine items: (1) to pay their rent, mortgage or utility bills; (2) to keep their home adequately warm; (3) to face unexpected expenses; (4) to eat meat or proteins regularly; (5) to go on holiday; (6) a television set; (7) a washing machine; (8) a car; (9) a telephone
Work related to pensions	Employment rate 55–64y	It is the ratio of the employed aged 55–64y to the working-age population
	Average length of working life	It measures the average number of years; a person aged 15 is expected to be active in the labour market throughout his/her life
Incomes related to pensions	Relative median income	It is the ratio of the median equivalized disposable income of people aged above 65 to the median equivalized disposable income of those aged below 65
	Aggregate replacement rate	It is the ratio of the median individual gross pensions of 65–74 age category relative to median individual gross earnings of 50–59 age category, excluding other social benefits
	Theoretical replacement rate	It is the individual pension entitlement divided by pre-retirement earnings, taking into account personal income taxes and social security contributions paid by workers and pensioners
Future incomes related to pensions	Future theoretical replacement rate	It is the individual pension entitlement divided by pre-retirement earnings, taking into account personal income taxes and social security contributions paid by workers and pensioners, using demographic and economic projections to a single time point
	Current and future benefit ratio	Defined as the median public pension income as a percentage of the whole salary of the country economy
	Gross median replacement rate	Defined as gross median pension entitlement divided by gross median pre-retirement earnings
Inequalities	Pensions gender gap	The difference in average wages between men and women expressed in percentage
	Inequalities of income distribution	The ratio of total income received by the 20% of the population with the highest income (top quintile) to that received by the 20% of the population with the lowest income (lowest quintile). Income must be understood as equivalized disposable income

Source: Compiled by authors from Eurostat Statistics Explained

In addition, the World Bank in the same report says that "... governments should not be required to provide the replacement rate indicated in its entirety to individual households...", indicating that these objectives should be achieved with a combination of compulsory contributions and voluntary pension schemes.

On the other hand, the OECD calculates the replacement rate data for an individual with the average salary, revalued annually, with a full career, using median income instead of average income, because the average one has a bias above due to individuals with higher income.

Thus, according to the OECD, although in 2012 it expressed an average net replacement rate of 70% of the net salary of the last year of employment (OECD 2012), nowadays it states the net replacement rate for an average worker is 66% of the average net working-age salary, as estimated on the basis of changes in the average net replacement rate for the 34 OECD countries analysed in the 2013 report (OECD 2013, pp.141) and the 2015 report (OECD 2015, pp.145). However, for those compulsory contribution systems, a target between 66% and 45% seems more reasonable, since the rate is proportionate in its vast majority by the public system.

Currently, researchers are working with the concept of "pension wealth", i.e. the total projected pension flow during the retirement period (see Fang et al. 2016; or Chlon-Dominczak 2016). From an individual point of view, pension wealth is "the discounted present value of future pension rights, taking into account the prospects of mortality" (Brugiavini et al. 2005).

The wealth of the gross pension can be defined as "the lump sum needed to buy an annuity giving the same flow of pension payments promised by the mandatory pension schemes" (OECD 2011). Also, wealth of net pension is defined as "the current value of the flow of pensions, taking into account taxes and social contributions that retirees have to pay for their pensions. It is affected by life expectancy and the age at which people retire, as well as indexation rules of each country" (OECD 2017). This indicator is measured as a multiple of annual gross earnings by gender.

The advantages of using pension wealth instead of replacement rates are many and consist primarily of taking into account the whole period in which the pension income will be received. In addition, there are several operating factors that are in favour of its use; for example, increased longevity increases the pension wealth, but does not affect the value of replacement rates; similarly, an increase in the retirement age decreases the pension wealth, while it does not lead to changes in replacement rates; in the same way, if pension income falls in relative value over time, the pension wealth would be less than if it remained constant, and on the other hand, the replacement rate says nothing about how it will evolve; finally, it can be argued that a reform that would change indexation would not change the replacement rate when retiring, but it would clearly show its effects when looking at the pension wealth. Consequently, it can be argued that the main advantage is that pension wealth measures the entire income flow, rather than focusing on a single payment over time.

The pension wealth is calculated normally by following one of the following two methods (Rajevska 2016):

- The empirical method, which implies the use of data from income and wealth surveys and therefore tends to be retrospective, reflecting the current rights and rules of the previous pension system.

- The institutional method, which uses a simulation approach: prospective pension rights are calculated for a series of "model cases" (with different careers, with or without interruption in employment, having or not having children, etc.), applying the parameters of the pension system and then calculating the outcomes.

8.4 Measuring with Synthetic Indicators

But now the information needed for decision-making comes not only from the choice of an indicator: once all the influential information in the study has been collected, the decision-making agent may find itself confronted with a broad set of simple measures on a series of situations, states, localities, regions, etc. which, in a disaggregated form, do not provide any clear or direct information useful for a better understanding of the current situation of each observation with respect to the others. It is therefore within this context that the *synthetic or composite indicators*, which are aggregated indices of simple indicators, are obtained by weighting and aggregating them with weights representing the relative importance of each one in the index. Ideally, this aggregation should measure multidimensional concepts that cannot be captured by single indicators individually.

In recent years, synthetic indicators have emerged as one of the most widely used analytical instruments in practice in many fields of social reality, and synthetic indicators are already commonly accepted as useful tools for decision-making and communication of information. According to the definition of OECD statistical terms, a synthetic indicator can be defined as "that combination or mathematical aggregation of indicators that represent the various components of the concept to be evaluated from a starting system, providing itself a multidimensional assessment" (Saisana and Tarantola 2002).

There are many reasons for the use of synthetic indicators. Briefly, they can be summarized in their ability to facilitate the interpretation of information by all users and at the same time to easily evaluate complex and multidimensional phenomena (Blancas et al. 2011). In any case, whatever the purpose for which a synthetic indicator is obtained, it must not constitute a purpose itself, but a tool that facilitates decision-making or clarifying information.

In the context of pensions, and specifically in terms of their adequacy, there are two synthetic indexes that currently stand out from the rest: the Allianz Retirement Income Adequacy Indicator, made by the insurance group Allianz, and the Melbourne Mercer Global Pension Index, conducted by the Australian consulting firm Mercer and the Australian Centre for Financial Studies, which, although it is a synthetic index of the performance of public pension systems, is made by three sub-indexes, one of them a specific sub-index of adequacy. Next, we will see both, and then they will be compared with the one made by Dr. Filip Chybalski, from the University of Lodz (Poland), who performed a complete and a very interesting adequacy synthetic indicator.

8.4.1 Global Pension Index (Mercer)

The Global Pension Index is a synthetic index, with annual data, published since 2009, and the last version is dated in 2016. It is formed by three sub-indices, also synthetic: adequacy (40% of the index weight), sustainability (35% of the index) and integrity (25% of the final weight of the index). They claim to cover almost 60% of the world's population, although it only offers data from 27 countries.

The composition of the adequacy sub-index is the one expressed in Table 8.3.

The development of the adequacy sub-index not only includes the pensions provided to both the middle and lower income but also includes the net rate of household savings and the rate of home ownership, and, as indicated, "... savings not related to pensions can represent an important source of financial security during retirement...".

The calculated values for the adequacy sub-index for the 2016 edition of the report are expressed in Table 8.4, where the value data obtained in the index for each country are provided and arranged according to the absolute ranking obtained between the countries analysed.

Table 8.3 Adequacy sub-index composition

Adequacy	Benefits
	Savings
	Tax support
	Benefit design
	Growth assets

Source: Mercer Global Pension Index Report

Table 8.4 Mercer Global Pension Index, adequacy sub-index, country values

Country	Mercer adequacy sub-index	Country	Mercer adequacy sub-index
Netherlands	78.2	China	58.2
Ireland	76.2	Poland	57.9
Australia	76.0	Chile	56.5
Denmark	75.8	UK	55.5
France	75.2	USA	53.5
Finland	70.6	Japan	48.5
Germany	70.4	Korea	46.5
Canada	68.0	Argentina	42.3
Brazil	67.9	Indonesia	41.0
Sweden	67.6	Malaysia	40.3
Austria	67.4	India	39.5
Italy	65.5	Mexico	38.5
Singapore	61.4	South Africa	34.0
Switzerland	60.5	*Average*	59.0

Source: Mercer Global Pension Index Report

8.4.2 Retirement Income Adequacy Indicator (Allianz)

Like the previous one, it is a synthetic index, first published in October 2015. It consists of two groups of sub-indicators selected for belonging to previously established categories: pension systems and other factors. Each of these categories is formed again by different sub-indicators. It provides data from 49 countries, and the report is divided by regional groups, due to regional coherence reasons at the time of the comparison, as indicated.

Significantly, the division of the "pension system" indicator by the three pillars of social security – where Pillar I is the pillar of social security, which provides both contributory and non-contributory pensions, and pillars II and III are respectively the pillars of corporate and individual forecast – is really interesting. But, for cross-country comparisons, in those where public pensions are based on a strong first pillar, countries in which pillars II and III are insufficiently developed, it is possible that pensions become adequate, but those countries appear in lower positions in this index ranking.

In the same way proposed by the Mercer index, each category has its specific weight in the final index, to form an adequacy ranking of the countries analysed. For that purpose, the report's authors divided the countries analysed in four regions in order to analyse homogeneous economies or at least with a high degree of similarity. The regions that divide countries are the following:

- Western Europe and North America
- Eastern Europe
- Asia
- Latin America and Oceania

The outcomes are categorized by the absolute ranking Allianz index gives each country and the ranking offered in each of the sub-indexes that comprise it, as we can see in Table 8.5. In each of the categories, the data of the position in the partial ranking each of the countries is provided are as follows (we choose Brazil as an example):

If we categorize the same countries for the outcomes from the two indexes, we obtain the following Table 8.6, where, except in the first country, we find big differences. For a better understanding of both rankings, and in order to facilitate the discussion on the differences, we present the following Table 8.6, where the positions of countries in both rankings are compared.

The ranking disparity is evident for all countries except for the Netherlands, first ranked in both. Country number 2 in one of the rankings is number 36 in the other;

Table 8.5 Example data outcomes

Country	Overall ranking	Pillar I	Pillar II/III	Non pension wealth	Spending needs	Transition from work
Brazil	16	4	35	43	34	34

Source: Retirement Income Adequacy Indicator report

Table 8.6 Compared country ranking outcomes

Countries	Mercer adequacy sub-index ranking	Allianz Retirement Income Adequacy Indicator Ranking
Netherlands	1	1
Ireland	2	36
Australia	3	35
Denmark	4	2
France	5	20
Finland	6	11
Germany	7	13
Canada	8	12
Brazil	9	16
Sweden	10	8
Austria	11	7
Italy	12	19
Singapore	13	41
Switzerland	14	4
China	15	44
Poland	16	33
Chile	17	40
United Kingdom	18	14
USA	19	6
Japan	20	5
Korea	21	*No data available*
Argentina	22	*No data available*
Indonesia	23	49
Malaysia	24	47
India	25	48
Mexico	26	46
South Africa	27	*No data available*

Source: Mercer Global Pension Index 2016 Report, Retirement Income Adequacy Indicator 2015

the one ranked number 15 in one ranking is ranked 44 in another and same for almost all of them.

The reason for this to happen is mainly due to the nature of the composite indicators. They are not absolute but relative measures, so that their reading and comprehension must be performed in a given context. On the other hand, it is due to the proper (or not) design of each index, as the sub-indicators that comprise it, as well as the relative weights of each one in the final index, where the disparities are accentuated.

Therefore, both indexes still remain representatives of measure, but they are a clear example of the enormous task faced by those who want to measure the adequacy, mainly due to difficulties to define.

Moreover, comparison between different moments in time is essential to measure the adequacy of pension systems, and that is something that none of these indices reflect.

8.4.3 Adequacy of Pension System Indicator (Dr. Filip Chybalski)

Another approach of measuring the adequacy of pensions is the one made by Dr. Filip Chybalski of the Lodz University of Technology, who computes one synthetic indicator (Chybalski 2012). He starts with the definition of three dimensions of adequacy: income, poverty and the differentiation of pensioners' material situation by gender. Next, the sub-indicators measuring the individual dimensions of adequacy are proposed, along with an aggregation procedure based on the tools of multidimensional statistical analysis. Then, the sub-indicators are aggregated into synthetic indicators for individual dimensions, and later the synthetic indicators for individual dimensions are aggregated into a single synthetic indicator to measure the adequacy of the pension system.

Chybalski concludes that in order to obtain comprehensive information on adequacy, one must use at least a few indicators, meaning that the issue must be approached in a multidimensional way. He further suggests introducing a synthetic indicator, derived from the following components:

- Pensioner income indicators: median relative income ratio of elderly people, aggregate replacement ratio, relative inequality of income distribution ratio and net pension wealth by gender.
- Pensioner poverty indicators: at-risk-of-poverty rate of older people and the change in at-risk-of-poverty rate of older people after retirement.
- Indicators of pensioners' gender differences: these are gender differences in the at-risk-of-poverty rate of older people, gender differences in the aggregate replacement ratio, change in at-risk-of-poverty rate of older people after retirement by gender, median relative income ratio of elderly people by gender and relative difference in net pension wealth by gender.

All the sub-indicators are taken from Eurostat and OECD data or computed by Chybalski himself. Every sub-indicator was assigned its relative weight and included into the formula developed by the researcher. He then used the formula to compute the aggregate APS (i.e. adequacy of pension system) indicator for EU-25 and Norway for 3 years, 2005, 2007 and 2009, and later ranked these 26 countries with the value of APS. The lower the APS is, the less adequate pensions are given by the system in a respective country. The APS outcome values varied from 0.22 (Latvia in 2009) to 0.85 (Luxembourg in 2007).

Again if we categorize the ranked countries the same countries by the outcomes from the three indexes, we obtain Table 8.7. It is, obviously, just a simple comparison not valid to assume absolute conclusions, made just to see if the three indexes

Table 8.7 Compared country ranking outcomes

Countries	Mercer adequacy sub-index ranking	Allianz Retirement Income Adequacy Index ranking	Chybalski adequacy of pension system indicator
Netherlands	1	1	4
Ireland	2	36	7
Australia	3	35	*No data available*
Denmark	4	2	18
France	5	20	3
Finland	6	11	17
Germany	7	13	5
Canada	8	12	*No data available*
Brazil	9	16	*No data available*
Sweden	10	8	19
Austria	11	7	6
Italy	12	19	15
Singapore	13	41	*No data available*
Switzerland	14	4	*No data available*
China	15	44	*No data available*
Poland	16	33	11
Chile	17	40	*No data available*
United Kingdom	18	14	13
USA	19	6	*No data available*
Japan	20	5	*No data available*
Korea	21	*No data available*	*No data available*
Argentina	22	*No data available*	*No data available*
Indonesia	23	49	*No data available*
Malaysia	24	47	*No data available*
India	25	48	*No data available*
Mexico	26	46	*No data available*
South Africa	27	*No data available*	*No data available*

Source: Mercer Global Pension Index 2016 Report, Retirement Income Adequacy Indicator 2015 report and Chybalski (2012)

can be comparable in order to measure the adequacy of pensions. And even more, it is not valid because Chybalski only computed European Union countries and because we take the APS last outcomes from 2009, while the other two indexes takes them from 2015.

It seems that Chybalski index is more compatible with the Mercer adequacy sub-index way to measure the pension adequacy than the Allianz one, only taking into account the country ranking, but at different time moments. The main reason why this happens is due to the choice of basic sub-indicators, closer in the case of Mercer and Chybalski ones, even if Chybalski includes the income gender gap in his index, insofar as they measure adequacy from different perspectives.

8.5 Conclusions

As we have seen during the development of the chapter, the adequacy of pensions is a concept with multiple edges, which escapes from a simple definition. But, making a synthesis of all the above, we can try to formulate one: the pensions of a particular country can be considered adequate if at the same time they protect the majority of the population from the risk of poverty and facilitate a standard of living similar to the one they had before retirement. This basic definition can be complemented in many ways, adding concepts, for example, like social justice, equity, reduction of gender differences and some other issues, but in this way expressed, it can facilitate its understanding and become an objective to focus by most of the countries with reasonable developed public pension systems.

On the other hand, as the second proposed objective of the chapter, it has been verified that the measurement of adequacy cannot be carried out with simple indicators, or with a single indicator, no matter how complete it may be, due to the different dimensions that the adequacy concept owns.

Traditionally, adequacy has been measured through the replacement rate indicator. It can be calculated both for countries and individuals, since it is an indicator widely used by all countries to give adequacy information and, even more, in order to facilitate comparison between them. However, due to the inclusion of more dimensions in the adequacy, in recent years many researchers have chosen to use synthetic indicators, which are the weighted sum of values and concepts that measure simple indicators.

The use of this type of indicators provides depth and tailored content to the adequacy measure and greatly helps decision-making in pension policy and public system reforms. In addition, comparisons over time have a greater wealth of data than those provided by the use of simple indicators.

The task we have, therefore, is to have great consensus on a single synthetic indicator, on a single method to construct it, or both, in order to achieve greater efficiency in the measure of the adequacy of the public pension systems.

References

Bajtelsmit, V., Rappaport, A., & Foster, L. (2013). Measures of retirement benefit adequacy: Which, why, for whom, and how much?. Society of Actuaries, 2013–1.

Banks, J., Blundel, R., & Tanner, S. (1998). Is there a retirement-savings puzzle? *The American Economic Review, 88*(4), 769–788.

Banks, J., Emmerson, C., Oldfield, Z., & Tetlow, G. (2005). *Prepared for retirement? The adequacy of retirement resources and distribution in England*. London: Institute for Fiscal Studies.

Bernheim, B. D., Forni, L., Gokhale, J., & Kotlikoff, L. J. (2000). How much Should Americans be saving for retirement? *American Economic Review, 90*(2), 288–292.

Beshears, J., Choi, J., Laibson, D., & Madrian, B. (2006). Simplification and saving. National Bureau of Economic Research Working Papers Series, Working Paper 12659, Massachusetts.

Biggs, A. G., & Springstead, G. (2008). Alternate measures of replacement rates for social security benefits and retirement income. *Social Security Bulletin, 68*(2).

Binswanger, J., & Schunk, D. (2011). What is an adequate standard of living during retirement? *Journal of Pension Economics and Finance., 11*, 203–222.

Blancas, J., Contreras, I., & Ramirez, J. (2011). Construcción de indicadores sintéticos: una aproximación para maximizar la discriminación. Annals of ASEPUMA, no. 19–0110.

Brugiavini, A., Maser, K., & Sunden, A. (2005), Measuring pension wealth. Paper prepared for a meeting of the Luxembourg Wealth Study held in January 2005: http://www.lisproject.org/lws/introduction/files/brugiavini_rev.pdf.

Chlon-Dominczak, A. (2016). Impact of Changes in multi-pillar systems in EEC Countries board individually on board wealth. *Journal of Pension Economics and Finance*. https://doi.org/10.1017/S1474747216000238.

Chybalski, F. (2012). Measuring the multidimensional adequacy of pension systems in European countries. Discussion Paper PI-1204, March 2012. The Pension Institute, London. http://www.pensions-institute.org/workingpapers/wp1204.pdf.

Chybalski, P., & Marcinkiewicz, E. (2015). The replacement rate: An imperfect indicator of pension adequacy in cross-country analyses. *Social Indicators Research, 126*(1), 99–117.

Duran-Heras, A. (2012). The Spanish pensions are adequate? Activities of the Social Protection Committee of the EU for evaluation. Budget and Public Expenditure 68/2012, (pp. 141–156). Madrid: Institute for Fiscal Studies.

European Commission (2003). Joint report by the commission and the council on adequate and sustainable pensions. (COM(2002) 737 - 2003/2040(INI))

European Commission, EC (2012a). White Paper: An Agenda for adequate, safe and sustainable pensions. SWD-2012.

European Commission, EC (2012b). Pension adequacy in the European Union 2010-2050. Directorate-General for Employment, Social Affairs and Inclusion of the European Commission and the Social Protection Committee, European Union, Publications Office, Luxembourg.

Fang, C., Brown, C., & Weir, D. (2016). Cohort changes in social security benefits and pension wealth. Ann Arbor: University of Michigan Retirement Research Center (MRRC) Working Paper WP 2016–350.

Fornero, E., Lusardi, A., & Monticone, C. (2009). Adequacy of saving for Old Age in Europe. In *Aging, Health and Pensions in Europe* (pp. 13–41). Springer and European Science Foundation.

Grech, A. G. (2013). How best to measure pension adequacy, CASE paper 172, London Centre for Analysis of Social Exclusion, London School of Economics, April 2013.

Harmer, J. & Australia Department of Families, Housing, Community Services and Indigenous Affairs (2008). *Pension review background paper*. Canberra: Dept. of Families, Housing, Community Services and Indigenous Affairs.

Holzman, R. & Hinz, R. (2005). Old-age income support in the twenty-first century: An International Perspective on Pension Systems and Reform. World Bank papers.

International Labour Organization, ILO. (1998). *Pension model ILO: A technical guide*. Geneva: Financial, Actuarial and Statistical Services.

Lusardi, A., & Mitchel, O. (2007). Financial literacy and retirement planning: New evidence from the Rand American Life Panel. Michigan Retirement Research Center Research Paper No. WP 2007–157.

Mercer. (2016). *Melbourne Mercer global pension index*. Melbourne: Australian Centre for Financial Studies and Mercer.

Munnell, A., Haverstick, K., & Sazenbacher, G. (2006). Job tenure and coverage board. CRR WP 2006–18. Center for Retirement Research at Boston College.

OECD. (2007). *Pensions at a glance: Public policies across OECD Countries*. Paris: OECD Publishing.

OECD. (2009). *Pensions at a glance 2009: Retirement income systems in OECD Countries*. Paris: OECD Publishing.

OECD. (2011). *Pensions at a glance 2011: Retirement - income systems in OECD and G20 Countries*. Paris: OECD Publishing.
OECD (2012): *OECD Pensions Outlook 2012*. OECD Publishing.
OECD. (2013). *Pensions at a glance: OECD indicators and G20*. Paris: OECD Publishing.
OECD. (2015). Pensions at a Glance 2015: OECD Indicators and G20. Paris: OECD Publishing (updated 2016).
OECD. (2017). Net pension wealth (indicator). https://doi.org/10.1787/c634eb4f-en in (Accessed on 19 January 2017).
Rajevska, O. (2016). Adequacy and equity of pensions as a function of institutional system board design: A case of the Baltic States. Doctoral Thesis. Riga, 2016.
Saisana, M., & Tarantola, S. (2002). State-of-the-Art Report on current methodologies and practices for composite indicator development. Joint Research Centre - European Commission.
Skinner, J. (2007). Are you sure you're saving enough for retirement? National Bureau of Economic Research Working Papers Series, Working Paper 12981, Cambridge.
Thaler, R. (1994). Psychology and savings policy. *American Economic Review Papers and the Proceedings, 84*(2), 186–192.
Van Derhie, J. (2006). Measuring retirement income adequacy: Calculating realistic income replacement rates. EBRI Issues Briefs No. 297, September 2006, Washington DC.
Whiteford, P., & Henman, P. (1998). Assessing budget standards: conceptual issues in the treatment of durables. *Social Security Journal, 1*.
World Bank. (1994). *Averting the old age crisis* (p. 295). Oxford University Press.

Chapter 9
Longevity Insurance Benefits for Social Security: International Experience

John A. Turner, Gerard Hughes, Agnieszka Chłoń-Domińczak, and David M. Rajnes

Abstract Longevity insurance benefits are deferred annuities that start payment at an advanced age at which a substantial proportion of the birth cohort has died. In high-income countries, that would mean that these annuities would start for people in their early 80s, but when social security programs were starting in many countries, the age at which longevity insurance annuities would start was substantially younger. Originally, public pension programs in a number of countries were structured as a longevity insurance program, with roughly 50% of those entering the workforce surviving to receive the benefits because of relatively high benefit eligibility ages. Over time, however, as life expectancy has improved, the benefits these programs provide have slowly transformed into benefits that most people entering the work force ultimately receive. This paper argues that reintroduction of a longevity insurance benefit as part of public pensions could be an important policy in particular because this benefit is generally not provided by the private sector. These annuities would benefit some older retirees, particularly in countries with modest public pension benefits, but the private sector has problems in providing them, particularly when they must be provided on a unisex basis. This chapter surveys countries that provide this type of benefit and also considers proposals for the provision of this benefit in the United States and Canada. The addition of these benefits to social

Research on Poland included in this paper was financed from research grant number UMO-2013/10/M/HS4/00466 from National Science Centre in Poland.

J. A. Turner (✉)
Pension Policy Center, Washington, DC, USA

G. Hughes
Trinity Business School, University of Dublin, Dun Laoghaire, County Dublin, Ireland

A. Chłoń-Domińczak
Warsaw School of Economics, Warsaw, Poland
e-mail: achlon@sgh.waw.pl

D. M. Rajnes
Social Security Administration, Bowie, MD, USA
e-mail: David.Rajnes@ssa.gov

M. Peris-Ortiz et al. (eds.), *Economic Challenges of Pension Systems*,
https://doi.org/10.1007/978-3-030-37912-4_9

security may be particularly desirable as part of a reform where other changes being made to maintain solvency are resulting in reduced generosity of benefits.

Keywords Annuities · Canada · China · Insurance · India · Ireland · Life expectancy · Longevity · Nepal · Old age · Public pensions · Poland · Social security · United States · Vietnam · Zanzibar

9.1 Introduction

Longevity insurance benefits are deferred annuities that start payment at an advanced age at which a substantial proportion of the birth cohort has died. While all annuities provide longevity insurance through pooling of annuity risks, longevity insurance annuities provide insurance targeted against running out of money at advanced ages. As people grow older, especially for those living past their life expectancy and for those relying on defined contribution plans, they risk having exhausted their sources of income other than their public pension. People with fixed income in retirement can see the real value of those income sources fall in half by their early 80s with inflation rates as low as 3%. People with low public pension benefits who are in their 80s and older are economically vulnerable. At that age, few are able to offset their low benefits by working. They may have used up their retirement assets other than their public pension benefit, and they may have increased expenses due to increased need for medical care.

Preventing people from falling into poverty as they age is a key goal of public pensions. Longevity insurance is one way to address the income needs of older people who have lived longer than they expected and have used up their retirement savings other than their public pension benefit. The addition of these benefits to social security may be particularly desirable as part of a reform where other changes being made to maintain solvency are resulting in reduced generosity of benefits.

This paper presents a survey of government-provided longevity insurance benefit programs around the world. It discusses longevity insurance benefits as a way for low-income countries to provide old-age benefits to their most vulnerable older populations.

9.2 Previous Literature

While all annuities provide retirees a degree of longevity insurance, in recent years the term longevity insurance has been used to refer to a particular type of deferred annuity. Longevity insurance is a deferred annuity that starts at an advanced age, such as 82. Longevity insurance annuities provide insurance against outliving ones assets, but only when that risk becomes substantial at advanced ages (Milevsky 2005).

Unless they choose some type of annuity, retirees with defined contribution plans in countries with social security systems that do not provide high replacement rates may face the difficult challenge of managing the spend down of their assets over a retirement period of uncertain length. With a longevity insurance annuity, the planning problem is greatly simplified. Instead of planning for an uncertain period, participants can plan for a fixed period—from the date of their retirement to the date at which they start receiving the longevity insurance benefit should they survive that long. Longevity insurance changes the planning problem from one with an uncertain end point (date of death) to one with a certain end point (the date at which longevity insurance begins providing benefits).

The age of purchase and the length of the deferral until benefits are received affect the level of benefits provided. For example, a longevity insurance annuity purchased with US$100,000 at age 70 would be expected to provide annual payments starting at age 85 of between $26,000 and $42,000 depending on the interest rate, whether a joint and survivor annuity was chosen and other factors. If the purchase was made instead at age 65 with the starting date at age 85, the $42,000 figure would increase to $51,000 (U.S. Department of the Treasury 2012). Alternative estimates indicate that an immediate annuity purchased with $100,000 and starting at age 65 would provide $6950 a year for life, compared to the same purchase with benefits starting at age 85 yielding $63,990 for life (Tergesen 2012). These benefits would be subject to inflation risk, but some policies allow for lower starting benefits with an automatic escalation. The amount of benefit depends on the interest rates prevailing at the time of purchase, with a risk associated with these annuities being that the purchase occurs at a time when interest rates are low. A strategy to deal with that risk would involve making smaller purchases of longevity insurance annuities over a period of several years.

Horneff et al. (2016) use a simulation model to show that the percentage of resources that a person would optimally annuitize increases over time during retirement and by age 80 would fully annuitize their financial wealth, other than wealth used for bequests. People who have some financial resources invested in equity can benefit from the equity premium early in retirement, gradually reducing their investment in equity and increasing the amount that is annuitized. A longevity insurance benefit does not follow that pattern of gradually increasing the share of assets that is annuitized, but it does capture some of the benefit of that strategy.

In the private sector, adverse selection may be more of an issue than for immediate annuities in that presumably only people with long life expectancies would purchase longevity insurance annuities. Also, potential purchasers may be concerned with the risk of life insurance company insolvency over a long time period.

Webb et al. (2007) argue that a longevity insurance annuity could be appealing to pension participants. They demonstrate that longevity insurance annuities can provide valuable insurance protection at an affordable cost. However, relatively few people have purchased them. One possible explanation may be that people are concerned that they might die before receiving a reasonable amount of their money back, and this concern would be substantially greater for longevity insurance annuities than immediate annuities because of their deferred payment start date. That approach to valuing annuities based on money back ignores the insurance benefit they provide for people who live to older ages. Iwry and Turner (2009) discuss adding a longevity annuity to target date funds as a way of encouraging their purchase through 401(k) plans in the United States. Ezra (2016) highlights that longevity annuities pool the greatest part of the longevity risk exposure—the part at the oldest ages—when longevity uncertainty is greatest relative to expected future longevity.

9.3 The Role of Longevity Insurance Benefits in the Early History of Social Security

Historically, many social security programs were designed as longevity insurance programs. Over time, they have gradually shifted to being retirement benefit programs. In the early development of social security, a number of countries initially established social security programs as longevity insurance benefit programs, with benefit eligibility ages as high as age 70 at a time when relatively few workers survived to those ages (Chen and Turner 2015).

Germany The original concept of social security under Chancellor Bismarck in Germany was a longevity insurance benefit, though that terminology was not used. The benefit was available at age 70 starting in 1889. While life tables are not available for that year, clearly less than half the population entering the workforce would be alive at that age. It was not until 27 years later (in 1916) that the retirement age was reduced to 65.

United States While US Social Security is now a benefit that most people who enter the workforce survive to receive, it was originally structured like a longevity insurance benefit. In 1940, when benefits were first provided in the United States, the benefit eligibility age was 65. Taking into account that people entered the workforce at earlier ages, from US life tables for 1910 for the population age 18 that year, at age 65, 54% of the population would still be alive (Glover 1921). Over time, two changes have fundamentally altered the nature of the benefits that social security provides in the United States and in other countries. First, benefit eligibility ages have been lowered. Second, longevity has increased. With these two changes, social security programs have transitioned from longevity insurance programs to programs providing old-age benefits for a substantial proportion of the population that entered the workforce in their youth.

Ireland and the United Kingdom When the means-tested old-age pension was introduced in Ireland and Great Britain in 1908, the retirement age was 70. In 1910–1912, life expectancy at birth for a male was age 51 (United Kingdom Office for National Statistics 2015). When the basic state pension was introduced in the

United Kingdom in 1946, the benefit eligibility age was 65 for men (60 for women) (Capretta 2007). When a social insurance-based Old Age (Contributory) Pension was introduced in Ireland in 1961, the retirement age was set at 70 and it remained at that age until the 1970s.

Norway, Iceland and Sweden In 1949, the benefit eligibility age was 70 in Norway and 67 in Iceland (Capretta 2007). When a universal old-age pension was established in Sweden in 1913, the eligibility age was 67 (Harrysson and Edebalk 2010).

Thus, in a number of countries, social security old-age benefits were first provided as longevity insurance benefits, providing benefits at an age where a substantial proportion of the population entering the workforce would have died. Social security has changed to a retirement benefit that most people receive rather than a longevity insurance benefit that is a form of insurance against living to an advanced older age.

9.4 Longevity Insurance Annuities Provided by the Government

From an economics perspective, the argument that the government should provide a benefit must be based at least in part on the conclusion that the private sector cannot provide such a benefit on equally favourable terms. In the United States, individually purchased longevity insurance annuities account for about 1% of the individual purchase annuity market (Panis and Brien 2016).

The government has several advantages over the private sector in providing longevity insurance benefits. First, it is able to limit its liability against the possibility of an unexpected improvement in life expectancy by indexing the age of eligibility for benefit receipt. While the private sector could do this prospectively for new clients, the government is able to do this for people nearing the age of entitlement for the benefit. For example, adjustments to benefit generosity are made at retirement age in Sweden for immediate annuities received at traditional retirement ages. The private sector could hedge against improvements in life expectancy by providing annuities whose generosity depended in part on changes in life expectancy.

Second, the government has a hedge against the liability to the extent that people work longer and pay more taxes due to improvements in health at older ages or due to raising the eligibility age for social security benefits. Currently, no assets exist for the private sector to invest in that provide a full hedge against unexpected improvements in life expectancy.

Third, the government does not have to deal with adverse selection because it provides the benefit to a preselected group. In the private sector, insurance companies would provide longevity insurance to people who self-select, in part based on their subjective expectation of long life expectancy.

Problems with the provision of longevity insurance benefits in the private sector, however, include that adverse selection may be more of an issue in that they presumably would only be purchased by people with long subjective life expectancies. Also, potential purchasers may be concerned with the risk of life insurance company insolvency over a long time period.

9.5 International Survey

This section surveys longevity insurance benefits provided by government public pension (social security) programs in a number of countries. The countries discussed are the full set of countries for which we were able to find longevity insurance programs. Life expectancy differs greatly by country, so the design of longevity insurance benefits in different countries would vary greatly by the age at which they would be available. While the difference between life expectancy at birth and life expectancy at age 20 is relatively small in high-income countries, the difference is substantial in low-income countries due to infant and youth mortality. Life expectancy at age 20 is a better measure for constructing a longevity insurance benefit because that benefit is for people who have worked. The life expectancy at age 20 gives the age at which roughly half of the population entering the workforce at age 20 would have died, and thus that statistic serves as an empirical measure as to whether an old-age benefits program would be classified as a longevity insurance program.

In the following international survey, we roughly classify longevity insurance benefits as starting at age 80 or later in high-income OECD countries, age 75 and older in middle-income countries and age 70 and older in lower-income countries. Further, we classify longevity insurance benefits based on the age at which they start and not on other correlates of those benefits, such as whether they are means tested, whether only social security beneficiaries are eligible or other issues. The international survey starts with a somewhat detailed explanation of programs in Ireland, Poland and China, followed by an explanation of a proposal for the United States, and less detailed explanations of programs in other countries.

In the following survey, the number following the name of the country is the life expectancy at age 20 (Word Life Expectancy 2015), which is a measure of roughly when a longevity insurance benefit might start.

Ireland (81.9) Ireland has had a non-contributory social assistance (anti-poverty) pension since 1908 and a contributory social security pension since 1961. Both pensions were originally available at age 70. The contributory social security pension provides flat rate (not earnings-related) pension benefits. The social assistance pension depends on income and assets in old age, and the social security pension depends on previous participation in the labour force.

Ireland pays a benefit of about US$550 a year at age 80, called the Age 80 Allowance. That benefit is automatically received by persons receiving Irish social security pensions once they turn age 80. The maximum flat rate value of the social security pension depends on having an annual average of 48 or more weekly contributions to the social insurance fund during one's working life. A sliding scale of average contributions is used to pay smaller pensions to those with average weekly contributions less than 48 per year. However, the Age 80 Allowance is not reduced for those with average weekly contributions less than 48 a year.

In Ireland's 1972 national budget, both the social assistance and contributory social security pensions were increased for older pensioners by introducing an age allowance for pensioners age 80 and over. All persons age 80 and older receiving either of those pensions automatically receive the age 80 Allowance. Thus, the age 80 Allowance is a social pension that is not separately means tested, but it is also not universal. The eligibility requirement excludes some higher-income persons who do not qualify for social assistance because of their income and do not qualify for a social security pension because of not having a sufficient history of work. The particular feature of it that we are focusing on as a model for other countries is that it starts at age 80. The administration of a social pension, such as in Ireland, that is not means tested is simpler and less costly than for a means-tested pension.

In his 1972 budget speech introducing the new pension benefit, the Irish Minister for Finance (Ireland 1972) George Colley said that the reason for introducing the allowance was that "I am especially conscious of the fact that very old persons are often at a disadvantage because of their inability to do things for themselves and shop around for the best value. In recognition of this, all non-contributory [and contributory] old age and blind pensioners age 80 and over will receive a further increase of 50p per week."

A further justification for the Age 80 Allowance is that data from Ireland show a substantial increase in medical expenses at older ages. Research by Redmond (2015) on the cost of medication by age shows that in 2012 average annual expenditure by those under age 65 was €406 compared with €1377 for those age 65–69 and €1772 for those age 75 and over.

While the relationship between the amounts of the Age 80 Allowance for the social security and social assistance pensions varied in the early years, since 1985 the allowance has been the same for both pensions. The nominal value of the allowance increased considerably in 2006, when it was increased to €10 per week, but it has not increased since then, thus declining in real value for the past decade. The cost of the benefit as a percent of GDP was 0.07% in 2011.

Poland (78.1) Poland has a relatively high pension coverage rate compared to other formerly communist transition economies. This result is achieved by a mix of contributory and non-contributory plans. The general social security pension system covers salaried workers and self-employed workers. Farmers are covered by a separate social security scheme, with a small contributory component (with contributions equivalent to 10% of the minimum monthly pension per month). Contributions cover less than 10% of the expenditure on farmers' pensions, and the rest is covered from general government revenues, which means that it is a quasi-social pension for this part of the Polish population. A social pension is a pension which is based on age and possibly income, but not on prior contributions. Old-age pensions are paid from ages 61 for women and 66 for men.

All people age 75 and over receive an additional benefit, financed from the national government budget. There are two types of such benefits. If a person receives a contributory pension (from the general social security plan or the farmers' plan), he or she receives a care benefit (*dodatek pielęgnacyjny*) that is paid on top of those benefits. If a person is not eligible for a social security pension, he or she receives a care allowance (*zasilek pielegnacyjny*) paid from the state budget by local community social services, based on the Polish Act on Family Benefits. Initially, the level of both social transfers was similar. Policy developments have led to a rising difference in the benefit levels. The care benefit is more generous due to its regular indexation that is guaranteed by law. The care allowance, financed from taxes and not indexed on a regular basis, was kept at a lower level as a part of the fiscal policy and budget savings.

The universal care benefit and allowance in Poland are factors contributing to the lower level of poverty among the population in the age group 75 years and older compared to those age 60 and older. According to Eurostat data (Turner et al. 2017), the poverty rate for people age 75 and older in Poland is the lowest among all age groups. This means that even a relatively small addition to income serves an important goal of reducing poverty at advanced ages.

Access to universal benefits for people age 75 and older reduces the risk of poverty at older ages. It provides an important addition to the income of people in the oldest age group. However, given the rising need for care services with age, it is still seen as insufficient (Szatur-Jaworska 2008).

China (77.2) Though, in some cities in China, an old-age allowance has been provided for those age 90 or 100, Ningxia province has taken the lead in providing an old-age allowance in the whole province and provides monthly benefits for those age 80 and older (Chen and Turner 2015). In May 2009, Ningxia province first started to provide the old-age allowance for those aged 80 and older in rural areas and those aged 80 and older with low income in urban areas. Thus, in urban areas, the old-age allowance is a means-tested program. China does not have a unified national social security program—program features vary across the provinces. Ningxia province is the first one to provide this benefit. The lowest benefit level as regulated by provincial government is as follows: those age 80–89 receive 300 yuan per month; those age 90+ receive 350 yuan per month. County or district governments can increase the benefit level according to their financial ability. In Shenzhen city (a developed city in China and the first city to develop a market economy at the end of the 1980s) of Guangdong province, the benefit level is as follows: those age 80–89 receive 200 yuan per month; those age 90–99 receive 300 yuan per month; those age 100+ receive 500 yuan per month.

Since 2009, more cities have established old-age allowance programs. In 2006, only 2.34 million people were receiving an old-age allowance, but by the end of 2010, 5.76 million people received the old-age allowance. From 2006 to 2010, the percentage of the population age 80 and older receiving old-age allowance benefits increased from 12.9% to 27.0%. In 2011, 14 provinces started to provide the old-age allowance. However, in general, the old-age allowance program is not universal for those age 80 and older in China.

In most cities, the old-age allowance is means tested and provides benefits to those with low income. In cities in Ningxia province, only those age 80 and older with per capita income of family members lower than 150% of the minimum living standard are eligible for old-age allowance. In Heilongjiang province and Jilin province, those age 80–89 with income lower than the minimum living standard are eligible for the old-age allowance (People's News 2012). For those age 90 and older, no means test is required. All eligible old-age persons can receive 100 yuan (US$16) per month. Thus, the old-age allowance programs in these two provinces are means tested for those age 80–89 while being universal for those age 90 and older (People's News 2012). In Shenzhen city, the old-age allowance is not means tested and is universal for those satisfying the age requirement.

United States (80.0) The United States does not have a social security longevity insurance benefit. Such a benefit was proposed in the Save Our Social Security Act of 2016 which would increase social security's actuarial deficit by 0.15% of taxable payroll, which means that it could be financed by raising the combined employer-employee payroll tax rate by 0.15%. Thus, the employee (and employer) contribution rate would increase by 0.075% of taxable payroll, which arguably would not be noticed by most workers and employers. The Act was introduced in Congress in 2016 by Representative Reid Ribble (Wisconsin-Republican) (U.S. Social Security Administration 2016b, c).

The benefit would be a flat benefit, meaning that everyone at a given age would receive the same amount. The benefit would phase in from ages 82 to 86 at 1% a year. That benefit increase at age 86 would equal 5% of the primary insurance amount (PIA) of a hypothetical worker with the same birth year who earned the average wage index wage (AWI) every year through age 61, which is the year prior to benefit eligibility at age 62. The primary insurance amount is the benefit a single person would receive if they retired at the normal retirement age for a person of their birth cohort. If the average worker had a replacement rate of 37%, the 5% point increase in their benefit would be an increase in their replacement rate of roughly 14% (5 divided by 37). The increase in replacement rates would be higher for workers with lower PIAs and lower for workers with higher PIAs. Because the PIA is a measure of lifetime wages, the benefit would be a progressive benefit that provided a relatively larger increase for lower-wage workers than for higher-wage workers.

In the future, the population age 80 and older is projected to grow more rapidly than the total population in the United States. The population age 80 and older was 3.7% of the total population in 2010 and is projected to increase to 5.0% of the total in 2030 and 7.4% of the total in 2050 (Vincent and Velkoff 2010). These projections indicate that the cost of a longevity insurance benefit will increase over time. That increase is partly due to improvements in life expectancy at older ages and partly due to the aging of the baby boom generation. Despite these increases, the social security actuaries project that the cost of the benefit in 2089 (the end of the 75-year projection period) would be 0.21% of taxable payroll (U.S. Social Security Administration 2016c).

Canada (82.7) A longevity insurance benefit has also been proposed in Canada. The Province of Québec maintains a social security program called the Québec Pension Plan, which is similar to the Canada Pension for the rest of Canada. An Expert Committee (2013) has proposed adding a longevity insurance benefit to the Québec Pension Plan that would be payable starting at age 75. Unlike the other social security benefits in Canada that are funded on a pay-as-you-go basis, the longevity benefit would be fully funded by contributions from workers and employers and would be provided on a defined benefit basis. Five years of benefits would be guaranteed, so that if a worker dies before age 75, a lump sum equal in present value to 5 years of benefits would be paid to a survivor. If the worker dies after age 75 but before age 80, a similar lump sum would be paid to bring the total payments up to 5 years' worth of benefits.

United Kingdom (81.7) Any person receiving a state pension in the United Kingdom receives a small benefit increase of £0.25 (=€0.35) per week at age 80. When it was introduced in 1971, it amounted to 4.2% of the basic state pension. The nominal amount was not increased over the years and it has now fallen to 0.3% of the basic state pension. The United Kingdom also provides the over 80 pension, which is a means-tested pension for those age 80 or older. It can also be paid as a top-up amount to a person's state pension when that person reaches age 80, if he or she receives the state pension at a lower rate than £71.50 or doesn't receive the basic state pension. Relatively few persons qualify for this benefit, however, because it has a low-income eligibility cutoff point.

Isle of Man (81.7) The Isle of Man provides at age 80 a supplement of £2 per week for anyone in receipt of a state pension (social security) and an old person's pension that begins at age 80. The Isle of Man is an internally self-governing crown dependency whose head of state is Queen Elizabeth, but it is not part of the United Kingdom. The old person's pension is "pension tested", meaning that qualification is based on receiving less than 60% of the basic state pension (social security) (U.S. Social Security Administration 2016a). The insured must be ordinarily residing in the Isle of Man and must have lived in the Isle of Man or the United Kingdom for at least 10 years in any 20-year consecutive period after age 60.

Germany (81.5) Riester pensions in Germany are voluntary defined contribution plans that were enabled by a pension reform taking effect in 2002 and named for the labour minister responsible for establishing them. They require that at retirement the participant purchase an annuity that begins payment by age 85 (Börsch-Supan and Wilke 2005). Thus, the Riester pension can be used as a longevity insurance annuity, but it is not specifically designed that way because benefits can start at earlier ages.

Vietnam (78.1) Vietnam implemented a non-contributory pension program in 2004 (Long 2011). Initially, the program provided a benefit of 65,000 dong (US$4.20) each month to persons age 90 or older who did not receive any contributory pension benefits. Over time, eligibility ages were reduced and the benefit amounts have increased. In 2007, the minimum eligibility age declined to 85 and, in 2010, to 80. Under current law, this old-age social pension (social assistance) is available to those age 60–79 who are "needy and living alone without family support" and to those age 80 or older and not receiving any contributory pension (US Social Security Administration 2015b).

The monthly benefit amount varies by age and health-related circumstances as follows: 180,000 dong (US$7.93) to those age 60–79 if needy and living alone without family support or older than age 80; 270,000 dong ($US11.90) if age 60–79, needy, disabled and living alone without family support or older than age 80, needy and living alone without family support; and 360,000 dong (US$15.87) if older than age 80, needy, disabled and living alone without family support. The benefit may be higher in provinces with greater fiscal capacity. According to various sources cited by the Asian Development Bank, more than two-thirds of eligible individuals had not received a benefit nor had many provinces implemented the program in recent years (Long 2011).

Nepal (72.7) Although social insurance coverage provided through the National Provident Fund is limited, an old-age allowance provides social assistance to an estimated 682,000 individuals who received the benefit in 2010. In December 1994, the government introduced a universal social pension for all Nepalis age 75 or older. Initial implementation of the program aimed to support older persons and their family-based support systems by providing cash payments of 100 rupees (US $2.21 in 1994$) per month to persons 75 years or older. In 1996, the government increased the benefit payable to people 100 years of age or older. In 2011, the program offered a monthly benefit of 500 rupees (around $US6) to all persons age 70 or older. On their 100th birthday, the benefit for beneficiaries increases to 1000 rupees. The program is funded through general taxation (Samson 2012).

The allowance provides national coverage, with some geographic variability in take-up rates. In most areas, the government aims to pay benefits every 4 months, equal to 2000 rupees (US$18.32) per payment. In remote rural areas with limited access to village development officers, however, the government struggles to make payments once a year, for the full entitlement of 6000 rupees (US$54.95) annually. In 2011, the population age 70 years or older was about 757,000 people, representing 2.6% of the total population. The senior citizens' allowance covered an estimated 640,119 older people in 2010, a small decrease from 646,461 beneficiaries in 2009 (Samson 2012). Currently, the monthly benefit still equals 500 rupees, but 1000 rupees are paid to members of certain ethnic groups (US Social Security Administration 2015a).

Kyrgyz Republic (73.1) The Kyrgyz Republic pays a pension supplement to persons age 80 or older. The benefit is also paid to World War II veterans, Chernobyl disaster workers and certain other groups (U.S. Social Security Administration 2014).

India (72.6) The city of Delhi provides a benefits program for low-income seniors starting at age 60, with a special supplement starting at age 70. In 2017, people age 60–69 receive a benefit of Rs 2000 a month, while those age 70 and older receive a benefit of Rs 2500 a month (Hindustan Times 2017).

Philippines (71.1) The Philippines has a program for low-income seniors that pays benefits starting at age 77 (Ronda 2015). The government has sought greater funding for the program so that it can extend the benefits to seniors who are younger than age 77.

Zanzibar (67.1) Zanzibar, a semi-autonomous country (in a union with mainland Tanzania), has recently launched a pilot program that offers both men and women age 70 or older 20,000 shillings (US$9.18) each month (Rebela 2016). The universal program was launched ahead of what is planned to be a similar universal pension program in Tanzania.

Lesotho (60.1) The old-age pension, which started in 2004, begins payment at age 70 (U.S. Social Security Administration 2015a). All persons age 70 and older are entitled to a monthly benefit equivalent to about US$40. The benefit is non-contributory, meaning that eligibility is not based on the person having made contributions. The cost of the benefit is equal to 1.7% of GDP (Ortiz et al. 2017). Lesotho provides an example of a low-income country that is able to provide old-age benefits by providing those benefits as a longevity insurance benefit, starting at a relatively old age, given the life expectancy in the country.

9.6 Comparison Across Countries

Table 9.1 compares characteristics of longevity insurance benefits programs for older people. Poland, Ireland, the UK and the Isle of Man have provided support for a long time for those age 75 or 80 under social insurance and social assistance programs. China (Ningxia and other provinces), Vietnam, Nepal, Kyrgyz Republic, the Philippines, Zanzibar and Lesotho provide support only under social assistance. Germany has provided support since 2002 when Riester individual DC pensions were marketed by private insurance companies. Recently, proposals have been made in the province of Quebec in Canada and in the United States that longevity support should be provided through social insurance programs.

The age of eligibility for a longevity insurance pension varies across countries depending on the life expectancy in the country. The age of eligibility in Nepal, Zanzibar and Lesotho is 70. In Quebec the proposed age is 75, and in the Philippines it is 77. In Ireland, the UK, the Isle of Man, China (Ningxia), Vietnam and the Kyrgyz Republic it is 80, and there is an increase in the allowance in Ningxia at age 90 and in Nepal at age 100. A proposal in the United States is that social security will phase in the full amount of a longevity benefit between the ages of 82 and 86.

Table 9.1 Comparison of longevity insurance by country and proposals for the United States and Canada

Country	Year introduced	Age of eligibility	Social insurance		Social assistance	
			Value per month	Contributions required	Value per month	Means test
Ireland	1972	80	€43.33 (=$46.36)	Automatic if receiving a state pension	€43.33 (=$46.36)	No means test for the supplement
Poland	1983	75	PLN 208.57 (=€50 =$53.50)	Automatic if receiving a contributory state pension	PLN 153 (=€37 =$39.59)	Not receiving a contributory pension
China (Ningxia)	2009	80–89			Yuan 300 (=€44.86 =$48)	Less than 150% of minimum living standard
		90+			Yuan 350 (=€52.34 =$56)	
UK	1971	80	£1.08 (=€1.52)	Automatic if receiving a state pension	£1.08 (=€1.52 =$1.62)	No means test for the supplement
		80			Top up to £311.02 (=€370.12 =$396.02)	No state pension or state pension of less than £71.50 per week
Isle of Man	1971	80	£8.70 (=€10.35)		£8.70 (=€10.35 =$11.07)	No state pension or less than 60% of basic state pension of £119.30
Germany	2002	85	Depends on capital value of Riester DC savings	Contributor to Riester voluntary DC personal account can buy an annuity payable at age 85		
Vietnam	2004	80			180,000–360,000 Dong = ($7.93 – $15.87 =€7.41 – €14.83)	Not receiving any contributory pension
Nepal	1994	70			Rupees 500 = ($6 =€5.60)	Not receiving any contributory pension
		100				

(continued)

Table 9.1 (continued)

Country	Year introduced	Age of eligibility	Social insurance		Social assistance	
			Value per month	Contributions required	Value per month	Means test
					Rupees 1000 = ($12 =€11.21)	
Kyrgyz Republic	2005	80			From 50% to 475% of the basic pension, depending on circumstances	Paid to persons age 80 and older, Chernobyl disaster workers and other groups
Philippines	2010	77			P500 = ($10.75 =€10.00)	Means test
Zanzibar	2016	70			Shillings 20,000 = ($9.18 =€8.58)	No means test
Lesotho	2004	70			Lesotho Malati 550 = ($40 =€37.4)	No means test
Proposals for Canada and the United States						
Canada (Quebec pension plan)	Proposed in 2013	75	For a worker who contributes for 40 years the value would be 20% of pensionable earnings	Would be fully funded by employers and employees on shared basis		
USA	Proposed in 2016	Phase in from 82–86	Five percentage points of primary insurance amount $64.29 (=€60.08)			

Note 1: Exchange rates on 4 December 2016 £1 = €1.19; €1 = U.S. $1.07; 1 Polish zloty = €0.24; I Yuan = €0.15
Note 2: Estimated value of US supplement on Old-Age and Survivors Insurance average monthly benefit is $64.29 (=$1285.87 × 0.05)
Note 3: 1 month = 4.35 weeks

The value of longevity insurance in Ireland is the same, €43.33 per month (US $46.36), whether it is paid under social insurance or social assistance programs. In Poland, it is about one-third higher under social insurance than social assistance, €50 v €37 or $53.50 v $39.59 per month. The value of the age 80 supplement for anyone in the UK and the Isle of Man who qualifies for a state pension is very modest, amounting to less than 2% of the basic state pension. However, in both jurisdictions there is a means-tested pension for anyone whose income is less than 50% of the basic state pension. The value of the payment in Germany is not uniform, as it would probably be under public programs for old-age pensions. The payment is provided by private insurance companies, and it varies according to the capital value of pension savings. In a radical proposal to reform the retirement system in Quebec, an Expert Committee (2013) proposed that the payment of longevity insurance should be 20% of pensionable earnings, which would be about four times higher than the average of around 5% of pensionable earnings which other countries pay. The proposed payment in the USA, 5% of pensionable earnings, is in line with what is provided by most other countries.

The cost of longevity insurance depends, among other things, on what level of benefits is offered and at what age. For most countries where the cost has been estimated, it is quite modest and would not impose a noticeable burden on employers and employees. In Ireland, the current cost amounts to 0.07% of GNP, and it would double to 0.16% in 2046, as the proportion of older people age 80 years and over increases faster than the people age 65 years and over. The proposal for the USA has been costed by the U.S. Social Security Administration (2016c), and if it were implemented, the current cost would amount to 0.15% of taxable payroll. By 2089, the cost would nearly double to 0.27% of taxable payroll, as people age 82 years and over would increase faster than those age 65 years and over. In Quebec province in Canada, the proposal to introduce longevity insurance which would pay 20% of pensionable earnings after 40 years of work would increase the cost of social insurance noticeably by 3.3% of pensionable earnings.

9.7 Conclusions

Longevity insurance benefits are deferred annuities that start at an advanced age. With current life expectancy, they generally start for persons in their 80s in high-income countries. A longevity insurance benefit is desirable in countries, such as the United States and Ireland, where social insurance old-age benefits are relatively modest, and people risk running out of other sources of retirement income at advanced older ages.

The government has several advantages over the private sector in providing longevity insurance benefits. First, it is able to limit its liability against the possibility of an unexpected improvement in life expectancy by indexing the age of eligibility for benefit receipt. While the private sector could do this prospectively for new clients, the government is able to do this for people nearing the age of entitlement for the benefit. For example, this is done at retirement age in Sweden for immediate annuities received at traditional retirement ages. Second, the government has a hedge against the liability to the extent that people work longer (and pay more taxes) due to improvements in health at older ages or due to raising the eligibility age for social security benefits. Currently, no assets exist for the private sector to invest in that providing a hedge against unexpected improvements in life expectancy. Third, the government does not face adverse selection because it provides the benefit to a preselected group. In the absence of coverage mandates in the private sector, insurance companies would provide longevity insurance to people who self-select, in part based on their subjective expectation of long life expectancy.

The survey presented in this paper indicates that a number of countries offer longevity insurance benefits as part of their public pension or social security benefits. These countries include some low-income and middle-income countries, as well as some high-income countries. In some countries, these benefits are supplements to either social security or social assistance benefits. In some low-income countries, longevity benefits are the primary social security benefit. Historically, in Germany, the United Kingdom, the United States and other countries, social security programs were first started as longevity benefit programs that provided benefits starting at an advanced age, relative to the life expectancy in those countries at the time.

Acknowledgements We have benefitted from collaboration on previous projects with David McCarthy, David Blake, Mark Iwry and Tianhong Chen.

References

Börsch-Supan, A. H., & Wilke, C. W. (2005). *Reforming the German public pension system*. http://www.rand.org/labor/aging/rsi/rsi_papers/2006_axel1.pdf

Capretta, J. C. (2007). *Global aging and the sustainability of public pension systems: An assessment of reform efforts in twelve developed countries*. A report of the aging vulnerability index project. Washington, DC: Center for Strategic & International Studies. http://csis.org/files/media/csis/pubs/pension_profile.pdf

Chen, T., & Turner, J. A. (2015). Longevity insurance annuities: China adopts a benefit innovation from the past. *International Social Security Review, 68*(2), 27–41.

Expert Committee on the Future of the Québec Retirement System. (2013). *Innovating for a sustainable retirement system: A social contract to strengthen the retirement security of all Québec workers*. http://www.rrq.gouv.qc.ca/SiteCollectionDocuments/www.rrq.gouv.qc/Anglais/publications/rapport_comite/rapport.pdf

Ezra, D. (2016). Most people need longevity insurance rather than an immediate annuity. *Financial Analysts Journal, 72*(2), 23–29. http://www.cfapubs.org/doi/pdf/10.2469/faj.v72.n2.3.

Glover, J. W. (1921). *United States life tables: 1890, 1901, 1910, and 1901-1910*. U.S. Bureau of the Census, U.S. Government Printing Office. http://www.cdc.gov/nchs/data/lifetables/life1890-1910.pdf

Harrysson, L., & Edebalk, P. G. (2010). *Employers and pension reform in Sweden from war to war*. Lunds University Working Paper. https://lucris.lub.lu.se/ws/files/3553576/1691648

Hindustan Times. (2017, January 6). Delhi Govt increases monthly pension of elderly, widows and disabled. *Hindustan Times*. http://www.hindustantimes.com/delhi/delhi-govt-increases-monthly-pension-of-elderly-widows-and-disabled/story-GM5KeCQHxdBgk62EyQ5CfK.html

Horneff, V., Maurer, R., & Mitchell, O. S. (2016). *Putting the pension back in 401(k) plans: Optimal versus default longevity income annuities*. SAFE Working Paper No. 150. https://papers.ssrn.com/sol3/papers.cfm?abstract_id=2853430

Ireland. (1972). *Financial statement, budget 1972*. http://oireachtasdebates.oireachtas.ie/debates%20authoring/debateswebpack.nsf/takes/dail1972041900020?opendocument

Iwry, J. M., & Turner, J. A. (2009). Automatic annuitization: New behavioral strategies for expanding lifetime income in 401(k)s. In W. G. Gale, J. M. Iwry, D. C. John, & L. Walker (Eds.), *Automatic: Changing the way America saves* (pp. 151–172). Washington, DC: Brookings Institution Press.

Long, T. L. (2011). Viet Nam: Pension system overview and reform directions. In D. Park (Ed.), *Pension systems and old-age income support in East and Southeast Asia: Overview and reform directions* (pp. 203–221). Asian Development Bank: Metro Manila.

Milevsky, M. A. (2005). Real longevity insurance with a deductible: Introduction to advanced-life delayed annuities (ALDA). *North American Actuarial Journal, 9*(4), 109–122.

Ortiz, I., Schmitt, V., & De Loveleen (Eds.). (2017). *Social protection floors: Volume 1: Universal schemes*. International Labour Organisation. https://papers.ssrn.com/sol3/papers.cfm?abstract_id=2895420

Panis, C. W. A., & Brien, M. J. (2016). *Innovations and trends in annuities: Qualifying longevity annuity contracts (QLACs)*. Advanced Analytical Consulting Group and Deloitte. October 24. https://www.dol.gov/sites/default/files/ebsa/researchers/analysis/retirement/innovations-and-trends-in-annuities.pdf

People's News. (2012). *Nine million people age 80 and older receiving old age allowance in China*. http://politics.people.com.cn/n/2012/0808/c1001-18693477-1.html

Rebela, M. (2016, November 23). Zanzibar pension scheme timely for poor elderly. *The Citizen*. http://www.thecitizen.co.tz/News/Zanzibar-pension-scheme-timely-for-poor-elderly%2D%2DVIDEO-/1840340-3460922-t823emz/index.html

Redmond, P. (2015). *Spending on medication increases with age*. http://www.publicpolicy.ie/spending-on-medication-increases-with-age/

Ronda, R. A. (2015). *DSWD wants bigger budget for indigent seniors' pension*. The Philippine star, updated September30.

Samson, M. (2012). In Nepal's senior citizens' allowance: A model of universalism in a low-income country context. In S. W. Handayani & B. Babajanian (Eds.), *Social protection for older persons: Social pensions in Asia* (pp. 214–246). Mandaluyong City: Asian Development Bank.

Szatur-Jaworska, B. (2008). Bezpieczeństwo socjalne – wybrane pieniężne świadczenia społeczne. [Social safety – selected cash social benefits]. In B. Szatur-Jaworska (Ed.), *Stan przestrzegania praw osób starszych w Polsce. Analiza i rekomendacje działań. [The status of respecting the rights of the older people in Poland. Analysis and recommendations for actions] Biuletyn RPO Materiały* (Vol. 65). Warsaw: Biuro Rzecznika Praw Obywatelskich.

Tergesen, A. (2012). *How to create a pension (with a few catches)*. Personal Finance, Wall Street Journal, April 9. http://www.wsj.com/articles/SB10001424052970204571404577253853314354494

Turner, J. A., Hughes, G., Chłoń-Domińczak, A., & Rajnes, D. M. (2017). Improving pension income and reducing poverty at advanced older ages: Longevity insurance benefits in Ireland and Poland as models for the United States. *Journal of Retirement, 4*(3), 96–110.

U.K. Office for National Statistics. (2015, September 1). English life tables no. 17, 2010-2012. *Statistical Bulletin*. http://www.ons.gov.uk/ons/rel/lifetables/decennial-life-tables/english-life-tables%2D%2Dno-17%2D%2D2010-12/stb-elt17.html

U.S. Department of the Treasury. (2012). *Longevity annuity contracts*. Federal Register 77 #23, February 3, pp. 5443–5454. http://www.gpo.gov/fdsys/pkg/FR-2012-02-03/pdf/2012-2340.pdf

U.S. Social Security Administration. (2014). *Kyrygystan. Social security programs throught the world: Asia and the Pacific, 2014.* https://www.ssa.gov/policy/docs/progdesc/ssptw/2014-2015/asia/kyrgyzstan.html
U.S. Social Security Administration. (2015a). *Lesotho. Social security programs throughout the world: Africa, 2015.* https://www.ssa.gov/policy/docs/progdesc/ssptw/2014-2015/africa/lesotho.pdf
U.S. Social Security Administration. (2015b). *Vietnam. Social security programs throughout the world: Asia and the Pacific, 2015.* https://www.ssa.gov/policy/docs/progdesc/ssptw/2014-2015/asia/index.html
U.S. Social Security Administration. (2016a). *The Isle of Man. Social security programs throughout the world: Europe, 2016.* https://www.ssa.gov/policy/docs/progdesc/ssptw/2016-2017/europe/isle-of-man.pdf
U.S. Social Security Administration. (2016b). *Proposals affecting trust fund solvency. Actuarial Publications.* https://www.ssa.gov/oact/solvency/
U.S. Social Security Administration. (2016c). *Representative ribble: Letter to the Honorable Reid Ribble.* https://www.ssa.gov/OACT/solvency/RRibble_20160713.pdf
Vincent, G. K., & Velkoff, V. A. (2010). *The next four decades. The older population in the United States: 2010.* Current population reports, P25–1128, U.S. Census Bureau, May. https://www.census.gov/prod/2010pubs/p25-1138.pdf
Webb, A., Gong, G., & Sun, W. (2007). *An annuity people might actually buy.* Center for Retirement Research at Boston College, issue in brief no. 7-10, July. http://crr.bc.edu/briefs/an-annuity-people-might-actually-buy/
World Life Expectancy. (2015). *Life expectancy by age.* http://www.worldlifeexpectancy.com/your-life-expectancy-by-age

Chapter 10
The French Mandatory Occupational Pension Scheme: History and Properties of a Point System

Frédéric Gannon, Florence Legros, and Vincent Touzé

Abstract This chapter deals with the French PAYGO mandatory occupational pension scheme for the private sector workers (AGIRC-ARRCO), one of the world's oldest pension point systems. In a first section, we trace the history of the setup of this system which relies on a particular mode of governance (joint administration by trade union and employers' respective representatives). The second section is dedicated to the analysis of the tax distortion properties of the calculation rule of this defined contribution supplementary pension system. We also discuss the similarities with the German and Swedish pension systems. Weakened by the 2008 economic crisis, this jointly administered French supplementary pension scheme had to undergo a severe adjustment in "emergency mode" (Turner, Social security financing: Automatic adjustments to restore solvency, Washington, DC: AARP Public Policy Institute, 2009), in October 2015. We detail this agreement and show how it restores medium term balance and enacts the principles of sustainable governance.

Keywords French supplementary pension system · Contributiveness · Tax distortion properties · Generational impacts

---

F. Gannon (✉)
University of Le Havre, Le Havre, France

OFCE-Sciences Po, Paris, France
e-mail: frederic.gannon@univ-lehavre.fr

F. Legros
ICN – Business School, Nancy, France
e-mail: florence.legros@icn-groupe.fr

V. Touzé
OFCE-Sciences Po, Paris, France
e-mail: vincent.touze@sciencespo.fr

M. Peris-Ortiz et al. (eds.), *Economic Challenges of Pension Systems*,
https://doi.org/10.1007/978-3-030-37912-4_10

10.1 Introduction

The French pension system is deeply marked by its Bismarckian origins: it is an insurance type scheme, with a certain proportionality between pensions (seen as an insurance compensation) and contributions (seen as an insurance premium), themselves being proportional to the wages.

Seventy percent of the French active population works in the private sector. Our analysis will consider only this sector and, more precisely, will focus on the second pillar of its pension system, which can be characterized by three key elements. First, it is organized as a pay-as-you-go pension scheme. That means that, at each period, the pensions are paid by the contributions. Second, it relies on two private associations: the AGIRC for the executives only and the ARRCO for both executives and nonexecutive employees. As these associations have been created on a professional basis, AGIRC and ARRCO pension schemes can be considered as the components of a second pillar, like the other professionally based schemes abroad (most of the time pension funds running with funding rules). Third, it has to be balanced and cannot borrow money because the access to the credit market is difficult not to say impossible without governmental guarantee.

In a first section, we trace the history of the setup of this system which relies on a particular mode of governance (joint administration by trade union and employers' respective representatives), accountable in the sense that this pension scheme prohibits itself from going into debt and thus must set up a reserve fund in order to prevent crisis situations caused by economic downturns and shortfalls in pension contribution revenues.

The second section is dedicated to the analysis of the tax distortion properties of the calculation rule of this defined contribution supplementary pension system. This is done, notably, by measuring the implicit marginal tax rate induced by the functional relationship between pension contributions and benefits. We also discuss its similarities with the German and Swedish pension system. On the opposite, we provide evidence that this supplementary pension system ensures lower tax distortion than would do a Swedish-like notional account, since by making the payment of point independent of the individual's age, it tends to benefit more to the older workers. Lastly, this system is deprived of any automatic – Swedish-like, again – adjustment mechanism that would force it to regularly adjust the level of pensions in order to stick to a sustainable trajectory.

In the third section, we present the most recent agreement, voted by social partners on 30 October 2015. This agreement provides for short-term and long-run measures that applies in full since 1 January 2019, after a 3-year transitory period during which specific actions have been taken.

10.2 Genesis and History

According to Charpentier (2014), the French universal coverage of retirement pensions is the outcome of a long path. If, during the nineteenth century, pension schemes have been devised for the employees of the public sector, the private sector has been much slower and reluctant to do so. Of course, private and optional retirement plans have been implemented, but a majority of workers could not contribute to these plans because of the low level or irregularity of their wages. On 5 April 1910, a law was passed relating to the workers and farmers' retirement, setting up France's first mandatory pension scheme. However, retirement was allowed only from age 65. Given the fact that life expectancy of the two social classes concerned was about 48, there were few potential beneficiaries.

On 30 April 1930, a law on social insurances was voted which established a mandatory social insurance (health, death, disability, retirement) for all the workers of the private sector whose wage is below a defined ceiling. Its financing was funded equally by employers and workers. Insurance companies, mutual societies and employers' funds shared this new market. Retirement pensions relied then on a capitalization funded scheme. The law stipulates that "the interest rates on investments mortality tables allow to define the 'old age insurance tariffs'" (Charpentier 2014). The wage ceiling implies the pension system is not universal and executives and engineers, notably, are excluded. This situation was to be corrected by the Matignon Agreements on 7 June 1936, which established the so-called "Collective Agreements", allowing the workers to negotiate "with the employers, at the level of industry federations, the implementation of private pension systems which will be used as models for the future executives pension system" (Charpentier 2014).

In 1945, the founding decrees of the social security imposed a pay-as-you-go pension system for all (Caisse Nationale d'Assurance Vieillesse, CNAV), up to a predefined wage ceiling, and cancelled the prevailing private pension systems below this ceiling. The CNAV pays a pension benefit from 65 years old which is computed by applying a replacement rate to an average wage. Executives opposed the suppression of their specific pension system. They lost their struggle for its generalization (below the ceiling) but obtained on 14 March 1947 the creation of a special system above the ceiling. This system built on three characteristics (Charpentier 2016):

1. Funding by capitalization was replaced by a pay-as-you-go scheme: the main justification of this shift was that a pay-as-you-go scheme allowed to pay without delay benefits to retirees who could not contribute to this same scheme (free lunch). A second justification was the distrust for the capitalization principle after its collapse due to the crisis of the 1930s, to the war and to the post-war soaring inflation. Also, the pay-as-you-go principle allowed for transfers between generations and the financial support of oldest people, who had undergone both the 1930s economic crisis and WW2.
2. A point system was set up (see infra) with executives contributing for the fraction of their wage above the social security ceiling.

3. The pension scheme relied on a collective agreement which was to be periodically renegotiated. In the absence of agreement, the pension system could be terminated.

The ruling of the pension system was organized according to three levels:

1. The legislative power is held by a national joint commission equally divided between employers and workers.
2. The executive power is in the hands of the "Association Générale des Institutions de Retraite des Cadres" (AGIRC).
3. Retirement institutions see to ensure a good management of the system. These institutions "develop at the industrial sector at the interprofessional levels with a great diversity of situations".

Retirement was allowed from age 55 and after a period of at least 10 contributing years. The normal retirement age was set at 65 and a malus coefficient was applied to pension in case of retirement before normal age. The scheme validated the working periods lying before 1 April 1947. The validation conditions were rather flexible. The validated years gave entitlement to a fixed amount of points.

The AGIRC scheme then expanded to sales and medical sales representatives, corporate executives, supervisors and technicians and similar workers. The expansion of the number of contributors along with economic growth allowed the system to be generous with the retirees. Charpentier (2016) recalls that, between 1952 and 1966, the administrators had decided "to collect only a fraction of the due contributions" and had not deemed useful to increase "the reserve funds beyond a year of contributions". A repurchase rate was introduced in 1952. It allows to collect more or less contributions than the facial payroll tax rate. COR[1] (2009) explains that the objective was "not to collect more contributions than was required by the pension expenditures, which was not intended to constitute reserves [...] The social partners agreed that it was better to leave this money in companies and wages rather than capitalize it at random market conditions". The call rate is thus less than 100% from 1952 (78%) to 1965 (95%).

The nonexecutives (workers and employees) drew from the AGIRC model but it took far more time to unify the pension plans. Numerous negotiations at different levels – companies, occupations, sectors – resulted in the creation of independent pension schemes. As many as 600 of them were accounted for by the Ministry of Labour in 1956. This uncontrolled development caused a great anxiety among social partners, if only for the simple reason that for a pay-as-you-go pension scheme to survive, it must operate in isolation.

On 15 May 1957, the social partners set up the UNIRS (Union Nationale des Institutions de Retraite des Salariés/National Union of Wage Earners Retirement Institutions). Its objective was to secure pension management within a unique

[1]The COR (Conseil d'Orientation des Retraites), created in 2000, is the official French advisory council on pensions, in charge of monitoring the middle- and long-term prospects of the pension system.

scheme, which led to a financial compensation between the different pension organizations, according to their relative demographic growth or decline. Membership of the existing schemes in the UNIRS is voluntary and the unique pension scheme would have to do without the main pension plans which had already structured themselves nationally. The march toward unity was slowed down by the fact that some plans refused to share their prudential reserve funds.

The UNIRS went through a period of strong growth of membership. On 8 December1961, the social partners established the "Association des régimes de retraite complémentaire[2]" (ARRCO). Initially, eighteen schemes, of which the UNIRS, coexisted with different operating parameters. It was mandatory for all companies to join one of the schemes. The agreement provided a retroactivity for wage earners who retired since 1927 with at least ten working years. Two contribution rates were applied: one below the social security wage ceiling and the other above.

The ARRCO pension scheme went through two significant changes:

1. A law voted in December 1972 required all the wage earners contributing to the General Social Security Scheme or to the Agricultural Social Mutual Fund to be covered by ARRCO; this mandatory coverage was extended to the executives for the fraction of their wages below the social security wage ceiling by a law passed in June 1973.
2. A unique scheme was finally adopted on 1 January 1999.

AGIRC and ARRCO schemes were, by construction, sensitive to the evolutions of the General Social Security Scheme (Caisse Nationale d'Assurance Maladie – CNAV).

In particular, AGIRC was very dependent upon the evolution of the fraction of the aggregate payroll above social security wage ceiling. If the latter grew faster than the average wage, the tax base on which relied this supplementary scheme was increased. Successive governments used this duality in relative growth to boost the increase of their receipts and cover the deficits of the General Social Security Scheme.

AGIRC and ARRCO proved also very sensitive to reforms. The right to retirement for all at 60, following a parliamentary mandate in March 1982, undermined the two schemes' financial balance. To address this risk, an intermediate financial structure was set up in 1998 the "Association pour la structure financière"[3] (ASF). Full pension age (without penalty) was maintained at 65. ASF was financed jointly by payroll taxes and by the state. It took at its expense the amount of penalties applied[4] by AGIRC and ARRCO in case of retirement before 65. ASF was terminated in 2000 to be replaced, in 2001, by the "Association pour la Gestion du Fonds

[2]Association of Supplementary Pension Schemes (translation by authors)

[3]"Association for the financial structure" (translation by authors)

[4]The maximum malus is 22%.

de Financement[5]" (AGFF). The AGFF charges a 2% (respectively 2.2%) contribution for the fraction of the wage below (respectively above) the wage ceiling. The reforms agreed at the beginning of the 2000s, progressively pushed up the normal retirement age for the General Social Security Scheme to 62, and the full pension age was delayed from 65 to 67, which improved the financial situation of the supplementary pension schemes.

Since 2002, the substantial surpluses of AGFF are allocated to AGIRC and ARRCO. On 18 March 2011, the social partners agreed to prorogate AGFF until 31 December 2018.

Relying on their obvious similarities, AGIRC and ARRCO have brought together the services and means of their federations in an economic interest group established on 1 July 2002, called GIE AGIRC-ARRCO. This management decision has promoted operative internal convergences. The final step of their co-evolution has been sealed by the 30 October 2015 agreement which provides for a unified scheme from 1 January 2019.

It is important to stress the fact that AGIRC and ARRCO's governance relies on negotiations between private organizations and actors: workers' trade unions on one hand, employers' trade unions on the other hand. These two supplementary pension schemes are private law entities. Legally, nothing should prevent them to be indebted, except the constraint imposed by the financial markets; that is, their ability to repay their borrowing. Without public guarantee, deficit is, de facto, not a possible option. This is why AGIRC and ARRCO have constrained themselves to financial balance on roughly 10-year horizon periods.

Their independence from the government leads them to elaborate intermediate long-run scenarios which are more prudent than those devised by the French public organism in charge to feed and monitor the debate and the reforms relating to pension schemes: the "Conseil d'Orientation des Retraites" (COR). For instance, in 2015, the "average" scenario (Var2) elaborated by GIE AGIRC-ARRCO assumes a 7% unemployment rate and a low convergence to 1.5% of the productivity growth rate (after 2035), whereas the COR's central (labelled scenario B) assumes respectively 4.5% and a faster convergence (after 2024).

Today, supplementary pension schemes play an important role, accounting for about 31% of total retirement for nonexecutives (ARRCO) and about 42% for executives (AGIRC). In 2015, ARRCO and AGIRC paid €45.5 and €23.8 billion pension benefits to 12.2 and 2.9 pensioners, respectively, i.e. 22.7% of national pension expenditures (24.7% with AGFF compensation). 18.2 million employees (4.2 for AGIRC) paid €47.9 billion in contributions. AGIRC and ARRCO have a reserve fund of €73 billion which generated €2 billion of financial income. AGFF surpluses also provided an additional resource (€4.7 billion), but the latter was insufficient and the two schemes reached a €3 billion deficit. According to Duc et al. (2016), these adjustments would reduce pension expenditures by €12.2 billion

[5]Association for the management of the financing fund (translation by authors)

and would increase the receipts by €5.8 billion. The 30 October 2015 agreement would concentrate 50% of expenditure reductions and 34% of increased receipts.

10.3 Pension Rules and Tax Distortion

10.3.1 General Principles

This second pillar is a scheme by points, i.e. a defined contribution pension scheme. Each contributor acquires points which are "capitalized" on an individual account.

The number of points acquired at each contribution period depends on the volume of contribution. That means that the contributions (in Euro) are divided by a "unit price" in order to be translated into points.

The contribution amount at each period results from product of a wage and an effective contribution rate which is itself the product of a facial contribution rate and a "call rate".

In other words, the number of points depends of the price of each point, the call rate and the facial contribution rate. This leads to a rather flexible scheme; any parameter can be modified in order to change the vested rights.

When people retire, the total amount of points is then fictively "sold" at a "unit price" (remember that it is a pay-as-you-go pension scheme); the pension is then determined.

The unit price of the point when the employee buys it is also called "reference wage"; its value as given in October 2016 is €16.1879 (for ARRCO) and €5.636 (for AGIRC). The rent values of one pension point as given in October 2016 are €1.2513 (for ARRCO) and €0.4352 (for AGIRC).

Contributions

There is a reference wage called "social security ceiling" (€24 per hour, i.e. €39,228 per year) which is the upper limit for the computation of first pillar and that is also used as a unit in order to fix the contribution rate.

The contribution rate varies according to the considered interval of revenue (see Cuvilliez and Laurent 2016). It is expressed in percentage of the gross wage. The contribution effective rates differ from the facial contribution rates and are computed as follows: effective contribution rate = facial contribution rate × repurchase rate. The repurchase rate is equal to 125%.

The wage limits for the computation of contribution rates define two wage brackets for ARRCO: for bracket 1 (fraction of the wage below the social security ceiling), the effective contribution rate is 7.75%. For bracket 2 (fraction of the wage lying between one and 3 social security ceiling), the contribution rate is 20.25%. For AGIRC, two wage brackets are defined: for bracket B (between one and 4 social security ceiling) and bracket C (between 4 and 8 social security ceiling), the contribution rate is 20.55%.

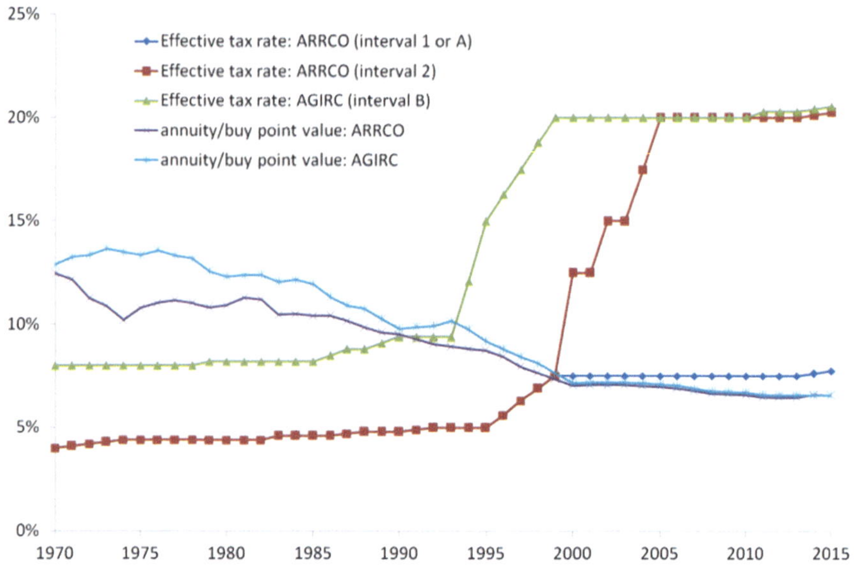

Fig. 10.1 Evolutions of AGIRC-ARRCO parameters

Nonexecutive workers contribute from ARRCO's bracket 1 to bracket 2 whereas executive workers contribute from ARRCO's bracket 1 to AGIRC's bracket C.

In addition to the contributions accruing to the worker's future pension, the supplementary pension plans apply an extra social tax rate, from 2.00% (bracket 1) to 2.20% (bracket 2 or B or C), to finance the AGFF, a structure dedicated to compensate the reduction in the pensions of people who retired before 65 or 67 after the 1983 reform. This contribution does not reward points. It is equal to 2% for fraction A and 2.2% for fraction B. Another exceptional 0.35% contribution without point (CET) applies.

The employer's contributive shares are 60% for ARRCO and 62% for AGIRC, respectively (bracket B). Figure 10.1 traces the evolutions of AGIRC-ARRCO parameters.

10.3.2 Computation Rules

In the supplementary pension schemes, the contribution allows the individual to buy points at price v_x^{buy}. In turn, each point of supplementary pension benefit confers a claim to an annuity of amount v_x^{ann}. The amount of pension depends on the number of points accumulated at the date of liquidation of the pension plan (Legros 2010):

$$P_R(W,I) = \rho(.) \cdot \sum\nolimits_{y=D}^{R-1} \left(\tau_y \cdot w_y / v_x^{\text{buy}}\right) \cdot v_x^{\text{ann}}$$

Coefficient $\rho(.)$ depends on the number of missing quarters compared either to the legal insurance period defined by the CNAV or to the age for which the length of insurance is not taken into account. The chosen solution is the most convenient for the worker. A 1% penalty applies for each missing quarter if the number of missing quarters is less than 12, then 1.25% until 20 missing quarters and 1.75% for each $\rho(.)$ is equal to one when the number of contributed quarters is just equal to the required one.

In practice, the supplementary pension plans apply a repurchase rate. That means the contribution paid does not fully qualify for points. The difference between the contributed rate and the applied rate can be considered as a tax. To simplify the notations, we will denote here:

$$v_x^{\text{buy}} = v_x^{\text{buy Agirc or Arrco}} \times \text{repurchase rate}$$

Before 2016, pensions were updated yearly on April 1. According to the agreement of March 18, 2011, pensions have been indexed on the evolution of the average wage of the contributors of the ARRCO and AGIRC plans minus 1.5 points, with the inflation rate as a minimum, which guarantees *a minima* to keep up with the purchasing power of the liquidated pension plans.

Since 2016, pensions are updated yearly on November 1 and the index will evolve as the inflation minus 1% with the inflation rate as a minimum.

10.3.3 Implicit Marginal Tax Rate: Definition and Computation

Implicit marginal tax rate is defined as the tax distortion with respect to actuarial neutrality (Feldstein and Samwick 1992; Gannon and Touzé 2013).

The likely present value (denoted hereafter LPV) of wages is the sum of the present values of the future wages under the survival condition:

$$\text{LPV}_x(\text{wages}) = \sum\nolimits_{y=x}^{R-1} \left(q_{y,x}/R_{y,x}\right) \cdot w_y$$

The LPV of contributions obtains similarly as:

$$\text{LPV}_x(\text{payroll taxes}) = \sum\nolimits_{y=x}^{R-1} \left(q_{y,x}/R_{y,x}\right) \cdot \tau_y \cdot w_y$$

The LPV of pension benefits takes into account the probability to be alive at the age of retirement, R:

$$\begin{aligned}\text{LPV}_x(\text{pensions}) &= \sum\nolimits_{y=R}^{120} (q_{y,x}/R_{y,x}) \cdot p_y(W, I_y) \\ &= p_R(W, I_R) \cdot \sum\nolimits_{y=R}^{120} (q_{y,x}/R_{y,x}) \cdot I^p_{y,R}\end{aligned}$$

where $I^p_{y,R}$ is the index factor of pension benefits, assumed to be independent of W.

Let $a_R = \sum_{y=R}^{120} (q_{y,x}/R_{y,x}) \cdot I^p_{y,R}$ be the value of 1 euro pension annuity perceived from age R, indexed by $I^p_{y,R}$.

Values of a_R are calculated under the following LR assumptions: 5% (discount rate) and 3.25% (nominal index rate). We use INSEE French prospective mortality tables (2007–2060).

The implicit marginal tax rate of pension contribution at age x is obtained from calculating the marginal additional contribution induced by a supposedly unique increase of wage at that age, net of the increase in pension benefit, divided by the variation of revenue:

$$\tau_{\text{marg},x} = \tau_x \cdot \Delta W_x - \Delta\text{LVP}_x(\text{pensions})/\Delta W_x$$

In the case of a permanent increase of wage, the marginal rate of pension contribution at age x is given by the following ratio:

$$\begin{aligned}\tau_{\text{marg},x} &= ((\Delta\text{LVP}_x(\text{payroll taxes}) - \Delta\text{LVP}_x(\text{pensions}))/\Delta\text{LVP}_x(\text{wages})) \\ &= \tau_x\left(1 - (q_{R,x}/R_{R,x}) \cdot \left(v_R^{\text{ann}}/v_x^{\text{buy}}\right) \cdot a_R\right)\end{aligned}$$

with

$$v_x^{\text{buy}} = v_x^{\text{buy Agirc or Arrco}} \times \text{repurchase rate} = \text{buying price of point}$$

$$v_x^{\text{ann}} = \text{annuity value of point}$$

Figure 10.2 compares three generations of workers (male and single), G1952, G1962 and G1973, born in 1952 (1962 and 1973, respectively) with full pension after 41 (42 and 43, respectively) contribution years and an entry on the labour market at 21 years old (22 and 23, respectively).

Note that from 1 January 2019, a 10% malus – reduced to 5% for low pensions – over 3-year period applies on pension for people opting out at full pension age (reference to first pillar) and 0 malus applies for people postponing by 1 year and bonus during 1 year if postponing by at least 2 years.

For the sake of simplicity, we compute the marginal tax rate applying with AGIRC rules. The profile obtained with ARRCO rules is similar all the more so since the parametric characteristics have converged. For future generations, the profiles will be identical.

For generations G1962 and G1973, the increase in marginal payroll tax rate after age 54 and 57 and 43 and 46, respectively, corresponds to a short-term hypothetical

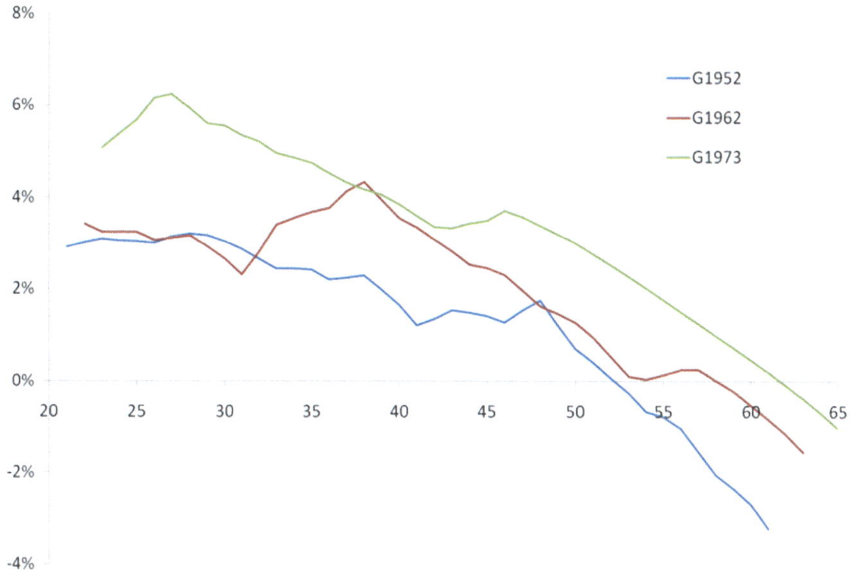

Fig. 10.2 AGIRC: implicit marginal payroll tax rate for three generations (1952, 1962 and 1973) (leaving at full pension age with 3-year 10% penalty)

increase in interest rate. For generation G1952, the marginal payroll tax rate is negative from age 52 on. The age where sign of the rate becomes negative depends crucially on financial and demographic hypotheses and more specifically on the longitudinal life table.

The global profile of marginal payroll tax rate with respect to age is decreasing. This property illustrates that the gap between the implicit return of the unfunded pension scheme, measured by $\left(v_R^{\text{ann}}/v_x^{\text{buy}}\right) \cdot a_R$, and the past and forecast financial return, measured by $(R_{R,\ x}/q_{R,\ x})$, is decreasing with age. For a given period, the point's price is the same at all ages which implies there is no mortality correction. This property benefits older workers closer to retirement age. The profile will be the same in German point system and in the Swedish NDC. Table 10.3 in appendix presents a detailed comparison of the three pension systems.

It is difficult to judge whether the unfunded pension return will be stronger in Sweden and Germany. In Sweden, the indexing of pensions below wage growth is conservative, which means that it will not be difficult to satisfy. In Germany, the demographic decline suggests heavy future adjustments notably by the demographic factor. However, the guarantees on the minimum replacement rate imply that the central government will have to intervene once the margins of adjustment by the increase in contributions will be no longer possible. Significant public aid from the German state, though, is financially credible due to the particularly satisfying quality of its public finances.

10.4 Governance in "Crisis Mode": A Focus on the 30 October 2015 Agreement

10.4.1 General Context and Sustainability Issues

In the absence of agreement, the expense/receipt dependency ratio, currently equal to 107.5%, would have reached about 116% in 2035 (Fig. 10.3). The AGIRC-ARRCO pension scheme relies on so-called variant 2 (see part 1), an intermediate scenario elaborated in 2015. At the end of the same year, the reserve fund of these two schemes amounted to €73 billion. In this medium-term perspective, sustainability is challenged, since in 2023 the pension schemes in deficit would be forced either to borrow (which is not feasible, because they would not benefit from public guarantee) or to take corrective rescue actions (Fig. 10.4).

10.4.2 Choice to Restore Solvency

According to GIE[6] AGIRC-ARRCO (Marais 2016), 30 October's agreement planned corrective actions 8 years before likely default in 2023. These actions impact expenditures (E) and receipts (R) either directly or indirectly.

The agreement provided for the merging of the two pension schemes from January 2019. An inter-branch agreement was due to be ratified before 1 January 2018.

The agenda provided a two-step procedure: immediate measures (I) coming into effect between the beginning of 2016 and the end of 2018, followed by delayed measures (D) (from 1 January 2019).

These measures can have short-term effects (ST = 2020) and/or long-term effects (LR = 2030). Let us describe succinctly the various impacts of the reform (see Table 10.1 for a detailed taxonomy of the different measures).

- Under-indexing of pensions (inflation rate minus 1 point) is fully effective as soon as inflation rate is strictly greater than 1% since scenario Var2 forbids nominal decrease in pensions. According to AGIRC-ARRCO, this amounts to a 2.5% decrease in total expenditures.
- From 2016, the yearly revaluation of pension is delayed from 1 April to 1 November.
- The increase of point's purchase value translates into its over-indexing with respect to its value. Until 2018, a threshold was imposed at 6% of the ratio: service value/(purchasing value × repurchase rate). The number of purchased points will decrease over time for a same amount of payroll tax. The relative

[6] *Groupement d'Intérêt Economique AGIRC-ARRCO*, an economic interest group established on 1 July 2002, is the common managing organization of AGIRC and ARRCO pension schemes.

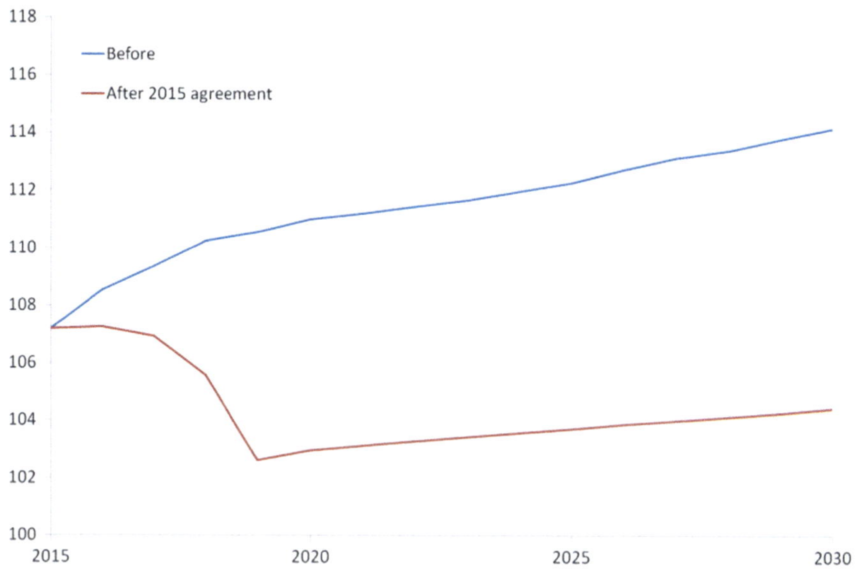

Fig. 10.3 Expenditure/receipt ratio (in percentage). (*Sources:* Authors' calculation from AGIRC-ARRCO public data)

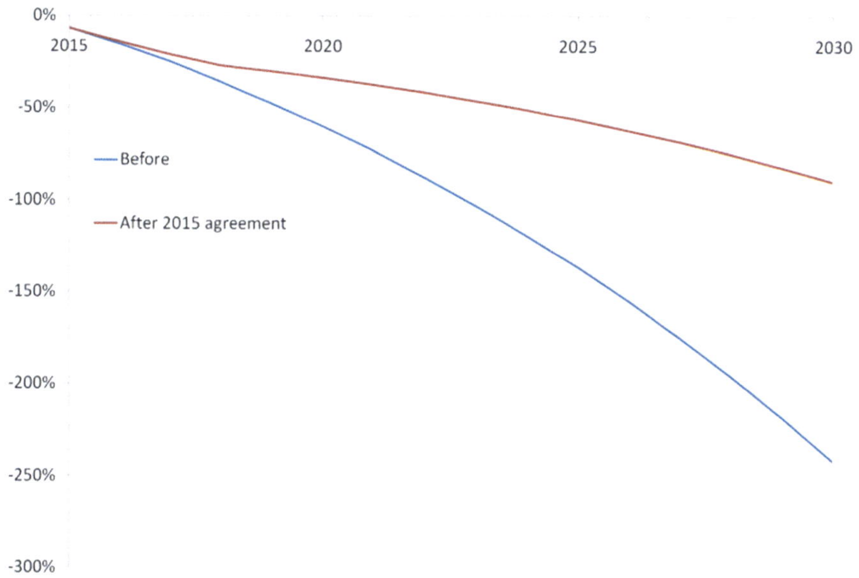

Fig. 10.4 Discounted cumulated deficit in % of current reserve fund from 2015 on. (*Sources:* Authors' calculation from AGIRC-ARRCO official forecast)

Table 10.1 Taxonomy of 30 October 2015 agreement's measures according to their impacts on expenditures (E), receipts (R), timing (immediate (I) or delayed (D) and duration (short term (ST) or long run (LR))

Measures	E	R	I	D	ST[a]	LR[a]
Under-indexing pensions (inflation – 1 point)	–		X		–2.5	–2.5
Delaying yearly revaluation of pensions by 7 months (1 Nov. 2016)	–		X		–1.5	–1.5
Increasing the purchase value of point (s.t. 6% threshold return rate)	–		X		–0.1	–1.1
Extension of AGFF contribution		+ + +	X		+0.1	+0.1
Solidarity coefficient	–	+		X	–0.6	–0.8
Management expenditures and social action	–			X	–0.3	–0.2
Increase in LR delivered pensions induced by the increase in the facial payroll tax rate to 17%	+ +		X		0	+0.2
Increase in adjustment factor (+2 points) + other contributions including the contributive payroll tax base merging and the facial payroll tax rate increase		+ + +		X	+2.4	+2.8
Total impact: expenditures					–4.8	–5.9
Total impact: receipts					+2.5	+2.9

Sources: authors' calculation from AGIRC-ARRCO official forecast
[a]In percentage of receipts or expenditures

magnitude of the long-run expected effect (reduction in expenditures) is 0.1% in 2020 and 1.1% in 2030.

- A leading measure applying to the future generations of retirees consists in inducing them to postpone by 1 year their retirement beyond full pension age. Otherwise, the mandatory occupational pension is reduced by 10% during 3 years before reaching 67. This pension reduction is limited to 5% for low pensions (under a specific tax ceiling). As early as 2019, the new retirees aged 62 will be penalized (by a reduction in their pension), which could induce them to delay their retirement, resulting in an increase of the overall contribution period and a corresponding shortening of their time spent in retirement. However, in its prospective scenario, the GIE foresees that 95% of the AGIRC-ARRCO contributors will not change their decision as to their retirement after the setting of the penalty just described. Its main impact will then be a decrease in pension benefits. The estimated residual gain is 0.8%, which corresponds to the difference between a gain (increase in contributions and decrease in pension benefits due to the reduction of time spent in retirement) and a loss (increase of pension benefits due to the acquisition of additional points and a yearly bonus of 10%, 20% and 30% for a two-year, a three-year and a four-year or more retirement delay, respectively).
- In 2019, increasing the repurchase rate (by 2 points) can be considered as equivalent to increasing payroll taxes by 1.6% (no additional pension points).

Table 10.2 Decomposition of the variation of the gain (in 2015 billion €)

Period	Expenditures	Receipts	Gain Δ(R–E)
2017	–1.6	+0.1	+1.7
2020	–4.2	+1.9	+6.1
2030	–6.0	+2.6	+8.6

Sources: Authors' calculation from AGIRC-ARRCO official forecast

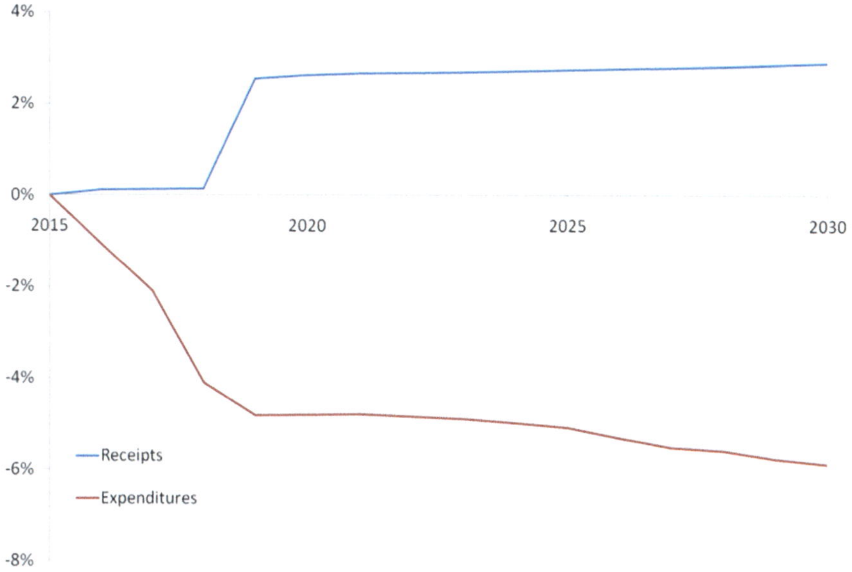

Fig. 10.5 Relative variations in receipts or expenditures. (*Source:* Authors' calculation from AGIRC-ARRCO official forecast)

The increase in the facial rate above the social security ceiling (past wage brackets 2 or B or C) to 17% leads to a 3.4% increase in contributions for AGIRC and 4.9% for ARRCO. The increase in the facial rate implies an increase in the LR delivered pension (additional attributed pension points). Added to other measures (merging of wage brackets 2, B and C, extension of AGFF above bracket C) aimed at increasing contributions, the overall effect leads to a roughly 2.8% increase in receipts in 2030.

The measures described above should lead to a reduction in 4.8% reduction in expenditures and a 2.9% increase in receipts between 2020 and 2030 (Fig. 2.5). The combined effects should reduce the deficit by €6.1 billion in 2020 and €8.6 billion in 2030 (Table 10.2 and Fig. 10.5).

It is worthy noticing that the results linked to the pension under-indexing are contingent to a greater than 1% inflation. Otherwise, this measure is obviously less efficient. For instance, according to official Insee data, in 2016, the observed inflation over the last 12 months was 0.2%, meaning the under-indexing was only 0.2% and not 1%.

The 30 October agreement is somehow disruptive, since, besides setting financial measures, it explicitly relies on fundamental principles about, first, viability and, second, governance organized from January 2019 ("Article 11. Mise en place d'un pilotage pluriannuel de la retraite complémentaire"/Implementation of a multi-year management of mandatory additional pension scheme), after the three-year transitory period.

The agreement includes the implementation of a strategic management scheme that relies on two principles and two instruments.

The two principles are as follows:

- Principle 1: Strategic decisions taken by the social partners in charge of AGIRC-ARRCO every 4 years.
- Principle 2: The latter must set the objectives in terms of trajectory.

The two strategic management instruments are as follows:

- 1. A measure of sustainability over a 15-year period: level of reserve funds, accompanied with a security ratio covering at least six-month pension benefits and/or the evolution of the expenditure/receipt ratio.
- 2. Control parameters, that is, the set of parameters used to control for receipts (contribution rate, adjustment factor, etc.) and for expenditures (service value of point in short term and long run, long-run purchase value of point, etc.). However, the use of some of these instruments is conditional upon both their authorized ranges and the evolution of the first pillar pension scheme.

Besides, a tactic management strategy sets each year the admissible ranges of certain parameters.

Also, an emergency procedure is established: "the Executive Board of the merged AGIRC-ARRCO scheme must warn the representative organizations [. . .] as soon as the constraints set for its strategic management are not respected".

The social partners are required to open "negotiations for the purpose of adjusting expenditures and/or charges of the merged occupational mandatory pension scheme"[7].

Hence, this procedure establishes the "crisis mode" governance of the pension scheme. This implies that solutions have to be found using discretionary tools (Turner 2009), in opposition to automatic balance mechanisms (Gannon et al. 2014, 2016).

Contrarily to Canada's, this emergency procedure does not require provisional measures such as pension freeze or automatic increase of contribution as long as the parliament has not voted adequate measures against default risk. The real threat for the AGIRC-ARRCO scheme would reach the point where its financial reserves are depleted, and to be forced to borrow on the financial markets to pay the pensions due,

[7]Translation by authors

which is most unlikely without state guarantee. Otherwise, a "fiscal cliff" procedure similar to the US one would be triggered. This is a credible threat point which the social partners must consider.

10.4.3 Impact on Implicit Marginal Tax Rate

How does this agreement modify the pension-contribution link and the implicit marginal tax rate?

The 30 October 2015 agreement's impacts vary according to generations. This can be assessed by studying how the agreement's measures affect the life cycle's implicit marginal rate of contribution for individuals of three successive generations.

The overall impact of the increase in the purchase price (increase in the price of the point and increase in the repurchase rate) reaches a maximum 8% increase in 2018 (see Fig. 10.6). For a given contribution rate, the number of points acquired each year should decrease by 8%. For a given point price, the increase in the facial contribution rate to 17% leads to an increase in the number of attributed pension points. According to our calculations, the two cumulative effects would lead to a reduction in the number of points acquired each year by about 2.5%.

The under-indexing of pensions (delaying of revaluation and the explicit under-indexing) rapidly led to an overall 3.8% decline in pensions in 2019 and then slowly declined to 4.5% in the long term (see Fig. 10.6). This slow decline reflects the fact

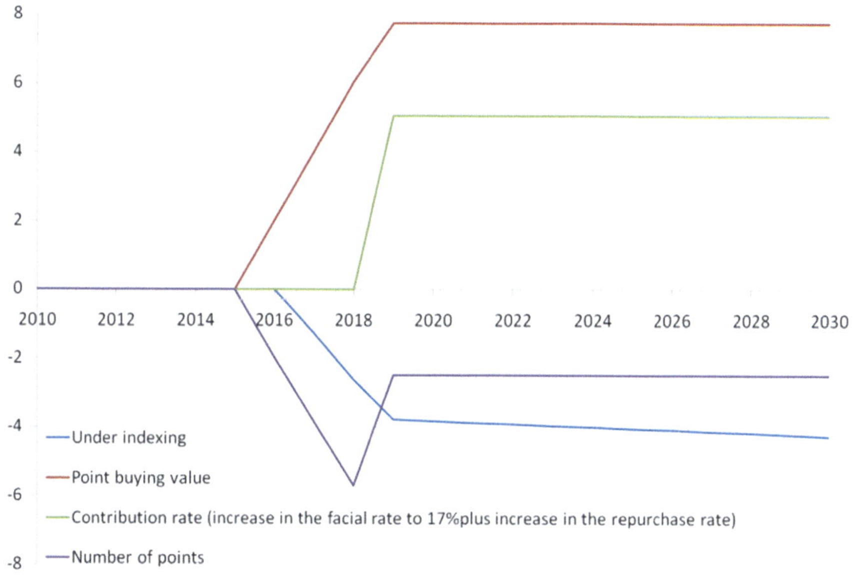

Fig. 10.6 AGIRC: relative changes in parameter values. (*Sources:* Authors' calculation)

that the pension indexation to productivity growth is delayed (November instead of April).

Considering the three-generation test cases presented earlier, we turn now to the temporal and generational impacts of the agreement's various measures. Figure 10.7a–c retraces the variations of the implicit marginal tax rate.

The 1952 generation (G1952) is only affected by the under-indexing of pension benefits (Fig. 10.7a). In retrospect, its implicit marginal contribution increases from 0.15 point at the beginning of its lifecycle to 0.6 point at its ending.

The 1962 generation (G1962) is also impacted by a comparable magnitude by the decrease in pension index (Fig. 10.7b). From age 54 (in 2016) then 57 (in 2019), the two successive increases in the point's purchasing price (by rent point value and point buying value) lead to a reduction of acquired points for a constant contribution. For a constant purchasing price, the contribution rate has a positive mechanical effect on the implicit marginal contribution rate, which turns negative when the underlying marginal rate is negative enough.

A similar evolution (Fig. 10.7c) is followed by generation 1973 (G1973). However, two differences are to be stressed:

1. The increase in the contribution rate occurs when workers are 46 compared with 57 for the 1962 generation. The 1973 generation will therefore be subject to longer tax increase.
2. The malus will stop only after 1 year against after 3 years for the 1962 generation, because we suppose that people will retire at 66, after 43 contributive years just 1 year before the full pension age 67 against 64 after 42 contributive years just 3 years before the full pension age 67.

From 2019, when AGIRC and ARRCO merged, mixing blue- and white-collar retirees may induce unequal tax distortion impact because of their life expectancy gaps. Moreover, white collars, though entering job market later, leave later and should be less impacted by "solidarity" penalty because of the 67-year-old limit. However, for the long careers, 62-year-old pension age will induce a 3-year-penalty.

10.5 Conclusion

This chapter has presented France's two occupational mandatory supplementary pension schemes for executives (AGIRC) and nonexecutives (ARRCO) of the private sector. They emerged after WW2, when the need and the will arose in many countries, including France, to opt for Beveridgean universal social protection systems. AGIRC and ARRCO were inspired from a Bismarckian tradition in the sense where, first, they were set up in the context of branch and interprofessional agreements and, second, they require contributions to deliver claims to pension. They also drew from the Beveridgean model, since they rely on a pay-as-you-go principle, which assumes a financial solidarity between generations and has permitted to grant pension rights to the first retirees who could not have contributed to the

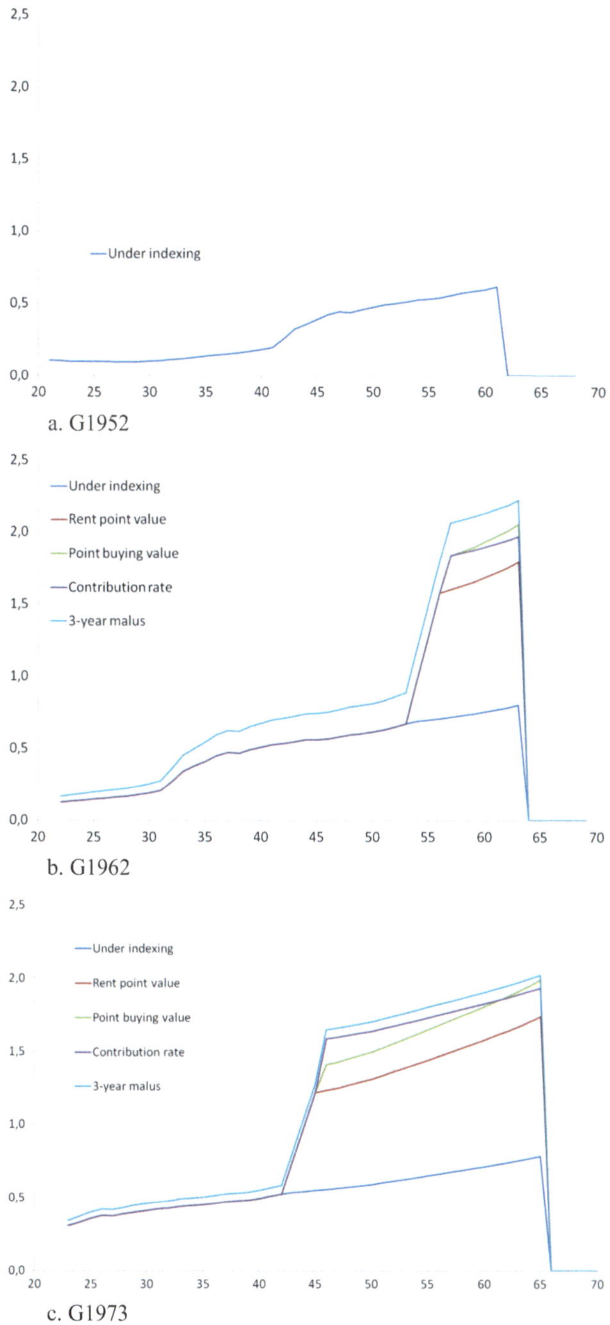

Fig. 10.7 AGIRC: variations of the implicit marginal tax rate (**a**) G1952, (**b**) G1962, (**c**) G1973

new scheme and whose pre-war pay-as-you-go retirement schemes were unable to pay them rents, after having undergone the Great Depression of the 1930s, the war period and, finally, post-war inflation.

These supplementary schemes result from agreements between employers and workers' trade unions. Starting small, they expanded to all the contributors to the General Social Security Scheme (Caisse Nationale d'Assurance Vieillesse – CNAV) to finally become mandatory.

Denied the possibility to revert to borrowing, they were compelled to achieve midterm financial equilibrium. Accordingly, they accumulated surpluses both to meet unexpected shocks and to smooth the effects of an aging population.

ARRCO and AGIRC schemes have, in the past, formed numerous links that give them a strong parametric homogeneity. Their co-evolution has been finalized by their merging, on 1 January 2019.

They rely on an actuarial logic that aims at connecting pension and contribution. Germany has adopted a similar system for its first pillar pension scheme. By using the "implicit marginal contribution rate" marginalist approach, we show that the pension-contribution relationship can be characterized by two kinds of distortions:

1. The purchase value of point is the same whatever the contributor's age and does not take into account mortality, which implies that the younger workers who will not retire before 40 years are disadvantaged compared to older workers due to retire in a few months.
2. The long-term rate of return of point (assuming a constant contribution rate) depends on the growth rate of the taxable total payroll, making it different from a financial return, which is generally greater in the long run.

Following the 2008 economic crisis and the ensuing rising unemployment, decline in economic growth and depreciation of financial assets, AGIRC and ARRCO supplementary pension schemes have been weakened because of the reduced growth of the payroll tax receipts and a decrease in their financial revenues. Since 2008, several adjustments have been necessary. The most recent one, the 30 October 2015's agreement, is particularly interesting because it is designed to last in the long term and provides the basis for automatic renegotiation triggered when solvency requirements are not met.

It is designed to last in the long term because its adopted measures should increase receipts by roughly 3% and durably reduce expenditures up to 6%, which guarantees equilibrium until 2023.

The inclusion in the agreement's provisions of the management of AGIRC-ARRCO pension scheme's financial equilibrium in the long run lays the groundwork of a genuine governance aimed at solvency. Though no *stricto* sensu automatic adjustment such as an ABM is provided for in the agreement, objectives and instruments are explicitly defined. Furthermore, a renegotiation principle (with an obligation of result) suggests that changes (decided in "crisis mode", hence discretionary) will take place.

Annex

Table 10.3 Comparison between France, Germany and Sweden: overall characteristics

	France	Germany	Sweden
Name	AGIRC and ARRCO	Abschnittsdeckungsverfahren	
Pension	Additional and compulsory	Basic and compulsory	Basic and compulsory
Governance	Employer and employees trade union	Federal government	Government
Coverage	Workers of the private sector	Workers of the private sector	All workers
Defined contributions	Points system	Points system	Notional account in currency
Year of creation	1947 (AGIRC) and 1962 (ARRCO) 2019 (fusion of AGIRC and ARRCO)	1957	1999
Sustainability objectives	Yes	Yes but not explicit	Balance ratio
Automatic balancing index	No	Sustainability demographic factor for the pensions (since 1999) and contribution rate for the receipts	Binding ABM
Automaticity of the balancing index	Irrelevant	Discretionary	Compulsory
Minimum guarantee	No	Obligation of result: replacement rate net >= 46% (2020) and >=43% (2030)	No
Contribution rate choice	Discretionary and fixed by agreement between social partners	Automatic if buffer fund <0.2 month but the maximum is fixed by the law: ceiling <20% (2020) and < 22% (2030)	"intention is to keep the contribution rate constant" (Barr 2013)
Buffer funds	Yes	Yes	Yes
Funding	Payroll taxes + returns on buffer funds	Payroll taxes and governmental transfers	Payroll taxes + returns on buffer funds
Rent coefficient conversion	Universal[a]	Universal[a]	Age and generation dependent
Penalty/ reward coefficient	Yes	Yes	No
Indexation of buy point price	Discretionary	Gross average wage	

(continued)

	France	Germany	Sweden
Annuity value indexation	Since April 2013: Max (growth rate of median wage 1.5; inflation) From Nov. 2016 to Nov.2018: max (inflation – 1.0)	Growth rate of average wage	3-year moving average nominal wage growth rate – 1.6%
Pension ages	From 57 y.o. with penalties until 65 y.o. (normal pension age of AGIRC-ARRCO) A specific fund pays the penalties between the normal pension age of basic scheme (CNAV), currently set at 62 and 65 y.o.	63 y.o. and 45 contribution years *or* from 65 y.o. (in 2012) to 66 (in 2023) and age 67 (in 2030)	61 y.o.
Widow/widower survivor	Yes	Yes	No

[a]Not explicitly linked to age and generation

References

Barr, N. (2013). The pension system in Sweden, Report to the Expert Group on Public Economics, Ministry of Finance.

Charpentier, F. (2014). Retraites complémentaires: Histoire et place des régimes Arrco et Agirc dans le système français 75 ans de paritarisme, Economica, 587p.

Charpentier, F. (2016). AGIRC-ARRCO: le troisième âge des retraites complémentaires, *Regards, 49*, 25–34.

Cuvilliez, J., & Laurent, T. (2016). The October 2015 agreement on France's complementary pension schemes for private-sector employees (AGIRC and ARRCO), *Trésor-Economics, 178.*

Duc, C., Martin, H., Trégulier, J. (2016). *Les réformes des retraites de 2010 à 2015*, Dossier de la DREES, n°9.

Feldstein, M., & Samwick, A. (1992). Social security rules and marginal tax rates. *National Tax Journal, 45*(1), 1–22.

Gannon, F., & Touzé, V. (2013). Pension rules and implicit marginal tax rate in France, proceedings of the 2013 Actuarial and financial mathematics conference (MichèleVanmaele et al., Eds), De KoninklijkeVlaamseAcademie van België, Brussels.

Gannon, F., Hamayon, S., Legros, F., & Touzé, V. (2014). Sustainability of the French first pillar pension scheme (CNAV): Assessing automatic balance mechanisms. *Australian Journal of Actuarial Practice, 1*, 33–45.

Gannon, F., Legros, F., Touzé, V. (2016). Sustainability of pension schemes: Building a smooth automatic balance mechanism with an application to the US Social Security, working paper OFCE, May 2016.

Legros, F. (2010). NDCs: A comparison of the French and German point systems. In *Pension reform: Issues and prospects for Non-Financial Defined Contribution (NDC) schemes*, edited by Robert Holzmann and Edward Palme, Proceedings of the NDC Conference in Sandhamn, Sweden, September 28–30, 2003.

Marais, S. (2016). Accord national interprofessionnel relatif aux retraites complémentaires Agirc-Arrco-Agff du 30 octobre 2015, Les Cahiers Etudes et Statistiques, n°1, February.

Turner, J. A. (2009). *Social security financing: Automatic adjustments to restore solvency*, Washington, DC: AARP Public Policy Institute.

Chapter 11
Last Lessons Learned from the Swedish Public Pension System

María del Carmen Boado-Penas, Poontavika Naka, and Ole Settergren

Abstract Retirement systems across the world are undergoing major reforms to adapt to continuously changing economic and demographic factors. Among these major changes are the so-called notional defined contribution pension schemes (NDCs), first developed about 20 years ago in countries such as Italy, Latvia, Poland and Sweden. These pension schemes attempt to reproduce the logic of a financial defined contribution pension plan within a pay-as-you-go framework. Among the countries with NDCs, Sweden is the only one where an automatic balancing mechanism goes hand in hand with the prior calculation of a financial solvency indicator that emerges from an actuarial balance sheet. This chapter describes the Swedish pension experience over the 2007–2015 period through its accounting method, together with the problems faced by the system and the policy responses.

Keywords Accounting · Balancing mechanism · Public pensions · Retirement · Solvency · Sweden

11.1 Introduction

Social security systems across the world are undergoing significant reforms to adapt their schemes to economic and demographic uncertainties.

M. del Carmen Boado-Penas (✉)
Department of Mathematical Sciences, Institute for Financial and Actuarial Mathematics (IFAM), University of Liverpool, Liverpool, UK
e-mail: Carmen.Boado@liverpool.ac.uk

P. Naka
Chulalongkorn Business School, Department of Statistics, Bangkok, Thailand
e-mail: poontavika@cbs.chula.ac.th

O. Settergren
Swedish Pensions Agency, Stockholm, Sweden
e-mail: ole.settergren@pensionsmyndigheten.se

M. Peris-Ortiz et al. (eds.), *Economic Challenges of Pension Systems*,
https://doi.org/10.1007/978-3-030-37912-4_11

In Europe, the common trend in the responses to the pension crisis is a wave of parametric adjustments that usually include changes in the contribution ceilings, increases in the retirement age or changes in the indexation of pensions[1]. Among the major changes carried out in pension reforms are the so-called notional defined contribution pension schemes (NDCs), first developed about two decades ago in countries such as Italy, Latvia, Poland and Sweden. Other countries, including Egypt, China and Greece, are seriously considering the introduction of NDCs[2].

NDCs, also known as defined contribution unfunded pension schemes, are ruled by a common principle; they attempt to reproduce the logic of a defined contribution pension plan within a pay-as-you-go (PAYG) framework. The notional account is a virtual one that records individual contributions, together with the fictitious return that they generate throughout each contributor's working life. The return that contributions earn is calculated on the basis of a macroeconomic index that tries to reflect the financial health of the system (i.e. changes in salaries and GDP growth), not market returns. The account balance is called notional because it is only used for record keeping (i.e. the system does not invest funds as the scheme is based on PAYG financing). When an individual retires, his or her accumulated contributions (or the notional account) are converted into a life annuity according to standard actuarial practice. Therefore, the amount of the initial pension depends on the mortality of the retiring cohort, potential future pension indexations and the technical interest rate used to discount the cash flows.

The notional model has some positive features, such as facing the ageing population more or less automatically or improving the relationship between contributions and pensions paid. However, these schemes do not guarantee sustainability due to the PAYG nature.[3] Valdés-Prieto (2000) shows that NDCs cannot generally provide financial equilibrium over the short term unless they are in the realistic steady state and have a notional rate equal to the covered salary bill. Hence, NDCs also require other financial modification mechanisms, such as government guarantees and repeated recourse to legislation – to be imposed in the same way as traditional defined benefit (DB) systems – or special measures, such as automatic balancing mechanisms (ABMs).

Sweden has gone beyond the NDC system that it implemented in 2001, in the sense that an income statement and a balance sheet[4] are annually published with the aim of analysing the system's solvency. Even so, an automatic balancing system that reduces the growth of the liabilities is triggered if the plan is not fully solvent. Sweden is claimed to be the only NDC country whose pension is financially

[1]See Whitehouse (2009), Whitehouse et al. (2009), and Organisation for Economic Co-operation and Development (2012).

[2]Interested readers can consult, for example, Lindbeck and Persson (2003), Williamson (2004), Börsch-Supan (2006), Holzmann and Palmer (2006), Vidal-Meliá et al. (2006), Auerbach and Lee (2009), Vidal-Meliá et al. (2010), Whitehouse (2010), Auerbach and Lee (2011), Chłoń-Domińczak et al. (2012), Holzmann et al. (2012).

[3]See Valdés-Prieto (2000) and Palmer (2013).

[4]Also called an actuarial balance sheet.

sustainable over the long term in the sense that it is not necessary to make changes to the contribution rate[5].

This chapter first presents and discusses the Swedish accounting method (income statements and balance sheets) over the 2007–2015 period, with special attention to changes in total assets and liabilities. Second, it describes and explains Sweden's policy responses to the negative effects of the financial and economic crisis on pension benefits and notional accounts, in combination with the effect of the new rules of automatic balancing.

The chapter is structured as follows. Section 11.2 describes the Swedish public pension system. Section 11.3 summarises the published balance sheets and income statements and analyses how they have evolved over the 2007–2015 period. Section 11.4 concludes with a discussion on the new responses to the economic crisis, which have been undertaken by the Swedish pension system since 2007.

11.2 Swedish Public Pension System[6]

The Swedish public pension system consists of two different earnings-related benefit schemes: an NDC pension (called the *inkomstpension*), on which this chapter focuses, and a fully funded financial defined contribution pension (the *premium pension*). A tax-financed guaranteed pension, annually adjusted according to the consumer price index, provides supplementary support for retirees with low NDC pensions.

Under the NDC scheme, both accounts and benefits are indexed by the change in the average income. When the initial pension is calculated – that is, when the notional account value is converted into an annuity – the pension is increased or front-loaded on the basis of an assumed annual real growth rate of 1.6% for the income index. This rate of advanced interest is then deducted every year from the increase in the income index. Thus, the NDC pension is indexed annually by the change in the income index reduced by 1.6%. In certain situations, exceptions to the regular income indexation of accounts and benefits apply. These exceptions are governed by the ratio of assets to liabilities (balance ratio[7]) as provided in the legislation on the balancing mechanism. The balance ratio is an indicator that

---

[5]According to Diamond (2004), a well-structured NDC system, with a decent-sized buffer stock of assets, will have little probability of needing legislative intervention as long as the economic growth is large enough.

[6]For a more detailed description of the Swedish pension system, see the Swedish Social Insurance Agency (2007, 2008, 2009, 2010, 2011, 2012, 2013, 2014, 2015) and Barr (2013). The latter paper also evaluates the pension system in Sweden against the goals established at the time of the reforms in the late 1990s.

[7]To indicate that the solvency ratio of a PAYG scheme is different from that of the *premium pension*, the *inkomstpension* system calls this ratio the balance ratio.

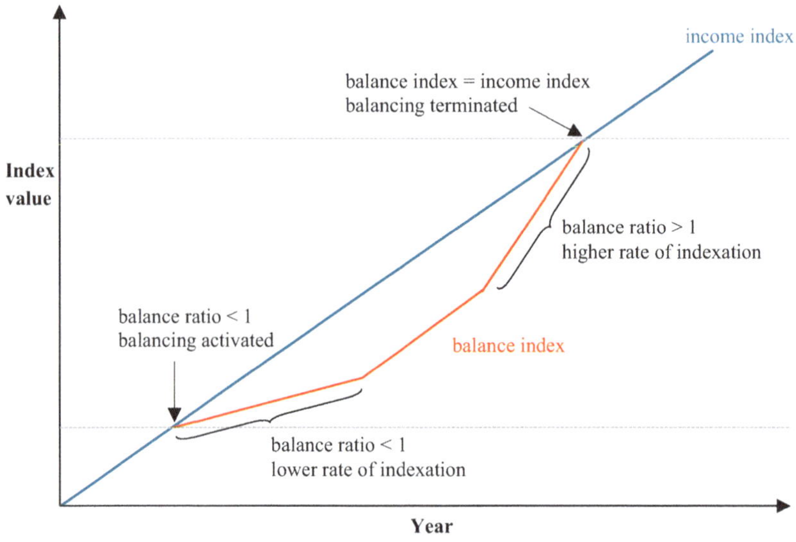

Fig. 11.1 Illustration of the balancing mechanism. (*Source:* The Swedish Social Insurance Agency (2015))

emerges from the actuarial balance sheet of the NDC scheme (presented in Sect. 11.3), expressed as:

$$\text{Balance ratio} = \frac{\text{Assets (e.g.fund assets + contribution asset)}}{\text{Pension liability}}$$

The balance ratio used in Sweden has a dual purpose – to measure whether the system can fulfil its obligations to its contributors and to decide whether an ABM should be applied.

Balancing Mechanism

Following Settergren's (2001) work, if, for some reason, the balance ratio is less than one, the ABM is triggered as shown in Fig. 3.1. This process basically consists of reducing the growth in pension liability (i.e. the pensions in payment and the pension account balances of the economically active population). Thus, the balance index (Fig. 11.1), rather than the change in the average income (expressed by an income or a salary index), is used to revalue the pensions in payment and the notional account of each contributor.

This ABM can be considered asymmetric as it is only triggered when the solvency ratio is lower than 1. However, the Swedish ABM allows for recovery. After a period of low returns as a consequence of the mechanism, a period of higher-than-normal returns follows (Fig. 11.1).[8]

[8]For more detailed explanations, see Barr and Diamond (2011).

11.3 Development of Solvency: Balance Sheets for 2007–2015

Sweden developed the new accounting rules with an almost identical discipline of the double-entry bookkeeping. The country also produces an actuarial balance sheet and an income statement every year. Its annual report has presented an overall picture of the financial health of the Swedish NDC pension system since 2001.

The balance sheet for the Swedish NDC pension system is a financial statement listing the pension system's obligation to contributors and pensioners on a particular date (also referred to as liabilities), together with the amounts of the various assets (financial assets and contribution amounts) that back up these commitments. The actuarial balance sheet mainly aims to provide a true and fair view of the pension system's assets and liabilities in the beginning and at the end of each fiscal year; by comparing these figures, it intends to determine the change in the net worth. The balance sheet also contributes to the management and disclosure of financial information because it is useful not only for the authority governing the system but also for contributors and pensioners in general and for the body that guarantees payment (i.e. the state and the contributors it represents) (Boado-Penas et al. 2008; Boado-Penas and Vidal-Meliá 2013).

The system's assets comprise the value of future pension contributions, referred to as the contribution asset and the buffer fund. The first entry on the asset side is called the contribution asset, which is the turnover duration (TD) multiplied by the value of the contributions made in a specific period. The TD is the expected average length of time between the payment of a monetary unit of contribution into the system and the disbursement of the corresponding credit in the form of a pension. It thus reflects the difference between the weighted average age of pensioners and the weighted average age of contributors, assuming that economic, demographic and legal conditions are constant. The TD[9] is also the sum of the pay-in duration and the pay-out duration as shown in Table 11.1.

Additionally, the contribution asset is equivalent to the present value of the perpetual future flow of contributions discounted with the inverse of the TD, called the implicit discount rate. If the TD increases (decreases), the implicit discount rate decreases (increases), and the value of the contribution flow increases (decreases). The implicit discount rate varied between 3.13 and 3.29 (see Table 11.1). The rate can also be regarded as the system's discount rate for contributions because it is defined by the contribution flows' capacity to amortise the pension debt.

The buffer fund[10], also called the fund asset, aims to stabilise pension disbursements and/or pension contributions in relation to economic and demographic

---

[9]After 2014, the disclosure about the TD has been calculated in terms of the difference between the weighted average ages of pensioners and contributors. See the Annual Report of the Swedish Pension System (2015), Appendix B, Formula B.3.1.

[10]Sweden is the only country using the NDC system that has created the buffer fund. Several countries with the PAYG state pension system (e.g. Canada, France, Ireland, Japan, Norway, Spain, etc.) have established the public reserve funds (Yermo 2008).

Table 11.1 Balance sheet of the Swedish NDC pension system on December 31, 2007–2015

Item	2007	2008	2009	2010	2011	2012	2013	2014	2015
Assets (% of GDP)									
Fund assets	27.2	20.9	25.1	25.4	23.9	26.0	28.1	30.1	29.4
Contribution asset	185.5	191.2	193.5	186.8	186.7	187.7	188.9	187.5	178.4
Total assets	212.7	212.1	218.6	212.2	210.6	213.7	217.0	217.6	207.8
Liabilities and results brought forward (% of GDP)									
Opening results brought forward	3.0	0.5	−7.4	−9.2	2.8	4.3	−2.1	3.2	10.1
Net income or loss for the year	−2.5	−7.7	−2.4	12.1	1.5	−6.4	5.5	7.5	−6.0
Closing results brought forward	0.5	−7.2	−9.8	2.9	4.3	−2.2	3.4	10.7	4.1
Pension liability	212.2	219.3	228.4	209.3	206.3	215.8	213.6	206.8	203.7
Total liabilities and results brought forward	212.7	212.1	218.6	212.2	210.6	213.7	217.0	217.6	207.8
Financial Indicators									
Balancing year	2009	2010	2011	2012	2013	2014	2015	2016	2017
Balance ratio, original definition[a]	1.0026	0.9672	0.9570	1.0138	1.0208	0.9901	1.0158	1.0521	1.0201
Balance ratio, modified legislation[b]	n.a.	0.9826	0.9549	1.0024	1.0198	0.9837	1.0040	1.0375	1.0067[c]
Pay-in duration (years)	21.07	20.88	20.83	20.62	20.55	20.56	20.41	n.a	n.a
Pay-out duration (years)	10.69	10.79	10.83	10.88	10.89	10.92	10.99	n.a	n.a
Turnover duration (years)	31.76	31.67	31.66	31.51	31.44	31.48	31.40	30.37	n.a
Smoothed turnover duration (years)	31.93	31.76	31.76	31.67	31.66	31.51	31.48	31.44	30.38
Implicit discount rate (1/TD) (%)	3.13	3.15	3.15	3.16	3.16	3.17	3.18	3.18	3.29
Income (or Balance) index (%)	4.5	6.2	−1.4	−2.7	5.2	5.8	−1.1	2.5	5.9
GDP (SKr billions)	3297	3388	3289	3520	3657	3685	3770	3937	4181

Source: Authors' compilation based on the data from the Swedish Social Insurance Agency (2007, 2008, 2009, 2010, 2011, 2012, 2013, 2014, 2015)

Note: *GDP* gross domestic product, *n.a.* not applicable

[a]The balance ratio calculated according to the previous definition (2007). It is calculated solely on the basis of the buffer fund's market value as of December 31 of the corresponding year, formerly called the financial position

[b]The balance ratio calculated according to the new definition (2008 onwards). It is calculated on the basis of a 3-year average of the buffer fund's market value

[c]The damped balance ratio is used instead of the balance ratio from 2015 onwards. It is equal to 1 plus one-third of the difference between the balance ratio fixed for that year and the number 1

changes. The buffer fund of the Swedish NDC system consists of five separate national pension funds (also known as *Allmänna pensionsfonder* [AP] funds): the First, Second, Third, Fourth and Sixth AP funds. Pension contributions are deposited equally to the First to the Fourth AP funds, which also equally finance the pension disbursements. In contrast, the Sixth[11] AP Fund is an evergreen one, which means that there are no contributions paid to and pension disbursements from the fund. The buffer fund's size is large, amounting to 20.9–30.1% of the GDP (see Table 11.1) and 9.5–14.5% as a share of the pension liability in 2007–2015.

In the balance sheet, the pension liability includes a liability to contributors and a liability to pensioners. The liability to contributors is the notional accumulated capital in the contributors' accounts. The liability to pensioners is the present value of the expected total of all pensions paid to current pensioners during their lifetimes, taking into account the current life expectancy and the real technical interest rate applied (1.6%) when the amount of the initial pension was calculated. The pension liability varies from 203.7% to 228.4% of the GDP (see Table 11.1).

Since the system was implemented in 2001, the contribution asset has always been less than the pension liability over time. For example, in 2015, the contribution asset accounted for SEK 7457 billion, in contrast to SEK 8517 billion in pension liability (see Table 11.3). The system would have been partially solvent. However, by including the buffer fund that absorbs the differences between the inflow of contributions and the outflow of pensions, the total assets will likely exceed the pension liability.

Figure 11.2 shows the evolution of the total assets, the pension liability and the balance ratio for the 2007–2015 period. Before 2008, the system's balance ratio was greater than 1, and the total assets and the pension liability had risen in diversity, with a rather higher growth in liabilities than in total assets. In 2008, the financial position of the pension system substantially deteriorated. The balance ratio dropped below 1 for the first time, amounting to 0.9672 due to a huge net loss of SEK 261 billion, equivalent to 7.7% of the GDP (see Table 11.1). According to the original legislation, balancing was activated with a 3.28% reduction of the indexation of notional accounts and pensions in 2009/2010. However, in 2009, the parliament modified the new rule on the basis of the three-year average of the buffer fund for calculating the balance ratio. As a result, the modified balance ratio increased to 0.9826, and the balancing effect was reduced to 1.74%.

In 2009, the system still faced financial deficit, but the loss (2.4% of the GDP) was not as large as that of the previous year. The total assets were less than 4.3% of the pension liability, for the balance ratio of 0.9549. The pension liability was 228.4% of the GDP, the highest value during the period. The negative indexation

[11]The Sixth National Pension Fund, known as the Sixth AP Fund, operates as a long-term investor in unlisted companies. Profits can be reinvested, and any losses must be covered by the fund capital. The owner (i.e. the Swedish Parliament) may, by changing the law, decide to allow funds to be paid into or withdrawn from the Sixth AP Fund. The Sixth AP Fund invests in the private equity market, while the First to the Fourth AP funds had identical investment rules and were allocated the same amount of capital in connection with the reorganisation of the AP funds in 2001.

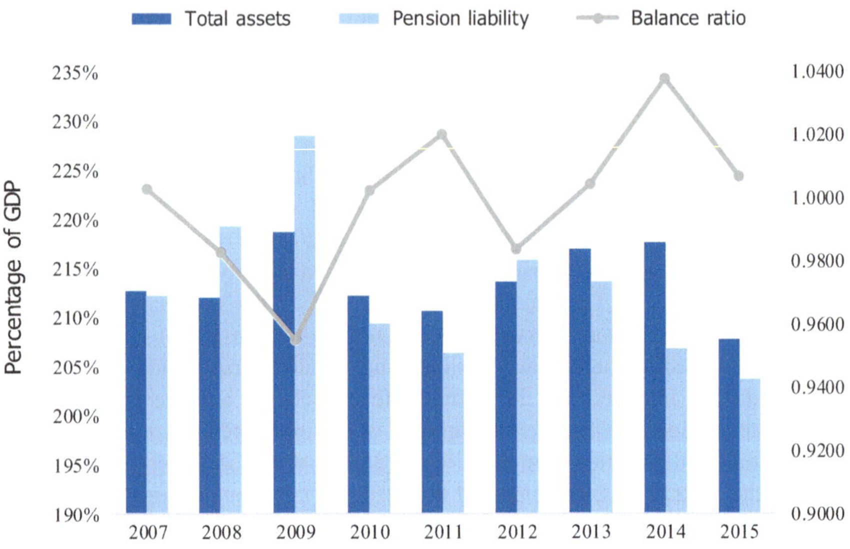

Fig. 11.2 Evolution of total assets, pension liability and balance ratio of the Swedish NDC pension system. (*Source:* Authors' compilation based on the data from the Swedish Social Insurance Agency (2007, 2008, 2009, 2010, 2011, 2012, 2013, 2014, 2015))

of notional accounts and benefits in 2009 and 2010 forced a significant drop in the value of the pension liability, and then, assets exceeded liabilities at the end of 2010. This surplus was equal to 0.0024%, for the balance ratio of 1.0024.

The pension system had been restored for a couple of years, and at the end of 2012, the pension liability exceeded the total assets again, for the balance ratio of 0.9837. Balancing was activated, and the indexation of pension balances and pension disbursements was decreased in 2013/2014. The pension liability has been revalued at a slower rate, and the pension system has been strengthened financially since 2013. The pension liability reached a value of 213.6% of the GDP in 2013 and 206.8% of the GDP in 2014, while the balance ratio increased to 1.004 in 2013 and 1.0375 in 2014. In 2015, with the aim of reducing the volatility caused by the indexation, the new form of smoothing the balance ratio (referred to as the damped balance ratio) was introduced and amounted to 1.0067. The damped balance ratio restricts balancing to one-third, resulting in less volatility in pension benefits when balancing is activated.

Figure 11.3 illustrates the relationship between the balance ratio and the income/balance index. When the balance ratio was less than 1, balancing was activated, and the income index was reduced in the next fiscal year. For example, in 2008 and 2009, the balance ratio was less than 1, and then, the income index was dropped in 2009 and 2010. After balancing was deactivated, the balance ratio was greater than 1, and the income index was increased. For instance, the balance ratio was higher than one in 2010 and 2011, and the income index rose in 2011 and 2012.

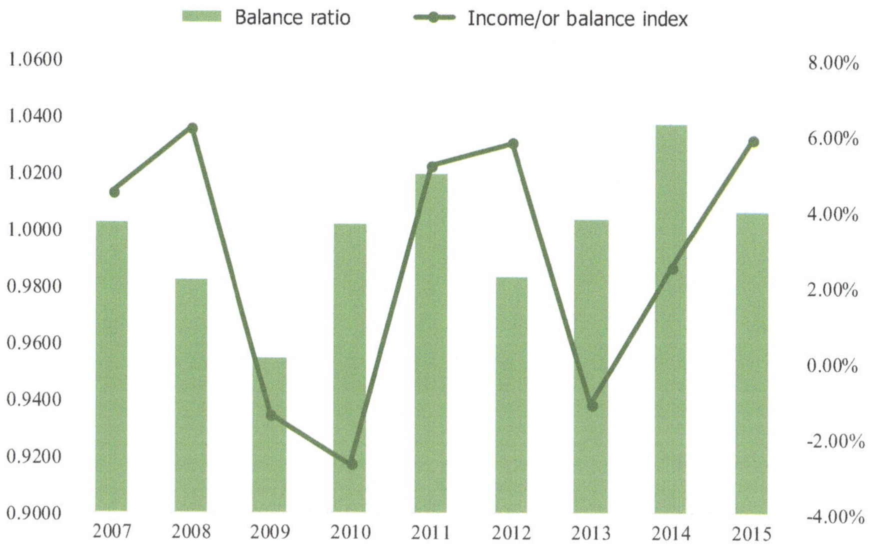

Fig. 11.3 Balance ratio and income/balance index of the Swedish NDC pension system. (*Source:* Authors' compilation based on the data from the Swedish Social Insurance Agency (2007, 2008, 2009, 2010, 2011, 2012, 2013, 2014, 2015))

Income Statements of the NDC Scheme

A full explanation of the reasons for the changes in the NDC system's solvency is specified and quantified in the income statement. It is divided into three sections: change in fund assets, change in contribution asset and change in pension liability, each presented as a percentage of the GDP over the 2007–2015 period (Table 11.2).

- Change in Fund Assets (Buffer Fund)

The total annual pension contributions and disbursements have amounted to approximately 6% of the GDP since 2007. In the first 8 years after the scheme was implemented, the net cash flow of the AP funds (the difference between contributions and disbursements, commonly referred to as the buffer fund entry) was positive. However, since 2009, the pension disbursements have become greater than the pension contributions. One reason for the growth in pension benefits is the huge number of cohorts born in the 1940s, who have recently retired (Swedish Social Insurance Agency 2010). The relatively substantial increase in the income index is another reason for the higher value of pension disbursements. For instance, in the beginning of 2009, the income index rose by 6.2% compared to 4.5% in the beginning of 2008, and then, the pension benefits grew by 9% in 2009, from SEK 199 billion in 2008 to SEK 217 billion in 2009.

However, the deficit of the net cash flow between pension contributions and benefits was offset by the returns on assets and capital in the buffer fund. From 2009 onwards, the positive return on capital has resulted in a relatively good overall change in fund assets; for example, the return on funded capital accounted for 3.76% and 1.60% of the GDP in 2014 and 2015, respectively. The variations in

Table 11.2 Income statement of the Swedish NDC pension system, 2007–2015

Item	2007	2008	2009	2010	2011	2012	2013	2014	2015
Change in fund assets (% of GDP)									
Pension contributions	5.76	5.99	6.17	5.82	5.91	6.02	6.02	5.99	5.88
Pension disbursements	−5.64	−5.87	−6.60	−6.25	−6.02	−6.40	−6.74	−6.48	−6.34
Return on funded capital	1.15	−5.73	4.14	2.41	−0.46	2.74	3.40	3.76	1.60
Administrative costs	−0.06	−0.03	−0.06	−0.06	−0.05	−0.05	−0.05	−0.05	−0.05
Total	1.24	−5.64	3.65	1.93	−0.60	2.31	2.65	3.23	1.10
Change in contribution assets (% of GDP)									
Value of change in contribution revenue	5.85	11.66	−3.50	6.59	6.97	3.26	5.70	6.76	7.96
Value of change in turnover duration	−0.67	−0.97	−0.03	−0.54	−0.05	−0.90	−0.16	−0.20	−6.12
Total	5.19	10.66	−3.50	6.05	6.92	2.36	5.52	6.53	1.84
Change in pension liability (% of GDP)									
New pension credits and ATP points	−5.88	−6.44	−6.51	−6.11	−5.66	−6.19	−6.42	−5.84	−5.88
Pension disbursements	5.64	5.87	6.60	6.25	6.02	6.40	6.74	6.48	6.34
Indexation or change in value	−8.13	−11.36	−1.95	4.69	−4.79	−10.94	−2.55	−2.34	−9.04
Value of change in life expectancy	−0.52	−0.80	−0.70	−0.71	−0.38	−0.35	−0.42	−0.51	−0.36
Inheritance gains arising	0.30	0.32	0.33	0.31	0.30	0.30	0.32	0.30	0.29
Inheritance gains distributed	−0.33	−0.35	−0.40	−0.37	−0.33	−0.35	−0.37	−0.36	−0.33
Deduction for administrative costs	0.06	0.03	0.03	0.03	0.03	0.03	0.03	0.05	0.02
Total	−8.89	−12.72	−2.55	4.12	−4.84	−11.10	−2.68	−2.24	−8.97
Net income or loss for the year (% of GDP)	−2.49	−7.70	−2.40	12.07	1.48	−6.43	5.49	7.52	−6.03

Source: Authors' compilation, based on the data from the Swedish Social Insurance Agency (2007, 2008, 2009, 2010, 2011, 2012, 2013, 2014, 2015)
A negative item (−) increases the pension liability, and a positive item decreases it (by the amount shown)
Note: *GDP* gross domestic product, *ATP Allmän tilläggspension*

the returns on the buffer fund reflect the volatility in the assets' prices allocated in each AP Fund. The investment strategies for the funds are broadly proportioned to 60% of equities and 40% of bonds.

The administrative costs are deducted annually from the pension funds, only until a retiree begins to draw a pension. At the current cost level, the deduction for costs reduces the value of the funds by approximately 1% of the GDP. The administrative costs reported in the income statement contain the costs of insurance administration and the National Pension Fund's operating expenses. Asset management fees, performance-based fees and transaction costs, such as brokerage commissions, are not reported as direct costs by the funds but have a negative effect on the section of the return on funded capital.

- Change in Contribution Asset

In the income statement, the change in the contribution asset is divided into the value of the change in the contribution revenue and the value of the change in the TD.

The value of the change in the contribution revenue, representing how much more (or less) the liability can be financed by a higher (or lower) level of contributions relative to the previous year, is the monetary value as expressed by the growth in the value of the contributions per capita multiplied by the growth of the labour force (Settergren 2013). Due to a gradual increase in pension contributions since the pension scheme was implemented, the value of the change in the contribution revenue has been positive and, in 2008, reached the maximum value of 11.66% of the GDP. In 2009, the contribution asset fell to SEK 6362 billion from SEK 6477 billion in 2008, resulting in a negative value of the change in the contribution revenue (−3.50% of the GDP). This drop in contributions was one reason for the loss incurred in the pension system and worsened the balance ratio. During the 2010–2015 period, the contribution revenue had slightly grown again at 3.26–7.96% of the GDP.

The value of the change in the TD, which is the two-year average of the smoothed contribution revenue[12] multiplied by the change in the TD, had dropped since 2005 and amounted to −6.12% of the GDP in 2015. The smoothed TD was 31.44 years in 2014 and 30.38 in 2015 (see Table 11.1). Therefore, the change in the TD dropped by 1.06 years, resulting in a sizable negative value of the change in the TD in 2015.

Taking into account the inverse relationship between the TD and the implicit discount rate, the marginally lower TD represents a slight increase in the implicit discount rate for the contribution flow, from 3.13% in 2007 to 3.29% in 2015 (see Table 11.1). The decreased TD and the increased implicit discount rate have reduced the contribution flow's capacity to finance the pension liability.

The pay-in duration, reflecting the difference in the number of years between the expected average age of earning a pension credit and the expected average age of retirement, had decreased from 21.07 years to 20.41 years over the 2007–2013

[12]As of the financial year 2015, a smoothed contribution revenue is no longer used.

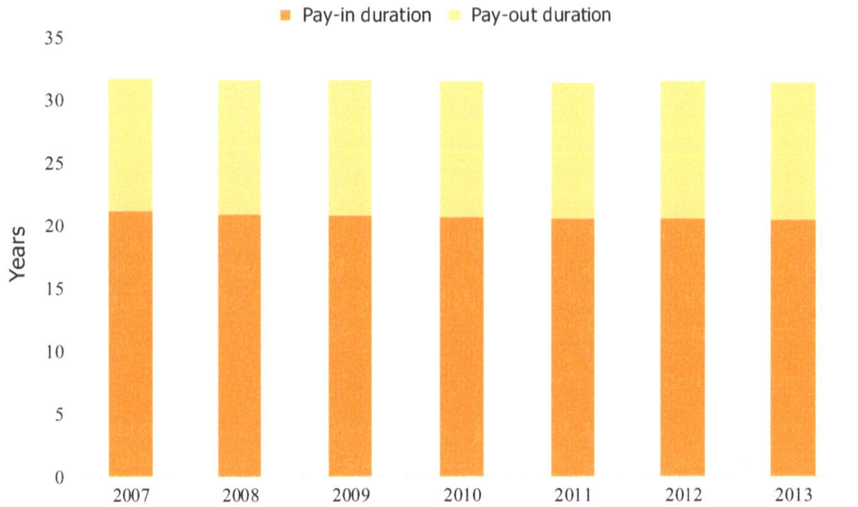

Fig. 11.4 Evolution of pay-in and pay-out duration of the NDC Swedish pension system. (*Source:* Authors' compilation based on the data from the Swedish Social Insurance Agency (2007, 2008, 2009, 2010, 2011, 2012, 2013, 2014, 2015))

period (see Table 11.1). This change represents an increase in the expected average age of contributors. However, the reasons for the negative trend have not been fully investigated[13] (Settergren 2013).

On the other hand, the pay-out duration, which is the difference in the number of years between the expected average age of retirement and the expected average age of pension recipients, had risen from 10.69 years in 2007 to 10.99 years in 2013 (see Table 11.1). This means an increase in the expected money-weighted average age of retirees because of longevity. The net effect of the change in the expected ages leads to a moderate drop in the TD. Figure 11.4 also illustrates the evolution of the TD, which is the sum of the pay-in and the pay-out duration.

The improvement in life expectancy has a direct effect on the increased pension liability and also changes the pension liability's structure – the time profile of payments – in a way that does not need to be fully financed in a PAYG pension system. The increased TD implies that the same flow of contributions can finance a larger pension liability (Settergren 2013). Besides, the net effect of the increase in life expectancy in a PAYG pension system, which is the difference of the increased value between the pension liability and the contribution flow, is associated with the higher TD. Settergren and Mikula (2005) and Vidal-Meliá and Boado-Penas (2013)

[13]Settergren (2013) points out that the ages of entry to the labour force market have increased slightly, and the relative wages of younger employees seem to have decreased. This situation could be explained, at least partially, by the increase in immigration to Sweden. The adult immigrants might have pushed up the average age of entry to the labour market; thus, there has been a decrease in the TD.

describe how cash flows, the stock of assets and liabilities of the PAYG pension system are affected by a shift in the mortality pattern.

- Change in Pension Liability

The changes in the size of the pension liability are caused by seven main items: new pension credits and *Allmän tilläggspension* (ATP) points, pension disbursements, indexation or change in value, value of change in life expectancy, inheritance gains arising, inheritance gains distributed and deduction of administrative costs as presented in the income statement (Table 11.2).

The new pension credits and the ATP points had risen by 5.66–6.51% of the GDP over the 2007–2015 period. The pension credits are accumulated in the notional account, whereas the ATP points corresponding to the estimated value of the new pension credits earned in the DB system are being phased out.[14] When the ATP points disappear completely, the value of this item will be identical with the pension contributions in the section of the change in fund assets. The equality between the contributions paid and the new pension credits earned is one common characteristic of an NDC or a defined contribution scheme (Settergren 2013).

As pension benefits are paid out by the AP funds and also constitute an amortisation of the pension liability, the amount of pension disbursements then reduces both the values of the fund assets and the pension liability. The value of the pension disbursements included in the change in the fund assets (Table 11.2) has the same value as the change in the pension liability.

The pension liability changes primarily with the annual indexation of pensions and pension account balances. The higher value of the indexation increases the pension liability. Indexation is determined by the change in the income index, in combination with the balance ratio in the years when balancing is activated, referred to as the balance index. In 2008, the indexation produced an increase in the pension liability, amounting to 11.36% of the GDP. Since balancing was activated in 2009 and 2010, the indexation was reduced. As a result, the pension liability decreased to approximately 4.69% of the GDP in 2010. In 2012, the pension liability increased to 10.94% of the GDP because of the high indexation, 5.8% of the income index, and the financial position of the system deteriorated with a negative balance ratio. The balancing mechanism was then activated, and the indexation was dropped to restore the system, which increased the pension liability by 2.55 and 2.34% of the GDP in 2013 and 2014, respectively.

Additionally, the pension liability is positively related to the change in the life expectancy. Life expectancy, as used in the income statement, refers to the assumed length of time for which an average pension amount is disbursed (the so-called economic life expectancy). For the NDC system, a higher life expectancy will increase only the pension liability to retirees. According to the projected negative impact on pensions of younger cohorts as presented in the 2010 Orange Report (Swedish Social Insurance Agency 2010), the monthly pension will be lower for

[14]Currently, the value of new ATP points (that corresponding to the old defined benefit (DB) pension system) is very small and will no longer be earned after 2017.

younger cohorts if they retire at a fixed age when life expectancy is improving. Therefore, the pension liability to active workers is unaffected by mortality changes. The value of the change in life expectancy (Table 11.2) is the difference between the pension liability calculated with the economic life expectancy used in the financial year and that used in the previous year. Over the 2007–2015 period, the value of the change in life expectancy had varied between −0.35% and −0.80% of the GDP.

The remaining accounting item in Table 11.2, inheritance gains, represents the notional account balances of participants who do not survive to retirement age, distributed to the survivors belonging to the same birth cohort. The items vary between 0.3% and 0.4% of the GDP. The inheritance gains distributed are not those actually arising but those expected to arise. Hence, both items are not offset perfectly.

The administrative costs are deducted from the notional accounts to finance the administrative and the fund management costs. On average, the deduction amount ranged between 0.02% and 0.06% of the GDP in 2007–2015 and did not exactly match the cash withdrawals from the fund assets in the administrative cost item.

Eventually, the net income/loss for the year is the sum of the totals of three sections: change in fund assets, change in contribution asset and change in pension liability. However, regarding the double-entry accounting system, the net income/loss is equivalent to the difference between the change in assets (fund assets and contribution asset) and the change in liabilities. Figure 11.5 shows the evolution of the change in assets, the change in pension liability and the net income/loss of the Swedish NDC pension system. The value had been volatile, ranging from the loss of 7.70% of the GDP in 2008 and the gain of 12.07% of the GDP in 2010.

Fig. 11.5 Evolution of change in assets, change in pension liability and net income/loss of the Swedish NDC pension system. (*Source:* Authors' compilation based on the data from the Swedish Social Insurance Agency (2007, 2008, 2009, 2010, 2011, 2012, 2013, 2014, 2015))

The imbalance of the system's financial position is chiefly caused by the change in the indexation of the pension liability.

11.4 Conclusions and New Responses to Economic Crisis

This chapter has described the Swedish experience in its NDC pension system over the 2007–2015 period, with special attention to the balance ratio under economic and financial uncertainties. It has shown how, in the post-2008 recession, the solvency of the Swedish NDC scheme dropped, and the balance ratio fell significantly below the unity, triggering the automatic balance mechanism in 2010. Pensions were reduced in 2010, 2011 and 2014.

Three different policy responses had been carried out in this respect, as follows:

The first was to smooth the value of the buffer fund used in the balance ratio. Thus, instead of using the value of the buffer fund as of 31 December in a specific year, the average of the value of the buffer fund as of 31 December in the last 3 years was used. This change was legislated despite (the predecessor to) the Swedish Pensions Agency's objection about the measure's inefficiency. The agency proposed that rather than smoothing the value of the buffer fund, the solvency deficit's effect on the pensions should be smoothed. According to the agency, this solution would result in a more efficient smoothing, partly due to considering all sources of solvency volatility, not only the volatility resulting from the value of the buffer fund.

The second policy response to the reduced pensions under the notional model was to cut taxes on pensions so as to counteract the net effect of the negative indexation. The retirees were more or less completely compensated for their losses in *inkomstpension* by the reduced taxes. This policy response implies that one of the main objectives of the NDC design – to insulate government finances from the development of the public pension plan – was not achieved.

Third, the volatility of the solvency measure – the balance ratio – triggered the Swedish Pension Agency's analysis of the reasons for the unanticipated level of volatility. This work revealed that the three-year smoothing of the income index caused a delay relative to the development of the contributions to the plan. This situation caused a significant real volatility in the ratio of the contribution asset to the pension liabilities. For example, a shift downwards in the nominal earnings growth would immediately result in a lower growth in the contributions and the contribution asset. The income index would fully react to this outcome with a four-year delay, causing a ceteris paribus permanent negative gap between assets and liabilities. The result would also be observed in traditional actuarial projections of the NDC plan.

This pre-crisis (unidentified but obvious from the experience) source of solvency volatility triggered the legislative attempt to eliminate or at least reduce the volatility caused by the indexation itself. The Swedish Pension Agency proposed measures that would eliminate the volatility caused by the indexation. Its main component was to eliminate the smoothing in the indexation and to make it slightly forward looking. Rather than using the change in income in the current year relative to the previous one, the (projected) change in income in the coming year relative to the current one should be used. The difference between the projected and the actual income growth should affect the indexation the following year. The agency claimed that combined with some compensating adjustments, this solution would completely eliminate the avoidable solvency volatility caused by the delay in indexation relative to the contribution development. To further reduce volatility, the agency proposed that balancing should only come into effect if the balance ratio was below the unity for 3 years in a row and that, in balancing, the indexation should yearly be reduced by only one-third of the adjustment necessary to achieve 100% solvency.

The pensions group (set up by the government to negotiate any changes to the political agreement on the pension reform in 1994) decided to propose to the parliament a simplified version of the technical adjustments recommended by the Swedish Pensions Agency. The smoothing of the income index was abolished, but the forward-looking design proposed by the agency was not enacted. The government/pensions group judged the forward-looking proposal (the increased use of projections in the indexation) as a risk and also disliked the technical changes forced by its design. Neither did the government/Pensions group adopt the agency's proposed rule of only using the balance mechanism if the solvency was less than 100% for three consecutive years. However, the new form of smoothing (reducing the indexation by only one-third of the necessary reduction to achieve 100% solvency) was implemented. The new indexation was used for the first time in 2015, and the new balance ratio was applied in 2016.[15]

The volatility of the indexation of pensions caused by the balance mechanism has been criticised by various groups in Sweden. Perhaps the most vocal critique has come from groups representing retirees, but other groups have also expressed disapproval. The political parties supporting the pension agreement have not criticised the balance mechanism's goal to secure an automatic, financially stable pension scheme. As evident from their legislative actions, they have disliked the volatility and tried to reduce it while adhering to the principle of automatic financial stability.

Somewhat surprisingly, there has been almost no professional or popular debate on the relevance of the solvency measure used. Considering the positive projections of the pension plan (the actual and the projected sizes of the buffer fund) – indicating that the present solvency deficit will be overcome without reducing pensions – the lack of debate is even more astonishing. This situation can possibly be attributed to the human tendency to accept a number as a fact, more or less regardless of the

[15]Another change in legislation addressed the inefficiency in the indexation/balance mechanism that implied that pension credits earned during a balancing period, and thus not subjected to a downward adjustment of the indexation, would still benefit from balancing the mechanisms upward. This inefficiency was already acknowledged by legislators when the balance mechanism was legislated in 2000, but at that time, no satisfactory solution to the problem was identified – partly due to time constraints. Barr and Diamond (2011) criticise this inefficiency.

underlying ambiguities of the calculation. Another or complementary interpretation of this absence of a more profound and philosophical critique is that the use of only factual transactions and events in estimating solvency, without any projections, has worked.

Annex A: Balance Sheets and Income Statements in Swedish Kronor

The balance sheets and income statements from 2007 to 2015 are shown in Swedish kronor in Table 11.3 and 11.4, respectively.

Table 11.3 Balance sheets, December 31, 2007–2015

Item	2007	2008	2009	2010	2011	2012	2013	2014	2015
Assets (SKr billions)									
Fund assets	898	707	827	895	873	958	1058	1184	1230
Contribution asset	6116	6477	6362	6575	6828	6915	7123	7380	7457
Total assets	7014	7184	7189	7469	7700	7873	8180	8565	8688
Liabilities and results brought forward (SKr billions)									
Opening results brought forward	100	18	−243	−323	103	157	−80	127	423
Net income or loss for the year	−82	−261	−79	425	54	−237	207	296	−252
Closing results brought forward	18	−243	−323	103	157	−80	127	423	171
Pension liability	6996	7428	7512	7367	7543	7952	8053	8141	8517
Total liabilities and results brought forward[a]	7014	7184	7189	7469	7700	7873	8180	8565	8688

Source: The Swedish Social Insurance Agency (2007, 2008, 2009, 2010, 2011, 2012, 2013, 2014, 2015)

[a]Total liabilities and result brought forward is the summation of "Opening results brought forward", "Net income or loss for the year" and "Pension liability"

Table 11.4 Income statements, 2007–2015

Item	2007	2008	2009	2010	2011	2012	2013	2014	2015
Change in fund assets (SKr billions)									
Pension contributions	190	203	203	205	216	222	227	236	246
Pension disbursements	−186	−199	−217	−220	−220	−236	−254	−255	−265
Return on funded capital	38	−194	136	85	−17	101	128	148	67
Administrative costs	−2	−1	−2	−2	−2	−2	−2	−2	−2
Total	41	−191	120	68	−22	85	100	127	46

(continued)

Item	2007	2008	2009	2010	2011	2012	2013	2014	2015
Change in contribution assets (SKr billions)									
Value of change in contribution revenue	193	395	−115	232	255	120	215	266	333
Value of change in turnover duration	−22	−33	−1	−19	−2	−33	−6	−8	−256
Total	171	361	−115	213	253	87	208	257	77
Change in pension liability[a] *(SKr billions)*									
New pension credits and ATP points	−194	−218	−214	−215	−207	−228	−242	−230	−246
Pension disbursements	186	199	217	220	220	236	254	255	265
Indexation or change in value	−268	−385	−64	165	−175	−403	−96	−92	−378
Value of change in life expectancy	−17	−27	−23	−25	−14	−13	−16	−20	−15
Inheritance gains arising	10	11	11	11	11	11	12	12	12
Inheritance gains distributed	−11	−12	−13	−13	−12	−13	−14	−14	−14
Deduction for administrative costs	2	1	1	1	1	1	1	2	1
Total	−293	−431	−84	145	−177	−409	−101	−88	−375
Net income or loss for the year (SKr billions)	−82	−261	−79	425	54	−237	207	296	−252

Source: The Swedish Social Insurance Agency (2007, 2008, 2009, 2010, 2011, 2012, 2013, 2014, 2015)

Note: *ATP* Allmän tilläggspension

[a]A negative item (−) increases the pension liability, and a positive item () decreases it, by the amount shown

Acknowledgements Maria del Carmen Boado-Penas is grateful for the financial support of the project MEYC ECO2015-65826-P.

References

Auerbach, A. J., & Lee, R. (2009). Notional defined contribution pension systems in a stochastic context : Design and stability. In J. R. Brown, J. B. Liebman, & D. A. Wise (Eds.), *Social security policy in a changing environment* (pp. 43–68). Chicago: University of Chicago Press.

Auerbach, A. J., & Lee, R. (2011). Welfare and generational equity in sustainable unfunded pension systems. *Journal of Public Economics, 95*(1–2), 16–27.

Barr, N. (2013). *The pension system in Sweden, report to the expert group on public economics 2013:7*. Stockholm: Ministry of Finance.

Barr, N., & Diamond, P. (2011). Improving Sweden's automatic pension adjustment mechanism, *Center for Retirement Research at Boston College*, Issue in Brief 11–2.

Boado-Penas, M. D. C., & Vidal-Meliá, C. (2013). The actuarial balance of the PAYG pension system: The Swedish NDC model versus the DB-type model. In R. Holzmann, E. Palmer, & D. Robalino (Eds.), *Non-Financial Defined Contribution (NDC) pension systems, volume 2: Gender, politics, and financial stability* (pp. 443–480). Washington D.C.: World Bank.

Boado-Penas, M. D. C., Vidal-Meliá, C., & Valdés-Prieto, S. (2008). The actuarial balance sheet for pay-as-you-go finance: Solvency indicators for Spain and Sweden. *Fiscal Studies, 29*(1), 89–134.

Börsch-Supan, A. H. (2006). What are NDC systems? What do they bring to reform strategies? In R. Holzmann & E. Palmer (Eds.), *Pension reform: Issues and prospects for Non-financial Defined Contribution (NDC) schemes* (pp. 35–55). Washington, D.C.: World Bank.

Chłoń-Domińczak, A., Franco, D., & Palmer, E. (2012). The first wave of NDC reforms: The experiences of Italy, Latvia, Poland, and Sweden. In R. Holzmann, E. Palmer, & D. Robalino (Eds.), *Nonfinancial defined contribution pension schemes in a changing pension world, volume 1: Rogress, lessons, and implementation* (pp. 31–84). World Bank: Washington, D.C.

Diamond, P. (2004). Social security. *American Economic Review, 94*(1), 1–24.

Holzmann, R., & Palmer, E. (2006). *Pension reform : Issues and prospects for non-financial defined contribution (NDC) schemes*. Washington, D.C.: World Bank.

Holzmann, R., Palmer, E., & Robalino, D. (2012). *Nonfinancial defined contribution pension schemes in a changing pension world, volume 1: Progress, lessons, and implementation.* Washington, D.C.: World Bank.

Lindbeck, A., & Persson, M. (2003). The gains from pension reform. *Journal of Economic Literature, 41*(1), 74–112.

OECD. (2012). Putting pensions on auto-pilot: Automatic-adjustment mechanisms and financial sustainability of retirement-income systems. In *OECD Pensions Outlook 2012*. OECD Publishing.

Palmer, E. (2013). Generic NDC: Equilibrium, valuation, and risk sharing with and without NDC bonds. In R. Holzmann, E. Palmer, & D. Robalino (Eds.), *Nonfinancial defined contribution pension schemes in a changing pension world, Volume 2: Gender, politics, and financial stability* (pp. 309–333). Washington, D.C.: World Bank.

Settergren, O. (2001). The automatic balance mechanism of the Swedish pension system: A non-technical introduction. *Wirtschaftspolitische Blätter, 48*(4), 339–349.

Settergren, O. (2013). A decade of actuarial accounting for the NDC scheme in Sweden: Quantifying change in the financial position of a PAYG pension plan. In R. Holzmann, E. Palmer, & D. Robalino (Eds.), *Nonfinancial defined contribution pension schemes in a changing pension world, Volume 2: Gender, politics, and financial stability* (pp. 361–391). Washington D.C: World Bank.

Settergren, O., & Mikula, B. D. (2005). The rate of return of pay-as-you-go pension systems: A more exact consumption-loan model of interest. *Journal of Pension Economics and Finance, 4* (2), 115–138.

Swedish Social Insurance Agency. (2007). *Orange report: Annual report of the Swedish Pension System 2007*. Stockholm: Swedish Social Insurance Agency.

Swedish Social Insurance Agency. (2008). *Orange report: Annual report of the Swedish Pension System 2008*. Stockholm: Swedish Social Insurance Agency.

Swedish Social Insurance Agency. (2009). *Orange report: Annual report of the Swedish Pension System 2009*. Stockholm: Swedish Social Insurance Agency.

Swedish Social Insurance Agency. (2010). *Orange report: Annual report of the Swedish Pension System 2010*. Stockholm: Swedish Social Insurance Agency.

Swedish Social Insurance Agency. (2011). *Orange report: Annual report of the Swedish Pension System 2011*. Stockholm: Swedish Social Insurance Agency.

Swedish Social Insurance Agency. (2012). *Orange report: Annual report of the Swedish Pension System 2012*. Stockholm: Swedish Social Insurance Agency.

Swedish Social Insurance Agency. (2013). *Orange report: Annual report of the Swedish Pension System 2013*. Stockholm: Swedish Social Insurance Agency.
Swedish Social Insurance Agency. (2014). *Orange report: Annual report of the Swedish Pension System 2014*. Stockholm: Swedish Social Insurance Agency.
Swedish Social Insurance Agency. (2015). *Orange report: Annual report of the Swedish Pension System 2015*. Stockholm: Swedish Social Insurance Agency.
Valdés-Prieto, S. (2000). The financial stability of notional account pensions. *Scandinavian Journal of Economics, 102*(3), 395–417.
Vidal-Meliá, C., & Boado-Penas, M. D. C. (2013). Compiling the actuarial balance for pay-as-you-go pension systems. Is it better to use the hidden asset or the contribution asset? *Applied Economics, 45*(10), 1303–1320.
Vidal-Meliá, C., Boado-Penas, M. D. C., & Settergren, O. (2010). Instruments for improving the equity, transparency and solvency of pay-as-you-go pension systems: NDCs, Abs and ABMs. In M. Micocci, G. N. Gregoriou, & M. G. Batista (Eds.), *Pension fund risk management: Financial and actuarial modeling* (pp. 419–472). Chapman & Hall/CRC Finance Series.
Vidal-Meliá, C., Domínguez-Fabián, I., & Enrique Devesa-Carpio, J. (2006). Subjective economic risk to beneficiaries in notional defined contribution accounts. *Journal of Risk and Insurance, 73* (3), 489–515.
Whitehouse, E. (2009). Pensions during the crisis: Impact on retirement income systems and policy responses, The Geneva Papers on Risk and Insurance - Issues and Practice, *34*(4), 536–547.
Whitehouse, E., D'Addio, A., Chomik, R. Reilly, A. (2009). Two decades of pension reform: What has been achieved and what remains to be done? The Geneva Papers on Risk and Insurance - Issues and Practice, *34*(4), 515–535.
Whitehouse, E. R. (2010). Decomposing notional defined-contribution pensions : experience of OECD countries reforms, *OECD Social, Employment and Migration Working Papers*, No.109.
Williamson, J. B. (2004). Assessing the pension reform potential of a notional defined contribution pillar. *International Social Security Review, 57*(1), 47–64.
Yermo, J. (2008). Governance and investment of public pension reserve funds in selected OECD countries, *OECD Working Papers On Insurance And Private Pensions*.

Chapter 12
The New Wave of Pension Reforms in Latin America

Carmelo Mesa-Lago and Diego Valero

Abstract In 1980–2005, 11 Latin American countries (out of a total of 20) implemented structural reforms ("privatization") in their pension systems, totally or partially shifting them from defined benefit, PAYG, and public administration toward defined contribution, fully funded financing, and private management. Initial design flaws and later modifications have required re-reforms ranging from full reversion to PAYG (Argentina and Bolivia) to improve the private system infusing social solidarity (Chile). Several countries that privatized their pensions have introduced parametric reforms (Colombia, Costa Rica, Mexico, and Uruguay), whereas others are discussing re-reforms (Dominican Republic, El Salvador, Panama, and Peru). Such reforms include adopting or expanding non-contributory pillars, increasing coverage, improving competition, and strengthening financial equilibrium, albeit with substantial differences between the countries. In this chapter, we review the implemented re-reforms, as well as those under discussion, and extract useful lesson for the region and the world.

Keywords Pensions · Latin America · Structural reforms · Re-reforms · Parametric reforms · Privatization · Social security principles

C. Mesa-Lago (✉)
Department of Economics, University of Pittsburgh, Pittsburgh, PA, USA

D. Valero
Departamento de Econometría, Estadística y Economía Española, University of Barcelona, Barcelona, Spain
e-mail: dvalero@novaster.net

M. Peris-Ortiz et al. (eds.), *Economic Challenges of Pension Systems*,
https://doi.org/10.1007/978-3-030-37912-4_12

12.1 Introduction

In 1980–2005, starting with Chile, 11 countries in Latin America implemented structural reforms[1] that totally or partially replaced previous "public" systems characterized by defined benefit (DB), pay-as-you-go (PAYG) or partial collective capitalization, and state- or social-insurance administration with "private" systems typified by defined contribution (DC), fully funded financing (FF), and private management (AFP[2]) based on individual accounts (see Table 12.1). The reforms adopted three diverse models: (1) substitutive, where the public system was closed and replaced by a private system (Chile, Bolivia, Mexico, El Salvador, and Dominican Republic); (2) parallel, where the public system stayed (with some parametric reforms) and a new private system was created, allowing both to compete (Peru and Colombia); and (3) mixed, where the public system was converted into a first pillar and a second private pillar established (Uruguay, Costa Rica, and Panama).

In general, the reforms had some positive effects: unification and standardization of some pension schemes with too generous benefits, strengthening of the relationship between contributions and pension level, improvement in the efficiency of individual accounts and their report and transparency, faster processing of benefits, significant increase in the pension-fund capital, and adequate capital returns, particularly at the start. Conversely, they generated negative effects often opposite to their initial promises: reduction/stagnation of population coverage, transfer of risks from the insured collectivity to the individual, elimination of social solidarity as individual accounts are not shared, accentuation of gender inequality, replacement rates and pension amounts being lower than expected, lack of/improper competition among AFP resulting in high management costs and profits, elimination of social participation in the pension administration, and transition costs being longer and higher than originally projected.

Some countries copied a model without its essential preconditions for success. The Chilean model worked because the country had a large formal labor sector and number of insured (facilitating several AFP), as well as a capital market founded at the end of the nineteenth century, and steady economic growth and fiscal discipline that generated a fiscal surplus. Conversely, in Bolivia and El Salvador, most of the labor force is informal and excluded from coverage; the small number of insured only permitted two administrators thus a duopoly without competition; lacking a stock market, the pension fund was invested mostly in state securities or bank deposits with a low capital return; and poor growth combined with lack of fiscal discipline led to substantial state debt.

---

[1]A structural pension reform totally or partially closes a public pension system, whereas a parametric reform maintains the system trying to improve it.

[2]*Administradoras de Fondos de Pensiones* (AFJP) in Argentina, *Operadoras de Pensiones Complementarias* (OPC) in Costa Rica, and *Administradoras de Fondos para el Retiro* (AFORE) in Mexico

Table 12.1 Taxonomy of pension reforms in private and public systems in Latin America, 2016

Model, country, year, and start of reform	System	Contribution	Benefit	Financing	Administration
Private (Structural reform)					
Substitutive model					
Chile (1981)					
Mexico (1997)	Private	Defined	Not defined	Fully funded	Private[e]
El Salvador (1998)					
Dominican Rep. (2003)[a]					
Parallel model	Public	Not defined	Defined	PAYG[g]	Public
Peru (1993)	or				
Colombia (1994)	private	Defined	Not defined	Fully funded	Private[e]
Mixed model					
Uruguay (1996)	Public	Not defined	Defined	PAYG[h]	Public
Costa Rica (2001)[b]	and				
Panamá (2005)	private	Defined	Not defined	Fully funded	Multiple
Private with Re-reform					
Chile (2008)	Private and	Defined	Not defined	Fully funded	Private
	solidarity	Not defined	Defined	PAYG	Public
Argentina (2008)[c]	Public	Not defined	Defined	PAYG	Public
Bolivia (2010)[d]	Public and	Not defined	Defined	PAYG	Public
	private	Defined	Not defined	Fully funded	Public
Public[e]					
Brazil[e]					
Cuba[e]					
Ecuador[f]					
Guatemala					
Haiti	Public	Not defined	Defined	PAYG	Public
Honduras					
Nicaragua[f]					
Paraguay[e]					
Venezuela[e]					

Source: Mesa-Lago (2008), updated with legislation from the countries

[a]Only the contributory program has been implemented; the other two programs were not operational in February 2017

[b]All insured are both in the public and private pillars within the mixed system

[c]Argentina had a mixed system in 1993–2008; the re-reform of 2008 nationalized the private pillar and integrated it with the remains of the public system

[d]Bolivia had a private system in 1996–2010; the system was nationalized and became public but retained existing individual accounts

[e]Recent parametric reforms; Costa Rica's public pillar had a parametric reform in 2005

[f]Ecuador and Nicaragua enacted privatization laws that were not implemented

[g]Public partial capitalization in the public pillars of Costa Rica and Panama, the public parallel systems of Colombia and Peru, and the public systems of Ecuador, Guatemala, Honduras, Nicaragua, and Paraguay

[h]Multiple administrations (private, public, or mixed) in Colombia, Mexico, and Dominican Republic as well as in the public pillar in mixed models

The explained quandaries, together with other initial design flaws and posterior changes, induced parametric reforms, insufficient to address the fundamental troubles. In 2008–2010 three countries enacted re-reforms of their private pension systems that significantly altered them: Chile (2008) kept the private system but with substantial modifications that addressed some of the problems, Argentina (2008) closed the private pillar and transferred all its insured and funds to the public system, and Bolivia (2010) followed the Argentinean approach and nationalized the private system but guaranteeing the existing individual accounts.

Among the nine remaining private systems, two mixed ones have introduced parametric reforms. Uruguay has the highest labor force coverage, whereas Costa Rica has the third (IADB 2016); the former has a segmented system while the latter has one of the most unified and standardized. Both have extended non-contributory pensions targeted on the poor that have significantly reduced poverty and also established compulsory coverage for self-employed. Both countries have social participation in the administration of the public pillar, and in the private pillar, they are public administrators that have stimulated competition with the private ones and cut managerial costs. Costa Rica implemented a parametric reform in 2005 that strengthened the actuarial equilibrium of the public pillar, but later a dispute ensued on the period of such equilibrium, between the superintendence and the social insurance entity (CCSS); a private actuary was hired to solve the dilemma, but his work was inadequate and discarded. An arbitration conducted by the school of mathematics at the national university concluded that the period of equilibrium was shorter than anticipated (UCR 2016), ensuing a debate and proposals of alternatives (Durán 2016). Uruguay substantially raised revenue in the public pillar through expansion of employment and real salaries and better control of evasion; but expenditures increased because of benefits improvement, aggravated by the most aged population in the region. A 2020–2065 projection forecasts a decline in fiscal transfers in the mid-term but rising thereafter reaching a deficit of 24% of GDP (Mesa-Lago 2014). Mexico improved competition in several ways: the superintendence must approve commissions and, if they are not submitted at the end of the year, then the lowest commission in the market is applied in the following year, and transfers should be channeled to the AFORES that offer better comparative quality (CONSAR 2010).

Currently, 11 Latin American countries have public systems (Table 12.1). Save for Argentina and Bolivia, we can only summarize their situation. Many of them face grave actuarial disequilibrium and some financial deficit. Brazil has one of the highest coverage in the region; parametric reforms of its two major schemes (private-sector workers' and civil servants') were introduced in 1999 and 2003, respectively; further reforms were implemented in 2012 and 2015, but still additional changes are required to close the gap between the two schemes and achieve financial-actuarial equilibrium. Cuba have virtual universal coverage and undertook a parametric reform in 2008 but not enough to cope with the most aged population in the region and insufficient contributions, which demand heavy state subsidies, whereas the real pension value halved in 1989–2015. Ecuador has a very fragmented pension system with various groups and separate schemes for the armed forces and the police. A parametric reform, enacted in 2015, introduced the following measures: (1) uniformed contributions in the three major groups (private sector, civil servants, and self-employed) but left unchanged the separate schemes, (2) eliminated the 40% state contribution to the pension scheme of social-security-institute employees but made the institute responsible for such pensions hence reducing its reserves, and (3) incorporated unremunerated working women in households into the old-age program, with the state paying part of the contribution (Resolución y Ley 2015). Venezuela's severe economic crisis and hyperinflation have depleted the pension reserves and devaluated the pensions. The least developed countries of Guatemala, Haiti, Honduras, Nicaragua, and Paraguay endure very low population coverage and face financial-actuarial imbalances.

This chapter describes the three re-reforms and assesses their effects, as well as ongoing discussions on re-reforms in Dominican Republic, El Salvador, Panama, and Peru. The evaluation is based on nine conventional social security principles shaped by ILO conventions, recommendations, and documents: social dialogue, universal coverage, uniform treatment, benefit sufficiency, social solidarity, gender equity, administrative efficiency and reasonable costs, social participation in the administration, and financial-actuarial sustainability (see Mesa-Lago 2008).

12.2 Description of the Re-reforms and Evaluation of Their Effects[3]

12.2.1 Chile[4]

The Chilean private system suffered several flaws. Labor force coverage decreased; affiliation of self-employed workers was voluntary and only 5% were covered. A non-contributory pension, targeted on the poor and means-tested, was restricted by waiting lists and available fiscal resources. At retirement, part of the insured either was ineligible for a minimum pension (lacked the 20 years of contributions) or the non-contributory pension (not meeting the means test). The armed forces were excluded from the reform and maintained separate programs with better pensions largely financed by the Treasury. The private system lacked endogenous solidarity; minimum and non-contributory pensions were state financed. Gender inequalities were accentuated: women received a lower pension than men because of frequent exits from the labor market to raise their children, an increase in the years of contribution required for the minimum pension, lower contribution density than men, a pension calculated on the fund accumulated in the individual account, and mortality tables differentiated by sex (having a lower capitalized fund and a higher life expectancy, women's annuity was lower than that of men). There were multiple

[3]See Mesa-Lago 2012

[4]Based on CAPSP (2015), Mesa-Lago and Bertranou (2016)

regulations and supervision entities. Commissions set as percentage of salary for managing the old-age and disability-survivor risks were high and stagnant in 1981–2007, and a fixed commission had regressive effects. Despite being the owners of individual accounts, workers didn't participate in the management of the system that was run by AFP. Contrary to the initial projections, transition costs accounted for 5% of GDP in 2006, after 28 years of the structural reform.

Chile's re-reform of 2008 added to the private system a solidarity pillar, PAYG, state managed and financed, which significantly improved social security principles badly eroded by the structural reform, as the following data for 2008–2014 shows. Coverage increased as follows: labor force from 62.8% to 64.8%, self-employed from 4% to 20%, women by 10%, and the elderly from 79% to 83.5%. Two new fiscally funded solidarity pensions (a basic non-contributory pension (PBS) for the poorest 40% of households and a state contribution (APS) for low-income pensioners) reduced poverty, doubled the number of beneficiaries, improved pension levels, and had progressive effects on distribution. The PBS real amount increased 50% while the average pension grew by 83%, favoring lowest-income pensioners. A maternity voucher is deposited in mothers' individual accounts for each child born alive; in case of divorce, up to 50% of the fund accumulated during marriage may be transferred from one spouse to the other. A biannual bidding process assigns new entrants in the labor force to the AFP offering the lowest commission hence cutting the average commission from 1.74% to 1.14% (0.47% in the lowest-fee AFP). A Commission of Users with wide representation of interested parties annually assesses re-reform performance and achievement of its goals. The state's role has been strengthened and all supervision agencies unified. The disability-survivors' premium, previously paid by the worker, was shifted to the employer, and the fixed commission was dropped. Total pension fund value increased from 52.8% to 69.6% of GDP in 2008–2015, 47% above the trough at the 2008 economic crisis. The re-reform is 0.7% of GDP (vis-à-vis 0.9% fiscal subsidy to the armed-forces and police-force schemes).

The long-term financial sustainability of the re-reform is ensured by a solidarity PAYG pension fund with a reserve to finance the added benefits; triennial actuarial studies of the fund and the solidarity pillar; mandatory allocation of fiscal resources in the budget law and annual reports on needed resources; 5-year actuarial studies to assess the effects of several factors on finances; an advisory board of experts that monitors the solidarity pension, its fiscal impact and sustainability, and the need for possible adjustment; and annual evaluation by the Commission of Users.

Despite the progress achieved, serious problems persist: 35% of the labor force (particularly the self-employed) and 16% of the elderly remain uncovered. The privileged and heavily subsidized (90%) armed-forces and police-force schemes continue. The solidarity pillar still has lacunas: 39% of women are uncovered, their replacement rate is 41% of that of men, their average pension amount is 43% of that of men, and gender-differentiated mortality tables diminish female pensions; 68% of pensions with a solidarity component are lower than the poverty line. About 81% of affiliates have not switched to the AFP with the lowest fees and remain affiliated to the most expensive three. Direct social participation in pension administration is still absent. Despite a decline, employers' evasion is still important and fines are very low. Employers do not contribute to the old-age scheme (together with Peru, the only two cases in the region) infringing the ILO minimum norm that the worker must not pay more than half of the total contribution. Capital returns show a declining trend and 44% of the portfolio is concentrated on foreign instruments.

In 2014, a Presidential Advisory Commission on Pensions was appointed and worked for 16 months to elaborate a diagnosis and propose changes to tackle the explained problems. Preceded by a remarkable social dialogue, in 2015 the Commission approved 58 recommendations; among them are to expand PBS access to 80% of the poorest households; augment by 20% the value of the PBS and APS; standardize with the general system the treatment of and contributions to the armed-forces and police-force schemes; implement unisex mortality tables, assign half of the contributions at the individual account to the legal or common spouse in case of divorce, and equally divide between spouses the fund accumulated during marriage; compensate unpaid work when caring for the elderly or incapacitated; establish a public AFP with the same operating rules as the rest and allow entry of not-for-profit entities; permit workers' participation in the board of directors and expand the functions of the Commission of Users; and develop new instruments of productive domestic investment, allow a greater share of investment in real assets, raise by 50% the cap on taxable income (with a progressive effect on distribution), heave the total contribution rate (and thus the deposit in the individual account) from 10% to 14% with 4% charged to the employer (in a 4-year period), and increase low penalties for employers that don't transfer the withheld worker's contributions. The cost of the 58 recommendations is 0.3% of GDP, totaling 1% of GDP combined with the 2008 re-reform cost.

The Commission also voted on three global models of re-reform: (A) substantially strengthen the solidarity pillar and significantly modify the individual capitalization pillar to correct many of its flaws, (B) create a mixed three-pillar system (the PBS, an intermediate social insurance pillar, and an individual capitalization pillar), and (C) return to a pure PAYG system. Models A and B, respectively, received 12 and 11 votes, whereas model C got one vote only and was judged as financially unsustainable. The Minister of Finance calculated that the cost of implementing the 58 proposals will be 0.4% of GDP (CAPSP 2015) and later reported that the cost of proposal B was 2.5% of GDP, almost four times the 0.7% that would cost proposal A (Bravo 2016). A Committee of Ministers was entrusted to study proposals A and B, as well as the 58 recommendations, to decide which ones to submit to executive and legislative powers. But 1 year elapsed without taking action, which in 2016 provoked massive demonstrations all over the country against the AFP. The government then submitted the proposals to the political parties, but a decision had not been made when this chapter was completed in February 2017.[5]

[5]Starting on January 1, 2017, PBS pensions were raised 10%.

12.2.2 Argentina[6]

The 1993 structural reform kept the pure public system and created a new mixed system with two pillars: the first (public) paid a basic pension while the second (private) added the largest pension. The system was afflicted by several flaws: decline in labor force coverage down to 45% in 2007, 35 years of contributions required to get a minimum pension and 70% of pensioners only receiving the minimum pension (the state had to pay a high proportion of benefits), non-contributory pensions targeted on the poor that didn't cover all of them (some of these pensions were arbitrarily granted by Congress), lack of indexation of pensions that prompted thousands of lawsuits, increase in commissions that took half of the wage deduction in 2007, elimination of social representation in the administration of the private system, banning the return to the public system after opting to change to the mixed system, limited competition (the number of AFJP was halved and transfers among them decreased), significant and growing deficit of the public system (financed by the state),[7] and severe losses of the pension fund in 2001 due to the devaluation of the peso vis-à-vis the US dollar and in 2008 resulting from the international financial crisis. Several parametric reforms, mainly in 2007, lessened some of the previous flaws.

The re-reform of 2008 had the support of the two main labor federations but not other groups; it failed to incorporate agreed guidelines from the 2001 to 2002 debate; it was enacted in 1 month, lacking inputs from experts, civil society and interest groups, as well as a serious debate in Congress that approved it by a majority of the ruling party.[8] The mandatory private pillar was closed—2.5 million insured (22% of total insured)—and US$25,545 million in the individual accounts were transferred to the public system (managed by a state agency: ANSES). Those funds were deposited in a Guaranteed Sustainability Fund (FGS), without separating the previous publicly insured from the newly transferred. Despite lack of approval of such transfer, there were no public protests due to the discredited private system and the AFJP.

The re-reform brought many positive actions and effects. Contributory coverage of the labor force rose from 45% to 53% in 2008–2014, whereas coverage of the elderly increased from 84% to 90%. This was achieved through better access to contributory pensions and extended non-contributory pensions for the needful elderly, disabled, and mothers, particularly benefiting low-income strata and reduc-

[6] Based on Mesa-Lago (2009), Hohnerlein (2012), and Bertranou et al. (2017)

[7] Public system revenues were drastically reduced because almost 80% of the insured and their contributions were shifted to the private pillar.

[8] Conversely, an extensive and serious debate took place during the 2001–2002 economic crisis that led to a series of well-thought recommendations.

ing poverty.[9] The private and public pension systems were merger and entitlement conditions/benefits standardized. Social solidarity improved with the shift from the private pillar without solidarity to the public system with strengthened solidarity. Better gender equity was achieved by extending contributory pensions to elderly women, eliminating gender-differentiated mortality tables, and granting a non-contributory pension to mothers with many children. All pension amounts were substantially enlarged and adjusted every 6 months to wages and total contribution revenue. Administrative commissions were eliminated, whereas disability-survivors premium became managed by the unified public system that doesn't charge fees. The elimination of social representation was lessened by an advisory council to monitor the reform with 38% of members from insured and pensioner representatives. The state role was strengthened and several public supervisory agencies were created.

On the other hand the re-reform had adverse effects. The public-system fragmentation subsists: 130 separate schemes continue, including the armed forces and some provincial/municipal civil servants, as well as restored privileged schemes, and fiscal subsidies carry on. There is urgent need to set a unified non-contributory means-tested scheme for the poor and terminate special pensions granted by Congress. ANSES is not truly autonomous and is supervised by multiple agencies; the FGS is managed by ANSES and monitored by a Congressional Commission with non-binding recommendations; there is not a single, autonomous, technical superintendence that regulates and oversees the general system and all separate pension schemes. Hundreds of thousands lawsuits have been filed against ANSES by insured for missed pension adjustments validated by the Supreme Court.

The huge flow of revenue in the PAYG system, resulting from the move of funds from individual accounts and other transfers, eliminated the public system deficit in the short run, but pension expenses significantly escalated and, in the long run, the public system faces substantial obligations from both the previous PAYG insured and those transferred from the private pillar. No actuarial assessment has been done on the system's long-term financial sustainability. The public-system deficit in 2010–2050 is projected to increase five times without fiscal subsidies. Due to the expansion of benefits, population aging, and life-expectancy increase, FGS revenue and returns could be insufficient to pay future obligations; in that case, the state will have to finance the deficit, increase contributions, cut benefits, and raise capital returns or a combination of all those measures. There are 1.36 contributors per one pensioner and the ratio is declining. Most separate schemes are actuarially imbalanced and take substantial fiscal resources. FGS funds are not invested with legal rules that maximize their capital return and minimize their risk; instead they have been used to pay the foreign debt and partly finance family allowances and state development projects. In 2014, 80% of all investment was in public debt and state development loans. Real capital returns have been either low or negative.

[9]"Pension moratoria" allowed workers and their beneficiaries to become eligible to pensions despite lacking the minimum number of contribution years.

12.2.3 Bolivia[10]

The structural reform copied the Chilean substitutive model, except for one feature explained below, with several adverse effects: labor-force coverage stagnated at 12%; the retirement age was raised to 65 for both sexes, very high for the country's life expectancy at retirement; the minimum pension was not guaranteed and the recognition bond was quite restricted; women coverage and their proportion of pensioners shrunk, whereas the female-male gap in pension levels expanded; the replacement rate was 20% of the average wage during the active life; there were two AFP (a duopoly) without competition[11]; social representation in the administration was abolished; the employer's contribution was eliminated while the worker's was increased violating the ILO norm; affiliates that contributed fell from 92% to 30%; 62% of the portfolio was concentrated in public debt; and transition costs were 2.5 times the initial projection. In a 2008 survey, 62% of affiliates/pensioners wanted a new system. A positive feature was that the reform was tied to the privatization of half of all public enterprises; 50% of their stocks financed an annual non-contributory flat benefit to part of the elderly (Bonosol).

Bolivia's Constitution of 2009 banned social security privatization and guaranteed the right to a non-contributory universal pension. The re-reform law of 2010 replaced the previous private substitutive system with a new integrated public PAYG system composed of three pillars: (1) The old-age contributory pillar, previously established, retained the individual accounts (for those already affiliated but not for new entrants) and is financed by contributions of workers and employers. (2) The semi-contributory pillar, the key innovation of the re-reform, covers the same risks as the contributory system, is financed by contributions and a new solidarity fund, and is publicly managed. (3) The non-contributory pillar; in 2007, 3 years prior to the re-reform, Bonosol was changed into *Renta Dignidad* (RD) and became truly universal: granted to all residents age 60 and above (5 years less than before), regardless of income, financed by the solidarity fund and publicly managed.

The re-reform stipulated that, 18 months after its enactment, a public administrator (*Gestora*) would be established to manage the entire system and make improvements such as the use of a national centralized system of affiliate registration, citizens' information, the collection of contributions and payments of benefits to simplify the processes and better delivery, as well as more efficient ways to detect evasion and payment delays, including incorporation into the Penal Code of crimes like employers' retention of workers' contributions and under-declaration of payrolls. High AFP profits would be eliminated and invested in the national economy. The *Gestora* was created in January 2015 to start operations by June 2016, but it was not ready and the start was postponed until September 2017. In the meantime, the

---

[10]Based on Mesa-Lago and Ossio (2012), Mesa-Lago (2017)

[11]Initially, the state assigned insured persons to the two AFP based on their place of residence and impeded changes between the two for 7 years; later such changes were allowed but only 0.3% of affiliates actually shifted.

two AFP continue operating and have ceased to invest in infrastructure and equipment (Bonadona 2017; Ortiz 2017).

The re-reform attained considerable improvements. Contributory coverage increased from 12% to 15% in 2010–2014; coverage of self-employed consultants became compulsory. Elderly coverage stayed at 98%, the highest in the region; the RD for those with a contributory pension was reduced by 25%; poverty in that group was cut by 14%. Retirement ages were diminished from 65 to 58 for both sexes and contributions from 15 to 10 years. Social solidarity was strengthened with the creation of the semi-contributory pillar and the solidarity pension, financed by a solidarity contribution partly paid by employers (that before only contributed the employment-injury premium) and partly by the insured (particularly those of higher incomes), with progressive effects on distribution. The minimum pension was finally guaranteed. Gender equity was enlarged with reduction of mothers' retirement age for each child born alive and a greater female share in the non-contributory pension. Commissions stayed the same; the 0.5% for AFP administrative cost is the lowest among private systems in the region[12]; it should be shifted to the *Gestora* and decrease because it would not have profits. Tougher sanctions were enacted for employers' debt, evasion of contributions, and other violations. In 2010–2014, capital in the fund climbed from 28% to 30% of GDP, and concentration of the portfolio in public debt was reduced from 62% to 34%; in addition, investment in foreign emissions previously banned was permitted but only had 3% of the total.

Despite those gains, the re-reform faces important challenges. Contributory coverage remains low and stagnant (15%, the smallest in the region) mainly due to 70% of the labor force being in the informal sector and continued formal-sector evasion. Generous conditions/benefits for the armed forces remain, with fiscal subsidies.[13] Administrative cost is still relatively low (0.5%), due to the lack of competition between the two AFP and the postponement of their replacement by the *Gestora*. Workers and employers don't participate in the system administration despite a constitutional mandate. The *Gestora* does not have full autonomy as it's beneath the tutelage of the Ministry of Economy and Finance and under the regulation of the Authority for Supervision and Control of Pensions and Insurances. The total contribution is higher than the previous one and, in the contributory system, workers pay from 2.7 to 4.8 times the employers' contribution thus infringing the ILO minimum norm. While the portfolio concentration on public debt declined in 2010–2014, the investment share in bank deposits jumped from 25% to 43% and its interest is very low or negative. As a result, the annual average real capital return dwindled from 6.8% in 2000–2010 to 0.5% in 2010–2014.

The pension system financial-actuarial sustainability is questionable, partly because of the reduced ages for retirement and the cost of the new solidarity benefits. According to the government, a study was conducted prior to the re-reform to

[12]Comparisons among private systems are based on AIOS (2016).

[13]The military pension is 56% higher than the average contributory pension and is granted based on years of service.

guarantee the sustainability of the system for 40 years, but it was not published. The re-reform law did not include an obligation to conduct periodic actuarial valuations, as in Chile. In September 2014, due to a request from the major labor federation, a private actuarial company was hired and its valuation was delivered in August 2015; the Ministry of Finance released a short report saying that such study had confirmed the projections done by the government (MEFP 2015). But the entire valuation had not been published by February 2017 (Ortiz 2017). A private study estimates present value of all PAYG obligations at 4.2% of GDP. The re-reform law set an active/passive ratio of ten to one; such ratio decreased from 3.4 to one in 2010 down to 2.8 to one in 2013, similar to the rate in the old PAYG and one-third of the goal set by the law.

12.3 Ongoing Re-reforms or Discussions

This section examines private pensions in four countries that are either undergoing re-reforms or immersed in a debate: Dominican Republic, El Salvador, Panama, and Peru.

12.3.1 Dominican Republic[14]

The Dominican Republic followed the substitutive model in 2003. Insured under age 45 were assigned to the new private system, whereas those older than 45 remained in the old public system (closed to new affiliates). Some special groups maintained their former DB schemes, and a few of them adapted to the reform; Congress and the judiciary kept their schemes intact.

Coverage before the reform was 30% (Mesa-Lago 2004) and it fell to 28% in 2016 (TSS 2017). Out of total affiliates, 58% are men and 42% women, and only 47.3% are active contributors (AIOS 2016). Coverage is limited because 53% of the labor force is in the informal sector, and collection of contributions is poor due to lack of resources and effective tools to control evasion by the Social Security Treasury (TSS 2017).

The reform law stipulated three regimes: contributory (for general workers), subsidized (for the poor), and contributory-subsidized (for self-employed). The contributory regime was established since the start, but the subsidized and contributory-subsidized regimes have not been implemented. Self-employed workers do not have a chance to affiliate to any regime.

Ages of retirement are among the lowest in the region: 55 for women and 60 for men. Women's life expectancy is 7 years longer and they retire 5 years younger than

[14]Based on Valero (2013), SIPEN (2016)

men, which combined with sex-differentiated mortality rates result in lower female pensions. The superintendence projects an overall replacement rate of around 36.5% over the last salary (SIPEN 2012), below the minimum set by ILO/OECD.

In the private system a solidarity pension is granted to insured that do not reach a pension above the minimum wage after 25 years of contribution. This benefit is financed by 0.4% of the salary included in the contribution of each affiliate.

The reform law stipulated a solidarity pension for the poor when meeting the quality of life index from SIUBEN.[15] The pension would be tantamount to 70% of the minimum wage at a cost estimated as 0.34% of GDP.[16] But that benefit is not in effect yet because the subsidized regime has not been implemented. The government is conducting a pilot to assess the cost and feasibility of said pension for 6% of the poor, despite the fact that 40% of the population is poor (SIUBEN 2012).

There are five AFP with limited competition among them. Annual transfers average 1.4% (the sixth highest among nine private systems) but are increasing. The two biggest AFP concentrate 60% of total assets. Administrative costs are 0.5% of wages plus an additional 25% on capital returns that exceed the index of bonds in the financing industry. Profits are 30.7% of net worth. The fees levels are disliked by the population. Participation of workers and employers in the administration of the private system does not exist.

Capital accumulated in the private fund reached 10.4% of GDP in 2016 (the lowest among private systems), all in local bonds (73.9% government bonds, 23.3% banking debt, and 2.8% non-financial bonds). The private system is the only one in the region without foreign investment. The real gross capital return in the last 10 years averaged 6.9% (AIOS 2016) and reached 9.0% in 2016 (SIPEN 2017).[17] Transition costs are not available because the recognition-bond cost has not been estimated.

At the end of November 2016, after more than 1 year of debate, the government submitted to the parliament a reform project under discussion in 2017. Major objectives are to increase coverage, strengthen the Treasury control powers, and reduce labor informality. Proposed measures are (1) to eliminate the contributory-subsidized regime and incorporate self-employed workers in the contributory regime, unless the worker meets the conditions of the subsidized regime (based on the contributive capacity instead of the labor condition), (2) to simplify the affiliation to micro-enterprises,[18] (3) to provide sufficient resources to the TSS to improve its oversight, and (4) to reduce AFP fees shifting from wage contributions to the balance in the individual accounts.

---

[15]Sistema Único de Beneficiarios, a database on the poorest families

[16]Own calculation based on ONE (2010), SIUBEN (2012), and CNSS (2013)

[17]SIPEN (2017), and own calculation

[18]The short-term goal is the affiliation to health services; contributions to pensions are delayed for 4 years.

12.3.2 El Salvador[19]

El Salvador also copied Chile's substitutive model without the necessary preconditions to be feasible. The debate was sparse and with a government bias; the reform was approved without debate in Congress by a large majority of the incumbent party. The system is fragmented: the remaining public system comprises two schemes for private-sector workers and civil servants with similar norms and the private system is DC, fully funded and privately managed by AFP. The armed-forces separate scheme has better entitlement conditions/benefits than all other systems/schemes.[20]

Coverage of the labor force decreased from 26.7% in 1998 (reform year) to 24% in 2014 and is declining, the third lowest among the nine private systems in the region, whereas affiliates that contribute have steadily shrunk to 25% in 2015, the lowest. Coverage of the self-employed is voluntary; regulations for their incorporation and that of other groups difficult to cover have not been implemented. Coverage of the population 65 years and over by contributory or non-contributory pensions is 17%. Ages of retirement are low by regional standards, 55 for women and 60 for men, which contribute to the disequilibrium of the system. About 78% of affiliates won't receive a minimum pension and 82% will have replacement rates between 39% and 43%, below the 45% minimum set by the ILO/OECD. There is no social solidarity in the private system but, outside of it, the state protects 25% of the labor force at the cost of 13% of GDP. In the private system, 10% of pensioners receive 33% of all pensions while 90% gets 67%. Women replacement rates average six percentage points less than men; female life expectancy is 4 years longer and they retire 4 years younger than men, which combined with sex-differentiated mortality rates result in lower women pensions. There are two AFP without real competition (zero affiliates changed AFP in 2013–2015); administrative costs are 2.2% of wages, the second highest among private systems, and AFP profits relative to the patrimony are 48.7%, the highest among such systems. Participation of workers/employers in the administration of the private system was abolished.

Capital accumulated in the private fund steadily rose to 34% of GDP in 2015 (second highest among private systems), but the stock market is incipient and the share of investment in public debt was 80%, the highest proportion (AIOS 2016). Furthermore, 59% of investment is in state securities (CIP) to pay the transition debt; CIP must be bought by AFP and pay very low interest; thus, the government has cheap credit at the cost of low future pensions. The real gross annual capital return in 1999–2014 averaged 8% but was very high at the start and thereafter declined to 3.4%. The pension debt took 13% of GDP in 2015 and is projected to 23% in 2027, while the actuarial deficit was 101% of GDP. In 2013, the ratio of contributors for one pensioner was 0.13 in the public system. IPSFA had a deficit of US$23 million in 2014, financed by the state.

[19]Based on Martínez et al. (2013), and Mesa-Lago (2014)

[20]Retirement is at 50 years (versus 55/60 women/men in the general system) and the replacement rate could be as high as 100% of the last salary.

Since 1998, 14 parametric reforms have been introduced to alleviate some previous flaws. In 2015 three re-reform proposals were presented by the government, and the final project in 2016 lacked an actuarial study. The private system would become a mixed system with two pillars: public and private; all insured should be in the former and only those earning more than two minimum wages would be assigned to the private pillar and contribute to it the excess of said amount. Drafted by the Ministry of Finance whose main objective was to balance de budget, all CIP and earned interests would be transferred to the state to eliminate the fiscal deficit; the state, in turn, would be responsible for deficit in public pensions (Presidencia 2016). The private-pillar fund would lose all the CIP (about US$600 million) reducing the resources needed for its financial sustainability and to pay adequate pensions. The proposal failed to address many major problems on the private system and was defeated in Congress. By the start of 2017, the situation and the flaws of the private system remained unchanged while the time of financial reckoning was imminent.

12.3.3 Panama[21]

The 2005 structural reform had scarce social dialogue; union demonstrations blocked the initial government proposal to strengthen the actuarially imbalanced public system,[22] prompting a political compromise: to close it and establish a new mixed system with two pillars—one public and another private.[23] The insured in the old public system until the end of 2007 continued in it (save those younger than age 35 that decided to move to the mixed system), while the insured that entered the system since 2008 are assigned to the mixed system. The old public system can't receive new affiliates and, together with the public pillar in the mixed system, is managed by social insurance (CSS), whereas the private pillar is by AFP. Civil servants have a voluntary separate private pillar (SIACAP). The employer's contribution was kept but at 32% of the total while the worker is 68% thus infringing the ILO minimum norm. Entitlement conditions and benefits in the old public system and the public pillar are alike; the same ages and contributions are required in the private pillar. A non-contributory pension targeted on the elderly and extremely poor began in 2009 and was extended in 2015.

The system is fragmented; in addition to CSS and SIACAP, there are separate generous schemes for armed forces and firemen, educators, and the Ministry of Social Development.[24] Prior schemes for the Ministry of Education and National Comptroller were closed to new affiliates. Separate schemes are totally/partly financed by the Treasury. Labor force total coverage was 48.7% in 2015 and elderly

[21]Based on AIOS (2013, 2016), OECD (2014), Mesa-Lago (2008, 2016c), and CONATO (2016)

[22]The solution required an increase of the very low contributions and retirement ages.

[23]The first US$500 of wages is assigned to the public pillar and US$500 and over to the private one.

[24]Military men and firemen can retire with 25–30 years of service and 100% of the last salary.

coverage was 83%, largely by the non-contributory pension; both percentages are the fifth highest in the region (IADB 2016). Retirement ages are 57 for women and 62 for man, low in the region relative to Panama's high life expectancy. The replacement rate in the public system/pillar is 60% of the average best 10 years of wages and it rises with additional contributions, but readjustment of pensions is discretionary. Five AFP in the private pillar jointly have scarcely 9% of the labor force, by far the lowest in all private systems, and annual transfers were 1.5% of affiliates.[25] Capital in all AFP is only 2% of GDP, the lowest among all private systems; gross capital returns averaged 6% since 2006 but declining to 4% in 2015.

The closed public system has 82% of total insured and all pensioners, whereas the mixed system has 18% of the insured and no pensioners; such low figures are explained by the latter having only 9 years of operation and the low income of most of the insured; only those with high income contribute to the individual accounts.[26] Some 33,000 enterprises have payment delays and the CSS can't prosecute them. The old public system faces a severe actuarial disequilibrium, aggravated since the reform because contributions have declined while expenses escalated as insured became pensioners. The reserve is rapidly declining and will be extinguished by 2024. A 2012 actuarial study internally done by CSS has not been published and the lack of actuaries impedes making a new one. A public debate began in 2016 to re-reform the system. CSS authorities argue that rising retirement ages and contribution rates, as well as tightening of too generous benefits, are not needed but that growing employment and wages, combined with better control of evasion/under-declaration/payment delays and more profitable investment, will do the trick, the same allegations that impeded a proper reform in 2005.

12.3.4 Peru[27]

The structural reform applied the parallel model—a public system (SNP) and a private one (SPP)—each with about half of the insured, competing between them. There was no social dialogue and the reform was approved by a congressional majority of the ruling party.

Labor force coverage is 26% and declining since 2012 (16th lowest in Latin America); only 43% of affiliates contribute (third lowest among nine private systems), partly due to the large informal sector (70% of the employed labor force), half of which is self-employed and uncovered[28]; 45% of the elderly is protected mainly

[25]No information is available on commissions. In SIACAP, only 27% of affiliates contribute.

[26]It's unknown what insured are in the closed public system and in the public pillar.

[27]Based on Defensoría del Pueblo (2014), Rojas (2014), Mesa-Lago (2016a, 2016b), and Cruz-Saco et al. (2017)

[28]A 2012 law mandated the gradual coverage of self-employed but it was later repealed.

by a non-contributory pension established in 2011.[29] The system is fragmented, with two major schemes that have diverse conditions, with various groups and a better separate scheme for armed forces, miners, and so forth. The retirement age is 65 for both sexes (high for the country) combined with 20 years of contributions in the public scheme, which is difficult to prove; hence, about 65% won't receive any pension. A minimum pension is guaranteed in the public scheme but quite restrictive in the private one. The latter lacks endogenous social solidarity; the state pays the recognition bond, the minimum pension in SNP, and the non-contributory pension. Only 37% of affiliates are women (the lowest proportion among private systems); they have lesser capital accumulation and higher life expectancy than men, and gender-differentiated mortality tables contribute to lower female replacement rates. Insured in SPP pay all contributions and commissions thus infringing the ILO norm; the AFP commission for old age (1.55%) is the second highest among private systems in the region; competition is scarce; only 0.4% of affiliates change AFP. There is no social participation in the administration of the AFP.

Fund capital accumulated was 20% of GDP in 2015, the fourth largest among private systems, but the Lima stock market is small and incapable of absorbing such sum; hence, 46% of total investment is in foreign instruments, the highest in the entire region. The real gross capital return averaged 7.5% annually in 1992–2014 but it was only 1.2% in 2015. The public scheme actuarial deficit amounted to US $25,000 million, which is growing and unsustainable. The active/passive ratio fell from three to one in 2014 to 2.8 to one in 2016.

The 24-year-old structural reform has been submitted to several parametric reforms; the latest in mid-2016 allowed the insured at SPP, at the age of 65, to withdraw up to 95.5% from the individual account and, at any age, 25% for housing; 71,000 insured had done so by mid-2016. The entire system is in danger: the public scheme is financially unsustainable and the private scheme runs the risk of depletion of all funds. A lively debate on re-reform alternatives is ongoing with several proposals, but none are supported by actuarial valuations. In October 2016 the newly elected president announced a re-reform and the appointment of a technical commission including international experts, expected to begin in 2017.

12.4 Conclusions and Lessons from the Re-reforms

The three re-reforms of private systems (Argentina, Bolivia, and Chile) have had diverse performance coping with the structural reform flaws; all improved most social features but the first two confront long-term actuarial disequilibria. The four countries that either tried a re-reform unsuccessfully (El Salvador) or have ongoing

[29]The non-contributory pension is granted to two-thirds of the extremely poor that don't get another pension and are submitted to a means test.

discussions (Dominican Republic, Panama, and Peru) face a strenuous situation that requires urgent solution.

Social dialogue was wide in the re-reform of Chile, partial in Bolivia, and none in Argentina; this is essential to have valuable inputs and legitimize any reform. Coverage of the labor force is low and declining/stagnant in Bolivia, El Salvador, and Peru, intermediate in the Dominican Republic, and relatively high in Chile, Panama, and Argentina (all expanding), largely the result of the size of the informal sector, ad hoc policies to incorporate the self-employed, and rigorous control of evasion and payment delays. All countries save the Dominican Republic have a non-contributory pension targeted on the poor or the extremely poor (with significant differences in extension and pension level); this benefit has increased elderly coverage and reduced poverty incidence; hence, it's crucial in countries that have a low contributory coverage. Bolivia has a universal albeit frugal pension granted to all the elderly; applying it to other countries could double costs at the current level of benefits. Social solidarity does not exist in private systems/pillars; the three re-reforms have developed a solidarity pillar able to cope with that vacuum; the other four countries need to do something similar. All countries keep a separate privileged scheme for the armed forces (and for other powerful groups) financed by the state (0.9% of GDP in Chile vis-à-vis 0.7% for the entire solidarity pillar); this costly inequality should be corrected. Gender inequality was reduced in the three re-reforms (still some problems persist), an important lesson for the other countries. Benefit sufficiency was improved by the re-reforms although low replacement rates (especially for women) remain; the situation is worse in the other countries (retirement ages are very low in Bolivia, Dominican Republic, El Salvador, and Panama). AFP commissions are relatively high in private systems/pillars and paid by workers; Argentina eliminated the AFP and the commissions, Chile reduced them, and Bolivia kept them unchanged albeit low; better competition is needed in all private systems/pillars (mainly in Bolivia and El Salvador) to cut administrative costs. In Chile and Peru, the employer does not contribute, whereas in Bolivia and Panama, the employer pays a minority of the total contribution hence infringing the ILO minimum norm. The theoretical discussion on who pays the employer contribution (himself, the insured or the consumer) is not entirely settled. The Chilean commission has proposed gradually charging 4% on wages to the employer, a policy to be considered by the other two countries. Social participation in the administration of the private system/pillar does not exist (but do so in public systems of Dominican Republic, Panama, and Peru); Argentina and Chile have advisory boards that attenuate such vacuum.

Long-term financial-actuarial equilibrium is a serious problem in all countries, saved for Chile that has taken measures to guarantee it; this is the foundation to sustain, in the long run, other aspects and should be professionally done, published, and discussed. Argentina has not conducted actuarial evaluations/projections while Bolivia allegedly did but without revealing the results; scarce data from both countries indicates a serious actuarial disequilibrium. El Salvador and Peru re-reform proposals are not based on actuarial valuations; Panama's latest actuarial study has not been released; those countries studying re-reforms must conduct the necessary actuarial work.

To improve feasibility, a re-reform should take into account the country's economic-social conditions; the major goal must be the improvement of social security principles (including financial-actuarial sustainability) instead of placing emphasis on capital accumulation; it is great if this is attained, but it should not be given priority as it has had questionable results.

References

AIOS (2016). Boletín Estadístico 2015, 29, December, and 30, June 2016.

Asociación Internacional de Organismos de Supervisión de Fondos de Pensiones—AIOS (2013). Seminario Internacional de Pensiones. Panama.

Bertranou, F., Centrángolo, O., Grushka, C., & Casanova, L. (2017). Argentine case. In I. Díaz (Ed.), *Reverting pension privatization in the world*. Geneva: International Labor Office.

Bonadona, A. (2017). Information on Bolivia to C. Mesa-Lago, La Paz, January 12.

Bravo, D. (2016). Information of Chile's President of the Commission to C. Mesa-Lago, Santiago de Chile, October 28.

CNSS (Consejo Nacional de Seguridad Social) (2013). Decreto n° 381-13: Reglamento de Pensiones Solidarias. December 24th. http://www.cnss.gob.do/app/do/doc_dec.aspx.

Comisión Asesora Presidencial sobre el Sistema de Pensiones—CAPSP (2015). Informe Final. Santiago de Chile.

CONATO (2016). Propuesta sobre un régimen de seguridad social. Ciudad Panamá.

CONSAR (2010). Acuerdo por el que se abrogan diversas disposiciones emitidas por la Comisión Nacional del Sistema de Ahorro para el Retiro. Diario Oficial de la Federación. June 2nd. http://www.gob.mx/cms/uploads/attachment/file/64755/Acuerdo_abrogatorio_CONSAR_100602.pdf.

Cruz-Saco, M., et al. (2017). *Demografía, Empleo, Gasto, Ahorro y Pensiones en el Perú*. Lima: Universidad del Pacífico.

Defensoría del Pueblo (2014). Las Pensiones en el Marco de la Seguridad Social en el Perú. Lima: Documento de Trabajo.

Durán, F. (2016). Entendiendo la sostenibilidad de pensiones IVM de la CCSS: Logros y desafíos. San José.

Hohnerlein, E. M. (2012). Pension re-reform in Argentina. In C. Mesa-Lago 2012, (pp. 201–233).

Inter-American Development Bank—IADB (2016). Dadabase SIMS, June www.iadb.org/en/databases/sims/home. 2017.hrml.

Martínez, I., et al. (2013). *Sistema Previsional de El Salvador: Diagnóstico y Propuesta de Reforma*. San Salvador: Equipo Técnico de la Superintendencia de Pensiones.

Mesa-Lago, C. (2008). *Reassembling social security: A survey of pension and health care reforms*. Oxford: Oxford University Press.

Mesa-Lago, C. (2009). Re-reforms of Latin American pension systems: Argentinean and Chilean models and lessons. *The Geneva Papers on Risk and Insurance Issues and Practice, 34*(4), 602–617.

Mesa-Lago, C. (2012). Re-reforms of privatized pensions systems. Munich: Zeitschrift für ausländisches und internationales Arbeits- und Sozialrecht, *23*(3), 189–316.

Mesa-Lago, C. (2014). Los modelos mixtos de pensiones en Costa Rica y Uruguay: Algunas lecciones para la re-reforma en El Salvador. Aportes al Debate sobre Políticas Públicas, *4*(6), 1–20.

Mesa-Lago, C. (2016a). Sugerencias para la re-reforma de pensiones en Perú. Lima: Apuntes Revista de Ciencias Sociales, *43*(78), 41–60.
Mesa-Lago, C. (2016b). Seguridad social, re-reformas de pensiones y recomendaciones para Perú. Lima: Seminario Internacional, Hacia un sistema integral de seguridad social, October 21.
Mesa-Lago, C. (2016c). *Reformas estructurales, y re-reformas de pensiones en América Latina: Lecciones para Panamá*. Panama: International Social Security Association, World Forum on Social Security.
Mesa-Lago, C. (2017). Reverting pension privatization in Bolivia. In I. Díaz (Ed.), *Reverting pension privatization in the World*. Geneva: ILO.
Mesa-Lago, C., & Bertranou, F. (2016). Pension reforms in Chile and social security principles, 1981- 2015. *International Social Security Review, 69*(1), 25–45.
Mesa-Lago, C., & Ossio, L. (2012). Pension re-reform in Bolivia, In C. Mesa-Lago 2012, (pp. 235–257).
Ministerio de Economía y Finanzas Públicas—MEFP (2015). Resultados del estudio matemático actuarial ratifican las proyecciones de sostenibilidad que hizo el MEFP. La Paz, August 14.
OECD/IADB/World Bank (2014). Pensions at a glance: Latin America and the Caribbean. Washington DC.
ONE (Oficina Nacional de Estadística) (2010). IX Censo Nacional de Población y Vivienda 2010. volumen 1 Informe General. Junio 2012. http://censo2010.one.gob.do/index.php?module=articles&func=view&ptid=2&p=6.
Ortiz, J. F. (2017). Information on Bolivia to C. Mesa-Lago, Mexico City, January 20.
Presidencia de la República (2016). Iniciativa de Ley de Reforma de la Ley del Sistema de Ahorro de Pensiones. San Salvador, February 16.
Resolución y Ley (2015). Reforma de pensiones, November and April. Quito.
Rojas, J. (2014). El Sistema Peruano de Pensiones. Lima: Fondo Editorial.
SIPEN (2016). Boletín Trimestral, 53. September 30. Santo Domingo. http://www.sipen.gov.do/index.php/publicaciones/boletines-trimestrales/category/boletines-trimestrales-2016.
SIPEN (2017). Resumen Estadístico Previsional al 31 de diciembre de 2016. http://www.sipen.gov.do/index.php/estadisticas/resumenes-estadisticos/category/resumen-estadistico-previsional.
Sistema Único de Beneficiarios—SIUBEN (2012). Calidad de vida. Estudio Socioeconómico de hogares en República Dominicana. http://www.siuben.gob.do/publicaciones/libro-calidad-de-vida/.
Superintendencia de Pensiones de República Dominicana—SIPEN (2012). Resumen de resultados Estimación Tasa de Reemplazo a 31 de diciembre de 2011 y 31 de diciembre de 2012. www.sipen.gov.do/.../Resumen_Resultados_Estudio_Tasa_de_Reemplazo_a_Dic_2011.
Tesorería de la Seguridad Social (TSS) (2017). Informe Estadístico 4° Trimestre. Departamento de Planificación y Desarrollo. December 31. www.tss.gov.do/pdf/inf_stats4tri-2015.pdf.
Universidad de Costa Rica---UCR (2016). Estudio Actuarial del Seguro de IVM Administrado por la CCSS. San José: Escuela de Matemática.
Valero, D. (2013). Planes de Pensiones complementarios en las empresas latinoamericanas. Una aplicación práctica para la República Dominicana. Saarbrüken: Ed. Publicia.

Chapter 13
Financial Sustainability of the Algerian Retirement System: A Perspective Analysis of the 50 Coming Years

Farid Flici and Frédéric Planchet

Abstract Maintaining retirement systems stability is nowadays a big challenge for all countries. Such sustainability is widely related to a set of time-varying elements that include population structure, longevity, employment, and affiliation to social security. For the case of Algeria, public retirement works according to the pay-as-you-go principle and equilibrium is maintained by public subsidy. But, population is now aging, and longevity is improving. The retired population is supposed to grow faster than the population at working age. Consequently, it will be harder to keep equality between retirement incomes and outcomes especially if we consider the weakness of the demand for social security among workers. The latter remains widely dependent on public employment; the employees of the private sector are less covered. In the present paper, we aim to simulate the future evolution of the demographic and economic factors affecting the stability of the Algerian retirement system in order to show their long-run effect. As a result, we found that it will be impossible to keep the retirement sustainability within its current design. The accelerating aging process imposes to undertake heavy reforms in the near future.

Keywords Retirement · Pay-as-you-go · Experience mortality · Contribution rates · Aging · Longevity

---

F. Flici (✉)
Centre for Research in Applied Economics for Development (CREAD), Algiers, Algeria
e-mail: farid.flici@cread.dz

F. Planchet
Institut de Science Financiére et d'Assurances (ISFA), Lyon, France
e-mail: frederic.planchet@univ-Lyon1.fr

M. Peris-Ortiz et al. (eds.), *Economic Challenges of Pension Systems*,
https://doi.org/10.1007/978-3-030-37912-4_13

13.1 Introduction

As a part of the social security system, a pension system aims to guarantee for elderly a basic income to satisfy their vital needs. The functioning of pension systems combines social protection and insurance principles (OECD 2005). This combination aims to integrate two main objectives: smoothing retirement benefits to individual saving efforts and to keep equity between individuals within the same population (Merton et al. 1987) for which we can add poverty alleviation (Bovenberg and Van Ewijk 2011a). The insurance component is set to cover people from the risk to survive to high ages. Aging results in reducing physical and intellectual capacities of people (Ilmarinen and Toumi 1992) which implies a loss of competitiveness in the labor market called loss of earning power (Wang et al. 2014). Longevity improvement weighs too heavy for pension funds especially if not associated with a parallel improvement of the healthy life expectancy (Bovenberg and Van Ewijk 2011b). Thus, the necessity to keep a pension plan sustainable is not only related to financial issues but more likely to protect low-earning people. That is why the intervention of the State is needed.

The allowance of contributions to pay retirement benefits can be managed in different ways. Pay-as-you-go system (PAYG) is the most classical way to finance pension schemes. This system was first founded in Germany starting from 1889 (Henke 2002; Lui 1998; Wong 2015). England followed up starting from 1892 (Wang et al. 2014). Following Wong (2015), a PAYG pension system is "a plan in which the current pension welfare of the elderly is financed by contributions from the current working population." The stability of a PAYG system is widely based on some proportionality of the population of retirees in regard to the contributing population. In 2015, the part of the population aged 60 and over in the world population is estimated at 12.3%. According to the projections of the United Nations Organization (UNO 2015), this part is expected to increase to 21.5% in 2050 and to 28.3% in 2100. This aging process is threatening the stability of the pension schemes financed by PAYG system. The number of people at working age which are theoretically supposed to contribute for one individual at retirement is falling down permanently. Thus, the design of pension schemes all over the world must undergo deep reforms. The World Bank, being conscious of the fact that PAYG systems will not resist to face population aging for the long run (Holzmann et al. 2008), proposed in 1994 a general framework of reform (WB 1994).The World Bank discussed a set of key elements in concern of the design of pension systems to convene the new economic and demographic constraints. In this sense, the main recommendation was to pass from a one-pillar system to a multi-pillar system. In the beginning, a three-pillar system was proposed:

1. First pillar: Mandatory, wages-linked, defined benefits system, and publicly managed
2. Second pillar: Mandatory, funded schemes, defined contribution system, and privately managed
3. Third pillar: Voluntary, fully funded, and privately managed

Each pillar is conceived to serve a well-defined function. The first pillar targets poverty alleviation; it can be a universal system offering a minimum income for the whole older population or a limited benefit system based on some eligibility criteria: needs-linked or employment-related incomes. The second pillar may endorse the saving-incomes smoothing. It encourages individual saving and economic capital accumulation. This second pillar can take two forms: individual savings plan or occupational plan. The third pillar allows high-wage earners to augment their saving effort in the intention to receive more incomes at retirement. All these three pillars are contributory. Later, the World Bank added two additional non-contributory pillars (Holzmann and Hinz 2005):

- Zero pillar: It is a non-contributory universal system which deals directly with the vulnerable old population by offering them a minimum protection level.
- Fourth pillar: It is an informal system based on intra-family solidarity, not necessarily based on financial supports. It can consist of social assistance as housing, health care, etc.

According to the World Bank suggestions, a multi-pillar system is very suitable with a multi-objective pension system (Holzmann and Hinz 2005). The formal one-pillar system is less flexible in this sense. Also, the World Bank does not propose a standard solution to be used in all circumstances but just a general framework to be adapted with the specificity of each country (Holzmann et al. 2008).

In order to ensure the long-run sustainability of a pension system, the underlying risks must be well known and well evaluated. Firstly, the nature of the risks to manage within a pension plan depends widely on the structure of the system itself. The PAYG system is very sensitive to demographic changes. Population aging results in an unbalance between the working population and the population at retirement age; longevity is traduced by the extension of the retirement age compared to the working age; also, the mortality function of retirees can be significantly different from that of the global population. In such a case, the use of the global population life tables for actuarial calculations can lead to mis-estimation of the risk function. On the other side, there is a part of the risk which is related to changes in the economic growth between the working period and the period of retirement: wages, employment, affiliation to social security, inflation, etc.

The Algerian retirement system[1] is still based on a single-pillar system (Pillar 1), as it is mostly the case in the Middle East and North Africa (MENA) region. Pension systems in MENA region are still in an early maturation stage. For a long time, the contributing population has been much more important than the population of retirees in this region. Considering the financial equilibrium of the system from the cash-flows point of view is not appropriate for sustainability evaluation. Robalino et al. (2005) focused on the structural problems that are known in pension systems in MENA region and averted the emergency to proceed to deep reforms. According to the same authors, even without taking into account the effects of population aging, the actual pension design in MENA region suffers from permanent inefficiencies (Robalino et al. 2005):

[1]This paper doesn't consider the law 16-15 of December 31, 2016 setting the minimum age of retirement at 60 years for men and 55 years for women.

1. The first problem is the abusive generosity of the system: While replacement rate of the working age income is almost 50% in average, MENA's pension systems offer a replacement rate of around 75%. The problem is that the promised pension benefits are large and seem to be unsatisfied without a significant intervention of the public treasury. Ben Brahem (2009) discussed the pension systems' generosity in North African countries (Tunisia, Algeria, and Morocco) and confirmed that the high generosity of the pension systems in the cited countries cannot be kept for the long run because of population aging.
2. The second element consists in how these systems were designed: The way that benefits are defined distorts labor market supply and saving decision. Linking benefits to the final wage rather than to the average earning conduces to systemic generous benefits and then to some manipulation in salary definition along the working career. The configuration of the system encourages evasion, discourages the individual saving efforts, and makes working population to prefer early retirement. For the case of Algeria, even if the age for retirement is fixed at 60 years by the regulation, a significant number of workers get retired long before. Also, the current system generates some inequalities in terms of benefits distribution in intra- and inter-generations (Mendil 2014).
3. Weakness in terms of administrative efficiency.
4. Modesty of coverage rates.

The fact that pension systems represent a long-term commitment requires efficient planning in all sides. It will be very difficult for MENA countries, including Algeria, to pay the promised benefits under the new demographic challenges mainly represented by population aging. A parametric reform will not be sufficient to keep the sustainability of the system. It is not easy to extend social security among working people in a short period. Such an alternative must focus on the determinants of social security demand (Merouani et al. 2016). A significant augmentation of contribution rates for social security will encourage evasion and will affect the labor market equilibrium. Reforms must be oriented to pass from a one-pillar to a multi-pillar pension system, by reducing the incidence of the unfunded schemes and to complete it by a funded scheme (Chourouk 2003).

The main objective of this paper is to address the effects of longevity, aging, and the retirees' specific mortality on the stability of the Algerian pension plan. The evaluation of the future engagement of the pension fund under PAYG system is directly related to the estimation of the mortality function of the pensioners and to predict its future reduction. In concern of the economic factors, we will suppose them to stabilize at their recent observed level or to continue evolving according to the recent observed trend. For this, we will start by presenting the elements which may affect the financial long-run stability of the Algerian pension system. The projection of retirement incomes/outcomes must be based on a population forecast. Unfortunately, Algeria does not have a population projection for the period beyond 2040. In a first part, we do a population projection by forecasting mortality and fertility while assuming a null migration balance. For mortality, we do a coherent mortality forecast by using the product-ratio method proposed by Hyndman et al.

(2013). For fertility, we use the Lee-Carter model adapted for fertility (Lee 1993) while supposing that the total fertility rate will fall down from three births per woman in 2015 to 2.5 in 2070. On the basis of the population forecast, we will define the expected evolution of the contributors and retirees' numbers. Then, we fix a scenario about salaries and pension amounts evolution. The mortality scheme of the retired population is supposed to be defined by the dynamic life tables calculated by Flici and Planchet (2019). Finally, the evolution of total expenses and total incomes are projected. On the basis of the obtained results, a set of recommendations are formulated.

13.2 Overview of the Algerian Retirement System

The Algerian retirement system is mandatory, financed by PAYG system, earning-linked defined benefits, and publicly managed. The regime dedicated for the self-employed population (employers and self-employed) is managed by "Caisse Nationale de Sécurité Sociale des Non Salaries (CASNOS)" while the employee's regime is managed by the "Caisse Nationale des Retraites (CNR)." Here, we will focus only on the second regime.

The monthly contribution is defined as a part of the salary. The retirement age was fixed at 60 years for employees. Retirement benefits are defined in function of the average of the 60 final wages W^* (or the average of the 60 best wages if more advantageous) and in order to attribute for each working year a validation rate of 2.5%. The retirement benefit (RB) is calculated as follows:

$$\mathrm{RB} = W^* * n * 2.5\%$$

With a number of contribution years n equal or higher to 32, the formula above leads to a replacement rate of 80% of the average of the best (/last) 60-month wage. This replacement rate is higher than the average in the MENA region which is evaluated at 70–75% and much higher than its level in developed countries (Robalino et al. 2005).

In the sense of the law, a working year is validated to give part in the pension benefits if it has led to, at least, 6 months of contribution. This last element with the fact of considering the best (or last) wages rather than the whole career average wage to define retirement benefits endorses the evidence of the relative high generosity which marks the Algerian retirement system already highlighted by Ben Brahem (2009). In addition, some bonuses are provided for some categories:

- A minimal pension equal to 75% of the national guaranteed minimal wage (NGMW).
- A bonus of 5 years is given for women with one additional year for each raised child with three as a limit.

- A bonus of 5 years is accorded for moudjahidine (former combatants of the Algerian liberation war 1954–1962). Years of participation in the war are doubly computed with a validation rate of 3.5% rather than 2.5%, a replacement rate of 100%, and a minimum equal to 2.5∗NMGW.
- A pension complement is provided for one spouse in charge.
- An early retirement for workers under nuisance conditions.

In addition to the normal age retirement (NAR), many other types of pre-retirement were proposed in order to smooth individual decisions and economic circumstances:

- Proportional retirement (PR): This type was introduced in 1997 to allow workers to retire before fulfilling the required conditions. Only 20 years of activity and a minimal age of 50 years are required.
- Early retirement (ER): This formula was introduced in 1994 to suit the case of workers who lost their job consequently to the economic crisis of the 1990s. The pensioner must be 50 years old and have accumulated 20 years of activity and 10 years of contribution at least. Also, the decision of getting retired must be supported by the employer who must pay the right opening contribution which is defined in function of the number of anticipated years.
- Retirement allowance (RA): The retirement allowance was proposed to allow those who have reached the age of 60 without fulfilling the requirements to have access to retirement, in order to benefit from a minimal earning for a minimum of 5 years of contribution.
- Retirement without age condition (RAC): When 32 years of contribution are accumulated, a worker can enjoy his retirement before reaching the legal age of retirement. In order to compensate for the loss resulting from his early retirement since he is still able to improve his final wage, his replacement rate is augmented by 2% for each year below age 60 years in the limit of 5 years.

The five types of retirement presented above can be grouped into one main category: the direct retirement (DR). Additionally, survivor's benefits are provided for the family members after the death of the insured worker/pensioner. We can distinguish two types of survivor's benefits: survivor's pension (for NAR, PR, ER, and RAC) and survivor's allowance (for RA). Survivor's benefits are provided to:

1. The spouse: In case of remarriage, the pension is transferred to the other rights holders.
2. Orphan: For males until 18 years old or 21 years if they are still studying or for females until occupation or marriage.
3. Parents: Only if their own pension is under 75% of NGMW.

In order to preserve the purchasing power of pensioners against inflation, retirement pensions and allowances are annually re-evaluated.

13.3 The Financial Balance of CNR: Evolution Overview

From 2000 to 2013, the global expenses of the CNR have grown from 117 to 687 billion *dzd* (Algerian dinar) with an annual exponential growth rate of 13.7%. On the other hand, the global incomes have passed from 114 in 2000 to 599 billion in 2013 with an annual exponential growth rate of 12.8%. Figure 13.1 draws their differential evolution.

This evolution resulted from a combination of a set of factors, principally the differential evolution of the populations of retirees and that of contributors and also the improvement of salaries and pension benefits.

First, we start by giving a short overview of the evolution of the Algerian population structure from the independence in 1962 till now. Then, the evolution of the economic factors will be shortly discussed.

13.3.1 *Population Growth and Structure*

The Algerian population has grown from about 11 million in 1962 to across 40 million in 2016. The evolution of the population at working age compared to that at retirement age allows us to give an indication about the theoretical ratio of contributors to retirees. In this sense, a comparative evolution for the Algerian population is shown in Fig. 13.2 according to population census data.

The ratio of the population at working age to the population at retirement age was at around 6.7 in 1966 and 8 in 1977 and has been varying between 8 and 9 starting from 1987.

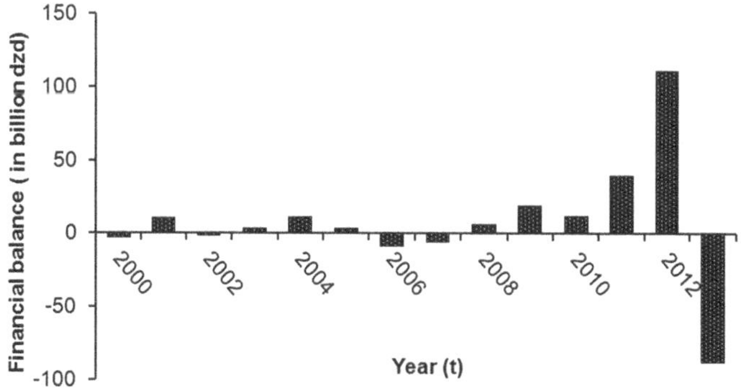

Fig. 13.1 Pension plan incomes vs. outcomes (2000–2013). (*Source:* CNR (2014))

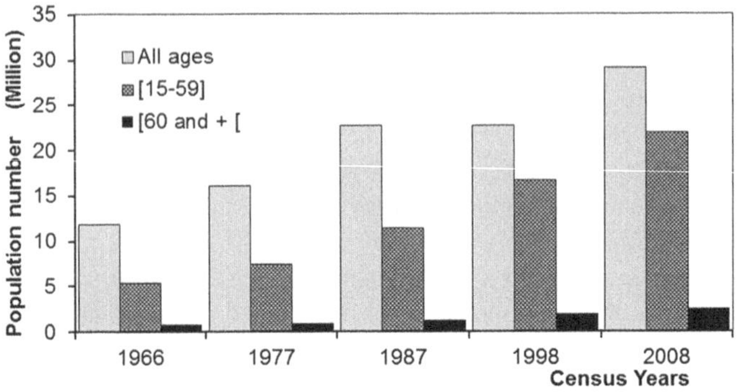

Fig. 13.2 Population at working age vs. population at retirement age. (*Source:* Algerian population censuses (1966, 1977, 1987, 1998, and 2008))

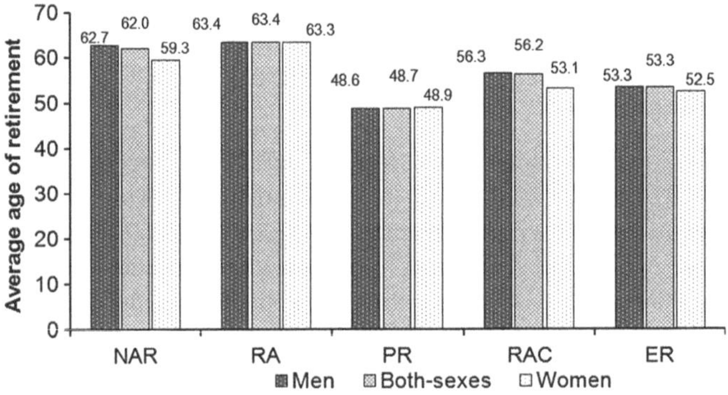

Fig. 13.3 Average retirement age for direct retirement (2013). (*Source:* Calculated from data provided by CNR (2014))

13.3.2 Average Age of Retirement

Even if, theoretically, the age of retirement is fixed at 60 years, many options exist to allow people to get retired earlier. These options bring down the average age of retirement. Figure 13.3 shows the average age of retirement for the direct retirement types (NAR, RA, ER, PR, and RAC) in 2013 (CNR 2014). There is no detailed data for other years.

For NAR and RA, for which a minimum age of 60 years is required, the average age of retirement in 2013 was, respectively, 62 and 63.4. For the other types, this age was equal to 48.7, 56.2, and 53.2 for PR, RAC, and ER, respectively. A slight difference is observed between men and women. Men retire later than women in all retirement types except for PR where the average retirement age for women is slightly higher than that of men: 48.6 for men and 48.9 years for women. When considering all the direct retirement types, it turns out that the average retirement age is 59 years for men and 57 years for women.

13.3.3 Retirement System Outcomes

A detailed analysis of the retirement expenses evolution requires analyzing two main elements: the evolution of the population of beneficiaries and the pension benefits amounts. Before all, we give, in Fig. 13.4, a summary about the types of retirement within the Algerian retirement system.

Retirement benefits in the Algerian system can be gathered into four main categories: the retirement pensions (RP), the retirement allowances (RA), complementary retirement (CR), and other allowances (OA). Each category comprises direct and survivor's benefits. There are no available details in concern of the other allowances which represent a part of nearly 0% from the direct retirement expenses as shown in Fig. 13.5.

Figure 13.5 shows the retirement expenses distribution by type of retirement. According to the item (a), around 98% of retirement expenses are used to pay retirement pensions while only 2% go to retirement allowances. The complementary retirement and the other allowances parts are near to 0%. Item (b) provides more details about this distribution; 74.9% are served as a direct retirement pension (DRP) and 22.8% as a survivor's retirement pension (SRP).

(a) Evolution of the number of pensioners

The total number of pensioners passed from 1.25 million in 2000 to 2.48 million in 2013 and to 2.77 million in 2015. Figure 13.6 shows this evolution by type of retirement.

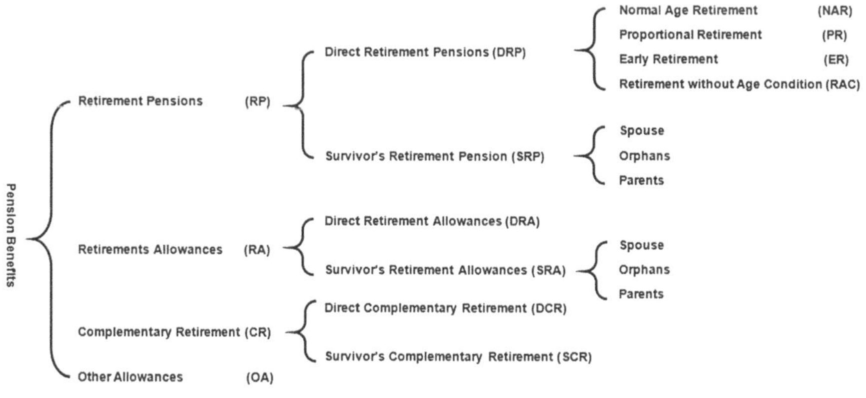

Fig. 13.4 Types of retirement in the Algerian retirement system

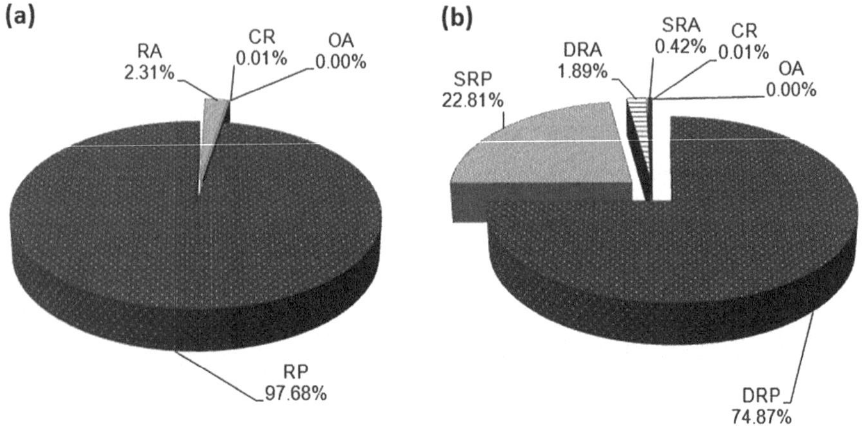

Fig. 13.5 Retirement expenses average distribution by type of retirement (2000–2013). (*Source:* Calculated from data provided in CNR (2014))

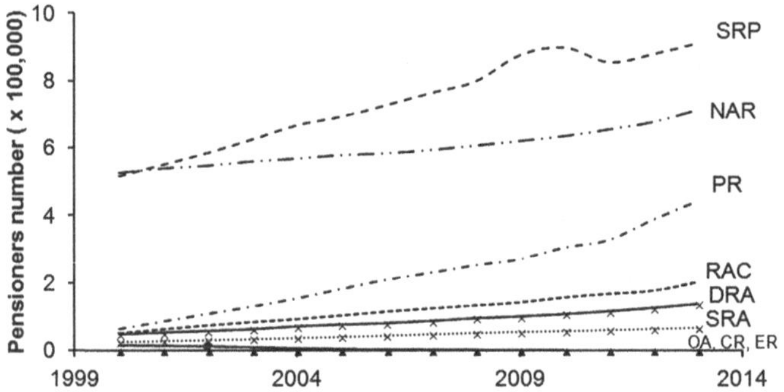

Fig. 13.6 Evolution of the number of pensioners by type of retirement (2000–2013). (*Source:* CNR (2014))

The numbers of NAR and SRP beneficiaries are very important compared to the other types of retirement. NAR beneficiaries passed from 525,000 in 2000 to more than 712,000 in 2013. For SRP, the evolution was from 515,000 to 910,000 beneficiaries. The PR beneficiaries have grown from 64,000 in 2000 to 442,000 in 2013. In 2013, the RAC, DRA, and SRA recorded, respectively, 203,000, 140,000, and 67,000 beneficiaries. The parts of the ER, CR, and OA are much smaller with around 1,200 beneficiaries in 2013.

(b) Part of retirees among the population at retirement age

Access to retirement requires contributing for social security during a minimum number of years varying from 5 years for the case of RA to 32 years for the case of RAC. To benefit from a NAR pension, a minimum of 15 years is required against 20 years for PR and ER. The contribution period can vary in duration and in nature

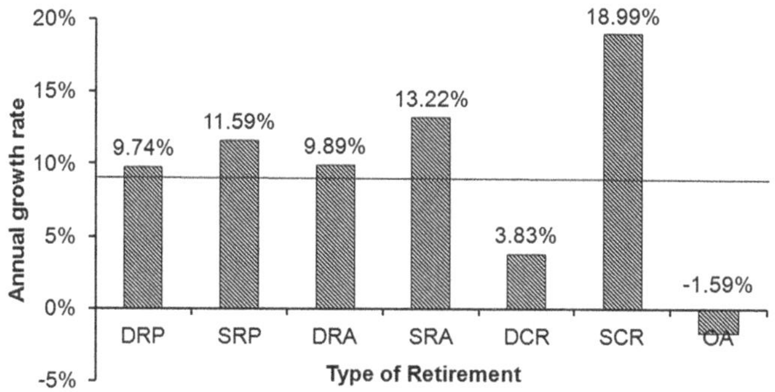

Fig. 13.7 Annual growth rates of retirement benefits in average (2000–2013). (*Source:* CNR (2014))

(continuous/discontinuous) according to the employment conditions, individual preferences, and social security design. Thus, the notion of coverage is different for workers and for people at retirement age. Social security coverage at working age determines retirement coverage, but there is no mathematical relationship between the two. In other words, if we know only the affiliation rate for social security, we cannot expect the number of retirees in the future. A part of the actual contributors will not be acceded to retirement if their whole contribution period falls down the required minimum. For that, in the absence of an individual contribution history, it is not evident to determine exactly the number of future retirees among a given generation.

(c) Pension benefit average amount evolution

The monthly pension benefit is defined by a combination of a set of elements: the final wage, the number of years of contribution, the annual revaluation rate, and the validation rate for each year of contribution. The average benefit amount by type of retirement is affected by the age structure of the retirees' portfolio. For that, its time evolution is tied to the entrance/exit movement in each portfolio. When wages are growing in time, it results that the younger retirees have higher pension benefits than the older ones.

According to Fig. 13.7, the average benefits in DRP have grown with an annual rate of 9.75%. For the other types, the average growth rate for all types was around 9.05%.

According to Fig. 13.8, the annual revaluation rate has stagnated during the period 1998–2009 between 4% and 5%. Starting from 2010, this rate passed beyond 8% and reached an exceptional level of 12% in 2014. Because of the new budgetary constraints imposed by the recent decline of oil prices, the revaluation rate was set at 5% in 2015 and at 2.5% in 2016.

The annual growth of pension benefits doesn't result only from the annual re-evaluation which aims to protect pensioners against inflation and the additional advantages provided to keep in line low pensions with a defined minimum, but also from the time evolution of wages. Thus, and in average, new retirees have higher retirement benefits compared to the oldest ones when wages grow in time.

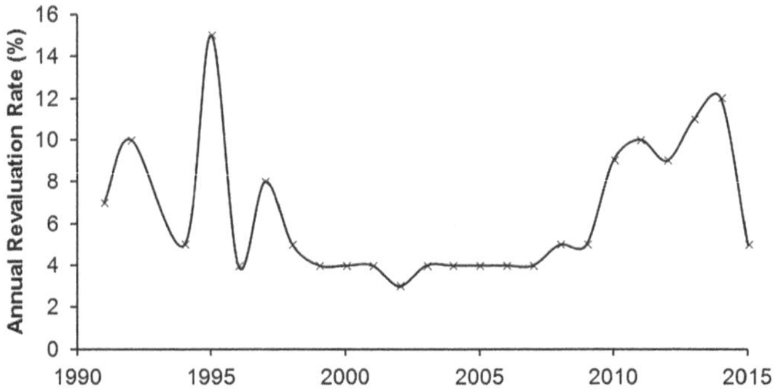

Fig. 13.8 Annual pensions benefits revaluation rate. (*Source:* From 1991 to 2013 – CNR (2014). From 2014 to 2015 – Official Journal of the Republic of Algeria, n°: 2014/25, 2015/24 (www.joradp.dz))

13.3.4 Retirement Incomes

In a PAYG system aimed at poverty reduction, public intervention is needed to adjust financial unbalances. For the period from 2000 to 2013, in average, the resources of the CNR come mainly from the contributions of the affiliated employees with a part of 75.6%. Public transfers represent around 23.6% while less than 0.8% come from the investment of contributions (CNR 2014).

(a) The population of contributors

Figure 13.9 shows a scheme of the process that goes from the global population to the contributing population passing through labor market, occupational choices, and social security.

It is not the whole population aged 15–59 which participate in the labor force, the total labor force records only the individuals supplying labor for the production of goods and services and it comprises the workforce and the unemployed population. The working population contains employees and employers/self-employed. At the end it is only the affiliated employees who contribute for CNR.

Figure 13.10 shows a comparative evolution of the population at working age, the active population, and the affiliated population in Algeria from 2005 to 2015. During the whole observation period, the part of population at working age contributing for social security has fluctuated in-between 20.15% and 22.75% with an average of 21.28%. That means that for five persons at working age, there is only one contributor for social security.

Even if men and women have equal parts in the population at working age, the rates of participation in the labor force and the workforce are different and males have the most important parts. In 2015, the activity rate was evaluated at 65% for men and only at 15% for women. The employment rate was at 90% for men and 83.5% for women. Unfortunately, data about affiliation to social security are not

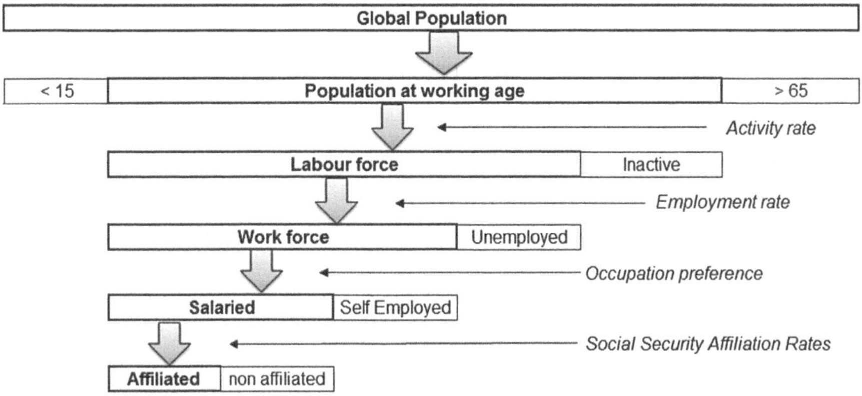

Fig. 13.9 Affiliation scheme

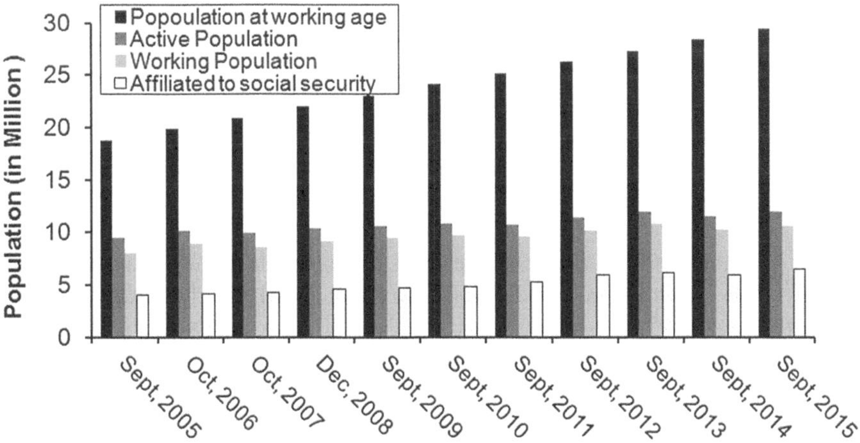

Fig. 13.10 Population at working age, active population, and affiliated population in Algeria. (*Source:* Population at working age was calculated by interpolation/extrapolation based on 1998 and 2008 census data and the ONS annual publications. Other indicators are issued from ONS (2015))

available by sex, and we suppose for simplification issues that affiliation rates are same for men and women.

(b) Monthly wage

In a wage-related defined benefits pension plan, contributions are calculated as a part of the monthly wage. The national guaranteed minimal wage (NGMW) can have a significant effect on the evolution of the monthly average wage. The NGMW is fixed by authorities in order to protect people earning very low salaries, and it

Table 13.1 Evolution of the NGMW in Algeria (1990–2012)

Revision date	NGMW (in Algerian dinar)
01/01/1990	1000
01/01/1991	1800
01/07/1991	2000
01/04/1992	2500
01/01/1994	4000
01/05/1995	4800
01/01/1998	5400
01/09/1998	6000
01/01/2001	8000
01/01/2004	10,000
01/01/2007	12,000
01/01/2010	15,000
01/01/2012	18,000

Source: ONS (2012)

represents guidance for the general evolution index of the other wage categories. The evolution of the NGMW in Algeria is represented in Table 13.1.

As shown in Table 13.1, the NGMW has been revised many times between 1990 and 2012 and has grown 18 times along that period. It has quadrupled in only 4 years between 1990 and 1994. After, the augmentation trend has known some moderation.

(c) Contribution rates

The contribution for retirement is paid as a part of the contribution for social security. The contribution rate for social security in Algeria has marked many revisions from 1985 till today. In 2015, the social security contribution rate has been fixed at 34.5% of the monthly wage. Twenty five percent are supported by the employer; 9% by the insured himself, and 0.5% represents a public subsidy. The contribution for retirement represents almost 50% of the contribution for social security. Its evolution over time is shown in Fig. 13.11.

The contribution rate for retirement (CRR) has marked important augmentations from 1985 to 2015 by passing from 5% to 18.25%. Two augmentations were highly significant; the revision of 1991 brought up the CRR from 5% to 11%. The three consecutive revisions of 1998, 1999, and 2000 allowed the CRR to increase to 16%. This fast augmentation has had the objective of maintaining the retirement regime financial balance.

13.4 Population Projection

We intend to study the stability of the Algerian retirement scheme during the 50 coming years. First, a population projection is needed. Then, the populations of contributors and retirees can be deduced by assuming some hypotheses about

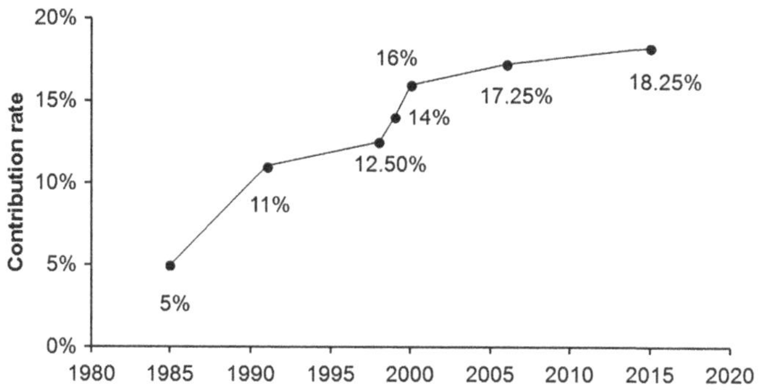

Fig. 13.11 Evolution of the contribution rate to retirement in Algeria. (*Source:* Official Journal of the Republic of Algeria, different editions www.joradp.dz)

activity, occupation, and affiliation to social security. Population projection is based on a set of hypothesis regarding the future trends of fertility, mortality, and immigration. The recent changes of life expectancy evolution and the total fertility rate (TFR) in Algeria need a longer time length to be assessed, and it is so difficult to assess if the recent observed trend will be maintained in the upcoming years or it will diverge from the general trend observed since the late 1970s. Conscious of all these elements, we do a population projection until 2070 only in the intention of evaluating the sustainability of the Algerian retirement regime without addressing any critical review of the goodness of the projection itself.

13.4.1 Baseline Population

Population structure is mainly given by population censuses. Data recorded by civil status allows drawing of the year-to-year population evolution. For population forecast purposes, a baseline population is needed. In this sense, we prefer to use the population structure issued from the latest Algerian population census of 2008 as a baseline population to perform our projection, rather than using the population structure published by the ONS in 2015 or 2016.

Figure 13.12 shows the single age pyramid of the Algerian population according to the 2008 census. Note that the population aged 75 years and over was broken down by a linear interpolation between 70 and 100 years, while the number of population aged 100 years and over is supposed to be equal to 0.

13.4.2 Mortality Forecast

To project the age-specific mortality rates (ASMRs) to the future, we achieved a coherent mortality forecast.

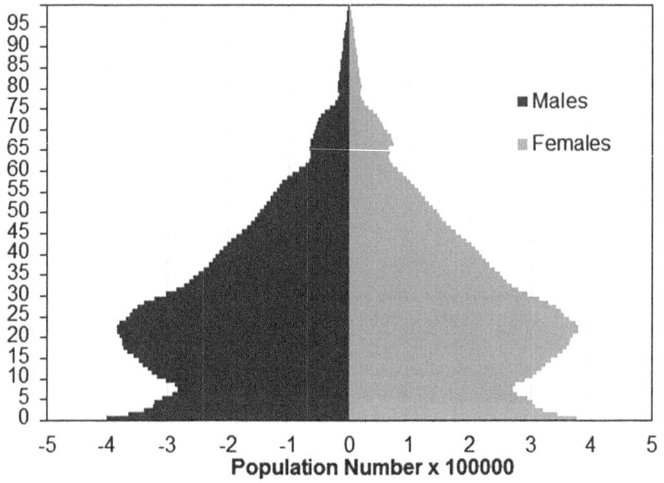

Fig. 13.12 Single age population pyramid (Algeria, 2008). (*Source:* General population census 2008; single age numbers were interpolated by Karup-King method)

The use of the Lee-Carter model (Lee and Carter 1992) to project the ASMRs independently for males and females leads to some incoherence regarding the mortality sex ratio by the horizon of the forecast (Flici 2016c). The use of the coherent approach allows us to avoid this kind of incoherence. Flici (2016b) compared two coherent mortality models to project ASMRs for males and females in Algeria: the product ratio method proposed by Hyndman et al. (2013) and the Lee-Carter model with an additive common component for males and females proposed by Li and Lee (2005). It turned out than, for Algeria, the first model leads to better results regarding the goodness of fit and the coherence. Figure 13.13 shows the resulting expected evolution of life expectancy at birth for males and females.

13.4.3 Fertility Forecast

To fix the future scenarios of fertility rate evolution in Algeria, we performed a probabilistic forecast incorporating experts' view. We aim to keep the population forecast results obtained in this paper within the framework of the national official projections methodology. The scenario of fertility evolution used for our projections were mainly derived from the discussions of the population projections subcommittee of the National Committee for Population (NCP) which depends on the National Health Ministry. Experts of the NCP judged that the TFR is expected to keep slightly decreasing toward a level of 2.5 children per woman by the horizon of 2030. In order

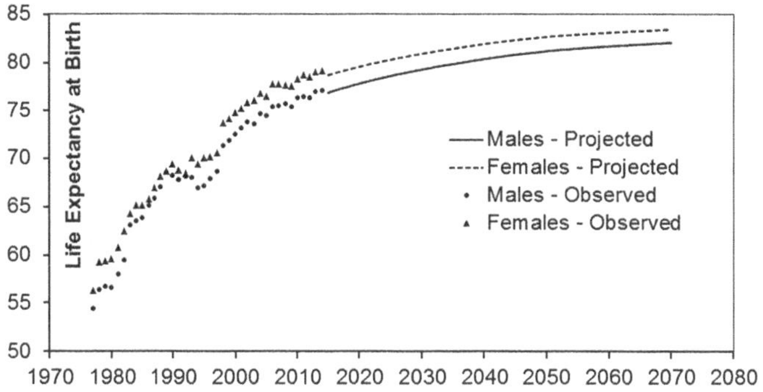

Fig. 13.13 Life expectancy coherent forecast for men and women. (*Source:* Flici (2016b))

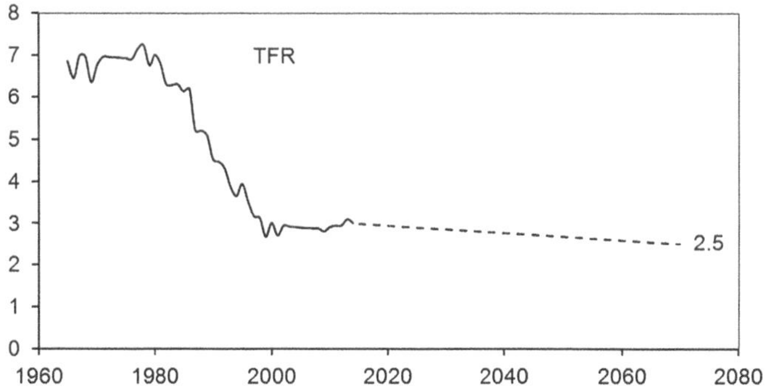

Fig. 13.14 Total fertility rate forecast. (*Source:* From 1964 to 2014 – Algerian official publications (various). From 2015 to 2070 – The future evolution scenario is issued from the working meetings of the National Committee for Population/population projections subcommittee)

to keep working within the same framework, we kept assuming an ultimate level of fertility of 2.5 by the horizon of 2070. Results are shown in Fig. 13.14.

13.4.4 Population Projection Results

Because immigration's data are missed or not available in the required format, we suppose the immigration sold to be equal to 0. The combination of the ASMRs and the age-specific fertility rates (ASFRs) applied to the baseline population provided by the population census of 2008 allowed us to obtain the global population evolution and its age and sex structure for the period 2008–2070. The population pyramids for the years 2020, 2030, 2040, 2050, 2060, and 2070 are shown in Fig. 13.15.

When we observe the transformation of the population pyramid from 2020 to 2070, we can deduce that the top of the pyramid is expected to enlarge faster than its

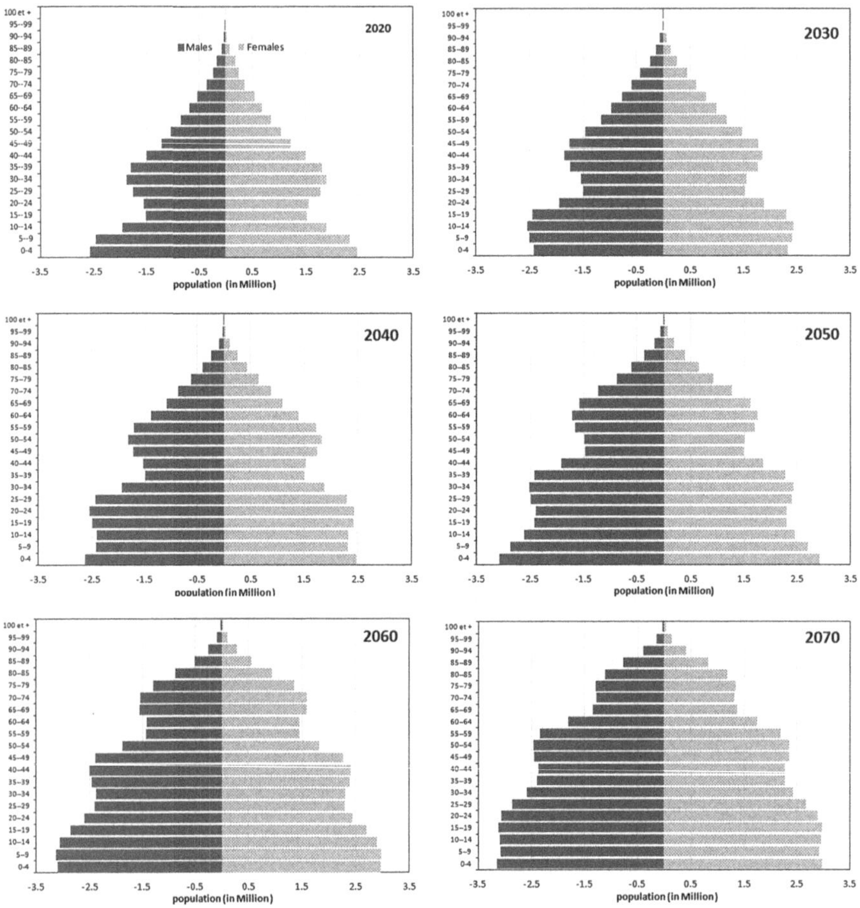

Fig. 13.15 Population pyramids for years 2020, 2030, 2040, 2050, 2060, and 2070

base. That reflects the aging process of the Algerian population during the 50 upcoming years. The part of the population aged 60 and over is expected to increase from around 8% in 2015 to keep around 20% starting from 2050.

13.4.5 The Evolution of the Populations at Working and at Retirement Ages

The population forecast allows us to deduce the populations at working age [15–59] and the population at retirement age [60 and over]. We observe that the global population is approximately equally divided between males and females. The population aged 15–59 is expected to grow from around 24 million in 2015 to

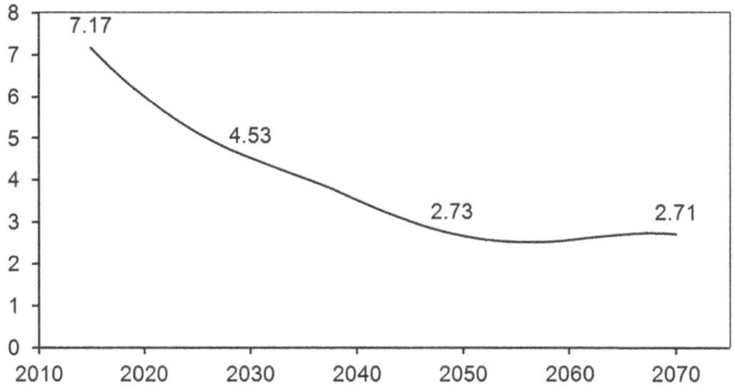

Fig. 13.16 Number of working people for one theoretical retiree (Projection results)

30 million in 2030 and to 45 million by 2070. On the other hand, the population aged 60 and over is expected to grow from 3.4 million in 2015 to about 16.5 million by 2070.

The analysis of this evolution in absolute terms does not highlight the effect of population aging on the financial balance of the retirement system. Figure 13.16 shows the expected evolution of the ratio of the population aged 15–59 to the population aged 60 and over which represents the number of individuals at working age corresponding to one theoretical retiree.

Figure 13.16 shows the expected decrease in the ratio of the population at working age to the population at retirement age. In 2015, we have more than seven individuals at working age corresponding to one individual at retirement age. This ratio is expected to fall to 4.5 in 2030 and to stabilize around 2.7 starting from 2050. If it is difficult to keep equilibrium between incomes and outcomes of the retirement regime within a theoretical ratio of 7, it will be more difficult to keep it under a value of 2.7. The main challenge will be to make a great part of the population at working age in occupation and then within the social security system.

In the following parts, we will try to consider these two last elements in order to define the long-term sustainability of the retirement system.

13.5 Economic Factor Future Evolution Scenarios

In concern of the economic factors, we suppose some simplistic scenarios. Activity rates, employment rates, occupation status preference, and affiliation to social security are supposed to remain constant over the projection period and also the annual revaluation rate of retirement benefits. Salaries will be supposed to keep evolving following their recent growth trend.

13.5.1 Labor Force, Workforce, and Affiliation to Social Security

During these last years in Algeria, there is only 40% of the population at working age who are offering their workforce in the labor market. This rate was around 53% in 2002. The employment rate has decreased from 44% in 2002 to 36% in 2015. 38.5% of the employed population is still not affiliated to social security. Figure 13.17 summarizes the recent evolution of these three elements.

In this paper, the labor force participation rate will be kept constant at the level of 40%. The employment rate will be supposed to be around 36% and the affiliation to social security will be fixed at 60%.

Affiliation rate for social security allows us to determine the population of contributors among working people while retirement coverage allows determination of the population of retirees among the population at retirement age. These two elements cannot be supposed to be fully dependent since the access for retirement requires a person to pay contributions for a minimal number of years. Accordingly, retirement coverage among a generation is directly related to the number of years of contribution among the same generation. An active person has to contribute during a minimum of 5 years during his whole working age to get access for retirement when he is 60 years old. During the working age length of a generation, especially when social security coverage is low, it is evident to have an important flow into/from social security system. In the absence of micro-data about the contributing history, it is not evident to fix any relationship between contribution rates and retirement coverage within a given generation. The future number of retirees is supposed to be more important than the average number of contributors among the same generation, because contribution rate represents just an average which does not address entrance and exit into/from the population of contributors. We conclude that even if we can estimate approximately the evolution of the number of contributors from year-to-year among a generation, we cannot easily conclude the future number of

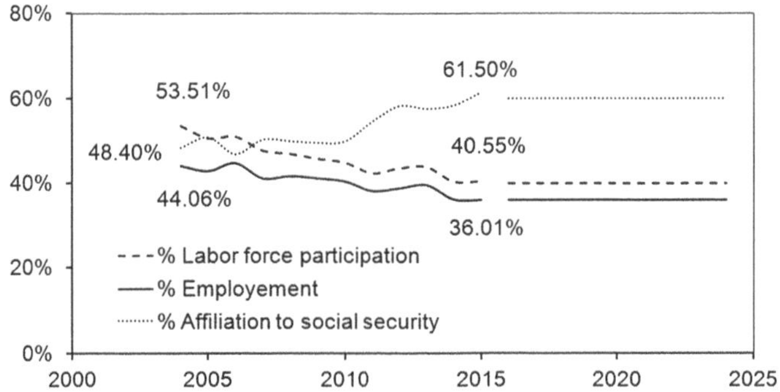

Fig. 13.17 Activity, employment, and affiliation to social security rates. (*Source:* Calculated from data provided by ONS (2015))

individuals who will be retired when they reach the retirement age. To avoid this mis-estimation problem, we proceed as follows:

- All the population at working/retirement ages will be supposed to be potential contributors/retirees. Hence, the evolution of the population number among the same cohort is only defined by the survival function.
- Data concerning activity, employment, occupation status preference (employees or self-employed), and affiliation to social security will be used to estimate the chance to be affiliated as an employee (affiliated to CNR) for all the individuals aged 15–59.
- The population forecast combined with the expected evolution of the average wage, the contribution rate, and the chance to be affiliated as an employee is supposed to allow estimation of the expected evolution of total contributions.
- The age-specific probability to contribute for CNR allows us to estimate the expected duration of contribution. Combined with the final wage, this allows us to estimate the average pension benefit (first retirement benefit). The annual revaluation rate of retirement benefits allows drawing of the evolution of retirement benefits over age and over time. Multiplied by the potential population of retirees, that allows us to estimate the total expenditure allocated to pay direct retirement pensions at time *t*.
- Because survivor's benefits require specific models and data without being our main objective in this paper, the survivor's pension total expenditure is calculated as a part of the direct pension expenditures. The sum of the two gives the total retirement expenses.
- The administrative fees are calculated as a percentage of the retirement expenses. The total gives the global outcomes of the retirement system.

In what follows, the elements cited above will be presented in more detail.

13.5.2 The Affiliation Rate Among the Population at Working Age

By assuming the population at working age to be potential contributors for CNR, we calculate, at each single age from 15 to 59, the rate to be affiliated as an employee among the population at working age. The estimation of this rate is based on a set of information, i.e., activity rates, employment rates, part of employees among the working people, and affiliation rate to social security. The workforce survey conducted by the ONS in 2013 (ONS 2014a) provides the data needed in our calculations. Data about activity and employment are arranged by sex and five age groups starting from 15–19 until 60 and over. Activity rate represents the ratio of the labor force to the population at working age. The employment rate is calculated by the working population divided by the population at working age. Activity and employment rates in Algeria in 2013 are presented in Fig. 13.18.

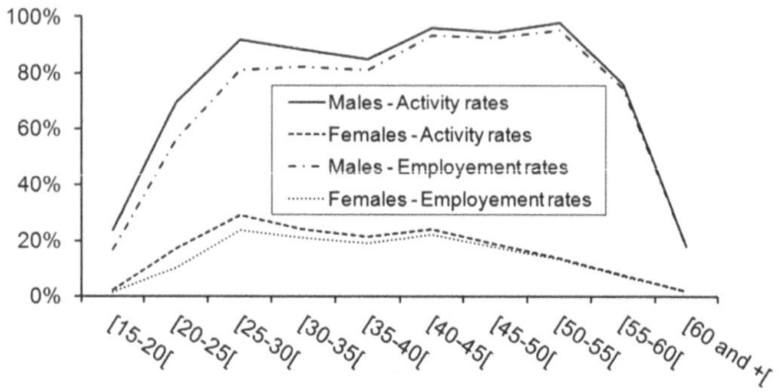

Fig. 13.18 Activity and employment rates by five age groups (2013). (*Source:* ONS (2014a))

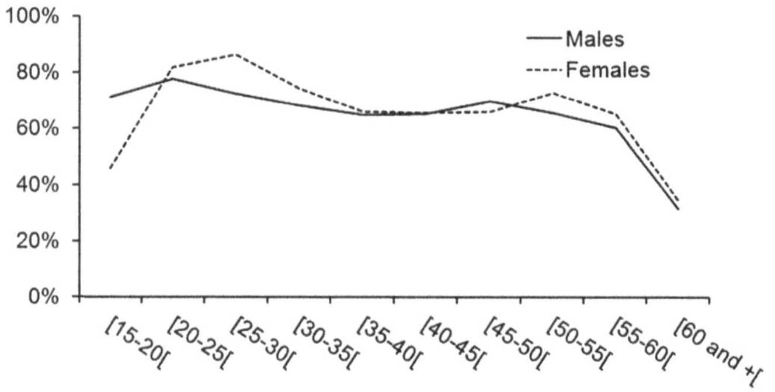

Fig. 13.19 Part of employees among workers by five age groups (2013). (*Source:* ONS (2014a))

The activity rate is around 44%, 71% for males and 16.6% for females. Between 25 and 55 years old, men are the most active during their working age with a rate of 92% while women are more active between 25 and 45 with an average activity rate of 21.5%. The curve representing employment follows nearly the shape of the curve of activity with a slight gap at young ages narrowing gradually with age. The employment rate for men is 65%; for women it is only about 14%.

In concern of the distribution of workers by occupation status (employees and self-employed), the part of employees is about 69% of workers, 68% for men and 73% for women. The part of employees among workers by age is shown in Fig. 13.19.

Data about affiliation to social security is given by type of occupation (employees or self-employed) or by sex but not by age. Affiliation rate to social security for the whole working population is 57.5%, 54% for men and 72% for women. Employees are well covered than self-employed people. The affiliation rate of employees is 70%, 65% for men and 92% for women. This difference is mainly due to the nature of the employer (private or public) and to the occupation status (employees or self-employed). Salaried women work more in the public sector compared to men with

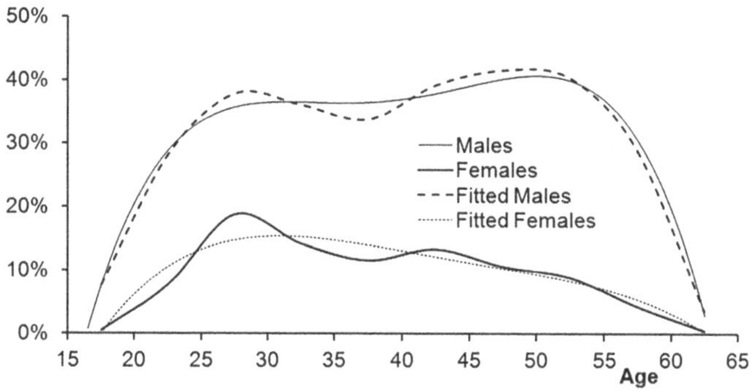

Fig. 13.20 Age-specific probability to contribute for CNR by age (2013). (*Source:* Calculated from data provided in ONS (2014a))

respective parts of 83% and 54%. Self-employment takes a part of 31% among men and 24% among women. The automatic affiliation to social security in the public sector makes the affiliation rate of the public employees equal to 100%. The coverage in the private sector is supposed to be much lower. This information is unfortunately missed in the ONS report (ONS 2014a).

By using all of the presented information, the part of the contributors for CNR among the population at working age can be deduced. The obtained results are shown in Fig. 13.20.

Figure 13.20 represents the part of contributors for CNR among the population at working age by age and sex. The interpolation at single ages was done by a polynomial fitting: a 5-degree polynomial for men and a 4-degree polynomial for women. Then, the fitted curves in Fig. 13.20 show the age-specific affiliation rates to CNR among people at working age that we denote as $AS^s_{x,t}$ with x representing age, t representing year, and s representing sex. This indicator can be used to estimate the distribution of contributors by sex and age among a given population (or a given cohort). The expected duration of contribution to CNR during a working career of each individual, denoted as EDC, can simply be approximated by summing the chances to contribute for CNR between 15 and 64 years. This can be written as:

$$\mathrm{EDC}_s = \sum_{x=15}^{64} \mathrm{AS}^s_x$$

It turns out that the expected duration of contribution to CNR is equal to 15 and 4.6 years respectively for males and females at working age. Then, the expected average of the first retirement benefits can be directly adjusted to the expected duration of contribution. If we consider a common retirement age of 59 years for men and 57 years for women, then the population reaching this age will be supposed to be potential retirees. Hence, the average of the first retirement benefit will be calculated on the basis of the expected duration of contribution and the final wage.

That will make possible to estimate the total retirement benefits (TRB) by only multiplying by the number of people reaching the average age of retirement.

13.5.3 Evolution of the Average Contribution

The evolution of the average monthly contribution is directly related to the evolution of wages and contribution rate. Here, the contribution rate will be supposed to remain constant. Wages are supposed to evolve following the recent observed trend. If we consider the period 2009–2013, the average growth rate of the net wages is 9.5%. From 1990 to 2013, the crude average wage has evolved by an annual growth rate of 10.7%. Here, we use a rate of 9.5% as an assumption of the future evolution of wages. In 2013, the contribution rate for social security was at 34.5% including 17.25% for retirement;10% are paid by the employer, 6.75% by the employee himself, and 0.5% by the government. Starting from 2015, the part required from the employer reached 11% and the contribution rate for retirement became 18.25%. This rate is used to project contributions for the period from 2015 to 2070. The contribution is calculated by multiplying the average crude monthly wage by the contribution rate for retirement. If we consider the average crude monthly wage of 2013 which is equal to 50,211 dzd, the annual average contribution of that year should be equal to:

$$50{,}211 \times 17.25\% \times 12 = 103{,}957.8 \text{ dzd}$$

For a number of contributors of 5,173,000, the total contribution to CNR during the year 2013 is evaluated at 537,773,825,900.68 dzd. The total income of CNR in 2013 is about 599 billion dzd; 430 billion come from contributions, 12 billion as investment returns, and 121 billion as public transfers. If we compare only the theoretical and the real total contributions, we can conclude that CNR may suffer a recovery problem evaluated at around 20%. It seems that some employers are not regular in paying the contributions of their employees. Also, the fact that a full year of contribution is validated when only 6 months of real contribution are proved may contribute to the cited gap between theoretical and real incomes.

13.5.4 Evolution of the Average Retirement Benefit

The evolution of the average retirement benefit results from the evolution of the duration of contribution, the annual revaluation rate, and the final wage. The evolution of the net wage over age reveals that in 2011, wage at 55–59 represents 1.11 of the average net wage. To make the relationship between wage and age, we proceeded to a polynomial fitting based on the data provided in ONS (2014b) which gives the evolution of the wages by large age groups such as <25, 25–39, 40–49, and 50 and over. The obtained results are shown in Fig. 13.21.

The retirement benefit amount is directly tied to the average wage of the last 5 years of the working career. If we admit that the average age for retirement is 59 years for men and 57 years for women, the wage to be considered in the calculation of the first retirement benefit corresponds to the average wage between 54 and 58 for men and 52 and 56 for women. In addition, the evolution of the retirement benefit amount is also affected by the annual revaluation as shown in Fig. 13.8. By including all these factors, we have shown in Fig. 13.7 that the average growth rate of the average retirement benefit was at 9.33% during the period 2000–2013.

13.5.5 Survivor's Retirement Expenses and Administration Fees

In addition to the direct retirement benefits, CNR provides survivor's benefits for spouses, orphans, and also parents. Modeling the expenses implied by survivor's benefits is complicated and can be separately treated by another work. Our idea is to consider the survivor's benefit expenses as a percentage of the direct benefit expenditures according to the recent observed trend. The evolution of the part of survivor's benefits expenses on the direct benefit expenses during the period 2000–2013 is shown in Fig. 13.22.

The part of survivor's benefit expenses represented 25% of the direct benefit expenses in 2000. This part has evolved to stagnate at around 31% starting from 2006. Here, we will suppose that this part will remain at this value during the upcoming years. In addition to retirement expenses (direct and survivor's benefits), the total outcome of CNR comprises administration fees. These expenses represent on average between 2006 and 2013 a proportion of 1.5% from the retirement expenses (CNR 2014), and we suppose that it will remain at this level during the upcoming years.

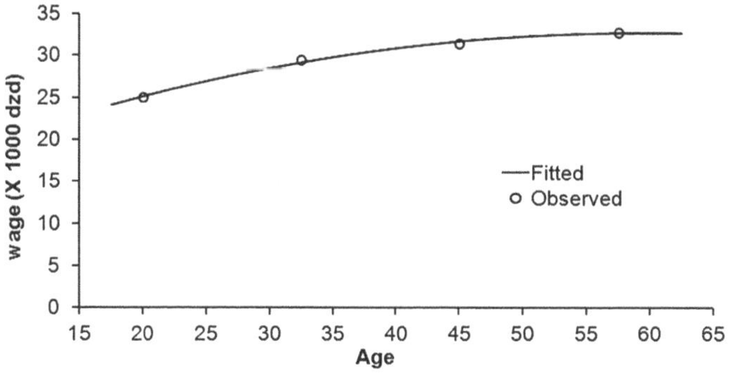

Fig. 13.21 Wage vs. age (2011). (*Source:* Calculated from ONS (2014b))

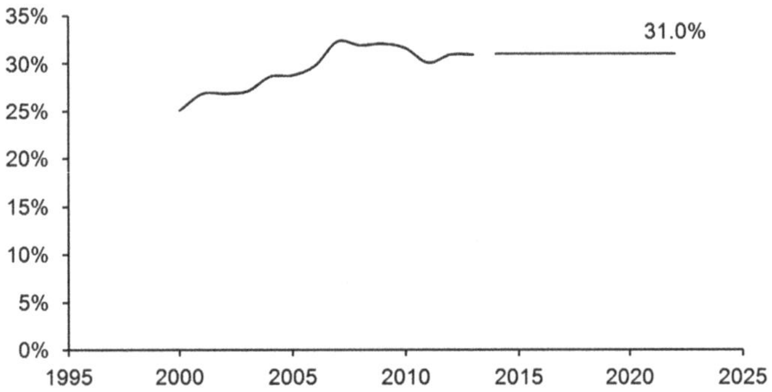

Fig. 13.22 Evolution of the ratio of the survivor's benefits on direct benefit expenses. (*Source:* Calculated from data provided by CNR (2014))

13.6 Incomes-Outcomes Projection

In order to predict the future evolution of incomes and outcomes of the employee's retirement scheme, we preferred to separate in our calculation the portfolio already in payment and the future generations including that of the current contributors. The actual portfolio of retirees will firstly be supposed to be closed for new entrances. Then, the late entrances will be addressed separatily. In contrast, the current portfolio of contributors can undergo some exits and entrances depending on the affiliation behavior of the working population. For that, calculation concerning this category will be done as part of that of the future generations.

The age of retirement will be supposed to be equal to the average age observed in 2013 which is 59 for men and 57 for women. Parallel to this, the working age will be extended until 64 years in order to take into account the individuals whose keep working beyond the average age of retirement. We remind that in this paper, the specificity of the retired population compared to the global population in terms of mortality will be considered in the outcomes projection. As shown in Flici and Planchet (2019), the prospective experience life tables were constructed and projected on the basis of the mortality experience of the retirees of CNR. It will be more convenient to use these tables to describe the survivorship of retirees rather than the use of the global population life tables.

As mentioned above, the minimal number of years of contribution which allows one to get access to retirement is 5 years (retirement allowance), while 32 years of contribution allow one to benefit from a full retirement. Such a detail is not addressed in our calculation and we suppose simply that workers contributing less than 5 years are compensated by those having contributed for more than 32 years.

13.6.1 Portfolio in Payment Phase

First, we will estimate the future evolution of pensions to be paid for the portfolio of retirees in payment phase according to the 2013 closing situation. The distribution by age groups and sex of the direct retirement beneficiaries in 2013 is shown in Fig. 13.23.

We observe that the age group 60–64 contains the most important number of retirees. Even if the minimal age for retirement is fixed at 50 for men and 45 for women, we observe that some men have retired before this age. This case represents an exception compared to the general rule. During the terrorism decade that Algeria experienced during the 1990s, the government created a security institution to protect the rural areas popularly known as *communal guards*. After the end of terrorism, this institution became useless and a part of the fired agents has benefited from an exceptional early retirement starting from 2012 (CNR, 2014).

In what follows, we will predict the time evolution of the total benefits of the presented portfolio. This evolution will result from the evolution of two parameters: (1) the survival function of retirees and (2) the evolution of the average retirement benefits. The evolution of survivals among the population of retirees is described by the experience prospective life table (EPLT-2013) constructed by Flici and Planchet (2019). In concern of the evolution of the average retirement benefits, we will suppose that the latter will keep being annually revaluated with an rate of 5%.

Formulation

Let $l_{x,t}^{s}$ denotes the surviving retirees at age x and year t for sex $s =$ male or female. Until now, the population of retirees is arranged by five age groups. To obtain the single age distribution, we use the Karup-King method to break down the five age populations into single age populations. This method is well explained in Flici (2016a). The open age group [95 and over] is supposed to be closed at 100 years. The weakness of the number of retirees in this age group permits such a hypothesis without affecting significantly the final results. Let ${}_{n}P_{x,t}^{s}$ denote the surviving

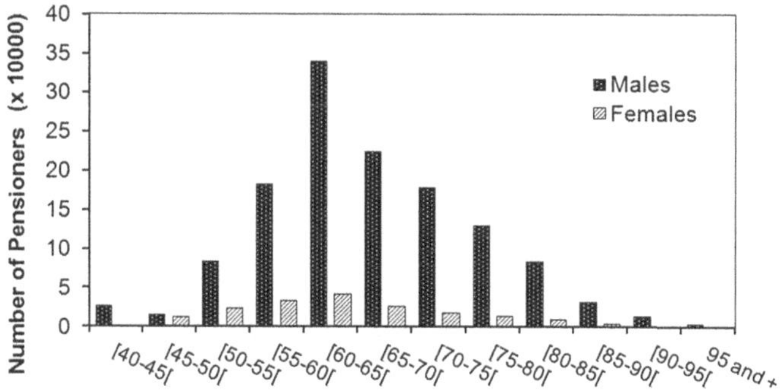

Fig. 13.23 Distribution of direct retirement beneficiaries by sex and age (2013). (*Source:* CNR (2014))

probability between ages x and $x + n$ between the year t and $t + n$ (EPLT-2013), and let $\overline{RB}_{m,t}$ to be the annual average direct retirement benefit growing with a rate $r = 5\%$. The total retirement benefits at year t related to the portfolio in payment can be calculated as:

$$\mathrm{TRB}(1)_t = \sum_{x=m}^{w} l_{x,t} * \overline{RB}_{m,t}(1 + r)^{t-2013}$$

Note that the number of surviving retirees is evolving from a year to another following the relationship $l^s_{x+1,t+1} = l^s_{x,t} * P^s_{x,t}$. The total retirement expense is calculated by summing the male's and female's retirement expenses:

$$\mathrm{TRB}(1)_t = \mathrm{TRB}(1)_t^{\text{males}} + \mathrm{TRB}(1)_t^{\text{females}}$$

13.6.2 Next Generation of Contributors and Retirees

The projection of the future incomes-outcomes related to the future generations of contributors and retirees must be principally based on the population projection results. As mentioned earlier, all the population at working age will be considered as a potential population of contributors. Then, the probability to be affiliated as an employee combined with the expected evolution of wages will allow us to estimate the average contribution by a single age between 15 and 64 years. In a similar way, the population at retirement age will be considered as potential retirees. Then, the average duration of contribution combined with the expected final wage will allow us to estimate the average of the first retirement benefit. We remind that the expected duration of contribution is 15 years for men and 4.6 years for women at working age.

(a) Expected contributions

The expected contributions are calculated on the basis of the evolution of the population aged 15–64 issued from the population forecast. The number of the population at age x at time t is denoted as $L^s_{x,t}$ with s = males or females, $t \geq 2014$, and $x = 15, 16, \ldots, 64$. The probability to contribute for CNR at age x is denoted as AS_x (see Fig. 13.20). We suppose that wages will keep growing with a rate of 9.5% during the future years. It gives:

$$\overline{W}_t = \overline{W}_{2013}(1 + 9.5\%)^{t-2013}$$

The total contributions during the year t (denoted as TC_t) is calculated by summing the contributions to be paid by different cohorts during the same year (denoted as C_{xt}). The formula can be written as:

$$\mathrm{TC}_t = \sum_{x=15}^{64} C_{xt} = l_{xt} * \mathrm{AS}_x * \overline{W}_t * 18.25\%$$

(b) Expected pension benefits

The calculation of the expected retirement benefits for the future generations of retirees returns to expect the average duration of contribution, the final wage evolution, the age of retirement, and the annual revaluation rate of retirement benefits. The average age of retirement is 59 for men and 57 for women. Then, the last five wages of the working years serve to calculate the pension benefit. Here, the wages between 54–58 and 52–56, respectively, for men and women will be considered to calculate the average first retirement benefits. For simplification issues, we replace the age intervals by the central ages. It means that the average wages corresponding to 56 and 54 years ($W_{56,\,t}$ and $W_{54,\,t}$) will be considered, respectively, for men and women. Because these details are not provided in the ONS publications, we estimate $W_{56,\,t}$ and $W_{54,\,t}$ from $\overline{W_t}$ according to the polynomial function shown in Fig. 13.21. We obtain $\overline{W}_{56,t} = 1.107 * \overline{W_t}$ and $\overline{W}_{56,t} = 1.104 * \overline{W}_t$.

The expected duration of contribution is supposed to be 15 years for men and 4.6 for women. The annual revaluation of retirement benefits will be supposed to remain at around 5%. First, it convenes to calculate the annual retirement benefit corresponding to the first year of retirement that we denote as $\overline{\mathrm{RB}}_{m,t}$($m$ denotes the retirement age) and is calculated by:

$$\overline{\mathrm{RB}}_{m,t} = \overline{W}_{m-3,t-3} * \mathrm{EDC} * 2.5\%$$

Then, the time and age evolution of the annual retirement benefit is supposed to keep growing with a constant annual revaluation rate of 5%:

$$\overline{\mathrm{RB}}_{m+n,t+n} = \overline{\mathrm{RB}}_{m,t}(1+5\%)^n$$

The total retirement benefit during a year t is calculated by a multiplication by the population number in each generation. If we consider $\Lambda_{x,\,t}$ as the population number at the age x during the year t issued from the population forecast, the survival function of this starting population will be estimated on the basis of the life table EPLT-2013. The total RB during a year t can be calculated by:

$$\mathrm{TRB}(2)_t = \sum_{x=m}^{w} \overline{\mathrm{RB}}_{x,t} * \Lambda_{x,t}$$

13.6.3 The Financial Stability of the Whole Portfolio

The evolution of the total retirement benefits is calculated by summing the retirement benefits of the portfolio in payment and the retirement benefits that will be distributed to the future generations. Here, there is a risk of double computation or an omission in concern of certain categories of retirees. The first group (portfolio in payment) is observed by the end of 2013, and it is constituted by retirees aged 40 and over. The second group (future generations) is constituted by the generations who will retire starting from 2014 when reaching the average age of retirement m. The risk of double computation concerns the individuals who are already retired before reaching the age m. In addition to the fact that they are already considered in the first group, those retirees will be computed again in the second group when they reach the age m. To avoid this double computation, we remove the retirees aged below the average retirement age from the first group. On the other hand, the current portfolio in payment is not supposed to be closed to new entrances. Some people belonging to the oldest generations (aged more than m in 2013) and haven't been retired yet are not considered in any group. To fix this missing information, the future entrances in the current portfolio of retirees between age m and 65 years must be estimated and added into account. To do this, a distribution of the probability of getting retired among the working population must be calculated for each age. Then, the retirement schedule will be addressed. The CNR report (CNR 2014) provides the distribution of workers getting retired in 2013 by five age groups as shown in Fig. 13.24.

The total number of the new retirees in 2013 is evaluated to 129,000; 90% are men and only 10% are women. We can observe that an important part of the total number of departure for retirement has occurred at 60–64 for men and women. Beyond the age of 65, the proportions are much less important. The numbers that we can observe between 40 and 49 for men represent a special case in concern of the years 2012 and 2013 (fired municipal guards). If we consider that the minimal age of retirement is 50 for men and 45 for women and 65 is an extension of the normal retirement age which is 60, the probability of getting retired at each age from 45 to 65 for men and from 50 to 65 for women can be calculated.

Costa (1998) tried to approximate the probability of retirement at single age from studying the labor force participation rates issued from census data. Here, we simply estimate this probability (rate) by dividing the number of workers getting retired in 2013 by the average number of affiliated employees during the same year with a distinction by sex and age. In Sect. 13.5.2, we approximated the distribution of the affiliated employees by age and sex. The number of workers getting retired in 2013 at each age group $[x, x + 5]$ divided by the structure of the affiliated employees by age gives the hazard rate of retirement for workers not yet retired as represented in Fig. 13.25.

Initial calculations gave the hazard rate for getting retired by five age groups between 50 and 65 for men and 45 and 65 for women. For our calculations, a description by single ages is needed. For that, we performed an interpolation of the rates at single ages. A change point can be observed starting from age 60 because the

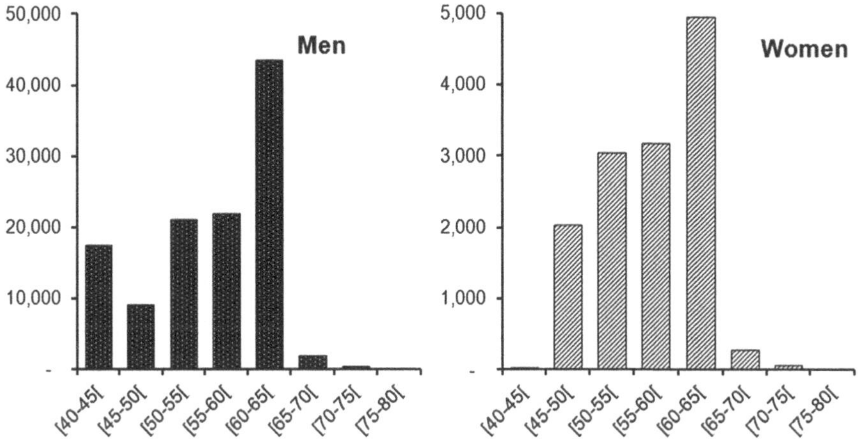

Fig. 13.24 Distribution of workers getting retired in 2013 by sex and age. (*Source:* CNR (2014))

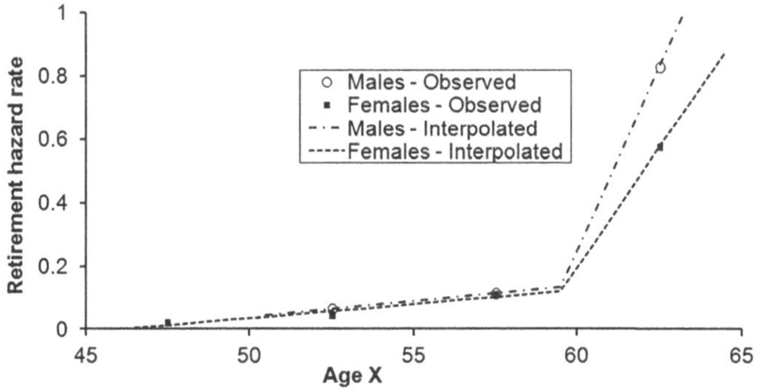

Fig. 13.25 Probability of retirement by age (2013)

legal retirement is fixed at that age, and the use of a unique interpolation function along the whole age range may lead to unsatisfactory fitting quality. The use of a junction of two linear functions allowed us to escape this disadvantage. However, and in order to make the interpolation results more adapted to reality, the junction point was extended until 60 years rather than to be the center of the age group 55–59 as shown in Fig. 13.25. In other words, it is more realistic that the probability of getting retired starts to rise starting from the age of 60 than starting from the age of 57.

In what follows, the retirement probability age pattern is supposed to remain constant in the future. That allows passing from an annual to a generational description of the age-specific retirement probability. These calculated retirement schedules will be used to estimate the future entrance to the portfolio in payment. Accordingly, the evolution of the number of retirees in each generation within the portfolio in payment is defined by the death (exit) and the decision of retirement (entrance).

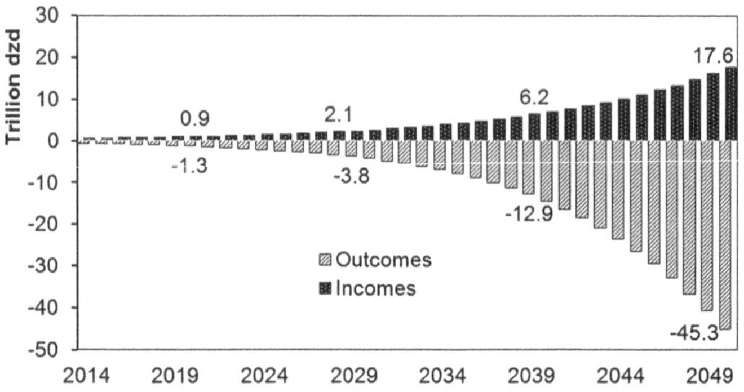

Fig. 13.26 Projected incomes-outcomes

The projection of the financial balance of CNR returns to project separately total incomes and total outcomes. Total outcomes are constituted from the total retirement expenses augmented by 1.5% representing the administration fees. Retirement expense gathers the direct retirement benefits plus 31% representing the survivor's benefits. The total incomes are principally constituted from the contributions of the affiliated population augmented by investment returns of about 2.86% of the total contributions. We remind that there is a difference between the theoretical total contributions and the real contributions of about 20% that we have assumed to be due to a problem of contributions recovery. The difference between the total incomes and the total outcomes is covered by public transfers. Figure 13.26 shows the projected total incomes and outcomes.

According to the projection results, total incomes in 2014 are evaluated at 519 trillion *dzd* against 703 trillion for total outcomes. Public transfers cover 25% of the total outcomes. By 2030, the part of the public transfer needed to keep the financial balance will pass to around 42% from total incomes and to 61% by 2050 as shown in Fig. 13.27.

The financial deficit of CNR in 2013 was at 24% and it is covered by public transfers. It is supposed to reach a total value of 27.7 trillion *dzd* in 2050. In such conditions, we wonder if the government can support this permanent growing gap for the long run and ensure inter-generational equality.

13.7 Conclusion

The importance of pension plans in poverty reduction and old population protection highlights the need to study their financial sustainability for the long run. Even if, in most pension schemes, pension benefits are somehow linked to the paid contributions following the insurance principle, public transfers are necessary to preserve the low-earning population in a social protection context. However, there is no evident

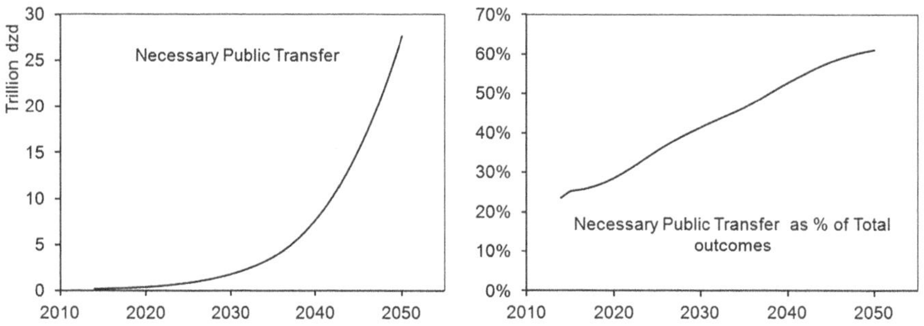

Fig. 13.27 Projection of public transfer in retirement system incomes

optimal combination between these two principles, and there is not an evident way to design a pension system adapted to the whole population. A preference for the insurance principle will result in a disadvantage for the low-earning population, and the adoption of a pure solidarity system will pluck the high earners out of the system. Maintaining the stability of the system for the long run requires public management. In some particular conditions, the private sector cannot support the temporary losses. The government may support the temporary deficit in order to save the well-being of the low-earning population and to encourage economic development for the long term.

In Algeria, the financial balance of the retirement system is still maintained by public transfers. The actuarial return rate of retirement contracts is almost superior to the return rates in financial markets (Mendil 2014). Even if the public budget is expected to recover the future unbalances, that must be equally distributed between the different generations. Admitting a fixed level of the State contribution in the retirement system incomes, the latter must be periodically evaluated and updated in order to ensure the sustainability of the retirement system. The generosity of the Algerian retirement system, as in North African countries, is supposed to fall down during the upcoming decades with the increase of the number of retirees and the relative decrease of the public incomes (Ben Brahem 2009). In such conditions, it will be difficult, but necessary, to ensure equality between the actual and the future generations.

We have shown in this work that the effect of longevity and aging on the retirement system sustainability is permanent and not temporary. The financial deficit is expected to rise continually to reach a level of 61% by 2050. For that, a parametric reform cannot be sufficient to ensure the long-run sustainability of the system. Augmenting the contribution rate or postponing the retirement age cannot be sufficient to reduce the financial gap for the long term. A large reform of the whole system is needed. If we intend that it will be possible to keep the public transfers at around 25% of the total outcomes, maintaining this part constant will be necessary to improve equity between the actual and the future generations.

In order to maintain the actual system as sustainable as possible for the long run, it will be necessary to revise the actuarial contributions-pensions linkage. Longevity improvement increases the duration of payment of retirement benefits. If the retirement age is not postponed, that leads to an unbalance between the working duration and the retirement duration. Population aging provokes a fall in the ratio of the population at working age to the population at retirement age. To keep total incomes at the level of total outcomes in a PAYG system, it will be necessary to ask more contribution efforts from working people while moderating the benefits distributed to retirees.

According to all these findings, it will be necessary to pass from a one-pillar to a multi-pillar system as was suggested by the World Bank (WB 1994). That will allow the reduction of financial deficit of the whole system and the restriction of public transfers in a way to ensure the long-run sustainability. It will be important to keep the actual system with some adjustments. Retirement pensions must be capped and public subsidies need to be more dedicated to the poorest part of the population . In the same chain of ideas, it will be a need to address a second pillar, mandatory, fully funded, and privately managed, in order to straighten the linkage between contributions and pensions. A third pillar, fully funded but voluntary, will encourage the individual contribution efforts and will allow high-wage earners to improve their retirement conditions. However, the second and third pillars need a strong financial market allowing efficient investment of contributions of the affiliated workers.

References

Ben Brahem, M. (2009). Pension system generosity and reform in Algeria, Morocco and Tunisia. *International Social Security Review, 2*(62), 101–120.

Bovenberg, A. I., & Van Ewijk, C. (2011a). *The future of multi-pillar pension systems*. Netspar Discussion Paper, Tilburg: Netspar.

Bovenberg, A. I., & Van Ewijk, C. (2011b). *Designing the pension system: Conceptual framework*. Netspar Discussion Paper, Tilburg: Netspar.

Caisse Nationale Des Retraites (CNR). (2014). *Recueil statistique Recettes Dépenses 2013*. Document non publié, sous-direction de la planification et des statistiques, Alger, Algérie.

Chourouk, H. (2003). Pensions in North Africa: The need for reform. *Geneva Papers for Risk and Insurance, 4*(28), 712–726.

Costa, D. L. (1998). The evolution of retirement. In *The evolution of retirement: An American Economic History: 1880–1990* (pp. 6–31). Chicago: University of Chicago Press.

Flici, F. (2016a). *Closing out the Algerian life tables: For more accuracy and adequacy at old age*. In Proceeding of the IAA-LS colloquium. Lisbon. https://www.actuaries.org/lisbon2016/papers/16.FaridFliciPaper.pdf.

Flici, F. (2016b). *Coherent mortality forecasting for the algerian population*. In Samos conference in actuarial sciences and finance. Samos, Greece, 18–22 May 2016, https://www.researchgate.net/publication/303821160/Coherent/mortality/forecasting/for/the/Algerian/population.

Flici, F. (2016c). *Projection de la structure de la mortalité par âges unitaires pour la population algérienne*. Centre de Recherche en Economie Appliquée pour le Développement CREAD, Working Paper: https://www.researchgate.net/publication/299441992/PROJECTION/DE/LA/STRUCTURE/DE/LA/MORTALITE/ALGERIENNE?ev=prf/pub.

Flici, F., & Planchet, F. (2019). Experience Prospective Life-Tables for the Algerian Retirees. *Risks*, 7(2):38.

Henke, V. (2002). Pension reform and life insurance in Germany. In *Regional meeting for the eastern and central European countries*. Document ° 5/Room 1, Tallinn, Estonia, 07-–08 February 2002.
Holzmann, R., & Hinz, R. (2005). *Old age income support in the 21st century: An international perspective on pension systems and reform*. Washington, D.C.: The World Bank.
Holzmann, R., Hinz, R. P., & Dorfman, M. (2008). *Pension systems and reform conceptual framework*. (Social Protection Discussion paper n° 0824). June 2008.
Hyndman, R., Booth, H., & Yasmeen, F. (2013). Coherent mortality forecasting: The product-ratio method with functional time series models. *Demography, 50*(1), 261–283.
Ilmarinen, J., & Toumi, K. (1992). Work ability of aging workers. *Scandinavian Journal of Work, Environment & Health, 18*(2), 8–10.
Lee, R. (1993). Modeling and forecasting the time series of us fertility: Age distribution, ranges, and ultimate level. *International Journal of Forecasting, 9*, 187–202.
Lee, R., & Carter, L. (1992). Modeling and forecasting U.S. mortality. *Journal of the American Statistical Association, 87*(419), 659–671.
Li, N., & Lee, R. D. (2005). Coherent mortality forecasts for a group of populations: An extension of the Lee-Carter method. *Demography, 42*(3), 575–594.
Lui, F. T. (1998). *Retirement protection: A plan for Hong Kong* (1st ed.). Hong Kong: City University of Hong Kong Press.
Mendil, D. (2014). *Le niveau de vie des retraités algériens et l'inégalité des retraites*. In Séminaire scientifique de la Caisse des Dépôts, Bordeaux, France, 3 Oct 2014.
Merouani, W., Hammouda, N. E., & El-Moudden, C. (2016). The microeconomic determinants of demand for social security: Evidence from the Algerian labour market. *Institutions and Economies, 8*(1), 25–61.
Merton, R. C., Bodie, Z., & Marcus, A. J. (1987). Pension plan integration as insurance against social security risk. In *Issues in pension economics* (pp. 147–172). Chicago: University of Chicago Press.
Office National des Statistiques (ONS). (2012). *Rétrospective Statistique 1962–2011: Salaires*. http://www.ons.dz/IMG/pdf/CH3-SALAIRES.pdf.
Office National des Statistiques (ONS). (2014a). *Enquête emploi auprès des ménages 2013, Collections Statistiques N 185, Série S: Statistiques Sociales*. Direction technique chargée des statistiques de la Population et de l'Emploi, Alger, Algérie. http://www.ons.dz/IMG/pdf/PUBLICATION/EMPLOI/2013/nal.pdf.
Office National des Statistiques (ONS). (2014b). *Revenus salariaux et caractéristiquesindividuelles -Enquête sur les dépenses de consommation et le niveau de vie des ménages 2011, Collections Statistiques N 189 Série S: Statistiques Sociales*. La Direction technique chargée des statistiques sociales et des revenus. http://www.ons.dz/IMG/pdf/pubnsal13-2.pdf.
Office Nationaldes Statistiques (ONS). (2015). *Activité, emploi et chômageau 4 ° trimestre 2015, collection statistique n ° 726*. http://www.ons.dz/IMG/pdf/DSEmploi0915.pdf.
Organisation for Economic Co-operation and Development (OECD). (2005). *Pensions at a glance: Public policies across OECD countries*. Paris: OECD Publishing.
Robalino, D. A., Whitehouse, E., Mataoanu, A. N., Musalem, A. R., Sherwood, E., & Sluchynsky, O. (2005). *Pensions in the Middle East and North Africa: Time for change*. Washington, D.C.: The World Bank.
United Nations Organization (UNO). (2015). *World population prospects: The 2015 revision, key findings and advance tables*. New York: Department of Economic and Social Affairs/Population Division.
Wang, P., Zhang, M., Chand, R., & Howell, K. E. (2014). *Retirement, pension systems and models of pension systems*. (Economics Working Paper n° 1402).
Wong, M. K. (2015). *Problems of PAYG pension scheme and pension reform – a note on overseas experience and international guidelines*. Working paper. http://www.hkeconomy.gov.hk/en/pdf/PAYG.pdf.
World Bank (WB). (1994). *Averting the old age crisis: Policies to protect the old and promote growth*. A World Bank Policy Research Report. New York, USA: New York, USA: Oxford University Press.

Chapter 14
Pension Design and Risk Sharing: Mixed Solutions Between Defined Benefit and Defined Contribution for Public Pension Schemes

Pierre Devolder and Sébastien de Valeriola

Abstract In classical pension design, there are essentially two kinds of pension schemes: Defined Benefit (DB) and Defined Contribution (DC) plans. Each scheme corresponds to a different philosophy of spreading risk between the stakeholders: in a DB, the main risks are taken by the organizer of the plan, while in a DC, the affiliates must bear all the risks. Especially when applied to social security pension systems, this traditional view can in both cases lead to unfair intergenerational equilibrium. The purpose of this chapter is to present alternative architectures based on a mix between DB and DC in order to achieve both financial sustainability and social adequacy. An example of this approach is the so-called Musgrave rule, but other risk-sharing approaches will be developed in a pay-as-you-go philosophy. These principles will be illustrated by the Belgian proposition of reform of the first pillar, based on a points system with a simultaneous automatic adaptation mechanism of the retirement age, the contribution rate, the replacement rate, and the indexation rate.

Keywords Public pension schemes · Hybrid pension scheme · Belgian public pensions · Social adequacy · Risk sharing · Pay-as-you-go

P. Devolder
Institute of Statistics, Biostatistics and Actuarial Sciences (ISBA), Université Catholique de Louvain, Louvain-la-Neuve, Belgium
e-mail: pierre.devolder@uclouvain.be

S. de Valeriola (✉)
ICHEC Brussels Management School, Laboratoire Quaresmi, Brussels, Belgium
e-mail: sebastien.devaleriola@ichec.be

M. Peris-Ortiz et al. (eds.), *Economic Challenges of Pension Systems*,
https://doi.org/10.1007/978-3-030-37912-4_14

14.1 Introduction

As in many countries, the first pillar of pension in Belgium, based on a pay-as-you-go mechanism and a Defined Benefit (DB) architecture, is under pressure and needs fundamental reforms to guarantee both long-term sustainability and social fairness. Even if some parametric changes have been made in recent years, no fundamental decisions have been taken to restore the long-term viability and the global coherence of the system (see, e.g. Devolder 2010).

The absence of global reforms contrasts greatly with the situation in other countries where fundamental reforms have emerged in the past few years, such as the Notional Defined Contribution (NDC) in Sweden (Holzmann et al. 2012; Palmer 2000; Settergren 2001), the introduction of a sustainability factor in Germany (Borsch-Supan et al. 2003), and other techniques of automatic adjustment (Vidal-Melia et al. 2006; Knell 2010). In Belgium, however, there have been no real reforms, despite the country's negative financial trend. The development of the expenditure is negatively affected not only by ageing and the 'baby boom' (as in many Western countries) but also by the low level of labour force participation (see, e.g. European Commission 2014). Nevertheless, after years of silence, there seems finally to be an increasing political awareness of the problem.

It was in this context, in 2013, that the Belgian government decided to ask a commission of academic experts to propose a new structure for Belgian public pensions. The results of this commission have been published in a report (Commission de réforme des pensions 2020-2040 2014). The aim of this chapter is to present some of the ideas proposed by this commission. In particular, we would like to address the problem of risk sharing between contributors and retirees. In a classical pension architecture, based on a DB philosophy (resp. a DC philosophy), all the risks are borne by the contributors (resp. the retirees). The idea presented by the commission is to create an automatic adjustment of the replacement rate and the contribution rate based on a sharing of the risks between contributors and retirees. One possible solution in this context is to use the so-called Musgrave rule based on a modified replacement rate. This rule is not related to the gross salary, but to the salary net of pension contributions. However, other sharing rules between the two generations are possible. The aim of this chapter is to present various sharing rules and to measure the level of solidarity generated by these adjustment techniques. To this end, we use a simple deterministic model, where the main driver is the dependence ratio (ratio between the number of retirees and the number of workers). In particular, we introduce two different ways to model the impact of a change in the dependence ratio on the contribution and the replacement rates. The first one is based on a ratio between the change in the contribution rate and the change in the replacement rate. The second one introduces a convex invariant (convex combination between the contribution rate and the replacement rate). In both cases, DB and DC schemes appear to be extreme solutions for the parameters, and the 'Musgrave rule' is one of the possible intermediate systems. Other examples of mix between DB and DC are proposed.

The chapter is organized as follows. Section 14.2 briefly summarizes the pension formula for the existing Belgian first pillar for employees. Section 14.3 explains the new points system proposed by the commission of experts. In Sect. 14.4, we illustrate the link between this system and a NDC scheme. In Sect. 14.5, we develop the 'Musgrave rule,' generating an intermediate system between DB and DC (a system called DM, or Defined Musgrave). In Sect. 14.6, we define the risk-sharing coefficient, which compares the variations of the contribution rate and the replacement rate in the event of change in the dependence ratio. In particular, in a Defined Musgrave (DM) scheme, the risk-sharing coefficient is not constant, and the values obtained suggest that in general this system is closer to DB than DC. The DM approach is generalized in Sect. 14.7, where we define a family of pension schemes indexed by a continuous parameter whose extreme values correspond to DB and DC and to which DM belongs. Section 14.8 presents a continuous time approach; the automatic adjustment can be seen then as a control on differential equations of the contribution rate and the replacement rate. In Sect. 14.9, we present some numerical illustrations based on real Belgian data. Section 14.10 introduces the concept of the sustainability factor and looks at the yearly adaptation of existing pensions. Finally, Sect. 14.11 concludes this chapter.

14.2 The Existing Defined Benefit System in the Belgian First Pillar

The existing first pillar of pension in Belgium is a classical combination of pay-as-you-go (PAYG) and Defined Benefit (DB). For instance, for employees, the pension formula is based on the average of indexed salaries; more precisely, the normal retirement age is 65, and the amount of pension is given by

$$P = 0.6\left(\frac{1}{45}\sum_{t=T-45}^{T} S_t\, h(t,T)\right),$$

where P is the pension amount, T is the retirement year, S_t is the salary of year t (with application of salary ceiling), and $h(t, T)$ is the indexation coefficient between years t and T.

This system presents many drawbacks: it is not transparent, its actuarial fairness is not ensured, its financial sustainability is under pressure, and too many incentives exist for early retirement.

14.3 A New Points System

The pension reform's commission has proposed to move from this DB framework to a new system having three main characteristics: PAYG financing, benefit computation based on a points system, and a risk-sharing mechanism between DB and DC.

In such a system, the pension formula is described as follows. During the active career, every contributor receives each year a number of points given by the ratio between his own salary and a reference salary, fixed each year. The reference salary could, for instance, be the mean salary of the economy:

$$n_t = \frac{S_t}{S_t^r},$$

where n_t is the number of points for year t, S_t is the individual salary of year t, and S_t^r is the reference salary of year t.

The total number of points accumulated at retirement year T by a pension participant, having a career of R years, is given by

$$N_T = \sum_{t=T-R}^{T} n_t.$$

For example, when $R = 45$, somebody earning exactly the reference salary each year will obtain exactly 45 points at retirement. The total number of points is therefore a sort of metric of the length of the career, corrected by the level of salary.

The pension at retirement age is given by the following formula:

$$P_T = N_T \, V_T \, \rho_T, \tag{14.1}$$

where N_T is the total number of points, V_T is the value of the point (expressed in euros), ρ_t is the actuarial coefficient.

The value of the point V is fixed every year simultaneously taking into account a number of different goals. It should ensure a sustainable individual pension based on an adequate replacement rate, while providing a relative stability to the contribution rate. Different political choices can be made regarding the risk sharing between contributors and retirees. This point will be addressed in detail in Sect. 14.5. The actuarial correction must take into account the retirement age and the length of the career (total or partial actuarial neutrality) and is based on life expectancies. The following formula can be considered:

$$\rho_T = \frac{e(x_{\text{normal}})}{e(x_{\text{real}})},$$

where $e(x_{\text{normal}})$ (resp. $e(x_{\text{real}})$) is the life expectation at the normal retirement age (resp. the real retirement age chosen by the affiliate). The normal retirement age can be defined explicitly (e.g. 65 years) or can take into account a reference length of career (e.g. age corresponding to 45 years of career). In the last case, the normal retirement age is not unique and depends on the start of the working career.

After retirement, the pension is indexed, taking into account changes in salaries and the sustainability of the regime:

$$P_{T+1} = P_T \, h_T \, \eta_T,$$

where h_T is the indexation coefficient and η_T is the sustainability factor.

As a first simple example of determination of the value of the point, consider a target in terms of replacement rate for a representative agent ('DB' philosophy). Let us assume an affiliate with a salary equal each year to the reference salary; in order to obtain a full pension, we ask this affiliate to work during a reference period denoted by N^*. We don't apply in this case any actuarial correction ($\rho = 1$) and the pension (14.1) becomes

$$P_T = N^* \, V_T.$$

The value of the point can be fixed by reference to a replacement rate denoted by δ:

$$P_T = \delta \, S_T^r.$$

The value of the point is then

$$V_T = \frac{\delta S_T^r}{N^*}. \tag{14.2}$$

For a replacement rate of 60% and a reference period for the career of 45 years, the value of the point is then equal to 1.33% of the reference salary.

14.4 Comparison with a NDC Scheme

There are clear analogies between this points system and a Notional Defined Contribution scheme (NDC). In a NDC scheme (see, e.g. Holzmann et al. 2012), the pension can be written (assuming a normal retirement age of 65)

$$P = \frac{1}{a_{65(T)}} \sum_{t=T-R}^{T} \pi \, S_t \, g(t,T),$$

where P is the pension, T is the retirement year, S_t is the salary of year t (with ceiling), π is the contribution rate, $g(t, T)$ is the revalorization based on notional rates and $a_{65(T)}$ is an annuity price fixed at retirement year T. It is easy to see that Formula

(14.3) can be seen as a particular choice of the general point Formula (14.1). Introducing the reference salary into Formula (14.3), we obtain

$$P = \frac{1}{a_{65(T)}} \sum_{t=T-R}^{T} \pi \, \frac{S_t}{S_t^r} \left(g(t,T) S_t^r \right).$$

If we assume, as is usual in NDC systems, that the revalorization coefficients are in line with the increase of the mean salary, we can write

$$g(t,T) S_t^r = S_T^r.$$

So finally we obtain

$$P = \frac{1}{a_{65(T)}} \, \pi \, S_T^r \, R.$$

The value of the point is then

$$V_T = \frac{\pi \, S_T^r}{a_{65(T)}}. \tag{14.3}$$

In particular, for a representative agent with a salary equal each year to the reference salary and a length of career equal to the requested duration N^*, the replacement rate is not constant anymore but is given by

$$\delta_T = \frac{\pi N^*}{a_{65(T)}}.$$

In this last formula, the contribution rate π usually remains constant (DC nature); then if the reference length N^* is not adapted and if the annuity price $a_{65}(T)$ increases because of the longevity effect, the replacement rate will automatically decrease.

14.5 Between DB and DC: The Musgrave Rule

The point system presented in Sect. 14.3 is a very flexible architecture and can be modelled using various calibrations. The key question is how to fix the value of the point and how to adapt the system automatically to exogenous shocks. We have already proposed two ways to define the point (Formula (14.2) in a DB philosophy and Formula (14.3) in a NDC context). The aim of this section is to introduce a third way in between and that is based on the Musgrave rule. Section 14.6 will generalize this approach by introducing a whole family of intermediate solutions between the two extremes DB and DC.

In a DB framework, there is an absolute guarantee for the retirees (fixed replacement rate) and the contributors must support the risks; in a DC framework, there is an absolute stability for the contributors (fixed contribution rate) and the replacement rate is adjusted. The points system can extend this polarity by allowing many other mechanisms of risk sharing between retirees and active workers.

Let us introduce the following notations:

π = contribution rate,
S = average salary,
P = average pension,
N_A = number of contributors,
N_R = number of retirees.

The equilibrium in pay-as-you-go is expressed by the pension equation:

$$\pi S N_A = N_R P.$$

The dependence ratio denoted by D is given by:

$$D = \frac{N_B}{N_A}. \tag{14.4}$$

In order to model the demographic risk, let us assume an initial stable situation (denoted by state 1) composed only of representative agents (same salary and same career) receiving a pension based on a replacement rate δ_1 (with $0 < \delta_1 < 1$) on the last salary and a contribution rate π_1. The system is then given by the two equations:

$$\begin{aligned} D_1 P_T &= \pi_1 S_T \quad \text{(budget equation)}, \\ P_T &= \delta_1 S_T \quad \text{(pension equation)}. \end{aligned} \tag{14.5}$$

Equilibrium between the parameters is obtained when the following classical condition is fulfilled:

$$\pi_1 = D_1 \delta_1. \tag{14.6}$$

According to Formula (14.2), the value of the point is given by

$$V_T = \frac{\delta_1 S_T^r}{N^*}.$$

Suppose now that the system moves to another stage characterized by another dependence ratio denoted by D_2. We will often assume that $D_2 > D_1$ (ageing of the population). We want to define the new parameters δ_2 and π_2, still linked by

$$\pi_2 = D_2 \delta_2.$$

Clearly, there are an infinite number of such solutions! The two polar situations are the well-known DB and DC schemes.

In a *DB scheme*, the replacement rate has to remain constant and the contribution rate must increase in case of ageing (risk is borne only by the contributors):

$$\delta_2 = \delta_1,$$
$$\pi_2 = \pi_1 \frac{D_2}{D_1}.$$

In a *DC structure* (e.g. NDC), the contribution rate has to remain fixed and the replacement rate will decrease in case of ageing (risk is borne only by the retirees):

$$\pi_2 = \pi_1,$$
$$\delta_2 = \delta_1 \frac{D_1}{D_2}.$$

Musgrave has proposed (Musgrave 1981) another invariant leading to a form of sharing of the risk between the two generations. Let us define the Musgrave ratio as the ratio between the pension and the salary net of pension contributions:

$$M_1 = \frac{P_T}{S_T(1-\pi_1)} = \frac{\delta_1}{1-\pi_1}. \tag{14.7}$$

This ratio, exactly as a classical replacement rate, compares the standard of living of retirees and contributors but now takes into account the effort of contribution borne only by active people.

In a DB structure, the Musgrave ratio increases when the dependence ratio increases:

$$M_2 = \frac{\delta_2}{1-\pi_2} = \frac{\delta_1}{1-\pi_1 \frac{D_2}{D_1}},$$

while in a DC structure, the Musgrave ratio decreases:

$$M_2 = \frac{\delta_2}{1-\pi_2} = \frac{\delta_1}{1-\pi_1} \frac{D_1}{D_2}.$$

Under the Musgrave rule, called here DM (Defined Musgrave), we want to stabilize this coefficient:

$$M_2 = M_1 = M.$$

In this philosophy, the new replacement rate can be easily obtained using (14.6):

$$M = \frac{\delta_2}{1-\pi_2} = \frac{\delta_2}{1-D_2\delta_2},$$

so that

$$\delta_2 = \frac{M}{1+MD_2}.$$

By using (14.6) again, the contribution rate becomes

$$\pi_2 = \frac{MD_2}{1+MD_2}.$$

We can also compare old and new values of the two parameters.

Values of the replacement rate For the replacement rate with the Musgrave rule, we compute

$$\delta_2 = \frac{M}{1+MD_2} = \frac{\frac{\delta_1}{1-\pi_1}}{1+\frac{\delta_1}{1-\pi_1}D_2} = \delta_1 \frac{1}{1+\delta_1(D_2-D_1)}.$$

In a DC scheme, the new replacement rate was given by

$$\delta_2 = \delta_1 \frac{D_1}{D_2}.$$

In a DB scheme, the replacement rate remains constant:

$$\delta_2 = \delta_1.$$

We can obtain the following rule, showing that Defined Musgrave can be seen as an intermediary scheme between Defined Benefit (no influence of the dependence ratio on the replacement rate) and Defined Contribution (full influence of the dependence ratio).

Proposition 14.1 If the dependence ratio increases ($D_2 > D_1$) and if the initial contribution rate is $0 < \pi_1 < 1$, then we have the following inequality:

$$\delta_2^{\mathrm{DB}} = \delta_1 > \delta_2^{\mathrm{DM}} = \delta_1 \frac{1}{1+\delta_1(D_2-D_1)} > \delta_2^{\mathrm{DC}} = \delta_1 \frac{D_2}{D_1}. \tag{14.8}$$

Proof On the one hand, as $D_2 > D_1$, we have

$$\delta_1 > \delta_1 \frac{1}{1+\delta_1(D_2-D_1)}.$$

On the other hand, we compute

$$\begin{aligned} 1 > \pi_1 &\Rightarrow D_2 - D_1 > \pi_1(D_2 - D_1) = D_1\delta_1(D_2 - D_1) \\ &\Rightarrow D_2 > D_1(1 + \delta_1(D_2 - D_1)) \\ &\Rightarrow \delta_1 \frac{1}{1 + \delta_1(D_2 - D_1)} > \delta_1 \frac{D_1}{D_2}. \end{aligned}$$

Values of the contribution rate For the contribution rate with the Musgrave rule, we compute

$$\pi_2 = \frac{MD_2}{1 + MD_2} = \frac{D_2 \frac{\pi_1}{D_1(1-\pi_1)}}{1 + D_2 \frac{\pi_1}{D_1(1-\pi_1)}} = \pi_1 \frac{D_2}{D_1 + \pi_1(D_2 - D_1)}.$$

In a DB scheme, the new contribution rate was given by

$$\pi_2 = \pi_1 \frac{D_2}{D_1}.$$

In a DC scheme, the contribution rate remains constant:

$$\pi_2 = \pi_1.$$

Then we have the following property similar to Proposition 14.1.

Proposition 14.2 If the dependence ratio increases ($D_2 > D_1$) and if the initial contribution rate $0 < \pi_1 < 1$, then we have the following inequality:

$$\pi_2^{\mathrm{DC}} = \pi_1 < \pi_2^{\mathrm{DM}} = \pi_1 \frac{D_2}{D_1 + \pi_1(D_2 - D_1)} < \pi_2^{\mathrm{DB}} = \pi_1 \frac{D_2}{D_1}. \tag{14.9}$$

Proof On the one hand, as $\pi_1 < 1$, we have

$$D_1 + \pi_1(D_2 - D_1) < D_2,$$

which leads to

$$\pi_1 < \pi_1 \frac{D_2}{D_1 + \pi_1(D_2 - D_1)}.$$

On the other hand,

$$\pi_1 \frac{D_2}{D_1 + \pi_1(D_2 - D_1)} < \pi_1 \frac{D_2}{D_1}$$

is a straightforward consequence of

Table 14.1 Contribution rate and replacement rate formulas in DB, DC, and DM

	Contribution rate	Replacement rate	Value of the point
DB	$\pi_2 = \pi_1 \frac{D_2}{D_1}$	$\delta_2 = \delta_1$	$V_2 = V_1 = \frac{\delta_1 S_T^r}{N^+}$
DC	$\pi_2 = \pi_1$	$\delta_2 = \delta_1 \frac{D_1}{D_2}$	$V_2 = V_1 \frac{D_1}{D_2}$
DM	$\pi_2 = \pi_1 \frac{D_2}{D_1 + \pi_1 (D_2 - D_1)}$	$\delta_2 = \delta_1 \frac{1}{1+\delta_1 (D_2 - D_1)}$	$V_2 = V_1 \frac{1}{1+\delta_1 (D_2 - D_1)}$

Table 14.2 Numerical comparison of the replacement and contribution rates in DB, DC, and DM

		$D_2 = 0.25$	$D_2 = 0.35$	$D_2 = 0.45$	$D_2 = 0.50$	$D_2 = 0.60$
DB	δ	0.50	0.50	0.50	0.50	0.50
	π	0.13	0.18	0.23	0.25	0.30
DC	δ	0.80	0.57	0.44	0.40	0.33
	π	0.20	0.20	0.20	0.20	0.20
DM	δ	0.54	0.51	0.49	0.48	0.45
	π	0.14	0.18	0.22	0.24	0.27

$$D_1 + \pi_1 (D_2 - D_1) > D_1.$$

Remark 14.1 If the population is getting younger rather than ageing (i.e. $D_2 < D_1$), the order relations given in properties 14.1 and 14.2 are reversed.

The Defined Musgrave approach can be seen as an intermediary scheme between DB and DC in terms of contribution rates and replacement rates. In a DM scheme, the two rates move together in opposite directions (increase of the contribution rate and decrease of the replacement rate). Contributors and retirees are affected by the demographic risk. Table 14.1 summarizes the three types of pension scheme (DB, DC, and DM).

Example 14.1 Let us assume an initial steady state characterized by the following parameters: initial dependence ratio: $D = 0.40$, initial replacement rate $\delta = 0.50$, and initial contribution rate $\pi = 0.40 \times 0.50 = 0.20$. Then Table 14.2 gives, for various values of the new dependence ratio, the new contribution rate and replacement rate in the three structures (DB, DC, and DM).

14.6 Risk-Sharing Coefficient

The Defined Musgrave mechanism can be considered as an intermediate scheme between DB and DC. In this section, we develop a new metric called risk-sharing coefficient which is based on the solidarity level between contributors and retirees in the event of shocks affecting the pension system. This measure will permit us to generate many other intermediate solutions between DB and DC.

We start from a steady state given by the equilibrium Eq. (14.6). A change in the dependence ratio D generates new values for the contribution rate and the replacement rate, which are still solutions of the equation

$$\pi_2 = D_2\delta_2. \tag{14.10}$$

We introduce the following notation:

$$\pi_2 = \pi_1(1 + \lambda_\pi), \tag{14.11}$$

$$\delta_2 = \delta_1(1 - \lambda_\delta). \tag{14.12}$$

The parameters λ_π and λ_δ represent the relative changes in the rates π and δ. Equilibrium Eq. (14.10) gives the following relation between these parameters:

$$(1 + \lambda_\pi) = \frac{D_2}{D_1}(1 - \lambda_\delta). \tag{14.13}$$

We can also introduce a risk-sharing coefficient, comparing the efforts supported by the contributors and the retirees:

$$\kappa = \frac{\lambda_\pi}{\lambda_\delta}. \tag{14.14}$$

If this coefficient is equal to 1, the risk is equally shared by the two generations. We first compute the values of these new parameters in the three systems introduced in Sect. 14.5.

Values of the parameters in a DB scheme In a DB scheme, we have by definition

$$\lambda_\delta = 0.$$

Equation (14.13) gives the other parameter:

$$1 + \lambda_\pi = \frac{D_2}{D_1} \quad \text{or} \quad \lambda_\pi = \frac{D_2 - D_1}{D_1}.$$

The risk-sharing coefficient is then, $\kappa = +\infty$.

Values of the parameters in a DC scheme In a DC scheme, we have by definition

$$\lambda_\pi = 0.$$

Equation (14.13) gives the other parameter:

$$1 = \frac{D_2}{D_1}(1 - \lambda_\delta) \quad \text{or} \quad \lambda_\delta = \frac{D_2 - D_1}{D_2}.$$

The risk-sharing coefficient is then, $\kappa = 0$.

Values of the parameters in a DM scheme In a DM scheme, we get, using Table 14.1, for the contribution rate,

$$\pi_2 = \pi_1 \frac{D_2}{D_1 + \pi_1(D_2 - D_1)} = \pi_1(1 + \lambda_\pi) \Rightarrow \lambda_\pi = \frac{(D_2 - D_1)(1 - \pi_1)}{D_1 + \pi_1(D_2 - D_1)},$$

and for the replacement rate,

$$\delta_2 = \delta_1 \frac{1}{1 + \delta_1(D_2 - D_1)} = \delta_1(1 - \lambda_\delta) \Rightarrow \lambda_\delta = \frac{(D_2 - D_1)\delta_1}{1 + \delta_1(D_2 - D_1)}.$$

The risk-sharing coefficient in a DM scheme is

$$\kappa = \frac{\lambda_\pi}{\lambda_\delta} = \frac{(D_2 - D_1)(1 - \pi_1)}{D_1 + \pi_1(D_2 - D_1)} \frac{1 + \delta_1(D_2 - D_1)}{(D_2 - D_1)\delta_1} = \frac{1 - \pi_1}{\pi_1} = \frac{1}{\pi_1} - 1. \tag{14.15}$$

For natural values of the contribution rate ($\pi < 0.5$), this sharing coefficient is higher than 1, showing that in a Defined Musgrave, contributors made a bigger effort than the retirees (system closer to DB than DC). In Example 14.1, this coefficient is equal to 4.

Let us remark that in a Defined Musgrave, this coefficient depends on the contribution rate. Therefore, successive applications of this rule will change the value of the risk-sharing coefficient (along with the change in the contribution rate), which is thus a variable metric in this context.

We can also look at other forms of risk sharing than those generated by the Musgrave rule. In particular, we can consider a constant value for the risk-sharing coefficient.

Values of the parameters in a scheme with a constant risk-sharing coefficient If the parameter κ remains constant, we get:

$$(1 + \lambda_\pi) = \frac{D_2}{D_1}(1 - \lambda_\delta),$$
$$\lambda_\pi = \kappa\, \lambda_\delta.$$

The solution is given by:

$$\lambda_\delta(\kappa) = \frac{D_2 - D_1}{D_2 + \kappa\, D_1},$$
$$\lambda_\pi(\kappa) = \kappa \frac{D_2 - D_1}{D_2 + \kappa\, D_1}.$$

The contribution rate and the replacement rate become:

$$\pi_2 = \pi_1 \frac{D_2\,(1+\kappa)}{D_2 + \kappa\, D_1},$$
$$\delta_2 = \delta_1 \frac{D_1\,(1+\kappa)}{D_2 + \kappa\, D_1}. \tag{14.16}$$

In particular, when the coefficient κ is equal to 1, we obtain a system with an equal risk sharing between retirees and contributors (called here DE for Defined Equal): the automatic adjustment generated by this choice is such that if for instance the contribution rate has to increase by 5% because of an increase of the dependence ratio, then simultaneously the replacement rate will also decrease by 5%. The contribution rate and the replacement rate are then given by:

$$\pi_2 = \pi_1 \frac{2\,D_2}{D_2 + D_1},$$
$$\delta_2 = \delta_1 \frac{2\,D_1}{D_2 + D_1}.$$

Example 14.2 Let us assume an initial steady state characterized by the following parameters: initial dependence ratio: $D = 0.40$, initial replacement rate $\delta = 0.50$, and initial contribution rate $\pi = 0.40 \times 0.50 = 0.20$. Then Tables 14.3 and 14.4 give for various values of the new dependence ratio the new contribution and replacement rates for different constant values of the risk-sharing coefficient κ, starting from DC schemes, finishing with DB schemes.

Table 14.3 Numerical comparison of the contribution rates for constant risk-sharing coefficients

	κ	$D_2 = 0.25$	$D_2 = 0.35$	$D_2 = 0.45$	$D_2 = 0.50$	$D_2 = 0.60$
DC	0	0.20	0.20	0.20	0.20	0.20
	0.5	0.17	0.19	0.21	0.21	0.23
DE	1	0.15	0.19	0.21	0.22	0.24
DM	4	0.14	0.18	0.22	0.24	0.27
	20	0.13	0.18	0.22	0.25	0.29
DB	∞	0.13	0.18	0.23	0.25	0.30

Table 14.4 Numerical comparison of the replacement rates for constant risk-sharing coefficients

	κ	$D_2 = 0.25$	$D_2 = 0.35$	$D_2 = 0.45$	$D_2 = 0.50$	$D_2 = 0.60$
DC	0	0.80	0.57	0.44	0.40	0.33
	0.5	0.67	0.55	0.46	0.43	0.38
DE	1	0.62	0.53	0.47	0.44	0.40
DM	4	0.54	0.51	0.49	0.48	0.45
	20	0.51	0.50	0.50	0.49	0.49
DB	∞	0.50	0.50	0.50	0.50	0.50

14.7 A Convex Invariant

Another way to generate intermediate solutions between DB and DC is to characterize a pension scheme by a quantity remaining constant through time. In a DC system, this invariant is given by the contribution rate; in a DB, by the replacement rate.

The Defined Musgrave is based on the following invariant (cf. Eq. (14.7)):

$$M = \frac{\delta}{1-\pi}.$$

This relation can be written

$$M = \delta + M\pi \quad \Leftrightarrow \quad \frac{1}{1+M}\delta + \frac{M}{1+M}\pi = \frac{M}{1+M}. \tag{14.17}$$

This last equation shows that, in a DM, the convex combination of the contribution rate and the replacement rate

$$\alpha\delta + (1-\alpha)\pi$$

with

$$\alpha = \frac{1}{1+M} = \frac{1-\pi}{1-\pi+\delta}$$

has to remain constant.

Relation (14.17) allows us to generalize the DM approach by choosing other values of the convex coefficient α. It is already easy to see that a DB scheme corresponds to the case $\alpha = 1$ and a DC scheme to the case $\alpha = 0$.

Considering the pension scheme in a two period model, a convex invariant risk sharing will be based on the following rule:

$$\alpha\delta_2 + (1-\alpha)\pi_2 = \alpha\delta_1 + (1-\alpha)\pi_1, \tag{14.18}$$

where α is a constant chosen between 0 (DC) and 1 (DB). This coefficient α can be seen as a measure of the importance given to the retirees, $1-\alpha$ being the measure of the importance given to the contributors.

From Eq. (14.18), together with the pension equation

$$\pi_2 = D_2\delta_2,$$

we obtain the new rates as a function of the convex coefficient:

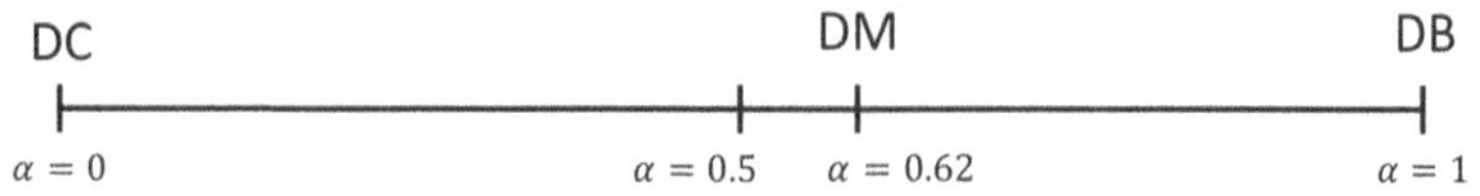

Fig. 14.1 Schemes generated by various convex combinations

$$\delta_2 = \delta_1 \frac{\alpha + (1-\alpha)D_1}{\alpha + (1-\alpha)D_2}, \tag{14.19}$$

$$\pi_2 = \pi_1 \frac{D_2}{D_1} \frac{\alpha + (1-\alpha)D_1}{\alpha + (1-\alpha)D_2}. \tag{14.20}$$

For instance, if $\alpha = 0.5$ (equal weight between contribution rate and replacement rate), we obtain

$$\delta_2 = \delta_1 \frac{1 + D_1}{1 + D_2},$$
$$\pi_2 = \pi_1 \frac{D_2}{D_1} \frac{1 + D_1}{1 + D_2}.$$

Figure 14.1 gives an illustration of the schemes family obtained using this convex combination. Using the parameters of Example 14.1, the coefficient α for DM is equal to 0.62, showing once again that DM is closer to DB than DC. In general, the convex parameter α of a DM will be greater than 0.5 if

$$\frac{1-\pi}{1-\pi+\delta} > \frac{1}{2} \quad \Leftrightarrow \quad \pi + \delta < 1,$$

or, using Eq. (14.6),

$$\pi < \frac{D}{1+D},$$
$$\delta < \frac{1}{1+D}.$$

The following property gives a link between this convex parameter α and the risk-sharing coefficient κ introduced in Sect. 14.6 (Formula 14.14).

Proposition 14.3 The risk-sharing coefficient κ given by (14.14) and the convex parameter α given by (14.18) are linked by the relation:

$$\kappa_2 = \frac{1}{D_1} \frac{\alpha}{1-\alpha}. \tag{14.21}$$

Proof Putting together definitions (14.11) and (14.12) and Eqs. (14.19) and (14.20) yields

$$\lambda_\delta = 1 - \frac{\alpha + (1-\alpha)D_1}{\alpha + (1-\alpha)D_2} = \frac{1}{D_1}\frac{\alpha(D_2 - D_1)}{\alpha + (1-\alpha)D_2},$$
$$\lambda_\pi = \frac{D_2}{D_1}\frac{\alpha + (1-\alpha)D_1}{\alpha + (1-\alpha)D_2} - 1 = \frac{(1-\alpha)(D_2 - D_1)}{\alpha + (1-\alpha)D_2}.$$

The result follows straightforwardly.

Remark 14.1 Relation (14.21) shows that if we look at a pension system in a multi-period model with successive changes in the dependence ratio and therefore successive applications of the automatic adjustment, the two coefficients α and κ cannot remain simultaneously constant across time, apart from the two limit situations of a DB or a DC. For instance, a DM scheme is characterized by a constant $\alpha = 1/(1+M)$ (see Eq. 14.17), but its risk-sharing coefficient given by (14.15) will change over time together with the contribution rate.

Extension to multi-period models When considering the pension scheme in a multi-period context, Eq. (14.18) can be written

$$\alpha\delta_t + (1-\alpha)\pi_t = C_\alpha, \tag{14.22}$$

where $C_\alpha \in (0, 1)$ is a constant which can be understood as the initial value of the convex combination.

Note that, using the budget equation, we can obtain for δ_t and π_t expressions as functions of D_t:

$$\begin{aligned} \pi_t &= \delta_t D_t \\ \alpha\delta_t + (1-\alpha)\pi_t &= C_\alpha \end{aligned} \quad \Rightarrow \quad \begin{aligned} \delta_t &= \frac{C_\alpha}{\alpha + (1-\alpha)D_t} \\ \pi_t &= \frac{C_\alpha D_t}{\alpha + (1-\alpha)D_t} \end{aligned}. \tag{14.23}$$

Example 14.3 Let us assume an initial steady state characterized by an initial dependence ratio $D = 0.40$, an initial replacement rate $\delta = 0.50$, and an initial contribution rate $\pi = 0.40 \times 0.50 = 0.20$. We suppose that after one period, the dependence ratio moves to a new value: $D = 0.50$. Then Table 14.5 gives for various values of the convex parameter α the new contribution and replacement rates.

Table 14.5 Numerical comparison of the contribution and replacement rates for constant convex parameters α

	Convex parameter α	Contribution rate	Replacement rate
DC	0%	0.20	0.40
	25%	0.22	0.44
	50%	0.23	0.47
DM	61, 54%	0.24	0.48
DB	100%	0.25	0.50

14.8 A Continuous Time Framework

In this section, we generalize the results obtained previously to a continuous time framework. We assume a pension scheme satisfying at any time the equilibrium equation:

$$\pi_t = \delta_t D_t.$$

Taking the log derivative of this budget equation yields

$$\frac{d\pi_t}{\pi_t} - \frac{d\delta_t}{\delta_t} = \frac{dD_t}{D_t}. \tag{14.24}$$

We now assume that there exists a function $\beta : [0, \infty) \rightarrow [0, 1]$ such that

$$\begin{cases} \dfrac{d\pi_t}{\pi_t} = (1 - \beta_t)\dfrac{dD_t}{D_t}, \\ -\dfrac{d\delta_t}{\delta_t} = \beta_t \dfrac{dD_t}{D_t}. \end{cases} \tag{14.25}$$

This function corresponds to an automatic adjustment mechanism of the contribution rate and the replacement rate in relation to the ageing of the population modelled by the log derivative of the dependence ratio.

Relation (14.25) suggests that a fraction β of the ageing effect will generate a decrease in the replacement rate, while a fraction $(1 - \beta)$ will generate an increase in the contribution rate.

Choosing the values taken by the function β leads to different kinds of pension schemes, among which we recover the schemes obtained in the discrete framework of the previous sections.

Defined Contributions Choosing $\beta \equiv 1$ leads to the equation

$$\frac{d\pi_t}{\pi_t} = 0 \quad \Rightarrow \quad \pi_t = C$$

for some constant C, and thus to the Defined Contributions scheme.

Defined Benefits Similarly, defining $\beta \equiv 0$ yields

$$\frac{d\delta_t}{\delta_t} = 0 \quad \Rightarrow \quad \delta_t = C$$

for some constant C. We therefore recover the Defined Benefits scheme in this case.

Defined Musgrave If β is chosen to be equal to the contribution rate π, the scheme obtained is the Defined Musgrave one. Indeed, we compute

$$
\begin{aligned}
d\log\left(\frac{\delta_t}{1-\pi_t}\right) &= d\log\delta_t - d\log(1-\pi_t) \\
&= \frac{d\delta_t}{\delta_t} + \frac{d\pi_t}{1-\pi_t} \\
&= -\pi_t\frac{dD_t}{D_t} + \pi_t\frac{dD_t}{D_t} \\
&= 0,
\end{aligned}
$$

so that the quotient $\delta_t/(1-\pi_t)$ is constant.

Constant proportion If β remains constant, we can obtain an easy form of the contribution rates and the replacement rates:

$$
\begin{aligned}
\pi_t &= A\,D_t^{1-\alpha}, \\
\delta_t &= A\,D_t^{\alpha},
\end{aligned}
\tag{14.26}
$$

where A is a constant generated by the initial conditions.

For a particular choice of the function β, we can also make a link between this approach and the convex invariant idea of Sect. 14.7.

Convex combination of the rates Defining $\beta = \gamma\pi$ for some constant γ leads to the scheme defined by a constant convex combination as in (14.22). We compute as previously

$$
\begin{aligned}
d\log\left(\frac{\delta_t}{1-\gamma\,\pi_t}\right) &= d\log\delta_t - d\log(1-\gamma\,\pi_t) \\
&= \frac{d\delta_t}{\delta_t} + \frac{d\pi_t}{1-\gamma\,\pi_t} \\
&= -\gamma\,\pi_t\frac{dD_t}{D_t} + \gamma\,\pi_t\frac{dD_t}{D_t} \\
&= 0.
\end{aligned}
$$

The corresponding quotient is thus constant, and the convex combination can be retrieved:

$$
\begin{aligned}
\frac{\delta_t}{1-\gamma\,\pi_t} = C &\Leftrightarrow \delta_t + C\gamma\,\pi_t = C \\
&\Leftrightarrow \frac{1}{1+C\gamma}\,\delta_t + \frac{C\gamma}{1+C\gamma}\pi_t = \frac{C}{1+C\gamma} \\
&\Leftrightarrow \alpha\delta_t + (1-\alpha)\pi_t = C_\alpha
\end{aligned}
$$

if we define

$$
\alpha = \frac{1}{1+C\gamma} \quad \text{and} \quad C_\alpha = \frac{C}{1+C\gamma} = \alpha\,C. \tag{14.27}
$$

Next, we define a continuous equivalent of the risk-sharing coefficient κ defined in the discrete framework (Sect. 14.6). Drawing our inspiration from the discrete expressions

$$\begin{cases} \lambda^{\pi} = \dfrac{\pi_2 - \pi_1}{\pi_1}, \\ \lambda^{\delta} = -\dfrac{\delta_2 - \delta_1}{\delta_1}, \end{cases}$$

which are equivalent to Eqs. (14.11) and (14.12), we define

$$\begin{cases} \lambda_t^{\pi} = 1 - \beta_t \\ \lambda_t^{\delta} = \beta_t \end{cases} \quad \text{and} \quad \kappa_t = \frac{1 - \beta_t}{\beta_t}.$$

It is interesting to note that λ_{π} and λ_{δ} are related to the risk sharing between active workers and retirees, as in the discrete framework. Indeed, we can rewrite the former as

$$\frac{\frac{d\pi_t}{\pi_t}}{\frac{dD_t}{D_t}} = \frac{d \log \pi_t}{d \log D_t}$$

and the latter as

$$\frac{\frac{d\delta_t}{\delta_t}}{\frac{dD_t}{D_t}} = \frac{d \log \delta_t}{d \log D_t}.$$

If we ignore the logarithms, these quantities thus give the variability of the rates with respect to the variability of the dependence ratio. The risk-sharing process therefore allows us to measure how the demographic risk is split between workers and retirees.

Using the definitions of the process β proposed in the previous points, we obtain values for κ which are similar to the ones obtained in the discrete framework. It is straightforward to see that in a Defined Contributions scheme, $\kappa_t \equiv 0$ and that in a Defined Benefits scheme $\kappa_t = +\infty$. The Defined Musgrave case leads to

$$\kappa_t = \frac{1 - \pi_t}{\pi_t},$$

similarly to (14.15). We also compute for the scheme defined by a convex combination of the rates that

$$\kappa_t = \frac{1 - \beta_t}{\beta_t} = \frac{1 - \gamma\pi_t}{\gamma\pi_t} = \frac{1 - \frac{1-\alpha}{\alpha\, C}\pi_t}{\frac{1-\alpha}{\alpha\, C}\pi_t} = \frac{1 - \frac{1-\alpha}{C_\alpha}\pi_t}{\frac{1-\alpha}{C_\alpha}\pi_t} = \frac{\frac{\alpha}{C_\alpha}\delta_t}{\frac{1-\alpha}{C_\alpha}\pi_t} = \frac{1}{D_t}\frac{\alpha}{1-\alpha},$$

Table 14.6 Functions β and κ obtained in the continuous framework (γ is a positive constant)

	Function β	Function κ
Defined contributions	1	0
Defined benefits	0	$+\infty$
Defined Musgrave	π_t	$\frac{1-\pi_t}{\pi_t}$
Convex combination of the rates	$\gamma\pi_t$	$\frac{1}{D}\frac{\alpha}{1-\alpha}$
Constant proportion	γ	$\frac{1-\gamma}{\gamma}$

using (14.22) and (14.27). Note that this result is the identical to (14.21). Finally, in the case of the constant proportion pension schemes, the risk-sharing process is constant:

$$\kappa_t = \frac{1-\gamma}{\gamma}.$$

Table 14.6 gathers the results we have obtained in the continuous framework.

14.9 Numerical Illustrations

We provide in this section numerical illustrations of the multi-period model. In order to show how the replacement rate, the contribution rate, and the risk-sharing coefficient evolve when the dependence ratio varies, we need a projection of the latter variable. We have chosen to compute it from the demographic forecasting 2015–2060 performed by Belgian public agencies (Federal Planning Bureau and Statistics Belgium 2016), as it is widely used for pension-related computations in Belgium. As it can be seen from Fig. 14.2, D goes from 30% to 45% for a time horizon of 50 years.

Using Eq. (14.23), we obtain the development of π_t and δ_t. The projection starts in 2015, so that the initial parameters (i.e. D_0 and δ_0) correspond to 2015 numbers. In Figs. 14.3 and 14.4, the projections of both rates are plotted, showing how the hybrid pensions schemes react when D increases. Their role as intermediates between DB and DC is clearly pictured. Note that these graphs confirm the fact that the DM scheme is closer to DB than to DC.

Finally, Fig. 14.5 shows the changes in the risk-sharing factor over the years, computed using formulas from Table 14.6.

14.10 The Sustainability Factor

Until now, we have considered a mean replacement rate for all the retirees, leading to automatic adjustment of the average pension amounts and the contribution level. We could introduce a new refinement based on the fact that the average pension is in fact

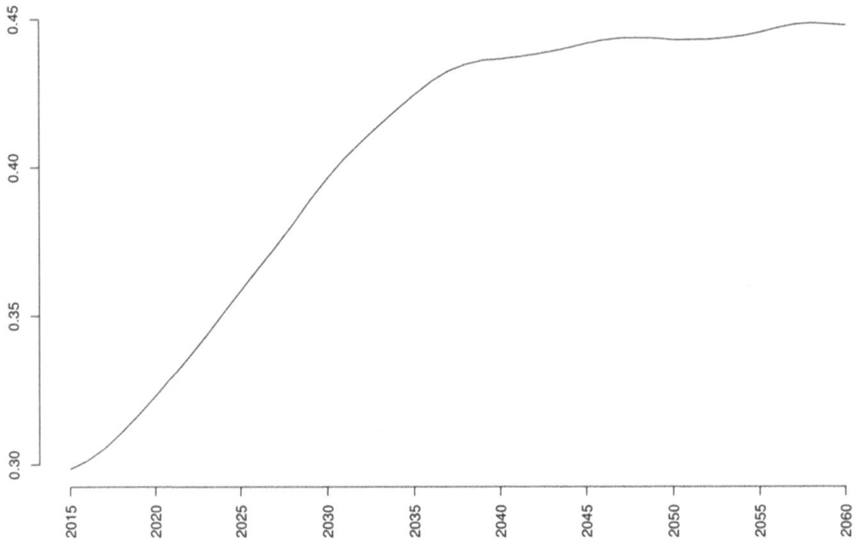

Fig. 14.2 Changes in the dependence ratio D according to the demographic projections performed by the Federal Planning Bureau and Statistics Belgium (2016)

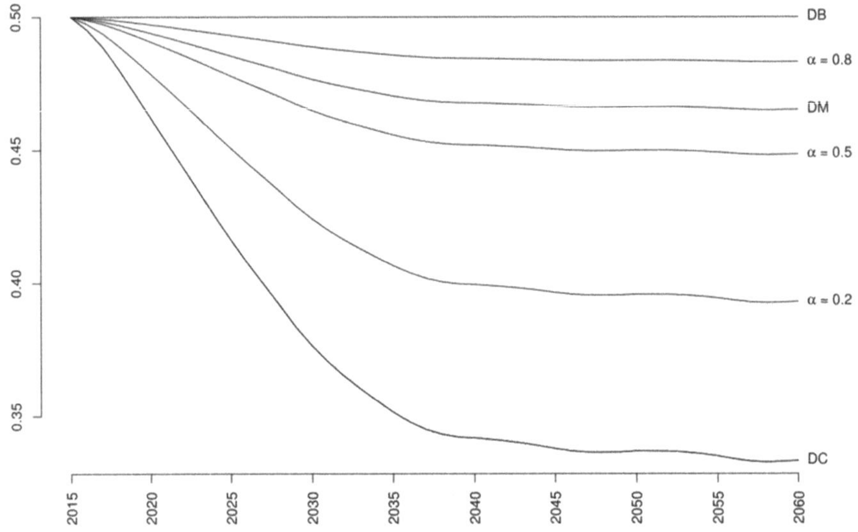

Fig. 14.3 Projection of the replacement rate δ

a mixture of two effects: the new pension level for the generation going into pension and the adaptation of the previous pensions for those that have retired earlier.

Instead of considering just the mean replacement rate, we could monitor the system in terms of benefits by decomposing these two effects and introducing two parameters:

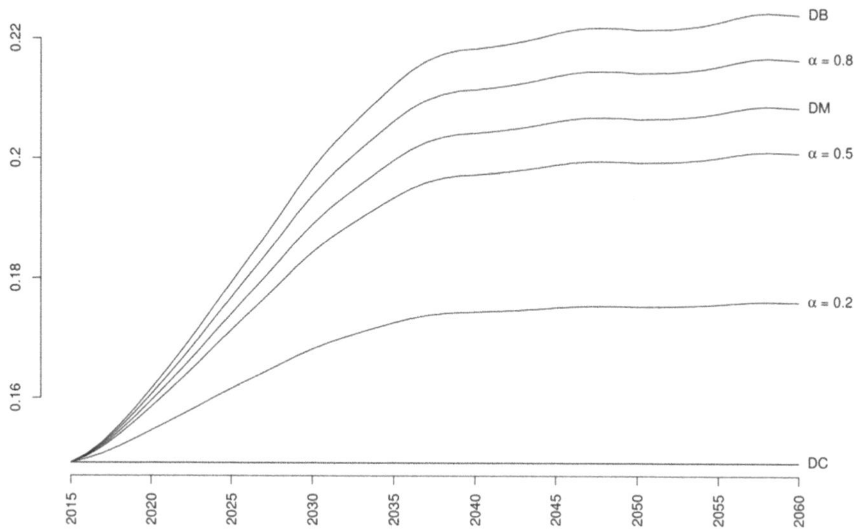

Fig. 14.4 Projection of the contribution rate π

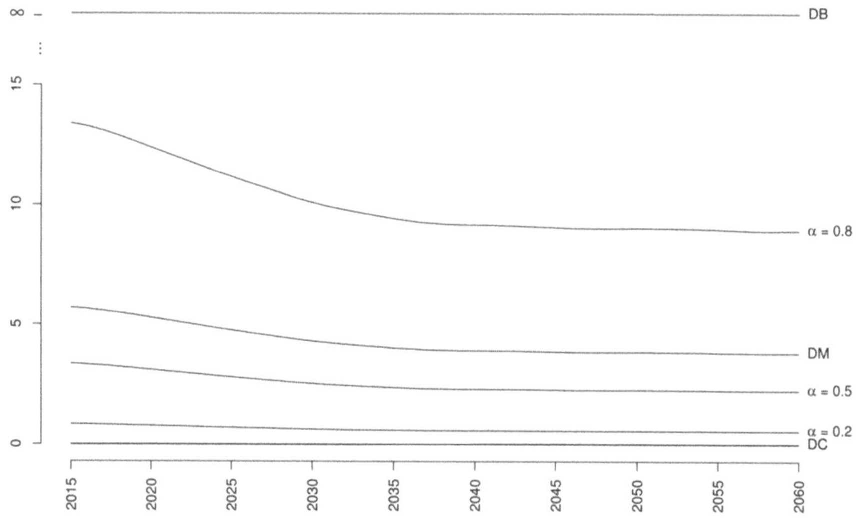

Fig. 14.5 Projection of the risk-sharing coefficient κ

- The replacement rate, but only for the new pensioners in order to compute their first pension amount,
- A sustainability factor that could affect the normal adaptation of their previous pensions on salaries (see Sect. 14.3).

Let us consider for simplicity a model with two generations of retirees in a discrete time context.

For the new generation of retirees, the pension is given by:

$$P_t^n = S_t\, \delta_t^n, \tag{14.28}$$

where

P_t^n = new pension for people retired at time t,
δ_t^n = replacement rate for people retired at time t.

For the generation already retired earlier, the pension is adapted in line with salaries but also takes into account a sustainability factor:

$$P_t^o = P_{t-1}^n \frac{S_t}{S_{t-1}} \eta_t, \tag{14.29}$$

where

P_t^o = pension for people retired before time t,
η_t = sustainability factor.

Taking into account (14.28), the pension (14.29) becomes:

$$P_t^o = \left(\delta_{t-1}^n\, S_{t-1}\right) \frac{S_t}{S_{t-1}} \eta_t = \delta_{t-1}^n\, S_t\, \eta_t. \tag{14.30}$$

If the sustainability factor is equal to one, the old pensions can be fully adapted along with the change in salaries. If this factor is lower than one, this adaption is only partial.

To monitor the pension scheme, we now have three main parameters: the contribution rate, the replacement rate for the new retirees, and the sustainability factor for the old retirees. By adapting these parameters each year, we can at the same time preserve the financial sustainability of the system and promote solidarity between the generations (intergenerational solidarity between the active workers and the retirees and also between the new retirees and the old ones).

In this architecture, the equilibrium equation between incomes and expenses becomes:

$$\pi_t\, S_t\, N_{A_t} = N_{R_t}^n\, P_t^n + N_{R_t}^o\, P_t^o, \tag{14.31}$$

where

N_A = number of contributors,
N_R^n = number of new retirees,
N_R^o = number of old retirees.

This equation can be expressed in terms of partial dependence ratios and replacement rates:

$$\pi_t = D_t^n\, \delta_t^n + D_t^o\, \delta_{t-1}^n\, \eta_t, \tag{14.32}$$

where

$$D_t^n = \frac{N_{R_t}^n}{N_{A_t}},$$

$$D_t^o = D_t - D_t^n = \frac{N_{R_t}^o}{N_{A_t}}.$$

We can also always consider the general equilibrium:

$$\pi_t = D_t\, \delta_t. \tag{14.33}$$

Equations (14.32) and (14.33) can be combined to obtain a relation between the average replacement rate for the whole population of retirees and the specific parameters of the two generations of retirees:

$$D_t\, \delta_t = D_t^n\, \delta_t^n + \left(D_t - D_t^n\right) \delta_{t-1}^n\, \eta_t. \tag{14.34}$$

In particular, the replacement rate for the new generations of retirees can be expressed in relation with the other parameters:

$$\delta_t^n = \delta_t + \frac{D_t - D_t^n}{D_t^n} \left(\delta_t - \delta_{t-1}^n \eta_t\right). \tag{14.35}$$

In this relation, the dependence ratio D is an exogenous factor; the average replacement rate has been defined previously (e.g. by applying the Musgrave rule). Then Eq. (14.35) can be used to obtain the specific factors of the two generations of retirees (δ_t^n and η_t). Different choices can be made with respect to the risk sharing between the new and the old retirees. Let us consider three possible choices corresponding to various additional constraints.

Case 1 Solidarity: $\delta_t^n = \delta_t$.

The replacement rate for the new generation of retirees in one specific year must be similar to the average replacement rate for all the retirees that year (a kind of solidarity between all the retirees). Then Equation (14.35) gives the sustainability factor:

$$\eta_t = \frac{\delta_t}{\delta_{t-1}}. \tag{14.36}$$

The sustainability factor corresponds to the change in the replacement rate, showing that this choice can be seen as an equilibrated solution between all the retirees.

Case 2 Protection of the new retirees: $\delta_t^n = \delta_{t-1}^n$.

The replacement rate for the new retirees has to remain constant; in this case, all the impact of the demographic change will affect the sustainability factor and hence the indexation of the old pensions. Then Equation (14.35) gives the following sustainability factor:

$$\eta_t = \frac{\delta_t}{\delta_{t-1}^n} - \left(1 - \frac{\delta_t}{\delta_{t-1}^n}\right) \frac{D_t^n}{D_t - D_t^n}. \tag{14.37}$$

Case 3 Protection of the old retirees: $\eta_t = 1$.

No sustainability factor is applied on the indexation of the old pension. In this other extreme case, all the impact of the demographic change will affect the replacement rate of the new retirees. Then Equation (14.35) gives the new replacement rate:

$$\delta_t^n = \delta_t + \frac{D_t - D_t^n}{D_t^n} \left(\delta_t - \delta_{t-1}^n\right). \tag{14.38}$$

In conclusion, we can model the global structure of a pension scheme as a two-step process reflecting the level of risk sharing and solidarity between the different generations:

- Step 1: general equilibrium between active people and retirees by defining a rule of automatic adaptation of the contribution rate π_t and the average replacement rate δ_t (based for instance on Formula (14.22)),
- Step 2: equilibrium between the new and the old retirees by defining a rule of automatic adaptation of the sustainability factor η_t and the replacement rate for the new retirees δ_t^n based on Formula (14.35).

As an example of implementation of this two-step process, let us develop the application of the Musgrave rule (Formula (14.7) combined with the solidarity case between retirees.

The first step gives the contribution rate and the mean replacement rate (Sect. 14.5) (M being the Musgrave constant):

- Contribution rate:

$$\pi_t = \frac{M\,D_t}{1 + M\,D_t},$$

- Mean replacement rate:

$$\delta_t = \frac{M}{1 + M\,D_t}.$$

In case 1 (solidarity), the replacement rate for the new retirees is equal to the mean replacement rate and taking into account (14.36), we get in the second step:

- Replacement rate for new retirees:

$$\delta_t^n = \delta_t = \frac{M}{1 + M\,D_t}, \tag{14.39}$$

- Sustainability factor:

$$\eta_t = \frac{1 + M\,D_{t-1}}{1 + M\,D_t}. \tag{14.40}$$

14.11 Conclusion

NDC and classical DB social security systems can be seen as extreme solutions in risk sharing between retirees and contributors. The 'Musgrave' technique (using a replacement rate expressed in terms of salaries, net of pension contributions) is an intermediate solution that has been considered in the proposition of reform based on a points system for Belgium. This approach seems to bring more solidarity and equity between the generations than in a pure DB or DC scheme, where only one generation bears the risk.

However, this Musgrave system is but one example of a mix between DB and DC and is based on a solidarity level that can be challenged. In this chapter, we introduce a natural way to extend these three systems into a continuous family of systems with an automatic adjustment mechanism based on some constraint.

We also introduce a convex mix between the replacement rate and the contribution rate. The Musgrave rule is a particular case of this last philosophy. These different formulas allow the State to decide the level of solidarity to be injected into the social security system.

Appendix: Another Family of Pension Schemes Defined through a Convex Invariant

The family of pension plans (indexed by parameter α) defined in Eq. (14.22) can be viewed as a 'line segment' linking DC (corresponding to the beginning of the segment: $\alpha = 0$) to DB (corresponding to the end of the segment: $\alpha = 1$). Of course, the straight line is not the only way of connecting these two points: we can obtain infinitely many such curves. Formally, any regular function

$$f : (0,1)^2 \times [0,1] \to (0,1) : (x, y, \alpha) \mapsto f_\alpha(x, y)$$

such that $f_0(x, y) = y$ and $f_1(x, y) = x$ leads to a family of pension plans by defining, for some fixed α,

$$f(\delta_t, \pi_t, \alpha) = C_\alpha$$

for some constant $C_\alpha \in (0, 1)$. Of course, we get back to Eq. (14.22) choosing $f(x, y, \alpha) = \alpha x + (1 - \alpha)y$.

Defining $f(x, y, \alpha) = x^\alpha y^{1-\alpha}$ leads to an interesting family of pension plans:

$$\delta_t^\alpha \, \pi_t^{1-\alpha} = C_\alpha \quad \Leftrightarrow \quad \alpha \log \delta_t + (1 - \alpha) \log \pi_t = \log C_\alpha.$$

The result is a log-linear combination of the replacement and contribution rates, i.e. the equivalent of (14.22) for the logarithm of the rates instead of the rates themselves.

Similarly to (14.23), in this case, we obtain from the budget equation the following expressions for the contribution and replacement rates:

$$\begin{cases} \pi_t = \delta_t \, D_t \\ \delta_t^\alpha \, \pi_t^{1-\alpha} = C_\alpha \end{cases} \Rightarrow \begin{cases} \delta_t = C_\alpha D_t^{\alpha-1} \\ \pi_t = C_\alpha D_t^\alpha \end{cases}.$$

References

Borsch-Supan, A., Reil-Held, A., & Wilke, C. B. (2003). *How to make a defined benefit system sustainable: The sustainability factor in the German enefit indexation formula*. Discussion paper of the Mannheim Institute for the Economics of Aging 37.

Commission de réforme des pensions 2020-2040. (2014). *Un contrat social performant et fiable*. URL: http://pension2040.belgium.be/fr/.

Devolder, P. (2010). Perspectives pour nos régimes de pension légale. *Revue belge de sécurité sociale, 4*, 597–614.

European Commission. (2014). *The 2015 Ageing Report: Economic and budgetary projections for the 28 EU Member States (2013-2060)*. https://ec.europa.eu/economy_finance/publications/european_economy/2015/ee3_en.htm

Federal Planning Bureau and Statistics Belgium. (2016). *Perspectives de population 2015-2060*. URL: http://www.plan.be.

Holzmann, R., Palmer, E., & Robalino, D. (2012). *Non-financial defined contribution pension schemes in a changing pension world*. World Bank: Washington, DC.

Knell, M. (2010). How automatic adjustment factors affect the internal rate of return of PAYG pension systems. *Journal of Pension Economics and Finance, 9*(1), 1–23.

Musgrave, R. (1981). A reappraisal of social security finance. In F. Skidmore (Ed.), *Social security financing* (pp. 89–127). Cambridge: MIT.

Palmer, E. (2000). *The Swedish pension reform model: Framework and issues*. Social Protection Discussion Paper of the World Bank 12.
Settergren, O. (2001). The automatic balance mechanism of the Swedish pension system: A non-technical introduction. *Wirtschaftspolitische Blätter, 4*, 339–349.
Vidal-Melia, C., Boado-Penas, M. C., & Devesa-Carpio, J. E. (2006). Automatic balance mechanisms in pay-as-you-go pension systems. *The Geneva Papers on Risk and Insurance-Issues and Practice, 34*(2), 287–317.

Chapter 15
Automatic Balancing Mechanisms for Pay-As-You-Go Pension Finance: Do They Actually Work?

María del Carmen Boado-Penas, Humberto Godínez-Olivares, and Steven Haberman

Abstract In pay-as-you go pension systems, automatic balancing mechanisms (ABMs) are designed to face adverse demographic and economic changes. In this respect, ABMs can be defined as a set of pre-determined measures established by law to be applied immediately as required according to an indicator that reflects the financial health of the system. The purpose of ABMs is, through successive application, to restore the sustainability of the pay-as-you-go pension system. First, adjustments can be made in benefit levels to reflect changes in life expectancy; second, adjustments can be made through the revaluation of the contribution basis of earlier years; and third, adjustments may occur through the revaluation of pensions in payment. Countries such as Finland, Portugal, Germany, Sweden and Japan, amongst others, have already legislated and included different types of mechanisms into their pension systems. This chapter aims to explore the different mechanisms that have been recently set up and analyse their effectiveness in terms of financial sustainability and adequacy of benefits.

Keywords Adequacy · Adjustment · Ageing · Public pensions · Sustainability

M. del Carmen Boado-Penas (✉)
Institute for Financial and Actuarial Mathematics (IFAM), Department of Mathematical Sciences, University of Liverpool, Liverpool, UK
e-mail: Carmen.Boado@liverpool.ac.uk

H. Godínez-Olivares
Arundo Analytics, Houston, TX, USA
e-mail: humberto.godinez@arundo.com

S. Haberman
Faculty of Actuarial Science and Insurance, Cass Business School, City, University of London, London, UK
e-mail: S.Haberman@city.ac.uk

M. Peris-Ortiz et al. (eds.), *Economic Challenges of Pension Systems*,
https://doi.org/10.1007/978-3-030-37912-4_15

15.1 Introduction

A pay-as-you-go (PAYG) pension system requires a balance between the expenditure on pensions and the income from contributions made by the active workers over time. In many countries, the recent decline in fertility rates, the recent increases in longevity and the current forecasts for the ageing of the baby-boom generation all point to a substantial increase in the age dependency ratio, and this will raise serious concerns about the sustainability of PAYG pension systems. This is a worldwide problem, and consequently, many European countries have already carried out some parametric reform, or even structural reform, of their pension systems.

In the meantime, some countries have decided to set up automatic balancing mechanisms (ABMs). ABMs are defined (Vidal Melia et al. 2009) as a set of predetermined measures established by law to be applied immediately as required according to an indicator that reflects the financial health of the system. Their purpose, through successive application, is to re-establish the financial equilibrium of PAYG pension systems without the repeated intervention of the legislator. The adjustments[1] can be made on benefit levels, revaluation of contribution bases and/or indexation of pensions in payments.

According to D'Addio and Whitehouse (2012), three main automatic mechanisms can be considered for changing pension values. First, adjustments can be made in benefit levels to reflect changes in life expectancy; second, adjustments can be made through revaluation of earlier years' contribution bases; and third, adjustments may occur through the indexation of pension payments. In fact, two-thirds of the pension reforms in OECD countries in the last 15 years contain measures that will automatically link future pensions to changes in life expectancy – this compares with only one country (Denmark) a decade ago.

According to European Commission (2012), a few EU Member States that reformed their pension systems in the recent past have formally introduced a sustainability factor and/or other reduction coefficients into the specification that determines the amount of pension benefits. This approach introduces a component that changes the size of the pension benefit depending on expected demographic changes at the time of retirement. In most of the cases, this leads to a reduction in pension entitlements, having a positive impact on the sustainability of the public pension system as well as on public finances. In practice, countries, such as Finland and Portugal, adjust the level of benefits in line with life expectancy at retirement age. Other countries like Sweden, Canada, Germany and Japan, amongst others, have a combination of risk-sharing adjustments that affect both the contributors and the pensioners of state pension systems.

During the last few years, organisations like the European Commission and the OECD have been recommending reforms that would lead to more financially sustainable PAYG pensions and also lead to stable and adequate levels of income in old age. There is an obvious trade-off between improving financial sustainability

[1]See D'Addio and Whitehouse (2012) and Godínez-Olivares et al. (2016a, b).

and pension adequacy at the same time, as increases in pension benefits (adequacy) will lead to a deterioration in pension finances (and, hence, worsen the sustainability).

With this in mind, this chapter aims to explore recent reforms (ABMs) that have been set up in some representative OECD member countries and analyse their effectiveness in terms of financial sustainability and pension adequacy. Following this introduction, the next section of the paper describes some general adjustments that might be carried out to improve sustainability and adequacy. Section 15.3 describes the ABMs implemented in Finland, Portugal, Germany, Sweden, Japan and Canada. Section 15.4 provides some concluding comments.

15.2 Pension Reforms: An Overview

According to the World Bank (2008), a reform of a pension system should be determined by applying the adequacy, affordability, sustainability and robustness criteria. Amongst these criteria, the World Bank perspective continues to assign a high priority to parametric reforms of unsustainable pay-as-you-go systems and to rely on diversification of instruments to manage long-term risks. Under this context, a sustainable system is defined as the one which is financially sound and can be maintained over a foreseeable horizon under a broad set of reasonable assumptions. OECD (2015, 2016, 2017) also put reforms of pension systems amongst their members and partner countries on the agenda. The pension reforms aim to achieve a more financially sustainable pension system, which could also provide an adequate income for pensioners.

Public pension expenditure (OECD 2015) accounts for 18% of total public spending across OECD countries, and it represents 9% of the total GDP. The projections also show that pension expenditures in the vast majority of the countries will keep increasing if no measures are taken. Most OECD countries have been active in changing their pension systems in the last few years and a majority of countries have already implemented reforms to improve the financial sustainability of their systems. As noted above, there is a trade-off between improving financial sustainability and pension adequacy at the same time. For example, increases (reductions) in pension benefits deteriorate (improve) financial balances. Countries like Australia, which have achieved an improvement both in sustainability and adequacy, took a combination of measures, such as increasing both the contribution rate and the retirement age. Some other countries have done so whilst maintaining or improving retirement income adequacy, at least for some population groups.

Below is a summary of the several measures[2] that have been carried out to improve the financial sustainability and adequacy.

Improving Financial Sustainability

---

[2]Based on OECD (2015).

- The most popular measure was to strengthen the incentives to work, thereby enlarging the total contribution base of the system. In fact, between September 2013 and September 2015, the focus in 14 OECD countries has been on increasing sustainability through the lengthening of working lives. This can be done through (i) increases in the statutory retirement age, (ii) tightening of early retirement provisions, (iii) higher financial incentives to delay the retirement age and (iv) greater possibilities to combine work and pensions.
- As an illustration of the above point, the retirement age of males entering the labour market at age 20 will increase from 64 years currently, on average across all OECD countries, to 65.5 years by the late 2050s.
- Very few countries have carried out extensive reforms through nominal benefit cuts. In Finland, Portugal and Spain,[3] the initial pension benefit paid to new retirees will be adjusted based on an indicator of the projected life expectancy gains.
- A much larger number of countries have changed the indexation of pension benefits to less generous uprating mechanisms. In Finland, the indexation of pensions was limited to 0.4%. Pension indexation has been frozen in Greece since 2011 and in Belgium since 2015. In Italy, pensions above a threshold for the period 2014–2016 are only increased by a fixed amount only. Other countries,[4] such as Spain, Canada or Luxembourg, have introduced automatic mechanisms to strengthen the link between pension indexation and the financial health of the system.
- Many countries have raised revenues for the financing of public pensions through higher contributions (without generating additional pension entitlements) in defined-benefit systems. For example, in Canada, the contribution rate is increasing from 9.9% in 2011 to 10.8% in 2017 whilst in France the contribution rate will increase by 0.3% by 2017 for both employees and employers.
- Measures to curb pension administration costs have been quite common. In general costs have been reduced and performance increased in a number of countries through the merging of the administration, the implementation of regulatory measures or the use of new technology.

Improving Retirement-Income Adequacy

- Several countries have taken measures to increase the coverage of voluntary private pension schemes. Thus, all OECD countries have set up mandatory or quasi-mandatory pension systems to achieve high coverage[5] in pension schemes. In Japan, for instance, from April 2017 the qualifying period for the national pension will decrease from 25 to 10 years, hence increasing coverage and benefiting short-career workers.

---

[3]Section 15.3 details the reforms carried out in Finland and Portugal. In Spain, the reform based on linking initial benefit to life expectancy will happen every 5 years from 2019.

[4]See OECD (2015) for more details.

[5]Countries with a large informal sector, such as Mexico, Chile and some G20 countries, may still have lower coverage levels even in mandatory schemes.

- Some countries have awarded retroactive pension credits or reduced the impact of missing years of contributions on pension levels targeting vulnerable groups.
- Some countries have reduced the taxation of pensioners' income. In Portugal, the extraordinary surcharge introduced in 2013–2014 will be limited to pensions exceeding EUR 4611 from 2015. Increased tax relief was given to older people in Sweden in 2014.
- In some defined-contribution schemes, contribution rates have been increased.
- In a number of countries, management costs have been lowered and several improvements have been made to the security of pension investments. For example in Canada, between 2013 and 2016, an automatic enrolment regime for the minimum pension (old age security) is being phased in, with the aim of lowering both the administrative burden on retirees and the pension administrative costs.

15.3 ABMs that Link Future Pensions to Changes in Demographic Factors

This section describes the ABMs implemented in some representative OECD member countries. In Finland and Portugal, the mechanism links the amount of the initial pension to changes in life expectancy. Sweden, Germany, Canada and Japan have a combination of risk-sharing adjustments that affect both contributors and pensioners of state pension systems.

15.3.1 Finland

The Finnish two-tier pension system consists of a basic state pension, which is pension-income-tested, and a range of statutory earnings-related schemes, with very similar rules for different groups. The schemes for private-sector employees are partially pre-funded whilst the public-sector schemes are PAYG financed with buffer funds that are intended to even out future increases in pension contributions.

According to Sect. 83 of the Employees Pensions Act (TyEL) that came into force as the beginning of 2007, the life expectancy coefficient is defined so that the capital value of the pension adjusted with the coefficient is the same when calculated with the available mortality rates for the previous 5 years as the unadjusted capital value of the pension in the base year 2009 calculated using the mortality rates over the period 2003–2007. In this way, the effect that changes in longevity have on the capital values of pensions is neutralised in the long run. If life expectancy were to increase, monthly pensions would be decreased, and if life expectancy were to decrease, monthly pensions would be increased.

In Finland, the life expectancy coefficient is determined at the age of 62 for each age group. When calculating the amount of the initial pension, the accrued pension is multiplied by an automatic balancing mechanism called the life expectancy coefficient. The purpose of the life expectancy coefficient is to limit the growth in pension expenditure due to the rising life expectancy. It also contributes to prolonged working lives by lowering the incentives to retire early.

Before the reform of 2017, the life expectancy coefficient for a particular year n (EAK^n) was calculated by dividing the longevity indicator (*EAL*) for the base year 2009 with the longevity indicator for n, i.e. using the following formula:

$$\mathrm{EAK}^n = \frac{\mathrm{EAL}_{62}^{2009}}{\mathrm{EAL}_{62}^{n}} \tag{15.1}$$

The longevity indicator[6] for a particular year n, EAL^n, is computed as follows:

$$\mathrm{EAL}^n = \sum_{x=62}^{100} 1.02^{-(x+0.5-62)} \frac{L_x^n}{l_{62}^n} \tag{15.2}$$

where

x is the age from retirement.

l_x^n is the number of persons alive at age x, in particular, $l_{62}^n = 1$; the number of persons alive at age $x + 1$ is obtained using the formula: $l_{x+1}^n = \left(1 - q_x^n/1000\right)\ l_x^n$ with q_x^n being the mortality rate at age x in year n.

L_x^n is the average number of persons alive in the cohort at ages $(x, x + 1)$, i.e. $L_x^n = \left(l_x^n + l_{x+1}^n\right)/2$.

The goals of the pension reform of 2017: The economic downturn of 2008 escalated discussion concerning the earnings-related pension scheme in Finland and, in particular, the incentives it offers employees to extend their working careers. As a result, the effective retirement age[7] should increase by 3 years in the next 17 years from the level of 59.4 years of 2008 to the level of 62.4 in 2025. Second, the fiscal sustainability of the government should be aided such that the fiscal gap decreases by one percentage point.

Other goals included stabilising pension expenditure ratios and setting pension contributions at a sustainable level. In order to achieve these goals, the social partners agreed that, after 2027, the general retirement age will be linked to life expectancy so that the ratio of the theoretical working career (time between the age of 18 and the general retirement age) to the theoretical time spent at retirement (defined as the life expectancy at the general retirement age) remains unchanged. Therefore the new life expectancy coefficient in year n is defined as:

[6]According to standard actuarial practice, this indicator can be defined as life annuity at age 62 with a technical interest rate of 2%.

[7]See Kannisto (2016).

$$\mathrm{EAK}^n = \frac{\mathrm{EAL}_{62}^{2009}}{\mathrm{EAL}_{62}^{2026}} \frac{\mathrm{EAL}_{65}^{2026}}{\mathrm{EAL}_{x_r}^{n}}, \tag{15.3}$$

with x_r being the current general retirement age.

This results in a mitigation of the life expectancy coefficient so that the rise in life expectancy is not taken into account twice. It follows from the formula that the mitigated coefficient is slightly undercompensating in terms of the capital value of the old age pension.

15.3.2 Portugal

Portugal is projected to face faster ageing than most EU Member States in the coming decades. In Portugal,[8] the initial pension of the earnings-related DB pension scheme is calculated according to the following formula:

Initial pension amount = reference earnings × accrual rate × sustainability factor.

The reference earnings measure was the best 10 out of the final 15 years. From 2017, this base has been redefined to be lifetime average earnings.

The accrual rate ranges between 2% and 2.3% depending on the year of earnings.

The sustainability factor is an automatic adjustment of the pensions system in response to changes in life expectancy and longevity and it is used to reduce the pension at retirement. This factor results from the relation between the average life expectancy at age 65 in 2006[9] and the one that will occur in the year before the pension claim. Therefore, the sustainability factor for year n can be computed as follows:

$$\frac{\mathrm{LI}_{65}^{2006}}{\mathrm{LI}_{65}^{n}}, \tag{15.4}$$

with LI being the average life expectancy at age 65.

Also, the normal retirement age has been raised from 65 to 66 years of age (or 43 years of contributions for a full pension) and it could be raised further, linked to changes in life expectancy at retirement.

---

[8]In Portugal, the occupational pension market is relatively small, mostly as a result of the generous public pension system.

[9]The new law foresees that the reference year may be changed in response to increased life expectancy or other contingent factors that make pensions unsustainable.

The Portuguese pension reform will also contribute to reduce the high net replacement rate,[10] OECD (2017), which was around 90% in 2014.

15.3.3 Germany

In Germany, the pension system relates the amount of retirement pension to the number of years contributed and the pensionable income for each of those years. This point-based system has undergone a series of reforms over the last years.

The pension point value[11] which is generally adjusted annually in relation to the gross wage growth can be altered further on (mainly lowered) by two additional factors: the *contribution factor* and the *sustainability factor*.

The *contribution factor* accounts for changes of the contribution rate to the statutory pension scheme and to the subsidised (voluntary) private pension schemes. An increase of contribution rates will reduce the adjustment of the pension point value. Also, an upper ceiling in the contribution provision was introduced in 2004.

As explained by Börsch-Supan (2007), the formula for revaluing pensions in payment in Germany includes a *sustainability factor*,[12] proposed by the *Rürup-Kommission*, that takes into account the system's dependency ratio. This *sustainability factor*, which measures the change of the number of standardised contributors in relation to the number of standardised pensioners, links the adjustment of the pension point value to the changes in the statutory pension scheme's dependency ratio, the ratio of pensioners to contributors.

Mathematically, the amount of the pension in year t, P_t, can be expressed as follows:

$$P_t = P_{t-1} \cdot \frac{\text{ANW}_{t-1}}{\text{ANW}_{t-2}} \cdot \underbrace{\left[\left(1 - \frac{\text{PQ}_{t-1}}{\text{PQ}_{t-2}}\right) \cdot \alpha + 1\right]}_{\text{Sustainability Factor (SF)}} \tag{15.5}$$

where

[10]The net replacement rate is defined as the individual net pension entitlement divided by the net pre-retirement earnings, taking into account personal income taxes and social security contributions paid by workers and pensioners.

[11]The pension point value is valid for newly retired and already retired pensioners.

[12]In 2005, Austria also introduced a so-called sustainability factor (Knell et al. 2006), but it is very different from the German one. The Austrian sustainability factor is to be applied if the trend in life expectancy deviates upwardly from the assumed demographic path.

PQ = [pensioners/(contributors + unemployed)] or the number of equivalent pensioners per number of equivalent contributors.[13]

ANW is the average earnings of all employees, net of taxes and social insurance contributions.

α is a parameter which redistributes the adjustment between pensioners and contributors, which means that its values will lie between 0 and 1. If α equals zero, the current benefit indexation formula remains unchanged and all the weight of the adjustment, generated by a higher proportion of pensioners in the population, would be shouldered entirely by the contributors. If α equals one, all the weight of the adjustment would fall on the pensioners. According to Börsch-Supan and Wilke (2006), the Commission fixed the value of α at 0.25, which was considered to respond to the objective of the *Riester* reform: to maintain the contribution rate below 20% until 2020 and below 22% until 2030. Furthermore, it was stipulated that the government would have to intervene if the pension level were to fall below 67% of net earnings.

Ferh and Habermann (2006) have simulated the effects of the *sustainability factor*, which measures changes in the dependency ratio, and of the *demographic factor*,[14] which takes into account changes in life expectancy. They concluded that both reform packages redistribute resources from currently living middle-aged generations to younger and future living generations. However, the redistribution is much stronger under the 'sustainability factor' than under the 'demographic factor'. Similarly, both reforms increase the risk exposure of currently middle-aged generations and reduce the risk for younger and future ones.

Additionally to the *contribution* and *sustainability factors*, Germany introduced a specific 'pension assurance law'. This states that the pension point value will not decrease in case of decreasing wages. Theoretical decreases of the pension point value are temporarily frozen and will be counterbalanced with future increases of the pension point value starting from the year 2011.

According to Sailer (2015), the increase in the contribution rates maintains adequate replacement rates whilst raising the retirement age[15] accounts for longevity increases. In this sense, the German pension system faces the challenge of an ageing population and achieves a balance between affordable coverage, adequate benefits and retaining sufficient financial reserves.

[13]It is worth noting that when determining the number of pensioners, an adjustment is made according to the number of people that receive the minimum pension. An adjustment is also made to the number of contributors according to the contribution bases, and the number of unemployed has been added to the formula in order to exclude cyclical effects on the dependency ratio.

[14]The former conservative government in Germany introduced a so-called *demographic factor*, which was supposed to reduce future benefits in accordance with the increase in future life expectancy. This reform was suspended soon after the change of government in 1998.

[15]In Germany, the statutory retirement age increases gradually from 65 in 2011 to 67 by 2030.

15.3.4 Sweden[16]

Sweden has a notional defined-contribution (NDC) scheme[17] and has published an actuarial income statement and balance sheet[18] every year since 2001. Also, the Swedes have gone further by triggering an automatic balancing system if the balance ratio that emerges from the balance sheet reveals that the pension system is partially solvent.

As shown by Valdés-Prieto (2000), it is only with strong restrictive conditions (constant productivity growth and a set demographic level) that automatic short-term financial viability, i.e. a constant cash-flow balance between benefits and contributions, can be maintained under a notional model. This is common sense if there is no provision for a buffer fund. The financial sustainability of the NDC scheme has to be supported by well-known conditions based on the growth in the number of contributors and real wages and, according to Settergren and Mikula (2005), by other not so well-known conditions such as changes in mortality patterns. Valdés-Prieto (2000) shows that, even when applying the most favourable formula, NDCs can only achieve this in a rather unrealistic steady state. Hence, NDCs also require other financial modification mechanisms (ABMs) to be imposed in the same way as traditional defined-benefit systems.

Following Settergren (2001), if, for some reason, the balance ratio[19] is less than one, the ABM is triggered. This consists basically of reducing the growth in pension liability, i.e. the pensions in payment and the contributors' notional pensions capital. Thus, the *balance index* rather than the change in average salary (expressed by an *income or salary index*) is used to revalue the pensions in payment and the notional account of each contributor.

The expression for calculating the *balance index* in year t, BI_t, the first year in a period when the balance ratio is less than one, can be expressed as follows:

$$\mathrm{BI}_t = I_t \cdot \mathrm{BT}_t^* \tag{15.6}$$

where I_t is the income index in year t, i.e. an index for the level of average income in year t, and BT_t^* is the damped balance ratio in year t, as a measure of the ratio between assets and liabilities.

In year $t + 1$ the balance index is equal to:

---

[16]See Chap. 11 for a more detailed description of the Swedish public pension system together with the compilation of the actuarial income statement and balance sheet.

[17]An NDC scheme reproduces the logic of a financial defined-contribution pension plan (accumulated contributions are converted into a life pension annuity taking into account life expectancy according to standard actuarial practice) within a PAYG framework.

[18]See Boado-Penas and Vidal-Meliá (2012) for more details on the Swedish actuarial balance sheet.

[19]Alonso-García et al. (2017) study the extent to which the balance ratio and also a liquidity ratio are affected by fluctuations in economic and demographic conditions and explore the introduction of an ABM into the NDC pension scheme.

$$\mathrm{BI}_{t+1} = \mathrm{BI}_t \cdot \left(\frac{I_{t+1}}{I_t}\right) \cdot \mathrm{BT}^*_{t+1} = I_{t+1} \cdot \mathrm{BT}^*_t \cdot \mathrm{BT}^*_{t+1} \tag{15.7}$$

At the end of year $t - 1$, the indexation of pensions in payment is calculated as the ratio between the balance index for year t and the income index for year $t - 1$ divided by 1.016. Indexation of notional pension capital is calculated as the ratio between the balance index for year t and the income index for year $t - 1$. At the end of year t, there is analogous indexation of the ratio between the balance index for year $t + 1$ and the balance index for year t.

Indexation by the balance index ceases when the balance index reaches the level of the income index. Therefore, if the balance ratio is greater than one when the mechanism is triggered, the revaluation of the contributors' notional pension capital and pensions in payment will be greater than the change in average salary. This means that after a period of low returns, as a consequence of this mechanism, a period of higher-than-normal returns follows.[20]

According to Barr and Diamond (2011), the Swedish mechanism has some undesirable results. First, it creates the likelihood of large shocks for retirees. Specifically, when the balance ratio fell below one for the first time in 2008, the adjustment to be made[21] in 2010 was so large that the government responded by altering the mechanims to reduce the initial impact on pensions in payment. Slower adjustment means that more adjustment will be needed later. Secondly, the authors state that the mechanism, whilst disadvantaging retirees, tends to advantage workers.

From 2011, several changes have been made affecting the ABM calculation. The first was to smooth the value of the buffer fund used in the balance ratio. Thus, instead of using the value of the buffer fund as of 31 December in a specific year, the average of the value of the buffer fund as of 31 December in the last 3 years was used. As stated in Chap. 11, this change was legislated despite the Swedish Pensions Agency's objection concerning the proposed measure's inefficiency. Also, from 2017 onwards, the balance index will be calculated using the *damped*[22] balance ratio, which is a new form of smoothing the balance ratio. In terms of the dimension of adequacy,[23] the government lowered taxes for pensioners to partially offset the negative effects of the automatic balancing. Also, Sweden continues to support and promote occupational and third pillar pension schemes.

---

[20]See Barr and Diamond (2011).

[21]The adjustment is being made 2 years after, reflecting lags in calculation and implementation.

[22]For more details on the damped balance ratio, see Chap. 11 and the Swedish Social Insurance Agency (2015).

[23]See The 2015 Pension Adequacy Report (2015).

15.3.5 Canada

In Canada, the first pillar is the old age security programme that provides a universal basic benefit payable at age 65 based on citizenship and year of residence. The second mandatory pillar consists of the earnings-related Canada and Québec Pension Plans (CPP and QPP). Both plans are financed by employer and employees' contributions and also by investment earnings. Funds not immediately required to pay benefits are invested in the markets by the respective plans' fund managers; therefore, these plans are partially funded. In Canada, according to Billig and Ménard (2013), the first two pillars replace about 40% of pre-retirement earnings for individuals with earnings at the average level.

In 1997, Canada introduced a sustainability clause and other changes in the Canada Pension Plan (CPP), converting it into a partially funded system. Bosworth and Weaver (2011) state that the mechanism provides a combination of benefit freezes and contribution increases in the event that the system is projected to go into long-term deficit.

The Chief Actuary reports the minimum[24] contribution rate that will sustain the plan to the federal and provincial Ministers of Finance for them to make recommendations as to whether the benefits and/or legislated contribution rate should be changed. The actuarial report, which is carried out every 3 years with a time horizon of 75 years, is based on the best-estimate assumptions. According Vidal Melia et al. (2009), if the actuarial review concludes that the plan is not financially sustainable, and the federal and provincial Ministers of Finance cannot reach an agreement to increase or maintain the legislated rate, a mechanism will be triggered to keep the actuarial deficit in check by increasing the legislated contribution rate by the amount necessary to cover 50% of the deficit, whilst the benefits are frozen for 3 years until a new actuarial valuation is carried out. At the next actuarial review, the minimum contribution rate is calculated based on the updated assumptions and the same process is repeated. This framework is called an *insufficient rates provision*. It was also established by law that any improvement or extension of benefits or pensions would have to be financed in advance, i.e. through a funded system.

According to Vidal Melia et al. (2009), unlike the Swedish system, in which the weight of the adjustment falls exclusively on the amount paid to current and future pensioners, given that the contribution rate is by definition fixed at a level of 18.5%, the Canadian mechanism shares the adjustment between pensions and contributions. Also, Sakamoto (2013) states that an important advantage of the Canadian ABM is that the burden of returning to sustainability is shared between workers, through higher contributions, and retirees, through slightly lower benefits.

[24]The minimum contribution rate consists of two components. The first component is applicable to the plan excluding the full funding provision for improvement or extension of benefits and is referred to the steady-state contribution. The second component of the minimum contribution rate consists of the full funding rate for increased or new benefits.

The main disadvantage of this type of mechanism is that the automatic adjustment occurs only if the Canadian Parliament cannot first decide on an adjustment, which is considered to be unlikely. The Canadian mechanism is really a semi-automatic balance mechanism.

The 27th CPP Actuarial Report, OSFI (2016) determines the minimum contribution rate to be 9.79% of contributory earnings for the year 2019 and thereafter,[25] i.e. below the legislated contribution rate. With the legislated contribution rate of 9.9%, total assets are expected to increase significantly over the near term and then will continue increasing at a slower pace. Contributions, at a rate of 9.9%, are projected to be more than sufficient to cover pension expenditures over the period 2016–2020. Thereafter, investment earnings will be more than sufficient to make up the difference between contributions and expenditures. The excess resulting from the legislated rate of the plan (9.9%) over the minimum contribution rate (9.79%) allows for the plan's assets to grow more quickly.

On June 2016, the Ministers of Finance of the provinces of Canada agreed to enhance the Canada Pension Plan; later this agreement was converted in the latest Pension Reform (Bill[26] C-26) to the CPP. The enhancement will have the following design features[27]:

- Increase the amount of the retirement pension, as well as the survivor's and disability pensions and the post-retirement benefit, subject to the amount of additional contributions made and the number of years over which those contributions are made.
- Increase the maximum level of pensionable earnings by 14% as of 2025.
- Provide for the making of additional contributions, beginning in 2019.
- Provide for the creation of the Additional Canada Pension Plan Account and the accounting of the funds in relation to it.
- Include the additional contributions and increased benefits in the financial review provisions of the Act and authorise the Governor to make regulations in relation to those provisions.
- Amend the *Canada Pension Plan Investment Board Act* to provide for the transfer of funds between the Investment Board and the Additional Canada Pension Plan Account and to provide for the preparation of financial statements in relation to amounts managed by the Investment Board in relation to the additional contributions and increased benefits.
- Amend the Income Tax Act in order to increase the Working Income Tax Benefit to help low-income earners and provide a deduction for additional employee contributions to help low-income earners.

---

[25]The legislated contribution rate of 9.9% applies to the first 3 years after the valuation year, i.e. to the current review period of 2016–2018.

[26]Parliament of Canada (2016).

[27]The 27th CPP Actuarial Report does not reflect the changes to the CPP resulting from this enhancement. A new actuarial report will be prepared that sets out the extent to which the enhancement affects the estimates contained in the 27th CPP Actuarial Report.

15.3.6 Japan

According to the Ministry of Health, Labour and Welfare (2014), Japan's demographic structure, which is already the world's most aged, is projected to age still further, with the proportion of the population aged 65 or older (i.e. the ageing rate) projected to reach 36.1% in 2040 (when the second-generation baby boomers reach the age of 65) and then climb still further to 39.9% in 2060.

The 2004 pension reforms (Ministry of Health, Labour and Welfare 2014) introduced an actuarial mechanism (also called financial stabiliser, macroeconomic indexation or modified indexation) for automatically balancing benefits and contributions. Moreover, in order to avoid imposing an excessive burden on people of active age in the future, a fixed cap was placed on contributions. Future benefit levels are then automatically adjusted in order to achieve equilibrium between benefits and contributions in the long term within the scope of the financial resources (including use of reserves) imposed by this cap. The mechanism is applied to both the revaluation of the contribution bases and the revaluation of pensions in payment. It takes into account both improvements in life expectancy and population increases or decreases.

Whether to continue to apply the modified indexation or not is determined on the basis of an actuarial valuation. The Japanese actuarial valuation, compiled at least every 5 years,[28] projects contribution revenues and pension expenditures over a period of 95 years based on changes in demographic structures, taking into account the financial stabiliser. The modified indexation system is activated if the financial projections of the social security pension schemes for the next 95 years, under the normal indexation regime, show financial imbalance. Japan applies what is known as the *limited balance* or *closed period balancing method*, i.e. the period of financial equilibrium is finite. As Sakamoto (2008) points out, the financial stabiliser gradually reduces the level of benefits until financial equilibrium is attained, i.e. once financial equilibrium is attained under normal indexation, the application of modified indexation is suspended.

According to Vidal Melia et al. (2009), the Japanese financial stabiliser was proposed as an adaptation of the Swedish ABM despite the large design differences between the two pension systems. Sakamoto (2013) states that the contribution programme was fixed to reduce the anxiety of younger generations that the contribution rate might be endlessly raised.

The modified indexation, to revalue the contribution bases until retirement, is the net growth in salaries, β, minus the modifier and can be computed as follows:

[28] Although the application of the modified indexation is determined every 5 years, the actual rate of modified indexation is determined every year on the basis of the past experience.

$$\beta - \underbrace{(\delta + 0.3\%)}_{\text{Modifier}} \tag{15.8}$$

with δ being the rate of decrease of the active participants in the social security pension systems (or zero if it is increasing).

For the indexation of pensions in payment, the modified indexation is as follows:

$$\text{CPI} - \underbrace{(\delta + 0.3\%)}_{\text{Modifier}} \tag{15.9}$$

In both formulae, 0.3% is defined as the increase rate of unisex life expectancy at the age of 65, i.e. the adjustment rate that compensates for the increase in costs deriving from the increase in longevity.

Furthermore, there are some conditions for the activation of the modifier. If the CPI or the salary growth is negative, the new indexation is not activated, i.e. the modifier is assumed to be equal to zero. Also, if the CPI or the rate of salary increase is positive but less than the modifier, the modified indexation is replaced by zero (Sakamoto 2013).

Since the modified indexation was introduced in 2004, it has only been activated once – in fiscal year 2015, i.e. only once for the last 13 years. Now, the Japanese government is concentrating all its efforts on revitalising the Japanese economy, and we note that prices have been trending upwards since the second half of 2013 and wages too exhibited growth in 2014 (Ministry of Health, Labour and Welfare 2014).

During the period 1999–2001 (Whitehouse 2009), prices fell in successive years by 0.3%, 0.7% and 0.7%. The government chose not to impose reductions in nominal benefits at the time. In part, this probably reflects the political difficulties of cutting nominal benefit levels. However, there was also an economic rationale: the government was keen to encourage household consumption as a means of boosting the economy. The overall increase[29] in real pensions – because of deflation – over the period 1999–2001 was 1.7%. However, adjusting pensions to reflect inflation but ignoring deflation has a 'ratchet' effect – pensions can go up but never down – which might pose fiscal problems. In order to avoid such problems, Japan will in future reduce benefits to claw back this gain. A factor of 98.3% (reflecting the overall 1.7% price fall) will be applied to future pension levels. Furthermore, as deflation continued, the policy was changed. Prices fell by 0.9% in 2002 and 0.3% in both 2003 and 2005. Benefits were reduced in line with the falls in these years.

Finally, three main aspects were identified in the report of the National Council on Social Security System Reform (published on August 2013) and the Act on Promotion of Reform to Establish a Sustainable Social Security System (Act No. 112 of 2013). The three aspects are as follows:

---

[29]These effects of keeping the benefit level at a point higher than the system presumes were nullified by the 2012 reform by gradually reducing the benefit level until the beginning of fiscal year 2015 (1 April 2015).

1. Full application of modified indexation even when prices and wages growth are low or negative. When these growth rates are low, the modified indexation may become negative after subtracting the modifier from the normal indexation. The proposal is that the negative modified indexation should be applied even in such a case. When these growth rates are negative, the modified indexation becomes even more negative. The proposal is that the greater negative modified indexation should be applied.
2. Further widening of the coverage of the pension plan amongst employees.
3. Lengthening of the contribution payment period and deferral of the age at which one starts to receive social security pensions.

These three aspects are being considered as a part of a new reform to the current pension system. However, they have not yet been incorporated.

15.4 Conclusions

This chapter has described the different automatic mechanisms that have been recently set up in six typical developed countries (Finland, Portugal, Germany, Sweden, Canada and Japan) to guide the system onto the road to long-term financial stability. Each of these ABMs aims to ensure the periodic monitoring of sources of pressure on pensions and to build public confidence. The ABMs analysed are implemented together with other measures such as an increase in retirement age for the case of Finland, Portugal and Germany. In the case of Sweden and Canada, the ABM is linked to a solvency indicator that derives from an actuarial balance whilst in Japan the ABM is included in the actuarial projections carried out every 5 years.

In Finland and Portugal, the automatic mechanism links the amount of the initial pension to changes in life expectancy, whilst in Sweden, Germany, Canada and Japan, there is a combination of measures that affect both contributors and pensioners. In some cases, such as Finland and Sweden, the ABM has already been through recent reforms. Other countries such as Japan are considering new changes to the mechanism. The Canadian Pension Plan has also been enhanced by increasing the amount of benefit amongst other measures and therefore increasing the pension adequacy. The fact of reforming ABMs and/or including other kinds of measures into the pension system does seriously question the effectiveness of the automatic mechanisms studied.

In pension systems, there is often tunnel vision (Barr 2013), defined as a tendency to consider adequacy and sustainability separately. In many countries, the Ministry of Finance worries about sustainability and the Ministry of Social Security worries about adequacy, with little dialogue occurring between the two agencies. In this regard, a link between retirement ages and life expectancy would present one effective form of increasing sustainability in public pension systems, and at the same time, by increasing retirement age, it would have a positive effect on pension adequacy. In fact, most countries have increased their statutory retirement ages based on current and projected increases in life expectancy. However, this parametric reform is not the panacea and is usually taken in combination with other reforms. Another solution for improving sustainability and adequacy simultaneously would be to decrease the amount of the pension benefit, through a sustainability factor, and at the same time increase the contribution rate. This is the kind of approach taken by Germany. Further research is needed to evaluate whether there the resulting adjustments are shared fairly between contributors and pensioners.

Acknowledgements Humberto Godínez-Olivares is grateful for the financial support from the National Council of Science and Technology (CONACYT) CVU-204504 and the IPE Pensions Scholarship Fund. María del Carmen Boado-Penas is grateful for the financial assistance received from the Spanish Ministry of Economy and Competitiveness (project ECO2012-36685 and ECO2015-65826-P).

References

Alonso-García, J., Boado-Penas, M. C., & Devolder, P. (2017). Automatic balancing mechanisms for notional defined contribution accounts in the presence of uncertainty. *Scandinavian Actuarial Journal*, 1–24. https://doi.org/10.1080/03461238.2017.1304984.

Barr, N. (2013). *The pension system in Finland: Adequacy, sustainability and system design*. Finnish Centre for Pensions: Helsinki.

Barr, N., & Diamond, P. A. (2011). Improving Sweden's automatic pension adjustment mechanism. *Center for Retirement Research Brief, 11*(2), 1–8.

Billig, A., & Ménard, J. C. (2013). Actuarial balance sheets as a tool to assess the sustainability of social security pension systems. *International Social Security Review, 66*(2), 31–52.

Boado-Penas, M. C., & Vidal-Meliá, C. (2012). Chapter 23: The actuarial balance of the pay-as-you-go pension system: The Swedish NDC model versus the US DB model. In R. Holzmann, E. Palmer, & D. Robalino (Eds.), *NDC pension schemes in a changing pension world, volume 2: Gender, politics, and financial stability* (pp. 443–489). Washington, DC: World Bank. ISBN (paper): 978-0-8213-9478-6 ISBN (electronic): 978-0-8213-9479-3 DOI: https://doi.org/10.1596/978-0-8213-9478-6.

Börsch-Supan, A. H. (2007). Rational pension reform. *The Geneva Papers on Risk and Insurance - Issues and Practice, 32*(4), 430–446.

Börsch-Supan, A. H., & Wilke, C. B. (2006). Chapter 22: The German public pension system: How it will become an NDC system look-alike. In R. Holzmann & E. Palmer (Eds.), *Pension reform: Issues and prospects for notional defined contribution (NDC) schemes*. Washington, DC: World Bank. ISBN-13: 978-0-8213-6038-5 eISBN-10: 0-8213-6038-X DOI: https://doi.org/10.1596/978-0-8213-6038-5.

Bosworth, B., & Weaver, K. (2011). *Social security on auto-pilot: International experience with automatic stabilizer mechanisms*. Center for Retirement Research at Boston College. CRR WP 2011-18.

D'Addio, A. C., & Whitehouse, E. (2012). *Towards financial sustainability of pension systems. The role of automatic-adjustment mechanisms in OECD and EU countries, report number 8/12*. Bern: Federal Social Insurance Office.

European Commission. (2012). *The 2012 ageing report: Economic and budgetary projections for the EU27 Member States (2010–2060)*. Joint Report prepared by the European Commission (DG ECFIN) and the Economic Policy Committee (AWG). http://ec.europa.eu/economy_finance/publications/european_economy/2012/2012-ageing-report_en.htm

Ferh, H., & Habermann, C. (2006). Pension reform and demographic uncertainty: The case of Germany. *The Journal of Pensions Economics and Finance, 5*(1), 69–90.
Godínez-Olivares, H., Boado-Penas, M. C., & Pantelous, A. A. (2016a). How to finance pensions: Optimal strategies for pay-as-you-go pension systems. *Journal of Forecasting, 35*(1), 13–33.
Godínez-Olivares, H., Boado-Penas, M. C., & Haberman, S. (2016b). Optimal strategies for pay-as-you-go pension finance: A sustainability framework. *Insurance: Mathematics and Economics, 69*, 117–126.
Kannisto, J. (2016). *Effective retirement age in the Finnish earnings-related pension scheme*. Statistics from the Finnish Centre for Pensions 03/2016.
Knell, M., Köhler-Töglhofer, W., & Prammer, D. (2006). The Austrian pension system – How recent reforms have changed fiscal sustainability and pension benefits. *Monetary Policy & the Economy, Q2*(06), 69–93.
Ministry of Health, Labour and Welfare. (2014). *Summaries of the 2014 actuarial valuation and reform options*. Pension Bureau. Sustainable and reliable pension system.
OECD. (2015). *Pensions at a glance 2015: OECD and G20 indicators*. Paris: OECD Publishing.
OECD. (2016). *The OECD pensions outlook*. Paris: OECD Publishing.
OECD. (2017). *Net pension replacement rates (indicator)*. Paris: OECD Publishing. doi: https://doi.org/10.1787/4b03f028-en (Accessed on 27 May 2017).
Office of the Superintendent of Financial Institutions (OSFI). (2016). *Actuarial report 27th on the Canada pension plan as of 31 December 2015*. Office of the Superintendent of financial institutions Canada – Office of the Chief Actuary.
Parliament of Canada. (2016). *Bill C-26*. First Session, 42nd Parliament, 64–65 Elizabeth II, 2015–2016, Statutes of Canada 2016, chapter 14. http://www.parl.gc.ca/HousePublications/Publication.aspx?Language=E&Mode=1&DocId=8708008. Assented 15 December 2016.
Sailer, M. (2015). *Adequate contribution rates for sustainable pension funding: Lessons from the German debate and actual practice, German pension insurance, Berlin*. Department for Research and Development.
Sakamoto, J. (2008). *Roles of the social security pension schemes and the minimum benefit level under the automatic balancing mechanism* (NRI Papers No. 125). Nomura Research Institute, Japan.
Sakamoto, J. (2013). *Automatic balancing mechanisms*. Preliminary draft, Nomura Research Institute. https://www.actuaries.org/lyon2013/papers/PBSS_Sakamoto.pdf
Settergren, O. (2001). The automatic balance mechanism of the Swedish pension system – A non-technical introduction. *Wirtschaftspolitische Blätter, 4*(2001), 339–349.
Settergren, O., & Mikula, B. D. (2005). The rate of return of pay-as-you-go pension systems: A more exact consumption-loan model of interest. *The Journal of Pensions Economics and Finance, 4*(2), 115–138.
Swedish Social Insurance Agency. (2015). *Orange report: Annual report of the Swedish pension system 2015*. Stockholm: Swedish Social Insurance Agency.
The 2015 Pension Adequacy Report. (2015). *Current and future income adequacy in old age in the EU*. Joint report by the Social Protection Committee (SPC) and the European Commission (DG EMPL).
Valdés-Prieto, S. (2000). The financial stability of notional account pensions. *Scandinavian Journal of Economics, 102*(3), 395–417.
Vidal Melia, C., Boado-Penas, M. C., & Settergren, O. (2009). Automatic balance mechanisms in pay-as-you-go pension systems. *Geneva Papers on Risk and Insurance - Issues and Practice, 34* (2), 287–317.
Whitehouse, E. R. (2009). *Pensions, purchasing-power risk, inflation and indexation* (OECD Social, Employment and Migration Working Papers, No. 77). OECD Publishing. https://doi.org/10.1787/227182142567.
World Bank. (2008). *The World Bank pension conceptual framework: World Bank pension reform primer series*. Washington, DC: World Bank. http://documents.worldbank.org/curated/en/389011468314712045/The-World-Bank-pension-conceptual-framework.

Chapter 16
The Role of Complementary Pensions

Mercedes Ayuso, Montserrat Guillen, and Diego Valero

Abstract Recent reforms of public pension systems implemented in various countries, including Spain, have sought to ensure the sustainability of benefits. However, achieving a structural budget balance (i.e. long-run equality between income and expenditure) may result in a decrease in the replacement rate or in the percentage that the pension represents of the last salary. The development of complementary pension schemes, both occupational and personal, is presented as a feasible alternative for increasing the adequacy of benefits. However, both systems face significant challenges in their further implementation, with business structures, on occasions, being highly concentrated in small and medium enterprises and under the significant influence of longevity, inflation and interest rate risks. This chapter presents a comprehensive analysis of the possibilities offered by the second and the third pillars to complement public pension systems and their possible innovations for increasing their level of penetration in different countries.

Keywords Sufficiency · Notional defined contribution · Occupational pension schemes · Individual pension schemes · Defined contribution schemes · Defined benefit schemes · Defined ambition schemes · Behavioural economics

M. Ayuso (✉) · M. Guillen
Riskcenter, Department of Econometrics, University of Barcelona, Barcelona, Spain
e-mail: mayuso@ub.edu

D. Valero
University of Barcelona, Barcelona, Spain
e-mail: dvalero@novaster.net

M. Peris-Ortiz et al. (eds.), *Economic Challenges of Pension Systems*,
https://doi.org/10.1007/978-3-030-37912-4_16

16.1 Introduction

The relentless increase in longevity is forcing governments around the world to rethink their pension systems. The dependency ratio of the EU-27 is set to rise from below 30% in 2010 to more than 50% in 2060 (UN 2013), and worldwide this growth is equally unstoppable, as can be seen in Fig. 16.1.

This phenomenon, coupled with budget tensions in various countries, has led many governments to adopt reforms aimed, primarily, at guaranteeing the financial sustainability of their public pension systems. Most of these changes operate over extremely broad time frames, so that whilst their effects are gradual, in the long run, their impact should be notable. Thus, the proportion of pensions paid out in relation to average wages, i.e. the pension benefit ratio, is set to fall on average by 9% in Europe in the period to 2060, whilst in some countries, most notably Spain, this fall is likely to be 20%, the third highest in Europe, behind only Cyprus and Portugal (EC 2015).

Public pension system reforms, by focusing their attention on sustainability, are likely to have a considerably negative impact on their adequacy, hence the fall in the replacement rate, i.e. the first pension as a share of the average wage at retirement. This rate is set to fall in Europe by 12.3% by 2060 and in particularly dramatic cases, such as Spain (the highest in Europe), by 30.4%, leaving the rate at 48.6% (EC 2015). The reforms also affect the later value of pensions, not only their initial value, with pension revaluation systems leading to losses in purchasing power: on average, between 8% and 10% a decade after receiving the first pension (reaching 14.5% in Portugal, the highest, and 10.5% in Spain).

Which of the measures adopted by these reforms have had such a dramatic effect on pension adequacy? In short, all those that impact the retirement age, in the form of (1) an increase in the absolute statutory retirement age; (2) an increase in the statutory retirement age linked to the evolution in life expectancy; (3) factors of sustainability, which encourage the prolongation of active working life by reducing

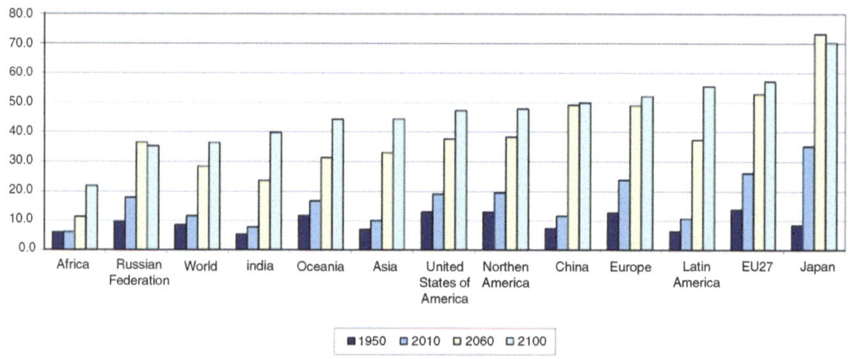

Fig. 16.1 Dependence ratio from 1950 to 2100. (*Source:* UN World Population Prospects: The 2012 Revision)

pensions; (4) notional defined contribution schemes,[1] which encourage the prolongation of active working life by granting rights linked to contributions; and (5) increases in the requirements to obtain a full pension, such as additional number of years of contribution.

Examples of countries in which these measures have been implemented include Denmark, which introduced a retirement age formula based on the evolution of life expectancy, which is recalculated every 5 years; the United Kingdom, which seeks to maintain a balance between those that are active and those that are passive (the latter being approximately one-third of the former), with reviews every 6 years; Portugal, which uses a criterion of automatic adjustment of the retirement age to two-thirds of the increase in life expectancy; Cyprus and Greece, which increase the retirement age by 100% of the increase in life expectancy, with 5-year and 3-year reviews, respectively; the Netherlands, which does the same, as long as life expectancy increases by more than 3 months per year; and Slovakia, which considers a 5-year moving average of life expectancy and makes automatic adjustments.

As mentioned, other systems have an indirect effect on the retirement age. In Europe, the main exponents of this are Sweden, Italy, Poland, Latvia and Norway, which adopted notional defined contribution schemes; Finland, which established a life expectancy coefficient for each age cohort at the age of 62 (the level of comparison for each year being that of 2009) applied to the pension; Spain, which approved a sustainability factor, similar to the one adopted in Finland, but with a 5-year review of life expectancy at the age of 65 in 2014, also applied to pensions; Germany, which introduced a sustainability factor based on an adjustment of pensions in course of payment to compensate for changes in the dependency rate; and France, which directly increased the statutory period of contributions.

In addition, there have been, in combination with, or independently of, the above measures, reforms that (1) affect the validation of pension rights; (2) increase the number of years taken into consideration for determining the pension, almost to the point of considering complete working lives; and (3) vary pension indexation, subjecting benefits to more restrictive criteria than simply inflation or wage increases.

In short, the numerous reforms that have been undertaken, mainly, but not exclusively, in Europe, have sought to guarantee the sustainability of pension schemes, at the expense of their adequacy. This has necessarily led people to seek other ways of guaranteeing themselves a pension to allow them the standard of living they want. What is true is that, accordingly, various States have begun to promote or improve private complementary pension systems with reforms that favour their development and which allow them to supplement public pensions and so guarantee adequate benefits.

[1] A broad definition of these systems can be found in Barr (2006).

16.2 Legislative Changes in Complementary Pensions in Europe

There are basically three ways to approach the development of complementary pension systems: (1) making them mandatory, (2) making them semi-mandatory and (3) introducing financial and/or tax incentives. Recent reforms in Europe have tended to follow one of these three paths. The first path has been taken by Bulgaria, Estonia, Croatia, Lithuania, Latvia and Romania, as they have established mandatory defined contribution plans for all workers. Austria, Belgium, Denmark, Malta, the Netherlands, Portugal, Sweden and Norway, in one form or another, require the existence of occupational pension plans, either by law or by collective agreement. All of these, in common with the semi-mandatory plans that we discuss below, are workplace pension plans and do not affect individual schemes.

The most obvious exponent of the quasi-mandatory formula is the United Kingdom, with its National Employment Savings Trust (NEST), a system of savings for corporate retirement that is founded on two basic principles of behavioural economics, which we shall return to later: auto-enrolment and the default option. In this system, all workers aged 22 and over are automatically enrolled in the scheme unless they expressly indicate otherwise or they are already part of an occupational pension scheme in which the contribution rate is higher than that established in the new system. This rate is 8% of the salary, financed on a tripartite basis (the employee contributes 3% of the salary and the employer 4% and the State grants 1% as a tax bonus).[2] Previously, and in other latitudes, New Zealand, with its KiwiSaver model, achieved remarkable increases in the coverage of its complementary plans. NEST's results could not be more promising in the 3 years since it has been running. The number of participating companies is 135,000, with more than 3.3 million workers and an asset volume close to one billion pounds. The average rate of exclusion (members who opt out of the plan) is 7%, but most are in the upper age cohorts (over 55) and correspond to those who believe it is not worth contributing to the scheme as they are due to retire shortly (NEST 2013).

Financial and/or tax incentives used to promote complementary systems form part and parcel of the German reform. Here, the so-called Riester plans provide direct subsidies to those who are unable to make contributions to complementary systems. The use of tax incentives is likewise the exclusive method used in Spain (albeit decreasingly so, given that the benefits have been reduced over time). One of the drawbacks of this system is that it has not been taken up by people with middle and low incomes, owing to the negligible impact that the tax deductions have on their tax returns and income levels, and in general these are the people who most need to have complementary savings.

As might be expected, those countries in which the systems are strictly voluntary present a lower uptake than those in which their introduction is mandatory or quasi-

[2]Details can be consulted at http://www.nestpensionguide.co.uk.

mandatory. Therefore, a commitment on the part of the States to impose, albeit in a soft fashion, occupational pension plans would appear to be an adequate solution to guarantee that the people save to cover the gap generated by the fall in benefits from the public systems.

16.3 Occupational Pension Plans

Occupational pension schemes[3] have traditionally been defined benefit plans, a consequence, in part, of their original design, which saw them as a means of supplementing public pensions. In these plans, the fundamental risks are borne by the sponsor, the company that promotes and finances them. The last 30 years have revealed the potential magnitude of these risks in various cases (insufficient returns on investments, increased longevity and falls in public coverage), with the result that companies have taken steps to change the basic structure of their pension plans by shifting towards defined contribution plans. With this swing of the pendulum, the risks have been fully assumed by the pension plan members, the workers, with the company retaining its commitment to paying a fixed contribution. The final benefit, however, is no longer guaranteed or predetermined, but is the result of the investment of the workers' fixed contributions, net of expenses.

In plans of this type, the benefits are typically received as a lump sum rather than as an annuity. Figure 16.2 shows the distribution of pension fund assets in 2013 between defined contribution and defined benefit plans, and in spite of the historical volume of defined benefit plans, in some countries, including Spain, the assets managed in defined contribution plans now constitute the majority. It should be pointed out that, for countries that have a basic pension system based on fully funded individual accounts, including most Latin American countries and various countries in Eastern Europe and Asia, these systems have been fully defined contribution plans from the outset.

The latest country of some significance in which pension systems have largely been converted to defined contribution plans (with certain distinctions that we shall discuss below) is the United Kingdom, traditional bastion of defined benefit plans. Spain initiated a shift in the same direction in the last decade of the last century.

In examining the pension systems that are now predominant, a number of preliminary reflections are required. First, we should stress the marked asymmetries of information and technical capacity that exist. In general, members of workplace pension systems lack the necessary technical and financial knowledge to undertake a proper evaluation of their pension plan and what it covers in relation to their needs. This fact, together with other characteristics that we shall describe in the next section when speaking of behavioural economics, means they face severe difficulties when it comes to taking decisions.

[3]For a detailed historical analysis of these systems, see Valero (2013).

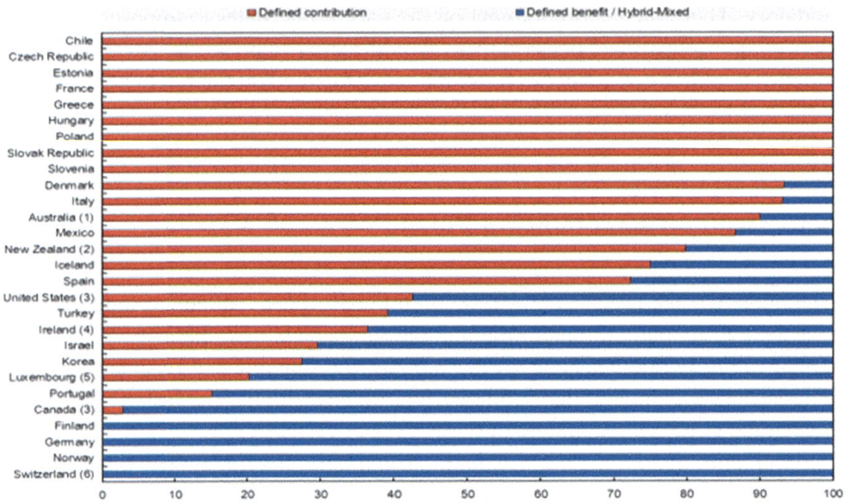

Fig. 16.2 Distribution of pension fund assets in 2013. (*Source:* OECD Global Pension Statistics (2013))

Antolín suggests a series of policy actions to address the problems arising from defined contribution models (Antolín 2013). He stresses ensuring that pension plan design is coherent between the accumulation and pay-out phases and with the overall pension systems, in particular the public system. He also stresses that risks should have an appropriate system of governance that allows them to be detected, measured and managed to minimise their negative consequences.

It is crucial that in these defined contribution systems the participation of the members is high, that is, that the plans extend to all the workers of a company and to all the companies of a country. As mentioned, mandatory or semi-mandatory systems, based on the principle of auto-enrolment, provide encouraging outcomes. Thus, what a system of auto-enrolment ensures is the automatic enrolment of all workers in the workplace pension plan. However, if some workers do not want to join the scheme, then it is they who have to expressly opt out from the plan. As we have seen with the NEST system, the exclusion rate is very low.

It is recommendable that the schemes are based on matching contributions: the workers choose a contribution and the company, according to predetermined rules, equals or improves it, up to a certain limit. This creates a symbiosis of interests, so that the member who contributes a higher level also sees how his company makes a proportional effort and vice versa.

Tax incentives have been used, unsuccessfully at times, as the driving force behind the decision to save. Although important, their impact on the decision-making process should not be critical. Incentives should be adequate and should be based on the premise that savings are rewarded, not that people save to obtain a prize.

The costs under which the systems operate are of special relevance. Barr and Diamond (2010) explain that a 1% annual commission can reduce total accumulation by approximately 20%. Valero (2013) estimates that in compulsory defined contribution pension systems in Latin America, almost 25% of contributions will not capitalise the pension, but go to cover administrative costs.

Pension systems need to be simple, low-cost (Barr and Diamond (2010) explain several examples of success in this regard) and understandable to their members.

Once designed, another critical point is the investment options that exist. Antolín (2013) advocates for default strategies based on investment according to life cycle criterion, which means an automatic adjustment of the investments to the risk profile of the member based on their age. The poor financial training of members can lead, all too frequently, to erroneous decisions that result in the reduction of pension rights. Therefore, the no decision[4] can be the best decision. Taleb (2012) also suggests that not making decisions or procrastination in these matters can be a natural defence.

Pension systems were originally designed so that their benefits took the form of an annuity. As discussed, the defined contribution design makes it easier to perceive the plan's lump sum, but it is convenient to return to the origins of the pension system and somehow guarantee that benefits are received periodically. To do this, it is necessary to innovate in the income market, moving beyond classic annuities, and to start using deferred annuities, programmed retirement or combinations of the two, including lump sum provisions. An interesting analysis can be found in Blake and Boardman (2010).

But even the simplest defined contribution models (those that are limited to establishing a contribution proportional to the equivalent wage for all members) still need to concentrate on the design phase. Blake and Dowd (2013) make a number of very useful considerations: when designing a plan, it is necessary to simulate stochastic models, which incorporate plausible, transparent and consistent hypotheses so as to know, in a probabilistic environment, the different arrival scenarios. Their calibration needs to be periodically reviewed both by auditing and by hypothesis testing and backtesting. All the scenarios that the members might face (level of contribution, growth of the contribution, alternative investments and arrangements) must have a map of quantitative consequences that can help them understand the foreseeable results of the decisions they have to make. The models cannot forget that not all the members will have the same characteristics and, therefore, they must be highly flexible so that their processes can be customised. Moreover, they must also keep in mind the expenses applicable in all phases of the savings and dissavings process. There should be no lack of scenarios and projections about the evolution of longevity and consequent life expectancies. The risk profiles of each member will influence the allocation of assets, which means that, when modelling, another of the variables to take into account is precisely these profiles. It is essential to

[4]This corresponds to the Taoist doctrine of wu wei, literally non-doing or passive achievement. Various editions of Tao Te Ching, ascribed to Lao Tzu, can be consulted; for instance Tzu (2016).

project the overall results up to retirement, but it is especially important to project them beyond retirement, to see how the system works not only at the exact moment of retirement but also in future projections (pension update). In the final phase of modelling, scenario analysis and stress testing are tests that must necessarily be incorporated.

Ambachtsheer (2013) introduces the Tinbergen principle (i.e. sustainable solutions need as many instruments as there are goals) to stress that not all members of an occupational pension plan have the same objectives and that this variety of goals should lead to the use of more than one instrument, or at least, to more than one implementation. Basically, the main objective of the younger participants is high investment returns, whilst for the older participants the main goal is pension payment certainty, both of which are not easy objectives to attain in a single instrument.

When it comes to designing a defined contribution plan, certain principles need to be incorporated to guarantee stability and ensure that the risk is shared (Van Galen et al. 2014). As Einstein claimed: 'Everything should be made as simple as possible, but not simpler'. The plan should offer a range of options that simplify choice. Thaler and Benartzi (2004) compare it to a good restaurant menu: it offers participants the tools (the menu) to adapt the solution (the food) to their needs, but without their having to be experts (chef).

If there is one thing that acts to demotivate the participants of a pension plan, it is that the returns are below expectations. This is why it is necessary to be prudent with the promises made in relation to the plan and to ensure that the returns are not unequal. In the long run, win-lose models do not work. The plan has to be win-win, as in the collaborative systems defined by the Nash equilibrium (Nash 1950). Models must also be robust to extreme situations and objectives and always provide adaptability. We should bear in mind that in a pension scheme not all risks are diversifiable (e.g. individual longevity) that can be shared amongst the group. Diversifiable risks should be shared, but non-diversifiable risks (young participants can tolerate more financial risk than their older counterparts) must be borne by each generating element.

There has been a recent growth in interest in so-called defined ambition plans (Department of Work and Pensions 2012). These are hybrid plans midway between defined benefit and defined contribution schemes. They seek to provide greater certainty in terms of eventual accumulated pension rights than is provided by a defined contribution plan, but with lower cost volatility for firms than under a defined benefit system. This can be achieved, on the foundations of a defined contribution model, by using different channels, some of them mutually complementary: contracting deferred income with defined contributions (thereby eliminating interest rate and longevity risks, at least in the part insured by the income), using surpluses above a desired level of return to constitute buffer reserves that can act when returns are lower (similar in this respect to the so-called cash balance plans) or contracting external guarantees of minimum (absolute or relative) returns, or final capital (similar to guarantee plans), which would lead, in short, to a greater protection of retirement income.

What every pension plan should contain is adequate information. In this regard, for example, current European legislation concerning regulations for institutions for occupational retirement provisions (IORP II), and in particular the Pension Statement, is a notable step forward in terms of the simplicity, comprehensibility and transparency of pension plans. This legislation, which supplements IORP I, stems from the need to strengthen corporate governance and the transparency of pension plans in a defined contribution world, especially after the recent economic crisis. It is a question of strengthening the growth of long-term savings, at a rate above the growth in longevity to which we referred earlier, and of recognising the importance of long-term institutional investment for the European economy. These regulations, approved at the end of 2016, aim to (1) improve the governance of pension plans, (2) strengthen risk management, (3) promote transparency, (4) foster cross-border activity and (5) establish a modern and appropriate framework for pension fund investments. They are comparable to the European insurance regulations known as Solvency II, but do not incorporate the capital requirement pillar, only those of governance and transparency.

The Pension Statement is a physical and electronic document of no more than two pages that provides members with the following information about where they stand in relation to their pension plan: (1) guarantees provided by the plan, (2) level of funding acquired, (3) amount of contributions of the employer, (4) details of all costs applicable to the plan, (5) details of the profitability, (6) possibility and means of making transfers, (7) accumulated level of rights in the plan and (8) pension projection.

In addition, for defined contribution plans, the statement should provide information about (1) accumulated capital; (2) projected capital, at the time of retirement and in subsequent years; (3) expected equivalent monthly income; (4) investment options; (5) graphic information of profitability and risk; (6) sufficient information, prior to withdrawal, to choose options for collection of benefits; and (7) options to receive those benefits.

16.4 Some Considerations Regarding Decumulation

Having referred on various occasions to the rise in longevity, we now examine the risks that derive from this increase, above all, in the decumulation phase. Not only do we need to consider the financial risks following retirement, but we also need to bear in mind those resulting from an unexpected increase in survival, the impact of which can be considerable. During this phase, in which people have to take decisions about their future and their stability, not only in financial terms but also in terms of their health, tax obligations and inheritance, having access to appropriate guidance that helps them make the right decisions is essential. Behavioural economics can help us considerably in seeing how to face these decisions, which all too often result in systematic errors (Valero 2015), as we shall see in the following section.

Some of these erroneous decisions are associated with perceptions of life expectancy. O'Brien et al. (2005) show how people tend to underestimate their future lifespan by about 6 years. More specifically, in the older age brackets (between 60 and 69), this underestimation is 3.5 years, whilst in younger ages, it reaches 10 years. It is worth mentioning that men underestimate their life expectancy by almost twice as much as women. The consequence of this is that if we believe we are going to live less than we actually will, our savings will be insufficient.

People have an inadequate understanding of the risk of longevity and, therefore, fail to assume the risk (Blake 2014). What they hope is that their retirement savings will be enough to sustain their level of consumption throughout their lives, but it is extremely difficult to measure what level of spending they can assume if they are to outlive their savings. To be able to do this, they need to have a knowledge of and a control over many variables, such as where to invest, what returns they can expect, what expenses are associated with the investment, how much erosion can be caused by inflation and, of course, the risk of living longer than expected (risk of longevity).

When deciding how to receive the pension plan benefits, the following points need to be borne in mind: (1) the person's overall financial situation, which will determine the level of wealth to provide for; (2) the financial needs foreseen in the future, which is fundamental for defining the initial level and the degree of pension growth; and (3) the immediate capital needs and the amount to set aside for inheritance (Valero 2013). Thus, the pension acquires a holistic dimension, insofar as it must satisfy all the needs in a global manner: providing sufficient income on which to live, coverage for all risk contingencies (death or disability) and sufficient capital to meet all unforeseen situations and the legacy to be left to heirs.

This seems to indicate the need, at least in part, that payments should be periodic and mandatory. Blake (2014) points out that the value of contracting an annuity is significantly greater than not having one after a certain age (75–80 for a healthy person), which is precisely when the cost of guaranteeing longevity grows exponentially. A longevity insurance could be mandatory after a certain age, within the plan itself (Berstein et al. 2015), but stipulated from the moment of reaching retirement, through deferred income.

Pension systems that allow various forms of payout (each member being free to choose) have to be subject to mechanisms that allow the best decision to be taken, in line, that is, with the member's characteristics and needs (Acuña et al. 2015). To this end, pension system regulations must guarantee that any choice is made within a framework that respects competition, transparency and simplicity and ensures low costs for members (FIAP 2015). When freedom of choice leads to a member making an erroneous choice, this is when the existence of mandatory and default options is most important.

To conclude, a scheme that combines temporary income with deferred annuities, in which the member retains ownership of part of his balance but with the other he assumes the longevity risk, is surely one that brings most value to the member in terms of social protection. This model strikes a balance between flexibility and protection: temporary income gives flexibility and liquidity to face any contingency, whilst the deferred life annuity insures against the risk of longevity, using only a small portion of the accumulated balance (Antolín 2008a, b).

16.5 Behavioural Economics Applied to Pensions

16.5.1 What Is Behavioural Economics?

Traditional economic postulates have proved insufficiently representative of reality when applied to decision-making processes under risk. Questions related to decision-making or people's preferences when making risky decisions, which underpinned the decision theory that dominated until the end of the last century, have undergone a radical change of perspective with the studies undertaken by Kahneman and Tversky and most specifically with the development of their Prospect Theory (Kahneman and Tversky 1979).

The foundations of classical decision theory, based on the maximisation of expected utility and principles of rationality in choice, have been called into question by Prospect Theory, which bases its analysis on the incorporation of principles of psychology and behaviour giving rise to behavioural economics. Prospect Theory shows how people derive utility from gains and losses, measured relative to a reference point, rather than from absolute values of wealth, so that the way people behave indicates that we are generally conservative when it comes to gains and risky when it comes to losses. This suggests that we are more affected by losses than we are by gains. Whereas classical theory regards people as *Homo economicus* in line with Becker (1976), that is, we always think and choose in a rational way and the predictions we make are bias-free, behavioural economics is based on a consideration of people as *Homo sapiens*. That is, we make mistakes and the forecasts we make can be biased and might not be correct.

The doctrine is therefore divided between classical economists who consider that there should be no intervention in the decision-making process and behavioural economists who believe that there should be some kind of help that facilitates decision-making, without this presupposing that someone or something should choose on our behalf. Behavioural economics considers that in the decision-making processes we adopt a series of heuristics, which generate biases that distance us from optimal choices. Thus, heuristics are a set of mental shortcuts that allow us to simplify the process of estimating the probability of the occurrence of an event and which, in fact, lead us to subjective estimates of that probability. It is obvious that such mental processes facilitate the task, but it is also evident that they lead us to make systematic mistakes. Biases are precisely the errors we incur by the repeated use of heuristics. In the end they are nothing more than traps that our mind sets itself and which distance us from a rational form of decision-making. Although we can always try to anticipate these traps, it is not always easy to see them.

This happens because our mental thought process is made up of two systems: system one (also known as the automatic system) is the system that makes us react quickly and instinctively; and system two (the reflective system) is the system that allows us to give thoughtful and controlled responses (Kahneman 2011). Our brain is designed for the basic purpose of survival, what from the neurological perspective is known as the 'reptilian brain', and we have shared this brain with most animals since the beginning of history. Only the evolution of our brain has allowed us to develop these reflective facets of intelligence that are exclusive to human beings.

Some of the biases that characterise our decision-making process are related to certain mental archetypes that, curiously, we consider logical. We have a notorious tendency to see patterns of behaviour where only chance exists, not to consider as extraordinary events that are, to allow ourselves to be influenced by the way in which things are presented to us and not to do things so as to avoid the associated risks and, hence, the errors that might arise from our intervention. In general, we do not like to move, if we can be still (what we call procrastination), and it hurts us to have to regret having done something.

We also have a special consideration of the concept of equity, since we make this quality dependent on the environment and the context, implying a subjectivity that displaces all objective considerations.

As human beings we are especially liable to overreact to the results of recent phenomena and to consider that our capacities to predict what might happen are superior to what they really are. To this extent, we understand that we can exercise a certain control over events. Likewise, we pass our opinions through the filter of our memories, so that our memory of something that happened is usually marked by a moment of maximum intensity during that event, especially of the way that event ended or of the memory that we retain of it. This happens because we are inhabited by two 'selves', the 'self' that remembers and the 'self' that experiences, with the former being clearly predominant.

When we consider pensions and the decisions that people must take about them, we have to think carefully about how to structure the architecture of decisions. The tree of options that we offer decision-makers must have a simple structure, with few, easily comprehensible choices. The key is to make the processes simple. To ensure that the options are properly sited in the mental process that leads to a decision being made, they have to enter through the automatic system of thought before moving into the reflective system. The options should not be neutral but the decision-maker should be presented with some form of guidance that shows them the best path to take. It should not be forgotten that decisions about pensions are extremely infrequent, that they have deferred effects that do not allow us to compare them or to use points of reference and that they do not allow us the immediate enjoyment of the consequences of the decision made. For this reason, it is absolutely essential that we are able to facilitate this decision-making process, by providing default options, by trying to facilitate an immediate perception of the decision made, by offering incentives that lead to the decision and, in short, by making the process as easy as possible.

It is extremely common, when dealing with pensions, to refuse to decide, or at least to put off the decision, to overestimate the short-term outcome, to be full of doubts in the decision made and to be subject to all kinds of influences to change it and, precisely because the question has not been understood, to give excessive consideration to everything that is already known.

What behavioural economics tells us is that the information architecture must make the options readily comprehensible, easy to take on board, incentivising, motivational and useful; moreover, it must lead the individual on the right path to building an adequate pension plan. One of the fundamental problems encountered is precisely the inability we all have to identify with our elderly selves. Thus, the postulates of this discipline indicate that we must have the capacity to transfer a person to his or her retirement so that they are able to visualise themselves in that position.

Hence, offering default options and giving recommended rates of contribution and incentives to remain in the pension system with increments agreed to in advance should all help the individual in the decision-making process. Individuals have to be presented with familiar elements that are likely to be received with gratitude and which allow them to start the process from a simple, readily acceptable origin. The information that is transferred from the outset has to be favourable, must generate security and must avoid substantial changes in the initial status quo.

Once the individual has understood or accepted that the process of saving for old age is necessary and begins to make contributions, we must continue facilitating the process. The information that is periodically delivered must also be clear, simple and transparent, and it must contain the elements that people really need to know: what benefits can they aspire to at the current rate of saving, in terms of future monthly income. It is often of little use for them to know what the accumulated capital is at any given date or even the capital they will have at the time of their retirement, because they are unable to convert this into a monthly income, which is really what they are interested in knowing. There is a danger that they suffer an illusion of wealth and consider that what is accumulated is enough to live out the rest of their days.

Information about the outcomes of their investments is in many cases useless, or at least insufficient, to really know how their savings are evolving. Information about the yields obtained in the last quarter, for example, can give a distorted picture of the real evolution, and what is worse is it can lead to totally erroneous decisions being taken based on the perception of recent events and the overvaluation that is mentally made of them. What people really care about is what the long-term performance is, what the average future performance may be and how it will affect their monthly pension.

When, amongst the options provided by a pension system, people are given the ability to choose the investments they want to make, it is vital that they be afforded the elements that facilitate their decision-making. Once more, default options are an indispensable tool. Life-cycle models play an important part in this approach, since they simplify the decision-making process in a rational way. In Latin America, for example, the multi-fund system has been and is being widely used as a proxy for the life-cycle system. With these models, individuals generally retain their ability to make their own decisions, but in global terms the best way forward is clearly indicated to them. In some cases there are limitations on choosing funds with a certain level of risk at certain ages; this is because governments have chosen to protect citizens and to protect themselves from their erroneous decisions which can lead to a significant undermining of their pension rights.

Another of the major questions associated with pension systems, and for which behavioural economics can provide solutions, is that of decumulation. There are multiple ways of receiving what has been accumulated on retiring, but undoubtedly some are more suited to the objectives that a pension system sets itself. Clearly, there is more than just one valid instrument, but by combining them appropriately, we can ensure that the reception of the pension meets the needs of the retiree. Combinations of immediate or deferred life annuities, programmed withdrawals and specific capital arrangements, if accompanied by adequate information and guidance, will be appropriate to ensure the decumulation process is successful, as anticipated.

Behavioural economics finds in neuroscience an exceptional complement, since it allows us to verify from a neurophysiological point of view what we have established from a psychological point of view. The techniques available to us today for studying brain reactions allow us to see how certain tasks performed by our brain react to impulses and decisions of an economic nature, such as the optimal allocation of scarce resources. Actually, what we are doing is locating psychological behaviours in neuronal processes, that is, giving a neuronal basis to the behavioural responses we give to the problems that the economy poses. This discipline of neuroeconomics explains the decision processes that arise as our brains are engaged in tasks of representation, anticipation, evaluation and making choices. For example, we are able to associate the process of saving for retirement to the activation of the brain's striate body, which is where the centre of pleasure and reward is located, and also to the medial prefrontal cortex, which is in the limbic system of our brain, in juxtaposition to the dorsolateral prefrontal cortex. Both brain pulsations are in opposition and dispute with each other the decision to save. The development of neurology to explain economic processes is still in its infancy, but is an area of vast potential and probably represents a fruitful field of study for the analysis of decision-making process in relation to pension schemes.

16.5.2 What Role Can Behavioural Economics Play in Improving Pension Systems?

Thaler and Benartzi (2004) highlight the potential of behavioural economics for promoting occupational pension plans in the United States, by applying their 'Save More Tomorrow' programme to the 401(k) plan.

In the United Kingdom, in seeking to provide supposed freedom of choice, the hitherto mandatory contracting of annuities at the age of 75 was annulled. But whilst Thaler and Sunstein (2009) coined the expression 'libertarian paternalism' to demonstrate the benefits of such decisions, Blake (2014) has criticised this measure most severely.

Behavioural economics provides a new perspective on the development of complementary pension systems. It analyses the systematic biases that the human mind weaves, above all, with regard to pensions (self-control restrictions, inertia and loss aversion); and it identifies the 'nudges' (small modifications of context to promote a certain behaviour) that can correct or take advantage of these biases.

Ultimately, there are three elements on which a behavioural strategy for saving should be developed: (1) using default options to make it as easy as possible, (2) helping to create habits and (3) establishing mechanisms to ensure saving is not painful.

From a behavioural perspective, it is imperative that an awareness phase be designed, providing clear explanations of potential scenarios backed up with decision maps. Generally speaking, the need exists, but people are not necessarily aware of it. For companies, it is important to exploit auto-enrolment schemes with flexible contributions, matching contribution schemes and plans in which the company provides the infrastructure and the members make their contributions in a collective framework. Establishing a process of synchronised contributions (i.e. increases agreed to in advance and executed automatically) ensures that the level of savings is constant and progressive, which after all is one of the great deficiencies in most pension systems.

16.6 Next Steps

We finish by returning to freedom of choice: clearly, it is desirable that people are free to choose their pension plan, but they must receive adequate help when making this decision. Choosing a pension is one of the most critical decisions we have to make in life, but at the same time one for which most people tend to be least prepared. A poor decision can have highly detrimental consequences for a person's future.

Seen from a behavioural perspective, the choice is not a simple question of satisfying a wish list. On the contrary, people need to be guided – be it mandatorily or by means of default options – towards what has generally been shown to be the best for the majority. Of course, there should always be room for those who, with sufficient information and criteria, want to opt out. People can be 'nudged' in the right direction, but they cannot be forced.

Most people suffer an asymmetry of information and this gives rise to a number of biases in their way of thinking. They tend to have a money illusion and so tend to overestimate a current lump sum when this is set against a lifetime of lower payments. Or, as result of the framing effect, i.e. the way the options are presented to them,[5] they are unable to take the best decision.

The applications of behavioural economics are, therefore, valid both at the level of occupational pension schemes, depending on the way in which companies present and manage their pension plans, and at that of individual schemes, depending on whether pension plan sponsors are able to motivate individuals to worry about their savings, that is, to show a concern for their future when they are no longer earning an income.

[5]See Benartzi et al. (2011) and their explanation of 'framing' in the case of annuitisation, in which they present the rents as 'consumption frames' and not as 'investment frames'.

Acknowledgements The study was supported by ICREA Academia, the Spanish Ministry of Economy and Competitiveness and the ERDF under grants ECO2015-66314-R and ECO2016-76203-C2-2-P.

References

Acuña, R., Palomino, M., Villar, L., Villagómez, A., & Valero, D. (2015). *Cómo fortalecer los sistemas de pensiones latinoamericanos. Experiencias, lecciones y propuestas*. Sura Asset Management, Estudio Internacional, Tomo I.

Ambachtsheer, K. (2013). *Designing 'Defined Ambition' pensions plans. A Frame for discussion*. Rotman ICPM (International Centre for Pension Management). Rotman School of Management, *5*(2).

Antolín, P. (2008a). *Ageing and the payout phase of pensions, annuities and financial markets*. OECD, Working Paper Series in Insurance and Private Pensions, 29.

Antolín, P. (2008b). *Policy options for the payout phase*. OECD, Working Paper Series in Insurance and Private Pensions, 25.

Antolín, P. (2013). *The OECD roadmap for the good design of defined contribution pension plans*. OECD DAF/FIN Pension Unit.

Barr, N. (2006). Non-financial defined contribution pensions: Mapping the terrain. In R. Holzmann & E. Palmer (Eds.), *Pension reform: Issues and prospects for non-financial defined contribution (NDC) schemes* (pp. 57–69). Washington, D.C.: The World Bank.

Barr, N., & Diamond, P. A. (2010). *Pension reform. A short guide*. Oxford: Oxford University Press.

Becker, G. S. (1976). *The economic approach to human behavior*. Chicago: The University of Chicago Press.

Benartzi, S., Previtero, A., & Thaler, R. H. (2011). Annuitization puzzles. *Journal of Economic Perspectives, 25*(4), 143–164.

Berstein, S., Morales, M., & Puente, A. (2015). *Rol de un seguro de longevidad en América Latina: Casos de Chile, Colombia, México y Perú*. Federación Internacional de Administradoras de Fondos de Pensiones (FIAP), Octubre. Available from: http://www.fiapinternacional.org/wp-content/uploads/2016/01/rol_de_un_seguro_de_longevidad_en_latam_casos_chile__colombia__mexico_y_peru__octubre_2015_.pdf.

Blake, D. (2014). *The consequences of not having to buy an annuity* (Discussion Paper PI-1409). Pensions Institute, Cass Business School, City University. Available from: http://www.pensions-institute.org/workingpapers/wp1409.pdf.

Blake, D., & Boardman, T. (2010). *Spend more today: Using behavioural economics to improve retirement expenditure decisions* (Discussion Paper PI-1014). The Pensions Institute, British Library.

Blake, D., & Dowd, K. (2013). *Good practice principles in modelling defined contribution pension plans*. London: Pensions Institute, Cass Business School.

Department of Work and Pensions. (2012). *Reinvigorating workplace pensions*. London: Stationery Office.

European Commission (EC). (2015). *The 2015 Ageing Report: Economic and budgetary projections for the 28 EU Member States (2013–2060)*. European Economy 3/2015. Available from: http://ec.europa.eu/economy_finance/publications/european_economy/2015/pdf/ee3_en.pdf.

Federación Internacional de Administradoras de Fondos de Pensiones (FIAP). (2015). *Modalidades de Pensión en los Sistemas de Capitalización Individual*. FIAP, Nota de Pensiones, 6, Septiembre. Available from: http://www.fiapinternacional.org/nota-de-pensiones-no-6-modalidades-de-pension-en-los-sistemas-de-capitalizacion-individual/.

Kahneman, D. (2011). *Thinking, fast and slow*. New York: Farrar, Straus and Groux.

Kahneman, D., & Tversky, A. (1979). Prospect theory: An analysis of decision under risk. *Econometrica, 47*(2), 263–291.

Nash, J. F. (1950). The bargaining problem. *Econometrica, 18*, 155–162.

National Employment Savings Trust Corporation (NEST). (2013). *Annual report and accounts 2013 to 2014*. London: NEST Corporation. Available from: https://www.gov.uk/government/publications/national-employment-savings-trust-corporation-annual-report-and-accounts-2013-to-2014.

O'Brien, C., Fenn, P., & Diacon, S. (2005). *How long do people expect to live? Results and implications*. Centre for Risk and Insurance Studies, Nottingham University Business School. CRIS Research Report 2005–1. Available from: https://www.nottingham.ac.uk/business/businesscentres/crbfs/documents/cris-reports/cris-paper-2005-1.pdf.

Organisation for Economic Co-operation and Development (OECD). (2013). *Pensions at a Glance 2013: OECD and G20 indicators*. Paris: OECD Publishing. Available from: http://www.oecd-ilibrary.org/finance-and-investment/pensions-at-a-glance-2013_pension_glance-2013-en.

Taleb, N. (2012). *Antifragille*. New York: Random House.

Thaler, R. H., & Benartzi, S. (2004). Save more tomorrow: Using behavioural economics to increase employee saving. *Journal of Political Economy, 112*, 164–187.

Thaler, R. H., & Sunstein, C. R. (2009). *Nudge*. New York: Penguin.

Tzu, L. (2016). Tao Te Ching. United States: Wisehouse Classics Edition.

United Nations. (2013). *World population prospects: The 2012 revision*. Population Division, Department of Economic and Social Affairs, United Nations, New York. Available from: https://esa.un.org/unpd/wpp/Publications/Files/WPP2012_HIGHLIGHTS.pdf.

Valero, D. (2013). Tendencias en materia de pensiones privadas. El papel de las rentas vitalicias. In J. A. Herce (Ed.), *Pensiones: una reforma medular* (pp. 175–189). Madrid: Fundación de Estudios Financieros y Círculo de Empresarios.

Valero, D. (2015). *Neuroeconomía y Economía del comportamiento de pensiones*. Livro Técnico Congresso 2015, Asociación Brasileña de Administradoras de Fondos de Pensiones (ABRAPP).

Van Galen, T., Kocken, T., & Lundbergh, S. (2014). Demystifying pension design: Clearer principles Foster. Better practices. *Rotman International Journal of Pension Management, 7* (2), 1–7.

Chapter 17
A Two-Regime Performance Test of the Mexican Public Pension Funds (SIEFOREs)

Oscar V. De la Torre-Torres, Evaristo Galeana-Figueroa, and Dora Aguilasocho-Montoya

Abstract In the present chapter, we measure the performance of the four types of SIEFOREs and their corresponding performance indices in a two-regime scenario. With the use of Markov-switching models, we found that the historical prices and performance of the SIEFOREs can be modeled with a two-regime geometric Brownian motion stochastic process, and we found that the conventional net-return index measured by CONSAR (the official authority in the pension system) is not sufficient for informational purposes. With our tests, we found that the good performers are not that good in crisis time periods, given the risk exposure with their management. Also, we found that some middle-table performers are the best in a two-regime scenario. With our results, we proved that it is preferable to measure performance in a two-regime scenario in order to increase informational efficiency among pension savers.

Keywords Pension funds · Pension fund performance · Markov-switching models · Portfolio back test and simulation · SIEFORE

17.1 Introduction

In 1997, Mexico reformed its pension system in order to reduce the budget pressure of the public pension system (the 1943 defined-benefit (DB) plan) that was caused by the increase in the elderly population and life expectancy. By following several international recommendations and the trend made by several developed and developing countries (Thomas and Spataro 2016), Mexico followed the Chilean example of creating a defined-contribution (DC) system with mutual-fund-type individual accounts in which the employee saves during her/his accumulation age

O. V. De la Torre-Torres (✉) · E. Galeana-Figueroa · D. Aguilasocho-Montoya
School of Accounting and Management, Saint Nicholas and Hidalgo Michoacan State University (UMSNH), Morelia, Mexico
e-mail: amontoya@umich.mx

M. Peris-Ortiz et al. (eds.), *Economic Challenges of Pension Systems*,
https://doi.org/10.1007/978-3-030-37912-4_17

and in which she/he will retire only with the saved proceedings plus the financial earnings, given the investment policy of the fund (known as SIEFORE[1]).

Since then, several studies have been made to test the benefits of the Mexican 1997 pension reform and the ones made in other countries. An example of the international studies are the aforementioned work of Thomas and Spataro (2016), who made a review of the tests made in several pension reforms in developed countries such as Australia, Canada, France, Germany, Iceland, Japan, the U.S., the U.K, Switzerland, and Spain[2] and some other developing ones such as Chile, Colombia, Gambia, Mexico, Papua New Guinea, Peru, and Uruguay. In their conclusions, they signal that the DC pension savers are prone to more job rotation than the DB ones for the fact that these have portable pension benefits. They also observe that the desire of retirement in the DB pension savers is determined by the incentives given to do so. This study also made a review and summary of the impact that several pension fund reforms have had in the development of their local financial markets. Their conclusions observe that development is noted primarily in the developed countries, given the level of informational efficiency and issues such as lower agent risk and free capital flows. These authors observe that the economic benefit of a given pension-system reform is due to parallel reforms in the fiscal, economic, educational, and legal institutions.

We also found the work of Chan-Lau (2005), who analyzes three subjects: (1) the determinant of asset allocation in developed countries, (2) the development of emerging financial markets given their pension system and reforms, (3) the determinants of pension fund performance. In the first factor, the author found that the transfer of pension risk from the company to the employees (in the case of developed countries such as the Europeans countries, Japan, or the U.S.) has changed the investment objective from an asset-liability immunization to a maximization of risk-adjusted returns, leading to a reduction of home bias in the asset allocation of pension fund portfolios. As a result of this, the author found that in the 1990s, some corporate (DB) pension funds faced some financial gaps in their plan given this home bias and due to losses incurred in their investments during the price contraction of technology companies' stock market. With this in mind (home bias reduction and also the switch to DC plans), global diversification plays an important role in pension fund performance and leads the author to conclude that the actual diversification in emerging financial markets is due to the reform or the change to DC plans in developed countries, along with the reforms made in these emerging countries.

In the Mexican case of interest herein, we can mention the work of Villagómez and Hernández (2009), who made the economic and fiscal impact analysis of the Mexican reform and observe the improvements to be made, as is the case of the reform of other pension plans, such as the ones of public universities and other public companies. In the same object of analysis, we found the work of Albo et al.

[1]The acronym of Sociedad de Inversión Especializada en Fondos para el Retiro or retirement mutual fund.

[2]Just to name a few of these cases.

(2007), who made a 10-year review of the 1997 reform and made some interesting proposals (some of them implemented today) to enhance the economic impact due to stronger funding and a proper pension level at retirement. Among these, we mention the reduction of home bias, along with the increase in the investment levels in other assets such as foreign stocks and debt, real estate, and commodities (a change formally made in 2008, as we will see next). As other potential improvements, the authors suggested increasing the savings percentage (in relation to the total salary paid) and the application of fiscal incentives to the pension savings made by independent entrepreneurs and workers. These proposals were tested in their validity to the Mexican reality by Villagómez and Hernández (2009), by Villagómez and Ramírez (2014), and by Villagomez (2014). This last proposal has been also tested with the use of longevity swaps, as Rodriguez-Reyes (2017) suggests. As noted, all the previous literature related to the benefits and improvements of the pension reform of 1997 has focused on the savings rate, universality, and the inclusion level of the Mexican people and also on the rate of formality in the labor market. Only a few of these have focused on the performance of SIEFOREs and in potential improvements in the allowed investment policy of these. Some of the main first steps to solve this can be found in De la Torre Torres et al. (2015a, b), who note that there is no public performance benchmark for measuring the performance of the SIEFOREs and suggest using a multiasset investment policy statement (IPS) benchmark. They observe that the minimum variance benchmark is a proper definition of a potential IPS benchmark to test the performance of the SIEFOREs.

In the original reform of 1997, the official investment policy of the SIEFOREs consisted of allowing these to invest only in Mexican government and corporate debt securities, but in 2004, a reform was made to allow them to invest in a Mexican equity component through structured notes or other investment vehicles such as ETFs or mutual funds. At that point, the existing single SIEFORE type was split into two types: one, for older people, that was not allowed to invest in stocks and a second one that was allowed to invest up to 15% in these types of securities. In that same time period, both types of SIEFOREs were allowed to invest in debt securities of another countries.

In 2007, the investment policy changed and started to follow a life-cycle investment (Merton 1969; Bodie et al. 1992) profile, and with this change, the SIEFOREs were allowed to invest even in international stocks and in real estate, leading to a five-type SIEFORE system in which the type 5 SIEFOREs (SB5) were the riskiest ones with the highest investment levels in equities and international debt and the type 1 (SB1) were the most conservative. In 2008, another change was made in the investment policy, and the SB4 and SB5 were merged into a single type 4 for people of 36 years of age or less. This type of SIEFORE is the most aggressive in its investment policy, being that type 1 (for people with more than 60 years of age) is the most conservative.[3] With this in mind, the actual investment

[3]Type 3 (SB3) are SIEFOREs for people that are 37 and 46 years old and type 4 (SB4) for people between 46 and 60.

Table 17.1 Investment policy, CONSAR

	SB0 (%)	SB1 (%)	SB2 (%)	SB3 (%)	SB4 (%)
Value at risk	0.70	0.70	1.10	1.40	2.10
Debt issued or endorsed by the Mexican government in MXN (mxBB to mxAAA)	100.00	100.00	100.00	100.00	100.00
Foreign securities (BBB- to AAA for debt)	0.00	20.00	20.00	20.00	20.00
Equity	0.00	10.00	30.00	35.00	45.00
Foreign currency	0.00	30.00	30.00	30.00	30.00
Securitizations	0.00	10.00	15.00	20.00	30.00
Structured securities	0.00	10.00	15.00	20.00	20.00
Mexican REITs (FIBRAs) and REITs	0.00	5.00	10.00	10.00	10.00
Inflation-protected securities (minimum investment allowed)	0.00	51.00	0.00	0.00	0.00
Commodities	0.00	0.00	5.00	10.00	10.00

Source: Own elaboration departing from the investment policy of CONSAR (2017)

policy allowed by the CONSAR for the fourth type of SIEFOREs at the moment of writing this chapter is the one shown in Table 17.1.

There is a fifth type of SIEFORE, known as the retirement SIEFORE (SB0), that is for retired people. This type of SIEFORE will not be of interest here for the fact that it does not invest in risky assets such as stocks, commodities, real estate, or other risky international securities that could generate more than one regime or state of nature in the stochastic process.

Departing from this issue, it is of interest and necessity to enhance the investment policy of the SIEFOREs because better returns lead to higher wealth at retirement. As we will mention in the brief literature review next, we noted that there are not any academic reviews about the performance of the SIEFOREs in normal and/or distress periods in financial markets.[4] All the previous tests on the SIEFOREs have been made in a single regime or state of nature time series, and these do not review if it is either proper to use a single regime performance test or a multiregime one. That is, these studies do not determine if it is proper to measure the risk and return level of a given SIEFORE by differentiating its performance in a normal (or good-performing) or in a crisis (or bad-performing) time period.

With this in mind, our core idea is to test if it is proper to model the performance of the SIEFOREs (the four basic types) in a two-regime scenario and to determine the level of expected return, risk exposure, and mean-variance efficiency in this context (a metric that it is not used in mutual funds or pension funds or SIEFOREs).

[4]For the sake of simplicity and setting aside the definition of "crisis" in Macroeconomics and Economic Theory (an issue that is not exempt of controversies) we will define a financial distress, bad-performing or crisis time period as that time in which the level of price fluctuation is wider and negative than more stable periods. A definition that is consistent with times such as the 2007–2008 financial crisis and 2011–2012 European debt crises time periods.

The present chapter is structured as follows: in the next section, we will mention a brief literature review, followed by our test and result review section. In the last section, we present our conclusions and potential extensions of the current review.

17.2 Literature Review

As previously mentioned, the literature review related to the study of the Mexican pension reform of 1997 is still scant but very important. The most related work to this chapter is the work of Calderón-Colín et al. (2009), who test the demand elasticity and competitiveness of the SIEFOREs and note that even if there were 10,000 SIEFOREs or more, the management cost would not lessen due to market or competition issues. They noted that the SIEFORE selection is noisy and uninformed and the particular SIEFORE selection is due to back-to-back practices or to marketing efforts instead of the performance of their investments. This last paper motivated the test made by De la Torre Torres et al. (2017), who test the level of homogeneity in the performance of the SIEFOREs as a potential cause of this uninformed and noisy SIEFORE selection. In their results, they found that given the official IPS given by CONSAR (2017), there is no alpha generation or difference in the performance of these types of pension funds in the long term, leading to a low level of competitiveness among these in terms of returns paid to the investor. This last work is one of the motivations of the present paper because we will test the level of mean-variance efficiency among SIEFOREs in a two-regime context.

Another study that motivates the work in the present chapter is the test that Martínez and Venegas (2014) made to the SB1 and SB2 types of SIEFOREs. In their paper, the authors performed an ARIMA-GARCH model (symmetric and asymmetric) and found the presence of asymmetries in the volatility or risk levels of both types of SIEFOREs. The authors also found that the level of risk in the riskier SB2 SIEFOREs does not justify the extra return paid in relation to the SB1s, leaving the door open to further studies and test on this issue (a test that we pretend to extend here). Later, the work of Santillán et al. (2016) reviews the performance of the four types of SIEFOREs tested herein, and they extend the work of Martínez and Venegas (2014) by incorporating the effect of long memory. That paper gives proof that the classical assumption of a geometric Brownian motion in the stochastic process does not hold for the SIEFOREs and it is more appropriate to model these with a long-memory fractional geometric Brownian motion. This last conclusion means that the influence of older price ($t + n$, $n > 1$) movements is still relevant, leading to a potential persistence in the risk levels.

Departing from these last two results, we want to test the performance of the SIEFOREs with a Gaussian Markov-switching model with two regimes due to the fact that we suspect that the potential fractional integration found by Santillán et al. (2016) could be the result of the presence of two or more regimes in the time series. In a clearer definition, we assume that the behavior of the time series of the returns (r_t) in the SIEFOREs should be modeled not with the unimodal probability density function but with a bimodal one with two Gaussian bells in the probability density function and the corresponding two means ($\mu_{s\,=\,i}$) and standard deviations ($\sigma_{s\,=\,i}$). Each bell and its corresponding parameters correspond to a regime or state of nature. For the case of the present chapter, we will assume that there are two regimes: one ($s = 1$) known as the *low-volatility*, *good-performing*, or *normal* time period (or regime) and another ($s = 2$) known as the *high-volatility*, *bad-performing*, or *crisis* period (or regime). As previously mentioned, in footnote 5, we will not discuss the definition of crisis because that is a subject in which the economic and macroeconomic theories have a lot to review. The present work is a financial econometrics test, and we will use the term *bad performing*, *high volatility*, or *crisis* to refer to the second regime ($s = 2$) indistinctly. With this in mind, it is expected that $\sigma_{s\,=\,2} > \sigma_{s\,=\,1}$. This last definition, and thus assumption, is in line with the results and proposals of Hamilton (1989, 1994, 1996) and also in line with several works such as the ones of Brooks and Persand (2001), Alexander and Kaeck (2007), Alexander and Lazar (2008), or Hauptmann et al. (2014), who use Markov-switching models in financial (active investing and asset-pricing) applications.

One of the main characteristics of Markov-switching models (henceforth MS) is that, contrary to normal-mixture models (which are also multimodal), the underlying and unobserved process of changing from one regime to another can be modeled in an s state Markovian process with its correspondent transition probability matrix (we present the two-regime case), which models the transfer from one regime ($s = i$) to another one ($s = j$) at $t + 1$:

$$\boldsymbol{\Pi} = \begin{bmatrix} \pi_{1,1} & \pi_{1,2} \\ \pi_{2,1} & \pi_{2,2} \end{bmatrix}, \pi_{i,j} = P(s_t = j | s_{t-1} = i, r_t, \boldsymbol{\theta}) \tag{17.1}$$

Also, another interesting output of this is the smoothed probability $\xi_{s\,=\,i,\,t} = P(s = i | r_t, \boldsymbol{\theta})$, which measures the likelihood of being in regime $s = i$ at t. With these definitions, Markov-switching models are useful for estimating the parameter vector, given the number of regimes with the next log-likelihood function (LLF):

$$\mathrm{LLF}_{\mathrm{MS}} = \sum\nolimits_{t=1}^{T} ln \left[\frac{\pi_{s=1}}{\sqrt{2\pi}\sigma_{s=1}} e^{-\frac{1}{2}\left(\frac{\Delta\% B_{i,t} - \mu_{s=1}}{\sigma_{s=1}}\right)^2} + \frac{\pi_{s=2}}{\sqrt{2\pi}\sigma_{s=2}} e^{-\frac{1}{2}\left(\frac{\Delta\% B_{i,t} - \mu_{s=2}}{\sigma_{s=2}}\right)^2} \right] \tag{17.2}$$

Aside from this brief literature review and the main motivation of testing the performance of the SIEFOREs in a two Gaussian-regime scenario, we will test if it is proper to model the performance of the return time series of the four types of SIEFOREs. With this, we will determine the observed level of expected return ($\mu_{s\,=\,i}$) and risk ($\sigma_{s\,=\,i}$) exposure in each regime, along with the observed mean-variance efficiency, estimated with a two-regime Sharpe ratio (1966)[5]:

[5]Given the mean 28-day CETES as the risk-free asset or *rf*.

$$SR = \frac{\mu y_i - \mu_{rf}}{\sigma y_i}, \quad SR = \frac{\mu y_{i,s=i} - \mu_{rf}}{\sigma y_{i,s=i}} \tag{17.3}$$

17.3 Econometric Test

In order to process the data and to make the econometric test, we used the daily historical prices (P_t) of each of the four types of SIEFORE published by CONSAR (2018). The dates that we downloaded were from March 1, 2005 (the date on which the investment in equities was allowed in the IPS), to July 30, 2018. This time period includes the effect of the upward trend of 2004–2007 in all the world's financial markets, given the monetary stimulus implemented by the United States in 2001 and also some bad-performing or crisis time periods such as the 2007–2008 financial crisis and the 2011–2012 European debt crisis. It also includes the observed shocks in Mexican capital markets such as the uncertainty of the Mexican FX, debt and equity markets due to the U.S., and the Mexican election processes, along with the NAFTA renegotiations in the 2016–2018 period.

With this historical data, we calculated the continuous time return given the next expression:

$$r_t = ln(P_t) - ln(P_{t-1}) \tag{17.4}$$

We also used the return price time series to calculate a base 100 value on March 1, 2005, to the end of the test period in order to determine the accumulated return paid for each SIEFORE.

Along with the historical SIEFORE prices, CONSAR (2018) also publishes some performance benchmarks of each SIEFORE. It is not clear if these benchmarks are equally weighted or are market-cap weighted indexes. Unfortunately, CONSAR, as the official authority and regulator of the Mexican public pension system, is not clear and quite accountable in their index valuation methodologies. This government commission publishes the net return index, which is a return calculation with a 36-month rolling window for calculation, and this is the only public and most widely used performance metric, setting aside the risk exposure and other more punctual performance metrics. Even if they publish these very useful indices with the "official" SIEFOREs prices, they do not make their levels public and they do not make public comparisons of the performance of each SIEFORE against their market peers (proxied as a market with these benchmarks). They also omit the methodology of how these benchmarks are calculated, leaving some questions open.

In order to solve this issue and to determine the methodology used, we used the price of each type of SIEFORE and we replicated the performance of each type of

SIEFORE index by using the price-weighted method. This was done in order to prove if this was the proper calculation method. We found small differences, and then we assumed that the methodology of these indices is a market-cap one by using either the net asset value or the total managed assets amount observed in each SIEFORE. This last conclusion is an issue the we left for CONSAR to answer, and by using this assumption as valid (that it is a market-cap performance index), we will analyze the individual performance of each SIEFORE and compare it with their corresponding SIEFORE type index, which we assume as "valid" for the fact that CONSAR (2018) is the one that makes these index values public.

We also performed the base 100 value and continuous time calculations in these indices. With the historical return time series, we calculated the expected return (μ_i) and risk (σ_i) parameters in a single-regime Gaussian context by using the next LLF:

$$\text{LLF} = \sum_{t=1}^{T} ln\left[\frac{1}{\sqrt{2\pi\sigma}}e^{-\frac{1}{2}\left(\frac{\Delta\%B_{i,t}-\mu}{\sigma}\right)^2}\right] \tag{17.5}$$

We also used Hamilton's (1989, 1994, 1996) filter in a Gaussian two-regime context as in (17.2) in order to determine the expected return ($\mu_{i,\ s\ =\ 1}, \mu_{i,\ s\ =\ 2}$) and expected risk ($\sigma_{i,\ s\ =\ 1}, \sigma_{i,\ s\ =\ 2}$) levels for the good-performing or normal ($s = 1$) and for the bad-performing or crisis ($s = 2$) time periods, respectively. With the LLFs given in (17.2) and (17.5), we calculated the Akaike (1974), Schwarz (1978), and Hannan and Quinn (1979) information criterions in order to determine if it is more appropriate to model the return time series in a single or in a two-regime scenario.

Once determined, we calculated the Sharpe ratio as in (17.3) for both the single and the two-regime parameters in order to know the level of mean-variance efficiency of the indices and the SIEFOREs.

Complimentary to this, we ran an accumulated return and a maximum-drawdown analysis in order to determine the accumulated performance and potential loss that each SIEFORE shows during the test period.

In order to organize our tests, we ran four pools of tests. One for each SIEFORE type, and in the type 1 (SB1) SIEFOREs, we included the analysis of the CONSAR (ALL) index, which measures the performance of the four types of SIEFOREs.

One issue that we have to sort is the presence of survivor bias by the fact that some SIEFOREs merged with other ones and some new participants in the market have shorter historical data that do not contemplate the effects of important time periods such as the 2007–2008 financial crisis. Given this, the SIEFOREs and indices that we will test here are briefly described in Table 17.2. In the original version of that table, we were going to include SIEFORE XXI Banorte, but we had to omit that SIEFORE because the quality of the historical data provided by CONSAR (2018) was doubtful and poor.

Now that we have described the main tests that we performed, we will present the review of observed results next.

Table 17.2 The SIEFOREs and performance benchmarks studied in the performance and econometric test

Studied benchmarks			
Ticker	*Name*		
SB_ALLindex	The performance index of all the types of SIEFOREs		
Ticker	*Name*	*Ticker*	*Name*
SB1index	Type 1 SIEFORE performance benchmark	SB3index	Type 4 SIEFORE performance benchmark
SB2index	Type 3 SIEFORE performance benchmark	SB4index	Type 5 SIEFORE performance benchmark
Studied SIEFOREs			
Ticker	*Name*	*Ticker*	*Name*
Azteca	SIEFORE Azteca	Principal	SIEFORE principal
Citibanamex	SIEFORE Citi-Banamex	Profuturo GNP	SIEFORE GNP
Inbursa	SIEFORE Inbursa	SURA	SIEFORE SURA
Invercap	SIEFORE Invercap		

Source: Own elaboration

17.3.1 Type 1 (SB1) SIEFOREs Test Results

For the specific case of type 1 SIEFOREs, we summarize in Table 17.3 the goodness of fit of a single and two-regime stochastic process of the performance benchmarks of all the types of SIEFOREs (*SB_ALLindex*), along with one of this type of SIEFORE (SB1). We also present the same results for the six studied SIEFOREs. As noted, the LLF and the three information criterions give strong proof for modeling the stochastic process of these SIEFOREs in a two-regime scenario.

Following this, we present the statistical summary and performance of the studied indices and SIEFOREs in Table 17.4 (annualized values are presented inside brackets). As noted, the accumulated returns paid by the SIEFOREs are practically equal among them, with the exception of Inbursa and Azteca, who, even if they are subject to the investment policy of Table 17.1, have poor management results given a potentially conservative investment strategy. We support this statement due to the fact that their accumulated returns are slightly higher than the 28-day CETES or risk-free asset. Despite this result, the mean daily returns in the single regime are very similar. This is an issue that is also observed in the good-performing or normal time periods in the two-regime scenario. The potential difference among SIEFOREs could be generated, as the results suggest, during the bad-performing or crisis periods. As noted in the second panel of Table 17.4, there are notable differences among these types of SIEFOREs during this scenario, an issue that could lead to accumulated return differences, especially in Inbursa and Azteca. Another issue of interest is the performance of Invercap. As noted in the accumulated and mean returns (a proxy of the actual ranking method of the net performance return used by CONSAR), this SIEFORE figures among the best performers, but if we analyze the

Table 17.3 The goodness-of-fit test of a Gaussian single-regime stochastic process in the studied SB1 index and SIEFOREs versus the two-regime one

Ticker	*LLF 1 regime*	*LLF 2 regimes*	*Akaike 1 regime*	*Akaike 2 regimes*
SB_ALLindex	13,890.24	14,949.29	−27,778.49	−29,892.57
SB1index	15,532.82	16,469.49	−31,063.63	−32,932.99
Azteca	15,600.54	16,625.69	−31,199.08	−33,245.38
Citibanamex	15,347.39	16,241.11	−30,692.78	−32,476.22
Inbursa	20,161.87	21,097.78	−40,321.74	−42,189.57
Invercap	13,770.86	15,385.93	−27,539.72	−30,765.86
Principal	15,440.22	16,294.68	−30,878.44	−32,583.36
Profuturo GNP	15,161.65	16,068.65	−30,321.30	−32,131.30
Ticker	*Schwarz 1 regime*	*Schwarz 2 regimes*	*Hannan-Quinn 1 regime*	*Hannan-Quinn 2 regimes*
SB_ALLindex	−27,772.36	−29,874.20	−27,775.84	−29,892.29
SB1index	−31,057.51	−32,914.61	−31,060.99	−32,932.70
Azteca	−31,192.95	−33,227.01	−31,196.43	−33,245.10
Citibanamex	−30,686.66	−32,457.85	−30,690.14	−32,475.94
Inbursa	−40,315.62	−42,171.19	−40,319.10	−42,189.28
Invercap	−27,533.59	−30,747.48	−27,537.07	−30,765.57
Principal	−30,872.32	−32,564.99	−30,875.80	−32,583.08
Profuturo GNP	−30,315.18	−32,112.93	−30,318.66	−32,131.02

Source: Own elaboration with data from CONSAR (2018)

performance given the risk exposure or the expected return in crisis or bad-performing time periods, the performance is totally different: this SIEFORE is the worst performer and the riskiest one during distress time periods.

This last comparison made in Table 17.4 is something that we strongly recommend to be done by CONSAR, that is, to compare the expected return in normal and crisis periods and to publish the level of risk exposure in those same periods. Also, we suggest publishing the mean-variance efficiency in the same two-regime context. As noted in the first panel of Table 17.4 and by setting aside the atypical case of Inbursa, the performance picture changes especially when a two-regime analysis is made. Some SIEFOREs that perform well in normal time periods are among the worst performers in the crisis ones. Cases such as Citibanamex change their ranking in this time period. With these results, we support our suggestion of publishing not only the returns paid but also the level of risk exposure and mean-variance efficiency in normal and crisis time periods.

17.3.2 Type 2 (SB2) SIEFOREs Test Results

For the case of SB2 SIEFOREs, in Table 17.5, we show the goodness of fit of their index and SIEFOREs. Similar to the previous type (SB1), we found a better

Table 17.4 Statistical and performance summary of the studied SB1 indices and SIEFOREs versus the two-regime one

Performance summary				
Ticker	*Accumulated return*	*Sharpe ratio one regime*	*Sharpe ratio two regimes*	*Max. drawdown*
SB_ALLindex	158.1844 (11.2989)	0.6199	2.0486/ −0.6271	−6.4604
SB1index	136.5629 (9.7545)	0.8061	2.4347/ −0.6091	−5.8634
Azteca	115.6333 (8.2595)	0.6036	2.2582/ −0.4276	−5.8937
Citibanamex	145.8214 (10.4158)	0.8485	2.1717/ −0.6180	−6.4713
Inbursa	115.4906 (8.2493)	2.3235	5.3320/1.2537	−0.6044
Invercap	140.1362 (10.0097)	0.5012	1.9472/ −0.4058	−9.4911
Principal	126.4565 (9.0326)	0.6866	2.2775/ −0.7324	−6.028
Profuturo GNP	134.5646 (9.6118)	0.7034	2.2315/ −0.6201	−5.6778
SURA	147.2030 (10.5145)	0.8324	2.3263/ −0.2824	−5.7019
CETES28D	114.8768 (8.2055)	—	—	0.0005
Statistical summary				
Ticker	*Mean one regime*	*Mean two regimes*	*Standard dev. one regime*	*Standard dev. two regimes*
SB_ALLindex	0.1355 (6.7750)	0.1945 (9.7272)/ −0.0706 (−3.5308)	0.9049 (6.3984)	0.5141 (3.6351)/ 1.6415 (11.6075)
SB1index	0.1230 (6.1503)	0.1571 (7.8537)/ −0.0466 (−2.3280)	0.6748 (4.7716)	0.3543 (2.5056)/ 1.4347 (10.1450)
Azteca	0.1098 (5.4886)	0.1399 (6.9964)/ 0.0168 (0.8417)	0.6744 (4.7691)	0.2993 (2.1164)/ 1.2517 (8.8506)
Citibanamex	0.1285 (6.4245)	0.1537 (7.6852)/ −0.0343 (−1.7142)	0.7089 (5.0123)	0.3902 (2.7590)/ 1.6516 (11.6782)
Inbursa	0.1097 (5.4839)	0.1168 (5.8406)/ 0.1017 (5.0853)	0.1451 (1.0257)	0.0627 (0.4434)/ 0.1999 (1.4137)
Invercap	0.1251 (6.2574)	0.1570 (7.8523)/ −0.0734 (−3.6725)	1.1710 (8.2800)	0.4917 (3.4766)/ 2.8885 (20.4246)
Principal	0.1168 (5.8384)	0.1522 (7.6080)/ −0.0771 (−3.8548)	0.7013 (4.9587)	0.3728 (2.6360)/ 1.5412 (10.8981)
Profuturo GNP	0.1218 (6.0897)	0.1601 (8.0063)/ −0.0665 (−3.3246)	0.7343 (5.1922)	0.3934 (2.7820)/ 1.5428 (10.9090)
SURA	0.1293 (6.4646)	0.1521 (7.6052)/ 0.0098 (0.4891)	0.7274 (5.1438)	0.4058 (2.8694)/ 1.5546 (10.9930)
CETES28D	0.1094 (5.4724)	—	0.0388 (0.2743)	—

Source: Own elaboration with data from the simulations and CONSAR (2018)

Table 17.5 The goodness-of-fit test of a Gaussian single-regime stochastic process in the studied SB2 index and SIEFOREs versus the two-regime one

Ticker	*LLF 1 regime*	*LLF 2 regimes*	*Akaike 1 regime*	*Akaike 2 regimes*
SB2index	2251.64	2515.13	−4501.27	−5024.26
Azteca	2286.52	2578.80	−4571.03	−5151.59
Citibanamex	2154.91	2451.64	−4307.83	−4897.27
Inbursa	3274.98	3482.77	−6547.96	−6959.54
Invercap	1921.17	2268.98	−3840.35	−4531.97
Principal	2260.63	2495.01	−4519.26	−4984.02
Profuturo GNP	2141.14	2416.46	−4280.28	−4826.93
SURA	2177.43	2433.59	−4352.86	−4861.17
CETES28D	4511.92	—	−9021.84	—
Ticker	*Schwarz 1 regime*	*Schwarz 2 regimes*	*Hannan-Quinn 1 regime*	*Hannan-Quinn 2 regimes*
SB2index	−4496.72	−5010.61	−4498.96	−5024.62
Azteca	−4566.48	−5137.94	−4568.72	−5151.96
Citibanamex	−4303.28	−4883.62	−4305.52	−4897.63
Inbursa	−6543.40	−6945.89	−6545.64	−6959.90
Invercap	−3835.79	−4518.31	−3838.04	−4532.33
Principal	−4514.71	−4970.36	−4516.95	−4984.38
Profuturo GNP	−4275.73	−4813.27	−4277.97	−4827.29
SURA	−4348.31	−4847.52	−4350.55	−4861.53
CETES28D	−9017.29	—	−9020.08	—

Source: Own elaboration with data from CONSAR (2018)

explanation level if we use a two-regime time series model to measure the performance of these types of pension funds.

Departing from this last result, we present the statistical and performance summary of these SIEFOREs (Table 17.6), and we found similar results to the ones observed the previous SB1 SIEFOREs. We noted the observable change in terms of risk exposure and mean-variance efficiency.

This issue leads us to observe that the publication of a mean-variance efficiency or risk exposure table that distinguishes the performance in good-performing and bad-performing time periods would be a useful tool for pension savers in order to make a less-noisy decision, as Calderón-Colín et al. (2009) et al. proved out as true.

17.3.3 Type 3 (SB3) SIEFOREs Test Results

The goodness of fit of a two-regime stochastic process is proved in the results in Table 17.7. The LLF and information criterion values give strong support to this conclusion, and following this, we present the performance and statistical summary in Table 17.8.

Table 17.6 Statistical and performance summary of the studied SB2 indices and SIEFOREs versus the two-regime one

Performance summary				
Ticker	*Accumulated return*	*Sharpe ratio one regime*	*Sharpe ratio two regimes*	*Max. drawdown*
SB2index	149.4969 (10.6783)	0.1542	0.6729/ −0.5669	−8.9604
Azteca	135.1441 (9.6532)	0.0972	0.4148/ −0.3406	−9.2684
Citibanamex	159.9139 (11.4224)	0.1713	0.7809/ −0.6236	−10.8044
Inbursa	116.2862 (8.3062)	0.0238	0.6819/ −0.3982	−1.6704
Invercap	143.4360 (10.2454)	0.0802	0.6313/ −0.5700	−13.2415
Principal	143.7054 (10.2647)	0.1314	0.7062/ −0.7500	−8.2166
Profuturo GNP	174.1785 (12.4413)	0.2155	0.7835/ −0.5785	−11.2203
SURA	168.3643 (12.0260)	0.2069	0.7694/ −0.4782	−9.5458
CETES28D	114.8768 (8.2055)	—	—	0.0005
Statistical summary				
Ticker	*Mean one regime*	*Mean two regimes*	*Standard dev. one regime*	*Standard dev. two regimes*
SB2index	0.1306 (6.5305)	0.1588 (7.9408)/ −0.0887 (−4.4374)	0.9708 (6.8643)	0.5188 (3.6683)/ 2.4723 (17.4816)
Azteca	0.1221 (6.1073)	0.1374 (6.8701)/ −0.0115 (−0.5750)	0.9236 (6.5307)	0.4765 (3.3695)/ 2.5109 (17.7544)
Citibanamex	0.1365 (6.8227)	0.1717 (8.5843)/ −0.1500 (−7.4983)	1.1146 (7.8814)	0.5635 (3.9848)/ 2.9414 (20.7987)
Inbursa	0.1102 (5.5102)	0.1197 (5.9857)/ 0.0884 (4.4194)	0.2250 (1.5911)	0.1064 (0.7527)/ 0.3740 (2.6446)
Invercap	0.1271 (6.3549)	0.1736 (8.6813)/ −0.2162 (−10.8106)	1.5565 (11.0058)	0.7189 (5.0834)/ 4.0400 (28.5670)
Principal	0.1273 (6.3628)	0.1631 (8.1530)/ −0.1400 (−6.9988)	0.9584 (6.7767)	0.5368 (3.7958)/ 2.3517 (16.6293)
Profuturo GNP	0.1441 (7.2044)	0.1766 (8.8280)/ −0.1396 (−6.9816)	1.1368 (8.0380)	0.6057 (4.2827)/ 3.0446 (21.5284)
SURA	0.1410 (7.0513)	0.1715 (8.5740)/ −0.0676 (−3.3807)	1.0793 (7.6320)	0.5701 (4.0313)/ 2.6184 (18.5147)
CETES28D	0.1094 (5.4724)	—	0.0388 (0.2743)	—

Source: Own elaboration with data from the simulations and CONSAR (2018)

Table 17.7 The goodness-of-fit test of a Gaussian single-regime stochastic process in the studied SB3 index and SIEFOREs versus the two-regime one

Ticker	*LLF 1 regime*	*LLF 2 regimes*	*Akaike 1 regime*	*Akaike 2 regimes*
SB3index	2154.74	2429.47	−4307.49	−4852.93
Azteca	2238.87	2507.83	−4475.74	−5009.65
Citibanamex	2063.64	2366.42	−4125.28	−4726.84
Inbursa	3112.30	3298.36	−6222.60	−6590.71
Invercap	1817.24	2195.51	−3632.48	−4385.02
Principal	2206.53	2444.72	−4411.07	−4883.45
Profuturo GNP	2049.07	2340.62	−4096.13	−4675.23
SURA	2078.36	2347.35	−4154.72	−4688.69
CETES28D	4511.92	—	−9021.84	—
Ticker	*Schwarz 1 regime*	*Schwarz 2 regimes*	*Hannan-Quinn 1 regime*	*Hannan-Quinn 2 regimes*
SB3index	−4302.94	−4839.28	−4305.18	−4853.29
Azteca	−4471.19	−4996.00	−4473.43	−5010.02
Citibanamex	−4120.72	−4713.19	−4122.96	−4727.20
Inbursa	−6218.05	−6577.06	−6220.29	−6591.07
Invercap	−3627.93	−4371.37	−3630.17	−4385.38
Principal	−4406.52	−4869.79	−4408.76	−4883.81
Profuturo GNP	−4091.58	−4661.58	−4093.82	−4675.59
SURA	−4150.17	−4675.04	−4152.41	−4689.05
CETES28D	−9017.29	—	−9020.08	—

Source: Own elaboration with data from CONSAR (2018)

In this riskier type of SIEFORE, the benefit of using a mean-variance analysis in a two-regime context instead of a single return-only one is noted with more emphasis. The ranking changes in terms of mean-variance efficiency and in terms of performance if we use the risk exposure and expected return parameters. This issue leads us to the same conclusions previously stated in the type 1 and type 2 SIEFOREs.

17.3.4 Type 4 (SB4) SIEFOREs Test Results

Finally, we present the goodness of fit and performance results in Table 17.9 and Table 17.10, respectively. As noted, the conclusions are very similar to the previous types of SIEFOREs: that is, the first places in terms of accumulated and mean return change when a two-regime filter is used. We reach the same conclusion in terms of mean-variance efficiency: the best performers do not hold their ranking position in crisis periods, and also the performance ranking is different in normal time periods. The goodness of fit results also give strong proof for modeling the stochastic process with a Gaussian two-regime Markov-switching time series model.

Table 17.8 Statistical and performance summary of the studied SB3 indices and SIEFOREs versus the two-regime one

Performance summary				
Ticker	*Accumulated return*	*Sharpe ratio one regime*	*Sharpe ratio two regimes*	*Max. drawdown*
SB3index	157.7017 (11.2644)	0.1635	0.7531/ −0.5497	−10.1528
Azteca	143.6313 (10.2594)	0.1271	0.5373/ −0.4018	−9.6801
Citibanamex	168.0378 (12.0027)	0.1749	0.8156/ −0.5668	−12.0912
Inbursa	123.7039 (8.8360)	0.1388	1.0025/ −0.3880	−1.8703
Invercap	147.4402 (10.5314)	0.0782	0.5603/ −0.4125	−16.9504
Principal	150.1378 (10.7241)	0.147	0.7573/ −0.7160	−8.778
Profuturo GNP	189.4484 (13.5320)	0.2311	0.8087/ −0.5320	−12.5183
SURA	182.4179 (13.0299)	0.221	0.8327/ −0.4566	−11.0146
CETES28D	114.8768 (8.2055)	—	—	0.0005
Statistical summary				
Ticker	*Mean one regime*	*Mean two regimes*	*Standard dev. one regime*	*Standard dev. two regimes*
SB3index	0.1352 (6.7617)	0.1700 (8.5004)/ −0.1029 (−5.1467)	1.1149 (7.8834)	0.5686 (4.0205)/ 2.7318 (19.3167)
Azteca	0.1272 (6.3606)	0.1487 (7.4326)/ −0.0324 (−1.6198)	0.9886 (6.9907)	0.5160 (3.6485)/ 2.4962 (17.6507)
Citibanamex	0.1409 (7.0426)	0.1810 (9.0511)/ −0.1482 (−7.4093)	1.2698 (8.9791)	0.6205 (4.3879)/ 3.2141 (22.7269)
Inbursa	0.1150 (5.7511)	0.1289 (6.4455)/ 0.0839 (4.1933)	0.2839 (2.0073)	0.1373 (0.9707)/ 0.4662 (3.2964)
Invercap	0.1294 (6.4714)	0.1713 (8.5660)/ −0.1611 (−8.0561)	1.8056 (12.7674)	0.7809 (5.5216)/ 4.6378 (32.7944)
Principal	0.1310 (6.5489)	0.1702 (8.5111)/ −0.1428 (−7.1409)	1.0354 (7.3212)	0.5674 (4.0124)/ 2.4913 (17.6159)
Profuturo GNP	0.1518 (7.5915)	0.1866 (9.3319)/ −0.1550 (−7.7498)	1.2966 (9.1680)	0.6749 (4.7725)/ 3.5150 (24.8548)
SURA	0.1483 (7.4158)	0.1842 (9.2090)/ −0.0823 (−4.1159)	1.2434 (8.7923)	0.6346 (4.4874)/ 2.9700 (21.0011)
CETES28D	0.1094 (5.4724)	—	0.0388 (0.2743)	—

Source: Own elaboration with data from the simulations and CONSAR (2018)

Table 17.9 The goodness-of-fit test of a Gaussian single-regime stochastic process in the studied SB4 index and SIEFOREs versus the two-regime one

Ticker	*LLF 1 regime*	*LLF 2 regimes*	*Akaike 1 regime*	*Akaike 2 regimes*
SB4index	2073.50	2346.51	−4145.01	−4687.02
Azteca	2228.19	2482.73	−4454.39	−4959.47
Citibanamex	1973.04	2279.89	−3944.07	−4553.77
Inbursa	2971.82	3156.00	−5941.63	−6306.01
Invercap	1798.76	2140.91	−3595.52	−4275.81
Principal	2152.50	2388.77	−4303.01	−4771.53
Profuturo GNP	1956.57	2254.77	−3911.14	−4503.54
SURA	1998.27	2260.84	−3994.54	−4515.69
CETES28D	4511.92	—	−9021.84	—
Ticker	*Schwarz 1 regime*	*Schwarz 2 regimes*	*Hannan-Quinn 1 regime*	*Hannan-Quinn 2 regimes*
SB4index	−4140.46	−4673.37	−4142.70	−4687.38
Azteca	−4449.83	−4945.81	−4452.08	−4959.83
Citibanamex	−3939.52	−4540.12	−3941.76	−4554.13
Inbursa	−5937.08	−6292.35	−5939.32	−6306.37
Invercap	−3590.97	−4262.16	−3593.21	−4276.17
Principal	−4298.46	−4757.88	−4300.70	−4771.89
Profuturo GNP	−3906.59	−4489.88	−3908.83	−4503.90
SURA	−3989.99	−4502.03	−3992.23	−4516.05
CETES28D	−9017.29	—	−9020.08	—

Source: Own elaboration with data from CONSAR (2018)

17.4 Conclusions

Since the reform of 1997, the Mexican pension fund system has evolved to a defined-benefit (DB) one and the pension liability has been transferred to pension savers. Since inception, the DB system works with the selection of individual pension savings mutual funds known as SIEFOREs,[6] in which the pension savers invest her/his proceedings during the active life cycle and use them at retirement. Departing from this reform, an issue of interest is to test the performance of the SIEFOREs in terms of return, risk exposure, and mean-variance efficiency.

Several studies have been made in order to explain and prove the benefits of the Mexican pension reform of 1997, but just a few of these review the performance of the SIEFOREs. The official authority for this pension system in Mexico, CONSAR,[7] calculates a net return index, which measures only the return paid (net of pension

[6]Sociedad de Inversión Especializada en FOndos para el REtiro or pension savings mutual fund.

[7]Comisión Nacional del Sistema de Ahorro para el Retiro or National Pension Savings Commission.

Table 17.10 Statistical and performance summary of the studied SB3 indices and SIEFOREs versus the two-regime one

Performance summary				
Ticker	*Accumulated return*	*Sharpe ratio one regime*	*Sharpe ratio two regimes*	*Max. drawdown*
SB4index	157.7017 (11.2644)	0.1635	0.7531/ −0.5497	−10.1528
Azteca	143.6313 (10.2594)	0.1271	0.5373/ −0.4018	−9.6801
Citibanamex	168.0378 (12.0027)	0.1749	0.8156/ −0.5668	−12.0912
Inbursa	123.7039 (8.8360)	0.1388	1.0025/ −0.3880	−1.8703
Invercap	147.4402 (10.5314)	0.0782	0.5603/ −0.4125	−16.9504
Principal	150.1378 (10.7241)	0.147	0.7573/ −0.7160	−8.778
Profuturo GNP	189.4484 (13.5320)	0.2311	0.8087/ −0.5320	−12.5183
SURA	182.4179 (13.0299)	0.221	0.8327/ −0.4566	−11.0146
CETES28D	114.8768 (8.2055)	—	—	0.0005
Statistical summary				
Ticker	*Mean one regime*	*Mean two regimes*	*Standard dev. one regime*	*Standard dev. two regimes*
SB4index	0.1352 (6.7617)	0.1700 (8.5004)/ −0.1029 (−5.1467)	1.1149 (7.8834)	0.5686 (4.0205)/ 2.7318 (19.3167)
Azteca	0.1272 (6.3606)	0.1487 (7.4326)/ −0.0324 (−1.6198)	0.9886 (6.9907)	0.5160 (3.6485)/ 2.4962 (17.6507)
Citibanamex	0.1409 (7.0426)	0.1810 (9.0511)/ −0.1482 (−7.4093)	1.2698 (8.9791)	0.6205 (4.3879)/ 3.2141 (22.7269)
Inbursa	0.1150 (5.7511)	0.1289 (6.4455)/ 0.0839 (4.1933)	0.2839 (2.0073)	0.1373 (0.9707)/ 0.4662 (3.2964)
Invercap	0.1294 (6.4714)	0.1713 (8.5660)/ −0.1611 (−8.0561)	1.8056 (12.7674)	0.7809 (5.5216)/ 4.6378 (32.7944)
Principal	0.1310 (6.5489)	0.1702 (8.5111)/ −0.1428 (−7.1409)	1.0354 (7.3212)	0.5674 (4.0124)/ 2.4913 (17.6159)
Profuturo GNP	0.1518 (7.5915)	0.1866 (9.3319)/ −0.1550 (−7.7498)	1.2966 (9.1680)	0.6749 (4.7725)/ 3.5150 (24.8548)
SURA	0.1483 (7.4158)	0.1842 (9.2090)/ −0.0823 (−4.1159)	1.2434 (8.7923)	0.6346 (4.4874)/ 2.9700 (21.0011)
CETES28D	0.1094 (5.4724)	—	0.0388 (0.2743)	—

Source: Own elaboration with data from the simulations and CONSAR (2018)

fund management fees) in a rolling time window of 36 months. This is the only official and public performance used nowadays, and there is no information that says what has been done, in terms of risk exposure, to achieve such return. Departing from this issue, we propose to measure the expected return, risk exposure, and mean-variance efficiency for each of the SIEFOREs in a single- and in a two-regime scenario. One regime corresponds to *normal* or *good-performing* ($s = 1$) time periods and another for *crisis* or *bad-performing* ($s = 2$) ones. We propose this regime differentiation by the fact that it is expected that the management and performance and risk-exposure results are different among SIEFOREs in crisis time periods.

In order to test our proposal, we used the historical prices of each of the four types of SIEFOREs[8] and their corresponding performance indexes. With the continuous time return of these, we used Hamilton's (1989, 1990, 1994) filter and we determine the expected return $\mu_{i,\ s}$, risk exposure $\sigma_{i,\ s}$, and Sharpe (1966) ratio in $s = 1$ and $s = 2$. The results and the goodness of fit of our tests suggest that it is appropriate to model the stochastic process of each SIEFORE (and index) with a two-regime Markov-switching geometric Brownian motion process, instead of with a single-regime (conventional) one. Departing from this result, we noted (especially in the riskiest SB3 and SB4 SIEFOREs) that the performance ranking changes if we assume two regimes and that the "best performers" with a single-regime return ranking are not always "best-performers" if we review their result in a *normal* or a *crisis* time period. As expected, the best performers in a single regime are not so "best" in a crisis regime because their level of risk exposure is higher compared to that of their "not-so best" peers.

Departing from these results, we propose to CONSAR to measure and publish the expected return, risk exposure, and mean-variance efficiency in a two-regime scenario of all the SIEFOREs, instead of only measuring the net return paid. With this, we expect to increase the informational efficiency among pension savers and to reduce the noisy and uninformed SIEFORE selection made nowadays, an issue that Calderón-Colín et al. (2009) proved as true for the Mexican case.

Some of the issues that we suggest extending in the present review is to determine the main driving factors that lead to the performance differences observed during crisis periods. Another one is to determine the reason of why some SIEFOREs, such as Azteca or Inbursa, have a significantly different performance than their peers even if they use the same official investment policy.

[8]Type 1, or SB1, is the most conservative and type 4, or SB4, is the most aggressive with higher investment limits in equities, international securities and commodities.

References

Akaike, H. (1974). A new look at the statistical model identification. *IEEE Transactions on Automatic Control, 19*, 716–723. https://doi.org/10.1016/J.CUB.2017.09.001.

Albo, A., González, F., Hernández, O., et al. (2007). *Hacia el fortalecimiento de los sistemas de pensiones en México*. BBVA-Research. http://www.bbvaresearch.com/KETD/fbin/mult/Haciaelfortalecimientodelossistemasdepensionesenmex_tcm346-189743.pdf?ts=1642013. Accessed 3 Feb 2012.

Alexander, C., & Kaeck, A. (2007). Regime dependent determinants of credit default swap spreads. *Journal of Banking & Finance, 32*, 1008–1021. https://doi.org/10.1016/j.jbankfin.2007.08.002.

Alexander, C., & Lazar, E. (2008). Markov Switching GARCH Diffusion (No. 44). ICMA Centre Discussion Papers in Finance 2008-01 (Vol. 44). Reading. Retrieved from https://www.researchgate.net/profile/Carol_Alexander/publication/46455390_Markov_Switching_GARCH_Diffusion/links/0f31752ff4a9e86a7c000000/Markov-Switching-GARCH-Diffusion.pdf.

Bodie, Z., Merton, R. C., & Samuelson, W. F. (1992). Labor supply flexibility and portfolio choice in a life cycle model. *Journal of Economic Dynamics and Control, 16*, 427–449.

Brooks, C., & Persand, G. (2001). The trading profitability of forecasts of the gilt–equity yield ratio. *International Journal of Forecasting, 17*, 11–29.

Calderón-Colín, R., Domínguez, E. E., & Schwartz, M. J. (2009). Consumer confusion: The choice of pension fund manager in Mexico. *Journal of Pension Economics & Finance, 9*, 43–74. https://doi.org/10.1017/S1474747209004004.

Chan-Lau, J. (2005). Pension funds in latinamerica. *Financial Markets, Institutions & Instruments, 14*, 107–134.

CONSAR. (2017). *Investment regime updated at 2017*. In: Financial data. http://www.consar.gob.mx/gobmx/Aplicativo/Limites_Inversion/?lang=en. Accessed 3 September 2018.

CONSAR. (2018). *SIEFORES historical prices*. In: Financial info. https://www.consar.gob.mx/principal/siefores%7B_%7Dbasicas/precios%7B_%7Dde%7B_%7Dbolsa%7B_%7Dde%7B_%7Dlas%7B_%7Dsiefores.xls%7B&%7Dsa=U%7B&%7Dved=0ahUKEwicpuOwpMDJAhWBGx4KHUBzA7o4ChAWCBcwCQ%7B&%7Dclient=internal-uds-cse%7B&%7Dusg=AFQjCNHxFAXKqu5OAd06A1jF. Accessed 23 August 2018.

De la Torre Torres, O. V., Galeana, E., & Aguilasocho, D. (2015a). An actual position benchmark for Mexican pension funds performance. *Economía: teoría y práctica, 43*, 133–154.

De la Torre Torres, O. V., Galeana, E., Martínez Torre-Enciso, M. I., & Aguilasocho, D. (2015b). A minimum variance benchmark to measure the performance of pension funds in Mexico. *Contaduría y Administración, 60*, 593–614. https://doi.org/10.1016/j.cya.2015.05.009.

De la Torre Torres, O. V., Galeana Figueroa, E., & Alvarez-García, J. (2017). The cost of homogeneity in life cycle pension funds: An explanation to demand's inelasticity of Mexican pension funds with a performance attribution test. *European Research on Management and Business Economics, 24*, 97–103. https://doir.org/10.1016/j.iedeen.2017.11.002.

Hamilton, J. D. (1989). A new approach to the economic analysis of nonstationary time series and the business cycle. *Econometrica, 57*, 357–384.

Hamilton, J. D. (1990). Analysis of time series subject to changes in regime. *Journal of Econometrics, 45*, 39–70. https://doi.org/10.1016/0304-4076(90)90093-9.

Hamilton, J. D. (1994). *Time series analysis*. Princeton: Princeton University Press.

Hamilton, J. D. (1996). Specification testing in Markov-switching time-series models. *Journal of Econometrics, 70*, 127–157. https://doi.org/10.1016/0304-4076(69)41686-9.

Hannan, E. J., & Quinn, B. G. (1979). The determination of the order of an autoregression. *Journal of the Royal Statistical Society, Series B, 41*, 190–195. https://doi.org/10.2307/2985032.

Hauptmann, J., Hoppenkamps, A., Min, A., et al. (2014). Forecasting market turbulence using regime-switching models. *Financial Markets and Portfolio Management, 28*, 139–164. https://doi.org/10.1007/s11408-014-0226-0.

Martínez, M. R., & Venegas, F. (2014). Análisis del riesgo de mercado de los fondos de pensión en México un enfoque con modelos autorregresivos. *Contaduría y Administración, 59*, 165–195. https://doi.org/10.1016/S0186-1042(14)71269-0.

Merton, R. (1969). Lifetime portfolio selection under uncertainty: The continuous time case. *The Review of Economics and Statistics, 51*, 247–257. https://doi.org/10.2307/1926560.

Rodriguez-Reyes, L. (2017). El manejo del riesgo de longevidad en los sistemas públicos de pensiones. Una propuesta de uso de swaps de longevidad para México. *El Trimestre Económico, LXXXIV*, 681–706.

Santillán, R., Martínez, M., & López, F. (2016). Análisis econométrico del riesgo y rendimiento de las SIEFORES. *Revista Mexicana de Economía y finanzas, 11*, 29–54.

Schwarz, G. (1978). Estimating the dimension of a model. *The Annals of Statistics, 6*, 461–464.

Sharpe, W. (1966). Mutual fund performance. *Journal of Business, 39*, 119–118.

Thomas, A., & Spataro, L. (2016). The effects of pension funds on markets performance: A review. *Journal of Economic Surveys, 30*, 1–33. https://doi.org/10.1111/joes.12085.

Villagomez, F. A. (2014). El ahorro para el retiro: Una reflexión para México. *El Trimestre Económico, 81*, 549–576.

Villagómez, F. A., & Hernández, I. (2009). Impacto de la reforma al sistema de pensiones en México sobre el ahorro. *Economía Mexicana Nueva Época, XIX*, 271–310.

Villagómez, F. A., & Ramírez, G. D. (2014). Pensión universal proporcional. Una propuesta para México. *El Trimestre Económico, LXXXI*, 839.

Chapter 18
Regime-Switching in the Volatility of Mexican Pension Fund Returns

Francisco López-Herrera, Marissa R. Martínez-Preece, and Roberto Joaquín Santillán-Salgado

Abstract Several Latin American countries reformed their retirement-pension systems during the 1980s and 1990s because the previous funded or pay-as-you-go systems were deemed insufficient to support the rapidly growing aging populations. Mexico was no exception, and in 1997 it replaced its traditional pay-as-you-go system with a privately managed scheme, in which contributions by or on behalf of active workers are deposited in individual accounts and channeled to a privately managed pension fund. The main function of these private pension fund managers is to invest active workers' contributions in financial securities portfolios to maximize returns and minimize risks, increasing the accumulation in individuals' accounts. The defined-contribution system, as it is known, manages workers' accumulated resources to support them upon retirement. According to government authorities, the system also has the advantage of increasing domestic savings due to the compulsory nature of workers' savings, and investing them to foster economic growth. Since the defined-contribution system was implemented in Mexico, its investment regime has undergone several changes. At the end of 2004, a new type of basic pension fund, SIEFOREs (Sociedades de Inversion Especializadas de Fondos para el Retiro), was created, and a new 2007 amendment allowed for the creation of three new different types of pension funds designed to serve workers pertaining to different age ranges, encompassing their complete life span. This chapter analyzes the conditional volatility of SIEFOREs' returns based on a model according to which GARCH

F. López-Herrera (✉)
División de Investigación de la Facultad de Contaduría y Administración, Universidad Nacional Autónoma de México (UNAM), Mexico City, Mexico
e-mail: flopez@fca.unam.mx

M. R. Martínez-Preece
Departamento de Administración, Universidad Autónoma Metropolitana-Azcapotzalco, Mexico City, Mexico
e-mail: mrmp@correo.azc.uam.m

R. J. Santillán-Salgado
Departamento de Economía y Finanzas, EGADE Business School, Garza García, Nuevo León, Mexico
e-mail: roberto.santillan@itesm.mx

M. Peris-Ortiz et al. (eds.), *Economic Challenges of Pension Systems*,
https://doi.org/10.1007/978-3-030-37912-4_18

parameters follow a two-regime Markov-chain process. Since all the available information for each SIEFORE is used, a thorough analysis is carried out, taking into account different critical facts that have influenced retirement pension fund risk. The study's results and conclusions are useful for retirement pension fund managers, as well as for the system's regulators and supervisors.

Keywords Pension funds · Markov-switching GARCH models · Return volatility · Risk returns

18.1 Introduction

Latin American countries[1] executed deep structural reforms to privatize their retirement pension systems during the 1980s and 1990s as a response to hard evidence that traditional *fully funded* or *pay-as-you-go* systems were insufficient to support an increasingly aging population and a declining contribution base. Before transforming the traditional public system to a private scheme, most shifted from a *funded* to a *pay-as-you-go* scheme since the former was expected to generate an operational deficit after some years. Notwithstanding, the latter did not resolve the retirement pension systems' liquidity problems because most workers' accumulation was not enough to fund their retirement due to long periods of unemployment and the coexistence of parallel and nontransferable pension regimes that workers joined and exited as they changed jobs.

Mexico's pension system was subject to similar problems, and in 1997, the country's government decided to replace the then existing *pay-as-you-go* system with a privately managed retirement pension scheme that followed the blueprint of the Chilean retirement pension system, which was introduced during the early 1980s and had proved successful after 15 years of operation. Under the new scheme, contributions by, or on behalf, of active workers are deposited in individual accounts, and all the resources in the individual accounts are channeled to privately managed specialized pension funds. Their objective is to invest the workers' contributions in financial securities portfolios to maximize returns and minimize risk. Fund administrators manage the savings so that the accumulation of periodic contributions plus retained earnings build up, and the balance at the end of a worker's working life is enough to support her in retirement. Different private funds compete in the market for the workers' savings with active publicity and promotion campaigns. However, the funds' performance, which should be one of the most powerful sale arguments, is made public by CONSAR[2] the industry's

[1]Peru in 1993, Argentina and Colombia in 1994, Uruguay in 1996, Bolivia in 1997 and El Salvador in 1998 (Martínez-Preece and Venegas-Martínez 2015)

[2]The acronym of Mexican regulatory entity for the Mexican pension system, especially for the supervision and regulation of SIEFORES: Comisión Nacional del Sistema del Ahorro para el Retiro or "National Retirement Savings Commission".

government supervisor, only once a month. That report contains very crude measures of return and volatility, and savers have to make their choice of SIEFORE based on it. The report's limited information is unquestionably insufficient to reveal the dynamic characteristics of the system and to support the analysis of SIEFOREs with decision-making objectives. The living conditions that Mexican workers will face upon retirement depends on the characteristics of the prevailing retirement pension system. Therefore, the analysis of retirement pension funds' performance in Mexico deserves greater attention, but very little research has been produced on it. The fundamental motivation of this work is to perform an in-depth study of SIEFOREs' evolution in recent times, including their performance during periods of high and low volatility.

This chapter analyzes the conditional volatility of SIEFOREs' returns using a model in which GARCH parameters switch between two regimes following a Markov-chain process. Each SIEFORE's available data is used in the analysis to consider critical facts that have influenced the pension funds' risk. The estimation results support several conclusions that are relevant for retirement pension fund managers, as well as for regulators and supervisors, and contribute to a better understanding of the characteristics of the industry, which, we hope, can enhance the long-term benefits enjoyed by future pensioners.

18.2 Literature Review

The significant progress observed in health sciences, as well as improvements in the living standards of vast population contingents in every region of the world, and the extraordinary solutions to a number of social, educational, and participation problems that are nowadays supported by modern technological breakthroughs, have together created a favorable environment for individuals across the world to live longer lives. At the same time, the world's population has experienced a slowdown in fertility rates, in some cases explained by intended demographic policies (as in China and other emerging countries), rapidly changing social values, the new role played by women in the labor force, and changing societal values.

However, living longer lives comes with the challenge of counting on adequate long-term funding to make them reasonably good and comfortable. Besides, diminishing birth rates imply fewer future contributors to traditional *pay-as-you-go* or *defined-benefit* retirement pension systems, posing a challenge to public policy designers responsible for retirement pension systems. As lucidly expressed by Barr and Diamond (2009), the traditional pension systems, with fixed contribution rates awarding monthly benefits at a given retirement age, are no longer congruent with the longer retirement period that comes with extended life expectancy and increased dependency rates associated to declining fertility.

The new demographic trends exert significant strain and raise relevant concerns for traditional defined-benefit pension schemes, posing the question of their long-term sustainability (see, for example, Verbič and Spruk 2014; Peinado and Serrano

2014). For these reasons, new ways and schemes to provide adequate retirement plans are currently under serious consideration all over the world.

Among other alternative schemes, a system that has attracted the attention of governments in several countries and deserved the scrutiny of serious academic studies due to its solid foundations and capacity to adapt to different demographic contexts is the *defined-contribution* pension system (Williamson et al. 2012). This system originated during the early 1980s, when the Chilean government opted for the first system of its kind, in the context of major structural reforms seeking to improve the performance of that country's economy, including a generalized privatization of state-owned firms (James 2005; Santillán-Salgado et al. 2010). The name given to the entities that comprised the new system was "Administradoras de Fondos de Pensiones" (AFP)—*pension fund managers*—and they brought significant macroeconomic and financial benefits to the country. Results were so satisfactory as to justify that during the following 20 years, the scheme was adopted in countries from Latin America, Eastern and Central Europe, and Asia (James 2005). However, the adoption of defined-contribution systems has not been limited to emerging countries as they have also been very successfully introduced in a number of developed countries, including Canada, Ireland, the United Kingdom, and the United States.

In recent decades, the literature expanded rapidly to study a wide variety of regulatory issues, operational challenges, microeconomic aspects, macroeconomic consequences, and, in recent years, the performance of pension fund investment portfolios. Some of the most influential works in the field of the defined-contribution retirement pension system include those of Orzag and Stiglitz (2001), Calderón-Colín et al. (2010), Fuentes et al. (2010), Alonso et al. (2015), De la Torre et al. (2015), Martínez-Preece and Venegas-Martínez (2014), and Santillán-Salgado et al. (2016).

Consistent with the aims of this study, the succinct literature review presented here centers on representative studies that address the financial performance of *defined-contribution* retirement pension funds. Paraphrasing Martínez-Preece and Venegas-Martínez (2014), neither savings nor economic growth is the ultimate objective of the design of pension programs (Diamond and Stiglitz 1974). However, it should be considered that the possibility of increasing total savings, even when it implies exposing workers to greater risks in order to make their savings support economic growth, is acceptable only if it has been carefully analyzed and if, ultimately, it results in greater well-being for the population.

Among the first studies interested in addressing the question of how successful defined-contribution plans would be in providing pensions to workers once they retire, Blake et al. (2001) make a significant contribution by describing the way pension provision systems undergo the transition from an unfunded social security scheme to a private funding framework and, within that category, from a defined-benefit system toward a defined-contribution system. In their work, they describe the huge transfer of risk from the previous bearers, namely taxpayers and corporate sponsors, toward the individual agents who participate in a defined-contribution system. To further the understanding of the implications of that transition, they estimate the value at risk (VaR) during the accumulation phase of defined-contribution pension plans implementing diverse asset-return models, such as models with stationary moments, or regime-switching models and at the same time explore different asset-allocation strategies, again using a variety of alternatives (static and dynamic). The authors reach four important conclusions, the first of which is particularly worrying because, according to the authors, defined-contribution plans can be "extremely risky" compared to a defined-benefit benchmark system. Their second conclusion is that VaR estimates are highly sensitive to what kind of asset-allocation strategy is followed by the fund managers. Interestingly, the third conclusion is that a static asset-allocation strategy that gives a high weight to equity assets achieves substantially better results than other dynamic strategies investigated. Lastly, their fourth conclusion, consistent with the previous one, is that less risky bond-based asset-allocation strategies require savers to make significantly higher contributions to achieve similar retirement pensions as riskier equity-based strategies.

The defined-contribution system that has prevailed in Mexico since 1997 is described in some detail by Martínez-Preece and Venegas-Martínez (2014). According to these authors, one of the main features of the system is that it is managed by the private sector through individual accounts that concentrate the contributions made by workers, employers, and the government. The minimum period that a worker needs to contribute to the system is 25 years, and the pension received will depend on the individual record of each worker. This means that the balance of the individual worker's SIEFORE upon retirement will depend on the time during which she has made contributions, of the amounts deposited and of the yields accumulated throughout her working life. This last feature is linked to financial market performance since the worker's savings are used to purchase financial securities. So the total accumulation in the worker's retirement account will depend on the assets' price changes and accumulated yield that have built up in the individual's investment portfolios. That fact justifies a detailed study of the market performance of SIEFOREs and exploring their risk-return characteristics. In order to study the market risk performance of two types of SIEFOREs, the SIEFORE Básica I (SB1) and the Siefore Básica 2 (SB2), during the period from July 1, 1997, to December 31, 2010, for SB1 and from September 1, 2004, to December 31, 2010, for SB2, Martinez-Preece and Venegas-Martínez use an equally weighted performance benchmark of each SIEFORE type and an ARIMA-GARCH model to examine their dynamic returns and volatility. The authors also analyze the risk premium of both types of funds. One of the most relevant findings reported by these authors is that the yields obtained by these two types of funds during the period of analysis are not sufficient to compensate for the additional risk assumed by pension funds, whose portfolios include a variable income component. More specifically, they show that, in terms of mean-variance efficiency measured with Sharpe ratios, the SB1s underperformed the most conservative SB2s due to the higher volatility of the former (as expected) and to the asymmetry of the GARCH process inherent to the time series. The authors conclude with a reflection that seems to be right given the compulsory nature of savings SIEFOREs for workers, analyzing their financial risk and, in particular, the market risk, is of utmost importance since precisely the latter is the one that affects the total value of the accumulated retirement funds upon which the workers will depend at the end of their working life. They also emphasize that there is an unsatisfied need for better SIEFORE financial performance measures.

A study by Tecnológico de Monterrey on the defined-contribution Mexican retirement pension system discusses at length its antecedents; its macroeconomic impact on the labor market, on the public finances of the country, and on savings; and several other economic aspects (Fuentes-Castro 2014). Among the many interesting results of the analysis of the system and of its impact on the Mexican financial system, the reported findings suggest that the recent pension reform has contributed to the development of the country's financial sector, augmented the depth of the long-term debt markets in Mexico, and contributed to reduce the cost of long-term funding. Also, based on the results a vector error correction model, the report indicates that the evolution of the SIEFORE Granger affects the Mexican stock index but not the other way around. In brief, one of the relevant conclusions of the study is that pension funds can influence the financial system. However, the conclusions of that study are particularly relevant for the present work. Firstly, the degree of diversification of the assets held by the SIEFOREs represents an area of opportunity for improvement. Furthermore, that analysis explores whether some SIEFOREs replicate the strategy of other SIEFOREs and concludes that the correlation between different SIEFORE returns show high degrees of association and that by using a Granger-causality analysis, it can be concluded that some of the SIEFOREs lead the rest. The study explores how active the SIEFOREs are in trading and if they buy and sell securities from each other. It also finds that assets' holdings augmented when their returns increased; i.e., there is a positive correlation between an asset purchase and its performance. The evidence is clear in the case of international stocks, domestic private debt, structured products, international bonds, and government bonds. The study concludes with a list of recommendations aimed to improve the accumulation of savings, the stability of the system, and a more conscious participation of the population.

Martínez-Preece and Venegas-Martínez (2014) again undertake the analysis of the financial performance of Mexican pension funds with the intention of analyzing its market behavior and, more specifically, the volatility of the yields of different types of pension funds during the period from April 1, 2008, through December 31, 2014 (i.e., daily information of the four types of pension funds for almost 7 years). The authors attempt to determine if the pension system in Mexico is sustainable, considering its endowment and operating conditions. In the empirical part of their study, the authors model the dynamics of SIEFOREs' yield volatility using the SIEFOREs' indices, which are quoted in the Mexican Stock Exchange and published by CONSAR for the stated period of analysis. To model the SIEFOREs' risk premium volatility, the authors chose a GARCH-M model. The output of the GARCH-M model shows that the SIEFORE yields' negative perturbations are larger than the positive perturbations; i.e., there is asymmetry in volatility. For that reason, the authors opt for an EGARCH model, whose adjustment is quite satisfactory, which confirms that there are no remaining GARCH effects that require further adjustments. The estimation results of the EGARCH model confirm the presence of significant asymmetry coefficients in all four SIEFOREs' risk premia. The conditional volatility obtained for the SB4 with the GARCH-M model is very high, almost 50% during the 2008 financial crisis. In contrast, the conditional volatility observed for the more conservative SB1 yields is the lowest with respect to its peers. Based on their statistical analysis, Martínez-Preece and Venegas-Martínez conclude that under a pensionary system with low contributions and an unstable labor market that results in a discontinuity of the workers' pension lifetime savings accumulation, the financial stability of the system becomes a key element to guarantee satisfactory pensions in the future. So they ask the question: how many of the workers in the system will accumulate enough savings so as to enjoy a retirement pension above the minimum guaranteed pension? To answer this question, they make a simple calculation that reveals that a typical worker must work and contribute to the system for at least 25 years, earning a salary equivalent to three and a half times the minimum wage during that period, and that the accumulated savings must yield a minimum of 12% annually with bimonthly composition. In contrast, the average historical rate of return of SIEFOREs is in the order of 7%, making the accumulation of a large proportion of the population unlikely to be enough upon retirement. Only an estimated 12% of the workers who contribute to the defined-contribution system will have enough accumulation to exceed the minimum guaranteed pension offered by the government. These conclusions must be considered when any proposal to reform the system is discussed. Evidently, the system needs an urgent revision that increases the accumulation rate for workers, employers, and the government.

Lastly, Santillán-Salgado et al. (2016) develop a study that analyzes SIEFOREs' performance since the defined-contribution system's original introduction and through different time subperiods (1997–2012, 2004–2012, and 2008–2012). They present the results of an econometric analysis conducted on yields and the volatility of the five Basic SIEFOREs (SB1, SB2, SB3, SB4, and SB5) created by the Mexican government to replace the defined-benefit system, which prevailed until 1997, and that are listed on the Mexican Stock Exchange. Their main objective is to verify the nature of the stochastic behavior of the performance and volatility series of the different SIEFOREs. Specifically, they propose two working hypotheses to determine the presence of long-term memory effects in both series: (a) "It is possible to model the yields of SIEFORES without considering the long-term memory," and (b) "It is possible to model the volatilities of SIEFORES without considering the long-term memory." Both hypotheses are soundly rejected by the analysis, and the reported results show evidence of fractional integration in both the yields and the volatility series. In the first case, the analysis is extended with ARFIMA models (p, d, q). The presence of high-persistence volatility is also confirmed, justifying the development of GARCH models with fractional integration, known as FIGARCH (p, d, q) models. The authors report that there are great similarities between SB3, SB4, and SB5 return volatility. It is evident that the turbulence that surged during 2008 and the first months of the following year related to the global financial crisis, as well as the new phase of uncertainty associated with the risk that Greece, Portugal, Ireland, and Spain could default on their sovereign debt in 2011, had an impact on all three newer SIEFOREs, whose portfolios incorporate greater-risk assets. The main implication of these findings is that in order to measure the long-term performance of SIEFOREs and to model their volatility (with, for example, risk management purposes), more elaborate econometric models are needed. The use of modern econometric techniques for the measurement and modeling of yields and volatility is of the highest importance to determine the levels of exposure and to design possible risk coverage strategies that will prevent patrimonial damages to Mexican workers.

This literature review did not find any other contributions that analyze the relationship of performance and risk dimensions of defined-contribution pension funds, confirming the opportunity to make original studies that will improve our understanding of how these systems work and how they can be improved, more so considering the important economic and social role they play in modern societies.

18.3 The Defined-Contribution System in Mexico

As mentioned before, in 1997, Mexico implemented a defined-contribution system to replace the *pay-as-you-go* scheme, which had prevailed since the second half of the twentieth century. Originally, the system was created for workers of the Mexican Social Security Institute (Instituto Mexicano del Seguro Social (IMSS)).[3] In 2008, it included the State Workers Social Security and Safety Institute (Instituto de Seguridad y Servicios Sociales para los Trabajadores del Estado (ISSSTE)). While the new pension system includes most of the formal active workers in the country, it still coexists with defined benefits or traditional pension systems.[4] Nevertheless, the current tendency is for all pension systems to evolve progressively to defined contribution systems, managed privately through individual account schemes.

The traditional pension system has been managed by the IMSS since 1943, as a *funded* system created with active workers' contributions, in such a way that once the workers retire, their pensions could be financed through the fund. This reserve mechanism functioned when the number of pensioned workers represented a small ratio with respect to the total active workers. Demographic factors and social security pension requirements, which significantly favored the workers in detriment of the funds,[5] and their deficient management—channeling significant amounts of money to finance other services for the workers, such as health services—contributed to making fund revenues insufficient to cover pensions. This situation caused the

[3]This Social Security Institute embraces most of the formal active workers in the country.

[4]Pension scheme offered by state-owned companies such as the Federal Electricity Committee (Comisión Federal de Electricidad, CFE), Mexican Petroleum Company (Petróleos Mexicanos, PEMEX), several state governments and the Mexican Army.

[5]For instance, allowing workers to retire too early, and therefore receiving a pension for long periods of time.

depletion of fund reserves and forced authorities to substitute the funded scheme with a *pay-as-you-go* system, where pensions are paid directly with contributions from active workers. Nevertheless, after functioning for some years, this scheme also showed imbalances between contributions and benefits received by pensioned workers, due to an aging population, and a reduced mortality rate, which made the ratio between pensioned and active workers increase and, therefore, the funded system unsustainable.

Around 1995, the IMSS forecasted that if pension systems continued unchanged, the balance between revenues and pensions could only be maintained until 2005. From that date on, the pension system would face a fast-growing deficit, which eventually would have to be covered with federal revenues, and around 2020 would become too expensive to finance. Even though there were different opinions about the size of the deficit from both the Social Security Institute and external analysts, they all agreed that if the defined-benefit scheme remained the same, it would hardly be feasible for more than 20 years without incurring heavy social costs (Espinosa-Vega and Yip 2002).

These considerations led to the replacement of the *pay-as-you-go* retirement pension system with a defined-contribution scheme. As explained before, under this new system, workers, employers, and the government deposit their contributions for at least 25 years in an individual account where savings by or on behalf of the workers are kept and managed privately by companies specialized in pension funds (Administradoras de Fondos para el Retiro, AFORE), so upon their retirement, workers can finance their pensions themselves. Under this system, each worker will create his or her own fund, and the accumulated amount before retirement will depend on the size of the contributions and the length of time during which they are made.[6] Additionally, the government will guarantee a minimum pension in cases where the worker has failed to save enough to finance his/her retirement. A significant factor that will impact the accrued amount in individual accounts will be the financial market conditions during the accumulation period, since contributions are channeled by pension fund managers to invest in a wide variety of financial securities.

The new pension system closely resembles the defined-contribution system prevailing in Chile. Even international institutions, such as the World Bank and the International Monetary Fund, consider the Chilean experience as a reference in this matter. Nevertheless, the reform made in the Chilean pension system in 2008 and the problems it currently faces have brought to light some flaws.

[6]The length of time during which savings are deposited in individual accounts is known as the accumulation period.

Table 18.1 Different types of pension funds (SIEFORE) (July 2011)[a]

Type of SIEFORE	Worker's age range
Basic 1	60 years old or more
Basic 2	From 46 years to less than 60 years old
Basic 3	From 37 years to less than 46 years old
Basic 4	From 27 years to less than 37 years old
Basic 5	Less than 27 years old

Source: Modifications to the Investment Regime (2011), CONSAR
[a]Modifications can be found in *Disposición de carácter general que establecen el Régimen de Inversión al que deberán sujetarse las SIEFORE*, published in the Mexican Federal Gazette (Diario Oficial de la Federación DOF) on July 27, 2011. These amendments are also known as *Circular Única Financiera* o CUF (Unique Financial Amendment)

Table 18.2 Types of SIEFORE (from October 2012)[a]

Type of SIEFORE	Worker's age range
Basic 1	60 years old or more
Basic 2	From 46 years to less than 60 years old
Basic 3	From 37 years to less than 46 years old
Basic 4	Less than 37 years old

Source: Modifications to the Investment Regime (2011), CONSAR
[a]According to the *Disposición de carácter general que establecen el Régimen de Inversión al que deberán sujetarse las SIEFORE*, published in the Mexican Federal Gazette on October 12, 2012. On November 23, BS4 and BS5 were merged

18.3.1 Types of Pension Funds and Main Characteristics

Retirement pension funds are designed for workers with different age ranges to encompass the complete life span of active workers, as shown in Table 18.1.

During the last semester of 2012, two new and very significant modifications to the investment policies were carried out. One of these amendments was the merger of Basic SIEFOREs 4 and 5, under the premises that the number of workers in the SB5 had decreased and that investment limits were practically the same for both types of funds, with the exception of securitized titles. Therefore, only four types of SIEFORE remained, as shown in Table 18.2.

The other modification concerned only the SIEFORE Básica 1 (SB1[7]). In this type of SIEFORE (Table 18.3), accumulated savings serve two different purposes: payment of pensions and accumulation of savings. So in order to separate both investment strategies included in SB1, a new SIEFORE to manage pensions was authorized. This new type of fund started in 2016, when the resources accumulated

[7]This SIEFORE caters to workers more than 60 years old, or to younger workers who freely choose this type of pension fund.

Table 18.3 Types of Basic SIEFORE (from December 2015)[a]

Type of SIEFORE	Worker's age range
BS0	60 years old or more nearing a total pension withdraw or with a negative pension
BS1	60 years old or more (still in the accumulation phase)
BS2	From 46 years old to less than 60 years old
BS3	From 37 years old to less than 46 years old
BS4	Less than 37 years old

Source: Modifications to the Investment Regime (2015), CONSAR

[a]According to *Disposición de carácter general que establecen el Régimen de Inversión al que deberán sujetarse las SIEFORE* published in the Mexican Federal Gazette on septiembre 24, 2015

became large enough to separate it from SB1, allowing SB1 to keep the savings of workers aged 60 or more years that are still in the accumulation period. The new fund will manage the savings of pensioned workers or from workers entitled to a guaranteed minimum pension. The objective of this modification is to ease and to improve the management of savings that are still in the accumulation phase while protecting retired workers whose savings are managed by AFOREs.

18.3.2 Investment Regime for Basic SIEFOREs

The purpose of the investment regime amendments is to allow workers to access securities that may yield high returns and to reduce the funds' risk through diversification.

The investment regime amendment carried out on April 30, 2004, allowed the division of SB1 into two, thus generating SIEFORE Básica 2 (SB2). Under this modification, SB1 was considered to be a mandatory fund, and each AFORE must manage at least one pension fund of this type. Due to this constraint, SB1 must be made up of securities that maintain workers' purchasing power. As mentioned before, until July 2011, SB1 targeted workers 56 years old or older, or younger workers who chose this type of pension fund because they did not want to assume high risks. During its first years, SB1 included only government and private securities. The incorporation of foreign securities was allowed as long as they did not exceed 20% of total assets. Even though the amendment published on December 10, 2002, approved investments in international securities, the 2002 amendment to buy international assets could not be enforced until the 2004 investment regime reform was implemented.

SB1 was also required to maintain at least 51% of total assets in debt securities with a face value in investment units[8] (UDIs) or Mexican pesos and interest rates the same as or higher than fluctuations in UDIs or than the national consumer price index. Also, SB1 can incorporate up to 100% of net total assets in debt securities with triple A investment grade or equivalent or up to 5% in debt securities with investment grade A. They can also operate with derivatives, as long as the maximum limits for debt securities with triple A, double A, and A investment grades are maintained, according to the underlying asset nature. SB1 can buy debt assets, both domestic and foreign, directly or indirectly through investment vehicles, as long as established limits are observed.

It is forbidden to buy debt securities, both domestic and foreign, that do not comply with the aforementioned investment grades. Buying foreign securities that grant rights or returns linked, directly or indirectly, to individual stocks, to a group of stocks or to price fluctuations of assets, or to commodities other than those authorized, is not allowed either.

Table 18.4 shows the limits established for different investment securities, considering market, credit, and concentration risks, as well as conflicts of interest according to the 2007 amendment. To date, SB1 continues to be the most conservative pension fund.

Investment regime modifications in 2011 included an increase in equity limits, with up to 5% of equity in Basic SIEFORE 1, and an increase in value at risk (VaR) limits, as shown in Table 18.5. Also, investments in commodities[9] were authorized, to serve as a natural hedge against inflation and to link this type of assets to the real economy, besides their association with financial markets.[10] However, these financial securities are forbidden for SB1, as well as structured securities of different types, such as infrastructure, housing, and other types of projects.

After 2011 structured securities limits in BS1 increased from 0% to 10% and the amount allowed for securitizations increased for all the Basic SIEFORE in 5%. The conditional value at risk (CVaR) is introduced as an additional measure of risk. In general, from 2011 to 2017, the total number of risky securities allowed in all types of pension fund increased. In some cases, the ranking of financial instruments

[8]"Mexico's Investment Units (UDIS) are units based on price increases and are used to settle mortgage obligations or commercial acts. They were created in 1995 to protect banks and focused mainly on mortgage loans. Banco de México publishes the value in pesos of the Mexico's Investment Unit for each day of the month in the Official Federal Gazette. On the tenth day of each month at the latest, Banco de México publishes the value of the Mexico's Investment Unit corresponding to days 11 and 25 of the month, and on the 25th of each month at the latest it publishes the value corresponding to the 26th day of that month through to the tenth day of the following month". Source: Banco de México.

[9]Commodities may be understood as gold, silver and platinum through the investment vehicles authorized by the Risk Analysis Committee, (Comité de Análisis de Riesgos, CAR), or the underlying assets in derivates used in the Banco de México operations that serve as commodities but that are different to those underlying financial assets, such as equity, interest rate, exchange rates, investment units and credits, among others.

[10]Annual Performance Report (Informe Anual de Labores) (2011).

Table 18.4 Investment regime (according to the 2007 investment regime amendment)

			Limit by typo of Basic SIEFORE			
Type of risk	Origin	Concept	1	2	3	4
Market risk		Value at risk (historical VaR)	0.60%	1.00%	1.30%	1.60%
		Equity (through stock indexes)	0%	15%	20%	25%
		Foreign currency (dollar, euros, yens, and currency index securities)	30%	30%	30%	30%
		Derivatives	Yes	Yes	Yes	Yes
Credit risk		Debt securities mxAAA and government debt securities	100%	100%	100%	100%
		Debt securities mxAA- and government debt securities	50%	50%	50%	50%
		Debt securities mxAAA and government debt securities	20%	20%	20%	20%
Risk by issuers and/or counterparties	Local	Debt securities mxAAA from one issuer or counterparty	5%	5%	5%	5%
		Debt securities mxAA from one issuer or counterparty	3%	3%	3%	3%
		Debt securities mxA from one issuer or counterparty	1%	1%	1%	1%
		Debt securities mxBBB+ from one issuer or counterparty	5%	5%	5%	5%
		Debt securities mxBBB- from one issuer or counterparty	3%	3%	3%	3%
	Foreign	Foreign securities A- from one issuer or counterparty	5%	5%	5%	5%
		From only one issuer	20%	20%	20%	20%
Other limits		Foreign securities (debt securities, mínimum A-)	20%	20%	20%	20%
		Securitizations	10%	10%	10%	10%
		Structured securities and subordinated debt	0%	0%	0%	0%
		FIBRAS (infrastructure and housing)	0%	0%	0%	0%
		Inflation-protected securities	(51% min)	No	No	No
Conflicts of interest		Securities by related entities	15%	15%	15%	15%
		Securities by entities with patrimonial affiliation with the AFORE	5%	5%	5%	5%

Source: Financial Data, Investment Regime (2007), CONSAR

Table 18.5 Investment regime (according to the 2011 investment regime amendment)

Type of risk	Origin	Concept[a]	Limit by typo of Basic SIEFORE[b]			
			1	2	3	4
Market risk		Value at risk (one-day historical VaR)[c]	0.70%	1.10%	1.40%	2.10%
		Equity (through stock indexes)[d, e]	5%	25%	30%	40%
		Foreign currency (dollar, euros, yens, and currency index securities)[f]	30%	30%	30%	30%
Risk by issuers and/or counterparties	Local	Ordinary debt from mxAAA to mxAAA or foreign currency from BB to AAA	5%	5%	5%	5%
		Subordinated debt from mxBB+ to mxBBB+ or foreign currency from B+ to BB-	1%	1%	1%	1%
	Foreign	Foreign securities A- from one issuer or counterparty	5%	5%	5%	5%
		From only one issuer[g]	--- maximum (35%, $300 mdp) ---			
Other limits		Foreign securities	20%	20%	20%	20%
		Securitizations[h]	10%	15%	20%	30%
		Structured securities[i]	0%	15%	20%	20%
		Infrastructure or housing	0%	10%	13%	13%
		Other	0%	5%	7%	7%
		Inflation-protected securities[j]	(51% min)	No	No	No
		Commodities	0%	5%	10%	10%
Conflicts of interest		Securities by related entities	15%	15%	15%	15%
		Securities by entities with patrimonial affiliation with the AFORE[k]	5%	5%	5%	5%
Mandates and contracts		Investment mandates	Yes	Yes	Yes	Yes
		Mutual funds	Yes	Yes	Yes	Yes
		Derivatives	Yes	Yes	Yes	Yes

Source: Financial Data, Investment Regime (2011), CONSAR

[a]As a percentage of assets directly managed by the SIEFORE

[b]Todos los límites son porcentajes máximos, excepto el límite de protección inflacionaria

[c]As total percentage of the SIEFORE, including assets managed by mandates or mutual funds

[d]Includes individual equity, IPOs, national equity and foreign indexes, and mandatory convertible securities in equity from national issuers

[e]Medium- and long-term issues, issuer, and collateral ratios. Repos and derivates are considered within this limits

[f]It includes all asset holdings by Basic SIEFORE managed by the same AFORE, to national and foreign debt and to structured securities. This limit maybe exceeded by CKDs (Capital Development Certificates) if they comply with the investment regime limits

[g]Securitization issued by an independent agent that ensure that investment regime guidelines are considered with these limits

[h]ICKDs and FIBRAS are included. Structured securities are divided in two: (1) infrastructure and housing and (2) other (private capital)

[i]Maximum limits for inflation-protected securities that guarantee an equal or higher return rate than inflation rate in Mexico

[j]Limit established in SAR Law, Article 48, fraction 10. Exceptionally a 10% is permitted. The limit is 0% when there are securities by entities with patrimonial affiliation

[k]All refer to maximum limits, with exception to inflationary protection, which refers to a minimum

included in the funds decreased, as it was the case of some foreign securities that changed their grade fromt A- to BBB-.

In 2013, REITs (real estate investment trusts) were introduced, but they did not account for the VaR as risky securities. Also, commodity derivatives were introduced.

In 2016, CERPIs and FIBRAE were introduced. CERPIs are certificates that allow investors to have access to a wide range of economic productive sector projects, and FIBRAEs are REITs for mature projects on energy and infrastructure sectors.

Eventually, on January 5, 2018, the amendment published in the Mexican Federal Gazette allowed pension funds to invest in foreign REITs and mutual funds with active strategies so they may beat the market. Also, ETS were introduced in the SIEFOREs' portfolios to track index funds (both national and foreign), as well as SPACs (special purpose acquisition companies). These certificates serve as an alternative equity designed to purchase companies with growth potential; nevertheless, these may turn out to be very risky if the enterprises do not grow as expected. In Table 18.6, modifications to the investment regime in 2018 are shown.

18.3.3 Pension Funds Behavior

The behavior of Basic SIEFORE through time is observed in Graph 18.1. The cumulative index of the funds are shown, as well as their returns. BS1 index grew with certain stability until the middle of 2008, when a large crash due to the 2008–2009 international market crisis is observed. After this period, BS1 tends to increase again; nevertheless, this growth stopped in 2014, and it was followed by a period of increased volatility, as it is shown in the SB1 return graph. The same behavior is observed in BS2. BS3 and BS4 show the same trend; nevertheless, BS4 grew at a faster pace than BS3, and therefore the volatility of the latter is higher than that of SB3.

18.3.4 Descriptive Statistic Parameters

Like many financial time series, the returns of pension funds and their volatility, measured through the price index, present some stylized facts such as leptokurtic distributions with heavy tails and volatility clusters.[11] The main descriptive statistic parameters from the returns of the Basic SIEFORE are shown in Graph 18.2.

[11]Mandelbrot (1963) was the first to notice the presence of volatility clusters while studying cotton prices, observing that large fluctuations are followed by large fluctuations, while small changes tend to be followed by small changes. Fama (1965) found similar results while analyzing 30 stocks belonging to the Dow Jones Index.

Table 18.6 Investment regime I (according to the 2018 investment regime amendment)

Type of risk	Origin	Concept[a]	Limit by typo of Basic SIEFORE 1	2	3	4
Market risk		Value at risk (one-day historical VaR)[b]	0.70%	1.10%	1.40%	2.10%
		Difference of the conditional value risk[b]	0.30%	0.45%	0.70%	1.00%
		Liquidity coverage ratio[c]	80%	80%	80%	80%
Risk by issuers and/or counterparties[d]		Debt issued or endorsed by the federal government	100%	100%	100%	100%
	Local[e]	SPE[e] debt from mxBBB to mxAAA or int'l currencies BB to AAA	10%	10%	10%	10%
		Debt from mxBBB to mxAAA or int'l currencies BB to AAA	5%	5%	5%	5%
		Subordinated debt mxBB+ to BBB- or int'l currencies B+ to BB-BB-	1%	1%	1%	1%
		Hybrid debt from mxBBB+ to mxBBB or int'l currencies BB+ to BB	2%	2%	2%	2%
	Foreign	Foreign securities from BBB to AAA from one issuer or counterparty[f]	5%	5%	5%	5%
		From only one issuer[g]	--- maximum (35%, $300 mdp) ---			
Asset class limits		Foreign securities[d]	20%	20%	20%	20%
		Equity[d,i]	10%	30%	35%	45%
		Foreign currency[d]	30%	30%	30%	30%
		Securitizations[d,i]	10%	15%	20%	30%
		Structured securities[d,j]	10%	15%	20%	20%
		Mexican REITs (FIBRAS) and REITs[k]	5%	10%	10%	10%
		Inflation-protected securities[l]	(51% min)	No	No	No
		Commodities	0%	5%	10%	10%
Conflicts of interest		Securities by related entities	15%	15%	15%	15%
		Securities by entities with patrimonial affiliation with the AFORE[m]	5%	5%	5%	5%
Vehicles and derivatives		Investment mandates	Yes	Yes	Yes	Yes

(continued)

Table 18.6 (continued)

Type of risk	Origin	Concept[a]	Limit by typo of Basic SIEFORE			
			1	2	3	4
		Derivatives	Yes	Yes	Yes	Yes

Source: Financial Data, Investment Regime (2018), CONSAR

[a]All the limits are maximum percentages, with the exception of the inflation protection limits

[b]As a percentage of the assets under management (AUM) directly managed by the SIEFORE. VaR will no longer be a regulatory limit once the AFORE satisfies the criteria set up in the Financial Provisions (CUF). The limits of the difference of the conditional VaR were determined by the Risk Analysis Committee (CAR), which might be stricter than the limits set up in the Investment Regime Provisions

[c]As a percentage of the high liquid assets of the SIEFORE. It is defined as the ratio between the value of the SIEFORE's reserves for derivative exposure and the value of high liquid assets

[d]As a percentage of the total AUM of the SIEFORE, including the assets managed by the specialized investment manager (Mandatario in Spanish)

[e]Rating of medium- and long-term issuances, as well as the issuer and/or endorser, in corresponding proportion. Repos and derivatives are computed in these limits as well. SPE stands for state productive enterprises

[f]The regulation permits investments in foreign securities with a credit rating below A- and equal or greater than BBB-. Nevertheless, the AFORE must abide by the Investment Regime Provisions and the Financial Provisions (CUF)

[g]Applies to the asset holdings of all pension funds of the same fund manager (AFORE) and for debt and structured securities. A CKD may exceed this limit if the issue meets certain conditions

[h]Includes individual stocks, IPOs, domestic and international equity indexes listed in the Index Lists, and mandatory convertible debt into share from Mexican issuers

[i]Securitizations fulfilling criteria established in Appendix R of the Financial Provisions (CUF) are computed in these limits and are considered as being issued by an independent issuer, as well as certificates that the source of income comes from real assets

[j]Includes CKDs and CERPIs

[k]Includes Mexican REITs (FIBRAS) and FIBRA-E. The latter is an issuer trust whose resources will be allocated for direct or indirect investment in companies, projects, or energy assets or infrastructure

[l]Minimum investment limit in securities that ensures a return equal or greater than the inflation rate in México

[m]The limits are written down in the SAR Law, Article 48, paragraph X. In exceptional cases, it could be increased up to 10%. The limit is 0% for financial entities with patrimonial affiliations

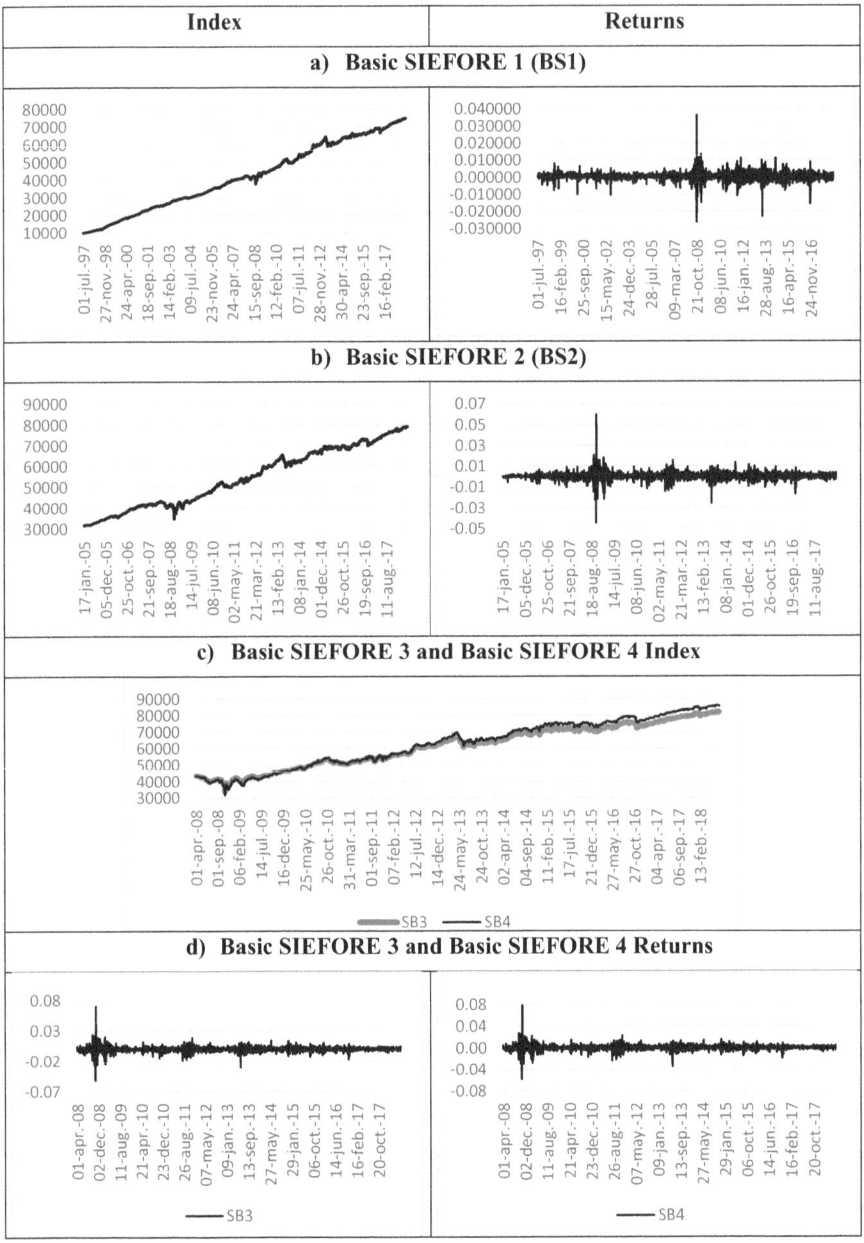

Graph 18.1 Basic SIEFORE cumulative index and returns. (*Source:* Prepared by the authors)

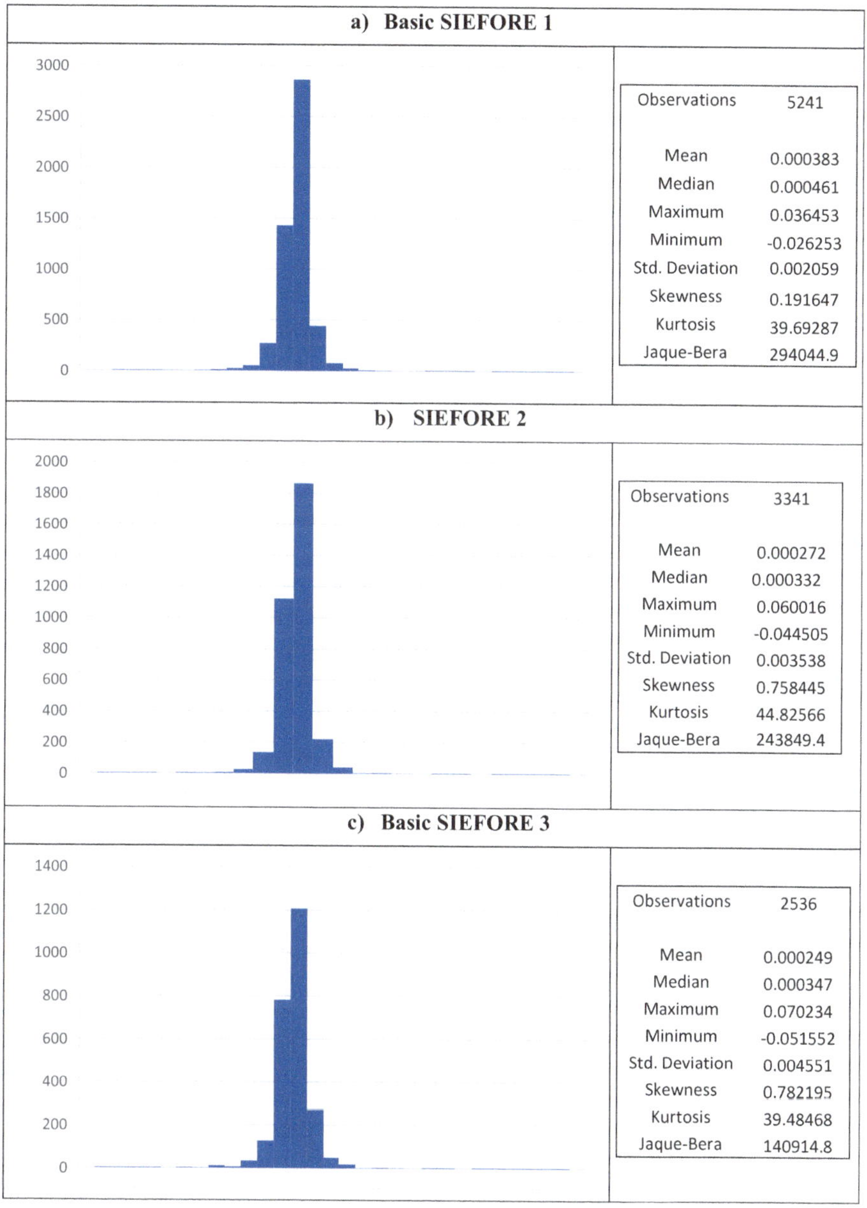

Graph 18.2 Descriptive statistic of the returns. (*Source*: Prepared by the authors)

d) Basic SIEFORE 4

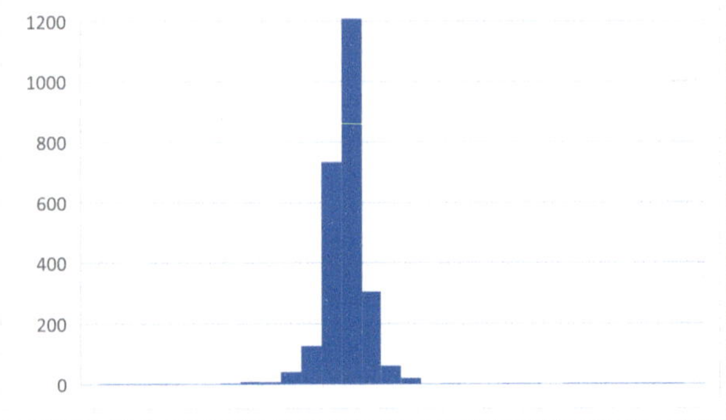

Observations	2536
Mean	0.000268
Median	0.00037
Maximum	0.078758
Minimum	-0.058124
Std. Deviation	0.005219
Skewness	0.675916
Kurtosis	36.86099
Jaque-Bera	121347

Graph 18.2 (continued)

18.4 Methodological Issues

According to Ardia et al. (2016), given y_t, $\mathbb{E}(y_t) = 0, \mathbb{E}(y_t, y_{t-r}) = 0, r \neq 0, t > 0$, the Markov-switching GARCH (MS-GARCH) model can be written in a general way as

$$y_t | (s_t = k, \Omega_{t-1}) \sim \mathcal{D}_k(0, h_{k,t}, \Xi_k), \tag{18.1}$$

$\mathcal{D}_k(0, h_{k,t}, \Xi_k)$ is continuous zero-mean distribution, with time varying variance $h_{k,\,t}$ and shape parameters gathered into vector Ξ_k; s_t is a stochastic state variable with whole values, defined in the discrete space $\{1, \ldots, K\}$, whose evolution goes according to a nonobserved ergodic, first-order homogeneous Markov chain, whose transition probability matrix is defined as

$$\mathbf{P} \equiv \begin{pmatrix} p_{1,1} & \cdots & p_{1,K} \\ \vdots & \ddots & \vdots \\ p_{K,1} & \cdots & p_{K,K} \end{pmatrix}_{K \times K} \tag{18.2}$$

$p_{i,\,j} \equiv \mathbb{P}(s_t = j | s_{t\,-\,1} = i)$ is transition probability; $0 < p_{i,\,j} < 1\ \forall\ i, j \in \{1, \ldots, K\}$; $\sum_{j=1}^{K} p_{i,j} = 1, \forall i \in \{1, \ldots, K\}$. $\Omega_{t\,-\,1} \equiv \{y_{t\,-\,i}, i > 0\}$ is the information set observed up to the previous period and, according with $\mathcal{D}_k(\cdot)$,

$$\mathbb{E}[y_t^2 | s_t = k, \Omega_{t-1}] = h_{k,t}; \tag{18.3}$$

$h_{k,\,t}$ is the variance of y_t conditional on $s_t = k$. Following Haas et al. (2004), $h_{k,\,t}$ is conducted by a GARCH process; i.e., the variance is conditioned by the regime or state, being a dependent function of the past realizations of y_t, past variances, and a vector of parameters that in turn depends on the regime:

$$h_{k,t} \equiv h(y_{t-1}, h_{k,t-1}, \Theta_k), \tag{18.4}$$

$h(\cdot)$ is a measurement function that defines the filter for the conditional variance ensuring nonnegativity.

The Bollerslev (1986) GARCH model is

$$h_{k,t} \equiv \alpha_{0,k} + \alpha_{1,k} y_{t-1}^2 + \beta_k h_{k,t-1}, k = 1, \ldots, K. \tag{18.5}$$

$\Theta_k = (\alpha_{0,\ k}, \alpha_{1,\ k}, \beta_k)'$, $\alpha_{0,\ k} > 0$, $\alpha_{1,\ k} > 0$, $\beta \geq 0$ and $\alpha_{1,\ k} + \beta_k \leq 1$ are required, respectively, to ensure that the variance in each regime is covariance-stationary and strictly positive.

The MS-GARCH model is complete with the conditional distribution of $\eta_{k,t} \equiv y_t / h_{k,t}^{1/2} \sim iid\mathcal{D}_k(0, 1, \Xi_k)$ for each regime. The normal probability density function is given as

$$f_N(\eta) \equiv \frac{1}{\sqrt{2\pi}} e^{-\frac{1}{2}\eta^2}, \quad \eta \in \mathbb{R}. \tag{18.6}$$

On the other hand, the probability density function of a variable distributed as a *t*-Student variable is given by

$$f_t(\eta; \nu) \equiv \frac{\Gamma\left(\frac{\nu+1}{2}\right)}{\sqrt{(\nu - 2)\pi\Gamma\left(\frac{\nu}{2}\right)}} \left(1 + \frac{\eta^2}{(\nu - 2)}\right)^{-\frac{\nu+1}{2}}, \quad \eta \in \mathbb{R}. \tag{18.7}$$

If $y \equiv (y_1, \ldots, y_T)'$ is the vector containing all the observations and $\Psi \equiv (\Theta_1, \Xi_1, \ldots, \Theta_K, \Xi_K, \mathbf{P})$ is the parameters set, then we have the likelihood function

$$\mathcal{L}(\Psi | y) \equiv \prod_{t=1}^{T} f(y_t | \Psi, \Omega_{t-1}), \tag{18.8}$$

$$f(y_t | \Psi, \Omega_{t-1}) \equiv \sum_{i=1}^{K} \sum_{j=1}^{K} p_{i,j} z_{i,t-1} f_{\mathcal{D}}(y_t | s_t = j, \Psi, \Omega_{t-1}).$$

$z_{i,\ t\ -\ 1} \equiv \mathbb{P}(s_{t\ -\ 1} = i | \Psi, \Omega_{t\ -\ 1})$ is the filtered probability of being in the state i in $t - 1$, which is obtained through the Hamilton filter (Hamilton 1989, 1994). If such is the case, $\widehat{\Psi}$, the vector of parameter of the model can be estimated by maximum likelihood methods.

Table 18.7 SB1 MS-GARCH models

	Normal	*S*-normal	*t*	$S-t$
$\alpha_{0,1}$	0.0001[a]	0.0001[a]	0.0002[b]	0.0004[a]
$\alpha_{1,1}$	0.0294[a]	0.0311[a]	0.0400[b]	0.0620[c]
β_1	0.9479[a]	0.9454[a]	0.9500[a]	0.9258[a]
ν_1			2.8196[a]	2.8155[a]
ξ_1		0.9793[a]		0.8988[a]
$\alpha_{0,2}$	0.0085[a]	0.0084[a]	0.0007[a]	0.0009[b]
$\alpha_{1,2}$	0.1718	0.1890	0.1810	0.1729
β_2	0.8262[a]	0.8087[a]	0.8188[a]	0.8207[a]
ν_2			6.0780[a]	6.7780[a]
ξ_2		0.8326[a]		0.9921[a]
$p_{1,1}$	0.9509[a]	0.9414[a]	0.9986[a]	0.9986[a]
$p_{2,1}$	0.2738[a]	0.3127[a]	0.0006	0.0009
p_1	0.8480	0.8421	0.3024	0.3914
p_2	0.1520	0.1579	0.6976	0.6086
Logl	2866.1875	2873.0456	2946.9992	2959.9666
AIC	−5716.3750	−5726.0911	−5873.9985	−5895.9331
BIC	−5663.8152	−5660.3914	−5808.2987	−5817.0934

[a, b, c]respectively, 1%, 5%, and 10% significance level

18.5 Analysis of Mexican Retirement Pension Fund Volatility

Table 18.7 reports the estimated parameters for SB1 two-regime volatility under four specifications: errors following distributions, normal and Student's *t*, and their corresponding skewed versions for both cases. Roughly speaking, almost all the parameters of all the estimated SB1 models look very similar. Nevertheless, when the two information criteria (Akaike and Bayesian) are taken into account, the studentized distribution options are the preferred specifications, especially the skewed one. The same conclusion is reached according to the log value of the maximum likelihood function. Considering both the nonskewed and the skewed *t*-Student models, the estimated parameters for the two regimes suggest that SB1 volatility can be regarded as a highly persistent process in a regime, accompanied by a less persistent volatility regime due to the nonsignificant (zero) squared past error coefficient shown by the four estimated models. At the same time, through the skewed estimated model, we can observe that the less persistent volatility regime corresponds to the more skewed period. The half-life of the volatility in the first regime is about 56 days, while for the second regime it is around 3.5 days.[12] The estimated probability of remaining at state 1 after being there is high in all the cases,

[12]The half-life of the volatility, i.e., the time that volatility takes to revert half of the way toward its unconditional mean after a deviation from the same, was estimated as usually: $\ln(0.5)/\ln(\alpha_{1,k} + \beta_k)$.

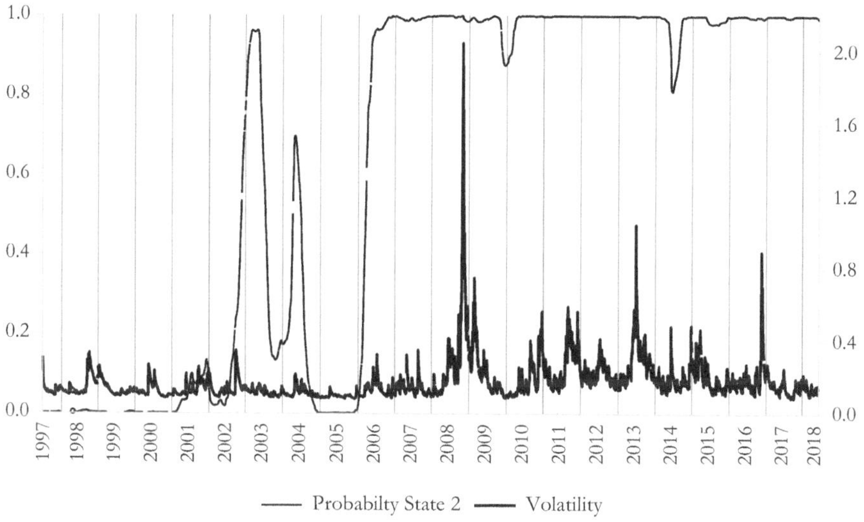

Graph 18.3 SB1 volatility and state 2 smoothed probabilities

Table 18.8 SB2 MS-GARCH models

	Normal	*S*-normal	*t*	$S-t$
$\alpha_{0,1}$	0.0001[a]	0.0001[a]	≈0	≈0[b]
$\alpha_{1,1}$	0.0249[a]	0.0238[a]	0.0002	0.0806[a]
β_1	0.9562[a]	0.9572[a]	0.9997[a]	0.9193[a]
ν_1			2.7683[a]	5.7774[a]
ξ_1		0.9994[a]		1.0198[a]
$\alpha_{0,2}$	0.0104[a]	0.0093[a]	0.0020[b]	0.0086[a]
$\alpha_{1,2}$	0.1782	0.1791	0.1468[c]	0.3687
β_2	0.8211[a]	0.8199[a]	0.8397[a]	0.6209[a]
ν_2			7.1128[a]	11.6205[b]
ξ_2		0.8826[a]		0.6853[a]
$p_{1,1}$	0.9327[a]	0.9247[a]	0.9960[a]	0.7844[a]
$p_{2,1}$	0.1702[a]	0.1698[a]	0.0007	0.5875[a]
p_1	0.7167	0.6927	0.1565	0.7316
p_2	0.2833	0.3073	0.8435	0.2684
Logl	58.0083	61.9199	84.2557	79.6442
AIC	−100.0166	−103.8399	−148.5114	−135.2884
BIC	−51.0352	−42.6132	−87.2847	−61.8164

[a, b, c] respectively, 1%, 10%, and 5% significance level

more so in the studentized specifications, where it looks almost like an absorbent state. Nonetheless, the estimated state probabilities suggest fair odds to alternate into states.

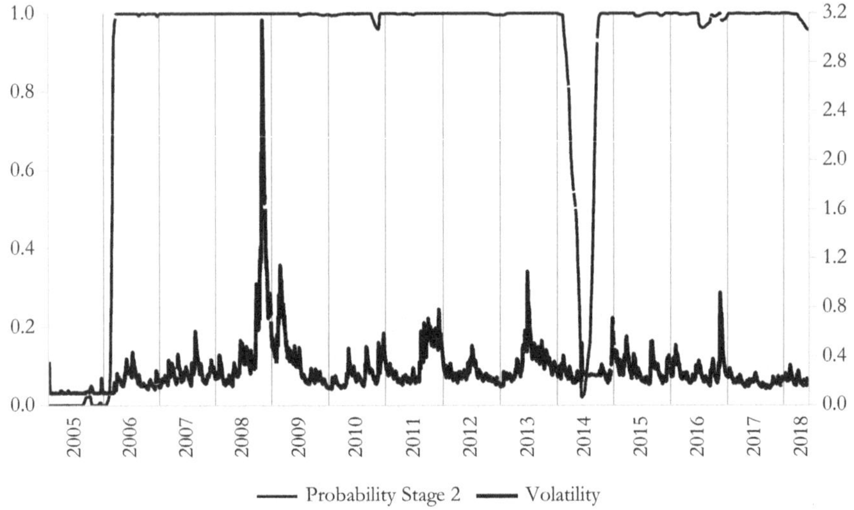

Graph 18.4 SB2 volatility and state 2 smoothed probabilities

As Graph 18.3 shows, a period characterized by lower volatility prevailed up to the middle of 2008. According to the estimated parameters of the MS-GARCH model with skewed t errors in both regimes, for almost all the years before 2006, a more skewed return distribution and a higher persistence level in volatility were observed. The notorious exception is the subperiod from the middle of 2002 to the last months of 2004, when both error distribution skewness and volatility persistence decreased. From 2006 to the end of the sample, Fig. 18.1 shows a general level of higher but less persistent volatility, accompanied by more skewed returns.

Table 18.8 shows the four estimated SB2 two-regime volatility models. We can see a few differences in some of the estimated parameters, but the Akaike and Schwarz criteria, and the value of the log-likelihood function, now suggest that the *t*-Student specification fits the data better. Nevertheless, it is worth noting that the skewness parameters estimated for the skewed normal and skewed-*t* specifications are highly significant. Under the assumptions of errors following a *t*-Student distribution in the two regimes, volatility seems very persistent, especially at the first state when it appears to correspond to an I-GARCH process, having a half-life of about 2310 days in the first regime and around 51 days in the second. Again, the probability of staying at state 1 is seen as an absorbent state, but the state probabilities suggest the possibility of switching from one regime to another.

Comparing the SB2 volatility shown in Fig. 18.2 with the aforementioned SB1 volatility, a similar pattern is observed for the common period. Before 2006, the volatility level is lower throughout the analyzed period, initiating an escalation in the first months of 2006 and, at the same time, changing the volatility process to regime two, in which it stays for all the remaining time minus a few months in mid-2014 (Graph 18.4).

The estimated SB3 models, Table 18.9, also provided similar values for the relevant parameters. Akaike criterion and Schwarz Bayesian criterion point out

Table 18.9 SB3 MS-GARCH models

	Normal	*S*-normal	*t*	$S-t$
$\alpha_{0,1}$	0.0007[a]	0.0006[a]	0.0003[b]	0.0002[b]
$\alpha_{1,1}$	0.0271[b]	0.0266[b]	0.0177[b]	0.0172[b]
β_1	0.9464[a]	0.9471[a]	0.9625[a]	0.9642[a]
ν_1			99.9836[a]	99.9826[a]
ξ_1		0.9745[a]		1.0323[a]
$\alpha_{0,2}$	0.0228[a]	0.0203[a]	0.0064[a]	0.0052[a]
$\alpha_{1,2}$	0.1643	0.1699	0.1600	0.1659
β_2	0.8297[a]	0.8249[a]	0.8380[a]	0.8327[a]
ν_2			6.8949[a]	7.2209[a]
ξ_2		0.8903[a]		0.8990[a]
$p_{1,1}$	0.9645[a]	0.9585[a]	0.9398[a]	0.9246[a]
$p_{2,1}$	0.1278[a]	0.1344[a]	0.0601[b]	0.0586[c]
p_1	0.7824	0.1344	0.4998	0.4371
p_2	0.2176	0.2362	0.5002	0.5629
Logl	−668.3394	−666.1323	−655.3594	−652.5671
AIC	1352.6788	1352.2646	1330.7188	1329.1341
BIC	1399.4796	1410.7656	1389.2198	1399.3354

[a, b, c]respectively, 1%, 5%, and 10% significance level

Table 18.10 SB4 MS-GARCH models

	Normal	*S*-normal	*t*	$S-t$
$\alpha_{0,1}$	0.0008[a]	0.0007[a]	0.0003[b]	0.0003[b]
$\alpha_{1,1}$	0.0310[b]	0.0302[b]	0.0176[b]	0.0166[b]
β_1	0.9433[a]	0.9444[a]	0.9637[a]	0.9655[a]
ν_1			99.9416[a]	84.3502
ξ_1		0.9585[a]		1.0179[a]
$\alpha_{0,2}$	0.0313[a]	0.0263[a]	0.0085[a]	0.0066[a]
$\alpha_{1,2}$	0.1790	0.1864	0.1563	0.1582
β_2	0.8158[a]	0.8095[a]	0.8414[a]	0.8401[a]
ν_2			6.9266[a]	7.3299[a]
ξ_2		0.8640[a]		0.8881[a]
$p_{1,1}$	0.9593[a]	0.9484[a]	0.9413[a]	0.9276[a]
$p_{2,1}$	0.1466[a]	0.1581[a]	0.0583[b]	0.0544[c]
p_1	0.7827	0.7539	0.4986	0.4288
p_2	0.2173	0.2461	0.5014	0.5712
Logl	−1046.0532	1042.2902	−1033.3296	−1029.5450
AIC	2108.1064	2104.5804	2086.6592	2083.0901
BIC	2154.9072	2163.0814	2145.1602	2153.2913

[a, b, c]respectively, 1%, 5%, and 10% significance level

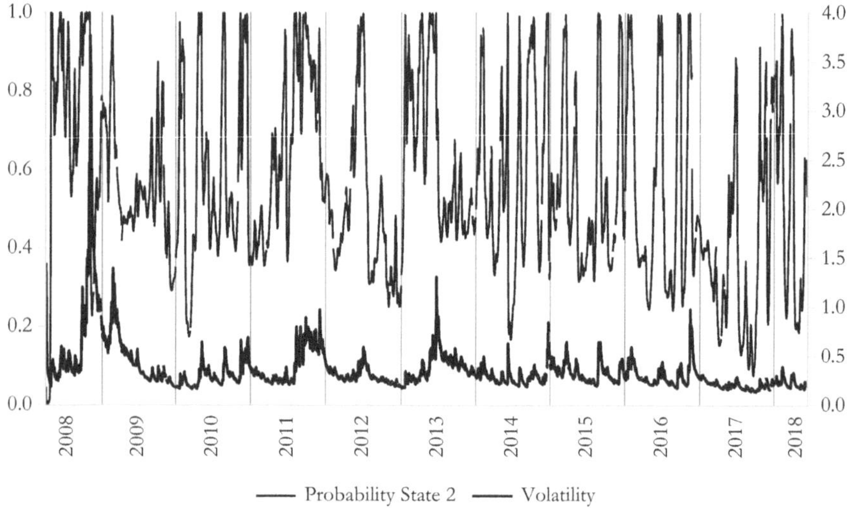

Graph 18.5 SB3 volatility and state 2 smoothed probabilities

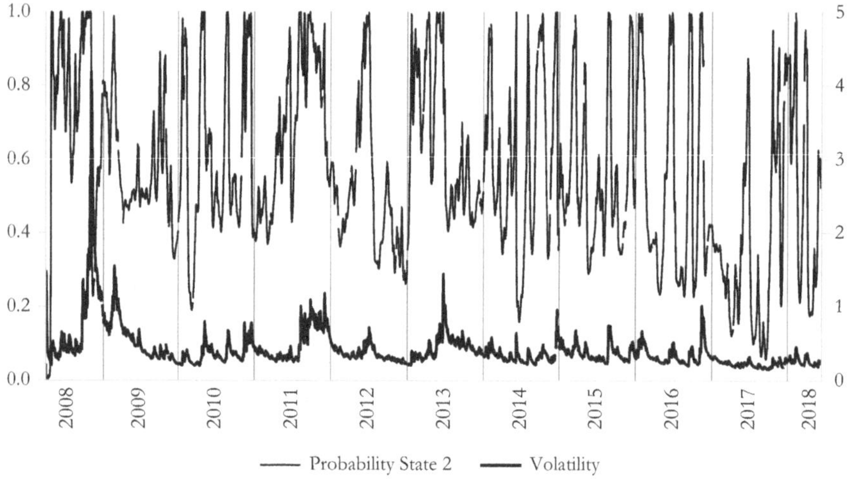

Graph 18.6 SB4 volatility and state 2 smoothed probabilities

different choices; the latter selects the *t*-Student model, while the former marginally prefers the skewed option. Since the maximized value of the log-likelihood function suggests the skewed-*t* model as the best fit, we will use it to continue the analysis. According to our model choice, we observe again a first regime with a highly persistent volatility process, which becomes notably less persistent in the second regime, simultaneously with a less skewed error distribution. The estimated half-life of the volatility for the first regime is about 37 days, but it is only around days for the second. The higher persistence period is also identified as the one with the more skewed error distribution. The probability of staying in the period of higher volatility persistence is a little lower than the previous cases. This, together with the state probabilities, suggests that the volatility process can switch from one regime to another more frequently, as can be seen in Fig. 18.3, which describes the behavior of the volatility and the smoothed probabilities for state 2 during the corresponding span of time. A similar pattern can be seen in Table 18.10 and Graph 18.5, which show, respectively, the estimated parameters of the four SB4 models and the behavior of the volatility and the state 2 smoothed probabilities (Graph 18.6).

18.6 Concluding Remarks

This chapter is devoted to the analysis of Mexican retirement pension funds' (SIEFOREs') volatility. The analysis is supported by a Markov-switching GARCH (MS-GARCH) model. In order to gain a better understanding of SIEFOREs' return volatility, we begin our study with a detailed description of the Mexican pension fund system.

Among the main factors that may have caused the volatility process of SB1 and SB2 to change from regime one to two in 2014 are the high levels of volatility in the international financial markets. This generalized increase in volatility was associated with the uncertainty surrounding interest rate increases by the Federal Reserve. Regarding the high volatility of SB3 and SB4, Greece's sovereign debt crisis and the uncertainty about what the consequences could be under a potential Brexit, and its conjunction with domestic economic circumstances, may explain it. After the 2008 financial crisis, SB3 and SB4 were characterized by high price return volatility due to the introduction of risky assets such as structured securities and REITs.

The increasing level of SB1 volatility is puzzling because this fund is the oldest one among those operating in the reformed Mexican pension fund system. Higher level of risk in pension fund returns are not good news for the people whose life after retirement depends on the balance accumulated as result of the yields provided by such pension funds. A natural claim is that the authorities should review the investment strategy scheme allowed by regulations and promote a better risk management. Constant performance appraisal of the pension funds is a must, heavily stressing the risk premia that are finally conveyed to the saver, that is, net of commissions and any other fees. As the analysis presented in this chapter suggests, similar advice could be applicable to the managers of the other SBs.

In general, the estimation of the MS-GARCH models shows that the volatility of Mexican pension fund returns is highly persistent, including levels that suggest explosive processes. Previous research has provided evidence of this fact and explains it as a consequence of the presence of long-memory processes, which, characterized by slowly decaying significant autocorrelations, pose several complications to understand and explain the behavior of the time series of financial asset returns because within the standard asset pricing theory, there is no satisfactory frame to explain financial asset volatility. The only way to learn more about the nature of SIEFOREs' return volatility is to continue exploring them with increasingly robust econometric models whose findings can be used by SIEFOREs' risk managers and protect the population's retirement savings while, at the same time, maximizing their accumulation.

Another subject of future studies is to improve our comprehension of the role of the restrictions that savers are forced to deal with. An outstanding restriction is that they cannot switch to another fund management company whenever they wish to, but they can only do so once a year. Studying if the fact that customers are, to some extent, captive as that restriction prevents pension fund managers from improving their performance because they are not subject to a real competitive challenge is another promising project.

References

Alonso, J., Hoyo, C., & Tuesta, D. (2015). A model for the pension system in Mexico: Diagnosis and recommendations. *Journal of Pension Economics and Finance, 14*(1), 76–112. https://doi.org/10.1017/S147474721400016X.

Ardia, D., Bluteau, K., Boudt, K., Catania, L., & Trottier, D-A. (2016). *Markov-Switching GARCH models in R: The MSGARCH package.* Allowable at SSRN: https://ssrn.com/abstract=2845809 or doi:https://doi.org/10.2139/ssrn.2845809.

Barr, N., & Diamond, P. (2009). Reforming pensions: Principles, analytical errors and policy directions. *International Social Security Review, 62*(2), 5–29. https://doi.org/10.1111/j.1468-246X.2009.01327.x.

Blake, D., Cairns, A. J. G., & Dowd, K. (2001). Pensionmetrics: Stochastic pension plan design and value-at-risk during the accumulation phase. *Insurance: Mathematics and Economics, 29*(2), 187–215. https://doi.org/10.1016/S0167-6687(01)00082-8.

Bollerslev, T. (1986). Generalized autoregressive conditional heteroskedasticity. *Journal of Econometrics, 31*(3), 307–327. https://doi.org/10.1016/0304-4076(86)90063-1.

Calderón-Colín, R., Domínguez, E., & Schwartz, M. (2010). Consumer confusion: The choice of pension fund manager in Mexico. *Journal of Pension Economics and Finance, 9*(1), 43–74. https://doi.org/10.1017/S1474747209004004.

De la Torre, Ó. V., Figueroa, E. G., Enciso, M. I. M. T., & Montoya, D. A. (2015). A minimum variance benchmark to measure the performance of pension funds in Mexico. *Contaduría y administración UNAM, 61*(3), 593–614. https://doi.org/10.1016/j.cya.2015.05.009.

Diamond, P., & Stiglitz, J. (1974). Increases in risk and risk aversion. *Journal of Economic Theory, 8*, 337–360.

Espinosa-Vega, M., & Yip, C. K. (2002). Government financing in an endogenous growth model with financial market restrictions. *Economic Theory, Springer; Society for the Advancement of Economic Theory (SAET), 20*(2), 237–257.

Fama, E. F. (1965). The behavior of stock-market prices. *Journal of Business, 38*(1), 34–105.

Fuentes, E., García-Herrero, A., & Escrivá, J. (2010). *Las Reformas de los Sistemas de Pensiones en Latinoamérica.* Retrieved from: http://www.bbvaresearch.com

Fuentes-Castro, H. J., Coordinator. (2014). *Impacto Macroeconómico de la Reforma Pensionaria en México.* Instituto Tecnológico y de Estudios Superiores de Monterrey Campus Ciudad de México. Centro de Estudios Estratégicos.

Hamilton, J. D. (1989). A new approach to the economic analysis of non-stationary time series and the business cycle. *Econometrica, 57*(2), 357–384. https://doi.org/10.2307/1912559.

Hamilton, J. D. (1994). *Time series analysis.* Princeton: Princeton University Press.

Haas, M., Mittnik, S., & Paolella, M. S. (2004). A new approach to Markov-switching GARCH models. *Journal of Financial Econometrics, 2*, 493–530. https://doi.org/10.1093/jjfinec/nbh020.

James, E. (2005). *Reforming social security: Lessons From 30 countries* (No. 277). NCPA policy reports (Vol. 75251). Dallas. www.ncpa.org/pub/st/st277

Martínez-Preece, M., & Venegas-Martínez, F. (2014). Análisis del Riesgo de Mercado de los Fondos de Pensión en México. Un Enfoque con Modelos Autorregresivos. *Contaduría y Administración, 59*(3), 165–195. https://doi.org/10.1016/S0186-1042(14)71269-0.

Martínez-Preece, M. R., & Venegas-Martínez, F. (2015). El mercado de los fondos de pensión en México: del reparto a la capitalización. *Estudios de Economía Aplicada, 33*(3), 903–928. Retrieved from https://ideas.repec.org/a/lrk/eeaart/33_3_13.html

Orzag, P. R., & Stiglitz, J. E. (2001). Rethinking pension reform: 10 myths about social security. In *New ideas about old age security: Toward sustainable pension systems in the 21st century*. Washington, DC: The World Bank.

Peinado, P., & Serrano, F. (2014). Fiscal crisis, social security reform and vulnerable population. *Panoeconomicus, 61*(SPEC. ISSUE), 129–143. https://doi.org/10.2298/PAN1401129P.

Santillán-Salgado, R. J., López, D., & Montenegro, J. (2010). Las Administradoras de Fondos de Pensiones y el Desarrollo del Mercado de Capitales en Chile. *Ensayos: Revista de Economía, XXIX*(2), 53–76. RePEc:ere:journl:v:xxix:y:2010:i:2:p:53-76.

Santillán-Salgado, R. J., Martínez-Preece, M., & López-Herrera, F. (2016). Análisis Econométrico del Riesgo y Rendimiento de las SIEFORES. *Revista Mexicana de Economía Y Finanzas, 11*(1), 29–54. https://doi.org/10.21919/remef.v11i1.76.

Verbič, M., & Spruk, R. (2014). Aging population and public pensions: Theory and macroeconometric evidence. *Panoeconomicus, 61*(3), 289–316. https://doi.org/10.2298/PAN1403289V.

Williamson, J. B., Price, M., & Shen, C. (2012). Pension policy in China, Singapore, and South Korea: An assessment of the potential value of the notional defined contribution model. *Journal of Aging Studies, 26*(1), 79–89. https://doi.org/10.1016/j.jaging.2011.08.002.

Chapter 19
Critical Issues of Public Pension System: The Italian Case

Roberta Melis and Alessandro Trudda

Abstract This chapter addresses the issue of the financial sustainability of public PAYG pension schemes. Criticalities and, in particular, demographic risks affecting those schemes have been analysed. A possible solution to reduce demographic risk impact is presented, that is the introduction of a funded component to balance the PAYG part when the ratio of contributors-pensioners is decreasing. A cost-benefit analysis is presented in order to verify how the sustainability of a public pension scheme improves, given the actual and future demographic trends, and to quantify the cost in terms of public debt. Finally, an application to Italian pension data is performed.

Keywords Public pension system · Demographic risk · Sustainability · Funded component

19.1 Introduction

In the last years, the debate on the sustainability of public pensions has assumed a fundamental role in many countries in the world.

According to the European Commission (European Commission 2017), pensions in Europe are mostly pay as you go (PAYG) and provide the main income for old age, and to accomplish this important role they must be sustainable and adequate.

Regarding the financing method, a pension scheme can be pay as you go (PAYG) or funded. In a PAYG scheme, the contributions from current workers are used to pay current pensions; in a funded scheme, the contributions paid from current workers are used to accumulate assets invested in the capital markets, and the accrued amount is used to pay benefits in the future. Public pension schemes are generally managed as PAYG, while private are funded.

R. Melis (✉) · A. Trudda
Department of Economics and Business, University of Sassari, Sassari, Italy
e-mail: romelis@uniss.it; atrudda@uniss.it

M. Peris-Ortiz et al. (eds.), *Economic Challenges of Pension Systems*,
https://doi.org/10.1007/978-3-030-37912-4_19

To be stable, a PAYG pension scheme compels an equilibrium between contributions and pensions, which is clearly influenced by demographic variables. The change in the demographic structure, in the last decades, has shaken this balance worldwide. The population-ageing phenomenon is a result, on one hand, of the decrease in fertility rates and, on the other hand, of the increase in life expectancy (on this topic, see Whiteford and Whitehouse 2006; Andersen 2012). This led to a decrease in the ratio of active-pensioners. Moreover unemployment and delayed entrance in work contribute to reducing this ratio. According to Borsch-Supan (2010), demographic change is a long-term process that lasts several decades, compared to a financial crisis, which is a short-term shock that lasts only a few years.

In order to improve this demographic and economic situation, numerous reforms have been developed above all in Europe and in OECD countries and also in the developing countries.

In many cases, governments carried out *parametric reforms*, in which the PAYG structure is maintained, while there is an adjustment of the benefit formula or of other parameters of the system, like the increase of the pensionable age, the rise of contribution rates (see Disney 2000, for a classification of pension reforms).

In the mid-nineties, Italy and Sweden independently implemented *notional defined-contribution* (NDC) systems, which are financed on a PAYG basis but where the pension is linked to the contributions paid during working life, with a notional account for each participant. An NDC scheme is a PAYG scheme that simulates a *funded defined-contribution* (FDC) scheme (see Auerbach and Lee 2009; Settergren 2001; Settergren and Mikula 2005; Gronchi and Nisticò 2008; Vidal-Melia et al. 2009). Other European countries, like Latvia and Poland and later Norway, adopted the NDC scheme.

Another possibility is the full or partial replacement of the PAYG structure with FDC. In the literature, usually it is referred to as *pension privatisation*, starting from Chile in 1981. According to Wang et al. (2016), there is a pension policy reversal in the developing countries due to low pension coverage, triple burden costs, tradeoff between pension reforms and social pension, and difficulties with annuitisation.

In this chapter, we present a mixed scheme for a public pension system with the introduction of a defined-contribution funded component. For the PAYG part, we adopt an NDC scheme, i.e. without the accumulation of resources but with defined contribution. We introduce a funded component, and we analyse how the financial sustainability improves with the partial accumulation of amount into a fund invested on capital markets. Furthermore, we measure the cost in terms of public debt and compare it with the benefit deriving from the improvement in sustainability. An application to the Italian pension system is developed.

19.2 The Demographic Structure

As highlighted in the Introduction, to be in balance, a PAYG system needs an equilibrium between active and retired. For this reason, the analysis of the demographic structure of a country is very significant in order to assess if in the future the system is sustainable.

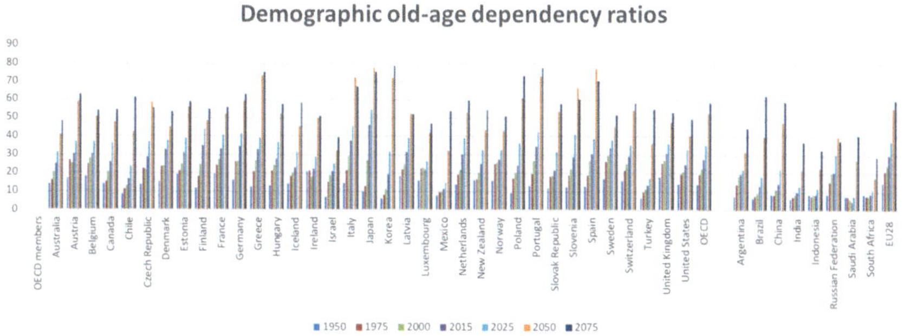

Fig. 19.1 Demographic old-age dependency ratios: historical and projected values, 1950–2075. (*Source:* OECD data (2017b))

A very important indicator is the *old-age dependency ratio*, which measures the number of those aged above 65 years (currently defined as old age) as a share of those between 15 and 64 years (currently defined as working age).

According to OECD (OECD 2017a), the population will decrease in the next decades. Figure 19.1 shows historical and projected values for the years 1950–2075 of demographic old-age dependency ratios for OECD countries (OECD 2017b). From the analysis of Fig. 19.1, the old-age-dependency ratio increased significantly from 1950 to 2015, and the projections also forecast a further increase. Considering the average value of the OECD countries, old-age-dependency ratio went from 13.9 in 1950 to 27.7 in 2015, and the projections forecast a doubling, reaching a value of 58.6 in 2075. In Italy, which in 2015 is in the second place after Japan, it will grow from 37.8 in 2015 to 67 in 2075.

According to the data released by the National Institute of Statistics (ISTAT) (ISTAT 2017b), in Italy in 2018, the average age of the population is over 45 (45.2), 22.6% of the population is over the age of 65, 64.1% are aged between 15 and 64, while only 13.4% are under the age of 15.

Figure 19.2a shows the pyramid of Italian population in 2018, while Fig. 19.2b shows the pyramid of Italian population in 2048, according to the forecasts of the Italian population elaborated by ISTAT (ISTAT 2017a).

According to ISTAT (2017b), future births will not be sufficient to compensate for future deaths. From the middle scenario, after a few years of forecasting, the natural balance (difference between births and deaths), will reach −200 thousand, then passing the threshold −300 and −400 thousand units in the medium and long terms. Survival is expected to increase. By 2065, the average life would grow up to 86.1 years for men and up to 90.2 years for women (in 2015, it was 80.1 for men and 84.6 for women). Fertility is expected to increase from 1.34 to 1.59 children per woman. The forecasts consider a positive migration balance.

From Fig. 19.2a, it is clear that the hump of the Italian population presents a peak between 40 and 60 years, given the presence of baby boomers. In the forecasts of

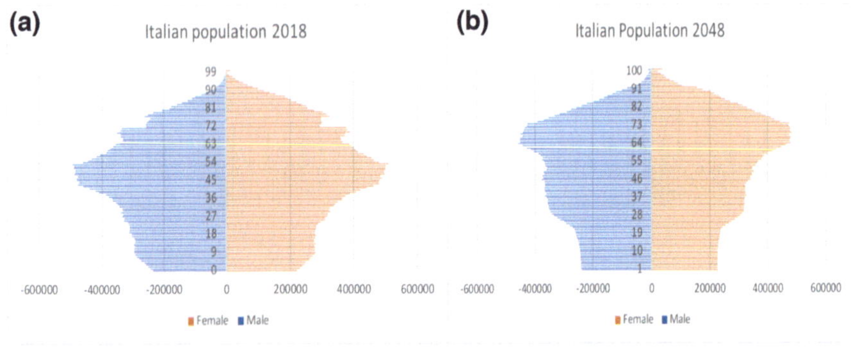

Fig. 19.2 (**a**) Pyramid of Italian population 2018 (**b**) Pyramid of Italian population 2048. (*Source*: ISTAT data (2017a))

2048, Figure 19.2b, the hump of the population will move from 57 to 76 years. This is also evident from the value of the old-age-dependency ratio in 2050 (72.4).

From the point of view of the sustainability of the pension system, this demographic phenomenon clearly determines a significant decrease in the contributory income and an increase in pension benefits. This will occur progressively in a few years, when the baby boomers begin to retire.

19.3 Pension Reforms in Italy

In the last three decades, the Italian pension system has undergone various reforms, with the aim of reducing public spending and allowing fairness in the calculation of benefits. The Amato Reform in 1992 increased the statutory retirement age by five years, cut the benefit formula and shifted indexation from real wages to prices (Castellino and Fornero 1999).

Law 335/1995 (the so-called Dini Reform) reformed the mandatory and complementary pension system with the aim of reducing the growth of the outlays and increasing equity both between and within the different working cohorts. These changes were necessary because the pension disbursement was taking a dangerous drift in terms of impact on the public budget: it was moved from a defined benefit to a defined contribution.

As already stated in the introduction, in the same period, in the mid-nineties, Italy and Sweden implemented an NDC system. In Sweden, there was also introduced a funded component into the scheme, with privately managed individual accounts (Palmer 2000); in Italy, the possibility of introducing a funded component was discussed but not implemented. Castellino and Fornero (1999) propose the introduction of a mixed pension system with the introduction of a funded component.

In PAYG defined-benefit schemes, the pension benefit is earnings based. Benefits are defined by a formula based on the product of three factors: the number of years of service, a percentage called the "accrual rate" and a conventional salary called 'pensionable earnings', which is the mean of the earnings obtained over the final years of work, revalued at a given rate. In the contributory-based scheme, the pension system is conceived as a virtual bank in which the contributions are deposited and from which the yearly pension instalments are withdrawn. Retaining the PAYG financial architecture means that the current pension expenditure is still financed by current contribution revenues. The new scheme switches over to the award and indexation formulas typical of a funded, defined-contribution system. For this reason, in Italy, this plan is called the 'contribution-based' scheme, whereas internationally it is called 'notional defined contribution', 'notionally funded' and 'notional accounts' (see Gronchi and Nisticò 2008).

However, the new rules were applied only to people entering in the labour market after 1995. Those who had at least 18 years of service as of 31 December 1995 were entirely subjected to the old rules. Finally, those workers who had less than 18 years of service in 1995 were subjected to a mixed system (pro rata). In this case, the pension is made up of two components: the first is calculated by the old rules (defined benefit) for the contributions paid until 1995; the second component is for contributions paid after 1995 and is computed on a contributory basis.

There was a long transition process that ended in 2012 with the *Fornero Law* (Law 214/2011), which imposed a pro-rata system for all retirees who entered into work force before 1996.

Other parametric reforms (increasing the retirement age or the contributory seniority) were approved. The main measures were Law 449/1997 (Prodi reform), which tightened the requirements for retirement pension and harmonised the requirements for early retirement of the public service with that of the INPS retirement pension. In addition, a portion of the current contribution rate relating to the end-of-service allowance for civil servants has been allocated to the supplementary pension scheme. Precisely because of this last forecast, with Legislative Decree 252/2005 (Maroni reform), the legislator intended to achieve the objective of removing the obstacles to the development of supplementary pensions.

19.4 The Pension Scheme

In this section, we describe the evolution of a PAYG scheme with the introduction of a funded component. The model explains a pension scheme for a social security system in a discrete time, with an age-structured population.

New Entrants

As already emphasised, the demographic variable new entrants, connected to their contribution capacity, assume a fundamental role for the evolution of a PAYG scheme.

In the literature, different stochastic models are used for the representation of the 'new entrants'. Colombo and Haberman (2005) analyse the impact of the stochastic evolution of the active membership population on the mismatch between assets and liabilities of a funded defined-benefit pension scheme and provide an exhaustive review of the literature.

Melis and Trudda (2010) use an ARMA (1,1) process to describe the 'new entrants' variation rate, splitting the population into males and females; Melis and Trudda (2012) use a mean-reverting process for the intensity of new entrants; in Devolder and Melis (2015), the increasing of new entrants is described by a lognormal process.

The risk related to the demographic variable 'new entrants' and to their future contribution capacity is a relevant component because a balance between the number of contributors and the number of pensioners is necessary for the sustainability of the fund.

Let $N(x, t)$ be the population aged x at time t, α is the entry age into the scheme, π is the age of retirement and ω is the extreme age.

At every time t, for each age x, the population evolves by multiplying the population aged $x - 1$ the previous year, $N(x - 1, t - 1)$, for the survival probability that a member aged $x - 1$ is alive after 1 year ($p_{x-1,1}$).

If $N(\alpha, t)$ is the number of people aged α at time t, the cohort of the new entrants evolves by multiplying new entrants at time $t - 1$, $N(\alpha, t - 1)$, by $(1 + d_t)$, where d_t is the rate of increase of new entrants at time t.

Thus, starting from new entrants at time 0, $N(\alpha, 0)$, and multiplying by the product of the rate $(1 + d_s)$, from $s = 1$ to t, we obtain $N(\alpha, t)$.

Contributions

The contributions paid by each member depend on the contribution rate and on the average income.

The function $w(x, t)$ is used to indicate the average wage for contributors aged x at time t. We consider an increasing income for each age class at the same rate g_t, the annual growth of income at time t.

By multiplying the contribution rate γ by the summation for each age class of the product of the wage function $w(x,t)$ and the number of contributors for each age $N(x, t)$ (with $\alpha \leq x \leq \pi - 1$), we obtain the total contributions at time t.

The total contribution $C(t)$ is calculated as follows:

$$C(t) = \gamma \sum_{x=\alpha}^{\pi-1} N(x,t) \cdot w(x,t) \tag{19.1}$$

Pensions

The same approach is used here for the total pensions $P(t)$ which is obtained by summing for each age, the product of the number of pensioners $N(x, t)$ (with $\pi \leq x \leq \omega - 1$), for the average pension $b(x, t)$. The total amount of the pensions is expressed by the following equation:

$$P(t) = \sum_{x=\pi}^{\omega-1} N(x,t) \cdot b(x,t) \tag{19.2}$$

After retirement, we assume that pensions are indexed at the same rate of salaries g_t. Thus, for people aged $\pi + 1$ at time $t + 1$ (retired at time t), the pension is obtained by the product of the pension of the previous year with $(1 + g_{t+1})$.

In our model, we assume the introduction of a funded component into a DC PAYG scheme (NDC). For the generation retiring at time t, the pension is the sum of two components: the former, $b_P(x, t)$, calculated with the PAYG system, and the latter, $b_F(x, t)$, calculated with the funding system.

Let us consider that a share of the contributions φ (with $0 \leq \varphi \leq 1$ is invested into a fund and the fraction $1 - \varphi$ is used to pay PAYG pensions.

In the NDC scheme, the pension is calculated by the conversion into annuity of the amount of the notional account of each worker. Thus, for the PAYG component, we calculate the value of the pension at the time of retirement ($b_P(\pi, t)$) by multiplying the fraction $(1 - \varphi)$ of the total contributory accrued amount (Mcj) by the annuity factor TC, the *transformation coefficient*, the annuitisation coefficient used for the conversion into annuity of the notional contribution amount accumulated by each worker. TC is function of the age, but in the present model it is constant because there is only one age to retire, π. The contributions accrue at the notional rate j, which is usually set by law. In Italy, the pension return is given by the 5-year moving average of GDP growth, calculated by ISTAT (see Baldacci and Tuzi 2003).

Thus, the PAYG component is calculated as follows:

$$b_P(\pi,t) = (1-\varphi) \cdot M_{Cj} \cdot \text{TC} \tag{19.3}$$

For the funded component, we use the same annuity factor because we are considering a social security pension scheme, but for the accruing of the contributions, we use the financial return on assets of the fund r instead of the notional interest rate.

For the funded component, we have

$$b_F(\pi,t) = \varphi \cdot M_{Cr} \cdot \text{TC} \tag{19.4}$$

If a component is capitalised every year, then $\varphi C(t)$ is invested into the fund, while $(1 - \varphi)\, C(t)$ is used to pay PAYG pensions.

Then we will have the recursive formula of the fund:

$$F(t) = F(t-1)(1+r_t) + \varphi C(t) - P_F(t) \tag{19.5}$$

where r_t is the return rate at time t of the amount invested in the fund and $P_F(t)$ indicates the total funded pensions paid at time t.[1]

[1]The total pensions paid at time t is the sum of the total PAYG and funded pensions at time t: $P(t) = P_{\text{PAYG}}(t) + P_F(t)$.

19.5 Performance Indicators

In this section, it has been analysed how much the cost of the public debt increases with the introduction of a funded component, and it is compared with the increase in the sustainability of the scheme. The goal is to assess if the rise in public spending for pensions is compensated by improvement in financial sustainability in the long run.

Let us define $Y(t)$ (with $Y(t) < 0$) as the part of public debt concerning the pension system. By starting from a certain public debt at time 0, in a generic time t it increases by multiplying the public debt the previous year, $Y(t - 1)$, for $(1 + \theta_t)$, where θ_t is the rate of the cost of public debt at time t, plus the difference between the contributions received and the pensions paid (pension balance), as follows:

$$Y(t) = Y(t-1)(1+\vartheta_t) + C(t) - P(t) \tag{19.6}$$
$$Y(0) = Y^* < 0$$

If we accumulate the fraction φ of the contribution $C(t)$ into a fund, then we have that, only the fraction $(1 - \varphi)$ is used to pay PAYG pensions. Thus, the pension public debt at time t becomes

$$Y(t) = Y(t-1)(1+\vartheta_t) + (1-\varphi)C(t) - P_{\text{PAYG}}(t) \tag{19.7}$$

Since starting from time 0 each generation invests a part φ of the contributions into a fund, in our evaluations we must take into account the lower revenues used to pay pensions and therefore the opportunity cost that must be parameterised on the public debt.

We want to verify at time T, our observation horizon, how much the public debt increases by increasing φ. We describe the cost indicator of the public debt at time T, with respect to infinitesimal variations of the rate φ. This indicator, which we call $\eta_{Y_T,\varphi}$, is expressed by the following equation:

$$\eta_{Y_T,\varphi} = -\frac{Y'_T(\varphi)}{Y_T(\varphi)} \tag{19.8}$$

We use the indicator $S_r(t)$, defined as the ratio between the fund value at time t, $F(t)$, and the actuarial liability[2] of the scheme at time t, AL(t), in order to measure how much the total liabilities are covered by the fund.

At the same time, we want to see how much the sustainability ratio increases with respect to φ. We define the indicator $\eta_{Sr_T,\varphi}$ as follows:

[2]AL(t) is the present net value of the benefits minus the present net value of the contributions.

$$\eta_{Sr_T,\varphi} = -S'_{r_T}(\varphi) \tag{19.9}$$

which represents the increase in the sustainability ratio at time T with respect to φ. It measures the sensibility of the sustainability ratio at the end of the horizon T to infinitesimal variations of the rate φ.

19.6 An Application to Italian Case

This section presents a numerical example of the model above applied to a pension system. Italian data from ISTAT are used. We take into account only the data from dependent workers.

The following assumptions are adopted:

- The pension is calculated with the NDC pension system for people starting to work after 1996, while for people starting before1996, pension is calculated using the mixed method, the so-called pro rata. Until 1996, the defined benefit (DB) formula is used, and the pension is calculated by multiplying the pensionable earnings, i.e. the mean of the earnings obtained over the final years of work, revalued at a given rate, by the number of years of contributions accrued in the DB system.
- Italian mortality tables 2017 were used (source: ISTAT).
- For new entrants, fixed entry age $\alpha = 25$, retirement age $\pi = 66$, $d = -0.02$.
- The inflation rate is fixed at 1.5%.
- The contribution rate is fixed at 33%.
- The last transformation coefficients have been employed.
- Salaries are appreciated at rate of inflation.
- Benefits are calculated with the mixed method.
- The return on assets is fixed at 2%.
- The rate of cost of public debt is fixed at 1%.
- The notional rate is fixed at 1.5%.

The pension scheme balance is projected for 50 years. We first consider the case of $\varphi = 0$, without the accumulation into the fund. The obtained results are summarised in Figs. 19.3, 19.4, 19.5, and 19.6.

Figure 19.3 shows the projection of the total contributions received by the pension system. As it is possible to observe, there is an initial increase, but after 16 years, there is a decrease in the total inputs. At the same time, by looking at Fig. 19.4, we can see that in the same period of time, there is an increase in the total pensions paid by the system. This situation causes a financial instability to the scheme because the system in the long run is not able to pay pensions without the public intervention to cover the pension liabilities.

In order to measure the level of individual performance, we calculate the replacement rate, the ratio of the first pension received to the last wage earned before the

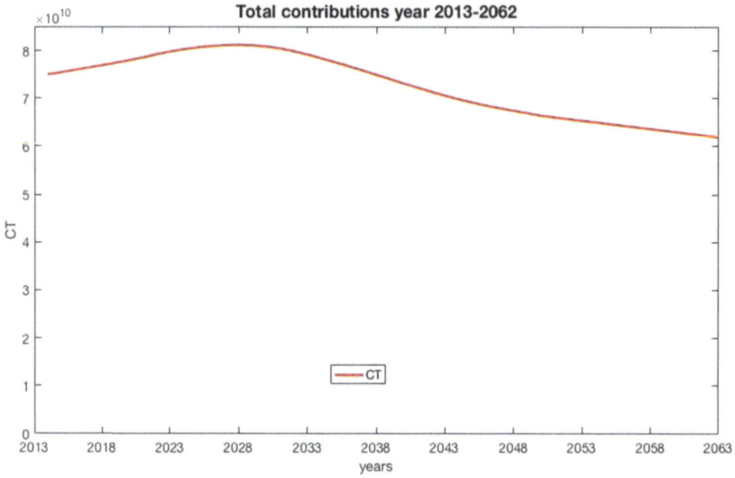

Fig. 19.3 Total contributions received in the years 2013–2062. (*Source:* Own elaborations)

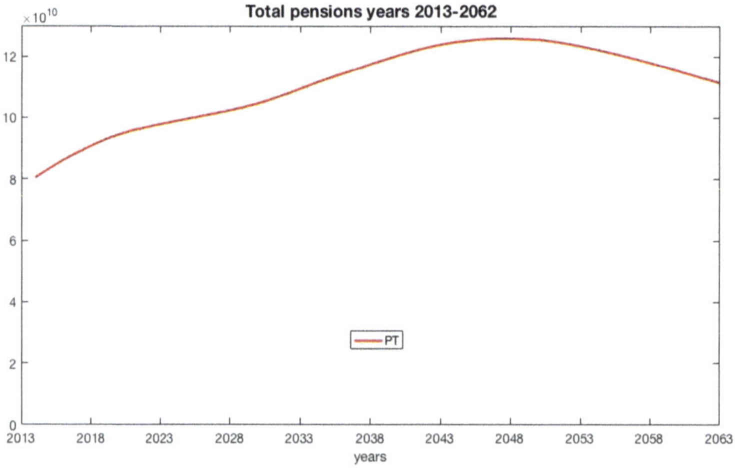

Fig. 19.4 Total pensions paid in the years 2013–2062. (*Source:* Own elaborations)

retirement. Figure 19.5 shows the projection of this indicator. As we can see, replacement rate is going to decrease, stabilising slightly above 50%.

We must stress that we consider only full careers, i.e. 40 years of contribution. If, instead, you do consider the unemployment and delayed entries into the working world, the replacement rate will be even lower, about 40%.

Then we consider the case in which a fraction φ of the contributions is invested into a fund. We calculated the overall balance for different values of φ in order to

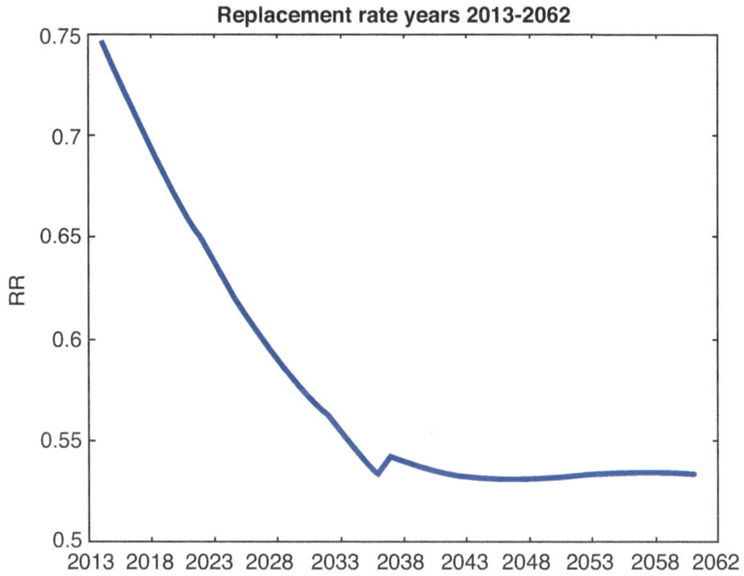

Fig. 19.5 Replacement rate in the years 2013–2062. (*Source:* Own elaborations)

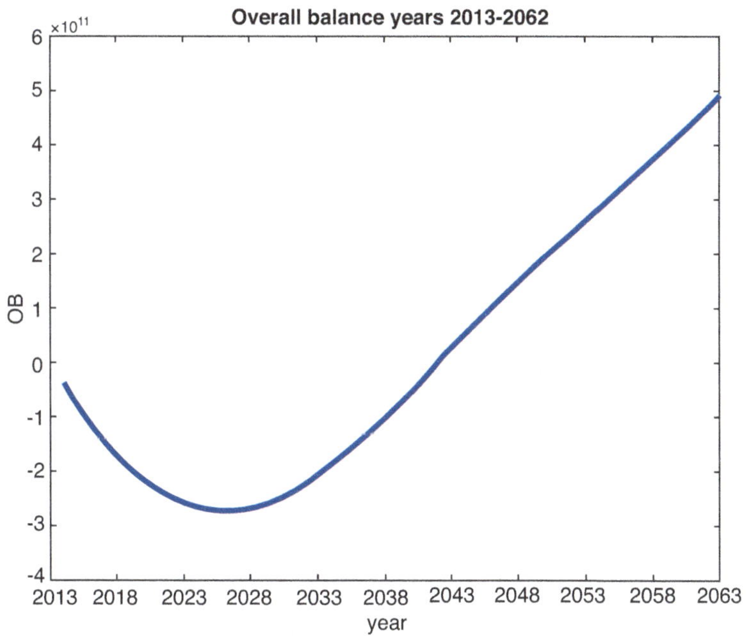

Fig. 19.6 Overall balance for $\varphi = 0.04$, years 2013–2062. (*Source:* Own elaborations)

find the number of years it will need to get the balance of the system and a state of autonomy without the intervention of the state to cover the negative balance.

Our findings are that the minimum φ that makes the system sustainable is 0.04, for which the balance is positive after 27 years. The results are shown in Fig. 19.6.

19.7 Conclusions

In this paper, we analysed the sustainability of a public pension scheme, focusing on the influence of the demographic structure in the long run. In particular, the Italian public pension system has been analysed.

A funded component in order to improve the sustainability has been introduced. The cost for the public budget is measured by the increase in the public debt. The model has been applied to Italian pension data of dependent workers.

For the public budget, if there is set aside a part of the contributions, after a number of years, it will get the balance of the system and a state of autonomy without the intervention of the state to cover the negative balance of social security.

The minimum component to be allocated, according to the assumptions used in the simulations of new contributors, the interest rate and cost of debt, is 4% of the contributions, which ensures an overall positive balance after about 27 years.

On the other hand, at the level of individual performance, the replacement rate increases with the introduction of a capitalisation component, but not significantly.

References

Andersen, T. M. (2012). Fiscal sustainability and demographics – Should we save or work more? *Journal of Macroeconomics, 34*, 264–280.

Auerbach, A. J., & Lee, R. (2009). Notional defined contribution pension systems in a stochastic context: Design and stability. In J. Brown, J. Liebman, & D. A. Wise (Eds.), *Social security policy in a changing environment* (pp. 43–68). University of Chicago Press, USA.

Baldacci, E., & Tuzi, D. (2003). Demographic trends and pension system in Italy: An assessment of 1990s reforms. *Labour, 17*, 209–240.

Borsch-Supan, A. H. (2010). *Social impact of the crisis - Demographic challenges and the pension system*. European Parliament's Special Committee on the Financial, Economic and Social Crisis, IP/A/CRIS/NT/2009–06 PE. 429.995.

Castellino, O., & Fornero, E. (1999). From PAYG to funding in Italy: A feasible transition? *The Geneva Papers on Risk and Insurance. Issues and Practice, 24*(4), 473–487.

Colombo, L., & Haberman, S. (2005). Optimal contribution in a defined benefit pension scheme with stochastic new entrants. *Insurance: Mathematics and Economics, 37*(2), 335–354.

Devolder, P., & Melis, R. (2015). Optimal mix between pay as you go and funding for pension liabilities in a stochastic framework. *Astin Bulletin, 45*(03), 551–575.

Disney, R. (2000). Crises in public pension programmes in OECD: What are the reform options? *Economic Journal Features, 110*, 1–23.

European Commission. (2017) Adequacy and sustainability of pensions. *European Semester Thematic Factsheets*.

Gronchi, S., & Nisticò, S. (2008). Theoretical foundations of pay-as-you-go defined-contribution pension schemes. *Metroeconomica, 59*(2), 131–159.

ISTAT. (2017a) *Previsioni della popolazione italiana 2017-2067, ISTAT.*

ISTAT. (2017b). *Il futuro demografico del Paese. Previsioni regionali della popolazione residente al 2065.* Statistiche report. ISTAT, https://www.istat.it/it/files/2018/05/previsioni_demografiche.pdf.

Melis, R., & Trudda, A. (2010). Demographic risk indicators in pay-as-you-go pension funds. *Problems and Perspectives in Management, 8*(4), 117–126.

Melis, R., & Trudda, A. (2012). Solvency indicators for partially unfunded pension funds. *Investment Management and Financial Innovations, 9*(4), 71–77.

OECD (2017a). *Pensions at a Glance 2017: OECD and G20 indicators.* Paris: OECD Publishing. https://doi.org/10.1787/19991363.

OECD. (2017b). Demographic old-age dependency ratios: Historical and projected values, 1950–2075. In *Demographic and economic context.* Paris: OECD Publishing. https://doi.org/10.1787/pension_glance-2017-table61-en.

Palmer, E. (2000). *The Swedish pension reform model: Framework and issues.* (Social Protection Discussion Paper 12, 23086), The World Bank.

Settergren, O. (2001). The automatic balance mechanism of the Swedish pension system. *Wirtschaftspolitishe Blatter, 4*, 239–249.

Settergren, O., & Mikula, B. D. (2005). The rate of return of pay-as-you-go pension system: A more exact consumption model of interest. *Journal of Pension Economics and Finance, 4*, 115–138.

Vidal-Melia, C., Boado-Penas, M., & Settergren, O. (2009). Automatic balance mechanism in pay-as-you-go pension system. *The Geneva Papers on Risk and Insurance. Issues and Practice, 34*(2), 287–317.

Wang, X., Williamson, J. B., & Cansoy, M. (2016). Developing countries and systemic pension reforms: Reflections on some emerging problems. *International Social Security Review, 69*(2), 85–106.

Whiteford, P., & Whitehouse, E. (2006). Pension challenges and pension reforms in OECD countries. *Oxford Review of Economic Policy, 22*(1), 78–94.

Chapter 20
Reinventing Social Security: Towards a Two-Step Mixed Pension System

Inmaculada Domínguez-Fabián, Francisco del Olmo-García, and José Antonio Herce-San Miguel

Abstract The literature has addressed the problem of pensions and has reached an almost unanimous conclusion that increased longevity is the main cause of the problem. However, in our opinion, longevity itself is not a problem and, therefore, should not be the cause of the problem of pensions. The real challenge for the sustainability of pension systems lies in a series of characteristic behaviours throughout the life cycle of a person that are motivated by increased longevity. The pension problem is therefore due to the lack of adaptation of pension systems to these vital behaviours and the fact of forgetting the initial purpose for which social security systems emerged: to ensure the 'great old age' and not properly determine the age of the 'great old age' and the needs associated with it. In this work, the limit between the active and passive phases of the life cycle is determined as the retirement age, which has maintained the rhythm of adaptation required by the ever-increasing longevity. Rebalancing resources and life cycle needs are also discussed, with particular attention to the economic needs from the current age of legal retirement. Given that neither the various reforms on the pay-as-you-go (PAYG) systems nor converting them to a funded system seems to solve the problem of sustainability and adequacy of pensions due to the various problems associated with each scheme, this work has been advanced and proposes the creation of a 'deferred mixed system'. This system is divided into two pillars, one defined as an individual capitalisation insurance that would cover pension between voluntary retirement age adopted by workers until the age of that 'great old age', so that until this age workers will finance their own pensions with their own savings or with a contribution by their full wage

I. Domínguez-Fabián (✉)
Financial Economics and Accounting, University of Extremadura, Cáceres, Spain
e-mail: idomingu@unex.es

F. del Olmo-García
Department of Economy and Business Management, Institute of Economic and Social Analysis (IAES)University of Alcala-Madrid, Madrid, Spain
e-mail: francisco.olmo@uah.es

J. A. Herce-San Miguel
Complutense University of Madrid-Análistas Financieros Internacionales (AFI), Madrid, Spain
e-mail: jherce@afi.es

M. Peris-Ortiz et al. (eds.), *Economic Challenges of Pension Systems*,
https://doi.org/10.1007/978-3-030-37912-4_20

salary (paid either by the employee or the employer), and another one structured as a system of public distribution with NDC, where the current workers finance the pensions of people who have passed the age of 'great old age' at the same time as they are accumulating actuarial rights for their state future pension.

Keywords Pensions · Longevity · Great old age · Deferred mixed system · Life cycle

20.1 Introduction and Major Results

The objective of Social Security is to protect workers against old-age and related risks, which they cannot cope with on their own. At the beginning of social security systems, which was at the end of the nineteenth century, these risks were experienced by workers (or their dependants) in this order: disability, widowhood and retirement. These risks had previously taken place in a context in which the working population had not been able to accumulate the necessary funds to generate incomes that replaced wages in the event of any of the mentioned contingencies.

Nowadays, after more than a century of valuable and immense service provided to society, Social Security everywhere is in a dilemma, which is characterised by three determining factors: the financial sustainability of benefit schemes, their sufficiency and the coverage of workers and their families. These three problems are generalised, at different levels, in all countries (Herce et al. 2017).

When the Prussia of Kaiser Wilhelm and Kanzler von Bismarck introduced Social Security, life expectancy at age 65, which was the retirement age that was then established, was less than 9 years. Only 30% of the population reached that age and protection was limited, mainly to illness, disability and support to orphans and widows. Retirement benefits for workers were merely secondary.

At present, retirement is the most relevant coverage of Social Security worldwide, and the effective retirement age is generally below 65 years, and the reference age (or legal age) for retirement does not exceed 68 years in any country. However, life expectancy at age 65 has more than doubled as compared with one century ago. This is undoubtedly causing the problem of sustainability of public pension schemes, which are often unmistakably attributed to low birth rates. It is simply a fact that with fixed or shorter working careers, we have each time longer retirement lives, which is causing an enormous imbalance in public pension systems, as well as in privately funded pension schemes, when it comes to sufficiency.

The risk of outliving your income or your savings leads directly to the poverty of pensioners or unsustainable pension systems or both. Once individuals are entitled to their pensions, they have very little capacity to deal with this risk and may also suffer loss in the purchasing power of their pensions, as well as entering long-term care phases that are very expensive in relation to their savings.

These risks must be mutualised and should not be left for individuals to face them alone because this is not very efficient and not everybody can do it. While Social Security was sustainable, it fulfilled this 'insurer's' role better than any other system, and somehow it must continue to fulfil this role. Social Security acts on a mandatory basis, and all workers are required to contribute to it. This ensures achieving the most efficient mutualisation of longevity risk. However, although the Social Security 'sells' life annuities to workers in the form of pensions, it stopped calculating these risks decades ago, if ever it strictly did so, using the actuarial technique. As a result, all public pension systems have become unsustainable, and increasingly so, as the life expectancy of pensioners increases without the retirement age or other system parameters (eligibility conditions, benefit amounts) being adjusted to the increase in life expectancy proportionally.

The private pension industry can also mutualise longevity risk using life annuities. But it cannot necessarily (and should not) force all individuals to acquire these life annuities, so they are currently more expensive than they would be if everyone were forced to acquire them from an insurance company. Moreover, if insurance companies could put a 'cap' on longevity risk, life annuities would be much cheaper. But longevity is a risk that cannot be easily pooled, such as fire or car insurance, and full insurance cannot be cheap as it requires huge savings, not just tiny premiums.

We find the main objective of this chapter in the preceding paragraphs. Social Security must reinvent itself to do exactly what it did a century ago: ensure 'grand age'. As can be seen below, this does not mean that individuals should retire at that grand age today, which would lie between 80 and 90, depending on the metrics adopted.

Now imagine that the Social Security is responsible for mutualising and securing the risk as from the grand age mentioned above, as it did more than a century ago, while the insurance industry is responsible for ensuring income from a retirement age freely chosen by workers until the so-called grand age. In this case, the industry would sell not life annuities but term annuities, which are much more efficient because Social Security is playing the role of insuring against longevity risk, in fact, almost in its entirety.

Workers, thus, would enjoy a continuous flow of retirement income, obtained in the most efficient way possible for each euro contributed to the different retirement schemes and could choose discretionally the moment of retirement or partially do so, etc. We would then be faced with a mixed system, but in two 'steps', in which the Social Security, re-scaled, sustainable and providing adequate benefits, would act in the final phase of workers' lives closing the protective model.

The problems mentioned in the previous paragraphs, namely the lack of adaptation of the retirement age to the objective of Social Security (avoiding lack or insufficiency of incomes at advanced ages) and insufficient savings to complement the public pension after retirement, are those that we aim to solve with the proposal that we present and develop in the present study: the introduction of a 'two steps' mixed pension system. The model we propose will be checked both in terms of individual financial solvency and in terms of financial sustainability of the aggregated system. We believe that this novel approach is a way out of current difficulties that combines methodologies that are generally not combined in the analysis of pensions.

The rest of the chapter continues as follows. Section 20.2 addresses a substantial problem created by increasing longevity that disproportionately diminishes the efficiency of a life annuity, whose market, moreover, suffers adverse selection problems and whose provider must cope with both problems. This is a first actuarial example that already establishes the greater efficiency of term annuities in contrast to life annuities given the much lower incidence of the longevity risk. In fact, our 'two-steps' solution for pensions arises from this first result.

Section 20.3 illustrates how increasing life expectancy is 'pulling' many individual and collective decisions and other relevant life-cycle milestones, such as the decision to extend the duration of the schooling period. It seems, however, not to affect the most relevant decision related to what interests us in this chapter, which is the retirement decision. This has consequences for the internal sustainability of the balance of resources and needs along the life cycle for everyone. Unfavourable individual balances, in the end, provoke unsustainability and/or benefit inadequacy in aggregate schemes, be these PAYG or fully funded.

In this sense, we state that the 'pensions problem' is not technical, not even political or institutional. All these layers are subordinated to the scarce and imperfect individual perception of the profound change that is taking place in the life cycle of each one of us. The problem is therefore of individual perception and acceptance, and the solution happens to be much simpler than commonly imagined.

Section 20.4 briefly describes the two-step mixed pension system we propose and introduces some basic notation on the contribution and benefit flows that are obtained in each of the stages. In addition, a line of research coinciding with the one we propose in the present study is discussed, which we have detected while writing this paper and which is reflected in some recent Chilean literature on the reform of its pension system.

In Sect. 20.5, we perform a comparative analysis, in terms of financial-actuarial solvency, of a defined benefit PAYG system and the two-step mixed system we propose. The illustrative exercise carried out on the internal rate of return (IRR) of the representative individual in both systems clearly shows that a PAYG system that protects workers at grand age and beyond is more sustainable because, without decreasing pensions (as shown in the following section), it provides benefits for a shorter period and is obviously more sustainable, always preserving benefits, the greater the grand age is. At the same time, the funded scheme, which is sustainable by definition, must be adjusted according to the individual's options regarding his or her ordinary retirement, as well as according to the options that the social security system of the second stage takes with respect to that grand age. Obviously, the longer the time span between ordinary retirement and the grand age is, due to individuals bringing the first one forward and/or because the Social Security delays the second one (which should happen pari passu with a longer life span), the more expensive the insured term income becomes, given the benefit amount, depending on the contribution rate, the contribution length and whether it is a defined benefit or a defined contribution scheme.

Section 20.6 analyses the aggregate balance of the Social Security grand age pension scheme for its demographic (affiliates and retirement pensions) and economic (income and expenditure, pensions and average contributions, contribution rates) flows and debt stocks; the latter referenced the GDP of the Spanish economy in the period 2016–2065. This analysis is carried out under three modalities: (i) in full consistency with the individual-based financial-actuarial solvency analysis performed in the previous section, (ii) by comparing the same indicators mentioned above for the current pay-as-you-go system and for the different simulations carried out on the grand age pay-as-you-go pension system and (iii) concerning the latter pension scheme, the simulations mentioned focused on constant contribution rates, variable contribution rates of balanced budget year by year, variable contribution rates of balanced budget in the projection period and, finally, contribution rates identical to the cases for this system in the financial-actuarial solvency analysis of the previous section.

Section 20.7 closes this chapter with a summary discussion of the main results.

20.2 The Impact of Increasing Longevity and Adverse Selection in the Life Annuity Market

Life expectancy at age 65 in Spain in 2015 was 20.8 years, an increase of 8 years compared with 1950 and 11.7 years compared with 1900. This leads, among other things, to increased expenditure on retirement pensions since these must be paid to individuals for more and more years. The retirement age, however, has not been adapted to this spectacular increase in life expectancy, and it is hard to imagine having to rely solely on this adjustment for the sustainability of Social Security at present, given the accumulated delay on this matter.

In fact, social resistance to an increase in retirement age linked to longevity, which would solve the sustainability and sufficiency problems of pensions, leads to the procrastination of political representatives in implementing policies based on this measure. In the absence of increases in birth rate (for pay-as-you-go systems), which ultimately would also be unsustainable, politicians opt for adjusting public pensions downwards to make them sustainable. Consequently, the need to implement supplementary retirement schemes arises.

However, unless we understand that the children we do not have are the number of months by which our life expectancy is increased each year (Herce 2017) and that part of this windfall gain should be dedicated to continue working. We will have no choice but to implement reforms based on cutting back on promised benefits that cannot be fulfilled (public pensions) and putting our savings to work for years to provide us with the complementary retirement income (private pensions) necessary to maintain the replacement rates observed today.

Thus, many countries have included the complementarity of public and private pensions in their pension system, seeking that the income that Social Security grants to pensioners, coming from the pay-as-you-go system, be supplemented with income generated by a private-defined contribution-funded system (Herce et al. 2017).

For income security reasons, the income that contemporarily complements the public system should be a life annuity similar in amount to that of Social Security benefits. This obliges the providers of the product and/or the benefit holders to be strongly exposed to the longevity risk since as life expectancy increases regularly, the value of the periodic income will be reduced, given the premium paid ex ante by the beneficiary. It is therefore necessary to make a relevant saving effort, a careful planning of such effort and a sound risk assessment to adequately complement for life the equally life-long provision of the Social Security from retirement age to death.

However, life annuities may be actuarially unfair to their holders even though the insurer suffers from an adverse selection problem: the healthiest and longest living individuals are those who subscribe to life annuities. This implies that annuitants receive payments whose present value is greater than the premium they paid to the insurer and leads the latter to overweigh general longevity in their mortality tables and benefit calculation formulae such that, finally, all annuity holders receive a lower amount than they should receive. This overcompensation is done by assuming a longer life expectancy of the product purchasers beyond what is indicated by the overall population mortality tables.

Mitchell et al. (1999) show that life annuities in the United States are between 15% and 25% lower than those obtained when using overall population mortality tables. Finkelstein and Poterba (2004) also show that life annuities in the UK, which are taken out by 65-year-old men, are between 10% and 15% lower than those that would be obtained using ordinary overall population mortality tables. Note that the problem that occurs when adverse selection and overweighted mortality are combined in the case of life annuities, it is significantly reduced in the case of term annuities.

As can be seen from the results of Table 20.1 below, which simulates the case of the individual represented in the upper part of the table, insurance companies use increased mortality tables, so that the resulting pension is lower than if ordinary mortality tables were used; this gap is greater when it comes to a life annuity than when it is a temporary annuity for the simple reason that a life annuity must face a substantially greater longevity risk.

Also, the desire to leave an inheritance weighs considerably on the decision of individuals when building up long-term savings. The results of the survey carried out by Costa et al. (2006) highlight the existence of a strong inheritance culture that tends to limit the market for life annuities and similar retirement products when these consume all the beneficiary's capital.[1] Up to 90% of those surveyed over the age of 50 plan to leave an inheritance, and this implies that their savings focus more on temporary movable assets, as well as on real estate assets.

[1]However, life annuities and other similar products are flexible enough to accommodate any of the saver's desire about the recovery of part, or all, of the premium contributed for the acquisition of the product. See Galdeano and Herce et al. (2017) for a complete characterisation of annuities.

Table 20.1 The impact of longevity risk on annuities (term versus life) using Spanish Mortality Tables

Hypothesis of analysis		
Starting age of contributions (with continuous contributions during the entire working life)	30	
Retirement age	67	
Grand age[a]	78	
Salary at the starting age of contributions	20,000 €	
Interest rate	3%	
Annual increase in wages	3%	
Expected inflation	2%	
Results	*Term annuity*[b]	*Life annuity*[c]
Annuity computed using the PERM/F 2000 table	33,593.76 €	20,299.95 €
Annuity computed using the ordinary mortality table	35,289.29 €	14,359.05 €
Annuity value gap due to compensation for longevity	4.80%	29.27%

Source: Compiled from Herce and del Olmo (2013)

[a]Age at which the Social Security initiates the payment of pensions in the two-step mixed system (see below)

[b]Term annuity that individuals obtain between the retirement age and the grand age, when the SS grants their life annuities

[c]Life annuity at retirement age

20.3 The Influence of Increased Longevity on Life-Cycle Changes: Understanding the 'Problem' of Pensions

The analysis of the 'problem' of pensions is a recurrent theme both in specialised literature and the media, given its social relevance and impact on public opinion. The sustainability problems of public pension systems, as a fundamental pillar of the welfare state, have motivated the study of their causes and possible solutions. There seems to be a certain consensus in accepting that greater longevity is the cause of the problem of sustainability of pensions, but a decreasing birth rate is often also mentioned, being the inversion of the population pyramid the maximum indicator of the combination of these two forces. It is often seen that the solution to this problem is going back to higher birth rates. In our opinion, however, calling for increased birth rates is a false solution to the problem.[2]

Given this diagnosis, particularly for the Spanish case, which is one of the most mentioned by international organisations due the unfavourable evolution of its pension system, the literature has proposed several alternatives to solve or at least

[2]In fact, each new worker entering the system will live longer than the worker he/she replaces and, given the current pension schemes that make the system already unsustainable in most countries, this will only increase this unsustainability.

alleviate the sustainability problem. In general, these measures focus on policies to increase system resources, reductions in benefits through stricter eligibility conditions and (modest) delays in the retirement age. In this regard, the influence of the birth system (e.g. Roig and Patxot 2005, among others), productivity (e.g. Alonso and Herce 2003; Conde-Ruiz and Alonso 2004; Belmonte et al. 2009, among others) or immigration (León 2004; Del Brío and González 2004; Izquierdo and Jimeno 2005; Conde et al. 2006; Jiménez-Ridruejo et al. 2009; González 2013, among others) on sustainability has been studied. Other proposals have focused on changing the funding system and shifting resources to it from general taxes (e.g. Zubiri 2012, among others) or modifying more intensively the parameters of the current system like the mandatory retirement age (Hernández de Cos et al. 2017, among others) or encouraging reforms that are more focused on the transition to a system non-financial defined contribution accounts (Hernández de Cos et al. 2017, and Eguiagaray et al. 2013, among others).

However, we consider that the pension problem is more profound since greater longevity seems to be affecting somehow other behaviours throughout the life cycle and that a priori are not usually related to the increase in life expectancy. To understand these behaviours and their implications, we focus on the evolution of the average age at which the main contingencies and/or vital milestones of a representative individual occur. These happen, for the typical subject, in the following order (Fig. 20.1).

In del Herce and del Olmo (2013); Olmo and Herce (2011) and in Domínguez at et. (2018), we firstly tracked statistically the average age at which these contingencies and/or life-cycle milestones occur in Spain. Figure 20.2 presents an updated version of that life-cycle map.

The first stage, the formative one, has increased in what is referred to as its effective completion age, from 17.3 years in 1999 to 20.3 in 2016. This does not

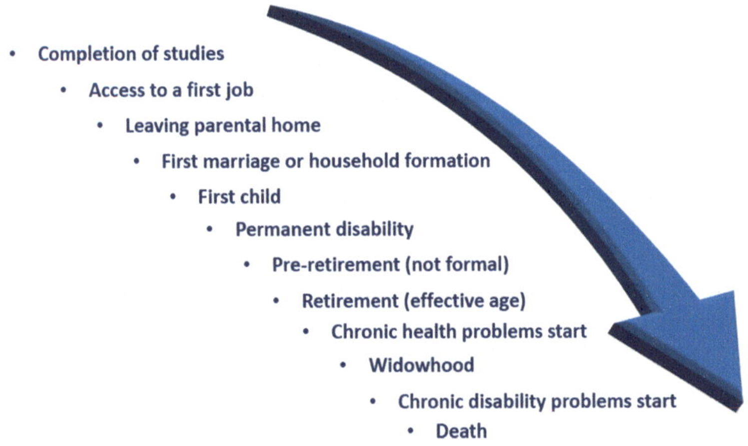

Fig. 20.1 Main milestones and contingencies across the life cycle. (*Source:* Herce and del Olmo (2013))

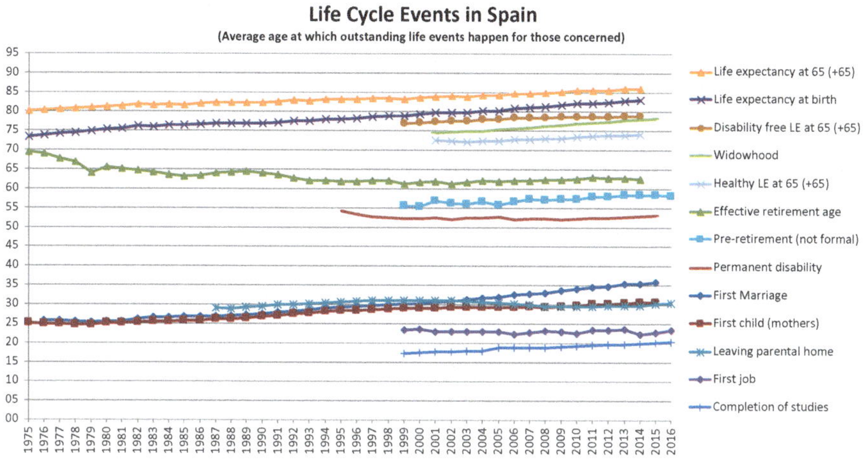

Fig. 20.2 Milestones of the life cycle in Spain (average age at which most relevant life-cycle events occur). (*Source:* Herce and del Olmo (2013); Del Olmo and Herce (2011), updated)

directly imply an increase in the entry age into the labour market, which has remained unchanged around 23.3 years, between 1999 and 2016, which, although worthy of a deeper study, could be due to unsuccessful job search or the realisation of non-formal training prior to entering the labour market in the early part of the period, shown in the graph.

The next important milestone is leaving parents' home, which did not have a uniform trend as between 1987 and 2001, the age at which this happened increased from 29.1 to 31.1) and then decreased from that year until 2011 (to 29.4 years). However, the crisis seems to force young people to stay in their parents' home, with the effective age increasing again to 30.4 years in 2016. This late quitting age also affects the age of the first marriage and that of the arrival of the first child (for mothers, at least), whose ages have also increased from 25.8 years in 1976 to 35.8 years in 2015 in the first case and from 25.3 years in 1975 to 30.7 years in 2015 in the second case.

The milestones that we are about to discuss next, unlike the previous ones, can occur at very different ages (except retirement). However, as shown by the average ages of occurrence, they usually occur in the second half or end of a typical life cycle.

In the case of permanent disability, we can see a slight decline in the average age at which it occurs: from 54.32 years in 1995 to 53.27 years in 2015. However, this figure has been used during severe economic crises to reduce registered unemployment by sending many redundant employees to early retirement. Again, it would be advisable to go deeper into analysing each of these events, whose eligibility requirements can sometimes be 'produced' by individuals themselves, who somehow are able to 'milk' the corresponding welfare system.

Regarding abandonment of productive activity, two key phenomena must be identified: pre-retirement and effective retirement. In relation to the former, which is not a statutory figure, the average age increased from 55.7 years in 1999 to 58.2 years in 2016. However, the evolution of the effective retirement age (with special emphasis on early retirement) is more relevant as it touches every worker reaching a certain age bracket. Although the statutory retirement age has traditionally been 65 years (67 when the last reform came into force), the effective age declined from 69.6 years in 1975 to 62.7 years in 2014. It is noteworthy to see how, as of 2004, the downward trend was reversed, although the effect was not intense, even though data available since the adoption of the 2011 reform (effective in January 2013) indicate that the average retirement age is rising slightly.

After retirement, the most relevant and vital milestones are related to people's personal autonomy and the end of the household that they formed in their adult life. It is in these contingencies that society's progress has been more relevant. Regarding life expectancy in good health for a person aged 65, it increased from the age of 72.6 in 2001 to the age of 74.0 in 2014. Additionally, the age at which widowhood occurs increased from 74.5 years in 2001 to 78.2 years in 2015, so life together with a partner is getting longer. On the other hand, and in view of the disability situation of a 65-year-old person, the disability-free life expectancy increased from the age of 76.9 in 1999 to the age of 79.0 in 2014. These data are consistent with a significant increase in life expectancy at age 65, from the age of 80.0 in 1975 to the age of 86.1 years in 2014, which in turn is accompanied by an equally significant declining mortality at ages below 65.

In summary, these data show how extended longevity affects a series of changes and behaviours throughout people's lives, which lie behind the real challenge for the sustainability of the pension system, besides carrying all kinds of personal, social and economic implications. At the same time, it can be seen how individuals increasingly delay their start of productive activities, but leaving the labour market is not experiencing that same delay.

Therefore, the 'pension problem' derives in fact from an incoherent 'vital algebra' problem, in which people contribute to the system fewer and fewer years and receive pensions for more and more years, and not simply from a problem of increasing longevity. We firmly believe that this is the real problem of pension and that neither children nor GDP growth (via productivity) will solve the problem. The 'pension problem', if the above is not taken into account, cannot be solved by parametric reforms of the system or by policies of increasing contributions or decreasing benefits.

The pension model that we have baptised as a 'two-steps mixed pension system', and that we have developed below, both theoretically and through quantitative illustrations, is based on the need to adapt pension schemes (public or private) to the longevity-induced behaviour of society and responds to those needs that workers cannot cope with individually when faced with ever-increasing longevity.

20.4 Description of the 'Two Steps Mixed Pension System'[3]

Pension systems are structured such that during the contribution phase, individuals contribute in relation to the salary they receive and do so until the retirement age x_j, so that later, during the retirement stage, they perceive a life pension from that system that is generated from their retirement until their death. This general scheme is run everywhere regardless of the system used, whether it is a PAYG, funded or mixed one.

Given the demographic risks that face pension systems and the fact that most of the reforms implemented lead to a reduction in the number of pensions, to make the schemes sustainable, this implies a problem of sufficiency of benefits and therefore a strong risk of impoverishment of retirees.

The vital algebra discussed in the previous section shows that individuals reduce the contribution period and increase the period in which they receive benefits, so that the new life pensions that are generated are higher than the pensions already being paid, which again poses a sustainability risk for the system.

The two-steps mixed system that we propose considers a period of active life, from the beginning of the working life to the moment of retirement (chosen with sufficient flexibility), and a retirement period, which is divided into two periods: one from ordinary retirement age to the so-called great age (or 'old age', as the one that the historical Social Security fixed at inception) and another one from that 'grand age' until the individual's death.

During active life, contributions will be made to two different schemes. Thus, the annual contribution made by the individual is divided into two parts:

- A part of the contribution generates a temporary actuarial financial income that the worker will receive from the moment he/she retires to the so-called grand age.

[3]During the last reviews of the present chapter to this volume we had the opportunity to learn about recent literature by Chilean authors (Larraín 2015; Larraín et al. 2017) showing simulations of the introduction of a system to ensure the 'fourth age', an identical concept to our 'grand age 'one in this paper. This literature has been published after the Herce and del Olmo (2013) paper and addresses the need to complement the Chilean system with a 'reinvented' Social Security that intervenes from that grand or fourth age, complementing the existing funding scheme, which makes the resulting mixed model very like the one we have been proposing since then, our two-steps mixed system in this paper. What we propose is to reduce the time scope of Social Security by introducing a previous scheme of temporary capitalisation income, and what the Chilean authors propose is to reduce the time scope of the funded system by reintroducing a Social Security pension scheme after the 'fourth age'. It is very encouraging that without previous direct or indirect contacts (as far as we know) between our two teams, we have both reached almost identical formulations that come to recognise, in short, the need to consider the problem of sufficiency of pensions by ensuring, but at the same time adapting to the twenty-first century, what is in fact the best longevity insurance ever invented: Social Security. This coincidence, and numerous contrasts with colleagues in informal debates, indicate that these ideas can open a new way of thinking about the design of pension systems that we believe and hope will gain room in the debate in the coming years.

- The other part finances pensions generated by a reinvented social security scheme, pay-as-you-go based, which consists of a life annuity from the mentioned grand age until the individual's death, hence the 'two steps'.

Therefore, when the individual retires, he/she will receive a temporary income from the retirement age that he/she has chosen within a greater flexibility until the grand age, based on capitalisation rules, age after which he/she will receive a retirement pension that is financed via a PAYG method until the moment of death.

This order of contribution and benefit flows ensures several crucial aspects of the arithmetic of pensions and the behaviour of workers at the same time, namely:

- First, between the ordinary retirement age and grand age (first step), an insured's temporary retirement income based on private capitalisation is involved. For this reason, each worker, depending on his long-term savings achieved, will be in the best conditions, duly informed, to even choose the ordinary retirement age to which he wants to stop working, or if he wants to make both statuses compatible. Temporary incomes will ideally be insured through actuarial products and, since they are not lifelong, will cover the survival risk (very limited up to grand age) very efficiently until that grand age. Their greater efficiency derives from the fact that they will not be designed to cover the longevity risk, which is high and increasing from grand age on and which is also very expensive to hedge, as seen in Sect. 16.2 above.
- Second, between grand age and death (second step), there is a retirement pension from Social Security, which, by definition, is an annuity and is calculated with strict actuarial criteria. However, this pension is financed through the pay-as-you-go method, so formally this second step is equivalent to the public system of notional individual accounts with defined contribution.

This way of presenting the sequence of contributions and benefits combined in time is what allows us to talk about the 'reinvention' of Social Security (Herce and del Olmo 2013).

The following chart shows the scheme that is followed in the current social security models, as well as the one followed in the case of the two-step mixed system that we propose (Fig. 20.3).

The two-step mixed model solves the vital algebra's consistency problem mentioned above since the pension funded by PAYG is paid from grand age until death, which means that the number of years that the system must pay benefits to any retiree are fewer that those under the current system. On the other hand, the fully funded scheme term annuities, payable since retirement until grand age, are marketed more easily than a life annuity since the former are significantly cheaper on unit terms as they must not be insured against longevity but in a small part of this risk (see Sect. 16.2 and the following sections). This product is thus more interesting for insurance companies and could eventually lead to a significant expansion of annuity markets everywhere in a natural way.

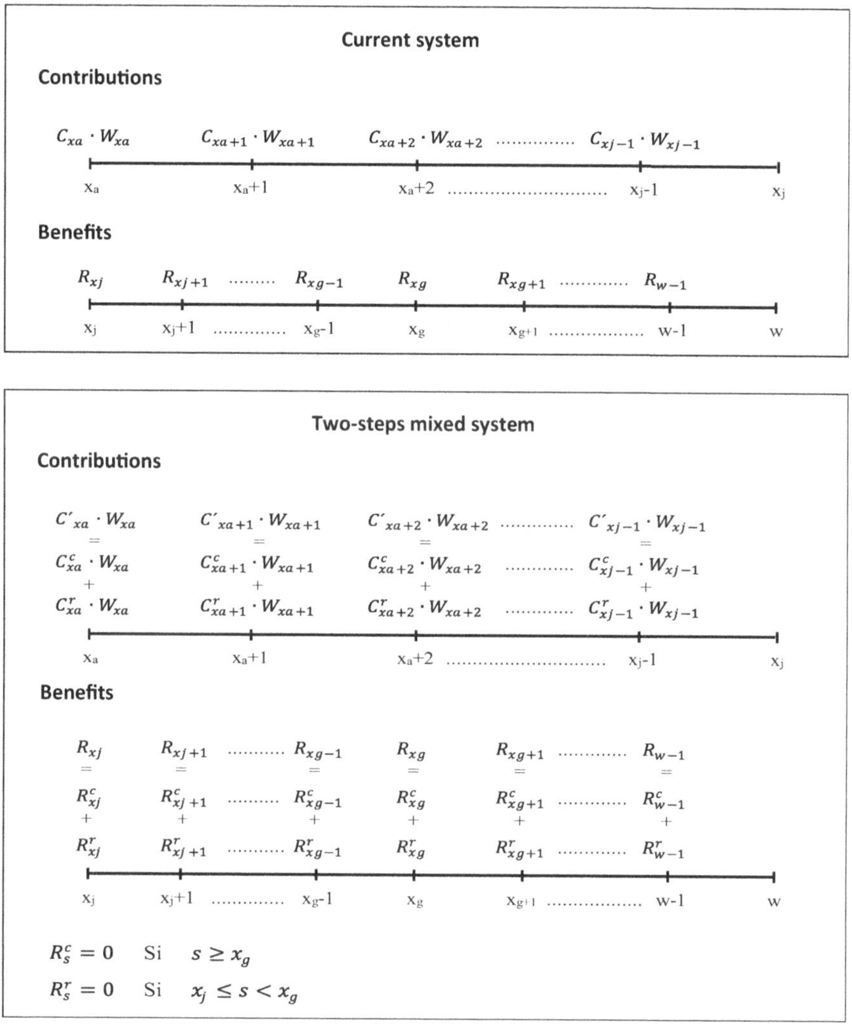

Fig. 20.3 Flow scheme of ages, contributions and benefits in current and mixed systems in stages Where

x_a: age of the individual when entering the labour market

x_j: age of the individual when taking ordinary retirement

x_g: age of the individual when reaching the so-called grand age

c_{x_a}: percentage of contribution at age x_a in the current system

c'_{x_a}: percentage of contribution at age x_a in the two-step mixed system; it includes both the contribution to the PAYG system $c^r_{x_a}$ and to the temporary income scheme $c^c_{x_a}$

R_{xj}: pension perceived by the individual at age x_j in the current system

R^c_s: pension perceived by the individual at age s generated within the funded system; this pension disappears at 'grand age' and is in fact a term annuity

R^r_s: pension perceived by the individual at age s generated within the PAYG system; this pension is null until grand age x_g and lasts for life once initiated

W_{x_a}: salary at age x_a, which is assumed to coincide, for simplicity, with the contribution base

In the following sections, the current PAYG-defined benefit system is compared against the two-step mixed system we propose. This comparison will be made following a dual perspective:

- An analysis of the financial solvency of both systems is performed through the internal rate of return for the representative individual.
- An analysis of the aggregate financial sustainability of both systems is performed through the analysis of total income and expenditure flows.

It should be noted that the dual approach of the internal rate of return and income and expenditure flows is rarely performed in the literature. In this study, we have combined them and performed both since we consider that both approaches, rather than being apart from each other, are complementary and therefore will provide greater robustness to the analysis.

20.5 Comparative Analysis of the Current Spanish PAYG System and the Two-Step Mixed System in Terms of Individual Financial Solvency

This section shows a comparative analysis, in terms of financial-actuarial solvency, of the PAYG system of defined benefit that exist today in Spain and the two-step mixed we propose to replace it in time. We will first describe the methodology and then carry out illustrative computations that will allow us to obtain conclusions aimed at renewing that current system in what should be in fact a reinvention of Social Security in the twenty-first century.

20.5.1 Methodology for Calculating the Internal Rate of Return

The relationship between the internal rate of return and the financial viability of a pension system has its origin in the seminal proposition by Samuelson (1958). According to this author, a pay-as-you-go system will remain in financial equilibrium if its internal rate of return is not greater than the sum of the rates of employment growth and wage growth. The methodology of the internal rate of return measures the relationship between the contributions made and the benefits received for the whole life cycle of an individual or group of individuals. The objective pursued in this method is to verify if in the pension system there is a financial-actuarial balance between the contributions made by everyone during his or her active years and the benefits that he/she will subsequently receive from the system when he/she retires.

For Devesa et al. (2002), the basic idea of Samuelson, still fully in force and frequently referred to in the literature, is that a pension system, financed through intergenerational transfers, will be sustainable in the long term provided that the IRR of the system does not exceed the average growth rate of real wages, plus the stable growth of the contributing population or, in other words, it does not exceed the growth of the system's fiscal base. Therefore, according to the IRR methodology, the financial viability of the pay-as-you-go system will be linked (Murphy and Welch 1998) with the average long-term sustainable economic growth and this will be the benchmark to establish the sustainability of the system. In the same vein, Jimeno and Licandro (1999) point out that in the long-term, the growth rate of real wages is given by the labour productivity growth rate, so for the PAYG system to be viable, the growth rate of the Gross Domestic Product must be at least equal to the average IRR of the system and never lower.

As in Devesa et al. (2002), this proposal, in which Aaron (1966) based his well-known paradox on Social Security, is complemented and developed, among others, by Keyfitz (1985a), who studies how the IRR is affected depending on the size of the cohort of individuals considered; Lapkoff (1985, 1988, 1991, who analyses how demographic instability affects the financial performance of different cohorts, has reached conclusions different from those by Keyfitz (1985b); Bravo (1996), who developed the demographic and economic elements and the rules that influence IRR. Some researchers, such as Boskin and Puffert (1987) or Leimer (1995), have been inclined to study the real rates of return effectively provided by the pay-as-you-go system, concluding, in the case of the United States and Canada, much higher values initially than at maturity. Schnabel (1997), in a similar vein, concludes that the generations born in the eighties in Germany will bear negative rates. Finally, Rofman (1993) studies the IRR within the same cohort or generation focusing on the effect of the different mortality rates on the IRR, which individuals are subjected to according to age, sex, race, level of education, income or place of birth.

Following Devesa et al. (2002), the IRR, for a contributor who joins the labour market at the age x_a, in a pure PAYG system, is defined as the value of parameter i of the compound capitalisation law, which actuarially equals to contribution flows with benefit flows.

The actuarial value of a worker's contributions over his active period (V_{COT}) is calculated as follows:

$$V_{\mathrm{COT}} = \sum_{t=0}^{x_j-1-x_a} P_{x_a}^t c_{x_a+t} W_{x_a} \prod_{i=t}^{x_j-1-x_a} (1+\alpha_i)(1+\beta_i)^{-1}(1+i)^{-t} \qquad (20.1)$$

where the notation used is

i: real internal rate of return.[4]

x_a: age of the individual when entering the labour market.

x_j: age of the individual when reaching retirement.

[4]The adjective real refers to being obtained from contributions and pensions calculated in real terms and not in nominal terms.

$P^t_{x_a}$: probability that a person of age x_a reaches the age $x_a + t$.

c_{x_a+t}: percentage of contribution at age $x_a + t$; it includes the contributions of both employers and employees.

W_{x_a}: salary at age x_a, which is assumed to coincide with the contribution base.

α_i: annual nominal growth rate of wages in the year in which the individual is aged i, which is assumed to be constant.

$W_{x_a+t} = W_{x_a}(1+\alpha^*)^t$: salary at age $x_a + t$.

β_i: annual inflation growth rate in the year in which the individual is aged i.

The current actuarial value of retirement benefits, discounted at rate i and according to the current Spanish legislation (simplified), is obtained as follows:

$$V_{Rx} = \sum_{t=x_j-x_a}^{w-1-x_a} R_{x_j} P^t_{x_a} (1+\lambda^*)^{t-(x_j-x_a)} (1+\beta)^{-t} (1+i)^{-t} \qquad (20.2)$$

where the notation used is

λ^*: cumulative annual rate of nominal pension growth.

w: age limit of the mortality table used.

R_{x_j}: initial retirement pension.

20.5.2 *Empirical Analysis Compared in Financial Solvency Terms*

To carry out the comparative analysis, the following assumptions are made:

Assumption 1. The ordinary retirement age (not to be confused with the grand age) is the same for the current PAYG system as for the two-step mixed system.

Assumption 2. In the two-step mixed system, grand age is introduced and properly defined; after this age, pension is granted by the reinvented PAYG Social Security scheme.

Assumption 3. The total duration and amount of retirement benefits in the current PAYG system and in the two-step mixed system is the same.

Assumption 4. In the two-step mixed system, a part of Pc social contribution by workers is allocated to the PAYG branch. That part is initially set at ½ of the total rate.

Assumption 5. In the two-step mixed system, management fees are charged on contributions during active life and term annuities perceived during retirement from the ordinary retirement age until grand age.

Assumption 6. The typical worker is a worker who started working at age 30 with an annual salary of € 20,000.

Assumption 7. Workers (opt to) retire at 67 with a replacement rate of 80% over their last salary, and grand age is set at 78 years.

Assumption 8. A wage increase of 3%, inflation at 2% and productivity growth at 1% are considered; pensions are updated annually with the Spanish Pension Revaluation Index, set at its minimum of 0.25% (we thus assume the unconstrained value of the PRI to be 'permanently' below this statutory floor).

Assumption 9. The contribution rate to the old-age retirement pension scheme has been estimated to be 17% in the current PAYG system.[5] In the two-step mixed system, the contribution rate needed to maintain the current retirement pension will be endogenously determined.

Assumption 10. The nominal interest rate is assumed to be 3%; management fees during the contribution period to the capitalisation scheme are 0.2% of assets and 1.5% during the decumulation period. These values can be adapted to the market situation.

Assumption 11. The Mortality Table 2015 for the Spanish population (Unisex), published by the Spanish Statistical Office (INE), is used.

Once the main assumptions have been established, the empirical analysis proceeds as follows:

Phase 1. The expected pension benefit flow of the public pension system is computed according to the current rules and assuming a replacement rate of 80%.

Phase 2. There are two time periods separated by the nature of retirement income received by the retiree: a first period where a term annuity is paid by the capitalisation pillar and a second period in which the retiree receives a Social Security pension. The first period spans from ordinary retirement to grand age and the second from grand age on.

Phase 3. Once the amount of the term annuity has been fixed, the contribution to be made during active life is determined so as to obtain this financial-actuarial income. According to assumption 9 above, the contribution to the current system, exclusively allocated to retirement benefits, is 17%. Thus, the contribution to the new PAYG system will be at least 50% of that 17%, that is 8.5%. If the total contribution required is higher than 17%, this will be increased, ensuring that 8.5 points are allocated to the new PAYG scheme and the rest to the capitalisation scheme.

With the strategy discussed, we will obtain the necessary contribution flows to finance the mixed two-step system we are proposing, as well as its benefit flows.

---

[5]The social security contribution rate in Spain is based on common contingencies, which include disability, widowhood, orphanage and retirement. Retirement expenditure in relation to all benefits generates that out of the total rate of 28.3% we can consider that 17% is the contribution rate for the retirement benefit.

These flows will allow us to calculate the internal rate of return of the new mixed system.

The results to be obtained out of the financial solvency analysis are individual 'internal rates of return' (IRR) offered by the current PAYG system, as well as the individual IRR offered by a mixed two-step system, the latter composed by the term (financial-actuarial) annuity IRR and the new Social Security life annuity IRR.

As a primer of the results that are discussed in what follows, the following Table 20.2 shows the results of the IRR calculation.

As can be seen, the IRR of the current system is 2.8%, which means that if GDP growth is 2%, there is a financial solvency problem of the system. This problem is reduced if the mixed system is introduced, in which case the IRR of the Social Security life annuity is 1.8%, i.e. lower than the long-term GDP growth. Both parts of the new system are more protected from unsustainability than the current system. Let us discuss now the baseline results that produce this IRR picture.

In the following tables, a sensitivity analysis of the parameters of retirement age and grand age is performed to see its impact on the individual IRR. As can be seen in Table 20.3, as the retirement age decreases, the IRR of the current system increases, making the insolvency of the system worse and reflecting the obvious fact that pensions must be paid for a longer period while contributions are received for a shorter period. In the case the mixed model takes the scene, the solvency of the system does not suffer because the cost of this decrease in the retirement age is financed through a corresponding increase in the contribution rate to the funded scheme if benefits must be kept.

Table 20.2 IRRs compared

Current system (no funded part)	2.8%
Two-step system (funded part)	0.5%
Two-step system (PAYG part)	1.8%

Source: Own computations

Table 20.3 Simulation 1: Change in the ordinary retirement age

Entry age (for working)	30	30	30
Grand age	78	78	78
Ordinary retirement age	60	65	70
Contribution years	30	35	40
Contribution rate to the current system	17%	17%	17%
Total contribution to the two-step system	42%	30%	21%
Contribution to the new PAYG system	8.5%	8.5%	8.5%
Contribution to the new funded system	33.5%	21.5%	12.5%
IRR current system	4.6%	3.3%	2.1%
IRR two-step system (funded part)	0.3%	0.5%	0.6%
IRR two-step system (PAYG part)	1.7%	1.7%	1.8%

Source: Own computations

Table 20.4 Simulation 2: Changes in the grand age

Entry age (for working)	30	30	30
Grand age	67	67	67
Ordinary retirement age	37	37	37
Contribution years	70	75	80
Contribution rate to the current system	17%	17%	17%
Total contribution to the two-step system	17.00%	22.02%	28.30%
Contribution to the new PAYG system	8.5%	8.5%	8.5%
Contribution to the new funded system	8.5%	13.52%	19.8%
IRR current system	2.82%	2.82%	2.82%
IRR two-step system (funded part)	0.72%	0.59%	0.48%
IRR two-step system (PAYG part)	3.28%	2.70%	1.14%

Source: Own computations

As the results of the previous table clearly show, retirement is very expensive, and delaying the adjustment of the retirement age as life expectancy increases is a great burden for the system, not to mention the reversal of the modest increases in the ordinary retirement age adopted to date or even decreasing the retirement age, as some parties are proposing in Spain and abroad. In the latter case, the IRR of the current system would be above 4.5%, making its insolvency worse, as discussed. But, in addition, the contribution rates for the funding scheme in the two-step mixed system we propose would rise disproportionately. However, ordinary retirement at age 70 greatly reduces the IRR of the current pay-as-you-go system, helping its sustainability decisively, while in the mixed system, the funding scheme, which should only fulfil benefit obligations for about 8 years, is significantly cheaper.

If, on the other hand, the grand age is lowered, the IRR of the PAYG scheme, in the mixed system, increases because the benefit period is longer, with contributions already due, while the contribution rate in the funded scheme decreases because of the shortening of the period in which capitalisation benefits must be paid (Table 20.4).

20.6 Comparative Analysis of the Sustainability of the Current PAYG System and the Two-Step Mixed System in Aggregate Terms to the 2065 Horizon

The sustainability of the system and the adequacy of benefits are the key to the current debate on pensions in Spain and in any other country. Our two-step mixed system proposal is, we believe, a way to solve these problems. As it must be clear to the reader by now, this proposal stands on two legs: (i) long-term savings to fund the term annuity and a much-delayed retirement (grand) age to make sustainable and sufficient the reinvented Social Security scheme. The result should be then both sustainability and adequacy of retirement income at the same or, even, lower cost.

We believe that this arrangement of pension schemes through time solves many of the current problems of pension systems around the world. It makes collective market insurance during step 1 efficient by avoiding the problem of 'open longevity' through providing term annuities, while Social Security in step 2 can be both sufficient and sustainable as it must deal with life benefits, even under a pay-as-you-go method, for a much shorter period for all retirees.

However, to defend the viability of this proposal, it is not enough to only demonstrate financial solvency at the individual scale in each of the two schemes that make up the mixed system, as was done in the previous section. The latter analysis must be complemented with an analysis of financial sustainability in aggregate terms, present and future, of the proposed system versus the current one in force in Spain now.

20.6.1 Methodology of Income and Expenditure Projection of the System

Exercises to project social security income and expenditure flows have been widely used in the literature since they allow to evaluate the expected income and expenditure trend of the system under different hypotheses of evolution of different variables that they depend on, such as the increase in life expectancy, changes in birth rates, migratory flows, policy changes, etc. These exercises have been carried out with varied methodologies, which, in general, belong to two types: accounting models and dynamic stochastic models, or a combination of both. Without the intention of being exhaustive, for the Spanish case, studies by Alonso and Herce (2003), Díaz-Saavedra (2005), Balmaseda et al. (2006), Jimeno et al. (2008), Gil et al. (2008), Moral-Arce et al. (2008), De la Fuente and Doménech (2009), Herce and Fernández (2009) and Sánchez-Martín and Sánchez-Marcos (2010) or reports by national and international bodies such as the Ministry of Employment and Social Security, the OECD or the European Commission (2015) can be highlighted. More recently, these exercises have been carried out to evaluate reforms implemented under the current Spanish pension system. In this sense, the studies by Conde Ruiz and González (2013), De la Fuente and Doménech (2013), Sánchez (2014), Díaz Giménez and Díaz Saavedra (2017) or Hernández de Cos et al. (2017) can be highlighted. For the empirical exercise contained in this section, an accounting model of the projection of expenditure and income of the Spanish system of contributory pensions was used.

20.6.2 Comparative Empirical Analysis in Terms of Sustainability

The projection of income and expenditure of the Spanish system of contributory retirement pensions is in line with that used in Galdeano et al. (2017). To carry out the projection, a population projection (INE) was combined with an ad hoc macroeconomic scenario for the period 2016–2065, which is shown in Table 20.5 below.

The macroeconomic scenario for this exercise shows assumptions about employment creation (the employment rate that is reflected is the ratio between the number of Social Security affiliates and the population of working age – between 16 and 64 years), and GDP growth can be derived combining assumptions on job creation and productivity growth, as it is also shown in Table 20.5.

These macroeconomic forecasts are consistent with the perspectives of the main institutions of analysis of the Spanish economy for the coming years, so that longer term projections represent a purely hypothetical, 'what-if' kind exercise.

Having said that, despite the data observed in recent years, the evolution of economic growth shows a trend change marked by a gradual deceleration in the coming years that will lead to a situation close to economic stagnation between 2038 and 2047 and will subsequently achieve very moderate economic growth. This statement, however, needs to be readily qualified.

It is important to understand that the dynamics of GDP is caused not by a prolonged economic crisis but by the significant decline in the labour force that even at saturation rates leads to the demographic projections used. It is a usual image in this type of exercises, and in no way does level GDP dynamics prevent GDP per capita from growing even at a healthy pace. This is already happening in countries such as Germany and Japan, economies in which the general population and the working population are already declining, level GDP is moderately growing and GDP per head is growing healthily.

In terms of employment growth, and in contrast to the latest data, the assumed scenario shows a downward trend, starting at the beginning of the 2030s towards a negative year-on-year employment growth, precisely because of the significant reduction in the working-age population, whose decline cannot be compensated even assuming a sharp increase in the activity rate that underlies the long-term macroeconomic framework. Thus, if one looks at the evolution of the employment rate, one can see a continuous growth that will lead to rates higher than 70% in 2065. This is also consistent with full employment in the medium to long term.

Finally, productivity developments will experience, we assume as a hypothesis, a slow growth trend until 2030, maintaining thereafter a steady and constant growth of 1% per year. It should not be forgotten, as stated by Alonso and Herce (2003), that productivity developments have no impact on the sustainability of the pension system since they affect wages and, consequently, pensions that are calculated on their basis (at birth, so to speak), so that their influence would be similar on income and expenditures, in the absence of other subsequent adjustments of the pension after it has been computed for the first time.

Table 20.5 Macroeconomic scenario of projections

	2016	2020	2025	2030	2035	2040	2045	2050	2055	2060	2065
Employment rate	57.8%	62.3%	65.9%	68.3%	69.4%	69.8%	70.1%	70.3%	70.6%	70.8%	70.9%
YoY growth rate of GDP	3.3%	1.7%	1.2%	0.8%	0.2%	−0.2%	−0.2%	0.3%	0.7%	0.8%	0.8%
YoY growth rate of employment	3.0%	1.6%	0.7%	−0.2%	−0.8%	−1.1%	−1.2%	−0.7%	−0.3%	−0.2%	−0.1%
YoY growth rate of productivity	0.2%	0.2%	0.5%	1.0%	1.0%	1.0%	1.0%	1.0%	1.0%	1.0%	1.0%

Source: Galdeano et al. (2017)

In turn, population trends were obtained from the latest official projections developed by INE until 2065. Based on these population projections, the dynamics of workers and pensioners of the system are developed together with existing pension and contribution formulas in the exercise reference year (2016). The normative changes that occurred in the last reforms of the Spanish pension system are thus already embedded in the model.

Once the macro-scenario that nurtures the projections has been defined, the system has then recognised affiliates in terms of effective employment at each moment and pensions for people over 60 years of age, although half of the workers retire in Spain at age 65.

As mentioned above, the model embodies the major normative changes introduced by the government in 2011 and 2013: (i) a gradual increase in the retirement age, (ii) a gradual increase in the pension computation period to form the 'pensionable wage base' (adopted in 2011 and in force since January 2014), (iii) the application of the sustainability factor as of 2019 and (iv) the annual update of all pensions through the Pension Revaluation Index (PRI) since January 2014 (adopted in 2013), among other minor measures. The PRI has been implemented in the model at 0.25% per annum, the minimum allowed under the current regulation as the exact formula of the PRI is expected to yield a lower value throughout the projection horizon.

The outstanding difference of the projections presented in this work compared to other models presented in the literature is the calibration of the model exclusively with the characteristics related to the contingency of retirement, excluding contributions, expenses and number of pensioners for contingencies such as survival and invalidity. This netting out will allow the comparison of the data of the existing system with the results obtained for the two-step mixed system we are also calibrating in this exercise.

To establish which part of the general contributions (28.3% of the salary) goes to the financing of retirement pensions, a general pension contribution of 17% has been assumed on wages.[6]

In this way, the demographic and economic variables of the Spanish system of contributory retirement pensions are obtained. The results are shown in Table 20.6 below.

The results presented in the table above do not lead to conclusions different from those shown in other studies in the literature, showing an increase in the population at retirement age of 62%, resulting in a 56% increase in the number of retirement pensions, compared to a reduction of 8% in the number of Social Security affiliations, caused by a 25% reduction in the working-age population and partially offset by an increase in the rate of employment and active participation of the working-age population.

[6]This rate has been calculated by obtaining the contribution rate weighted by the cost ratio of expenditure on retirement pensions on the total benefits expenditure of the system.

Table 20.6 Summary projection for the existing Social Security PAYG system

Demographic flows	*2016*	*2035*	*2050*	*2065*	*Ratio 2065/2016*
Total population (1 July) (thousands)	46,441	45,617	44,192	41,179	0.89
Population 16–64/66	30,474	28,438	24,012	22,871	0.75
Population of 60–64/66	2854	4952	3590	3476	1.22
Population of 65/67 and +	8197	11,546	14,523	13,298	1.62
Retirement pensions (thousands)	5693	7912	9681	8897	1.56
Affiliates (thousands)	17,599	19,742	16,890	16,259	0.92
Economic flows (euros 2015)					
Contributory expenses of the system (million euros)	84,248	110,489	134,811	125,273	1.49
Average annual retirement pension (euros)	14,510	13,692	13,652	13,612	0.94
Average annual contribution (euros)	3701	4115	4756	5497	1.49
Replacement rate (registered for pension)	135,7%	114,1%	105,1%	97,7%	0.72
Replacement rate (average pension)	111,0%	94,2%	81,2%	70,1%	0.63
Contribution income (million euros)	65,131	81,239	80,333	89,380	1.37
Surplus (+)/deficit (−) of system (million euros)	−19,117	−29,250	−54,478	−35,893	–
Reserve fund (+)/debt (−) (million euros)	6028	−336,911	−1,004,804	−1,702,658	–
In percentage of GDP					
Total income	5.82	5.82	5.82	5.82	1.00
Total expenditure	7.53	7.91	9.76	8.15	1.08
Surplus/deficit	−1.71	−2.09	−3.95	−2.34	–
Reserve fund/debt	0.54	−24.13	−72.76	−110.82	–
Ratio affiliates/pensions	3.09	2.50	1.74	1.83	0.59
Pro memoria (euros 2015)					
GDP (million euros)	1,119,573	1,396,464	1,380,895	1,536,401	1.37
GDP per worker (euros)	63,617	70,737	81,758	94,497	1.49
GDP per inhabitant (euros)	24,108	30,613	31,248	37,310	1.55

Source: Own computations

The most relevant effect of these transitions, in our view, is the sharp reduction in the ratio of affiliates to retirement pensions from 3.09 in 2016 to 1.82 in 2065.

Figure 20.4 shows the projections of expenditure, income and surplus/deficit of the new PAYG system, reflecting the persistent deficit in which the retirement pension system is in throughout the projection period, given the set of assumptions adopted for this simulation.

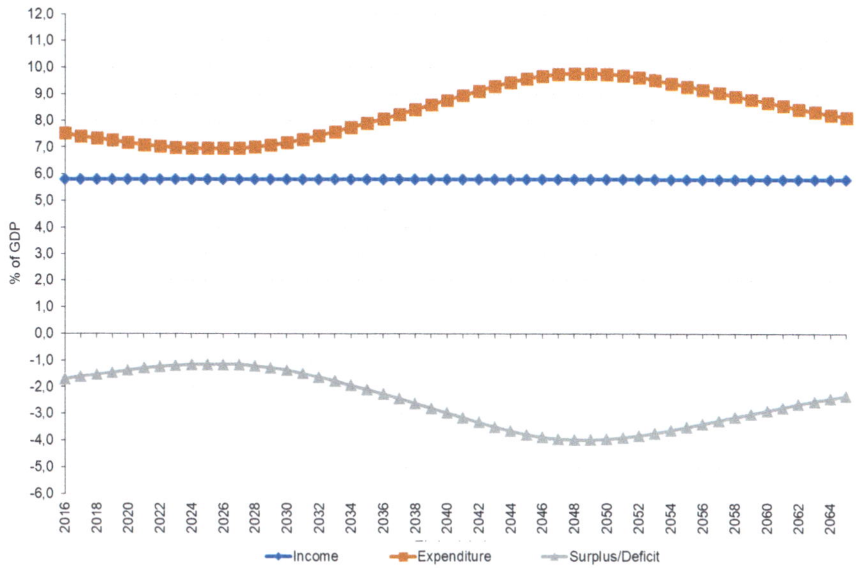

Fig. 20.4 PAYG system of defined benefits. (*Source:* Own computations)

It is evident that the demographic dynamics, intensified by the life-cycle behaviours derived from a greater longevity, make the system's income remain below 6% of GDP, while the expenditure increases to cover the needs of a greater number of retirement pensioners, who moreover live longer, being higher than 8% of GDP in 2065, but having left behind at that time a long history of expenditure ratios on GDP between 8% and 10%, which leaves its mark on the annual deficit of the system and especially the accumulated debt at the end of the projection period (110% of GDP in 2065, see Table 20.6 above).

Therefore, the structural deficit of the system will experience an upward trend as the 'baby boom' generations retire and a peak at between 2045 and 2055, returning gradually afterwards to levels close to 2% in 2065, slightly higher than those of 2016.

The evolution of the accounts of the current system of retirement pensions is problematic. In view of this more than probable eventuality, the adoption of a mixed system may be advisable, more specifically the two-step kind of system we are advocating in this paper. It can be shown that in this way, the public system will be able to absorb the increase in longevity by severely limiting the structural deficit and avoiding the dramatic accumulation of debt, which would destabilise it.

The simulations of the two-step mixed system (GAYG part) presented below are based on the same demographic and macroeconomic scenario presented previously and coincide with those of the existing system in the computation of contribution income since the affiliated population and the contribution percentage will be the same as in the current system. The big difference comes from the expenditure side.

Table 20.7 Projection of the new grand age Social Security pillar – no deficit

Demographic flows	*2016*	*2035*	*2050*	*2065*	*Ratio 2065/ 2015*
Total population (1 July) (thousands)	46,441	45,617	44,192	41,179	0.89
Population of 78 and +	3185	4983	7499	8348	2.62
Retirement pensions (thousands)	2036	2983	4397	4880	2.40
Affiliates (thousands)	17,599	19,742	16,890	16,259	0.92
Economic flows (euros 2015)					
Contributory expenditure of the system (million euros)	25,306	36,654	52,689	55,060	2.18
Average annual retirement pension (euros)	12,183	12,045	11,749	11,637	0.96
Contribution rate	6.61%	7.67%	11.15%	10.47%	1.58
Average annual contribution (euros)	1438	1857	3120	3386	2.36
Contribution income (million euros)	25,306	36,654	52,689	55,060	2.18
Surplus (+)/deficit (−) of system (million euros)	0	0	0	0	–
In percentage of GDP					
Total income	2.26	2.62	3.82	3.58	1.59
Total expenditure	2.26	2.62	3.82	3.58	1.59
Surplus/deficit	0.00	0.00	0.00	0.00	–

Source: Own computations

While in the existing system pensions cover the needs of people retired at an age generally around 65, the system proposed allows people to retire at the age they wish to under a funded pillar, while the new PAYG pillar of individual (i.e. notional) accounts will cover the needs only of people who reach and exceed grand age.

Under these premises, the projections of the PAYG pillar of the new system would be as shown in Table 20.7 below. However, in order for the new PAYG scheme to reach financial sustainability through time, we impose an endogenous (adjustable) contribution rate.

As can be seen in the above table, under the assumption of a continuous budget balance of the system, the expenditure amount of the system is reduced to a third of what is shown in Table 20.7 for the current system. This is due to the following reasons:

- In the new PAYG pillar, the pension is paid for a shorter number of years since it starts at the age of 78 instead of 65.
- The pension benefits of those who are 78 years old or more are lower than the pension benefits of those who have just retired as newborn pensions are higher than pensions produced years before.
- On the other hand, retirement pensions at 2016 are not fully impacted by measures included in the recent reforms, such as the pension calculation period, which will be gradually growing until 25 years in 2023, or the sustainability factor, which intervenes in 2019 and beyond. However, these parameters do

affect the calculation of pension expenditure in the years mentioned and increasingly, above all in what concerns the sustainability factor, later.

In the simulation presented in the previous table, the balanced budget restriction (zero deficit every year) is fixed, but in exchange, the contribution rate must be endogenous to this objective. This implies that problems such as uncertainty in labour for employers and equity problems can arise since contributions would be different from one year to the next and for different cohorts of workers.

For this reason, it would also be interesting to simulate a fixed contribution rate to finance retirement pensions of the PAYG pillar in order for the scheme not to accumulate too much debt in the medium and long term, thus ensuring general sustainability through time. This simulation is shown in Table 20.8 below. The fixed rate is set at 8.50% of the salary, and it can be observed that after some surplus years, there are deficit years and, at the projection horizon, accumulated debt amounts to a very low percentage of GDP. In fact, it is immediate to find the contribution rate that would bring Social Security current debt in 2065 to null.

Table 20.8 Projection of the new grand age Social Security pillar – fixed contribution rate and approximate sustainability

Demographic flows	*2016*	*2035*	*2050*	*2065*	*Ratio 2065/ 2015*
Total population (1 July) (thousands)	46,441	45,617	44,192	41,179	0.89
Population of 78 and +	3185	4983	7499	8348	2.62
Retirement pensions (thousands)	2036	2983	4397	4880	2.40
Affiliates (thousands)	17,599	19,742	16,890	16,259	0.92
Economic flows (euros 2015)					
Contributory expenditure of the system (million euros)	25,306	36,654	52,689	55,060	2.18
Average annual retirement pension (euros)	12,183	12,045	11,749	11,637	0.96
Contribution rate	8.50%	8.50%	8.50%	8.50%	
Average annual contribution (euros)	1850	2058	2378	2749	1.49
Contribution income (million euros)	32,565	40,620	40,167	44,690	1.37
Surplus (+)/deficit (−) of system (million euros)	7260	3966	−12,522	−10,370	–
Accumulated surplus (+)/deficit (−) of system (million euros)	7260	154,418	73,176	−134,632	–
In percentage of GDP					
Total income	2.91	2.91	2.91	2.91	1.00
Total expenditure	2.26	2.62	3.82	3.58	1.59
Surplus/deficit	0.65	0.28	−0.91	−0.67	–
Accumulated surplus (+)/deficit (−) of system	0.65	11.06	5.30	−8.76	–

Source: Own computations

Table 20.9 Projection of the new grand age Social Security pillar – fixed contribution rate and no debt at 2065

Demographic flows	*2016*	*2035*	*2050*	*2065*	*Ratio 2065/2015*
Total population (1 July) (thousands)	46,441	45,617	44,192	41,179	0.89
Population aged 78 and +	3185	4983	7499	8348	2.62
Retirement pensions (thousands)	2036	2983	4397	4880	2.40
Affiliates (thousands)	17,599	19,742	16,890	16,259	0.92
Economic flows (euros 2015)					
Contributory expenses of the system (million euros)	25,306	36,654	52,689	55,060	2.18
Average annual retirement pension (euros)	12,183	12,045	11,749	11,637	0.96
Contribution rate	9.07%	9.07%	9.07%	9.07%	
Average annual contribution (euros)	1976	2197	2539	2934	1.49
Contribution income (million euros)	34,767	43,365	42,882	47,711	1.37
Surplus (+)/deficit (−) of system (million euros)	9461	6711	−9807	−7349	–
Accumulated surplus (+)/deficit (−) of system (million euros)	9461	205,229	164,861	0	–
In percentage of GDP					
Total income	3.11	3.11	3.11	3.11	1.00
Total expenditure	2.26	2.62	3.82	3.58	1.59
Surplus/deficit	0.85	0.48	−0.71	−0.48	–
Accumulated surplus (+)/deficit (−) of system	0.85	14.70	11.94	0.00	–

Source: Authors' computations

This is exactly what a final simulation, shown below in Table 20.9, does. In this case, the constant contribution rate has been adjusted so as to achieve exact financial equilibrium at the end of the projection period. Thus, even if the demographic dynamics during that period makes the existence of specific imbalances inevitable, the system would accumulate a reserve fund large enough to absorb the deficit generated in the years with the highest expenses.

20.7 Final Comments

In this chapter, we have carried out an individual and aggregate assessment exercise of what we have called a 'two-steps mixed pension system' for Spain. This system consists of two pillars that are introduced over time. First is a private funded pillar (which may be compulsory or affiliation 'by default' or *self-enrolment*) and would provide temporary retirement income to workers from the time of retirement until the 'grand age'. At that moment, the Social Security would therefore pay the worker a life annuity.

The workers would choose the age at which they wish to retire freely, depending on their retirement savings to the first pillar, and may even choose not to retire until the grand age and could also choose to combine retirement income compatible with labour income. The grand age would be determined by the Social Security, but it would neither be compulsory, and the workers could combine their public pension with other labour income. Social Security would provide actuarial life annuities either defined contribution or defined benefit adjustable to meet sustainability goals.

Both pillars would be financed through specific contributions made during the working life, but the term annuities of the private funded pillar that would intervene in the first 'step' could also be financed by a single premium. Even this pillar could be extended in parallel to the Social Security intervention by acquiring an actuarial life annuity supplementary to that of the Social Security, thus reinforcing economic capacity from the grand age onwards.

Herce and del Olmo (2013) had already proposed this scheme in an approach that is considerably improved with the present one, which addresses both its internal (individual) and aggregate (system) coherence in terms of profitability, sufficiency and sustainability of the new mixed system. Indeed, it is shown that by adjusting actuarially the income derived from both pillars, a more efficient management of the longevity risk, very limited until the grand age, but considerably greater from there onwards, by the form in which each pillar of insurance intervenes.

The Social Security intervenes when the retiree has less years of life to cover, and therefore his or her budget and financial needs are severely limited, as well as the unsustainability risk, while maintaining the adequacy of benefits and a more careful planning of their economic-financial flows can be made. Individuals do not pay more than with the existing system; however, while they have more time to plan their long-term savings and to decide how their quitting from work activity should be. Workers also immediately receive the reward from a longer permanence in their work activity, being able to also evaluate ex ante, with greater transparency, the consequences of an early retirement.

A variant of this scheme has also recently been proposed for Chile (Larraín 2015; Larraín et al. 2017) due to the need for reintroducing the Social Security pillar into the mandatory funded system with a single pillar existing in this country, which usually ends up being manifestly insufficient to provide retirees with adequate life annuities. Although the resulting design ends up being the same, the interesting thing is that while in our design we turn to the introduction of the first pillar (the funded system) to make the income of the second one (a reinvented Social Security) adequate, in the case mentioned, the introduction of the second pillar (the Social Security) is invoked to make the income of the first pillar (funded system) sufficient. Both pillars are sequenced in time (two-step) around the 'grand age' or, as Larraín and his colleagues call it, the 'fourth age'.

We believe that such proposals to achieve both sustainability and sufficiency of pension systems, integrating the private and the public schemes into a common tax/benefit effort during the lifecycle, is novel and can be valuable in 'reinventing' Social Security and providing effective and efficient protection for workers in the twenty-first century.

References

Aaron, H. (1966). The social insurance Paradox. *Canadian Journal of Economic Review, 32*(3), 371–374.

Alonso, J., & Herce J. A. (2003). Balance del Sistema de Pensiones y Boom Migratorio en España. Nuevas Proyecciones del Modelo MODPENS a 2050. Documento de Trabajo 2003–02, *FEDEA*.

Balmaseda, M., Melguizo, A., & Taguas, D. (2006). Las reformas necesarias en el sistema de pensiones contributivas en España. *Moneda y Crédito, 222*, 313–340.

Belmonte, L. J., Corrales, A. J., & Ruiz, J. (2009). La sostenibilidad del sistema de pensiones en España. *European Journal of Education and Psychology, 2*(2), 113–129.

Boskin, M., & Puffert, D. (1987). *Social Security and the American Family*. NBER Working Paper No. 2117.

Bravo, J. (1996): La tasa de retorno de los sistemas de reparto. Estudios de Economía. *Universidad de Chile 23*(1), 115–135.

Comisión Europea. (2015). The 2015 Ageing Report: Economic and budgetary projections for the 28 EU Member States (2013-2060). European economy 3|2015, European Commission. Directorate-General for Economic and Financial Affairs.

Conde-Ruiz, J. I., & Alonso, J. (2004). El futuro de las pensiones en España: Perspectivas y lecciones. *Información Comercial Española (ICE), 185*, 155–174.

Conde-Ruiz, J. I., Jimeno, J. F., & Valera, G. (2006). Inmigración y pensiones: ¿Qué sabemos?, Documento de trabajo de la Fundación BBVA.

Conde Ruiz, J. I., & González, C. (2013). Reforma de pensiones 2011 en España. *Hacienda Pública Española/Review of Public Economics, 204*(1/2013), 9–44.

Costa, J., Gil, J., & y Mascarilla, O. (2006). Preferencias de la población ante la financiación de la dependencia: La Hipoteca Inversa en España. Estudios sobre la Economía Española, 233, FEDEA.

Del Brío, J. F., & González, M. C. (2004). Una proyección del gasto de pensiones en España: Análisis de su viabilidad. *Revista Internacional de Seguridad Social, 3*(57), 105–124.

Del Olmo, F., & Herce, J. A. (2011). Cambios en el ciclo vital: retraso de decisiones individuales y contingencias biográficas. *Panorama Social, 13*, 86–97.

De la Fuente, A., & Doménech, R. (2009). Ageing and real convergence: Challenges and proposals. In J. F. Jimeno (Ed.), *Spain and the Euro: the first ten years* (pp. 191–273). Banco de España.

De la Fuente, A., & Doménech, R. (2013). The financial impact of Spanish pension reform: A quick estimate. *Journal of Pension Economics and Finance, 2*, 111–137.

Devesa, E., Lejarraga, A., & Vidal, C. (2002). Modalidades de pensión y jubilación en las parejas. Documento de trabajo del IVIE.

Díaz-Saavedra, J. (2005). A parametric reform of the Spanish public pension system. Department of Business Administration, Universidad Carlos III de Madrid, Mimeo.

Díaz Giménez, J., & Díaz Saavedra, J. (2017). The future of Spanish pensions. *Journal of Pension Economics and Finance, 16*(2), 233–265.

Domínguez, I., Devolder, P., del Olmo, F., & Herce, J.A. (2018). A two step mixed pension system. *Retirement security, 7*,(1), 31–40.

Eguiagaray, J. M. et al. (2013). Un sistema de cuentas nocionales para España. Por un sistema de pensiones solidario, sostenible y transparente. Grupo Consultivo de Reflexión sobre Políticas Públicas.

Fernández, J. L., & Herce, J. A. (Dir.) (2009), Los retos socio-económicos del envejecimiento en España. Informe realizado por Afi para UNESPA: www.unespa.es/adjuntos/fichero_3009_20100125.pdf

Finkelstein, A. & Poterba, J. (2004). Adverse Selection in Insurance Markets: Policyholder Evidence from the U.K. Annuity Market. *Journal of Political Economy, 112*(1), 183–208.

Galdeano, I., Herce, J. A., et al. (2017). *Soluciones para la Jubilación. Naturaleza, ventajas, defensa y fomento de las rentas vitalicias en España*. UNESPA. Forthcoming.

Gil, J., López García, M., Onrubia, J., Patxot, C., & Souto, G. (2008). SIPES, Un modelo de simulación del sistema de pensiones contributivas en España: proyecciones de gasto a largo plazo. Estudios de Hacienda Pública. Ministerio de Economía y Hacienda e Instituto de Estudios Fiscales.

González, C. I. (2013). El sistema de pensiones español ante un escenario migratorio cambiante. *Economía española y Protección Social, 5*, 115–143.

Herce, J. A. (2017). Longevity and the 'greyny boom'. Manna is raining and (almost) nobody seems to realize it. Mi Jubilación. BBVA Pensiones. Downloadable at https://www.jubilaciondefuturo.es/recursos/doc/pensiones/20160516/en/longevity-and-the-greyny-boom.pdf

Herce, J. A., Galdeano, I., et al. (2017). *Pensiones en transición*. AVIVA. March 2017. Downloadable at http://blog.institutoaviva.es/pensiones-en-transicion-sistemas-de-pensiones/

Herce, J. A., & del Olmo, F. (2013). Reinventar la Seguridad Social asegurando la gran edad. En José A. Herce (Dir.). *Pensiones: Una reforma medular*. Ed. Fundación de EstudiosFinancieros y Círculo de Empresarios, pp. 191–209. Downloadable at https://www.fef.es/publicaciones/papeles-de-la-fundacion/item/273-estudio-pensiones-una-reforma-medular.html.

Hernández de Cos, P., Jimeno, J. F., & Ramos, R. (2017). El sistema público de pensiones en España: situación actual, retos y alternativas de reforma. Documentos ocasionales Banco de España, 1701.

Izquierdo, M., & Jimeno, J. F. (2005). Inmigración: desarrollos recientes y consecuencias económicas. Boletín Económico del Banco de España, pp. 41–49.

Jimeno, J.F & Licandro, O (1999). La tasa interna de rentabilidad y el equilibrio financiero del sistema español de pensiones de jubilación. *Investigaciones Económicas, 23*(1), 129–143.

Jimeno, J. F., Rojas, J. A., & Puente, S. (2008). Modelling the impact of aging on social security expenditures. *Economic Modelling, 25*(2), 201–224.

Jiménez-Ridruejo, Z., et al. (2009). El efecto de la inmigración en la sostenibilidad a largo plazo del sistema de pensiones en España. *Hacienda Pública Española, 188*, 73–124.

Keyfitz, S. (1985a). *Applied mathematical demography* (2nd ed.). New York: Springer-Verlag.

Keyfitz, N. (1985b). The demographics of unfunded pensions, *European Journal of Populations, 1*, 5–30.

Lapkoff, S. (1985). *Pay-as-you-go retirement systems in nonstable populations*. Working Paper, U.C. Berkeley Demography Group.

Lapkoff, S. (1988). Intergenerational flows of time and goods: Consequences of slowing population growth, with Ronald Lee. *Journal of Political Economy, 96*,(3), 618–651.

Lapkoff, S. (1991). A research note on Keyfitz's: The demographics of unfunded pension. *European Journal of Population, 7*, 159–169.

Larraín, G. (2015). Tomando en serio la longevidad: Un pilar de reparto para la cuarta edad. Presentación de Audiencia en la Comisión Asesora Presidencial sobre el sistema de pensiones.

Larraín, G., Ballesteros, S., & García, S. (2017). Longevidad y pensiones: una propuesta de seguro para la cuarta edad. Serie de Documentos de Trabajo de la Facultad de Economía y Negocios de la Universidad de Chile, SDT 441, Santiago de Chile.

Leimer, D (1995). *A guide to social security money's worth issues*. Social Security Administration. Office of Research and Statistics. Working paper Series. Number 67.

León, B. (2004). La inmigración: ¿Una opción ante el envejecimiento? Estudios sobre la Economía Española, FEDEA, 182.

Mitchell, O. S., Poterba, J. M., Warshawsky, M. J. & Brown, J. R. (1999). New evidence on the money's worth of individual annuities. *American Economic Review 89*(5), 1299–1318.

Moral-Arce, I., Patxot, C., & Souto, G. (2008). La sostenibilidad del sistema de pensiones. Una aproximación a partir de la MCVL. *Revista de Economía Aplicada, 16*(E-1), 29–66.
Murphy, K. & Welch, F. (1998). Perspectives on the social security crisis and proposed solutions. *The American Economic Review, 88*(2), 142–150.
Rofman, A. (1993). Las economías regionales. Un proceso de decadencia estructural.
Roig, G. A. & Patxot, C. (2005). Sistemas de pensiones y fecundidad. Un enfoque de generaciones solapadas. Documento de Trabajo Fundación BBVA, 3.
Samuelson, P. (1958). An exact consumption-loan model of interest with or without the social contrivance of money. *Journal of Political Economic, 66*(6), 467–482.
Sánchez-Martín, A. R., & Sánchez-Marcos, V. (2010). Demographic change and pension reform in Spain: An assessment in a two-earner, OLG model. *Fiscal Studies, 31*(3), 405–452.
Sánchez, A. R. (2014). The automatic adjustment of pension expenditures in Spain: An evaluation of the 2013 pension reform. Documento de trabajo del Banco de España, 1420.
Schnabel, R. (1997). Rates of return of the German pay-as-you-go pension system. No 98–56, Sonderforschungsbereich 504, University of Mannheim.
Zubiri, I. (2012). Reforma y sostenibilidad del sistema de pensiones: Una valoración crítica. *Economía Española y Protección Social, 4*, 59–105.

Index

M. Peris-Ortiz et al. (eds.), *Economic Challenges of Pension Systems*,
https://doi.org/10.1007/978-3-030-37912-4

The manufacturer's authorised representative in the EU is Springer
Nature Customer Service Centre GmbH, Europaplatz 3, 69115 Heidelberg,
Germany. If you have any concerns regarding our products, please
contact ProductSafety@springernature.com

Printed and bound by CPI Group (UK) Ltd, Croydon, CR0 4YY
30/09/2026
02225647-0014